The Addison-Wesley Series in Economics

Abel/Bernanke
Macroeconomics

Allen
Managerial Economics

Berndt
The Practice of Econometrics

Bierman/Fernandez
Game Theory with Economic Applications

Binger/Hoffman
Microeconomics with Calculus

Boyer
Principles of Transportation Economics

Branson
Macroeconomic Theory and Policy

Brown/Hogendorn
International Economics: Theory and Context

Browning/Zupan
Microeconomic Theory and Applications

Bruce
Public Finance and the American Economy

Burgess
The Economics of Regulation and Antitrust

Byrns/Stone
Economics

Canterbery
The Literate Economist: A Brief History of Economics

Carlton/Perloff
Modern Industrial Organization

Caves/Frankel/Jones
World Trade and Payments: An Introduction

Cooter/Ulen
Law and Economics

Eaton/Mishkin
Reader to accompany The Economics of Money, Banking, and Financial Markets

Ehrenberg/Smith
Modern Labor Economics

Ekelund/Tollison
Economics: Private Markets and Public Choice

Filer/Hamermesh/Rees
The Economics of Work and Pay

Fusfeld
The Age of the Economist

Ghiara
Learning Economics: A Workbook

Gibson
International Finance

Gordon
Macroeconomics

Gregory
Essentials of Economics

Gregory/Ruffin
Economics

Gregory/Stuart
Russian and Soviet Economic Structure and Performance

Griffiths/Wall
Intermediate Microeconomics

Gros/Steinherr
Winds of Change: Economic Transition in Central and Eastern Europe

Hartwick/Olewiler
The Economics of Natural Resource Use

Hogendorn
Economic Development

Hoy/Livernois/McKenna/Rees/Stengos
Mathematics for Economics

Hubbard
Money, the Financial System, and the Economy

Hughes/Cain
American Economic History

Husted/Melvin
International Economics

Invisible Hand Software
Economics in Action

Jehle/Reny
Advanced Microeconomic Theory

Klein
Mathematical Methods for Economics

Krugman/Obstfeld
International Economics: Theory and Policy

Laidler
The Demand for Money: Theories, Evidence, and Problems

Lesser/Dodds/Zerbe
Environmental Economics and Policy

Lipsey/Courant
Economics

McCarty
Dollars and Sense

Melvin
International Money and Finance

Miller
Economics Today

Miller/Benjamin/North
The Economics of Public Issues

Miller/Fishe
Microeconomics: Price Theory in Practice

Miller/VanHoose
Essentials of Money, Banking, and Financial Markets

Mills/Hamilton
Urban Economics

Mishkin
The Economics of Money, Banking, and Financial Markets

Parkin
Economics

Phelps
Health Economics

Riddell/Shackelford/Stamos
Economics: A Tool for Critically Understanding Society

Ritter/Silber/Udell
Principles of Money, Banking, and Financial Markets

Rohlf
Introduction to Economic Reasoning

Ruffin/Gregory
Principles of Economics

Salvatore
Microeconomics

Sargent
Rational Expectations and Inflation

Scherer
Industry Structure, Strategy, and Public Policy

Schotter
Microeconomics

Sherman/Kolk
Business Cycles and Forecasting

Smith
Case Studies in Economic Development

Studenmund
Using Econometrics

Su
Economic Fluctuations and Forecasting

Tietenberg
Environmental and Natural Resource Economics

Tietenberg
Environmental Economics and Policy

Todaro
Economic Development

Waldman/Jensen
Industrial Organization: Theory and Practice

Zerbe/Dively/Lesser
Benefit-Cost Analysis

Industrial Organization

THEORY AND PRACTICE

Don E. Waldman
Colgate University

Elizabeth J. Jensen
Hamilton College

 **ADDISON-WESLEY**

An imprint of Addison Wesley Longman, Inc.

Reading, Massachusetts • Menlo Park, California • New York • Harlow, England
Don Mills, Ontario • Wokingham, England • Amsterdam • Bonn
Sydney • Singapore • Tokyo • Madrid • San Juan • Milan • Paris

To our families,
Lynn, Abigail, and Gregory
Bob, Ben, and Annie

Sponsoring Editor: Denise Clinton
Senior Development Manager: Sylvia Mallory
Production Supervisor: Heather Garrison
Marketing Manager: Quinn Perkson
Production Services: Ruttle, Shaw & Wetherill, Inc.
Cover Photo: Christie's Images/SuperStock

Library of Congress Cataloging-in-Publication Data

Waldman, Don E.
    Industrial organization: theory and practice / Don E. Waldman,
Elizabeth J. Jensen.
        p.   cm.
    Includes bibliographical references and index.
    ISBN 0-321-01443-X (hc)
    1. Industrial organization (Economic theory)   2. Industrial
organization.   3. Industrial policy.   I. Jensen, Elizabeth Jane.
    II. Title
HD2326.W349   1997
338.9—dc21   97-21718
                                                          CIP

ISBN: 0-321-01443-X

1 2 3 4 5 6 7 8 9 10—MA—01 00 99 98 97

About the Authors

*D*on E. Waldman is the Richard M. Kessler Professor of Economic Studies at Colgate University. He has taught at Colgate since 1981 and has served as chair of the economics department and director of the division of social sciences. Before arriving at Colgate, he received outstanding teaching awards at Cornell University and the University of Maryland, Baltimore County. Professor Waldman received a B.A. in mathematics from Temple University, an M.A. in economics from Brown University, and a Ph.D. in economics from Cornell University. He is the author of two other books, *Antitrust Action and Market Structure* and *The Economics of Antitrust: Cases and Analysis,* as well as numerous articles, comments, and book reviews. Professor Waldman has also served as a consultant and expert witness on legal cases, specializing in antitrust, for both the government and private firms.

In addition to teaching a wide variety of courses at Colgate, Professor Waldman has twice led a group of honors students to study economics for a semester in London. He has been teaching courses on industrial organization and public policy for more than twenty years. Professor Waldman lives in Hamilton, New York, with his wife and their two children.

Elizabeth J. Jensen is Associate Professor of Economics at Hamilton College. She has taught at Hamilton since 1983 and has been chair of the economics department since 1992. Professor Jensen received a B.A. in economics from Swarthmore College and a Ph.D. in economics from the Massachusetts Institute of Technology. Before coming to Hamilton, she worked at the Council of Economic Advisers. Professor Jensen's primary research interest is in the economics of research and development with particular emphasis on the pharmaceutical industry.

Professor Jensen, who fondly remembers her first course in industrial organization at Swarthmore College as being the course that made her decide to become an economist, has been teaching courses on industrial organization since she came to Hamilton College. She lives in Clinton, New York, with her husband and their two children.

Brief Contents

Contents

Part II   MODERN INDUSTRIAL ORGANIZATION: GAME THEORY AND STRATEGIC BEHAVIOR 133

Preface

*Just as eating against one's will is injurious to health, so study
without a liking for it spoils the memory, and it retains nothing.*

Leonardo da Vinci

We wrote this book to help students learn about industrial organization. As the field of industrial organization has changed over the past two decades, the industrial organization courses we teach at Colgate University and Hamilton College have evolved as well; this book reflects much of what we have learned by teaching. Industrial organization has moved from being primarily empirically oriented to relying more extensively on sophisticated theoretical models. In keeping with this change, this text uses game theory as a unifying method of analysis of firm and industry conduct. Yet, as the transition from an empirical to a theoretical orientation has occurred, we have feared a loss of the valuable empirical tradition on which the field had been built. Over time we have become convinced that our students have learned best when we presented them with both the modern theory of industrial organization and an array of empirical examples of industry behavior and performance.

Our ultimate goal has been to write a comprehensive text that would be theoretically up-to-date and sophisticated yet rich in empirical examples of interest to students. We have also wanted to present competing views of the field and to encourage students to compare and contrast differing interpretations. In *Industrial Organization: Theory and Practice* we believe we have accomplished these goals.

Industrial Organization: Theory and Practice is aimed primarily at undergraduates who have completed at least a one-semester microeconomics course. The level of technical mathematics necessary to understand virtually all of the material is equivalent to the mathematics necessary to understand a standard intermediate microeconomics text. We have avoided calculus except in footnotes; whenever possible, we have used numerical examples rather than more generalized mathematical forms to make a point. Over the years we have been amazed at how much more quickly our students comprehend a numerical example. For our students at least, a linear demand curve such as $p = 100 - q$ is much less intimidating than a demand curve written as $p = a - q$.

Industrial Organization: Theory and Practice can also be used as the primary text in policy-oriented economics or business courses, and can serve as a background reference text for graduate courses in industrial organization or public policy toward business.

We want to highlight several features of the text. First, because of the importance of understanding the empirical techniques used in industrial organization, Chapter 2 presents a simple introduction to econometrics. Basic concepts such as R^2 and *t-statistic* are introduced in Chapter 2 and then used in subsequent chapters.

The analysis of oligopolistic conduct begins with Chapter 6, entirely devoted to the essentials of game theory. Following that chapter, we employ a simple game theory approach as the primary, but not the sole, framework for the remaining chapters on oligopolistic conduct. Using game theory as a basic framework helps our students understand the common relationships between different models of oligopolistic behavior. Without this framework, students have often told us that the differing models of oligopolist behavior appear disjointed and confusing.

The text devotes an entire chapter, Chapter 23, to international trade and industrial organization. This is a blossoming subfield in economic theory and research, and today's students should be aware of the importance of this new development.

Another strength of the text is the detailed discussion of many cases, including a wide variety of antitrust cases. Industrial organization is a field full of good stories and informative case studies. Throughout this book we present many examples to help students understand the close connection between theory and the real world. We use certain industries repeatedly, including the oil, automobile, airline, computer, and food distribution industries. As a result, students should gain not only an understanding of theory and statistical work in industrial organization, but also an appreciation of the importance of case studies in expanding our knowledge of the field.

We hope that incorporating many stories directly in the text will ensure that the book reads easily and that it will hold the interest of most undergraduate students. Despite its accessibility, the text should equip students with the necessary theoretical sophistication to enable them to gain a great deal of insight into firm behavior and public policy issues such as antitrust, regulation, deregulation, and international trade.

The study of industrial organization can be organized in many different ways. We have divided this text into four main parts:

I. The Basics of Industrial Organization

In Chapter 1 we present a brief history of the field and explain the differences between the two generally accepted approaches to industrial organization: the structure-conduct-performance approach and the Chicago School approach. Chapter 2 reviews basic microeconomic theory and briefly explains the statistical tools used in industrial organization. Chapter 3 examines the modern theory of the firm, including a discussion of the boundaries of the firm. Chapters 4 and 5 consider the structure of markets in the United States and market entry and exit. In Chapter 5, we emphasize the importance of both entry and exit barriers and of potential as well as actual competition.

II. Modern Industrial Organization: Game Theory and Strategic Behavior

Chapters 6–12 are the core chapters examining conduct, primarily, but not entirely, from a game theory perspective. We have worked hard to make even sophisticated game theory models, such as the Milgrom and Roberts limit pricing model and the Kreps and Wilson predatory pricing model, accessible to undergraduate students. We have devoted all of Chapter 9 to case studies of collusion and Chapter 11 to nonpricing strategies to deter entry, such as raising rivals' costs and product proliferation. Chapter 12 delves into more advanced versions of the Milgrom and Roberts limit pricing model and Tirole's presentation of the product proliferation model.

III. Business Practices

Chapter 13 explores product differentiation and advertising, and Chapter 14 investigates the relationship between market structure and the rate of technological advance. In Chapter 13, we focus on the welfare effects of product differentiation and advertising. Chapter 14 includes a fairly detailed look at Schumpeter's theory of creative destruction and also considers the United States patent system. Chapters 15 and 16 explore price discrimination and vertical integration, respectively, from a theoretical perspective. We have included in appendices several more advanced topics, such as the welfare effects of price discrimination with nonlinear demand curves and the problem of input substitution in the absence of vertical integration. In Chapter 17 we pause to review the major conclusions regarding the relationship between market structure and economic performance and to consider the interpretation of the empirical regularities established over the past 30 years.

IV. Public Policy and International Trade

Chapters 18–22 focus on public policy toward structure and conduct, with an emphasis on antitrust policy. Topics in these chapters include monopolization, collusion, mergers, price discrimination, and vertical restraints. These five chapters include contemporary antitrust cases that will be of interest to students, such as the *Ivy League Group* and the *NCAA* cases. Chapter 23 examines the interactions between the field of industrial organization and the field of international trade, with an emphasis on strategic trade policy in theory and practice. Finally, Chapter 24 presents the traditional theory of public utility regulation as well as recent developments in the area of deregulation. The book concludes on the note that the history of regulation and deregulation in the United States suggests that competition rather than regulation is the best method of achieving economic efficiency.

We have tried to write a flexible text that can be covered in full or in part in a variety of ways. Ideally, the entire book would be covered in two semesters or three quarters. An instructor teaching a one-semester or one-quarter course will probably have to decide whether to emphasize theory or policy. The following are possible course outlines:

In a two-semester course, cover Chapters 1–11 and 13–14 in the first semester and Chapters 15–24 in the second semester. Chapter 12 is advanced and should be included in courses emphasizing theory.

In a one-semester course emphasizing theory, cover Chapters 1–8, 10–17, and, if there is time, 23–24.

In a one-semester course emphasizing policy, cover Chapters 1–6, 8–9, 17–22, and 24. If time remains, cover one or more of Chapters 15, 16, and 23.

In a one-semester course on public policy toward business, or in business school courses, cover Chapters 1–6, 8–9, 18–22, and 24. If time allows, cover one or more of Chapters 13, 15, and 16.

To facilitate review and learning, we have included a summary at the end of each chapter to recap the important points. Each chapter also offers questions for discussion as well as problems. The answers to the odd-numbered problems are presented at the end of the book. And a glossary is included at the end of the text in case a student forgets, for example, the difference between *certain information* and *complete information*.

We wish to thank many for their help in preparing this book. John Greenman of HarperCollins worked with us throughout the preparation of the first draft of the manuscript and showed great wisdom and patience in his approach toward the project. We owe a great deal to Jack. Denise Clinton and Sylvia Mallory at Addison Wesley Longman have been tremendously helpful and encouraging in the past year. Peg Markow at Ruttle, Shaw & Wetherill did a wonderful job during the final production stages of the text. We would also like to thank Randal Reed of the University of Montreal and Leola Ross of East Carolina University for class-testing the manuscript.

We owe our gratitude as well to the many reviewers who offered fine guidance at various stages of the evolution of the manuscript. They are:

Donald L. Alexander, Western Michigan University

Gary Biglaiser, University of North Carolina, Chapel Hill

Erwin A. Blackstone, Temple University

James W. Brock, Miami University of Ohio

Michael R. Butler, Texas Christian University

Kathleen A. Carroll, University of Maryland, Baltimore County

Coldwell Daniel III, University of Memphis

Robert M. Feinberg, American University

Gary M. Galles, Pepperdine University

Claire Hammond, Wake Forest University

Dan Kovenock, Purdue University

Luther D. Lawson, University of North Carolina, Wilmington

Jim Lee, Fort Hays State University

Nancy A. Lutz, Virginia Polytechnic Institute and State University

Richard L. Manning, Brigham Young University

David E. Mills, University of Virginia

Randal Reed, University of Montreal

Stanley S. Reynolds, University of Arizona

David Rosenbaum, University of Nebraska, Lincoln

Leola B. Ross, East Carolina State University

Rochelle Ruffer, Youngstown State University

Frank A. Scott, Jr., University of Kentucky

Joseph Shaanan, Bryant College

Doris F. Sheets, Southwest Missouri State University

John M. Vernon, Duke University

Natalie J. Webb, Naval Postgraduate School

Everett E. White, Loyola University of New Orleans

Our students at Colgate University and Hamilton College deserve our thanks, not only for tolerating partial early drafts as their only textbook, but also for suggesting many fine improvements and pointing out more than one error. Our colleagues and friends—economists and non-economists alike—gave us much tangible and intangible help. Finally, our spouses, Lynn Waldman and Robert Turner, and our children, Abigail and Gregory, and Ben and Annie, deserve the greatest praise for their support and patience.

D. E. W.

E. J. J.

PART I

THE BASICS OF INDUSTRIAL ORGANIZATION

Chapter 1

Introduction

In the beginning there was perfect competition. And economists
saw that it was good. So they assumed perfect competition.

Anyone who has studied microeconomics at the introductory level can appreciate the preceding statement, as can anyone who has taught an introductory microeconomics course. In the authors' introductory courses students often ask why we assume perfect competition when we analyze the automobile, television, or oil industries. Students ask: How can you assume that there are a large number of sellers in those industries? How is it possible that no firm or group of firms has any control over price? How can you assume a homogeneous product in the automobile industry? When those questions arise, we tell our students that they are asking excellent questions and that economists use the perfectly competitive model as an approximation of the real world, but that it is obvious that those industries do not conform strictly to the assumptions of the model. We also tell students interested in learning more about such issues to take a course in industrial organization.

The field of industrial organization developed as an offshoot of traditional microeconomics. Microeconomics courses examine the interactions among consumers, producers, and government, with an emphasis on two traditional models: *perfect competition* and *monopoly*. While some courses also touch on models of **monopolistic competition** and **oligopoly**, most traditional courses pay relatively little attention to these models.

The perfectly competitive model assumes a large number of buyers and sellers, each of which is a price taker. The monopoly model assumes the opposite: one seller with complete control over price. While these models are easy to work with theoretically, neither is an accurate depiction of most real-world markets. Perfect competition accurately describes some markets, such as agriculture, retailing, some service industries, and the stock market. However, perfect competition is rare in manufacturing and mineral extraction.

Monopoly is also rare in the real world. Examples include public utilities such as the electric company, the natural gas company, the local telephone company, the cable television company, and in small isolated towns, the local food market or gasoline station. In its pure form, however, monopoly is even less prevalent than perfect competition. Structurally most markets are neither perfectly competitive nor monopolistic but fall somewhere in between. Such "in between" industries are classified as either oligopolies or monopolistic competition. *Oligopoly* refers to a market structure where a relatively small number of firms control the market. The prevalence of oligopoly is indicated by the fact that in 1987 the U.S. Bureau of the Census calculated that the top four firms controlled at least 20 percent of national sales in 81.5 percent of the 453 government-defined manufacturing industries.[1]

The field of industrial organization recognizes that the models of perfect competition and monopoly do not accurately depict most real-world markets. Nevertheless, the field has its roots in the traditional theory of the firm developed by Adam Smith in the eighteenth century and Alfred Marshall in the nineteenth century. The first important theoretical advances in the area of oligopoly theory were made by Augustin Cournot and Joseph Bertrand in the nineteenth century.[2]

Historically, a very important theoretical advance was made with the development of the theory of monopolistic competition by Edward Chamberlain in the early twentieth century.[3] *Monopolistic competition* is characterized by a large number of buyers and sellers, easy entry, and a differentiated product. Examples of monopolistically competitive markets include furniture, costume jewelry, textiles, and restaurants. Chamberlain's theory differed from the theories of Smith and Marshall by focusing attention on product differentiation and the study of the *firm* instead of the *industry*. One of the driving forces behind Chamberlain's work was a belief that previous models were poor predictors of the real world. Chamberlain believed that real world firms competed not only on the basis of price but also on the basis of product differentiation. The theory of monopolistic competition was a major breakthrough because it helped to fill the glaring gap between theory and empirical observations of how markets operated. The theory of monopolistic competition was, therefore, quickly incorporated into mainstream economic thought, and within a decade included in every microeconomics theory textbook.

Unfortunately the model of monopolistic competition turned out to have as many problems as the models of perfect competition and monopoly. The model has very limited predictive capability, and its few predictions are susceptible to serious criticisms. Despite drawbacks, monopolistic competition introduced into economic theory the concepts of product differentiation and a downward sloping demand curve associated with product differentiation, and highlighted the crucial role of entry. Chamberlain's model provided the first theoretical link between perfect competition and monopoly and ultimately led to renewed interest in oligopoly theory and development of the traditional industrial organization paradigm connecting structure, conduct, and performance.

In his seminal work, Chamberlain also discussed oligopoly, but in far less detail than he discussed monopolistic competition. Examples of oligopoly are numerous and include manufacturing industries such as automobiles, steel, pharmaceuticals, cereals, soft drinks, and beer. Early theoretical work on the relationship between oligopoly and economic performance resulted in few strong conclusions but led economists, among them Joe Bain, to test the relationship empirically.[4] Early empirical studies found that increased market control by a few firms in an industry was associated with higher industry profits; this was interpreted as an indication that the firms had colluded to raise price.

The evolution of industrial organization into a major area of economics has also been closely linked to the development of the modern theory of the firm. In the standard models of perfect competition and monopoly the firm has no discretion over its behavior. In both models, *all* firms maximize profits, and *all* firms increase price in response to an increase in costs. Industry case studies in the 1920s, however, suggested that real-world firms did not respond in such mechanistic ways. To the contrary, case studies indicated that firms had considerable discretion over price, output, and advertising expenditures. Berle and Means, for example, found that oligopolists followed behavioral objectives other than profit maximization.[5] The recognition that oligopolists had discretion over key economic variables led to a new series of questions. Could oligopolists engage in strategic behavior with regard to pricing, research and development, advertising, merger activity, and collusion to influence future market structure and economic performance?

Once economists recognized that *firms* have discretion over key choice variables, the primary focus for analyzing the relationships among structure, conduct, and performance shifted away from the industry and toward the firm. Economists who emphasized the discretionary freedom of firms often rejected the profit-maximizing hypothesis and placed great emphasis on the ability of firms to select alternative behavioral objectives.

As the above discussion implies, courses in microeconomic theory usually emphasize theoretical rigor at the expense of real-world accuracy. Industrial organization courses tilt the balance in the opposite direction, emphasizing an accurate depiction of the real world. As you will learn, however, industrial organization courses do not ignore theory. In fact, in recent years theory has played an increasingly important role in the field. Industrial organization economists, however, will not analyze the cereal industry by assuming it is perfectly competitive or monopolistic. Instead, the industrial organization economist recognizes that the best way to analyze the cereal industry, both theoretically and empirically, is as an oligopoly.

◢ Two Approaches to the Study of Industrial Organization

THE STRUCTURE-CONDUCT-PERFORMANCE (SCP) APPROACH

In the last two decades, the field of industrial organization has become much more theoretical. The **structure-conduct-performance (SCP)** industrial organization paradigm, however, was primarily empirical in its orientation. The SCP paradigm was developed by Professors Mason and Bain in the 1940s and 1950s.[6]

Mason, Bain, and their followers hypothesized that there is a direct relationship between *market structure*, *market conduct*, and *market performance*. Microeconomics courses emphasize this link without *overtly* recognizing it. Consider, for example, the link between structure and performance in microeconomic theory. In perfectly competitive markets, an atomistic *market structure* results in efficient *economic performance* with price equal to marginal cost, inefficient firms driven from the market, and long-run economic profits equal to zero. With a monopoly market *structure*, economic *performance* is poor: price exceeds marginal cost, inefficient firms can survive in the long run, and economic profits are greater than zero.

The SCP paradigm extends the structure-conduct-performance relationship to oligopoly. Figure 1.1 depicts the paradigm. The heavy arrows on the right show the primary relationships: basic market conditions determine market structure; market structure determines conduct; and conduct determines performance. In addition, government policies have a direct impact on structure, conduct, and performance. The thin arrows on the left depict the feedback effects of conduct on structure and of performance on conduct and structure.

An example may help explain Figure 1.1. Consider the ready-to-eat cereal industry. In terms of *market structure*, the cereal industry is an oligopoly, with Kellogg, General Mills, General Foods (Post), and Quaker Oats dominating the market. In 1982 these four firms controlled 86 percent of ready-to-eat cereal sales.[7] There are a small number of sellers and product differentiation through the production of many different brands is extremely important. The significance of product differentiation results in *conduct* that includes a great deal of advertising and a product strategy where each firm is constantly attempting to develop new brands. In 1987, for example, Kellogg spent $374,142,000, or 16.5 percent of its sales revenues, on advertising.[8] This compares with a national average of less than 1 percent for all manufacturing industries in 1977, the last year for which comprehensive data are available for all manufacturing industries.[9] This conduct results in *performance* that is characterized by price being greater than marginal and average cost with the cereal industry consistently ranked among the most profitable industries in the United States.[10]

The cereal industry analysis becomes more complicated when the feedback arrows on the left of Figure 1.1 are considered. Performance includes high profits, and these profits may result in increased advertising and increased investment in new product development. In this way *performance* may have an impact on *conduct*. In addition, the high advertising expenditures may make entry into the market more difficult (i.e., increase **entry barriers**) and reduce the number of sellers. In this way *conduct* may have an impact on *structure*. When analyzing the cereal industry industrial organization economists consider all these effects.

In the 1960s and 1970s SCP industrial organization economists studied the relationships suggested by Figure 1.1 in detail. A majority of this work was empirical. Many case studies as well as numerous statistical studies utilized data across industries. Common questions addressed in these studies included:

1. Is there a relationship between market structure and profitability?
2. Do increased entry barriers result in increased profits?
3. What are the most important entry barriers?

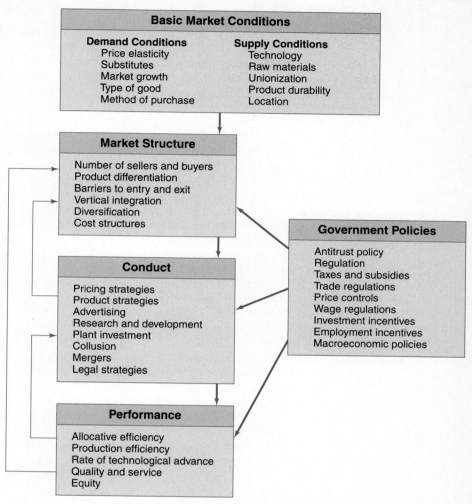

Figure 1.1 The structure-conduct-performance paradigm.

4. How does market structure affect the rate of technological advance?
5. What market structure(s) are associated with effective collusion?
6. How does market structure affect pricing strategies?
7. How does government regulation affect economic efficiency?
8. What is the impact of mergers on economic efficiency?
9. Does increased market power result in increased advertising, or does increased advertising result in increased market power?
10. Should the law permit collusion?
11. Should the government regulate monopolies?

THE CHICAGO SCHOOL APPROACH

The SCP paradigm provides one important approach to the study of real-world markets, but it is not the only valid way to approach the study of industrial organization. Economists associated with the **Chicago School of economics** have long argued that price theory models should be the primary tool for analyzing markets.*[11] Followers of the Chicago School rely heavily on price theory models to make predictions about expected conduct and performance and to design empirical tests of their theories. We have already noted that in the nineteenth century economists used theoretical models to analyze oligopoly behavior long before the development of the SCP paradigm. The Chicago School's theoretical approach to oligopoly, therefore, predates the SCP approach to the field.

In the 1960s and 1970s Chicago School economists questioned many of the major empirical conclusions reached by followers of the SCP approach. For example, SCP economists claimed that there was strong empirical evidence suggesting a positive relationship between monopoly power and profits. According to the SCP economists, increases in market power resulted in increased profits. Chicago School economists, however, argued that the true relationship might well be that increased *efficiency* led to increased market power and increased *profits*. Similarly, SCP industrial organization economists provided empirical studies suggesting that increased advertising raised entry barriers and resulted in increased profits. Chicago School economists, however, used theory and empirical evidence to suggest that advertising often provided information and that this improved information resulted in lower prices. SCP adherents also argued that high capital costs associated with entering a market erected entry barriers, but Chicago School economists argued that capital markets functioned efficiently, and therefore all potential entrants had equal access to capital. The debate between the followers of the two schools has been extremely important to the positive development of the field. Both camps have had a major influence by introducing many important new concepts into the economics profession.

Over the past 15 years a good deal more consensus has developed among economists who specialize in industrial organization.[12] The basis for much of the consensus is the application of **game theory** to models of oligopoly behavior. Game theorists view competition among oligopolists as a game. Of course, the game's outcome depends on the game's assumptions, and economists have attempted to devise oligopoly games that come closer and closer to approximating the real world. While the introduction of game theory has reduced the theoretical differences between advocates of the two schools, it has not reduced their differences regarding the interpretation of empirical evidence or their views concerning the necessary role of government intervention in the economy. This text relies heavily on the use of game theory to provide a theoretical framework for understanding oligopoly but also relies heavily on empirical evidence to support the theoretical conclusions.

---

*The Chicago School refers to a school of thought rather than geographic location. Chicago School economists believe in the efficiency of markets in the absence of governement intervention. Generally, Chicago School economists argue that markets take on structures that are efficient. Academic centers for the followers of this tradition include the University of Chicago, UCLA, and the University of Rochester, but followers are found at most universities.

Static versus Dynamic Models

Another important distinction between microeconomics courses and industrial organization courses is the emphasis industrial organization places on **dynamic performance**. Most microeconomics courses emphasize **static models** that deal with a moment in time. Short-run marginal and average cost curves shown in a textbook figure represent a snapshot of the industry at a precise moment in time. *Dynamic models* deal with changes *over time*. Dynamic models are strategic and tend to emphasize technological change more than static models do.

Static efficiency requires price to equal marginal cost and long-run average cost. Dynamic efficiency requires an optimal rate of technological advance and can exist even if price exceeds marginal and average cost. Courses in industrial organization tend to place considerable emphasis on dynamic models and dynamic efficiency. While this makes industrial organization analysis more complex and intricate than traditional microeconomic analysis, it provides valuable insight into what really constitutes efficient economic performance. Most economists recognize that even if an industry achieves static efficiency, its performance may be poor if it fails to invest in research and development at an optimal rate.

Theory and Empiricism

Many of the major questions in industrial organization yield ambiguous theoretical conclusions. For example, economic theory hypothesizes that increased advertising could have a positive economic impact by providing increased information or that increased advertising could have a negative economic impact by making entry more difficult. There is no theoretical way to prove which relationship is dominant. Under such circumstances the only way to provide insight into the economic impact of increased advertising is to rely on empirical studies.

Industrial organization relies heavily on the use of both case studies and statistical analyses. Case studies provide detailed examinations of specific industries. Studies of the beer, cereal, eyeglass, and soup industries have shed important light on the economic impact of advertising. Statistical studies of the advertising-competition relationship have also provided important evidence. Statistical studies suggest, for example, that the relationship is different depending on the types of goods being considered. Empirical evidence on the advertising-competition relationship is presented throughout the text, and an overview of the relationship is presented in Chapter 13.

As you begin the study of industrial organization, it is important to bear in mind that the field requires a thorough understanding of both theory and empirical work. In the 1950s, 1960s, and 1970s, traditional industrial organization economists tended to rely too heavily on empirical findings, while the Chicago School economists typically relied too heavily on standard price theory. We try to balance theory and empirical evidence throughout this book.

Government and Industrial Organization

Industrial organization analysis is crucially linked to government intervention in markets. An understanding of industrial organization is necessary for policymakers in the areas of antitrust, regulation, deregulation, and international trade. For example, when the government used antitrust to break up the American Telephone and Telegraph Company (AT&T), it relied on the advice of industrial organization economists who studied the telecommunications industry and argued that AT&T's monopoly reduced the rate of technological advance (note that the break-up was based on *dynamic* inefficiency). An industrial organization economist, Alfred Kahn, was the most instrumental person in speeding up the rate of deregulation of the airline industry. More recently the Telecommunications Act of 1996 that deregulated the telecommunications, broadcasting, and cable television industries was based on industrial organization analysis. A debate continues in industrial organization about the merits and demerits of antitrust policies that prevent price fixing, price discrimination, and mergers.

The second half of this text emphasizes the relationship between government and market performance. Should a modern economy rely on *laissez-faire* policies with minimal government intervention, or should the government be actively involved in the conduct and performance of specific industries? Alternatively, a middle ground that relies on antitrust policy to encourage and support competition could be the major goal of government. Addressing these types of questions is critical to making correct policy decisions and is one of the primary reasons for studying industrial organization.

The Global Economy and Industrial Organization

Until recently courses on industrial organization typically ignored international trade theory, whereas courses on international trade characteristically ignored industrial organization theory and dealt strictly with models of perfect competition. The recent trend toward a global economy, where American companies produce and sell abroad and foreign companies produce and sell in the United States, has dramatically changed this view. Industrial organization economists can no longer treat the international sector as a minor sidelight. Fortunately conditions have changed rapidly in both fields in the past 15 years with the introduction of many industrial organization models applied to situations of international competition. We deal with these new international realities in depth in Chapter 23.

General Approach of This Book

The study of industrial organization can be organized in several different ways. In this text we combine the structure-conduct-performance and price theory approaches to the field, with an emphasis on game theory. The book begins with a review of basic microeconomic theory in Chapter 2, which also presents a brief explanation of the statistical tools used in industrial organization. Chapter 3 examines the modern theory of the firm. Chapters 4 and 5 discuss the structure of markets in the United States and market entry and exit. Chapters 6 through 12 examine conduct, mostly, but not entirely, from a game theoretic perspective. Chapter 13 explores product differentiation and advertising, and Chapter 14 investigates the relationship between market structure and the rate of technological advance. Chapters 15 and 16 explore price discrimination and vertical integration, respectively, from a theoretical perspective. In Chapter 17 we pause to review the major conclusions regarding the relationship between market structure and economic performance. Chapters 18 to 22 emphasize public policy toward structure and conduct. Topics in these chapters include monopolization, collusion, mergers, price discrimination, and vertical restraints of trade. Chapter 23 examines the interactions between the field of industrial organization and the field of international trade. Finally, Chapter 24 surveys recent developments in the areas of regulation and deregulation.

SUMMARY

1. The field of industrial organization developed as an offshoot of microeconomic theory.
2. Industrial organization emphasizes the behavior of firms as compared with the behavior of industries more than does traditional microeconomic theory.
3. The two generally accepted approaches to the study of industrial organization are the structure-conduct-performance approach and the Chicago School approach. The structure-conduct-performance approach originally was primarily empirical in its orientation, whereas the Chicago School approach emphasized the use of price theory.
4. Modern industrial organization emphasizes the use of game theory to explore oligopoly behavior.
5. Industrial organization economists place great emphasis on dynamic efficiency, or the optimal rate of technological advance.

KEY TERMS

Chicago School of economics	monopolistic competition
dynamic performance	oligopoly
entry barriers	static models
game theory	structure-conduct-performance paradigm

DISCUSSION QUESTIONS

1. Why do you think traditional microeconomics courses emphasize the perfectly competitive and monopoly models and pay relatively little attention to oligopoly?

2. In what important way(s) does the structure-conduct-performance approach to industrial organization differ from the Chicago School approach?

3. Can you suggest a few industries where it appears that performance has had a feedback effect on structure?

4. What two types of empirical studies are used in industrial organization? Why do you think it is important to use both types of studies?

5. How can the study of industrial organization help policymakers arrive at better decisions?

NOTES

1. Authors' calculations based on U.S. Bureau of the Census, *1987 Census of Manufacturers, Concentration Ratios in Manufacturing,* MC87-S-6 (Washington, D.C.: U.S. Government Printing Office, 1992).

2. Adam Smith, *An Inquiry into the Nature and Causes of the Wealth of Nations* (New York: Modern Library edition, 1937); Alfred Marshall, *Principles of Economics,* 8th ed. (London: Macmillan, 1920); Augustin Cournot (1938) *Recherches sur les principes mathematiques de la theorie des richesses* Paris: M. Riviere & Cie., 1938. Translated in *Researches into the Mathematical Principles of Wealth* (New York: A. M. Kelly, 1960); and Joseph Bertrand, book review of "Recherches sur les Principes athematiques de la Theorie des Richesses," *Journal de Savants* 67 (1883): 499–508.

3. Edward H. Chamberlain, *The Theory of Monopolistic Competition* (Cambridge, MA: Harvard University Press, 1933).

4. Joe S. Bain, *Barriers to New Competition* (Cambridge, MA: Harvard University Press, 1956); Joe Bain, *Industrial Organization* (New York: John Wiley & Sons, 1959); Richard Caves, *American Industry: Structure and Performance* (Englewood Cliffs, NJ: Prentice-Hall, 1964); and Willard F. Mueller, *A Primer on Monopoly and Competition* (New York: Random House, 1970).

5. Adolf A. Berle and Gardiner Means, *The Modern Corporation and Private Property* (New York: Macmillan, 1932).

6. Edward S. Mason, "Price and Production Policies of Large-Scale Enterprise," *American Economic Review* 29 (March 1939): 61–74; Edward S. Mason, "The Current State of the Monopoly Problem in the United States," *Harvard Law Review* 62 (June 1949): 1265–1285; and Joe S. Bain, *Barriers to New Competition* (Cambridge, MA: Harvard University Press, 1956).

7. U.S. Bureau of the Census, *1982 Census of Manufacturers,* "Concentration Ratios in Manufacturing (Washington: D.C., U.S. Government Printing Office, 1986), MC82-S-7.

8. *Advertising Age,* September 24, 1987, p. 162.

9. Federal Trade Commission, *Statistical Report: Annual Line of Business Report, 1977* (Washington, D.C.: Government Printing Office, 1985).

10. F. M. Scherer, "The Breakfast Cereal Industry," in Walter Adams, ed., *The Structure of American Industry* (New York: Macmillan, 1986), pp. 192–193.

11. See George J. Stigler, *The Organization of Industry* (Homewood, IL: Richard D. Irwin, 1968). Also see Richard A. Posner, "The Chicago School of Economic Analysis," *University of Pennsylvania Law Review* 127 (April 1979); and Melvin W. Reder, "Chicago Economics: Permanence and Change," *Journal of Economic Literature* 20 (March 1982).

12. Jean Tirole, *The Theory of Industrial Organization* (Cambridge, MA: MIT Press, 1988), Chapter 1.

Chapter 2

Basic Theory

A standard microeconomic theory course or textbook emphasizes the economics of firms in perfectly competitive and monopolistic industries. As we will see, however, very few—if any—industries in the real world fall into either of these extreme market structures. Therefore, we direct most of our efforts in this book at examining firms' behavior in industries that are neither perfectly competitive nor monopolistic. Yet it is important to understand the perfectly competitive model because it will serve as an important reference point for examining other industry structures. Similarly, the monopoly model highlights how a firm with market power chooses its price and output level, as well as the welfare consequences of that choice.

This chapter begins by reviewing how a profit-maximizing firm chooses its output level. Next we consider some cost concepts that are used throughout the book. Then, we turn to the economics of three of the market structures introduced in Chapter 1: perfect competition, monopoly, and monopolistic competition. The importance of perfect competition as a reference is highlighted in a welfare comparison between perfect competition and monopoly. The final section introduces some important statistical tools used by industrial organization economists to examine various hypotheses about firm behavior.

The Profit-Maximizing Output Level

In previous economics courses you undoubtedly assumed that firms are interested in earning the largest possible profits. We examine the assumption of profit maximization carefully in Chapter 3. Throughout this chapter, we continue to assume that profit maximization is the objective of each firm.

Profits π are defined as total revenue (TR) minus total costs (TC). Profits depend on the quantity of output produced because both total revenue and total costs depend on output.* In deciding how much output to produce, any profit-

---

*We express this mathematically as $\pi(q) = TR(q) - TC(q) = P(q) \cdot q - TC(q)$, where P is the market price. Writing price as a function of quantity allows for the possibility that the price the firm receives might be affected by the quantity of output it sells.

maximizing firm, regardless of industry structure, must consider how a change in its level of output will affect its profits. Suppose a firm is deciding whether to increase output by one unit. To find the effect of this increase on its profits, the firm compares its **marginal revenue** (MR), the change in total revenue resulting from selling an additional unit of output, to its **marginal cost** (MC), the change in total cost resulting from producing that additional unit of output. If marginal revenue is greater than marginal cost, then selling one more unit of output will increase profits. On the other hand, if marginal revenue is less than marginal cost, selling another unit of output will reduce profits, and the firm should consider cutting back on its level of output. Using this kind of incremental reasoning, the firm eventually arrives at the output level for which marginal revenue is equal to marginal costs. This is the profit-maximizing level of output.*

To understand the implications of the profit-maximizing rule, we need to consider its two parts: marginal revenue and marginal cost. Because demand determines marginal revenue, it is necessary to specify the market structure before discussing marginal revenue. We therefore turn first to an examination of marginal cost.

Cost Concepts

ACCOUNTING COSTS VERSUS ECONOMIC COSTS

Before discussing the theory of costs, we have to clarify what economists mean by "costs," distinguishing between **accounting costs** and **economic costs**. *Accounting costs* are the costs reported by firms in their financial reports following various bookkeeping conventions. The *economic cost* of an input is defined as the payment that input would receive in its best alternative employment. The definition of economic costs draws on the concept of the **opportunity cost** of a good: the value of the resources used to produce that good in the best alternative use. Consider a car. Suppose that producing bicycles is the best alternative use of the inputs, including labor, used in producing cars. If 10 bicycles could have been made from the resources used to produce one car, then the opportunity cost of a car is 10 bicycles. For convenience, opportunity cost is often expressed in monetary units so the opportunity cost of a car would be the dollar value of 10 bicycles.

It is economic costs that are relevant for economic theory of firm behavior. A good way to understand the distinction between the two definitions of costs is to use each to measure the costs of various inputs.

---

*This result can also be shown using calculus. To find the value of q that maximizes profits, set the derivative of profits with respect to q equal to 0:

$$\frac{d\pi}{dq} = \frac{dTR}{dq} - \frac{dTC}{dq} = 0$$

so the first-order condition for a maximum is that $\frac{dTR}{dq} = \frac{dTC}{dq}$. This is simply the mathematical statement of the result that a necessary condition for maximizing profits is to choose q such that marginal revenue equals marginal cost.

For some inputs, the cost as measured by accountants and the cost as measured by economists are the same. An example is labor hired at some hourly wage rate. Suppose that a firm hires four workers at the going wage rate of $12 per hour. An accountant would measure the cost of labor as the out-of-pocket expenditures of $48. To calculate the opportunity cost, an economist would assume that the going wage rate of $12 per hour is the amount that the labor services would earn in their best alternative employment. The opportunity cost of hiring four workers for one hour would thus also be $48.

For other inputs, accounting costs and economic costs differ considerably. Two important categories are capital and labor inputs supplied by the owners of a firm. Consider first a machine that is owned by a firm. An accountant would determine how much of the original price of the machine to charge to current costs by applying a standard depreciation formula to the historical cost of the machine. Economists, however, want to know the opportunity cost of using that machine for one hour of production. This implicit cost is the **rental rate**: the amount that another firm would be willing to pay for the use of the machine for an hour. By continuing to use the machine, the firm is implicitly choosing to give up the rental income it could earn from another firm.

A similar distinction between accounting cost and economic cost arises in the case of labor services supplied to a firm by its owner. An accountant would not count the value of the owner's services as part of cost. An economist, however, would ask what an owner (or "entrepreneur") could have earned in the best alternative employment. This opportunity cost would be included as part of economic costs.

Because accounting and economic costs differ, accounting profits and economic profits differ. Economic profits are typically smaller than accounting profits because accountants do not count the value of any labor and capital inputs supplied by the owners of the firm. In fact, it is worthwhile for a firm to continue producing as long as economic profits are equal to *zero*. If economic profits equal zero, then revenues just cover economic costs, indicating that all resources are receiving their opportunity cost.

SHORT-RUN COSTS OF PRODUCTION

As we saw above, the profit-maximizing rule tells a firm to equalize marginal revenue and marginal cost, where marginal cost was defined as the addition to total costs resulting from the production of one additional unit of output. But what are "total costs"? The answer depends on the time period under consideration.

Economists customarily distinguish between the "short run" and the "long run."* Short-run total costs have two components: fixed costs and variable costs. In the short run, the level of use of some inputs, such as land, buildings, and equipment, cannot be changed. The costs of these inputs are **fixed costs** (F). Fixed costs do not vary with the level of output but are the same whether the firm

---

*Dividing time into just two periods is a simplifying assumption. In reality, there are many short runs, with increasingly more adjustment possible as we move from the shortest period toward the long run. In the very shortest run, all inputs are fixed.

produces a large or small amount of output. Examples include rent and property taxes.

Consider a firm that signs a contract to rent equipment for $300 per year, paid at the beginning of the year. This $300 is a fixed cost because the rental fee does not vary with the level of output. If the firm decides to go out of business at the end of the year, it would not sign a rental contract for the next year. But what would happen if the firm decides to stop production partway through the year? Can it get a refund of part of the $300 by returning the equipment? The answer depends on the terms of the contract. Suppose the rental agreement specifies that if the equipment is returned within the year, the firm will receive $100 back. The $200 is a **sunk cost**: it is that portion of fixed costs that is not recoverable. Because sunk costs cannot be recovered once they have been paid, they *should not* affect any subsequent decisions. The $100 that the firm could receive by returning the equipment within the year, however, *should* affect the firm's decisions; it is a recoverable cost.

Variable costs (VC) are the costs associated with those inputs that can be varied to change the level of output being produced.* Examples of variable inputs are labor, raw materials, and energy. The sum of variable costs and the recoverable part of fixed costs is called **avoidable costs** because the firm will not pay these costs if it produces no output.

Decisions about how much output to produce in the short run could be made using total costs. Often, however, it is preferable to use per-unit costs. To understand the relationships among various short-run costs, we will work through a numerical example, shown in Table 2.1.

Total fixed costs are given in the second column. In this example, all fixed costs are assumed to be sunk; the firm must pay $50 per month even if it produces no output.†

The third column shows total variable costs. To produce more output in the short run, the firm must use more of the variable inputs such as labor, electricity, and raw materials. Because the usage of variable inputs increases with the level of output, so do variable costs.

Table 2.1 identifies five additional types of short-run costs. All of these additional measures of cost are derived from the total fixed costs and the total variable costs. The other costs are just different ways of expressing the same basic information.

Total cost (TC) is the sum of fixed costs and variable costs. For example, look at the row in Table 2.1 for an output level of 6 units per month. Fixed costs are $50 and variable costs are $124, yielding total costs of $174. Because variable

---

*Variable costs are usually written as a function of output, VC(q), to show that they change as the level of output changes.

†If the firm could recover part of the fixed cost if it went out of business, then only the nonrecoverable part of fixed cost would be associated with an output level of zero. For example, suppose that in order to produce and sell output, a firm needs a license that costs $50 per month. If $10 of the $50 is refundable, then the relevant cost for an output level of zero is $40; the fixed cost for any output level greater than zero is $50.

TABLE 2.1   An Example of Short-Run Costs

Output (units per month) (1)	Total Fixed Cost ($ per month) (2)	Total Variable Cost ($ per month) (3)	Total Cost ($ per month) (4)=(2)+(3)	Marginal Cost ($ per unit) (5)	Average Fixed Cost ($ per unit) (6)=(2)/(1)	Average Variable Cost ($ per unit) (7)=(3)/(1)	Average Total Cost ($ per unit) (8)=(4)/(1)
0	50	0	50				
1	50	30	80	30	50.00	30.00	80.00
2	50	49	99	19	25.00	24.50	49.50
3	50	65	115	16	16.67	21.67	38.33
4	50	80	130	15	12.50	20.00	32.50
5	50	100	150	20	10.00	20.00	30.00
6	50	124	174	24	8.33	20.67	29.00
7	50	150	200	26	7.14	21.43	28.57
8	50	180	230	30	6.25	22.50	28.75
9	50	215	265	35	5.56	23.89	29.44
10	50	255	305	40	5.00	25.50	30.50
11	50	300	350	45	4.55	27.27	31.82
12	50	360	410	60	4.17	30.00	34.17

costs increase with the level of output and fixed costs are constant, total costs increase as the firm produces more output.

As defined earlier, short-run marginal cost (MC) is the change in short-run total cost resulting from a one-unit change in output.* When output increases from 4 to 5 units, for example, total cost increases from $130 to $150. The marginal cost of the fifth unit of output is thus $20. Because variable cost is the only part of total cost that changes with the level of output, marginal cost can also be calculated from variable costs. Variable cost rises from $80 to $100 when output increases from 4 to 5 units, again giving marginal cost of the fifth unit of output as $20. For many of a firm's decisions, marginal cost is the most important cost to consider.

Table 2.1 also shows three measures of average cost per unit of output. **Average fixed cost** (AFC) is fixed cost divided by output. Because fixed cost is constant, average fixed cost falls as output increases. For example, the average fixed cost associated with 2 units of output is $25 per month, whereas it is $5 per month for 10 units of output.

Average variable cost (AVC), shown in column seven, is variable cost di-

---

*Using calculus, short-run marginal cost, SRMC $= \dfrac{dc(q)}{dq}$.

vided by output. Short-run **average cost** (or average total cost) (AC), shown in column eight, is total cost divided by output. Average total cost can also be defined as the sum of average fixed cost and average variable cost.* For example, total cost of 10 units of output is $305, so average cost is $305 divided by 10, or $30.50. Alternatively, for 10 units of output, average fixed cost is $5 and average variable cost is $25.50, so average total cost is the sum, $30.50.

So far we have simply defined the various measures of short-run costs and explained the arithmetical relationships among them. But what is behind the various cost relationships? What factors determine how cost varies with the level of output a firm produces?

A firm's costs depend both on the level of inputs being used to produce a given level of output and on the prices that the firm must pay for those inputs. The existing technology dictates what inputs must be used to produce a given level of output. The relationship between inputs and output is represented by a **production function**, a mathematical relationship that identifies the maximum quantity of a good that can be produced per time period by a specific combination of inputs. In the short run the firm cannot change the levels of the fixed inputs. The short-run production function therefore indicates the relationship between the level of output and the quantity of the variable inputs.

Figure 2.1 shows the short-run per-unit cost curves for a firm. The shapes of these curves are consistent with the data in Table 2.1 and, in fact, are the typical shapes for short-run cost curves. It is important to note first that the prices of inputs are held constant in drawing these curves; we assume that the firm can hire any quantity of an input at a given price per unit. The cost curves would shift up if the price of an input, such as labor, increased.[†]

Short-run marginal cost in the numerical example of Table 2.1 and in Figure 2.1 is U-shaped. At first, the cost of additional units of output falls as the firm adds more units of labor, the variable input. The firm benefits from specialization and division of labor. In the example of Table 2.1, marginal cost falls until the firm is producing 4 units of output per month. Eventually, however, the fixed plant and equipment begin to be overutilized; the workers start to get in each other's way. At this point, short-run marginal cost starts to increase.[‡] Average fixed cost (AFC) falls over the entire range of output because the fixed amount is spread over larger and larger quantities of output. Average variable cost (AVC) is

---

*Short-run average cost,

$$\frac{C(q)}{q} = \frac{VC(q) + F}{q} = \frac{VC(q)}{q} + \frac{F}{q} = AVC(q) + AFC(q).$$

[†]An increase in the wage rate paid to labor would not cause the average fixed cost curve to shift up because labor is assumed to be a variable input.

[‡]The shape of the short-run marginal cost curve is inversely related to the marginal product of the variable input. As long as the marginal product is increasing, marginal cost falls. In the short run, economists usually assume that the law of diminishing marginal returns is relevant. This law is a generalization of empirical evidence that indicates that increasing the variable input, or inputs, while holding technology and other inputs constant, will eventually result in smaller and smaller increases in total product. When the marginal product of the variable input begins to fall, short-run marginal cost increases.

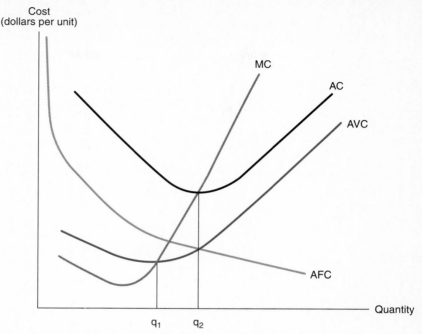

Figure 2.1   Short-run per-unit cost curves for a hypothetical firm.

U-shaped for the same reason as marginal cost; beyond some point, the constraint of the fixed factors of production—typically assumed to be the plant and equipment—makes each additional unit of labor less productive than the previous one. Workers' tasks become redundant and it gets more and more expensive to produce output within a given plant.

Average cost (AC), or average total cost, is the sum of AFC and AVC. AC is also U-shaped. The minimum of AC occurs at a higher level of output than the minimum point of AVC because AC reflects the steadily decreasing average fixed cost in addition to AVC.

The relationship between marginal and average, a frequently used relationship in economics, is the same for all curves. Consider the case for which MC is less than AC as output expands. AC reflects the costs of all units of output produced so far, whereas MC measures the cost of producing an additional unit of output. If the cost of producing one more unit is below average cost, average cost is pulled down by producing that unit. [You can understand this relationship by thinking of performance in a course. If the grade on the most recent exam in a course (the "marginal grade") is below the average grade before the exam, the exam pulls down the course average.] Of course, if MC is greater than AC, then average costs are increasing. If marginal and average costs are both U-shaped, the relationship between marginal and average implies that they are equal at the minimum of the average cost curve. This is shown in Figure 2.1: MC equals AVC at q_1, the minimum of AVC, and MC equals AC at q_2, the minimum of AC.

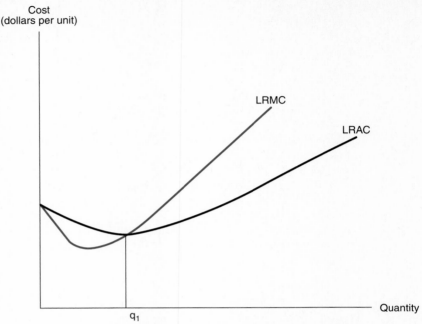

Figure 2.2   Long-run per-unit cost curves for a hypothetical firm.

LONG-RUN COSTS OF PRODUCTION

In the short run some inputs are fixed; the firm has to do the best it can with a given capital stock and plant size, for example. In the long run, however, the firm can buy new equipment and move into a different plant. In fact, all inputs are variable in the long run; the firm can choose that combination of inputs that allows it to produce a given level of output at the lowest possible cost.

Because all inputs are variable in the long run, there are fewer long-run cost curves to worry about. In the short run we have to distinguish among three total cost curves: fixed cost, variable cost, and total cost. Each short-run total cost curve corresponds to a short-run average cost curve. In the long run there is only one total cost curve and one average cost curve.

Figure 2.2 shows long-run marginal and average cost curves for a hypothetical firm. The relationship between average and marginal again implies that if the long-run average cost curve is U-shaped, MC equals AC at the minimum of AC, shown as q_1 in Figure 2.2.

Why would a long-run average cost curve be U-shaped? In the short run the average variable cost curve and the average total cost curves are U-shaped because some input or inputs are fixed. This same explanation does not apply in the long run because all inputs are variable.

Underlying the long-run curves is a characteristic of the firm's production function called **returns to scale**. A production function exhibits *constant* returns to scale if a proportionate increase in all inputs causes output to increase in the same proportion; for example, tripling all inputs leads to exactly three times as much output. A production function is subject to *increasing* returns to scale (or **economies of scale**) if a proportionate increase in all inputs results in a more than proportionate increase in output; that is, output more than triples when all inputs are tripled. The final possibility is that a proportionate increase in all inputs leads to a less than proportionate increase in output. This third case is *decreasing* returns to scale (or **diseconomies of scale**).

Returns to scale dictate the shape of the long-run average cost curve.* If a production function is characterized by economies of scale, the long-run average cost falls as the volume of output increases. Constant returns to scale imply a horizontal long-run average cost curve, while long-run average cost increases with output if the production function exhibits diseconomies of scale.† Long-run average cost will be U-shaped, therefore, if the firm's production function exhibits economies of scale at low levels of output and diseconomies of scale at higher levels of output. To see why this might be the case, we now consider the sources of economies and diseconomies of scale.

SOURCES OF ECONOMIES OF SCALE[1]

Economies of scale can exist at the *product* level, at the *plant* level, and at the *multiplant* level. At the product level, specialization is an important source of economies of scale. Often, firms can reduce the time required to produce one unit of output considerably by utilizing specialized machinery, but the setup time required for specialized machinery is usually high. Because of the extensive setup time, a firm producing relatively small quantities of output may find it cheaper to forgo the investment in specialized machinery and to use more general-purpose machinery instead. As the quantity of output increases, firms find it profitable to incur the larger setup time by investing in the cost-reducing technology in order to realize savings in running time.

---

*We continue to assume that the firm can hire any quantity of each input at a given price per unit.

†To see the relationship between returns to scale and long-run average cost, suppose the production function is given by $q = f(L,K)$. Choose any levels of labor L, and capital, K, say L_1 and K_1. Then $q_1 = f(L_1,K_1)$ and the long-run average cost associated with this level of output is $AC_1 = \dfrac{wL_1 + rK_1}{q_1}$. Here w represents the wage and r represents the rental rate of capital. We can rewrite this as $(AC_1)(q_1) = wL_1 + rK_1$. Now consider a proportionate increase in L and K and let $q_2 = f(aL_1,aK_1)$. The long-run average cost associated with this level of output is

$$AC_2 = \frac{waL_1 + raK_1}{q_2} = \frac{a(wL_1 + rK_1)}{q_2} = \frac{a(AC_1)\,q_1}{q_2}.$$

With increasing returns to scale, q_2 is greater than aq_1 and AC_2 is less than AC_1. You should be able to show that AC is constant with constant returns to scale and that it increases with the level of output in the case of decreasing returns to scale.

Similar savings can result from specialization and division of labor. As the number of employees producing a particular product increases, tasks can be more narrowly defined, giving workers the opportunity to become better at their tasks through repetition. Total labor time and cost will thus fall as the quantity of output increases.

At the plant level, economists have identified economies of scale resulting from increases in the size of processing units. This is important for industries such as petroleum refining and cement and chemical manufacturing in which production requires capital equipment such as tanks and pipelines. For such equipment the laws of geometry tell us that doubling surface area with a consequent doubling of materials costs leads to more than double the volume. In fact, a rough rule of thumb indicates that a firm can double the capacity of a processing unit such as a pipeline for an increase in capital costs of approximately 60 percent.*

As plant size increases, economies of scale can also result from *economies of massed reserves.*[2] All firms hold inventories of some machines or important replacement parts so that production will not be interrupted by a random breakdown. However, a large firm operating several specialized machines does not need to hold reserves for *each* machine in operation. Average costs thus decrease as the cost of holding replacement parts is spread out over a larger volume of output.

Similar savings from spreading overhead over a larger volume of output can be realized in other functions performed by a firm. These include auditing, marketing, finance, personnel, and research and development.†

Multiplant economies appear to be particularly important in certain types of industries. One is an industry that produces a product with relatively high transportation costs relative to value, such as steel or cement (see Sources of Diseconomies of Scale). In this case, if the geographic market is large, a firm may be able to achieve lower costs if it has several plants, each serving a single region, than if it has only one plant. A second type of industry in which multiplant economies of scale are likely to be important is one in which each firm produces multiple products. Here, specialization is again the source of economies of scale; it may be possible to achieve savings by having each plant specialize in a particular product line. Still a third type of industry is one in which multiple plants permit firms to advertise nationally instead of locally and enable firms to utilize national or world capital markets instead of local markets. Access to national

---

*In general, if capacity is increased by a factor of x, the *two-thirds rule* indicates that capital costs will increase by a factor of $x^{0.67}$.

†There are overlaps between economies of scale at the product level and at the plant level. Some economies at the plant level, such as spreading of overhead, could be realized by a large plant that produced a single product or by a large plant producing multiple products. Especially if demand for a single product is insufficient to justify production at a large enough volume to realize plant-specific economies, a firm may choose to produce more than one product in the same plant.

advertising and capital markets can significantly reduce costs.* A firm that operates only one plant may not have access to such national markets, but a firm operating several plants in different areas of the country may.

SOURCES OF DISECONOMIES OF SCALE

Eventually, economies of scale will be exhausted. The savings in unit cost associated with spreading setup time and overhead over larger and larger volumes of output decrease as the quantity of output produced increases. Similarly, economies of massed reserves become relatively less important as firm size grows. These arguments suggest that long-run average cost curves should eventually flatten.

Further arguments suggest that, as Figure 2.2 shows, long-run average cost may increase beyond some quantity of output. At first, this may seem somewhat odd. Surely, even if there are no further gains from specialization, a firm should be able to double all inputs, reproducing exactly what it had done before, and produce twice as much output. This would imply that the long-run average cost curve should be horizontal. Economists have suggested at least two reasons for increasing average cost beyond some quantity of output.

First, even in the long run, some input may actually be fixed, or at least scarce, and therefore not able to be increased proportionately with other inputs. A common example of such an input is managerial ability or entrepreneurship. Organizational difficulties associated with increasing size might then lead to less than proportionate increases in output. In fact, firms have devoted considerable attention to organizational structure in an attempt to avoid diseconomies associated with large-scale management. General Motors was an early leader in moving away from a centralized structure to a multidivisional one, splitting itself into five independent divisions—Buick, Cadillac, Chevrolet, Oldsmobile, and Pontiac—in the 1920s. Such decentralization aims to reduce the number of decisions and amount of coordination on the part of the chief executive officer. Today most large firms are multidivisional. Of course, even with decentralization, firms need an ultimate decision maker, whose talents and time can be stretched only so far.

Overall economies of scale depend not only on the production function but also on other functions of the firm. Thus a firm may realize economies of scale in production for reasons such as those discussed above, yet still experience overall diseconomies of scale. The most important source of diseconomies of scale at the plant level is transportation costs. As a plant expands, its requirements for raw materials increase. Also, to sell its output, the finished products must typically be shipped to a larger geographic area. As the geographic area expands, transportation costs per unit sold may increase. This is especially true for bulky, low-value

---

*Most of the cost savings discussed in this section represent real economies as opposed to pecuniary economies. **Real economies** are those that reflect actual savings of resources, such as reduction of transaction costs. Society benefits from the realization of real economies. **Pecuniary economies** are savings that are purely redistributive, increasing the welfare of one group and reducing the welfare of another. The differential in capital costs across firms reflects both real and pecuniary savings. Interest rate differentials across firms are discussed in more detail in Chapter 5.

products such as cement, sand, and steel. For these products, transportation costs rise quickly enough to lead to overall diseconomies of scale, limiting the geographic market that can be efficiently served by one plant.*

THE SHORT RUN AND LONG RUN REVISITED

In the long run all inputs are variable; the firm can choose its plant size, its stock of equipment, and the size of its labor force so that it can produce a particular quantity of output at the lowest possible cost. In the short run, however, the firm's choices are limited. Once a firm builds a plant, its options in the immediate future are constrained by the short-run cost curve associated with that plant size. Therefore, the long-run average cost must always be at least as low as the short-run average cost.

The relationship between long-run average cost and short-run average cost is shown in Figure 2.3. Suppose that there are only four plant sizes to choose among. Associated with each plant size is a short-run cost curve, shown as $SRAC_1$, $SRAC_2$, and so on. The optimal plant size depends on the output level being produced: the firm should use plant size 1 for output of q_1 but plant size 2 for output of q_2. The long-run average cost curve is the red portion of each of the short-run curves, because each of these segments shows the lowest possible average cost for the corresponding level of output.

Typically, a firm has many more than four plant sizes to choose among. As the number of possible plant sizes increases, the long-run average cost curve becomes smoother. Eventually, it becomes a smooth curve with each point on the curve associated with a different possible plant size. The black curve in Figure 2.3 is the long-run average cost curve.

The Economics of Perfect Competition

The material discussed so far applies to all firms, regardless of the market structure in which they operate. Any firm striving to maximize profits will choose to produce the level of output for which marginal revenue equals marginal cost. And nothing in our review of cost concepts depends on the market structure. The underlying determinants of costs are input prices and production functions for both a monopolist and a perfectly competitive firm.

To complete the model of output determination, we need to specify the demand conditions facing the firm. The demand conditions determine the revenues the firm can earn by selling various quantities of output. Unlike costs, the demand conditions depend on the market structure. We begin by considering the economics of perfect competition. Even though real-world markets rarely, if ever, exhibit all the characteristics of a perfectly competitive market, this model is important as an ideal against which other markets can be compared.

---

*It may be possible for a firm to overcome diseconomies of scale arising from transportation costs at least partially by operating multiple plants in different areas of the country.

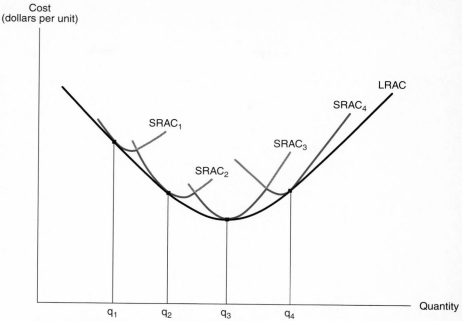

Figure 2.3   The relationship between short-run and long-run average costs.

THE ASSUMPTIONS OF PERFECT COMPETITION

In everyday usage, competition refers to intense rivalry among firms, such as that between the Coca-Cola Company and Pepsico or between Toyota and Subaru. Firms that are competitors in this sense recognize that their decisions affect other firms. Therefore, in making decisions such as how much output to produce or what advertising campaign to adopt, a firm considers the effect on competitors and their likely response.

Perfect competition as modeled by economists is quite different from the everyday view of competition. Each firm in a perfectly competitive market recognizes that its effect on the overall market is insignificant. Therefore, perfectly competitive firms do not view other firms as rivals; they make business decisions without considering the actions or reactions of other firms in the industry. Each firm views the market price as independent of its own level of output.

Formally, the long-run characteristics of perfect competition are as follows:

1. *Large number of buyers and sellers.* A perfectly competitive market contains many buyers and sellers, each small relative to total purchases or sales.
2. *Homogeneous product.* Firms in a perfectly competitive market produce a homogeneous, or identical, product. Because consumers cannot distinguish one firm's product from another's, they are indifferent about their supplier.
3. *Perfect information.* All economic agents (firms and consumers) have all of the information they need to make economic decisions. Consumers know the

price and quality of the product produced by each firm, and firms know their production functions and the prices of all inputs and outputs.

4. *No transaction costs.* Transaction costs are the costs of using the market, such as the costs of negotiating and monitoring a contract. In a perfectly competitive market, transaction costs are zero for both buyers and sellers.*

5. *Free entry and exit.* Adjustments to changing market conditions require that resources enter or leave the industry. In a perfectly competitive market these adjustments occur without firms having to incur any special costs; there are no barriers to entry or exit.

The characteristics of a perfectly competitive market ensure that firms and consumers are *price takers*. Because consumers are indifferent about their supplier, have perfect information about price, and incur no transaction costs in switching to a different seller, any firm that raises its price above the market price will immediately discover that it cannot sell any output. On the other hand, no perfectly competitive firm has any incentive to price below the market price because it can sell as much output as it wants at the going price. Therefore, buyers view the market price as beyond their control; they cannot find any firm willing to sell output at a price below the market price.

Figure 2.4 shows the demand curve facing a perfectly competitive firm. The vertical portion of the demand curve reflects the firm's belief that it will sell nothing if it charges a price higher than the market price, P*. The horizontal portion of the demand curve shows that the firm can sell whatever amount it wants if it charges the market price. It is important to emphasize that this figure shows the demand curve facing an *individual* firm in a perfectly competitive market. The market demand curve, which shows the relationship between the market price and the *total* amount of output demanded by consumers, is still assumed to be downward sloping.

The **price elasticity of demand**, often called simply the *elasticity of demand*, is a measure of how sensitive quantity demanded is to a change in price. It is defined as the percentage change in quantity demanded divided by the percentage change in price. The higher the absolute value of the elasticity of demand, the larger the change in quantity resulting from a change in price.† For example, an elasticity of -0.3 indicates that a 10 percent increase in price will reduce quantity demanded by only 3 percent (-3 percent/10 percent $= -0.3$). We would say that demand is inelastic since $|-0.3| < 1$. If the elasticity is -3, a 10 percent increase in price will reduce quantity demanded by 30 percent (-30 percent/10 percent $= -3$). In this case demand is elastic since $|-3.0| > 1$.

The elasticity of demand can be calculated as

$$\frac{\frac{\Delta Q}{Q}}{\frac{\Delta p}{p}} = \left(\frac{\Delta Q}{\Delta p}\right)\left(\frac{p}{Q}\right).$$ Note that $\frac{\Delta Q}{\Delta p}$ is the inverse of the slope of the demand curve.

---

*The importance of transactions costs is discussed in detail in Chapter 3.

†For any downward-sloping demand curve, the elasticity of demand is negative because a decrease in price will lead to an increase in quantity demanded.

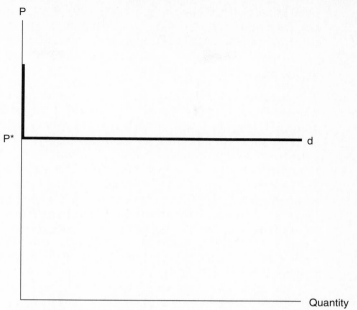

Figure 2.4   The demand curve facing a perfectly competitive firm.

For a horizontal demand curve, $\Delta p = 0$ everywhere, implying that $\dfrac{\Delta Q}{\Delta p} = \dfrac{\Delta Q}{0}$ and therefore that the elasticity of demand is infinity. The demand curve facing an individual firm in a perfectly competitive market is thus said to be *infinitely elastic*.

THE FIRM'S SUPPLY CURVE

The profit-maximizing rule tells a firm to produce that quantity of output for which marginal revenue equals marginal cost. In the special case of a firm in a perfectly competitive industry, marginal revenue always equals price. To understand why, remember that a perfectly competitive firm can sell another unit of output without having to lower its price. For example, consider a firm that is selling 10 units of output at a price of $2 per unit. Its total revenue is $20. If this firm sells 11 units of output at a price of $2 per unit, total revenue increases from $20 to $22; marginal revenue is $2, the market price.*

Combining the profit-maximizing rule with the fact that price equals marginal revenue for a perfectly competitive firm, we conclude that if a perfectly competitive firm wants to produce any output, it will choose the level for which

---

*Mathematically, marginal revenue = $MR(q) = \dfrac{d[P(q) \cdot q]}{dq} = P + q \cdot \dfrac{dP}{dq}$. Because a perfectly competitive firm's actions do not affect the market price, $\dfrac{dP}{dq}$ equals 0, and MR = P.

price equals marginal cost. Sometimes, however, a competitive firm may choose not to produce any output. To understand why, it is necessary to analyze the firm's supply decision in both the short run and the long run.

Short Run

A firm should choose to produce in the short run if its total revenue is greater than or equal to its avoidable costs, defined earlier as the sum of variable costs and the recoverable part of fixed costs. Consider first the case in which *all* fixed costs are *sunk*—that is, the firm's only avoidable costs are its variable costs. Even if a firm decides to produce zero units of output in the short run, it must still pay its fixed costs. In the short run, therefore, a profit-maximizing firm will choose to produce some output as long as the revenue it gets from selling that output—its **total revenue** (TR)—is greater than or equal to the costs of the variable inputs it must hire to produce that output—its **total variable costs** (TVC). If the firm more than covers its TVC, it can apply the revenues above total variable costs toward its fixed costs so that its short-run loss will be less than TFC. If all fixed costs are nonrecoverable, therefore, a profit-maximizing firm will produce some output in the short run as long as price is greater than or equal to average variable cost.* To summarize, in the short run, a perfectly competitive firm will produce the output for which price equals marginal cost *as long as that price is greater than or equal to average variable cost*. The point at which P = AVC is called the **shutdown price**. Because of the relationship between marginal and average, the point at which P = AVC = MC is the minimum point on the AVC curve.

   Figure 2.5 shows the firm's short-run supply curve. P_0 is the shutdown price for the firm; above P_0 the short-run supply curve is the marginal cost curve. Note that for prices below P_1 but above P_0 the firm produces output in the short run even though its economic profits are negative.[†] Economic profits are shown as the area of a rectangle with length equal to the quantity of output being produced and width equal to the difference between price and average cost at that quantity. For example, profits at q_2 equal the red rectangle in Figure 2.5.

   Now consider the case in which some fixed costs are *not* sunk costs. For example, assume that a firm rents equipment for $300 per year but can return the equipment within the year and receive $100 back. The fixed cost is $300; the sunk cost is $200. Now the firm's avoidable costs equal its variable costs *plus* $100, the recoverable portion of its fixed costs. To produce in the short run, total revenues must be greater than or equal to avoidable costs, raising the shutdown price.

   In general, the higher the recoverable portion of fixed costs, the further the

---

*TR > TVC implies that $(q \cdot P) - (q \cdot AVC) > 0$. This can be rewritten as $q(P - AVC) > 0$, or $P > AVC$.

[†]Profits = TR − TC, where TR is total revenue and TC is total costs. Because TR = P·q and TC = AC·q, profits can be written as q(P−AC). In Figure 2.5, if price is above P_0 but below P_1, P < AC, implying that economic profits are negative.

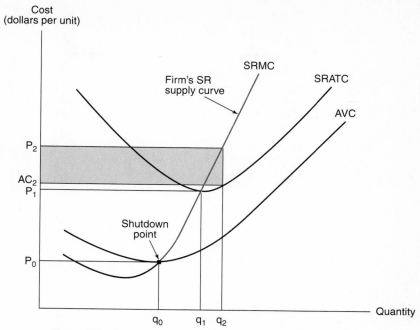

Figure 2.5   A perfectly competitive firm's short-run supply curve.

shutdown price is above average variable costs. In the extreme case all fixed costs are avoidable, and price must equal average cost in order for a firm to produce in the short run.

Long Run

In the long run, all inputs are variable and a firm will leave an industry if it is earning negative economic profits. In the long run, therefore, a profit-maximizing firm will produce only if total revenue is greater than or equal to total costs; that is, the firm produces in the long run only if price is greater than or equal to long-run average costs. The firm's long-run supply curve, shown in Figure 2.6, is its marginal cost curve above the minimum point on the long-run average total cost curve. Note that for any price above P^*, the minimum point on the average total cost curve, the firm is earning positive economic profits. For any price below P^* the firm will not produce in the long run.

THE MARKET SUPPLY CURVE AND EQUILIBRIUM

The short-run market supply curve is derived simply by choosing a price and adding up the quantities of output produced by each firm at that price. (Remember that the number of firms in the industry in the short run is fixed.) Market equilibrium is the intersection of the market demand and market supply

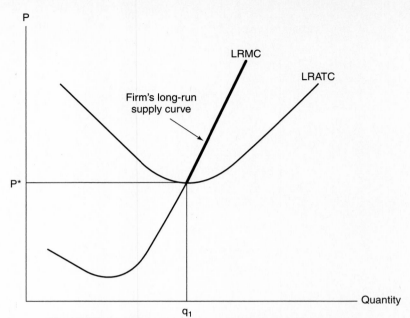

Figure 2.6   A perfectly competitive firm's long-run supply curve.

curves. At the equilibrium price, the quantity supplied by producers is equal to the quantity demanded by consumers. Figure 2.7 shows short-run equilibrium for the market and for a representative firm. In this figure, P_1 is the minimum of the firm's average variable cost and P_E is the equilibrium price. The equilibrium quantity produced by each firm is q_E and the equilibrium quantity for the market is Q_E.*

In the short run a perfectly competitive firm may be making positive, negative, or normal (zero) economic profits. In Figure 2.7, for example, the firm is earning excess (above normal) economic profits because price is greater than average total costs.

Because resources are mobile, however, no firm can make either positive or negative economic profits in the long run. Positive profits induce entry, which increases supply and reduces price, whereas negative profits cause firms to leave. Exit decreases supply and increases price. In long-run equilibrium, therefore, price must equal average cost so that economic profits equal zero. But remember that price is also equal to short-run *and* long-run marginal cost at the profit-maximizing level of output for the perfectly competitive firm. The long-run equilibrium price must thus equal P*, where short-run marginal cost, long-run marginal

---

*$Q_E = nq_E$, where n is the number of firms in the industry.

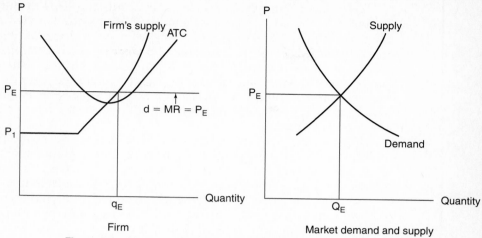

Figure 2.7   Short-run equilibrium for a representative firm and the market.

cost, short-run average cost, and long-run average cost are all equal. Figure 2.8 shows long-run equilibrium.

PROPERTIES OF COMPETITIVE EQUILIBRIUM

The perfectly competitive model serves as a valuable reference point because of the desirable properties of long-run equilibrium. The equilibrium resource allocation in a competitive economy is *efficient*, meaning that no possible reallocation of resources will make one market participant (consumer or firm) better off without hurting another. All mutual gains from trade have been achieved.

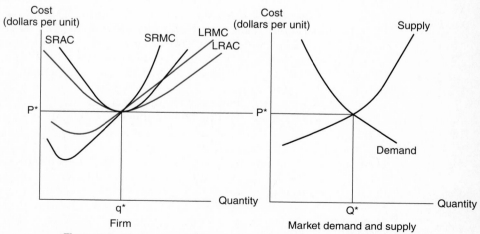

Figure 2.8   Long-run equilibrium for a representative firm and the market.

One important type of efficiency concerns the level of output being produced and purchased. Efficiency in the level of output, called **allocative efficiency**, requires that the marginal benefit of producing another unit of output equal its marginal cost. If the marginal benefit is greater than marginal cost, too little of the good is being produced; if marginal benefit is less than marginal cost, too much is being produced. In competitive equilibrium, price, a measure of the value a consumer places on the *last* unit bought, equals the marginal cost to society of producing that last unit. This ensures that the socially optimal quantity of the good is produced.

Competitive equilibrium also exhibits **efficiency in production**. Figure 2.8 indicates that in long-run equilibrium each firm is producing at the minimum point on its average cost curve. Output is produced using the least costly combination of inputs. Furthermore, high-cost firms will be forced to exit the market.

A third characteristic of competitive equilibrium is that each perfectly competitive firm earns zero economic profits in long-run equilibrium. Therefore, resources are earning only their opportunity cost.

Introduction to Welfare Economics

The perfectly competitive model serves as an important reference point for industrial organization economists. To study the economic cost of a departure from perfect competition, economists use the two related concepts of **consumer surplus** and **producer surplus**. For example, economists often evaluate the welfare effects of changes in market structure or of government policies by looking at changes in consumer and producer surplus.

Consumer surplus is the difference between the maximum amount consumers are willing to pay for a good and the amount they actually pay. Suppose a consumer is willing to pay a maximum of $50 for a sweater but is actually able to purchase the sweater for $40. She would receive $10 in consumer surplus. In general, the demand curve indicates the value to consumers of consuming additional units of a good. We thus measure consumer surplus by the area bounded above by the market demand curve and below by the market price, as shown by triangle ABC in Figure 2.9. Note that no consumer surplus is associated with the fiftieth unit of output; that unit of output would not be purchased at any price higher than $40. For the demand curve pictured in Figure 2.9, consumer surplus equals $1000: ($\frac{1}{2}$(50 × $(80 − 40)).

Producer surplus is analogous to consumer surplus. *Producer surplus* is the difference between the market price the producer receives for selling a unit of output and its marginal cost. For example, if it costs $20 to produce the first sweater and the market price is $40, the firm earns a producer surplus of $20 on that sweater. If the marginal cost of the second sweater is $30, then producer surplus on that unit would be $10. Because the supply curve represents the marginal cost of producing, producer surplus is the area bounded above by the market price and to the left of the supply curve. This is shown on Figure 2.9 as triangle BCD; producer surplus equals $500, the area of this triangle: ($\frac{1}{2}$(50 × $(40 − 20)).

The Economics of Monopoly

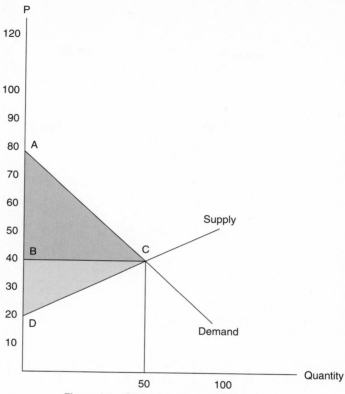

Figure 2.9 Consumer and producer surplus.

The Economics of Monopoly

THE RELATIONSHIP BETWEEN MARGINAL REVENUE AND PRICE

A **monopoly** is the sole producer of a good for which there are no close substitutes. Thus, a monopolist *is* the industry and faces the market demand curve for its product. That demand curve, like any market demand curve, slopes downward, and the monopolist can operate at any point along that market demand curve. It can choose a high price and sell a relatively small quantity of output, or it can choose a lower price and sell more output.

A monopolist, like any profit-maximizing firm, will choose to produce the quantity for which marginal revenue equals marginal cost. Unlike a perfectly competitive firm, however, marginal revenue for a monopolist does *not* equal price. To understand why, recall the definition of marginal revenue: the additional revenue a firm obtains from selling one additional unit of output. Because a monopolist faces the downward-sloping market demand curve, the only way it

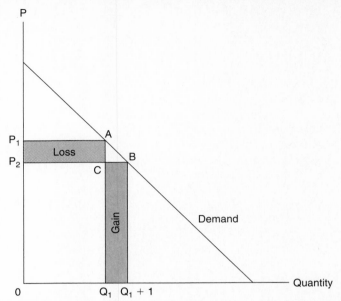

Figure 2.10 Changes in a monopolist's total revenue resulting from a price cut.

can sell an additional unit of output is by lowering the price on *all* units.* Although it gains revenue from the additional unit of output, it loses revenue on those units previously sold at a higher price. Figure 2.10 shows the trade-off faced by a monopoly. At P_1 the monopoly sells Q_1 units of output, and total revenue is the area of the rectangle OP_1AQ_1. To sell $Q_1 + 1$ units of output, the monopolist must lower price to P_2 ; total revenue becomes the area $OP_2B(Q_1 + 1)$. The monopoly gains area $Q_1CB(Q_1 + 1)$ in total revenue. The width of this rectangle is 1 and its height is P_2, so the area of the gain in revenue is P_2. However, by lowering price, the monopoly also loses area P_1ACP_2, which is the original quantity sold, Q_1, times the change in price. Marginal revenue is the sum of the two areas. Thus for a monopoly marginal revenue is always less than price. The precise relationship is given by:[†]

$$MR = P + Q\frac{\Delta P}{\Delta Q} = P\left(1 + \frac{Q}{P}\frac{\Delta P}{\Delta Q}\right)$$

---

*This argument assumes that the monopolist is not able to practice price discrimination. Price discrimination is considered in detail in Chapter 15.

[†]To derive this relationship, begin with TR = PQ. For a small change in quantity,

$$\Delta TR = P\Delta Q + Q\Delta P, \text{ so } MR = \frac{\Delta TR}{\Delta Q} = P + Q\frac{\Delta P}{\Delta Q}.$$

Using calculus, $MR = \dfrac{dTR}{dQ} = P + Q\dfrac{dP}{dQ} = P\left(1 + \dfrac{Q}{P}\dfrac{dP}{dQ}\right).$

and because

$$e_D = \frac{\Delta Q}{\Delta P}\frac{P}{Q'}$$

we have   (1) $$MR = P\left(1 + \frac{1}{e_D}\right) = P\left(1 - \frac{1}{|e_D|}\right)$$

where e_D is the price elasticity of demand.

Graphically, the marginal revenue curve lies everywhere below the market demand curve. Figure 2.11 shows that Q_M is the profit-maximizing quantity of output for the monopolist; here $MR = MC$. The profit-maximizing price corresponding to this quantity is P_M, which is found from the market demand curve.

Figure 2.11 also illustrates a relationship that we will use extensively later in this book. If the demand curve is linear, then the marginal revenue curve is also linear. Furthermore, the marginal revenue curve has the *same vertical intercept* as the demand curve but is *twice as steeply sloped*, so that the horizontal intercept of the marginal revenue curve is half the horizontal intercept of the demand curve.

To see the relationship between a linear demand curve and its marginal revenue curve, begin with the formula for marginal revenue given above:

$$MR = P + Q\left(\frac{\Delta P}{\Delta Q}\right)$$

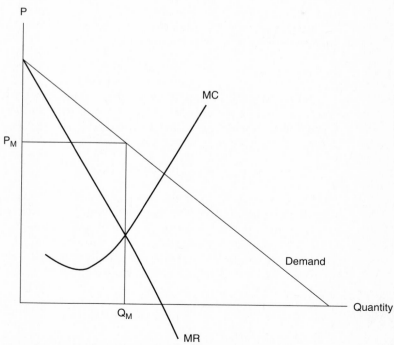

Figure 2.11 Profit-maximizing price and quantity for a monopolist.

If the linear demand curve is given by the equation P = a − bQ, then:*

$$MR = (a - bQ) + Q\left(\frac{\Delta P}{\Delta Q}\right)$$

Since $\frac{\Delta P}{\Delta Q}$ is the slope of the linear demand curve, it equals − b and:

(2) $MR = (a - bQ) + Q(-b) = a - 2bQ$

If, for example, the demand curve is P = 100 − 3Q, then MR = 100 − 6Q. In later chapters we will refer to this relationship between demand and marginal revenue as the "twice as steep rule."

ELASTICITIES, THE DEGREE OF MARKET POWER, AND THE LERNER INDEX

Throughout this book we make use of the concepts of elasticity, market power, and the Lerner index. This section shows how these concepts relate to one another.

Any firm that has the ability to set price above marginal cost, the perfectly competitive equilibrium price, is said to have *market power* or *monopoly power*. While we know that the monopolist will choose the profit-maximizing price-quantity combination on the market demand curve, we do not know how high that price will be in relation to marginal cost. How much can the monopolist raise price above marginal cost? What constraints does it face on raising price significantly above marginal cost?

We can answer these questions by examining the relationship between marginal revenue and price introduced earlier:

$$MR = P\left(1 - \frac{1}{|e_D|}\right)$$

Combining the formula for marginal revenue with the fact that marginal revenue equals marginal cost at the optimum price quantity combination and rearranging terms yields a measure of the degree of market power called the **Lerner index**, or the monopoly markup:

$$\text{Lerner index} = \frac{P - MC}{P} = \frac{1}{|e_D|}$$

The Lerner index indicates that even a monopolist has only limited control over price. If the price elasticity of demand is high, as illustrated in Figure 2.12(a), then a monopolist's profit-maximizing price is still relatively close to its marginal cost. A less elastic demand curve such as that shown in Figure 2.12(b) results in a larger monopoly markup. If the elasticity equals −10, for example, the Lerner index equals 0.1 and the gap between price and marginal cost is quite low. If the elastic-

*Using calculus, TR = (a − bQ) Q = aQ − bQ² so $\frac{dTR}{dQ} = a - 2bQ$.

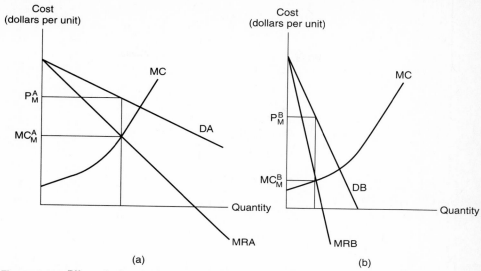

Figure 2.12 Effect of price elasticity of demand on the gap between profit-maximizing price and marginal cost.

ity equals −1.5, however, then the Lerner index is 0.67 and the gap is considerably larger.

Welfare Comparison

Earlier we noted that equilibrium in a perfectly competitive market exhibits several highly desirable characteristics. How does monopoly compare? Why do economists worry about market power? The major concern is that monopoly misallocates resources by producing the "wrong" amount of a good, where price does not equal marginal cost. In other words, monopoly is *always* allocatively inefficient. Figure 2.13 compares a market under perfect competition and under monopoly, assuming costs are the same under both industry structures. In this figure the perfectly competitive output is Q_{PC} and the perfectly competitive price is P_{PC}. Consumer surplus under perfect competition is shown by ABC. There is no producer surplus in this market under perfect competition. Under monopoly, with price P_M and quantity Q_M, consumer surplus is the much smaller triangle ADE. The difference between the two, area CEDB, can be broken into two parts: a rectangle (CEDF) and a triangle (DBF). The rectangle, monopoly profits, represents a transfer from consumers of the good to the owner(s) of the monopoly. Thus this area is *not* a loss from society's point of view, although we may be concerned about the effects of this transfer on the distribution of income. The area of the triangle DBF, however, represents a loss of social welfare. This area, called the **deadweight loss triangle**, is a measure of the misallocation of resources from monop-

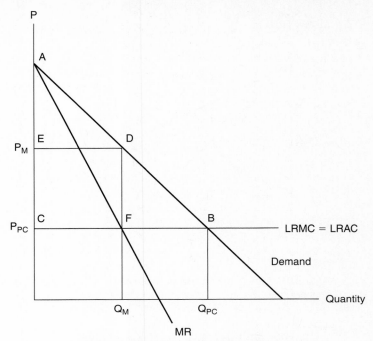

Figure 2.13   Welfare loss due to monopoly.

oly. By producing where price is greater than marginal cost, the monopoly produces too few units of the good.

It is very important to understand that this problem arises because the monopoly price is *greater* than the marginal cost of the good. Consumers would be willing to pay more for an additional unit of the good than it would cost society to produce that unit, yet the monopolist does *not* produce it. This is the fundamental problem associated with monopoly power.

MEASUREMENT OF THE COSTS OF MARKET POWER

How large is the welfare loss due to the misallocation of resources resulting from market power? The first economist to attempt to measure the magnitude of the deadweight loss was Arnold Harberger.[3] He recognized that the deadweight loss (DWL) could be measured by the formula $DWL = -\frac{1}{2}r^2 Se_D$, where $r = \frac{P_M - P_{PC}}{P_{PC}}$, $S = P_{PC} \cdot Q_{PC}$ (revenue), and e_D is the elasticity of demand. Using data on profit returns on capital from 73 manufacturing industries from 1924 through 1928, Harberger estimated that the deadweight loss due to monopoly power in the United States was less than 0.1 percent of GNP.

As you might imagine, Harberger's conclusion that deadweight loss was such a small percent of GNP resulted in much criticism and many further calculations.[4] Economists have examined Harberger's assumptions and his calculations, arguing that they led to an underestimate of the magnitude of deadweight loss. Critics assert that Harberger's assumed price elasticities of demand were too low* and that his assumed competitive rate of profit was too high.† Additionally, using industry profit rates causes an aggregation bias by averaging high monopoly profit rates with losses of other firms in the industry. Some of the revised estimates put the deadweight loss as high as 4 to 7 percent of GNP.[5]

Economists have identified other important possible costs of monopolization in addition to the deadweight loss, arguing that significant rent-seeking costs are involved in trying to gain and maintain monopoly power. A monopoly, for example, may spend "too much" on advertising, product differentiation, or investment in excess production capacity. Tullock and Posner argue that the welfare costs of monopoly include expenditures on lobbying and campaign contributions intended to obtain tariff protection, patent protection, and other preferential government treatment.[6] In the extreme, a firm would be willing to spend an amount up to the potential monopoly profits to become a monopolist. Such rent-seeking activities would increase the welfare costs of a monopoly.

Two economists who considered this issue carefully, Keith Cowling and Dennis Mueller, used advertising expenditures to approximate the costs of monopolization to society.[7] Adding these costs to their estimate of deadweight loss, they estimated that the welfare cost of monopolization may be as high as 13 percent of GNP.

Finally, we note that in less competitive markets, there is less pressure on firms to use inputs efficiently. Inefficient monopolists may not be driven out of the market even in the long run. We consider this effect on costs, called **X-inefficiency**, in more detail in Chapter 3. Figure 2.14 illustrates the welfare implications of a monopolist operating under higher costs than a competitive industry. If monopolization raises costs, the deadweight loss triangle is larger. In addition, the costs of producing the monopoly output level are higher. The important welfare point is that if increasing competition in monopolized markets would lead to reduced costs, then estimates of welfare losses based on deadweight loss triangles such as Harberger's will be far too low.[8]

While the controversy over the welfare cost of market power has not been resolved, it is possible to step back and make three observations. First, even a relatively small percent of GNP represents a considerable amount of resources. In a

---

*Harberger assumed that price elasticities of demand in all industries were equal to 1 (in absolute value). This assumption implies that the firm is not maximizing profits because a profit-maximizing monopoly will always operate at a level of output for which the elasticity of demand is greater than 1.

†Harberger used the average profit rate of his sample industries as a measure of the competitive profit rate. Critics contend that this method automatically led to an underestimate of the deadweight loss because of the characteristics of Harberger's sample. His sample was limited to manufacturing industries, a sector that tends to have a higher rate of return than other sectors, such as agriculture, retail, and service. According to Harberger's critics, because many manufacturing industries are somewhat monopolistic, averaging profit rates across manufacturing industries would lead to an overstatement of the "competitive" profit rate.

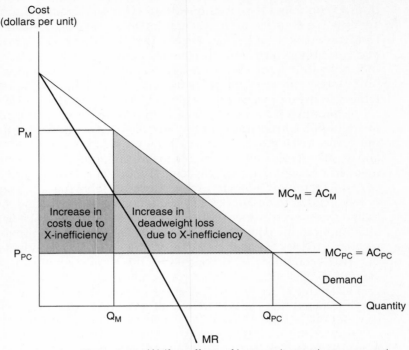

Cost (dollars per unit)

P_M

P_{PC}

$MC_M = AC_M$

Increase in costs due to X-inefficiency

Increase in deadweight loss due to X-inefficiency

$MC_{PC} = AC_{PC}$

Demand

Quantity

Q_M Q_{PC}

MR

Figure 2.14   Welfare effects of increased costs due to monopoly.

$6 trillion economy, 1 percent is $60 billion! Second, any strategic behavior on the part of firms intended to obtain or protect their monopoly positions raises the costs of monopolization substantially. Third, in some industries, the potential gains to society from decreasing monopoly power are large.

The Economics of Monopolistic Competition

Just as they generally agree on theoretical models of perfect competition and monopoly, economists tend to agree on the model of monopolistically competitive markets. The two important characteristics of monopolistic competition to keep in mind are product differentiation and easy entry and exit.

Product differentiation gives each monopolistic competitor some degree of market power and implies that it faces a downward-sloping demand curve, rather than the horizontal demand curve faced by a perfectly competitive firm. Short-run equilibrium for a monopolistically competitive firm is shown in Figure 2.15(a). Because the industry contains many firms, each firm's market power is limited and the firm's demand curve is less steeply sloped than the market demand curve. Figure 2.15(a) shows the usual profit-maximizing choice: produce the quantity of output, q_{SR}, for which marginal revenue equals marginal cost. The

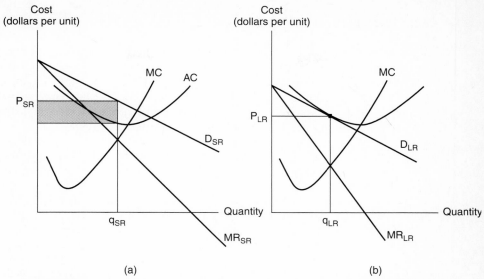

Figure 2.15   Short-run and long-run equilibrium for a monopolistically competitive firm.

corresponding price, P_{SR}, is above average cost, and thus the firm earns a positive economic profit.

As in perfect competition, this positive economic profit cannot persist in the long run. Attracted by profit, new firms will enter the industry. Entry shifts the firm's demand curve to the left, as shown in Figure 2.15(b). Entry continues until economic profits reach zero. In long-run equilibrium, the firm will produce q_{LR}, where marginal revenue equals marginal cost *and* where price equals average cost. Even though each firm has market power, the ease of entry and exit drives economic profits to zero.

Economists have identified two sources of inefficiency in a monopolistically competitive market. First, at the firm's profit-maximizing choice of output in both the short and long run, price is greater than marginal cost. Therefore, as in a monopoly, there is a deadweight loss in a monopolistically competitive market. Second, note from Figure 2.15 that in equilibrium the firm does not operate at the minimum of its average cost curve. This situation, in which the monopolistically competitive firm produces a smaller output level than that which minimizes average cost, is often described as "excess capacity." If fewer firms were in the industry, each could operate at a larger scale and a lower average cost. Note, however, that consumers undoubtedly value the opportunity to choose among a variety of products with different characteristics. The "variety" benefits of product differentiation must be considered in addition to the costs of the inefficiencies in formulating public policy.*

---

*The optimal amount of product differentiation in a monopolistically competitive market is analyzed in detail in Chapter 13.

Cautions

So far we have reviewed the theories of perfect competition, monopoly, and monopolistic competition. We have also looked at the welfare comparison between perfect competition and monopoly and between perfect competition and monopolistic competition. At this point it is useful to consider certain complicating factors—reasons why policymakers might not want to attack firms with market power as aggressively as simple theory might suggest.

One important reason for allowing a firm to possess at least some degree of market power is the existence of economies of scale in production. If a firm's long-run average cost curve decreases significantly as the quantity of output it produces increases, then it would be inefficient to have output produced by many small firms. In the extreme case, called a **natural monopoly**, one firm can serve the market at lower average cost than can more than one firm. We examine the empirical evidence on economies of scale in much more detail in Chapter 5.

A second reason to hesitate before recommending that policymakers stamp out all monopoly power is concern about the rate of technological change. Our simple welfare comparison of perfect competition and monopoly is a static comparison—a comparison at one specific point in time. As we shall discover, theory suggests that firms possessing market power may be more innovative than perfectly competitive firms. Perfectly competitive firms, for example, may lack the resources necessary to invest in research and development (R&D). Consider farmers, who do not typically do agricultural research. If there is a connection between market power and innovation, we might willingly accept some deadweight loss today in return for the considerable benefits associated with new products and new production techniques in the future. Recent antitrust policy has given increasing weight to concerns about technological change. Technological change is discussed in much greater detail in Chapter 14.

Finally, our comparison of perfect competition and monopoly must be reconsidered in light of the second-best theorem. There are many instances in the real world in which perfect competition is not feasible or even desirable. Inputs such as raw materials and managerial talent may be scarce, so that there cannot be many firms in an industry. Substantial economies of scale may dictate an industry structure in which firms possess at least some market power. Lipsey and Lancaster examined the welfare considerations of imposing perfect competition in some but not all markets in the economy.[9] Their second-best theorem states that overall welfare *may* improve by selectively achieving perfect competition—but it may not. In a second-best world, it is impossible to give general advice to policy makers.

Statistical Tools

Throughout this book we use economic theory to organize information about how firms ought to behave in various circumstances. Theory, however, can take us only so far. Theory can almost never tell us the magnitude, and sometimes cannot even predict the direction, of an expected response to some change in economic conditions. Therefore, economists turn to empirical techniques. The most widely used statistical technique in economics is **regression analysis**. This is a way of quantifying economic relationships and using economic data to test hypotheses about the relationships between economic variables.

Suppose that an economist wants to investigate the relationship between market structure and profits. The theories of perfect competition and monopoly suggest a simple hypothesis: economic profits increase as markets become more concentrated.* Let X_1 stand for a measure of market structure and Y for a measure of economic profits. (We examine the relationship between market structure and economic profits in detail in Chapter 17.)

We can graph a simple relationship between these two variables using a scatter diagram. Each point in this diagram represents an observation for a firm or an industry. Because our simple hypothesis is that an increase in concentration leads to an increase in economic profits, values of X_1 are plotted on the horizontal axis and values of Y are graphed on the vertical axis. If the hypothesis about the relationship between market concentration and economic profits is correct, a scatter diagram of data on X_1 should look like Figure 2.16(a): as the value of X_1 (market concentration) increases, so does the value of Y (profits). If the hypothesis is not correct, a scatter diagram might look like Figure 2.16(b), where there is no relationship between the values of X_1 and Y.

We can also express the hypothesis about the relationship between market structure and profits using a simple linear equation:

$$Y = \alpha_0 + \alpha_1 X_1$$

Here Y is called the **dependent variable**, X_1 is the **independent** or **explanatory** variable, and αs are the **parameters** of the equation. In this equation of a straight line α_0 is the vertical intercept and α_1 is the slope. If the hypothesis about the relationship between market structure and profits is correct, α_1 should be positive.

If no other factors affected profits, then all of the observations of X_1 and Y would lie exactly on the line. Profits, however, are likely to depend on many other variables, including some unobservable factors such as management skills. These unobservable factors are represented in the equation by ϵ, an error term:

$$Y = \alpha_0 + \alpha_1 X_1 + \epsilon$$

Because of the omitted factors, actual observations do not lie on a straight line but around it, as Figure 2.16(a) shows. The vertical distance between each data point and a straight line fitted through the observations is called the *residual*. AB shows the residual for the observation located at point A.

It is possible to sketch more than one line through the observations. Therefore, we need to decide which of these lines is "best." The most common method for fitting the line through data points is least squares regression. This

---

*Roughly speaking, the more concentrated a market, the closer it is to being a monopoly. Measures of market concentration are discussed in Chapter 4.

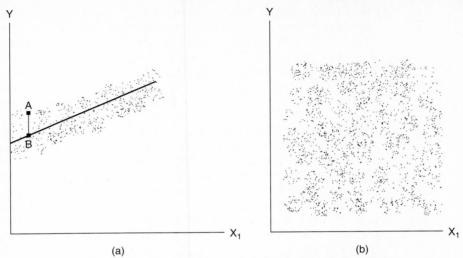

(a)   (b)

Figure 2.16   Hypothetical scatter diagrams of data on Y and X.

technique chooses values of α_0 and α_1 such that when all the residuals are squared and added together, the resulting sum is minimized. Note that least squares treats positive errors (where the actual observation lies above the fitted line) and negative errors (where the actual point lies below the fitted line) symmetrically. It also gives greater weight to larger residuals.

Least squares regression can also be used when theory suggests that more than one independent or explanatory variable exists, although graphing such relationships quickly becomes very difficult. For example, economies of scale may be a second important determinant of profitability. Letting X_2 represent economies of scale, the equation becomes:

$$Y = \alpha_0 + \alpha_1 X_1 + \alpha_2 X_2 + \epsilon$$

Now, α_1 measures the effect of an increase in market concentration on profits with the effect of economies of scale held constant. Similarly, α_2 measures the effect of an increase in economies of scale on profits with the effect of market concentration held constant. To get meaningful results, it is important to include all relevant variables in the model. Otherwise, some effects that are due to an omitted variable might be mistakenly attributed to the included variable(s). For example, if economies of scale were left out of the estimated equation, the least squares estimate of α_1 would reflect not only the effects of market concentration on profits but also the effects of economies of scale on profits. Economic theory is the guide in deciding which variables should be included in a model.

Economists typically do not have data on an entire population, such as all of the firms within an industry. They therefore use data from a sample—a fraction of the relevant population—to calculate estimates of various parameters. The least squares estimates of the parameters of the model depend on the particular sample of observations used for the estimation. Using a different sample of firms would give different estimates of the parameters. Because of this, we want to know how close the estimates from any sample are to the true values—those that would be obtained from using the entire population—of the parameters. We want to be able to reach conclusions about the contribution of each independent variable to changes in the dependent variable and about how well the estimated equation fits the data.

Fortunately, simple statistical tests allow us to answer these questions.* Suppose that we have estimated a regression equation and want to know whether our estimate of α_1 indicates a true relationship between market concentration and profits, or whether the estimated coefficient is an artifact of the sample. Roughly speaking, we want to know whether α_1 is zero or whether it is greater than zero, as theory suggests. To test the hypothesis that a true parameter is actually equal to zero, we can look at a test statistic called the *t-statistic*.† The t-statistic is defined as:

$$t = \frac{\hat{\alpha}}{\text{standard error of } \hat{\alpha}}$$

where $\hat{\alpha}$ is the least squares estimate of α and the standard error of $\hat{\alpha}$ is a measure of the dispersion of estimates of α around its mean.

High absolute values of t-statistics (a rough rule of thumb is a t-statistic greater than or equal to 2 in absolute value) indicate that it is unlikely that the true value of α is zero. In such a case, we would have evidence for a true relationship between the explanatory variable and the dependent variable, and we would say that α is statistically significant. Low absolute values of t-statistics, however, provide evidence that the true value of α may well be zero, indicating that the independent variable does not help explain variation in the dependent variable. Coefficients with small t-statistics are said to be not statistically significant.‡

In addition to examining the effect of a specific independent variable on the dependent variable, we may want to know how closely the estimated regression line fits the data. A statistic that provides information about the overall goodness-of-fit of the regression is called R-squared, written R^2. This statistic measures the percentage of the total variation of the dependent variable around its mean value that is explained by all of the independent variables included in the model. Its value ranges from 0, meaning that the independent variables account for none of the variation in the dependent variable, to 1, indicating that the independent variables completely explain the variation in the dependent variable.

---

*The validity of these tests depends on certain assumptions about the error term. A course in econometrics examines these assumptions in detail and considers the implications of violations of the assumptions.

†Economists typically use one of several standard statistical computer packages that estimate least squares parameters and report information about the regression such as the t-statistics.

‡In some cases estimated coefficients have large standard errors, and thus low t-statistics, even though the true values of the parameters are not zero. This occurs as a result of a problem called **multicollinearity**. In this situation two or more of the independent variables are very highly correlated, meaning that they tend to move together. This makes it hard to separate the independent effects of the variables.

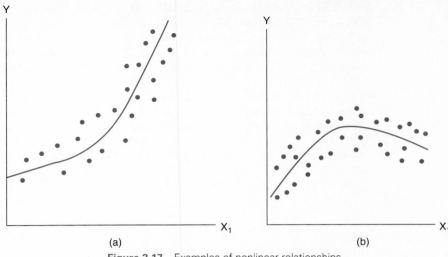

Figure 2.17   Examples of nonlinear relationships.

As an example, suppose we collected data on profits and a measure of market concentration and ran a regression, obtaining the following results:

$$Y = 2.65 + 0.567X_1$$
$$(3.46)$$

$$R^2 = 0.27$$

The number in parentheses is the t-statistic for the coefficient $\alpha_1 = 0.567$. These results would suggest that there is a positive and statistically significant relationship between market concentration and profits. The R^2 of 0.27 indicates that market power explains only 27 percent of the total variation in profits.

Because it is so easy to look at the R^2 as a summary statistic, we caution against putting too much emphasis on R^2. A high R^2 is not sufficient evidence to conclude that the variables included in the model are the appropriate ones. For example, even if a regression of sales of new homes on the price of soda happened to yield a high R^2, our knowledge of economics should lead us to question the validity of the results. In fact, adding additional explanatory variables will increase R^2, regardless of the economic importance of the variables. Economic theory should always serve as a check on the interpretation of empirical results.

Finally, several issues should be kept in mind when looking at the results of any regression. First, is the specification of the model correct—that is, does the model leave out any variables that theory suggests should be included? Earlier we noted that omitting a relevant variable biases the estimation. A second issue concerns the functional form of the equation. The equations discussed thus far assume that all of the explanatory variables affect profits in a linear fashion. While this is a convenient assumption, it is not the only possibility. The relationship between an independent variable and the dependent variable may be nonlinear. Figure 2.17 shows two common nonlinear shapes. To estimate a relationship of the form shown in Figure 2.17(a), a researcher can use a log-linear functional form, estimating a regression in which the dependent variable is log y rather than y. A relationship such as that shown in Figure 2.17(b) can be estimated using a quadratic functional form, in which both X and X^2 are included as explanatory variables. A third issue is the quality of the data. Industrial organization data are often of less than ideal quality. Problems with data include market definitions that are too broad or too narrow from an economic perspective, accounting data that do not accurately measure the relevant economic variables, and measurement errors due to various incentives facing those filling out the forms to inflate or deflate reported figures.

SUMMARY

1. While very few industries can be classified as either perfectly competitive or purely monopolistic, examining these theoretical extremes is useful. The perfectly competitive model serves as an important reference point for examining other industry structures, and the monopoly model shows how a firm with market power chooses its price and output level.

2. Any profit-maximizing firm, regardless of industry structure, will choose the quantity of output for which marginal revenue equals marginal cost.

3. It is important to distinguish between accounting costs and economic costs. Although accounting costs are reported by firms in their financial reports, it is economic costs that are relevant for a firm's decisions.

4. A firm's cost curves differ depending on the time period under consideration. In the short run, at least one of the firm's inputs is held constant; total short-run cost can thus be divided into fixed cost and variable cost. The shape of the short-run cost curves is determined by the marginal product of the variable input with an inverse relationship between the marginal product and the marginal cost.

5. In the long run, all inputs are variable and the firm can choose whatever combination of inputs allows it to produce a given level of output at the lowest possible cost. The shape of a firm's long-run average cost curve depends on the returns to scale. Increasing returns to scale, or economies of scale, imply a negatively sloped long-run average cost curve, whereas a positively sloped long-run average cost curve corresponds to decreasing returns to scale.

6. Economies of scale can exist at the product, plant, and multiplant levels. Sources of economies of scale include specialization, increases in the size of processing units, economies of massed reserves, spreading of overhead, and access to national capital or advertising markets.

7. Because of the characteristics of a perfectly competitive market, each firm takes price as given by the market equilibrium of supply and demand. It thus chooses output under the assumption that it faces a hori-

zontal demand curve for its own output, making the demand curve and the marginal revenue curve the same.

8. In the short run, a perfectly competitive firm will produce the output for which price equals (short-run) marginal cost as long as that price is greater than the average avoidable cost. If all fixed costs are sunk, average avoidable cost is identical to average variable cost.

9. In the long run, profit-maximizing perfectly competitive firms choose the output level at which price is equal to long-run marginal cost.

10. Market equilibrium is the intersection of the market demand and market supply curves. In the short run a perfectly competitive firm may be making positive, negative, or zero economic profits. In the long run, equilibrium price must equal average cost so that economic profits equal zero.

11. In long-run equilibrium in a competitive industry performance is allocatively efficient. Competitive equilibrium also exhibits efficiency in production, with each firm producing at the minimum point on its average cost curve.

12. A monopoly is the only producer of a product that has no close substitutes. Because the monopoly faces the market demand curve, marginal revenue is less than price. This implies that at the monopoly's profit-maximizing level of output, price is greater than marginal cost.

13. A monopolist's ability to charge a price that is above marginal cost depends on the elasticity of market demand. The less elastic the demand, the greater the market power the monopoly has.

14. The deadweight loss triangle is a measure of the misallocation of resources from monopoly. Many economists have estimated the size of the deadweight loss. Their estimates range from as low as 0.1 percent of GNP to as high as 13 percent of GNP.

15. A monopolistically competitive market is one in which products are differentiated and in which entry and exit are easy. In equilibrium in a monopolistically competitive market, price is greater than marginal cost, resulting in deadweight loss. Also, in long-run equilibrium, monopolistically competitive firms are not operating at the minimum of their average cost curves. However, consumers undoubtedly value the opportunity to choose among a variety of products with different characteristics.

16. The simple comparison of competition and monopoly highlights the resource misallocation associated with market power. However, policy makers need to keep a few cautions in mind. In particular, significant economies of scale or dynamic considerations concerning technological change may warrant a more lenient attitude toward monopoly power than the simple model suggests.

17. The final section of the chapter summarizes some basics of regression analysis, the most widely used statistical technique in economics. Empirical work is an important component of industrial organization.

KEY TERMS

accounting cost	multicollinearity
allocative efficiency	natural monopoly
average variable cost	opportunity cost
average cost	parameters
average fixed cost	pecuniary economies
avoidable cost	perfect competition
consumer suplus	price elasticity of demand
deadweight loss	producer surplus
dependent variable	production function
diseconomies of scale	profits
economic cost	real economies
economies of scale	regression analysis
efficiency in production	rental rate
explanatory variable	returns to scale
fixed cost	shutdown point
independent variable	sunk cost
Lerner index	total cost
marginal cost	total revenue
marginal revenue	total variable cost
market power	variable cost
monopoly	X-inefficiency

DISCUSSION QUESTIONS

1. "Accounting rules determine the dollar value of a firm's profits. Therefore, a firm should be concerned with accounting costs rather than economic costs." Discuss.

2. The owner of a small plant store does her own accounting work. Discuss how to measure the cost of her time.

3. Explain why the purchase price of a machine is not the relevant price for a firm trying to decide how much labor and how much capital to use in producing output.

4. Suppose you know that a firm's long-run average cost curve decreases as output increases up to 2,000 units of output, and is constant beyond that level of output. What do you know about returns to scale for the firm's production function? Explain your reasoning.

5. Consumer theory tells us that, other things being equal, consumers normally buy more of a good as its price falls. Given this, explain how we can say that the demand curve facing a perfectly competitive firm is horizontal.

6. Why would a firm that is making negative economic profits in the short run choose to produce rather than shut down? Explain the relevance of fixed and sunk costs for this decision.

7. Why would a profit-maximizing firm choose to enter an industry in which it expected to earn zero long-run profits? Why would it stay in such an industry?

8. What do economists mean by the statement that perfect competition leads to efficiency?

9. Explain why price is greater than marginal revenue for a monopoly. What implication does this have for the relationship between price and marginal cost at the profit-maximizing level of output?

10. Explain why the Lerner index can be viewed as a measure of monopoly or market power. What determines the magnitude of the Lerner index for a profit-maximizing monopoly?

11. Describe Harberger's approach to measuring the deadweight loss of a monopoly. Why might his estimate have been too low? too high?

12. "Allocative inefficiency and productive inefficiency are the 'price' of product variety." Discuss.

PROBLEMS

1. Consider the owner of a small lawn-mowing service. She can use one of two methods to mow lawns. The first is to purchase a tractor that costs $200 a year to own and then spend $1 (for labor and gas) for every acre of grass cut. The second is to spend $40 on a used push mower that will last one year and then spend $5 (for labor) for every acre of grass cut.

   a. Write down the total cost functions for the two methods, letting q represent the number of acres of grass cut per year.

   b. Find the average cost function and the marginal cost for each of the two methods.

   c. Assume first that the tractor has no resale value. What is the smallest number of acres of grass cut per year for which she should buy the tractor?

   d. Now assume that the tractor has a positive resale value. How does this change affect the decision about which method of mowing lawns should be chosen?

2. A perfectly competitive firm has the following short-run cost function:

$$SRTC = q^2 + 30q + 400$$

   The corresponding short-run marginal cost function is given by:

$$SRMC = 2q + 30$$

   a. If the market price is $50, how much output will this firm produce? Is $50 a long-run equilibrium price? Explain your reasoning.

   b. Find the equation of this firm's short-run supply function.

3. Consider a perfectly competitive firm with a total cost function given by TC = $q^2 + 100$, where q is the level of output. The marginal cost function is given by MC = 2q.

   a. If the price of output is $60, how much output should the firm produce?

   b. Find the firm's profits at this level of output.

   c. Find the equation of the firm's short-run supply curve.

   d. If there are 100 identical firms in the market, find the equation of the industry supply curve.

4. A monopoly can produce at constant average and marginal costs of AC = MC = 5. The market demand curve is given by:

$$P = 53 - Q.$$

   a. Use the twice as steep rule to find the equation of the marginal revenue curve corresponding to the market demand curve.

   b. Calculate the profit-maximizing quantity of output for the monopoly. What price will it charge?

   c. Find the monopoly's profits.

   d. Find the consumer surplus under monopoly.

   e. What level of output would be produced by this industry under perfect competition? What would the perfectly competitive price be?

   f. Find the consumer surplus under perfect competition.

   g. What is the value of the deadweight loss from monopolization of this industry?

   h. Verify that the sum of consumer surplus under monopoly, monopoly profits, and deadweight loss is equal to consumer surplus under perfect competition.

5. Consider a monopolist with the following costs:

$$TC = 2Q^2$$

$$MC = 4Q$$

   The market demand curve is given by:

$$P = 96 - 6Q$$

   a. Use the twice as steep rule to find the equation of the marginal revenue curve corresponding to the market demand curve.

   b. Determine the price the monopolist will charge and the quantity of output it will produce.

   c. Find the monopolist's profits.

REFERENCES

1. This section and the section on empirical estimates of economies of scale draw upon work done by F. M. Scherer and his colleagues. References include F. M. Scherer, "Economies of Scale and Industrial Concentration," in Harvey J. Goldschmid, H. Michael Mann, and J. Fred Weston (eds.), *Industrial Concentration: The New Learning*

(Boston: Little, Brown, 1974), pp. 16–54; F. M. Scherer, Alan Beckenstein, Erich Kaufer, and R. D. Murphy, *The Economics of Multi-Plant Operation: An International Comparisons Study* (Cambridge, MA: Harvard University Press, 1975); and F. M. Scherer and David Ross, *Industrial Market Structure and Economic Performance,* 3rd edition (Boston: Houghton Mifflin, 1990), Chapter 4.

2. The phrase comes from E. A. G. Robinson, *The Structure of Competitive Industry,* rev. ed. (Chicago: University of Chicago Press, 1958), pp. 26–27.

3. Arnold C. Harberger, "Monopoly and Resource Allocation," *American Economic Review*, Papers and Proceedings, 44 (May 1954): 77–87.

4. A summary of the methodological and empirical controversies surrounding the calculation of welfare loss is found in Frederic Jenny and Andre-Paul Weber, "Aggregate Welfare Loss Due to Monopoly Power in the French Economy: Some Tentative Estimates," *The Journal of Industrial Economics* 22 (December 1983): 113–29.

5. David R. Kamerschen, "An Estimation of the Welfare Losses from Monopoly in the American Economy," *Western Economic Journal* 4 (Summer 1966): 221–36; and Keith Cowling and Dennis C. Mueller, "The Social Costs of Monopoly Power," *Economic Journal* 88 (December 1978): 724–48, with comment by S. C. Littlechild, *Economic Journal* 91 (June 1981): 348–63, and reply by Cowling and Mueller, *Economic Journal* 91 (September 1981): 721–25.

6. Gordon Tullock, "The Welfare Costs of Tariffs, Monopolies and Theft," *Western Economic Journal* 5 (June 1967): 224–32, and Richard A. Posner, "The Social Costs of Monopoly and Regulation," *Journal of Political Economy* 83 (August 1975): 807–27.

7. Cowling and Mueller, *Supra* note 5.

8. Comanor and Leibenstein (William S. Comanor and Harvey Leibenstein, "Allocative Efficiency, X-Efficiency and the Measurement of Welfare Loss," *Economica* 36 [August 1969]: 304–9), estimate that the pure X-inefficiency effect of monopoly may be as high 9 percent of net national product.

9. R. G. Lipsey and Kelvin Lancaster, "The General Theory of Second Best," *Review of Economic Studies* 24 (1956): 11–32.

Chapter 3

Objectives of the Firm

Throughout this book we will spend much time analyzing the actions of firms in oligopolistic industries and examining the consequences of those actions for market behavior and performance. How is price set in an oligopoly? What factors determine expenditures on advertising? Do firms in an oligopoly spend proportionately more or less on research and development than firms in a competitive industry? Before considering these questions, it is necessary to examine the structure of a modern firm and look carefully at the important assumption of profit maximization. Throughout the review of the economics of perfect competition and monopoly in Chapter 2, we assumed that firms maximized profits. Now it's time to question whether this assumption makes sense for real-world firms.

The Neoclassical Firm

Suppose that at the beginning of your first microeconomics course, your professor had asked you to name some firms. Your list might have included General Motors, Exxon, IBM, Xerox, Coca-Cola, and Procter & Gamble. All of these firms are among the fifty largest U.S. Industrial Corporations as ranked by *Fortune*. You probably noticed in your microeconomics course that a "firm" in economic theory appeared to be quite different from these real-world large corporations.

Microeconomists usually model a firm as a single entity with a clear goal that it pursues without any wasted effort. The traditional neoclassical firm is represented by a production function that summarizes the relationship between inputs and output given the current technology. Regardless of industry structure, each firm is assumed to maximize profits, making it possible to precisely predict its output and pricing decisions. Because all firms are assumed to maximize profits, any differences in performance—such as across industries or over time within the same industry—must be due to factors external to the firm, such as the structure of the market or technology. In Chapter 2, for example, economic theory predicted that the price set by a monopolist would be above the perfectly competitive price for that same industry. The higher monopoly price resulted from the difference in industry structure and *not* from any difference in the firms' objectives. Monopolists and perfectly competitive firms were striving equally hard to achieve the same goal: the highest possible profits.

Real-world firms are much more complex than the neoclassical firm of microeconomic theory. Firms today often operate in many different product and geographical markets and are characterized by many operating divisions and levels. Recognizing the complex structure of present-day firms, economists have begun to think more carefully about the firm.[1]

This chapter examines work on the theory of the firm and explores the reasonableness of the profit-maximization assumption in light of that work. Some critics of profit maximization have focused on the role of corporate managers in daily business decisions, asking what motivates these managers. Other critics have pointed out the implications of large size and structural complexity for the realism of the assumption of profit maximization. Analyzing firm conduct becomes much more complicated without the assumption of profit maximization. Once the assumption of profit maximization is abandoned, for example, analyzing firm decisions such as pricing and advertising strategies requires an examination not only of market structure but also of the objectives of the firm, and the already challenging task of predicting strategies of oligopolistic firms becomes even more formidable.

The Theory of the Firm

A number of economists have focused attention on the theory of the firm, recognizing that the firm, unlike the consumer, is not an individual decision maker. Rather, the firm can be regarded as a series of contracts between a number of parties, including the workers, the managers, and the suppliers of capital. Some of these contracts are explicit; an example is the contract between Ford and the United Automobile Workers. Other contracts are implicit, reflecting managers' and workers' understandings about the conditions of work. As you can imagine, contracts vary widely across different types of firms. The theory of the firm examines the reasons for different types of explicit and implicit contracts and considers how these types of contracts affect the operation of the firm.

This chapter examines two aspects of the theory of the firm. The first is the scope of the firm. What factors determine whether production takes place within or outside of a firm? Why are some activities coordinated by the price signals of the market and others by the managers of firms? The modern theory of the firm tries to answer questions such as these.

After reviewing the main types of firms in existence today, we turn to the second issue: managerial contracts and the possible conflicts between the goals of the owners and those of the managers of a firm. Here we'll also consider possible incentives that can be created to encourage profit maximization as well as constraints on managerial behavior.

A FIRM'S BOUNDARIES

As early as 1937, Ronald Coase recognized that the firm and the market were alternative ways of organizing production.[2] Consider, for example, the production of a VCR. One possible way to produce a VCR is to have a firm perform only one stage of production, such as assembly. Such a firm would buy all the necessary parts from independent suppliers, assemble the VCR, and then turn the completed product over to another firm for marketing. At the other extreme, production of all parts, assembly, and marketing could be done within one large firm. How does a firm decide when it will produce a necessary input internally and when it will rely on the marketplace?

Coase argued that a firm would expand until the costs of undertaking a transaction internally were just equal to the costs of using the market to handle that transaction. The costs of using the market are called **transaction costs**. Williamson has built upon Coase's point, writing extensively on the importance of transaction costs and the types of organizational structures that have been developed to minimize transaction costs.[3]

Advantages of the Market

Williamson points out three production cost advantages of using the market.[4] First, suppose production of some input is subject to substantial economies of scale, yet suppose also that an individual firm requires only a relatively small quantity of that input. By aggregating the demands of many such small firms for that input, a single producer can realize economies of scale and produce at a lower average cost. Similarly, markets may aggregate related demands, allowing realization of **economies of scope** not available to a single firm.* A third production cost advantage associated with the market is reduction of risk. If there are uncertainties in demand for a single firm's product, a market can reduce risk by pooling demands over many firms.†

Using the market also enables a firm to take advantage of competitive pressures to control its costs. After all, as we discussed in Chapter 2, a competitive market allocates resources efficiently and results in production at the lowest possible cost. In Williamson's words, "Markets promote high-powered incentives and restrain bureaucratic distortions more effectively than internal organization."[5] Assuming there are a number of potential suppliers, a firm can search for the lowest cost producer by purchasing rather than making an input.

Advantages of the Firm

Given the advantages of using the market to procure inputs, why would a firm ever choose to produce some inputs internally? Coase and Williamson point out that there are also costs of using the market, and that in certain circumstances, these costs are high enough that they outweigh the production cost advantages of markets. Specifically, if transaction costs are high, firms are likely to turn to internal production.

---

*Economies of scope occur when it is less costly to produce two products together rather than producing each separately. Economies of scale and scope are discussed in detail in Chapter 5.

†The risk reduction benefit of pooling occurs as long as the individual firms' demands are not perfectly correlated.

Transaction costs arise from activities such as searching for a supplier, negotiating with the supplier about contract terms, arranging for delivery, and monitoring the quality of the input. Two assumptions are important in transaction cost economics. The first is **bounded rationality**. The assumption of bounded rationality recognizes that limits on knowledge, foresight, skill, and time constrain individuals' ability to solve complex problems.[6] Because of bounded rationality, a firm cannot write a contract ahead of time that covers all contingencies.*

Williamson notes, however, that even an incomplete contract that does not cover all possible outcomes could be used to carry out transactions if it were not for the second assumption of transaction cost economics: the presence of **opportunism**. In Williamson's words, opportunism is "self-interest seeking with guile."[7] Opportunism involves the usual behavioral assumption that individuals act to maximize their utility. But, in addition, opportunism postulates that economic agents will try to mislead, disguise, and confuse others if it is to their advantage to do so and if they think such activities cannot be detected easily. Because of opportunism, economic agents are not completely trustworthy.

As noted earlier, a firm is likely to rely on internal production rather than use the market when transaction costs are high. This is likely to occur when it is difficult to write a contract that eliminates the potential for opportunistic behavior. Three dimensions of transactions are important in identifying these circumstances: their frequency, the amount of uncertainty associated with transactions, and the degree of asset specificity.[8]

Frequency. Imagine a firm negotiating for the services of a machine. If these services will be needed only once or a few times, the firm can use the market. On the other hand, if these services will be needed repeatedly, the transaction costs of using the market will be high because of the frequent renegotiation costs. The more frequent a firm's need for an input, the more the firm can save on transaction costs by internal production.

Uncertainty. Williamson discusses three kinds of uncertainty. Primary uncertainty arises because circumstances can change and no one can predict the future perfectly. Secondary uncertainty is caused by lack of communication. One decision maker may simply not know what plans are being made by others, and transferring information accurately and completely is a difficult task. Finally, Williamson recognizes a third kind of uncertainty, behavioral uncertainty, that can result from strategic—or opportunistic—decisions about disclosure of information.

Whatever the nature of uncertainty, the conclusion of transaction cost economics is that the higher the degree of uncertainty, the higher are the transaction costs. A firm can provide adaptability to changing circumstances at lower cost than can the market.

Asset Specificity. **Asset specificity** refers to the degree to which some assets are of value primarily to one firm. Assets can be specific as a result of geographic location, physical characteristics, or specialized human capital. A professor who

---

*Using the terminology of the theory of the firm, bounded rationality implies that contracts are of necessity incomplete.

can teach industrial organization well is of value to any institution (or "firm") that wants to offer that course. However, a computer classroom set up on a specific campus is of value only to that institution because it cannot be transported elsewhere. Other examples of specialized assets are a pipeline from an oil refinery to an isolated distribution terminal and brand-name capital.

Transactions that involve highly specialized assets are likely to be costly. Once the investment in a specialized asset has been made, buyer and seller are in a bilateral relationship in which each side has few other options. This is likely to lead to difficult and expensive negotiations, possibly involving considerable bargaining and bluffs on each side. If the firm owns the specialized asset, however, the incentive for opportunistic behavior is reduced, lowering the associated transactions costs.

In summary, Williamson's expansion of Coase's original insight still maintains the usual assumption that a firm is interested in minimizing costs. The addition is that costs are recognized as the sum of the usual production costs and transactions costs. The more frequent a transaction, the greater the uncertainty, and the higher the degree of asset specificity, the more likely it is that an activity will be performed internally rather than across the market for any given level of production costs.

The Structure of Modern Firms

Having thought about the theoretical aspects of external versus internal procurement, we now turn our attention to the way in which modern firms are actually organized. Firm ownership takes several forms, with the most common in the United States being sole proprietorships, partnerships, and corporations.* Until the end of the nineteenth century, almost all firms were organized as sole proprietorships or partnerships. Two characteristics of proprietorships and partnerships became increasingly disadvantageous as technology and industry structure began to change in the years between the end of the Civil War and the beginning of the twentieth century.[9] One was *unlimited* liability. If a proprietorship or a partnership fails, the owner(s) can lose *all* assets, both business and personal. Also, proprietorships and partnerships both have *finite lives*. If one member of a partnership leaves or dies, the entire firm is automatically dissolved and a new partnership must be formed to continue the business.

By number, sole proprietorships and partnerships are still the dominant form of organization of firms in the United States. About 80 percent of businesses today are proprietorships or partnerships. These firms, however, are typically small and undergo a high rate of turnover each year. Proprietorships and partnerships account for only 10 percent of total sales in the United States.[10]

The vast majority of sales in the United States today are made by corporations. A corporation is a separate legal entity, created by government charter and given certain powers, privileges, and liabilities. An idea of the magnitude of some of today's largest corporations is shown in Table 3.1.

---

*Other forms of ownership include labor-managed firms and not-for-profit firms.

TABLE 3.1   **Ten Largest U.S. Industrial Corporations in 1995**

Firm	Industry	1995 Sales ($ millions)	1995 Assets ($ millions)
General Motors	Motor vehicles and parts	168,828.6	217,123.4
Ford Motor	Motor vehicles and parts	137,137.0	243,283.0
Exxon	Petroleum refining	110,009.0	91,296.0
Wal-Mart Stores	General merchandisers	93,627.0	37,871.0
AT&T	Telecommunications	79,609.0	88,884.0
IBM	Computers	71,940.0	80,292.0
General Electric	Electronics, electronic equipment	70,028.0	228,035.0
Mobil	Petroleum refining	66,724.0	42,138.0
Chrysler	Motor vehicles	53,195.0	53,756.0
Philip Morris	Tobacco	53,139.0	53,811.6

Source: Fortune, April 29, 1996, p. F1.

An important advantage of a corporation is that its owners have limited liability. Ownership of a corporation takes the form of holding of shares of stock which can be bought or sold. The owners, the shareholders, are liable only for the amount they paid to buy the shares of stock initially. This limit on the amount an owner can lose makes it less risky to invest in the firm than if the owner could also lose his or her personal assets. Also, a corporation has an infinite life; it is not automatically dissolved when an owner decides to leave the business. Because of these advantages, corporations can raise large sums of money more easily than can proprietorships or partnerships. The ability to raise large sums of money became increasingly important in the late 1800s as the minimum efficient size of firms grew.* Since then the corporate form of organization has gained steadily in prominence.

SEPARATION OF OWNERSHIP AND CONTROL

Before the 1900s, when most firms were organized as sole proprietorships or partnerships, ownership and control of the firm were combined in the hands of one or a few people. The person who made the day-to-day decisions was also the person who received any profits from the firm's operations. As corporations developed, however, ownership and control became increasingly separated.

The owners of a corporation are its stockholders, and a large corporation typically has many, many owners. General Electric, for example, has over 500,000 shareholders, IBM has over 700,000, and AT&T has over 2.5 million. While there

---

*Minimum efficient size, or minimum efficient scale, is the smallest level of output for which long-run average cost is at its lowest level. This concept and its importance are considered further in Chapter 5.

are many owners in the modern corporation, the day-to-day corporate business decisions are made by a relative handful of professional managers. In theory, the stockholders elect a board of directors to oversee the managers, ensuring that the owners' interests are represented. In practice, however, the candidates for the board of directors for the vast majority of corporations are selected by the managers. Few stockholders typically attend a corporation's annual meeting. Instead they give the managers their proxies, or permission to vote on behalf of the nominated candidates. Consequently, many corporate boards of directors are more of a rubber-stamping body than an independent group vigilantly examining the decisions made by management and protecting the interests of the owners.[11] In fact, over 80 percent of the largest 200 nonfinancial corporations in the United States today are considered to be controlled by management.[12]

MANAGERIAL OBJECTIVES

Why does it matter whether a firm is controlled by its owners or by managers? Let's start by accepting a central assumption of microeconomic theory: individuals try to maximize their own utility, the total satisfaction or benefit from consuming a good. This principle applies to people when operating firms as well as when behaving as consumers. The people who run firms will maximize profits *as long as* profit maximization is in their best interest. When the firm is run by its owners, profit maximization and utility maximization are consistent goals, because the main source of income for the owners is the firm's profits.*[13]

When ownership and control are separate, however, profit maximization and utility maximization may conflict as managers pursue objectives other than maximizing profits. Some important theories of managerial behavior are considered below.

Sales Maximization

In an early alternative to profit maximization, William Baumol hypothesized that managers attempt to maximize sales revenue.[14] Managers may focus on sales rather than on profits if managing a "large" company adds to their sense of status and prestige. Rankings such as the Fortune 500 are typically made on the basis of sales. Also, salaries may be more closely tied to sales or to the growth rate of sales than to profits. Commissions based on sales, for example, provide an incentive to focus on maximizing revenues rather than profits.

Figure 3.1 compares the profit-maximizing output level to the sales-maximizing output level for a monopolist facing a linear, negatively sloped market demand curve. By definition, a sales maximizer wants to produce and sell another unit of output as long as doing so increases total revenue, that is, as long as marginal revenue is positive. Maximum total revenue occurs at the quantity for which marginal revenue equals zero. In Figure 3.1, this is q_2. As Figure 3.1 shows, the sales-maximizing level of output is higher than the profit-maximizing level of

---

*If owner-managers also value nonpecuniary benefits, economic theory predicts that, in equilibrium, some expenditures will be made on benefits.

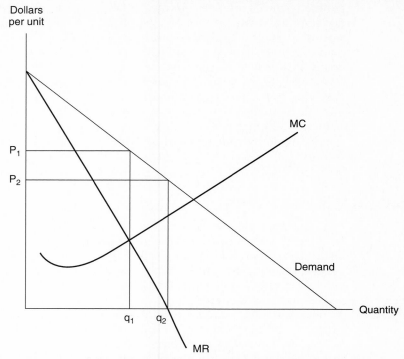

Figure 3.1 Sales maximization versus profit maximization by a monopolist.

output, q_1. It is important to note that because sales maximization increases the level of output chosen by the monopolist, the welfare loss due to monopoly is lessened. To sell this higher level of output, the sales-maximizing monopolist will set price below the profit-maximizing level, decreasing the gap between price and marginal cost.

The sales maximization model is frequently modified by introducing a minimum profit constraint.* Figure 3.2 shows the effects of such a constraint. Maximum profits occur at q_1, where the vertical distance between the total revenue and total cost curves is greatest and the "profit hill" reaches a maximum. This is also the quantity for which marginal revenue equals marginal cost, as shown in Figure 3.1. Output q_2 is the sales-maximizing quantity of output, where TR reaches its maximum or, equivalently, where marginal revenue is equal to zero, as shown in Figure 3.1. A very "tight" profit constraint, such as OA, will in fact force managers to maximize profits. A somewhat looser constraint such as OB will force managers to produce an output less than q_2, although they will produce an output greater than q_1. Finally, a very loose constraint on profits such as OC

*The arguments for such a constraint include consideration of stockholders, who might notice and be unhappy about profits well below the maximum attainable level, and the threat of takeover. Concerns such as these are discussed in more detail later in this chapter.

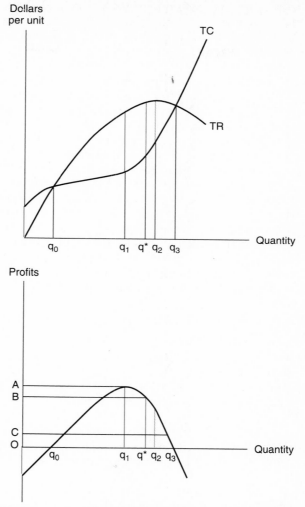

Figure 3.2 Effect of a minimum profit constraint on sales-maximizing behavior.

will not affect the sales maximizer's choice of output level; q_2 will be produced. Especially if the profit hill is rather flat, sales-maximizing managers may choose much higher output levels than profit-maximizing managers even under a minimum profit constraint.

Managerial Utility

Oliver Williamson has also analyzed the implications of utility-maximizing managers.[15] Williamson believes that managers' utility depends in part on profits; output will still be chosen by equating marginal revenue to marginal costs.

However, Williamson theorizes that managers also get satisfaction from executive perks such as fancy offices, executive jets, and "power breakfasts." Thus costs are higher than in the profit-maximizing model because money is spent on nice carpeting and art for the corner offices.*

In a world in which managers have some discretion over costs, costs may also be higher due to **X-inefficiency**. If managers are interested in living a quiet, peaceful life, they may not continually strive to find the least costly way of organizing production, handling materials, and, in general, doing business. As a result, costs are higher than necessary. Harvey Leibenstein, the originator of the term X-inefficiency, defines it as "the extent to which a given set of inputs do not get to be combined in such a way as to lead to maximum output."[16]

Finally, managers may care most about protecting their jobs. Does an interest in job security conflict with profit maximization? Not surprisingly, the answer is ambiguous. If a manager perceives that the best way to avoid being fired is to earn the highest possible profits, then there is obviously no conflict with neoclassical theory. Managers, however, probably face asymmetric returns to risky decisions.[17] The downside risk of a bad decision is extremely large—a manager can lose her or his job.[18] The reward for a good decision is far less dramatic—a manager might receive a bonus. Because of this asymmetry, managers of large corporations may avoid high-risk, high expected profit projects.[19]

FEASIBILITY OF PROFIT MAXIMIZATION

Rather than emphasizing the separation of ownership and control, some economists have focused their attention on the large size and structural complexity of modern firms. These economists have developed their theories primarily through observation of corporations and corporate decision makers.[20] Separation of ownership and control is not inconsistent with the predictions of these economists, however.

Most large corporations have thousands of employees, often organized into multiple functional components. Some specialize in production, some in finance, some in research and development, and some in environmental protection. This list could be extended almost indefinitely. Some economists argue that it is unrealistic to expect each of these thousands of employees to be striving in unison toward the goal of maximum profits. Different specialists are likely to have different goals or at least different ideas about how to achieve maximum profits. Engineers may be interested in new technological developments, while marketing staff may want to focus on products with great appeal to consumers. It is the top managers' job to choose among conflicting objectives. Managers, however, cannot know everything known by the employees under them in the chain of command. Furthermore, it is often notoriously difficult to accurately convey information. Because of these problems, top managers may simply be unable to choose the profit-maximizing strategy.

---

*Remember from Chapter 2 that if costs are higher under monopoly than under perfect competition, the welfare loss is also larger.

Satisficing and Rules of Thumb

Some argue that, because of organizational size and complexity, managers opt for "**satisficing**" instead of profit maximizing. The satisficer sets a minimum acceptable level of performance below which he or she does not want to fall. Once this level is reached, the satisficer can relax. In short, the satisficer does not strive to be the best that he or she can be but settles for something less.

Satisficing implies that firms use a variety of rules of thumb to guide their decisions. In this section, we consider the theory and empirical evidence on rules of thumb, or full-cost pricing.

Two types of formulas have been identified by economists. The first is based on the dominant firm's objective of earning a fixed rate of return on invested capital. Suppose, for example, a firm sets a target rate of return of R_0, where:

$$R_0 = \frac{TR - TC}{K} = \frac{Q(P - AC)}{K} \qquad [3.1]$$

and K represents total invested capital. To make this pricing system workable the firm must assume it will sell some quantity of output Q. Suppose the firm assumes it will sell 80 percent of its capacity. In that case, Q and AC are identified, and because the firm already knows K, the only remaining variable in equation 3.1 is P. All that remains to be done is to solve equation 3.1 for P.* If demand is particularly strong, sales will exceed 80 percent of capacity, Q will increase, AC will fall, and R_0 will exceed 10 percent. That of course is a preferred outcome for the firm. If demand is weak, however, Q will decrease, AC will rise, and R_0 will fall below 10 percent.

Another variation of **rule-of-thumb pricing** has firms setting prices as a fixed markup over invoice costs. For many years department stores such as Macy's and Bloomingdales simply priced by charging a fixed percent markup over the invoice cost of an item. If the markup was 100 percent, then $\frac{P - MC}{MC} = 1$ and $\frac{P - MC}{P} = 0.5$.

If a blouse cost Macy's $50.00, the retail price was set at $100.00, and if a suit cost $300.00, it was priced at $600.00. If all of the major department stores followed this cost-plus pricing system, it would keep them from competing too aggressively on the basis of price. The system is extremely operational and worked well for many years until discount stores such as Marshall's, T.J. Maxx, and Loehmann's began to underprice the major department stores by 20 to 50 percent.

Early empirical evidence suggested that rule-of-thumb pricing is a common phenomenon. Hall and Hitch discovered that 30 of 38 British firms surveyed in the 1930s claimed to use some rules to set prices.[21] Fog found similar results for

---

*For example, suppose that the target rate of return is 10 percent so $R_0 = 0.10$. If capacity is 1,000,000 units, 80 percent of capacity is 800,000 units. If AC = 10 for a production of 800,000 units and total invested capital K = 100,000,000 then:

$$R_0 = \frac{Q(P - AC)}{K} \Rightarrow 0.10 = \frac{800,000\ (P - 10)}{100,000,000}$$

Solving for P yields P = 22.5.

Danish firms.[22] In the United States the theory first received widespread attention when Kaplan, Dirlam, and Lanzillotti discovered that half of a sample of 20 large firms used some rules to set prices.[23] Kaplan and colleagues suggested that large corporate giants such as General Motors, International Harvester, Alcoa, Du Pont, Standard Oil of New Jersey, Johns-Manville, General Electric, General Foods, US Steel, and Union Carbide all priced to achieve a target rate of return.[24] Furthermore, they concluded that "[t]arget return on investment was probably the most commonly stressed of company pricing goals."[25]

Despite the apparent strength of Kaplan and coworkers' findings, their results raised some serious questions concerning rule-of-thumb pricing techniques. In their survey, 10 large corporations claimed to use some target rate of return to set prices, yet these targets varied widely from 20 percent on invested capital for Alcoa, General Electric, and General Motors down to just 10 percent for International Harvester and 8 percent for US Steel.[26] Furthermore, in most cases the firms actually earned rates of return that were significantly greater than the targets. General Motors, for example, averaged a 26 percent return between 1947 and 1955.

If the target rate of return was used by such powerful corporations, why were the target profit rates so variable? The simplest explanation is that because these firms faced widely differing elasticities of demand, they targeted widely differing returns on investment. Along these lines, Heflebower looked at the empirical evidence available on full-cost pricing and concluded:

> [F]urther consideration of these cost explanations of prices shows that the cost rules themselves contain, or in application are modified for, demand influences. In direct relation to the height of cross elasticities of demand among rivals' products, the gross margin used by the individual firm reflects not its own indirect costs but rather the margin it finds by experience to be desirable in light of costs and market conduct of rivals.[27]

To see the connection to the elasticity of demand, e_d, recall that:

$$MR = P\left(1 - \frac{1}{|e_d|}\right)$$

As shown in Chapter 2, profit maximization requires the equating of marginal revenue to marginal cost, implying that:

$$MC = MR = P\left(1 - \frac{1}{|e_d|}\right) = P - \frac{P}{|e_d|}$$

or

$$\frac{P}{|e_d|} = P - MC \Rightarrow \frac{P - MC}{P} = \frac{1}{|e_d|}$$

Thus, reviewing from Chapter 2 again, profit maximization requires price-cost margins to be inversely related to the elasticity of demand. If demand is highly elastic, price-cost margins will be small, while if demand is highly inelastic margins will be high. In the present context, this equation implies that firms that claim to be using a full-cost pricing method may be maximizing profits. In the words of Alfred Kahn, "In many situations, target-return pricing simply does not make sense except as an *ex post* rationalization of profit maximization."[28]

Another serious criticism of the rule-of-thumb theory is that even in industries in which surveys have revealed the existence of target pricing, more detailed studies have shown that other factors have a far greater effect on price.[29] In one such study of the Canadian cotton textile industry, McFetridge tested to see whether prices were altered by short-run changes in demand. He discovered that they were and therefore completely rejected the rule-of-thumb model.[30]

What can we conclude about the use of rules-of-thumb pricing methods? First, there is little doubt that many firms claim to use such methods. Second, these methods are almost always augmented by careful consideration of demand conditions. And, finally, such rules may be fully consistent with profit-maximizing behavior if the rules merely reflect the best the firm can *expect* to achieve given current demand and cost conditions.

Constraints on Managers

Criticism of the assumption of profit maximization has led its defenders to assert that, in fact, both constraints and incentives exist that keep managers from straying too far from the straight and narrow path of profit maximization. These activities are not without cost, of course. The magnitude of the costs varies from firm to firm, depending on factors such as the complexity of the operations, the tastes of the managers, and the costs of devising a monitoring system. In this section we consider the effectiveness of various constraints and incentives.

One constraint is the possibility of **stockholder revolt**. After all, owners always have the option of selling shares of stock if they are unhappy with a company's performance. Some argue that this form of indirect control encourages managers to treat stockholders carefully and keep their interests in mind.

A counterargument is that owners are unlikely to have complete information about alternative policies available to a firm.[31] They can try to determine whether profits are being maximized by watching how similar firms perform. Because no two firms are exactly alike, however, this kind of monitoring provides incomplete information. Available evidence confirms that indirect control through stockholder revolt is only a weak constraint on managers' behavior.[32]

A more serious constraint arising from financial markets is the threat of a **takeover**.[33] Many takeovers result from the **market for corporate control**. Suppose that current management is not maximizing profits. This will result in a firm's stock selling for less than it would under profit-maximizing management because stockholders are willing to pay no more than the present discounted value of the income, or profits, earned by the firm.* In such a case, different man-

---

*Present discounted value, or simply present value, refers to the value today of money received in the future. The present value of $1 received t periods in the future is $1/(1 + i)^t$, where i is the interest rate received per period. To understand this, recognize that if you deposited this amount (the present value) in the bank today, you would have a balance of $1 in t periods.

agement could purchase the firm's stock, fire the incumbent management, and begin to pursue a profit-maximizing strategy, thereby earning large capital gains as the value of the firm rises well above the purchase price. Assuming financial markets work well, such a takeover should occur whenever the potential gain in profits is greater than the costs of the takeover.*

What are the costs of a takeover bid? First, there are planning and legal costs. Also, once a poorly managed firm has become a target, its stock price may be driven up considerably both by speculative purchases by investors hoping to make a quick profit and by competition among acquiring firms.[34] In addition, transaction costs arise from information problems. Insiders, such as the current management, have the most accurate information about whether profit is being maximized. An outsider may have trouble distinguishing between low profits due to poor management and low profits due to events outside the firm's control.† Stockholders must also evaluate the claims of the group attempting a takeover, keeping in mind that the group has an incentive to reveal only information favorable to their attempt.

Because of these costs, the threat of takeover is unlikely to be a completely effective constraint on managers.‡ Exactly how much room managers have for non–profit-maximizing behavior is an empirical question. We will examine the evidence shortly.

The *product market* may also constrain managers' behavior. A firm that is not maximizing profits faces the possibility of being forced out of a competitive market as long as at least some other firms in the industry *are* striving for the highest possible profits. A highly competitive market, therefore, disciplines a firm to minimize costs and pick the profit-maximizing output level.

Finally, we note that in addition to the "sticks" of stockholder revolt and takeover threats, "carrots" may also encourage managers to maximize profits. One such incentive is to tie executive compensation to profits through bonuses or stock options. A study of compensation and stock holdings of 461 top executives in U.S. corporations found that executives' stock holdings averaged thirteen times their annual salary plus bonus.[35] Presumably, these executives are well aware of the link between the value of their companies' stock and their own wealth.

Theory cannot tell us conclusively whether or not an assumption of profit maximization is realistic. It is necessary, therefore, to turn to a consideration of the vast quantity of empirical work on managerial incentives and performance.

---

*Current management will be concerned about the threat of a takeover if the loss of their jobs results in loss of income or of "rents" attached to managerial jobs such as prestige or reputation.

†Because of this kind of information problem, it is not unusual to see current or former members of a firm's management involved in a takeover attempt.

‡This conclusion is reinforced when we recognize that managers have many ways of protecting themselves from hostile takeover bids. These tactics include the scorched earth, the poison pill, the staggered board, and protective acquisitions. See R. A. Walkling and M. S. Long, "Agency Theory, Managerial Welfare, and Takeover Bid Resistance," *Rand Journal of Economics* 15 (1984): 54–68.

Empirical Evidence

Despite the voluminous empirical evidence on the issues discussed in this chapter, the major issues remain unsettled. In this survey of the empirical literature the testable hypotheses that emerge from the theoretical literature are explored and an attempt is made to summarize the current "bottom line" on each issue.

In part there is a lack of consensus because the issues are difficult to test. Most of the available evidence comes from statistical tests. The data are often poor and a careful test requires many explanatory variables. For example, the list of explanatory variables in one comprehensive study on profitability includes the proportion of common shares held by the top five managers, the control position of outside owners, the firm's market share, its size, its diversification, industry structure, industry advertising, and a measure of industry propensities to innovate.[36] Most studies use only subsets of these explanatory variables, risking biased results.* Remember, however, that the alternative to biased results is often no results at all.

Finally, because theory does not always yield clear predictions, the data can be consistent with more than one theory. This has become especially true as theorists have tried to make their theory more realistic by introducing dynamic elements and constraints on managers' behavior.

Having sounded this warning, what can we learn from empirical work? First, a number of studies have examined the relationship between managerial compensation and various measures of a firm's performance.[37] If managerial compensation is most closely tied to profits, then the link between managerial utility maximization and firm profit maximization is restored. While evidence that managers are rewarded for increasing profits would not prove that they actually achieve the highest possible profits, it would at least lead us to believe that they have a strong incentive to focus on profitability as they make decisions. If, on the other hand, managerial compensation is more closely tied to another measure of performance, such as the growth rate of sales, managers may not even strive for maximum profits.

Reports in the business press such as the *Wall Street Journal* and *Business Week* may lead you to believe that managerial compensation is most closely linked to company size. After all, aren't the highest salaries paid managers of the largest firms? We must remember, however, that correlation does not prove causation. It is likely that running one of the Fortune 500 companies is more complex than running a small, local business. A manager of a larger company may receive higher compensation in recognition of her or his managerial ability, thereby creating a positive correlation between size and compensation. Ideally, a researcher needs to examine the determinants of compensation *within* a firm. In the studies that try to control for this size effect, most of the available evidence indicates that as profits increase, so does compensation. Moreover, there is a tighter link be-

---

*Remember from the discussion of regression analysis in Chapter 2 that omitting a relevant explanatory variable from a model causes the estimated coefficients to be biased.

tween compensation and profits than between compensation and sales or growth rate. Managers who want to maximize their compensation should therefore keep a close eye on profits.

Other studies compare firms with different ownership structures in an attempt to gather direct evidence on performance. Economists have compared choice of output level, profit rate, growth rate, and costs of firms under owner control to those of firms under management control.

Most of the studies looking at choice of output level have examined whether firms are maximizing sales or profits. Remember that sales maximization implies a higher output level and lower price than profit maximization. Almost all of the existing evidence rejects the hypothesis that firms pursue maximum sales, finding instead support for either profit or growth maximization.[38]

More than 20 studies have been published comparing the profitability of firms under management control to those of firms under tighter control by their owners.[39] If management is pursuing a strategy other than profit maximization, we should find a significantly lower rate of return for the firms run by managers. Sorting through these studies, we find no clear consensus. Results differ depending on the sample, the explanatory variables included in the model, and the statistical technique. A tentative "bottom line" for the studies on profitability indicates weak support for the hypothesis that profits in managerial controlled firms are lower on average than profits in owner-controlled firms. This difference, however, has not been found in all studies, and the gap is fairly narrow.

Fewer studies have compared the growth rate of firms under different forms of control.[40] The available evidence is again mixed, with less indication of differences in growth rate between firms under control by owners and those run by managers than for differences in profits.

Economists have also looked at cost differences across firms by type of control. Williamson's theory of expense preference, Leibenstein's X-efficiency, and various theories of satisficing all suggest that managers may not minimize costs. Many anecdotes and case studies suggest that managers may spend "excessive" amounts on various perks.[41] For example, consider Xerox, long protected from competition because of important patents. Eventually, however, Xerox's patents expired and Xerox faced competition from new entrants, which led to falling profits. In response to this unusual pressure, Xerox undertook its first drive to cut costs in 1975. The company fired eight thousand employees, postponed construction of a new headquarters, and decided not to build a new plant. Sales increased![42] IBM's experiences when they faced competition for the first time in the 1970s and 1980s were similar. A final example is AT&T, which has dramatically reduced costs in response to competitive pressures that arose after the firm was broken up by antitrust action.

Because of the availability of good data, several studies have examined the effects of managerial control in the banking industry.[43] These studies find evidence that firms under managerial control have higher expenditures on equipment, furniture, and personnel than do owner-controlled firms. As theory suggests, this is especially true in those cases where competition in the product market is weak.

Finally, an extensive body of literature examines takeovers and the effectiveness of the **market for corporate control**. It may not surprise you to learn that the evidence on the effectiveness of the threat of takeovers in constraining managers' behavior is not conclusive. One question economists have examined is the performance of those companies targeted for takeover in the years preceding the takeover. Some studies have found evidence that targets perform relatively poorly before initiation of a takeover, suggesting that managers who do not maximize profits will indeed be found out and penalized.[44] Martin and McConnell examined the turnover of top executives following a takeover and found that the top executive was more likely to be removed from office after a takeover if the firm was performing below the industry average. They note that, "If we assume that one important mechanism for correcting nonvalue maximizing behavior by the managers of target firms is to remove them from office, the results are consistent with the view that the takeover market plays an important role in disciplining top corporate executives."[45]

Other studies, however, do not support the conclusion that targets performed relatively badly before takeover. At worst, these studies find that the takeover targets were only slightly less profitable than similar nontargeted firms.[46] Further questions about how effective takeovers are as a disciplinary mechanism comes from a study by Ravenscraft and Scherer of firms' *post*merger performance. Their evidence indicates that mergers on average neither improved nor worsened profitability of the acquired units.[47]

A "bottom line" for the evidence on takeovers is that takeovers probably serve as only an *imperfect* constraint on managers. In an early study, Robert Smiley tried to estimate how tight this constraint is. He concluded that the market value of a firm can fall to 87 percent of its profit-maximizing value before a takeover attempt is likely to occur.[48] Managers thus seem to have some leeway to pursue non–profit-maximizing behavior, especially with regard to minimizing costs.

Where does all of this lead us? Profit maximization appears to be a reasonable first assumption to make in many cases. We must recognize, however, that many exceptions to profit-maximizing behavior exist.

SUMMARY

1. Many modern firms bear little resemblance to the traditional firm of microeconomic theory. They are large, complex entities that often operate in many different product and geographical markets.

2. The modern theory of the firm builds on Ronald Coase's fundamental observations that the firm and the market are alternative ways of organizing production and that costs are associated with either way of organizing production.

3. Advantages of using the market include the ability to aggregate demands of many small firms, allowing a producer to realize economies of scale or economies of scope. In addition, using the market can reduce production costs by reducing risk.

4. When transaction costs are high, firms are likely to rely on internal production rather than using the market. Three dimensions of transactions are important in identifying circumstances when transaction costs are

likely to be high: their frequency, the amount of uncertainty associated with them, and the degree of asset specificity.

5. If a firm is organized as a sole proprietorship or a partnership, ownership and control of the firm are combined in the hands of one or a few people. In a corporation, however, ownership and control are typically separated.

6. The separation of ownership and control in corporations gives managers the freedom to pursue objectives other than profit maximization. Possible managerial goals include sales maximization, pursuit of a high growth rate, utility maximization, and a focus on job security.

7. Some economists argue that the size and complexity of modern firms make it difficult for managers to choose the profit-maximizing strategy. They hypothesize that managers opt for satisficing behavior rather than profit-maximizing behavior. Satisficing behavior implies that firms use a variety of rules of thumb to make their day-to-day business decisions.

8. Defenders of the assumption of profit maximization argue that managers are both constrained and encouraged to maximize profits. Among the constraints are the possibility of stockholder revolt, the threat of takeover, and competitive pressure from the product market. Incentives such as bonuses and stock options encourage managers to pay attention to profits.

9. The empirical evidence on whether firms maximize profits is extensive, yet somewhat inconclusive. Firms may do a better job of selecting the profit-maximizing price than of choosing the cost-minimizing levels of production, employment, or perks. The assumption of profit maximization is most likely to hold in the longer run and in those markets where firms face competitors.

KEY TERMS

asset specificity	satisficing
bounded rationality	separation of ownership and control
economies of scope	stockholder revolt
market for corporate control	takeover
opportunism	transaction costs
rule-of-thumb pricing	X-inefficiency
sales maximization	

DISCUSSION QUESTIONS

1. Ronald Coase won the Nobel Prize in economics in 1991 for his insights about the factors that influence the organization of firms. Suppose your

friend, who is very bright but who has not studied economics, asks you to explain Coase's theory to her. What would you say?

2. Explain how using the market helps a firm control its costs.

3. Explain what is meant by "bounded rationality." What role does this assumption play in the theory of the firm?

4. Does the presence of opportunistic behavior contradict the assumption of utility maximization? Explain your reasoning.

5. U.S. automobile manufacturers have traditionally been highly vertically integrated, not only assembling parts into automobiles but also producing the parts. Japanese automobile manufacturers, in contrast, are much less highly integrated. They rely on a network of supplier firms for parts.

   a. Discuss the advantages and disadvantages of the U.S. system in comparison with the Japanese system.

   b. Japanese firms sometimes share technical personnel with their suppliers. Can you explain this using the theory of the firm? What concerns would motivate the firms to share personnel?

   c. Recently U.S. automobile manufacturers have turned to "outsourcing," relying on suppliers for parts rather than producing the parts internally. Not surprisingly, this move has caused tension with the United Automobile Workers union. Explain why automobile manufacturers are willing to risk labor disputes in order to rely on outside suppliers for parts.

6. Give some examples of job-specific skills and explain why transactions costs are higher if workers have job-specific skills.

7. "A policy-maker will be less concerned about the adverse effects of monopoly power if the monopolist is a sales maximizer rather than a profit-maximizer." Discuss this statement.

8. Suppose you are writing the contract for a manager of a large corporation. How might you structure the contract to take the owners' interests into account?

9. A 1985 study of 130 stock purchase plans found that, on average, these plans offered about 8 percent of the corporation's stock to its managers at a discount of 12 to 15 percent off the market price.* Typically, the plans allowed the managers to borrow funds at very low interest rates to buy the shares.

   a. Explain the purpose of these stock purchase plans.

   b. The stock market generally views the institution of such a plan positively. Following the announcement of a plan, the value of a firm's shares rose, on average, 3 percent above the market trend. What does this say about the stock market's evaluation of the effectiveness of the stock purchase plan?

*Sanjai Bhagat, James A. Brickley, and Ronald C. Lease, "Incentive Effects of Stock Purchase Plans," *Journal of Financial Economics* 14 (June 1985): 195–215.

10. "Insider trading" refers to stock transactions that allow individuals with insider knowledge of a firm (such as its managers) to profit. Many people regard this as an unfair advantage and argue that insider trading should be illegal. Can you make an argument *in favor of* insider trading?

11. Your inquisitive friend (from question 1) is back. She has read something about the "market for corporate control" and asks you to explain what that is and how it helps enforce profit-maximizing behavior on firms. What do you say to her?

12. Suppose you are trying to gather evidence on whether firms maximize profits. What methodological approach would you use? Discuss the strengths and weaknesses of your approach.

NOTES

1. Recent surveys include Beth V. Yarbrough and Robert M. Yarbrough, "The Transactional Structure of the Firm," *Journal of Economic Behavior and Organization* 10 (1988): 1–28; Paul Milgrom and John Roberts, "Economic Theories of the Firm: Past, Present, and Future," *Canadian Journal of Economics* 21 (August 1988): 444–458; and Roger Clarke and Tony McGuinness (eds.), *The Economics of the Firm* (Oxford: Basil Blackwell, 1987).
2. Ronald H. Coase, "The Nature of the Firm," *Economica* 4 (November 1937): 386–405.
3. References include Oliver E. Williamson, "Transaction Cost Economics," in Richard Schmalensee and Robert D. Willig (eds.), *Handbook of Industrial Organization* (Amsterdam: North-Holland, 1989); *The Economic Institutions of Capitalism: Firms, Markets, Relational Contracting* (New York: Free Press, 1985); "The Modern Corporation: Origins, Evolution, Attributes," *Journal of Economic Literature* 19 (December 1981): 1537–1568; "Transaction-Cost Economics: The Governance of Contractual Relations," *Journal of Law and Economics* 22 (October 1979): 3–61; and *Markets and Hierarchies—Analysis and Antitrust Implications: A Study in the Economics of Internal Organization* (New York: Free Press, 1975). See also Armen A. Alchian and Harold Demsetz, "Production, Information Costs and Economic Organization," *American Economic Review* 62 (1972): 777–795 and Benjamin Klein, Robert G. Crawford, and Armen A. Alchian, "Vertical Integration, Appropriable Rents, and the Competitive

Contracting Process," *Journal of Law and Economics* 21 (October 1978): 297–326.
4. See, for example, p. 1547 in Williamson, "The Modern Corporation: Origins, Evolution, Attributes."
5. Oliver E. Williamson, "Transaction Cost Economics," p. 150
6. The notion of bounded rationality is attributed to Herbert A. Simon. References include Herbert A. Simon, *Models of Man* (New York: John Wiley and Sons, 1957) and "Theories of Decision-Making in Economics and Behavioral Science," *American Economic Review* 49 (June 1959): 253–283.
7. Oliver E. Williamson, *The Economic Institutions of Capitalism: Firms, Markets, Relational Contracting* (New York: Free Press, 1985), p. 47.
8. This discussion draws upon Williamson, "Transaction Cost Economics," pp. 142–144.
9. See the discussions in Glenn Porter, *The Rise of Big Business, 1860–1920* second edition (Arlington Heights, IL: Harlan Davidson 1992), and Alfred D. Chandler, Jr. *The Visible Hand: The Managerial Revolution in American Business.* (Cambridge, MA: Harvard University Press, 1977).
10. *Statistical Abstract of the United States.*
11. Robert Larner, *Management Control and the Large Corporation* (New York: Dunellen, 1970), p. 3.
12. Edward S. Herman, *Corporate Control, Corporate Power* (Cambridge: Cambridge University Press, 1981), pp. 58–64.
13. R. Joseph Monsen, Jr., and Anthony Downs, "A Theory of Large Managerial

Firms," *The Journal of Political Economy* 73 (June 1965): 221–236.

14. William J. Baumol, *Business Behavior, Value and Growth* (New York: Macmillan, 1959).

15. Oliver E. Williamson, *The Economics of Discretionary Behavior: Managerial Objectives in a Theory of the Firm* (Chicago: Markham, 1967).

16. Harvey Leibenstein, "Competition and X-Efficiency," *Journal of Political Economy* 81 (May 1973): 766.

17. William Fellner, *Competition Among the Few* (New York: Knopf, 1949), pp. 172–173.

18. A manager's performance may be judged by looking at the trend of profits over recent years. Evidence suggests that corporate presidents' tenure is shortened if profits deviate from trend. See W.M. Crain, Thomas Deaton, and Robert Tollison, "On the Survival of Corporate Executives," *Southern Economic Journal*, vol. 43 (January 1977), pp. 1372–1375; Michael S. Weisbach, "Outside Directors and CEO Turnover," *Journal of Financial Economics* 20 (January/March 1988): 431–460; and Jerold B. Warner, Ross L. Watts, and Karen Wruck, "Stock Prices and Top Management Changes," *Journal of Financial Economics* 20 (January/March 1988): 461–492.

19. See R. Schramm and R. Sherman, "Profit Risk Management and the Theory of the Firm," *Southern Economic Journal* 40 (January 1974): 353–363; and Kenneth J. Boudreaux, "Managerialism and Risk-Return Performance," *Southern Economic Journal* 39 (January 1973): 366–372.

20. Important contributions include R.M. Cyert and J.G. March, *A Behavioral Theory of the Firm* (Englewood Cliffs, N.J.: Prentice-Hall, 1963); Herbert A. Simon, "Rational Decision Making in Business Organizations," *American Economic Review* 69 (September 1979): 493–513; K.J. Cohen and R.M. Cyert, *Theory of the Firm* (Englewood Cliffs, N.J.: Prentice-Hall, 1965); and J.C. March and H.A. Simon, *Organizations* (New York: John Wiley, 1958).

21. R.L. Hall and Charles J. Hitch, "Pricing Theory and Business Behavior," *Oxford Economic Papers* 2 (May 1939): 12–45.

22. B. Fog, *Industrial Pricing Policies* (Amsterdam: North-Holland, 1960), p. 217.

23. A.D.H. Kaplan, J.B. Dirlam, and R.F. Lanzillotti, *Pricing in Big Business* (Washington, D.C.: Brookings Institution, 1958); see also R.F. Lanzillotti, "Pricing Objectives in Large Companies," *American Economic Review* 48 (December 1958): 921–940.

24. Kaplan et al., *Ibid.*, pp. 130–165; and Lanzillotti, *Ibid.*, pp. 924–927.

25. Kaplan et al., *ibid.*, p. 130.

26. Lanzillotti, "Pricing Objectives in Large Companies."

27. R.B. Heflebower, "Full Costs, Cost Changes, and Prices," in National Bureau of Economic Research conference report, *Business Concentration and Price Policy* (Princeton: Princeton University Press, 1955), p. 366.

28. Alfred E. Kahn, "Pricing Objectives in Large Companies: Comment," *American Economic Review* 49 (September 1959): 674.

29. Heflebower, *Supra* note 27: 374–375.

30. D.G. McFetridge, "The Determinants of Pricing Behavior: A Study of the Canadian Cotton Textile Industry," *Journal of Industrial Economics* 22 (December 1973): 141–152.

31. Monsen and Downs, "A Theory of Large Managerial Firms," p. 25.

32. Oliver Williamson, *Corporate Control and Business Behavior* (Englewood Cliffs, NJ: Prentice-Hall, 1970); and Brian Hindley, "Separation of Ownership and Control in the Modern Corporation," *Journal of Law and Economics* (April 1970): 185–210.

33. References include Robin Marris, "A Model of the 'Managerial' Enterprise," *Quarterly Journal of Economics* 77 (May 1963): 185–209; Marris, *The Economic Theory of "Managerial" Capitalism* (London: Macmillan, 1964); Henry G. Manne, "Mergers and the Market for Corporate Control," *Journal of Political Economy* 73 (April 1965): 110–120; and the Symposium on Takeovers in *The Journal of Economic Perspectives* 2 (Winter 1988): 2–82.

34. Ravenscraft and Scherer offer evidence that, on average, acquiring firms lose money on their acquisitions. See David J. Ravenscraft and F.M. Scherer, *Mergers, Sell-offs, and Economic Efficiency* (Washington, D.C.: Brookings Institution, 1987) and "Life After Takeover," *Journal of Industrial Economics* 36 (December 1987): 147–156.

35. William A. McEachern, *Managerial Control and Performance* (Lexington: Heath, 1975), pp. 77–84.

36. Dennis C. Mueller, *Profits in the Long Run* (Cambridge: Cambridge University Press, 1986).

37. These studies include W.G. Lewellen and B. Huntsman, "Managerial Pay and Corporate

Performance," *American Economic Review* 60 (September 1970): 710–720; Robert Masson, "Executive Motivations, Earnings, and Consequent Equity Performance," *Journal of Political Economy* 79 (November/December 1971): 1278–1292; George K. Yarrow, "Executive Compensation and the Objectives of the Firm, in *Market Structure and Corporate Behavior*, edited by Keith Cowling (London: Gray-Mills, 1972), pp. 149–173; Geoffrey Meeks and Geoffrey Whittington, "Directors' Pay, Growth and Profitability," *Journal of Industrial Economics* 24 (September 1975): 1–14; William A. McEachern, *Managerial Control and Performance* (Lexington: Heath, 1975); David H. Ciscel and Thomas Carroll, "The Determinants of Executive Salaries," *Review of Economics and Statistics* 62 (February 1980): 7–13; John R. Deckop, "Determinants of Chief Executive Officer Compensation," *Industrial and Labor Relations Review* 41 (January 1988): 215–226; and Daryl N. Winn and John D. Shoenhair, "Compensation Based (Dis)incentives for Revenue-Maximizing Behavior," *Review of Economics and Statistics* 70 (February 1988): 154–158.

38. B.D. Mabry and D.L. Siders, "An Empirical Test of the Sales Maximization Hypothesis," *Southern Economic Journal* (January 1967): 367–377; M. Hall, "Sales Revenue Maximization: An Empirical Examination," *Journal of Industrial Economics* 15 (April 1967): 143–156; J.W. Elliot, "A Comparison of Models of Marketing Investment in the Firm," *Quarterly Review of Economics and Business* 11 (Spring 1971): 53–70; and Samuel Baker, "An Empirical Test of the Sales Maximization Hypothesis," *Industrial Organization Review* 1 (1973): 56–66. A study that disagrees with the above is C.L. Lackman and J.L. Craycroft, "Sales Maximization and Oligopoly: A Case Study," *Journal of Industrial Economics* 23 (December 1974): 81–96.

39. See Table 3–4 in Douglas F. Greer, *Industrial Organization and Public Policy,* third edition (New York: Macmillan, 1992), p. 83, for a nice classification of the results of many of these studies.

40. Some references include H.K. Radice, "Control Type, Profitability, and Growth in Large Firms: An Empirical Study," *Economics Journal* 81 (September 1971): 547–562; Peter S. Steer and John R. Cable, "Internal Organization and Profit: An Empirical Analysis of Large U.K. Companies," *Journal of Industrial Economics* 27 (September 1978): 13–30; Robert Sorenson, "The Separation of Ownership and Control and Firm Performance: An Empirical Analysis," *Southern Economic Journal* 41 (July 1974): 145–148; Peter Holl, "Effect of Control Type on the Performance of the Firm in the U.K.," *Journal of Industrial Economics* 23 (June 1975): 257–271; John J. Kania and John R. McKean, "Ownership, Control, and the Contemporary Corporation: A General Behavior Analysis," *Kyklos* 29 (1976): 272–291; and P.J. Thonet and O.H. Poensgen, "Managerial Control and Economic Performance in Western Germany," *Journal of Industrial Economics* 28 (September 1979): 23–37.

41. See Williamson, *The Economics of Discretionary Behavior*, pp. 35–135, for discussion of several case studies.

42. *Business Week*, April 5, 1976, pp. 60–66.

43. Cynthia Glassman and Stephen A. Rhoades, "Owner vs. Manager Control Effects on Bank Performance," *Review of Economics and Statistics* 62 (May 1980): 263–270; T.H. Hannan and F. Mavinga, "Expense Preference and Managerial Control: The Case of the Banking Firm," *Bell Journal of Economics* 11 (Autumn 1980): 671–682; and James A. Verbrugge and John S. Jahera, Jr. "Expense-Preference Behavior in the Savings and Loan Industry," *Journal of Money, Credit, and Banking* 13 (November 1981): 465–476.

44. References include Randall Morck, Andrei Shleifer, and Robert W. Vishny, "Characteristics of Targets of Hostile and Friendly Takeovers," in Alan J. Auerbach (ed.), *Corporate Takeovers: Causes and Consequences* (Chicago: University of Chicago Press, 1988); Mark L. Mitchell and Kenneth Lehn, "Do Bad Bidders Become Good Targets?" *Journal of Political Economy* 98 (April 1990): 372–398; and Kenneth J. Martin and John J. McConnell, "Corporate Performance, Corporate Takeovers, and Management Turnover," *The Journal of Finance* 46 (June 1991): 671–687.

45. Martin and McConnell, "Corporate Performance, Takeovers, and Management Turnover," p. 681.

46. David J. Ravenscraft and F.M. Scherer, "Life After Takeover," *Journal of Industrial Economics* 36 (December 1987): 147–156; Arthur T. Andersen and T. Crawford Honeycutt, "Management Motives for Takeovers in the Petroleum Industry," *Review of Industrial Organization* 3 (1987): 1–12; and Timothy Hannan and Stephen A. Rhoades, "Acquisition Targets and Motives: The Case of the Banking Industry,"

Review of Economics and Statistics 69 (February 1987): 67–74.

47. Ravenscraft and Scherer, "Life After Takeover," pp. 150–154.

48. Robert Smiley, "Tender Offers, Transaction Costs, and the Theory of the Firm," *Review of Economics and Statistics* 58 (February 1976): 22–32.

Chapter 4

Market Concentration

Chapter 3 looked at the firm, considering its structure and objectives. Recall from microeconomics that firms are grouped together into markets. The structure of markets—the number of firms and their size distribution—varies widely from one theoretical extreme, perfect competition, to the other, monopoly. Some industries, like automobiles, disposable diapers, or breakfast cereals, contain only a few large firms, while others, like tennis rackets, shaving cream, or supermarkets, have many more firms.

As we said in Chapter 1, industrial organization is a blend of empirical and theoretical work. In the next several chapters, we examine the determinants of market entry and exit and the conduct of firms in oligopolistic industries. To put the theory into perspective, this chapter summarizes some evidence on the structure of industries in the United States. We begin by looking at the extent of aggregate concentration. Do large firms dominate market activity? What has happened to aggregate concentration over time? How much turnover is there among the largest firms?

After considering the evidence on aggregate concentration, we turn to individual markets. Policy makers usually focus on individual rather than aggregate markets because of concerns about monopoly or market power, a firm's ability to set price above marginal cost. Recall from the welfare comparison of perfect competition and monopoly in Chapter 2 that pricing above marginal cost leads to a misallocation of resources: at the profit-maximizing output level, the value to society of another unit of output, price, is greater than the cost of producing that extra unit of output, marginal cost. This allocative inefficiency is a key reason why economists and policy makers are concerned about firms with market power.*

---

*Allocative efficiency is only one dimension of performance. Other important dimensions include the distribution of income and the possibility of X-inefficiency, considered in Chapter 2, and technological progress, discussed in Chapter 14.

Traditionally, a measure of market share or concentration has been used as a proxy for market power, although recent work has shown that it is important not to associate market share with market power blindly. As the next chapters will show, other factors such as barriers to entry and potential competition may be more important than market share in determining market power. Nonetheless, it is useful to understand how market concentration can be measured and to look at the trends and current levels of market concentration in various industries. Several statistical measures of concentration within a market are available; our discussion examines the strengths and weaknesses of these measures and considers issues of market definition.[1]

Aggregate Concentration

Aggregate concentration statistics measure the role played by large companies in the economy as a whole rather than measuring the extent to which, for example, Kellogg's dominates the breakfast cereal industry. Policy makers often worry about aggregate or economy-wide concentration and about possible abuses of the political system by very large firms.[2] The largest firms, with sales and assets amounting to hundreds of billions of dollars, may indeed have considerable political influence and may use this influence to gain legislative favors.*

A number of empirical studies have examined whether large firms abuse the political system. In one of the more sophisticated studies, Salamon and Siegfried examined the relationship between firm size and the ability to avoid corporate income taxes.[3] Their results suggested that larger firms had a statistically significant ability to avoid the corporate income tax. Baldani and Waldman reexamined the Salamon and Siegfried results by controlling for the opportunity costs of lobbying activities and still found a significant positive relationship between firm size and corporate income tax avoidance.[4] Baldani and Waldman found, however, that firms generally turned to lobbying against taxes only when they were unable to invest their discretionary funds profitably in the marketplace.

Policy makers also worry about aggregate concentration because of possible connections between aggregate and market concentration. Although even the largest firms do not necessarily dominate their particular markets, many do. Examples of large firms that also have large market shares within their individual markets include General Motors, Ford, IBM, and General Electric. In addition, large firms may be highly diversified or vertically integrated. Some hypotheses suggest that diversification and vertical integration can enhance a firm's power within an individual market.

---

*Assessing the alleged abuses of size is difficult. White (*Journal of Industrial Economics*, March 1981) uses the example of the Big Three automobile producers to make this point. One hypothesis is that size has not helped these firms because substantial regulations have been imposed on them. On the other hand, perhaps the firms did use their lobbying power to weaken the regulations or delay their imposition. Further anecdotal evidence of an advantage of being big is provided by the government bailout of Chrysler.

TABLE 4.1   **1992 Aggregate Concentration Shares Using Alternative Measures of Size**

Size Measure	Share of 50 Largest Manufacturing Corporations (percent)	Share of 100 Largest Manufacturing Corporations (percent)	Share of 200 Largest Manufacturing Corporations (percent)
Value added	23.7	32.1	41.7
Employment	13.0	17.5	24.2
Payroll	17.4	22.6	29.7
Value of shipments (plant sales)	23.0	31.8	41.4
New capital expenditures	21.8	32.6	45.0

Source: U.S. Bureau of the Census, "Concentration Ratios in Manufacturing," *1992 Census of Manufactures.*

Despite political concern about large size and aggregate concentration, data for the entire economy are scarce.[5] Typically, evidence is anecdotal or pertains to individual sectors. Furthermore, any conclusions about aggregate concentration are affected by the method used to measure size. As shown in Table 4.1, using employment data to measure size implies considerably less aggregate concentration than is evident using other measures. This reflects the tendency for large companies to have a higher capital-labor ratio than small companies. Payroll data, on the other hand, may be biased upward to the extent that large firms pay relatively high wages and salaries. While value added data are perhaps the least biased measure, these data are available only for the manufacturing sector.* In discussing aggregate concentration, therefore, a researcher must balance concerns about bias with the reality of the availability of data.

TRENDS IN AGGREGATE CONCENTRATION

The best available data on aggregate concentration are for the manufacturing sector. Table 4.2 shows what has been happening in manufacturing in the post–World War II period, using value added as the measure of size. These data show an increase in aggregate concentration in manufacturing between 1947 and the mid to late 1960s. Lawrence White attributes most of this increase to rapid growth in the demand for products that were produced in industries dominated by large firms.[6] Examples include motor vehicles, petroleum, aircraft, and electrical equipment. Since the 1960s, however, the figures based on value added show virtually no increase in aggregate concentration in manufacturing.

Value added is basically revenues minus the outside cost of materials, fuel, and power.

TABLE 4.2 **Aggregate Concentration in the Manufacturing Sector**

Share of Value Added (percent)	1947	1954	1958	1963	1967	1970	1972	1977	1982	1987	1992
50 Largest Firms	17	23	23	25	25	24	25	24	24	25	24
100 Largest Firms	23	30	30	33	33	33	33	33	33	33	32
200 Largest Firms	30	37	38	41	42	43	43	44	43	43	42

Source: U.S. Bureau of the Census, "Concentration Ratios in Manufacturing," *1982 and 1992 Census of Manufactures*, Table 1.

Asset data, by contrast, exhibit an upward trend since the mid 1960s. One reason for the difference between these two series is that asset data include operations of U.S. corporations' overseas subsidiaries, whereas value-added data do not. Large U.S. manufacturing firms have increasingly invested in overseas operations and have done so at a higher rate than have smaller firms. Aggregate concentration measures that include foreign assets, therefore, show an upward trend even though concentration in domestic manufacturing activities has been relatively stable. A second reason for the difference between the value-added and the asset data is that asset data include companies' activities in nonmanufacturing fields such as mining and transportation. Value-added data include only manufacturing activities. Again, greater diversification on the part of the largest firms leads to an increase in aggregate concentration using the asset data but not the value-added data. White argues that the asset data are seriously biased and should not be used as evidence of increasing aggregate concentration in the past 30 years.

While the best available data are for the manufacturing sector of the economy, this sector has become relatively less important in the United States economy. Today, manufacturing accounts for slightly less than one quarter of value added. Unfortunately, because value-added data are not available for other sectors of the economy, less can be said about levels and trends of aggregate concentration in these sectors.

White's survey of evidence from a variety of sources shows increases in aggregate concentration in some nonmanufacturing sectors and decreases in others during the 1960s. Aggregate concentration rose during that decade in electric and gas utilities, retail trade, and transportation; it fell in the banking and life insurance sectors. For the 1970s, however, aggregate concentration increased only in transportation. Other nonmanufacturing sectors showed either stable aggregate concentration or slight declines.

Turning to the entire private sector of the economy, rather than individual sectors, aggregate concentration can be measured using data on employment, after-tax profits, and assets. Table 4.3 shows that concentration in the private sector has apparently not increased during the past two decades and may actually have decreased slightly.

TABLE 4.3   **Aggregate Concentration in the Private Sector**

	Share of Non-Farm, Private Sector Employment (percent)			
	1970	**1975**	**1980**	**1984**
Largest 25	10.2	9.9	8.9	7.4
Largest 100	18.8	17.7	16.6	15.1
Largest 200	24.5	23.3	22.1	20.5
	Share of Assets of Non-Financial Corporations (percent)			
	1970	**1975**	**1980**	**1984**
Largest 25	16.8	17.0	16.0	12.7
Largest 100	29.1	29.2	28.0	26.6
Largest 200	37.9	37.7	35.9	34.1

Source: Golbe and White (1988, Table 9.4) in Alan J. Auerbach (ed.), *Corporate Takeovers* (Chicago: University of Chicago Press, 1988).

TURNOVER AND MOBILITY AMONG THE LARGEST FIRMS

Further information about the overall structure of the economy comes from studies of turnover among the largest U.S. firms. An early study by Collins and Preston looked at the 100 largest manufacturing, mining, and distribution companies in 1909, 1919, 1929, 1935, 1948, and 1958.[7] They found that only 36 of the 100 largest firms in 1909 were among the top 100 in 1958. An update of their study showed that by 1976 only 21 of the original 100 largest remained in the top 100.[8]

Other studies have also found considerable turnover among the largest firms over time.[9] Mueller's evidence showed that, in fact, many of the largest firms go out of business over time: 417 of the 1,000 largest U.S. manufacturing companies in 1950 were no longer operating in 1972. Most of the firms were no longer ongoing due to merger; a few had exited as a result of liquidation in bankruptcy proceedings. This result—that mergers rather than liquidation have been the main reason for firm disappearances over time—is consistent with the results of other studies of turnover.

Looking more closely at the firms that disappeared compared to those that survived, Mueller found that survivorship appears to be strongly correlated with initial size. The survival rate of the manufacturing firms ranked between 501 and 1,000 in 1950 was less than 50 percent, whereas 84 percent of the largest 200 firms in 1950 were still operating in 1972.

What conclusions can be drawn from the information on trends in aggregate concentration and in turnover? The information on turnover suggests that there is mobility among the largest firms, although the very largest are the most likely to survive. It is fair to conclude that aggregate concentration has probably not increased over the past 20 or 25 years and may even have decreased a bit. Having observed this, however, we cannot conclude that aggregate concentration is not a current problem. Hypotheses about political abuses and possible links between market concentration and aggregate concentration give little guidance about what aggregate concentration level constitutes a serious problem for society. Without a better theory of the problems associated with bigness, all we can do is observe trends.

Concentration in Individual Markets

While there are possible reasons to be concerned about aggregate concentration, most work within industrial organization looks at concentration within individual markets. Seller concentration within a particular market is regarded as a significant aspect of market structure because of its hypothesized relationship to market power and, ultimately, to behavior and performance. Although this structuralist model has been criticized, it still underlies much public policy toward business.* Antitrust authorities who worry about "competitiveness" usually have the structure of specific markets in mind. They are, for example, more likely to challenge mergers in a "concentrated" market than in an unconcentrated one, where concentration is measured by one of the statistical measures discussed below.

STRUCTURE-BASED MEASURES

Several statistical measures of seller concentration within an individual market are available. No measure is perfect; which one is used in any given situation depends on data availability and the questions being examined.

One possible measure of seller concentration is simply the number of firms in an industry. Economic theory indicates that, if everything else is equal, competition ought to increase as the number of firms within an industry increases. A monopolistic industry, of course, consists of only one firm, whereas perfectly competitive or monopolistically competitive industries contain many firms. In between are oligopolies, with a few firms.

The number of firms is most useful as a measure of concentration in the extreme cases of perfect competition and monopoly. If there are a few firms in the industry, however, a measure of concentration that also reflects market share is desirable. Imagine two industries, each containing five firms. Suppose that in one

---

*The structure-conduct-performance model and criticisms of it are discussed in detail in Chapter 17.

industry, the market is equally divided and each firm has a market share of 20 percent. In the second industry, suppose that one firm controls 80 percent of the market and the remaining four firms each have market shares of 5 percent. It seems likely that pricing and other behavior will be different in these two industries, suggesting that a good measure of concentration should somehow account for inequality of market shares.

Two measures of concentration take both the number of firms and the distribution of market shares into account. The first is the **concentration ratio**. The concentration ratio is the cumulative share of the K largest firms in the market, where typical values of K are 4, 8, and 20. Thus, the four-firm concentration ratio (CR4) is the sum of the market shares of the largest four firms in the industry. The most common measure of market size is sales, although concentration ratios can also be calculated using other measures of size such as value added, employment, or assets.

Concentration ratios have the advantage of being relatively easy to understand.* Furthermore, for the manufacturing sector at least, data on concentration ratios are readily available.

Because the concentration ratio has been so widely used in empirical studies and in antitrust cases, it is important to understand its limitations. First, any given concentration ratio describes the percentage of market shares held by a specific number of firms. Because of this, the concentration ratio will not be affected by changes in market share outside the largest firms. Also, the concentration ratio will not necessarily give consistent rankings of the degree of competition within an industry. It is possible, for example, that one industry appears to be more concentrated than a second using the four-firm concentration ratio but less concentrated using the eight-firm concentration ratio.†

Another problem is that the concentration ratio provides no information about the distribution of market shares *among* the top firms. Knowing that the top four firms control, for example, 60 percent of the market tells us something but does not indicate whether there is one dominant firm with 40 or 50 percent of the market or four fairly large firms each with approximately 15 percent. Similarly, changes in market share among the top firms will not change the reported concentration ratio.

An index called the **Herfindahl-Hirschman Index** (HHI) takes into account both the number of firms and the inequality of market shares.‡ The HHI was orig-

---

*Concentration ratios range from a value of slightly greater than 0 for a perfectly competitive industry to a value of 100 for a monopoly.

†A simple example illustrates this possibility. Suppose the market share of each of the largest eight firms in Industry A is 10 percent; let the distribution of market shares of the largest eight firms in Industry B be 20, 20, 5, 5, 2.5, 2.5, 2.5, and 2.5 percent. The CR4 for Industry A is 40 compared to a CR4 of 50 for Industry B. By contrast, the CR8 shows Industry A to be more concentrated: 80 for Industry A compared with 60 for Industry B.

‡The HHI was invented independently by two economists, Albert Hirschman and Orris Herfindahl. See A. O. Hirschman, "The Paternity of an Index," *American Economic Review* (September 1964): 761, for historical detail.

TABLE 4.4   **Calculation of Four-Firm Concentration Ratio and HHI for Two Hypothetical Industries**

Market Share (percent)	Industry A	Industry B
Firm 1	30	70
Firm 2	25	10
Firm 3	20	5
Firm 4	15	5
Firm 5	4	4
Firm 6	3	3
Firm 7	2	2
Firm 8	1	1
CR4	90	90
HHI	2180	5080
Numbers-equivalent	4.59	1.97

inally defined as the sum of the squares of individual firms' market shares, expressed mathematically as

$$HHI = S_1^2 + S_2^2 + S_3^2 + \ldots + S_K^2 = \sum_{i=1}^{K} S_i^2$$

where K is the number of firms in the industry.

While the original definition of the HHI used market shares, antitrust practitioners have typically moved the decimal point two places to the right, using percentages of the market instead.* We will follow this practice. Using this convention, the HHI approximates 0 for a perfectly competitive industry and equals 10,000 for a monopoly.

In general, the more firms there are in an industry, the lower is the value of the HHI, *ceteris paribus*. One way to see this is to use the fact that, in an industry with N firms of equal size, the value of the HHI is 10,000/N. The value of N is referred to as the **numbers equivalent**. The HHI for an industry containing three firms each with one third of the market is thus 3333, while an industry with four firms of equal size has an HHI of 2500.

The numbers equivalent relationship is sometimes used to give insight into the meaning of a particular value of the HHI. For example, for an HHI of 1,000, the numbers equivalent is 10:

$$N = \frac{10,000}{1,000} = 10$$

A market with 10 firms of equal size would thus have an HHI of 1,000.

The HHI increases as the market shares of a given number of firms become less equal. The simple example shown in Table 4.4 illustrates this property of the

---

*As discussed in Chapter 20, current antitrust policy, beginning with the 1984 merger guidelines, is based on the HHI.

HHI and shows the advantage of the HHI compared to the concentration ratio. Although both hypothetical industries have a four-firm concentration ratio of 90, the HHI for Industry B is higher, reflecting the less equal distribution of market shares among the four largest firms in each industry. Note that in calculating the four-firm concentration ratio, data on only the four largest firms are used, whereas data on all firms in the industry are used to calculate the HHI.

Finally, we note that the HHI is very sensitive to the market shares of the largest firms, due to the squaring of market shares. For example, $50^2 = 2,500$ while $25^2 + 25^2 = 1,250$. For this reason, it is very important to have accurate data on the market shares of the largest firms in an industry, but it is of much less concern if accurate data on the smallest firms are not available.

Beginning in 1982, the Census Bureau has reported the HHI for U.S. manufacturing industries. Table 4.5 shows four-firm concentration ratios and HHI's for some selected manufacturing industries.* This table suggests that there is a high correlation between the two measures of market power. Industries with high four-firm concentration ratios tend to have high HHIs, and low four-firm concentration ratios are typically associated with low HHIs. Kwoka confirmed this relationship, finding a correlation of +0.929 between CR4 and the HHI and of +0.961 between CR2 and the HHI.[10] While this evidence suggests that the choice of concentration measure might not matter, Kwoka has also shown that, even if they are highly correlated, different measures of market power can have considerably different explanatory power when used in a regression.[11] In summary, it is fair to say that no single measure of seller concentration is best for all purposes. The choice depends on the availability of data and on the questions being asked.

DEFINITION OF THE RELEVANT MARKET

A more crucial issue than the choice of concentration measure may well be the definition of the market. Many antitrust cases center around market definition. A properly defined market includes all firms that compete with each other but excludes all noncompetitors. To identify competitors, substitutability on the part of both consumers and producers should be considered. If two products are used for similar purposes by consumers, the firms making those products ought to be regarded as competitors. Also, if two goods are produced using similar production processes, then their producers are also competitors.†

Including too few firms results in a market definition that is too narrow, leading to measures of market power that are overstated. Including too many firms, on the other hand, leads to a definition that is too broad, with the result that reported measures of market power tend to be biased downward. In both cases, re-

---

*Market definition is discussed shortly. Table 4.5 uses industry definitions developed by the Bureau of the Census.

†Consider two firms, one producing widgets and one producing gadgets. Assume that the production processes are very similar, although consumers do not view widgets and gadgets as substitutes. If the widget manufacturer begins to earn excess profits, the gadget manufacturer is likely to switch to producing widgets also. Thus, the two firms are competitors.

TABLE 4.5 **1992 Concentration Ratios and HHI of Selected Industries***

SIC Code	Industry Name	Four-Firm Concentration Ratio	HHI for 50 Largest Companies
2022	Cheese, natural and processed	42	819
2024	Ice cream and frozen desserts	24	293
2035	Pickles, sauces, and salad dressings	41	661
2037	Frozen fruits and vegetables	28	313
2052	Cookies and crackers	56	1169
2082	Malt beverages	90	N/A
2111	Cigarettes	90	N/A
2251	Women's hosiery, except socks	55	1567
2321	Men's and boys' shirts	28	315
2335	Women's, misses', and juniors' dresses	11	61
2451	Mobile homes	35	491
2621	Paper mills	29	392
2721	Periodicals	20	180
2771	Greeting cards	84	2922
2841	Soap and other detergents	63	1584
2851	Paints and allied products	29	305
2911	Petroleum refining	30	414
3011	Tires and inner tubes	70	1743
3161	Luggage	43	767
3211	Flat glass	81	1988
3241	Cement, hydraulic	35	472
3271	Concrete block and brick	7	30
3312	Blast furnaces and steel mills	37	551
3334	Primary aluminum	59	1456
3411	Metal cans	56	1042
3524	Lawn and garden equipment	62	1085
3571	Electronic computers	45	680
3621	Motors and generators	36	447
3632	Household refrigerators and freezers	82	1891
3651	Household audio and video equipment	39	585
3711	Motor vehicles and car bodies	84	2676
3911	Jewelry, precious metal	16	95

Source: U.S. Bureau of the Census, 1992 *Census of Manufactures, Concentration Ratios in Manufacturing.*
*Using value of shipments

ported measures of market power are not very useful for purposes of prediction or of evaluation of performance.

In the United States, the basic system for classifying the output of manufacturing firms is the Standard Industrial Classification (SIC). This system, developed by the U.S. Bureau of the Census, uses numerical codes (**SIC codes**) to define markets. The broadest level is the two-digit level, called the *major industry group*. There are 20 major industry groups within manufacturing; examples include "Tobacco products" (21), "Apparel and other textile products" (23), "Petroleum and coal products" (29), and "Transportation equipment" (37). Each two-digit group is divided into three-digit *industry groups*, which are then further subdivided into narrower and narrower categories. The seven-digit level, the *product*, is the narrowest classification. Table 4.6 shows an example of the SIC divisions.

Most firms, of course, produce more than one product; many operate in more than one industry. Statisticians at the Bureau of the Census must first assign the sales figures of each firm to the various levels of classification. They can then calculate total sales and firm shares for each level. Because of requirements to maintain confidentiality of individual firm data, the Bureau of the Census does not publish the market shares of individual firms. For manufacturing, concentration ratios are published at the four- and five-digit levels; Herfindahl-Hirschman Indexes have been published at the four-digit level beginning with the 1982 Census of Manufactures.

Industrial organization economists have typically used information at the four-digit industry level in their studies. In part, this is because the data at that level are most readily available. Also, among publicly available data sources, these industries seem to correspond most closely to economic markets.

SIC categories are, however, far from perfect. They tend to emphasize producer substitutability more heavily than consumer substitutability. This leads to some market definitions that are too narrow and some that are too broad.

Some examples of industry pairs that are too narrowly defined include glass containers (3221) and metal cans (3411); cane sugar refining (2062) and beet sugar refining (2063); and broadwoven fabric mills, cotton (2211) and broadwoven fabric mills, wool (2231). In each of these pairs of industries, the products compete with each other in many uses, yet the manufacturers are classified as being in noncompeting industries. As noted earlier, concentration ratios in such in-

TABLE 4.6   **An Example of SIC Categories**

SIC Code	Designation	Name
20	Major Industry Group	Food and kindred products
208	Industry Group	Beverages
2082	Product Group or Industry	Malt beverages
20822	Product Class	Bottled beer and ale case goods
2082224	Product	Beer: Returnable bottles: 12 oz. bottles

dustries will overstate actual market concentration. For example, the four-firm concentration ratio in glass containers in 1992 was 84; in metal cans it was 56. In actuality, because producers in each industry compete with each other, effective market concentration is less than the published concentration ratios suggest.

Several SIC industries are obviously too broadly defined. A good example is pharmaceutical preparations (2834). Included in this industry are a wide range of therapeutic groups such as anesthetics, anticancer agents, antibiotics, and cardio-vascular hypotensives. Clearly these products are not substitutes from the consumer's point of view. The reported 1992 four-firm concentration ratio of 26 therefore understates actual market concentration. Other examples of industries that are too broadly defined include soaps and detergents (2841), with a 1992 four-firm concentration ratio of 63, and motors and generators (3621), with CR4 equal to 36 in 1992. The motor on a Cessna is a very different product from the motor on a washing machine, with very different machine tooling requirements; their manufacturers are not truly competitors.

Often, the best evidence on market definition comes from antitrust cases in which each side presents detailed data. Werden used evidence from cartels to examine the accuracy of four-digit SIC industries.[12] He concluded that, on balance, four-digit SIC industries tend to be too broadly defined, including firms that do not actually compete with each other.

The issues of market definition discussed so far concern proper definition of the *product market*. Concerns about the *geographic market* are also relevant. The two main issues here are the exclusion of imports and exports from Census calculations and the assumption that the geographic market is national.

Publications from the Bureau of the Census report only information for manufacturers located in the United States. This causes an upward bias in measures of market concentration in those industries in which competition from imports is important. A classic example of such an industry is SIC 37111, Passenger cars. Because there are only three major U.S. producers, General Motors, Ford, and Chrysler, the reported four-firm concentration ratio for this five-digit product class is close to 100. For consumers, however, imported automobiles are a close substitute for automobiles produced by U.S. firms and, thus, there is more competition than the reported concentration ratio suggests.* Other examples of industries in which imports are important include textile machinery, women's shoes, and TV sets.

The Census calculations implicitly define the geographic market as national. If the relevant market is regional or local, the reported measures understate the actual market concentration. This is most likely to be the case for products with a high ratio of transportation costs to value, such as cement, petroleum refining, and concrete, or for products that are highly perishable such as ice cream and fluid milk.[13] In such cases, the nationwide concentration ratio may be quite low,

---

*Output produced by a foreign manufacturer in a plant located in the United States is counted in the value of shipments for that industry. Thus, the trend toward production of cars in the United States by foreign companies such as Toyota and Volkswagen has decreased the bias in concentration ratios associated with ignoring imports.

while individual firms have considerable market shares within their particular markets.

In summary, we note that industrial organization economists must make use of the best data available. This frequently means accepting government figures and market definitions but using these data with care. For broad cross-sectional studies, government concentration ratios can sometimes be adjusted to reduce the bias or extremely biased observations can be eliminated. For detailed industry analyses such as those used in antitrust cases, however, researchers often conduct their own studies.

Market Concentration: Levels and Trends

Now it is time to look at some evidence. How concentrated are markets in the United States today? What has happened to concentration over time? Unfortunately, because evidence is scarce, we can only comment sketchily on concentration in many sectors of the economy. Data on the manufacturing sector, however, are more complete; we begin our survey by looking at that sector.

CONCENTRATION IN MANUFACTURING

The manufacturing sector represents approximately 20 percent of gross domestic product and is one of the largest sectors of the economy. Because of its importance and because the most complete data are available for this sector, the manufacturing sector is the most carefully studied sector of the economy.

Table 4.7 summarizes the most recent published evidence on market concentration in manufacturing, as measured by 1992 four-firm concentration ratios. One thing that is apparent from this table is that monopoly is very rare in the United States today. Only 4.6 percent of all manufacturing industries have four-firm concentration ratios of 80 or above. In fact, less than 1 percent of all manufacturing industries have four-firm concentration ratios between 90 and 100. At the opposite end of the spectrum, extremely competitive industries are also rela-

TABLE 4.7   Market Concentration in U.S. Manufacturing Industries, 1992

Range of Four-Firm Concentration Ratios	Number of Industries	Percent of All Industries	Percent of Value of Shipments Contributed by these Industries
0–19	77	18.8	17.7
20–39	156	38.1	42.0
40–59	110	26.9	21.8
60–79	47	11.5	11.1
80–100	19	4.6	7.3

Source: Authors' calculations based on U.S. Bureau of the Census, *1992 Census of Manufactures, Concentration Ratios in Manufacturing.*

tively rare. Four-firm concentration ratios vary from 0 to 19 for 18.8 percent of all industries with only 4.4 percent having four-firm concentration ratios below 10. The evidence in Table 4.7 shows that most manufacturing industries in the United States today fall into the intermediate ranges of concentration ratios.

How has industry structure in manufacturing evolved over time? Has the distribution of market shares always looked more or less like the current distribution, or has competition increased or decreased noticeably throughout the years? Not surprisingly, the earliest available evidence is incomplete and inconclusive. The period from the end of the Civil War until the early part of the 1900s has been described by economic historians as the "rise of big business." As one researcher notes,

> [In the spring of 1861] there was only one sector in the economy that included firms that could legitimately be called big businesses. . . . That was the railroads. . . . By [1911], much of the American economy was dominated by big businesses. They had come slowly at first, appearing here and there in manufacturing by the 1880s. . . . The pace then quickened, and they came in a torrent in the last years of the nineteenth and the first years of the twentieth century.[14]

Although the term "big business" encompasses issues of both firm size and market concentration, the clear evidence is that the last decades of the 1800s brought considerable increases in market concentration. Part of this was a result of the massive number of mergers that occurred in the first merger wave, discussed in Chapter 20.

What happened to market concentration in manufacturing between the end of the first merger wave, roughly around 1910, and the end of the Second World War, is less clear. Some evidence suggests that concentration tended to increase through World War II. Oligopolistic industries produced 16 percent of total product value in 1909, 21 percent in 1929, 28 percent in 1939, and 26 percent in 1947.[15] Other evidence, however, indicates that concentration fell from the end of the first merger wave until 1947.[16]

Between 1947 and 1963 a definite increase occurred in market concentration in manufacturing, with a slower rise from 1963 to 1972 and not much change during the period from 1972 to 1977.[17] Since then, competition in the manufacturing sector of the economy has increased considerably. Shepherd found that, as of 1980, an estimated 69 percent of manufacturing industries were effectively competitive, compared with 55.9 percent in 1958 and 51.5 percent in 1939.*[18] Corresponding to this increase in effectively competitive industries is a drop in the percentage of industries that are noncompetitive. Shepherd estimated that 6.3 percent of manufacturing industries were controlled by dominant firms in 1958, compared with 3.9 percent in 1980. Tight oligopolies, industries with four-firm concentration ratios above 60, stable market shares, medium or high barriers to entry, and a tendency toward cooperation, represented 37.5 percent of manufacturing industries in 1958 but only 27.1 percent in 1980.

---

*Shepherd defined effectively competitive markets as markets with four-firm concentration ratios below 40 percent, unstable market shares, and flexible pricing. Barriers to entry and profit rates in these industries are low and there is little collusion.

Several factors appear to be responsible for this recent increase in competition in the manufacturing sector of the economy.[19] The first is increased competition from imports in many industries, including steel, automobiles, aircraft, tires, television sets, cameras, copiers, and vacuum cleaners.* Shepherd estimated that import competition increased in at least 13 significant industries comprising 3.8 percent of national income in 1980; increased import competition was responsible for about one sixth of the trend toward increased competition between 1958 and 1980.[20] Part of the explanation for increased competition for imports is superior foreign technology and design, factors that push U.S. manufacturers to change their technology.

A second factor contributing to increased competition is antitrust actions. Industries affected by antitrust include telephone equipment, long-distance telephone service, photographic equipment and supplies, and shoe machinery. Antitrust actions account for between 23 and 57 percent of the rise in competition.† It is also worth mentioning that antitrust actions are likely to have a "spillover" effect: firms in industry A may change their behavior because of an antitrust case in industry B that established a general precedent.

A third source of increased competition in recent years is deregulation, although it is hard to separate the effects of deregulation from those of antitrust actions in many cases. Antitrust cases, for example, led to deregulation in the telephone sector and in banking. Major industries in which deregulation has played some role in increasing competition include telephone equipment, service, and long distance; railroads; trucking; airlines; banking; and security and commodity brokers. Shepherd estimated that the sectors affected by deregulation account for about 4 percent of national income.

The final factor considered by Shepherd was reductions in the importance of economies of scale. The growth in market size over time has decreased the minimum efficient scale of firms as a percent of market size in many industries, particularly since 1968. Minimum efficient scale (MES) is the smallest quantity of output for which long-run average cost is minimized. Shepherd does not quantify the overall importance of decreases in economies of scale in the rise of competition.‡

CONCENTRATION IN NONMANUFACTURING INDUSTRIES

Unfortunately, less detailed data are available for the nonmanufacturing sectors of the economy. Beginning with the 1987 Census, the Bureau of the Census be-

---

*Remember that published concentration ratios neglect imports. Shepherd used a variety of additional evidence to decide whether an industry was monopolistic, controlled by a dominant firm, controlled by a tight oligopoly, or effectively competitive.

†Many industries have been affected by both antitrust and deregulation. If all industries affected by both are excluded, the estimate of the effects of antitrust actions is 23 percent.

‡It is worth noting that in the years since Shepherd's study, computer technology has developed rapidly. Advances in computer technology are likely to have brought down the MES for many industries, thereby increasing the degree of "competitiveness."

TABLE 4.8 **1994 Gross Domestic Product by Sector**

Sector	Percent of GDP
Agriculture, Forestry, and Fisheries	1.8
Mining	1.5
Construction	3.8
Manufacturing	17.7
Transportation and Public Utilities	8.9
Wholesale Trade	6.8
Retail Trade	9.1
Finance, Insurance, and Real Estate	18.1
Services	18.9

Source: Economic Report of the President, February 1995, Table B-11.

gan publishing data that can be used to calculate concentration ratios for industries in some nonmanufacturing sectors. These industries are classified using Enterprise Industrial Categories (EIC). These categories correspond to the two-digit, or major industry group, level and, thus, are at a high level of aggregation. We can use these data along with evidence from various detailed industry studies to say a bit about market power in nonmanufacturing sectors of the economy. To help put these figures in context, Table 4.8 shows the percent of GDP produced by each sector.

Agriculture, Forestry, and Fisheries

EIC data are not published for industries in these sectors of the economy. All available evidence indicates that these sectors, which account for only approximately 2 percent of GDP, are and always have been competitive. Shepherd estimated that the share of this sector that was effectively competitive was 91.6 percent in 1939, 85 percent in 1958, and 86.4 percent in 1980.[21]

Mining Industries

The evidence on concentration in the mining industries is mixed. Using the 1987 Enterprise Statistics, the four-firm concentration ratio in metal mining is approximately 53. Coal mining and nonmetallic minerals have four-firm concentration ratios of 26 and 22, respectively, while the four-firm concentration ratio for oil and gas extraction is slightly less than 9. Several complicating factors also deserve mention, most of which suggest that market power in mining is greater than the concentration ratios suggest. One is the role of government in these markets; intervention is likely to reduce competition. Also, relevant markets for some mining industries are regional or local, rather than national. A final factor is the role of OPEC in the crude oil market. This cartel has been successful at keeping the price of crude oil above competitive levels for substantial periods of time since its formation in 1973.

Construction Industries

Construction industries account for about 4 percent of GDP. These industries have become increasingly competitive since the 1930s and can now be placed among the atomistic industries. The 1987 Enterprise Statistics show that the four largest companies accounted for only 2.9 percent of sales in general building contractors, 13.8 percent in heavy construction, excluding building, and 1.3 percent in special trade contractors. Among all companies in construction industries, the four-firm concentration ratio was 2.5 in 1987.*

Transportation and Public Utilities

The government has played a major role in many of these industries, controlling competition through regulation. Within the past two decades, deregulation and antitrust policy have increased competition in some industries in this sector considerably. Shepherd estimated that the share of this sector that was effectively competitive increased from 26.1 percent in 1958 to 39.1 percent in 1980.[22] EIC data are reported for only selected transportation industries, showing a 1987 four-firm concentration ratio of 13.6 in trucking and warehousing, 14 in water transportation, and 3.6 in transportation services. Market power in some other industries in this sector is considerably higher. Air transport, railroads, and intercity bus lines have moved from being highly regulated oligopolies to largely unregulated oligopolies. Because of natural monopoly considerations, gas and electricity distribution has been relatively untouched by changes in antitrust and regulation policy. Until very recently, natural monopoly considerations also were important for local telephone service. This industry, however, is in the midst of an enormous change, and customers in some areas are beginning to choose their own local telephone service. Further increases in competition are likely.

Wholesale and Retail Trade

Wholesale and retail trade comprise about 16 percent of GDP. Shepherd's statistics show that effective competition was predominant in these sectors during the period from 1939 to 1980. In fact, he estimated that by 1980 more than 90 percent of this sector was effectively competitive.[23] The EIC data in general confirm Shepherd's statement. The 1987 four-firm concentration ratio for all companies in wholesale trade is 1.7; for all companies in retail trade, it is 4.3. Within retail trade, however, a few industries have higher four-firm concentration ratios, particularly general merchandise stores with a CR4 of 32.8. Also, for many wholesale and retail trade industries, the relevant market is not national, so reported concentration ratios understate the true market power of firms. Most retailing indus-

---

*These figures may understate concentration somewhat, however, because construction is a local or regional rather than a national industry.

tries can probably be categorized as monopolistically competitive, although some are loosely oligopolistic.

Finance, Insurance, and Real Estate

This sector of the economy is one of the largest after manufacturing and accounts for approximately 18 percent of GDP. Shepherd's statistics show an increase in the share of this sector that was effectively competitive from 61.5 percent in 1939 to 63.8 percent in 1958 to 94.1 percent in 1980.[24] Banking and insurance, however, are primarily local markets, so it is likely that national figures understate actual concentration. It is hard to make a definitive statement because EIC data are not published for companies in these industries and because the existing detailed industry studies are fairly old.[25] Because of recent deregulation of the banking sector, statistics from these studies do not summarize the degree of competition that exists today. Also, many states regulate insurance rates, complicating the picture.

Services

The service sector is another large sector of the economy, accounting for approximately 19 percent of the GDP in 1994. This sector includes industries such as hotels, automotive repair, motion pictures, and health and legal services. EIC data show the four-firm concentration ratios to be quite low in most industries: about 14 in hotels; 12 in automotive repair, services, and parking; 6.6 in health services; and 1.4 in legal services. In motion pictures the four-firm concentration ratio is slightly higher at 28.6. Shepherd estimates that by 1980 approximately 78 percent of the output in this sector was produced under conditions of effective competition. Again, there is likely to be more market concentration than aggregate statistics indicate. Product differentiation and asymmetric information (in repair services, for example) give firms some market power. Overall, however, most service industries can be placed at the competitive end of the spectrum.

It is not possible to summarize the extent of market concentration in the entire United States economy in a simple way. The most recent attempt is Shepherd's; he estimated that, in 1980, 76.7 percent of output was produced under effectively competitive conditions, 18.0 percent was produced by firms in a tightly oligopolistic industry, 2.8 percent in industries categorized as dominant firm industries, and 2.5 percent under conditions approaching pure monopoly. The trend in most industries over time has been toward increasing competition, although the pace of change has been more rapid in some industries than in others.

SUMMARY

1. Aggregate concentration statistics measure the role played by large companies in the economy as a whole, rather than measuring market share within an individual market. Aggregate concentration is a concern because of possible abuse of the political system by large firms and because of possible connections between aggregate and market concentration.

2. Data on turnover indicate that there is mobility among the largest firms over time, although the very largest firms are the most likely to survive.

3. The available evidence indicates that aggregate concentration has probably not increased and may have decreased somewhat during the past 25 years.

4. Most work within industrial organization looks at concentration within individual markets. Traditionally, a measure of market share has been used as a proxy for market power. Although recent work has shown that it is important not to associate market share with market power blindly, measures of market concentration still play an important role in public policy.

5. Several statistical measures of seller concentration within an individual market are available. The two most commonly used measures are the concentration ratio and the Herfindahl-Hirschman Index.

6. Regardless of which measure of concentration is used, an important issue is the definition of the relevant market. A properly defined market includes all firms that compete with each other but excludes all noncompetitors. The market definitions used by the Bureau of the Census are less than perfect.

7. Available data indicate that both perfectly competitive industries and pure monopolies are very rare within manufacturing industries in the United States today. Most manufacturing industries have four-firm concentration ratios ranging from 20 to 75.

8. Market concentration within manufacturing industries in the United States has varied over time. Within the last 20 years, competition within the manufacturing sector of the economy has increased considerably. Reasons for this increase in competition include increased competition from imports, antitrust actions, deregulation, and reductions in the importance of economies of scale.

9. Although less detailed data are available on the nonmanufacturing sectors of the economy, evidence suggests that these sectors have also tended to become more competitive in recent years.

KEY TERMS

aggregate concentration

concentration ratio

Herfindahl-Hirschman index

numbers equivalent

SIC code

DISCUSSION QUESTIONS

1. Should policy makers be worried about the level of aggregate concentration in the economy? Think about both theoretical reasons and the available empirical evidence.

2. What is the point of examining turnover among the largest U.S. firms?

3. Discuss the relative advantages and disadvantages of four-firm concentration ratios compared to Herfindahl-Hirschman Indexes.

4. The case of *United States v. Continental Can Company* involved a merger between Continental Can, the nation's second largest manufacturer of metal containers, and Hazel-Atlas Glass Company, the third largest producer of glass containers in the country. Both can and bottle production were relatively concentrated industries. The two largest can manufacturers accounted for approximately 70 percent of can sales, while the three largest bottle makers accounted for about 55 percent of bottle sales.

   Market definition was a crucial issue in this case. Three alternative market definitions were considered:

   a. A narrow definition that considered metal containers and glass containers as separate markets

   b. A broad definition that combined metal and glass containers

   c. A still broader definition that included paper and plastic as well as metal and glass

   What evidence would you examine to decide which of these three definitions is the best?

5. Discuss the principal biases introduced by using Census data to measure market concentration. Which of these apply to the following four-digit SIC industries?

   a. (2026) Fluid milk

   b. (2711) Newspapers

   c. (2834) Pharmaceutical preparations

   d. (3085) Plastics bottles

   e. (3143) Men's footwear, except athletic

   f. (3651) Household audio and video equipment

6. Summarize the factors that Shepherd identified as responsible for increases in competition over recent decades and explain the role played by each factor.

PROBLEMS

1. Consider an industry that has eight firms with the following market share percentages: 30, 20, 12, 10, 10, 8, 7, and 3.

   a. Calculate the four-firm concentration ratio for this industry.

   b. Calculate the Herfindahl-Hirschman Index for this industry.

2. Consider an industry that has eight firms with the following market share percentages: 20, 20, 16, 16, 9, 8, 6, and 5.

   a. Calculate the four-firm concentration ratio for this industry.

   b. Calculate the Herfindahl-Hirschman Index for this industry.

3. Use your answers to questions 1 and 2 to discuss the advantages of the HHI over the four-firm concentration ratio.

4. Calculate the numbers equivalent for each of the following values of the HHI.

    a. 1,000

    b. 1,250

    c. 1,428

    d. 2,500

    Explain what the numbers equivalent tells us about a market. What information is *not* conveyed by the numbers equivalent?

5. Compute the HHI values for the following two industries, each of which contains four firms:

    Industry A: 70, 10, 10, 10

    Industry B: 25, 25, 25, 25

    What do these values tell you about market dominance? Do you think the HHI is a good indicator of market power? Explain your reasoning.

NOTES

1. An examination of market structure could also include looking at the extent of product line diversification and vertical integration of corporations. Empirical evidence on the extent of diversification and vertical integration in the United States is scarce. For the most comprehensive summary of the evidence that is available, see F.M. Scherer and David Ross, *Industrial Market Structure and Economic Performance*, 3rd edition (Boston: Houghton Mifflin, 1990), pp. 90–96.

2. See, for example, L.M. Salamon and J.J. Siegfried, "Economic Power and Political Influence: The Impact of Industry Structure on Public Policy," *American Political Science Review* 67 (September 1977): 1026–1043; and Jeffrey Baldani and Don E. Waldman, "Market Structure, Opportunity Costs and Tax Avoidance," *Review of Industrial Organization* 5 (Spring 1990): 1–29.

3. Salamon and Siegfried, *Supra* note 2.

4. Baldani and Waldman, *Supra* note 2.

5. This discussion draws heavily on Lawrence J. White, "What Has Been Happening to Aggregate Concentration in the United States?" *Journal of Industrial Economics* 29 (March 1981): 223–230.

6. White, *Supra* note 5, p. 226.

7. Norman R. Collins and Lee E. Preston, "The Size Structure of the Largest Industrial Firms, 1909–1958," *American Economic Review* 51 (December 1961): 986–1011.

8. Robert J. Stonebraker, "Turnover and Mobility Among the 100 Largest Firms: An Update," *American Economic Review* 69 (December 1979): 968–973.

9. References include Stanley E. Boyle and Joseph P. McKenna, "The Mobility of the 100 and 200 Largest U.S. Manufacturing Corporations: 1919–1964," *Antitrust Bulletin* 15 (Fall 1970): 505–519; Richard C. Edwards, "Stages in Corporate Stability and the Risks of Corporate Failure," *Journal of Economic History* 35 (June 1975): 428–457; Ronald S. Bond, "Mergers and Mobility among the Largest Manufacturing Corporations," *Antitrust Bulletin* 20 (Fall 1975): 505–519; and Dennis C. Mueller, *Profits in the Long Run* (New York: Cambridge University Press, 1986).

10. John E. Kwoka, Jr., "The Herfindahl Index in Theory and Practice," *Antitrust Bulletin* 30 (Winter 1985): 915–947.

11. John E. Kwoka, Jr., "Does the Choice of Concentration Measure Really Matter?" *Journal of Industrial Economics* 29 (June 1981): 445–453.

12. Gregory J. Werden, "The Divergence of SIC Industries from Antitrust Markets," Department of Justice Economic Analysis Group Discussion Paper, EAG 88–9 (1988).

13. See David Schwartzman and Joan Bodoff, "Concentration in Regional and Local Industries," *Southern Economic Journal* 37 (January 1971): 343–348.

14. Glenn Porter, *The Rise of Big Business: 1860–1920*, second edition (Arlington Heights, IL: Harlan Davidson, Inc., 1992).
15. Alfred D. Chandler, Jr., "The Structure of American Industry in the Twentieth Century: A Historical Overview," *Business History Review* 43 (Autumn 1969): 257.
16. G. Warren Nutter, *The Extent of Enterprise Monopoly in the United States: 1899–1939* (Chicago: University of Chicago Press, 1951).
17. Bruce T. Allen, "Average Concentration in Manufacturing, 1847–1972," *Journal of Economic Issues* 10 (September 1976): 664–673; William G. Shepherd, *The Economics of Industrial Organization* (Englewood Cliffs, NJ: Prentice-Hall, 1979).
18. William G. Shepherd, "Causes of Increased Competition in the U.S. Economy, 1939–1980," *Review of Economics and Statistics* 64 (November 1982): 613–623.
19. This discussion is based on Shepherd, *Supra* note 18, Tables 3 and 4.
20. Shepherd, *Supra* note 18, Table 3.
21. Shepherd, *Supra* note 18, Table 2, p. 618.
22. Shepherd, *ibid.*
23. Shepherd, *ibid.*
24. Shepherd, *ibid.*
25. See, for example, Federal Deposit Insurance Corporation, *Summary of Accounts and Deposits in All Commercial Banks, June 30, 1970* (Washington, D.C.: FDIC, 1970); and J.D. Cummins, H.S. Denenberg, and W.C. Scheel, "Concentration in the U.S. Life Insurance Industry," *Journal of Risk and Insurance* 39 (June 1972): 177–199.

Chapter 5

Entry and Exit

Entry and exit conditions are important determinants of existing firms' market power. A firm with a large market share may not be able to set price much above marginal cost if entry into the industry is relatively easy. Additionally, microeconomic theory predicts that entry and exit are important for selection. New capital is attracted to an industry by the prospect of earning economic profits. Old, inefficient capital is forced to leave an industry due to losses. Both barriers and incentives affect entry into and exit from an industry, as we discuss in this chapter.

We begin our consideration of entry and exit by looking at some evidence on patterns across industries. Then we turn to a discussion of the various types of barriers to entry. Entry is also affected by incentives, particularly expected profitability and market growth. After considering the theory, we examine the empirical evidence, on both impediments and incentives, to entry.

Following our discussion of entry, we turn to more recent work in industrial organization. This includes a consideration of the determinants of exit and an analysis of the interaction between entry and exit. We end the chapter with a discussion of a relatively recent theoretical development, the theory of contestable markets.

Patterns of Entry and Exit

Before looking in detail at possible determinants of entry and exit, let's examine some evidence about actual patterns of entry and exit of firms in the U.S. economy. In 1988 Dunne, Roberts, and Samuelson published one of the most detailed studies of entry and exit available.[1] They used Census data on firms in manufacturing industries in the years 1963, 1972, 1977, and 1982 to identify entrants into an industry and follow their growth or decline over time. They found several interesting results. First, on average, turnover among firms in manufacturing industries was fairly substantial. In each census year almost 39 percent of the firms producing in each industry were new entrants since the previous census year.* The

---

*Not all of these firms had been created in the time since the previous census. Some firms entered by diversification, either building a new plant or changing the outputs produced in existing plants. On average, slightly more than half the total number of entrants in each industry were new firms entering by constructing new plants.

statistics on exit are similar: an average of approximately 31 percent to 39 percent of existing firms left each industry between one census year and the next.

The statistics on entry and exit are slightly misleading, however. Looking more closely at their data, Dunne, Roberts, and Samuelson noted that both the entering and exiting firms were, in general, considerably smaller than existing firms. Averaging across industries, only about 16 percent of industry output was produced by entering firms and 16 percent by exiting firms, even though these firms constituted approximately one third of the total number of firms. In addition, new firms had high rates of failure. More than 60 percent of all entrants, on average, left an industry within five years of the census in which they first appeared, and almost 80 percent exited within 10 years.* Thus, successful entry seems to be more difficult than the statistics on the percent of an industry comprised of new firms indicate. In Dunne, Roberts, and Samuelson's sample, at least, entrants tended to be small relative to all firms in an industry, and they failed at a high rate. These facts suggest considerably more movement on the fringes of an industry than at its center.

Disaggregation of the data reveals a considerable variation in entry and exit patterns across industries. An average of 60 percent of firms in the instruments industry were new entrants, whereas only 20.5 percent in the tobacco industry were new. Despite the variation across industries, the correlation between average entry and exit rates is high. Industries with high entry rates tend to have high exit rates, and low entry rates are associated with low exit rates.

How can we explain the observed patterns of entry and exit? The answer is complicated, and we begin with a discussion of entry.

 *Entry*

Theory tells us that entry into an industry can facilitate adjustment to changes in demand and input prices, increase competition, and put pressure on existing firms to operate as efficiently as possible. New products or new technology may also be introduced through entry. In considering the determinants of entry, it is necessary to think about both factors that make entry difficult and factors that increase the incentives for entry. We consider impediments, or barriers to entry, first.

BARRIERS TO ENTRY

Definition

There are several alternative definitions of barriers to entry. Literally, a barrier to entry is any factor that prevents instantaneous entry. For practical purposes, such a definition is unworkable. As we saw in Chapter 2, even firms in a perfectly competitive industry can earn positive economic profits in the short run. It is only in the long run that profits encourage firms to enter, driving economic profits to

---

*The size of the surviving entrants increased relative to all firms in the industry over time.

zero. Thus, in talking about barriers to entry, we are in fact considering *long run* factors.

Bain, one of the first economists to do considerable work in industrial economics, defined barriers to entry as market conditions that allow incumbent firms to raise prices above the competitive level without attracting entry.[2] According to Bain's definition, a barrier to entry exists if a new firm cannot achieve the same level of profits after entry that an incumbent earned before entry occurred.*

Other economists do not accept Bain's definition of barriers to entry. Stigler defined a barrier to entry as ". . . a cost of producing (at some or every rate of output) which must be borne by firms which seek to enter an industry but is not borne by firms already in the industry."[3] For Stigler, an entry barrier exists only if the conditions of entry are more difficult for new entrants than they were for established firms.

For our purposes, a key distinction between Bain's and Stigler's definitions is whether economies of scale constitute a barrier to entry. Bain argued that economies of scale can and sometimes do act as an important barrier to entry into an industry. Stigler does not regard economies of scale as an entry barrier as long as both incumbents and potential entrants can operate on the same cost curve; he views the cost disadvantage faced by an entrant forced to produce at suboptimal levels as a consequence of demand conditions. In Stigler's words, "Some economists will say that economies of scale are a barrier to entry meaning that economies explain why no additional firms enter. It would be equally possible to say that inadequate demand is a barrier to entry."[4]

Other definitions have also been proposed. Von Weizsacker qualified Stigler's definition by requiring that a barrier to entry must lower consumer welfare: a barrier to entry exists if a cost differential between incumbents and entrants "implies a distortion in the use of economic resources from the social point of view."[5] According to Gilbert, a barrier to entry is the additional profit a firm can earn due solely to being an incumbent.[6] Gilbert's definition is similar to Bain's, although it focuses only on the incumbent firm.†

Our discussion of entry barriers uses Bain's determinants of the conditions of entry as a starting point. Bain basically considered static barriers to entry, including structural or technical conditions facing a firm over which it has no control. Most structural barriers involve cost differences of some kind between incumbents and potential entrants.

The literature on entry and exit has evolved considerably over the past 40 years, becoming increasingly complex. Economists have introduced the concepts of exit barriers, impediments to firms leaving an industry, and of behavioral barriers to entry. Behavioral or strategic **barriers to entry** are based on the notion of

---

*Bain's definition is complicated by the fact that not all potential entrants are equally advantaged. Bain suggested considering those barriers that would face the "most advantaged" potential entrant. These barriers would then serve as a minimum estimate of the height of barriers facing *any* entrant. (Bain, *Barriers to New Competition* [Cambridge: Harvard University Press, 1956], pp. 9–11)

†Gilbert's analysis also emphasizes the behavior of incumbents and their strategic responses to entry or the threat of entry.

strategic entry deterrence with economists realizing that existing firms might deliberately behave in ways that decreased the probability of entry by other firms.[7] Exit barriers are considered later in this chapter, and strategic entry deterrence is considered in Chapters 10 through 12 following the development of a game theoretic framework for use in the analysis.

Static or Structural Barriers to Entry

Bain identified four elements of market structure that act as barriers to entry: economies of scale, absolute cost advantages, capital cost requirements, and product differentiation advantages. Each of these is considered in turn, although product differentiation is sufficiently important and complex to warrant further attention later.

ECONOMIES OF SCALE

Theory

As we saw in Chapter 2, economies of scale exist if the long-run average cost falls as the volume of output increases. This relationship is illustrated in Figure 5.1 for output levels below q_1. In this figure, q_1 is the **minimum efficient scale** (MES). This is the smallest level of output for which average cost is at its minimum. Figure 5.1 also illustrates the two further theoretical possibilities of constant returns to scale and decreasing returns to scale, or diseconomies of scale. Between q_1 and q_2, increasing output brings no changes in unit cost; the long-run average cost curve is horizontal. For output levels greater than q_2, average costs rise with increases in output.

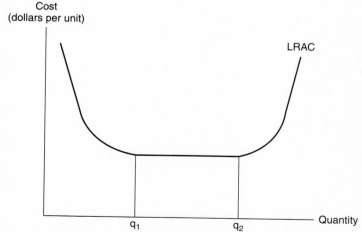

Figure 5.1   Hypothetical long-run average cost curve illustrating increasing returns to scale, constant returns to scale, and decreasing returns to scale.

How do economies of scale act as a barrier to entry?* Assume for the moment that capital markets work perfectly so that entrants can raise sufficient capital to finance entry as long as entry is profitable. Also, assume that all firms have access to the same technology. Under these conditions, economies of scale act as a barrier to entry if there is room in an industry for only a small number of firms, each of which produces enough output to minimize average cost. If each firm has the long-run average cost curve shown in Figure 5.1, it must produce and sell at least q_1 units of output, the MES, to produce at the lowest possible cost. How many firms of at least the MES can exist in an industry depends on the position of the market demand curve.

Figure 5.2 shows two possible market demand curves with the same long-run cost curve. In Figure 5.2(a) demand is sufficiently low that one firm can satisfy demand at the lowest average cost. In Figure 5.2(b), however, several firms could produce and sell enough output to minimize average cost. Thus, economies of scale are a more significant barrier to entry in the first case than in the second.

The key to understanding the argument about economies of scale as a barrier to entry is to recognize that existing, or incumbent, firms have already built MES plants. When the MES is large relative to demand, potential entrants must think carefully about the effect of entry on the market price of the product. They must guess how incumbent firms will react to entry.

Bain assumed that incumbent firms would choose to hold output constant at preentry levels even after entry. This "output maintenance assumption" is highly controversial among economists today, but we will maintain it for now.[†]

If incumbents continue to produce the same amount of output after entry as they did before entry, entry of another firm at the MES may well drive price below average cost, leading to economic losses. The losses will be large if the MES represents a large percent of the output of the relevant market and if a firm incurs a significant cost disadvantage by producing at a suboptimal scale. In addition, if a firm has to incur substantial sunk costs to enter an industry, the possibility of sustaining economic losses may deter entry.

EMPIRICAL ESTIMATES OF ECONOMIES OF SCALE

Many attempts have been made to estimate MES in various industries. Economists have used three techniques to estimate economies of scale: statistical cost analysis, survivor studies, and engineering analysis.

In a **statistical cost analysis**, the researcher runs a regression with cost as the dependent variable and output volume as one of the independent variables. To control for the effects of other factors that influence costs, variables such as the age of the equipment, the capacity utilization rate, and input prices must also be included as independent variables in the regression.

---

*Remember that some economists do not consider scale economies as barriers to entry. Stigler and others have argued that barriers to entry do not exist if there is no *postentry* difference between firms. This would be the case once an entrant had built an MES plant.

[†]Bain's model, the limit pricing model of entry deterrence is considered carefully in Chapters 10 and 12, along with criticisms and modifications.

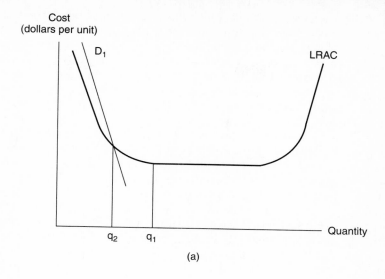

(a)

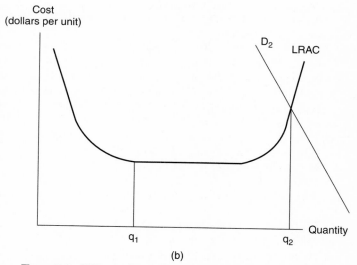

(b)

Figure 5.2   Different demand curves with identical LRAC curves.

The advantage of such a study is the ability to use high-powered statistical techniques. The primary disadvantage, however, is that these studies require extensive data that are often hard to obtain. Because of the constraint imposed by data availability, statistical cost analyses have primarily been done for regulated industries for which regulatory agencies require firms to report detailed and fairly uniform accounting data. Examples include electric power, railroads, and telecommunications.[8] It is important to note that these industries typically have been regulated *because* they were believed to be natural monopolies: the average cost curve was believed to be decreasing over a large quantity of output. It is hard, therefore, to make generalizations about economies of scale based on the studies that have been done on regulated industries.

The **survivor test**, developed by George Stigler, is a second technique for estimating economies of scale.[9] The idea underlying the survivor test is simply that, over time, the firms that "survive," supplying constant or increasing fractions of an industry's total output, must be efficient. A decreasing share of output over time is evidence of relative inefficiency; firms or plants of this size are not surviving.

As Stigler notes, the survivor test covers more than just efficiency in production; survival entails dealing successfully with a range of problems, such as relationships with labor and the government. The appeal of this method is its simplicity and the availability of necessary data. Because of this, many studies since Stigler's have used the survivorship technique.[10]

Hibdon and Mueller's examination of petroleum refining shows how the survivor technique is used.[11] Hibdon and Mueller used annual data on every refinery in the United States for the period 1947 through 1984. Following Stigler's methodology, they first divided plants into 10 different relative-size categories based on the proportion of industry capacity produced by each plant. They then calculated the share of industry capacity accounted for by each size class and watched what happened to this share and to the number of refineries in each class over time.

Hibdon and Mueller found decreases in the share of output over time produced by plants in the size categories at both ends of the range. The decreases were sharper in the smallest size categories than in the largest, leading them to conclude that, "The average cost curve has a pronounced negative slope at small capacities, a mildly positive slope at the largest sizes, and is relatively flat over the very wide range of in between sizes."[12]

Hibdon and Mueller also argued, however, that it is more appropriate to define size categories based on absolute size, here barrels per day, than on relative size, as Stigler had done. Using this alternative definition of size categories, they found a decreasing long-run average cost curve for the refining industry over the period. The results are thus sensitive to the way in which size is defined.

Interpreting the results of survivor studies is somewhat tricky.[13] For one thing, factors other than size, such as input costs, product mix, and age of equipment, may differ across firms. Economies of scale, however, refers to decreases in costs as output increases *with all other factors held constant*. Also, the results are sometimes ambiguous and confusing, with different researchers finding different patterns of survival, or, as in the study of the petroleum industry, different results depending on the exact technique used. Sometimes the smallest and largest firms in an industry "survive," while the fraction of output produced by intermediate size firms decreases over time. It is hard to know what such a result says about economies of scale.

Because of problems with both statistical cost analyses and survivor studies, some economists have used **engineering studies** to estimate economies of scale. This approach uses interviews, questionnaires, and surveys to gather information from engineers who are responsible for designing and planning new plants. These industry experts are asked how costs vary with the amount of output produced and what factors lead to economies or diseconomies of scale. Their responses are then used to estimate the minimum efficient scale plant. Largely because of the enormous amount of work involved in conducting a careful engineering study, relatively few have been undertaken.[14]

Table 5.1 shows the results of one of these studies. The first column lists MES as a percentage of 1967 U.S. demand for each industry. This column shows whether a plant needs to produce a large fraction of total industry output to realize existing economies of scale. For the 12 industries examined in this study, the MES plant is generally small relative to the national market. The only exception is the refrigerator industry, in which a firm in the mid 1960s would have needed 14 percent of the national market to realize economies of scale at the plant level.

Column 2 gives additional information about the height of the entry barrier

TABLE 5.1   **Minimum Efficient Scale Plants, Costs of Suboptimal Plants, and Concentration Ratios in Selected United States Manufacturing Industries, Circa 1967**

Industry	(1) MES Plant Size as a Percentage of 1967 U.S. Output	(2) Increase in Unit Cost at 1/3 MES (%)	(3) "Warranted" Concentration Ratio	(4) Actual Concentration Ratio, 1967
Beer brewing	3.4	5.0	13.6	40
Cigarettes	6.5	2.2	26.4	81
Broad-woven cotton and synthetic fabrics	0.2	7.6	0.8	36
Paints, varnishes, and lacquers	1.5	4.4	6.0	22
Petroleum refining	1.9	4.8	7.6	33
Shoes (other than rubber)	0.2	1.5	0.8	26
Glass containers	1.5	11.0	6.0	60
Cement	1.7	26.0	6.8	29
Integrated wide strip steel works	2.6	11.0	10.4	48
Ball and roller bearings	1.4	8.0	5.6	54
Household refrigerators and freezers	14.1	6.5	56.4	73
Storage batteries	1.9	4.6	7.6	61

Source: F. M. Scherer, Alan Beckenstein, Erich Kaufer, and R. D. Murphy, *The Economics of Multi-Plant Operation: An International Comparisons Study* (Cambridge: Harvard University Press, 1975), Chapter 3, pp. 80, 91.

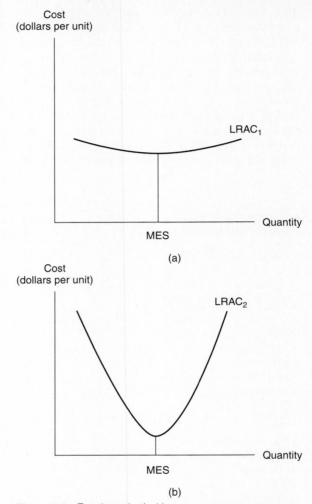

Figure 5.3   Two hypothetical long-run average cost curves.

posed by economies of scale. To understand the relevance of this column, imagine two industries. A firm in one industry has the long-run average cost curve shown in Figure 5.3(a). While economies of scale exist in this industry, the unit costs increase only slightly for output levels below the MES. A representative firm in the industry shown in Figure 5.3(b) has the same MES as in Figure 5.3(a), yet average costs rise steeply for a firm producing less than the optimal amount of output. A potential entrant might well be more reluctant to enter industry (b) than industry (a) because of the much greater increase in cost associated with entering at a small scale.

Column 2 of Table 5.1 gives estimates of the severity of the cost disadvantage of a firm that produces at only one third the MES. A large percentage increase in costs, such as that for cement, indicates a steeply sloped long-run average cost curve. This table shows that for a considerable number of the industries examined, the cost disadvantage of operating at less than MES is *not* severe, which suggests that real-world long-run average cost curves are much more gently sloped than those typically drawn in microeconomics textbooks or on classroom blackboards.

Another way to interpret the information on MES in various industries is to consider the percent of national output that would be produced by four firms, each of which operated an MES plant.* A high figure suggests that in order to realize economies of scale, an industry can consist of only a few large firms, whereas a low figure indicates that there is "room" in the industry for a large number of MES firms. To calculate this number, called the **warranted concentration ratio**, the figures in column 1 are simply multiplied by 4. Column 3 of Table 5.1 shows the results of this calculation, while column 4 shows the actual 1967 four-firm concentration ratios for each industry. Note that for most industries, the actual concentration ratio in column 4 is higher than the warranted concentration ratio reported in column 3.

The results of the few other engineering studies are generally consistent with the results reported in Table 5.1. Most industries in the United States can support a fairly large number of MES firms. Exceptions include turbogenerators, diesel engines, and civilian aircraft production. In other industries, such as synthetic rubber, cigarettes, and transformers, each MES plant accounts for somewhere between 5 and 10 percent of total national output. Overall, however, as summarized by Scherer, the conclusion of engineering studies is "that nationwide oligopoly and high seller concentration cannot be viewed primarily as the inevitable consequence of production scale economies at the plant level."[15]

This conclusion provides important information to policy makers. It suggests that in many cases least cost production is not inconsistent with an industry structure containing many firms. Often, concern about achieving production efficiency is *not* a reason to sacrifice competitive industry structure.

Because of the importance of this conclusion, we need to consider some qualifications. First, note that the engineering estimates are estimates of economies of scale at the *plant* level. If *multiplant* economies of scale are important, then the estimates of MES as a percent of total output shown in column 1 of Table 5.1 are too low. It would thus follow that industries would need to be more concentrated than the calculations shown in column 3 indicate.

A second problem with the estimates in Table 5.1 is that they assume a national market. This assumption is problematic for industries with high transportation costs, for which the relevant market is regional or even local. Again, in this case, the figures in Table 5.1 underestimate the degree to which economies of scale act as barriers to entry.

The severity of these problems is difficult to measure accurately. The best information indicates that taking multiplant economies of scale and transportation costs into account does not change the conclusion that economies of scale act as

---

*The reason for choosing four firms, rather than three or five or some other number, is the widespread use of the four-firm concentration ratio in empirial work, as discussed in Chapter 4.

only a moderate barrier to entry in most U.S. manufacturing industries. Actual concentration in many cases is higher than required by economies of scale.[16]

Chicago School economists have advanced more serious criticisms of the engineering estimates of MES.*[17] For one thing, they argue that such studies are backward-looking, based on the experience of the industry experts surveyed, and thus are quickly out of date in any industry in which production technology is changing. Also, the engineering data cover only technical processes, thereby omitting many important functions of the firm connected with efficiency. Examples of these functions are personnel decisions such as recruitment and promotion, product design, cost and quality control, and marketing.

The most serious criticism made by Chicago School economists is a philosophical one. They argue that trying to estimate MES and make inferences about the extent to which existing concentration is explained by economies of scale is fundamentally of little value to economists. John McGee has argued, for example, that "in the absence of artificial structures there is a strong presumption that the *existing* structure of industry is the *efficient* structure."[18] According to this view, firms get big because they are efficient; if any firm grows so large that it becomes inefficient, both internal and external pressures will act to correct the inefficiencies and reduce the firm's size.

◢ A Related Theoretical Development: Economies of Scope

At this point we digress somewhat from our consideration of Bain's structural barriers to entry to examine some recent theoretical work in the field of industrial organization. This work, on economies of scope, is an extension of work on economies of scale.

Most real-world firms are multiproduct firms, producing more than one product.[19] One obvious explanation for the existence of multiproduct firms is that it may be less costly for one firm to produce several products than for the same production to occur in several single-product firms. Economists have named the cost savings that result from producing joint products **economies of scope**.[20] Formally, let q_1 and q_2 represent two specific quantities of two different goods. An economy of scope exists if $C(q_1,q_2) < C(q_1,0) + C(0,q_2)$, where C is the cost function.

What are the sources of economies of scope? One is a fixed factor of production, such as a specialized machine. As discussed earlier, such a fixed factor is a classic source of economies of scale. If demand for a single product is not great enough to exhaust the economies of scale, the firm may look for other products that can utilize the same fixed factor of production. An example is railroad track. A railroad may offer both freight and passenger service if demand for either product does not fully utilize the track.[21]

---

*They also are critical of estimates of MES derived from statistical analysis.

Another example of a firm being able to realize cost savings by offering more than one product is in the airline industry.* Economies of scale in this industry are considerable: the passenger cost per mile is much lower on large airplanes than on small ones. Demand, however, in many city-pair markets is too low to warrant flying a large plane. Airlines therefore have turned to networking to take advantage of scale economies. As you probably know, many airlines have one or more hubs. Passengers originating in one relatively small city, such as Syracuse, are put on a single larger plane, even though they have a variety of destinations. These passengers are flown to a larger airport, such as Pittsburgh. Meanwhile, planes from other smaller airports are also routed to Pittsburgh. All flights are scheduled to arrive in Pittsburgh within a short enough time period that passengers can be regrouped according to final destinations, again flying on larger planes than would be warranted without networking.

The sharing of an input also gives rise to economies of scope. A farmer who is raising cows may choose to sell both the hide and the beef, rather than raising some cows just for the beef and others for the hide. Here, because two products can share the same input, economies of scope exist even in the absence of scale economies in any stage of production.

An important type of shared input is an intangible asset such as research knowledge or business know-how about production. As discussed in Chapter 3, transaction costs of obtaining new information initially, as well as of transferring information from one firm to another, are high. If several products require similar know-how, the high transaction costs associated with information transfer may make it less costly to produce all products within a single firm.

Empirical evidence on the importance of economies of scope is scarce. As shown by the technical definition of economies of scope, a researcher needs to calculate the cost of producing a specific level of each of at least two products separately, as well as the cost of producing those specific levels of the products together. In one carefully done study, Friedlaender, Winston, and Wang noted that estimating multiproduct cost functions leads to "formidable data problems."[22] Nonetheless, their work indicates the kind of information that can be obtained from such a study.

Friedlaendaer and colleagues estimated a multiproduct cost function for each of the three largest U.S. automobile producers, using data from the period from 1955 to 1979. They found wide variability in the measures of economies of scale and scope at different levels of output, indicating the inappropriateness of broad generalizations. They did find that, for all of the firms, economies of scope could be obtained by combining the production of large cars with small cars and trucks. A firm that already produced small and large cars, however, did not realize further economies of scope from also producing trucks. In general, they concluded that although economies of scope are undoubtedly important in some industries, it is difficult to evaluate their importance using current empirical evidence.

---

*A "product" in the airline market is a flight from one city to another, referred to as a "city-pair market."

ABSOLUTE COST ADVANTAGES

A second barrier to entry identified by Bain is an **absolute cost advantage**. Such an advantage is illustrated in Figure 5.4. For simplicity we have assumed that average cost is constant for both incumbent firms and potential entrants but that a typical established firm can produce at a lower average cost for any given level of output. Consider any price above P_1 but below P_2. At such a price an established firm makes positive economic profits, ordinarily an inducement for new firms to enter the industry. With its higher average cost curve, however, a potential entrant cannot make a profit unless price rises above P_2. Thus, the absolute cost advantage of incumbent firms acts as a barrier to entry.

What factors could lead to a gap between the average costs of established firms and potential entrants? Firms already in the industry may control a crucial input, may be able to borrow investment funds at lower interest rates than potential entrants, or they may have access to superior production technologies, perhaps protected by patents. They may have built plants in the most desirable locations, forcing new firms to ship raw materials or the final product greater distances. Also, entrants may have to pay more for scarce inputs, such as raw materials, managerial talent, or research personnel.*

As with each of Bain's original structural determinants of barriers to entry, recent theoretical work has considered how strategic decisions by incumbents affect cost asymmetries. Firms may, for example, try to prevent entrants from gaining access to inputs by negotiating contracts with suppliers or by buying existing supplies of a scarce raw material.† Another example is incumbents' use of "sleeping patents," which are held by a firm on a particular technology even though it is not using the technology. Such patents are valuable to incumbents because they prevent competitors from using a specific technology. This kind of strategic behavior is considered carefully in Chapters 10 through 12.

The empirical evidence on absolute cost advantages is scarce. Studies on the determinants of entry across industries typically do not include a variable to measure this barrier because of a lack of data. What we are left with, therefore, are some stories about industries in which established firms are at an advantage be-

---

*Gilbert ("Mobility Barriers and the Value of Incumbency" in R. Schmalensee and R. Willig [eds.], *Handbook of Industrial Organization* [New York: North Holland, 1989], pp. 494–495) argues that any scarce factor of production has an opportunity cost that should be included in the calculation of economic profits accruing to incumbents. Access to a scarce input by established firms, therefore, creates a barrier to entry only if the existing firm earns positive economic profits *after accounting for the opportunity cost of the resource*. For example, consider a firm with a key patent, such as Xerox's patent on xerography. Gilbert points out that such a patent is not necessarily a barrier to entry if the value of the resource in its next best use (i.e., its opportunity cost) is equal to its value to the holder of the patent. In this case, the patent should be sold, making the technology available to any firm willing to pay the price. However, if resources are specific to firms, then a patent may have a higher value to its holder than to any other firm, creating an absolute cost advantage for the patent holder.

†A classic example of such strategic behavior is Alcoa's alleged deliberate attempt to acquire deposits of bauxite ore to make it more difficult for new firms to produce aluminum. *U.S. v. Aluminum Company of America*, 148 F.2d 416 (1945).

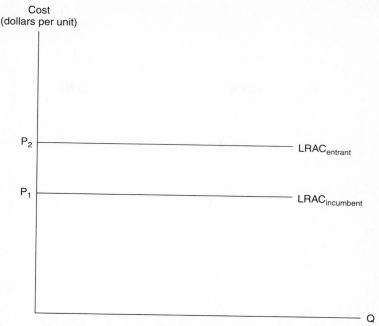

Figure 5.4 Absolute cost advantage of an incumbent firm.

cause of their ownership of the best (i.e., most easily accessible, lowest cost, or highest quality) supplies of an important input. Examples include ownership of ore deposits by Alcoa and International Nickel, control of supplies of tobacco leaf by the American Tobacco Company, Kodak's ownership of important patents, and Microsoft's ownership of the most widely used operating system software.[23] Perhaps not surprisingly, stories of absolute cost advantages often come from antitrust cases in which the government charges firms with monopolization of an industry. While absolute cost advantages are undoubtedly a barrier to entry in some industries, it is difficult to generalize about their overall importance. As we will see shortly, however, they tend to be important in industries where patents are significant or where capital costs are very high.

CAPITAL COSTS

High capital costs, the third structural barrier to entry, could have been included with the absolute cost advantage barrier discussed above. By focusing on high capital costs separately, we can emphasize a distinction from the absolute cost advantages discussed so far. As Figure 5.4 shows, the other absolute cost advantages are not necessarily associated with the scale of production. The horizontal average cost curves indicate that the per unit advantage of established firms is the same at small and large quantities of output. Capital costs, by contrast, are closely connected with economies of scale.

In general, the larger the minimum efficient scale, the larger will be the amount of financial capital required to enter at the MES. The higher the capital costs associated with entry, the less likely it is that one entrepreneur (even with a little help from her or his friends) can finance entry out of savings. A potential entrant in an industry with high capital costs must therefore turn to the capital market for funds.*

Now comes the connection to an absolute cost advantage.† If new firms have to pay a higher interest rate on borrowed funds than established firms, then they face a barrier to entry. Furthermore, the effect of this differential in interest rates will be greater the more capital investment a firm needs to finance to enter at the efficient size.

Why might new firms have to pay more for borrowed funds than established firms? Economists have identified at least three reasons for such a differential: risk, transaction costs, and loan market imperfections. Creditors may charge new firms a higher interest rate to compensate for a higher risk of bankruptcy and default on loans. Remember that Dunne, Roberts, and Samuelson found that the failure rate of new firms is indeed high.‡ Their evidence also shows that entrants tend to be small relative to all firms in an industry. A relationship between risk and firm size would thus be another reason for financial markets to charge entrants a risk premium. Theory suggests such a relationship: larger firms are more likely to be able to spread risks, protecting themselves from adverse events such as a price war, an increase in the cost of an important input, or a drop in demand. Larger firms spread the risk in several ways, including multiplant production and diversification across geographic and product markets.

Transaction costs are also related to firm size. Smaller firms pay a higher interest rate than larger firms. Fixed transaction costs are associated with issuing new securities. Large firms can spread these fixed costs over a larger volume of securities because they tend to issue new securities in relatively large amounts. Spreading fixed costs over a larger quantity reduces the per unit cost.

Theory suggests that market power in the loan market may also lead to an interest rate differential between small and large firms. Two assumptions are needed for this to occur. First, assume that concentration in local and regional banking markets is higher than in the national market. Especially in the past, this was

---

*The deterrent effect of high capital costs is greater for some potential entrants than for others. Consider entry by two firms into the steel industry: General Motors and Waldman and Jensen's newly formed steel company. Capital costs would be a considerably more formidable barrier for the second of these companies than for the first.

†In fact, Bain stated that one implication of the absence of an absolute cost advantage for an established firm is "that established firms should have no price or other advantages over entrants in purchasing or securing any productive factor (*including investible funds*)." (Bain, 1956, p. 12; italics added)

‡Some potential entrants, of course, will be able to enter a market successfully. However, as discussed in Chapter 3, it is difficult to accurately convey information. Poor risks are likely to behave opportunistically, distorting information about the risk of default. Because lenders cannot distinguish between potential entrants who have the ability to succeed from those who will fail, the cost of capital is higher for *all* new firms.

likely to be true because of regulatory restrictions on interstate branching. Second, assume that large firms tend to borrow in the national or international market, whereas small firms are more likely to look for funds in the local market. To the extent that these assumptions are true, local banks will use their market power to charge small firms interest rates somewhat higher than the competitive rates available to large firms.

The available empirical evidence mostly examines interest rate differentials across firms of different sizes. Evidence from the 1960s and 1970s suggests that small firms do pay a higher interest rate than larger firms and that this differential persists even when comparing relatively large firms. For example, Scherer and his colleagues found that corporations with assets of $1 billion could borrow funds at an average interest rate 0.34 percentage points lower than firms with assets between $200 million and $1 billion. At the time, this was a significant difference relative to average long-term interest rates.[24] Some, but not all, of this differential can be explained by risk; small firms seem to pay a higher premium on their loans than is warranted by their higher risk of default.[25]

Studies of the banking industry support the predictions of the loan market imperfections hypothesis. The more concentrated a local banking market is, the higher the interest rate paid by small firms. As theorized, concentration in a local banking market does not affect the interest rate paid on business loans to large firms because they are able to borrow in the national market.[26]

The bottom line is that small firms undoubtedly pay a higher interest rate on business loans than do large firms. Because new firms tend to be smaller and because of the greater uncertainty associated with new firms, entrants also pay a premium on borrowed funds. The greater the capital investment needed to operate a minimum efficient scale plant, the higher the barrier to entry will be.

The welfare implications of this differential in the cost of raising funds are complicated. The differential reflects both real and pecuniary savings. Remember from Chapter 2 that real economies reflect actual savings of resources, while pecuniary economies are savings that are purely redistributive, increasing the welfare of one group and reducing the welfare of another. A small firm pays a higher interest rate for its capital, and an investor in that firm earns a higher rate of return. Loan market imperfections create largely pecuniary economies.

PRODUCT DIFFERENTIATION

The final element of market structure identified by Bain as a barrier to entry is product differentiation. Consumers view products as imperfect substitutes for a variety of reasons, including differences in quality, in performance, or in reputation. In addition, costs may be associated with switching from one brand to another, in which case products that are initially seen as identical become differentiated once a consumer has purchased a particular brand. We consider product differentiation in much more detail in Chapter 13. For now the relevant issue is how product differentiation can act as a barrier to entry.

Remember from Chapter 2 that product differentiation gives individual producers some market power because each firm can raise its price without losing all of its customers. Product differentiation, however, does not necessarily allow incumbent firms to raise prices above the competitive level without attracting entry. Recall that the long-run equilibrium in the model of monopolistic competition is characterized by differentiated products and zero economic profits. Even though entrants cannot imitate the products of established firms perfectly, they are still able to attract buyers. Product differentiation does not, therefore, necessarily create an advantage for established firms relative to newcomers.

Although product differentiation does not *necessarily* lead to established firms earning positive long-run economic profits, evidence suggests that it often does result in excess profits. Indeed, Bain's early evidence frequently identified product differentiation as the single most important factor in determining whether incumbents could earn excess profits. More recent theoretical and empirical work supports Bain's results.

Product differentiation activities by firms can take many forms, including advertising, efforts by sales forces, offering service contracts and warranties, and making style changes. Our discussion focuses on advertising, although it can be extended to other product differentiation activities as well.

Economists have identified at least three ways in which advertising can create an advantage for incumbents.* These three channels are familiar ones: (1) advertising can contribute to an absolute cost advantage of existing firms; (2) advertising may exhibit economies of scale; and (3) advertising can increase the capital costs of entry.[27]

Absolute Cost Advantage

The key to whether advertising can create an absolute cost advantage for incumbents is whether the effects of advertising carry over from one period to the next. If *past* advertising does not affect *current* demand, then both established firms and entrants have to start over each period in terms of advertising, and an entrant faces no disadvantage relative to incumbents.

Suppose, on the other hand, that advertising is cumulative and its effects last over time. A winter advertising campaign might still be generating sales in the summer or fall. This could be the case, for example, if a specific ad persuades a consumer to try a product and if the consumer then develops brand loyalty toward the product. Another explanation for a carryover or lagged effect is that a consumer may need to hear or see a series of ads, say 10, before deciding to purchase a product. In this case, although the tenth ad triggers the sale, it is not wholly responsible.

If the effects of advertising last over time, then advertising can be viewed as an investment. In this case a new firm will have to spend more on advertising than an established firm in order to reach a comparable demand curve. Even if

---

*It is important to note that advertising can be procompetitive rather than anticompetitive. After all, for a competitive market to function, consumers must have good information. In some cases, advertising can be an effective way for a new firm to let consumers know about its product. Our discussion of the circumstances under which advertising is likely to be procompetitive as well as an examination of the empirical evidence about advertising is postponed until Chapter 13.

the established firm spends *nothing* on advertising in the current period, it still "inherits" some stock of advertising from previous periods. An entrant has to spend advertising dollars in the current period to catch up to the established firm. To the extent that past advertising affects current demand, advertising creates an absolute cost advantage for incumbents.

We can use a simple example to show the advantage to an incumbent of advertising carryover. Suppose that each established firm in a market spends $15 million on advertising and that the established firms have equal sales. Assume that the carryover effect of advertising expenditures is 0.2 so that having spent $15 million on advertising *last* year is equivalent to spending $3 million *this* year (0.2 × $15 million) and having spent $15 million on advertising *two* years ago is the same as spending $0.6 million this year (0.2 × 0.2 × $15 million). The total value of advertising per year for an established firm is thus $15m + $3m + $0.6m + 0.12m + . . . which is equal to $18.75 million.*

What this simple example shows is that a new firm would have to spend $18.75 million during its first year to match the effect of a $15 million expenditure by an established firm. Even if the established firms spend nothing on advertising in a particular year, an entrant would have to spend $3.75 million on advertising. For the first year, at least, the entrant's advertising costs per unit of sales will be greater than the established firms' costs per unit of sales at every level of sales.

Of course, the advantage to the established firms depends on the extent of carryover. A higher rate of carryover in the simple example above would lead to higher total annual value of advertising expenditures for established firms. How much carryover exists from one period to the next varies across industries and across types of products.[28] For low-priced, frequently purchased products, advertising depreciation rates seem to be fairly high. One study found that 90 percent of the cumulative effect of advertising on sales for such products takes place within three to nine months of the advertisement.[29] For other types of products, however, the cumulative effects of advertising on sales do not occur for two to three years. This is especially true for higher-priced, infrequently purchased products such as automobiles, appliances, and tires. The greater the carryover effect, the larger is the advantage for established firms.

Economies of Scale in Advertising

Advertising can also create an advantage for incumbents if economies of scale in advertising are important. Economies of scale in advertising may exist for several reasons. First, there may be a threshold below which advertising has no effect on sales. The cost of this minimum amount of advertising, like any other *sunk* fixed cost, leads to decreasing average cost as the quantity of output increases. A threshold exists if consumers have to hear a message several times in order to be affected by it or if a firm must buy a specified minimum amount of advertising.

------

*$15 (1 + 0.2 + 0.2^2 + 0.2^3 + . . .) = $15 $\left(\frac{1}{1-0.2}\right)$ = $18.75.

For example, consider a firm that wishes to buy advertising on national television, perhaps because its market is national. Such a firm faces a considerably higher fixed cost than one that can use local media to enter a regional market.

Increasing returns to advertising over some range also occur if volume discounts are given for advertising. The evidence on this is somewhat mixed, although some discounts do exist. Magazine advertisers are often offered volume discounts, and the cost per second of a television commercial decreases as the length of the time bought increases.* [30] Also, the cost per viewer of a television ad is much less at the national level than at the local level. One study found that "[n]etwork rates range from approximately 10 to 70 percent of the sum of individual station rates, with the discount varying by time of day and season. This means that a potential entrant cannot effectively utilize spot advertising in a limited area to counter network advertising."[31]

The importance of economies of scale in advertising is difficult to estimate. Undoubtedly, the magnitude differs across industries. Products for which repetition contributes to the effectiveness of advertising and products that must be advertised nationally are likely to exhibit economies of scale.

Effect on Capital Cost of Entry

The third way in which advertising can create an advantage for incumbents is connected to the first two. If the effects of advertising carry over substantially from one period to the next or if economies of scale in advertising are important, entry costs will include not only the cost of physical plant and equipment but also funds for advertising. Capital markets are likely to regard investment in advertising as particularly risky. It is difficult to predict the success of an advertising campaign, and advertising does not typically result in tangible assets that could be resold if the firm failed.[32] The riskiness of investment in advertising would result in entrants paying a high interest rate for such funds.

Incentives to Enter

Economists recognize that entry decisions depend on incentives as well as barriers. Much less work, both theoretical and empirical, has been done on incentives than on impediments, however. Empirical work on entry has focused primarily on two incentives: expected profitability and market growth.

EXPECTED PROFITABILITY

Microeconomic theory predicts that profit-maximizing firms will enter an industry if the net present value of expected profits, appropriately adjusted for risk, is positive. Entry decisions thus depend on expected post-entry revenues, expected entry costs, and expected post-entry operating costs. A key part of understanding

---

*Note that this discount may particularly benefit producers of more than one product who can divide a 30-second spot into commercials for two distinct products.

entry is, therefore, understanding how firms form expectations. The simplest model—one you learned in microeconomics—is that potential entrants look at the current economic profits of incumbents and enter if those profits are positive.

Some economists have developed more complex models of the formation of expectations. Highfield and Smiley hypothesized that potential entrants look not just at the level of current profits but also at the trend in profits over recent years.[33] Falling profits may discourage entry even in an industry in which incumbents' current profits are high. Still more sophisticated models require potential entrants to consider not only the effect of their own entry on prices and profits, but also the possible reactions of rivals to entry.[34] This kind of modeling gets quite complicated; most of the empirical work on entry, therefore, uses some fairly simple measure of past industry profits as a proxy for expected profitability.

MARKET GROWTH

Market growth is generally hypothesized to be positively related to entry. The higher the rate of growth of market output, the more "room" there is in the industry for an entrant and the less price will be driven down by the entrant's production, given a specific rate of supply expansion by established firms.* Also, potential entrants may expect it to be easier to sell their product to new customers than to take sales away from an incumbent in a market in which demand is stable or decreasing. Finally, new firms may have more flexibility, and thus lower costs, in adjusting to increased demand than do established firms.[35]

Empirical Evidence on Entry

We have covered a tremendous amount of ground thus far. Entry clearly plays an important role in models of market structure and performance. Before considering the empirical evidence on entry, it is worth emphasizing that it is the *joint* effect of all barriers that matters. Some individual barriers are strengthened considerably by their interaction with other barriers. If the relevant geographic market is local or regional, modest economies of scale become a more formidable barrier than they would be in a national market. Another example occurs in an industry in which it is important for a firm to provide service on the products it sells. In such a case, a potential entrant into manufacturing must also develop a service network. The necessity of entering more than one stage increases the capital costs associated with entry. As discussed earlier, even a slight differential in interest rates between incumbents and entrants can become a serious barrier if capital costs are high.[36]

Despite the theoretical work on entry and the recognition of its importance in influencing market structure and performance, surprisingly little work was done until approximately 20 years ago. A few early studies on entry focused on a

---

*It is possible that incumbents might respond more aggressively to entry in a market in which demand growth is high, however, since they would have more to lose in such a market. As noted before, we ignore this kind of strategic consideration in this chapter.

TABLE 5.2 **Bain's Evidence on Relative Heights of Specific Entry Barriers in 20 Industries (higher numbers denote higher entry barriers)**

Industry	Scale Economy	Product Differentiation	Absolute Costs	Capital Requirements
Automobiles	3	3	1	3
Canned goods	1	1 to 2	1	1
Cement	2	1	1	2
Cigarettes	1	3	1	3
Copper	n.a.	1	3	n.a.
Farm machinery	2	1 to 3	1	n.a.
Flour	1	1 to 2	1	0
Fountain pens	n.a.	1 to 3	1	1
Gypsum products	n.a.	1	3	1
Liquor	1	3	1	2
Meat packing	1	1	1	0 or 1
Metal containers	n.a.	2	1	1
Petroleum refining	2	2	1	3
Rayon	2	1	1	2
Shoes	2	1 to 2	1	0
Soap	2	2	1	2
Steel	2	1	3	3
Tires and tubes	1	2	1	2
Tractors	3	3	1	3
Typewriters	3	3	1	n.a.

Source: Bain, Joe S., *Barriers to New Competition* (Cambridge: Harvard University Press, 1956), p. 169.

relatively small number of industries, using questionnaires and other evidence on past entry to identify and evaluate individual barriers to entry. This method was pioneered by Bain.[37]

Table 5.2 shows Bain's evidence for 20 major U.S. manufacturing industries during the late 1940s and early 1950s. This table shows that product differentiation was the most important barrier to entry, closely followed by capital costs.* Bain found economies of scale to be very high barriers in three industries and substantial in seven. Absolute cost barriers were moderate to low in most industries, with the exception of copper, gypsum products, and steel.

*In Table 5.2 a "3" denotes a very high barrier to entry, a "2" represents substantial barriers, and a "1" moderate to low barriers. Bain classified an industry as having very high barriers to entry if existing firms could raise price 10 percent or more above the competitive level without attracting entry. Substantial barriers corresponded to the ability to raise price 7 percent, while moderate to low barriers allowed firms to raise price no more than 4 percent.

More recent evidence comes from a survey by Karakaya and Stahl of executives from 49 major U.S. corporations about the entry opportunities in 32 hypothetical market situations.[38] The survey assessed the importance of six barriers to entry:

1. Cost advantages of incumbents, including both economies of scale and absolute production costs
2. Capital requirements associated with entry
3. Product differentiation advantages of incumbents due to brand loyalties
4. Customer switching costs
5. Limited access to distribution channels
6. Government policy, such as licensing requirements or regulations

The barrier to entry ranked as important by the highest percent of executives in U.S. corporations was cost advantages of incumbents. Capital costs were ranked as important by the second highest percent, while product differentiation was in third place. These results differ from Bain's in terms of what the most important barrier to entry was.

To assess the joint effect of barriers to entry using Bain's method, the researcher uses the evidence on the height of individual barriers to classify each industry on an overall scale. Bain, for example, ranked automobiles, an industry with high scale economies, high product differentiation, high capital requirements, and low absolute cost barriers, as having very high overall barriers to entry. He put cigarettes in the same overall category as automobiles, even though cigarettes had high product differentiation, high capital requirements, low scale economies, and low absolute cost barriers. The steel industry, however, was ranked as having substantial barriers to entry, although it had high absolute cost barriers, high capital requirements, medium scale economies, and low product differentiation. Obviously, the judgment and expertise of the researcher are important in arriving at an overall assessment of the height of entry barriers into a specific industry. Table 5.3 shows Bain's results on overall barriers to entry.

Most of the empirical work on the determinants of entry has used regression analysis. A canonical study by Dale Orr was published in 1974.[39] Orr used annual data on 71 Canadian manufacturing industries over the period 1963–1967 to estimate a basic equation of the form:

$$logE = B_0 + B_1\pi_p + B_2X + B_3logK + B_4A + B_5R + B_6r + B_7C + B_8G + B_9logS + e_1$$

where E = a measure of *gross entry*, the average annual increase in the number of corporations in an industry

π_p = average level of past industry profit rate

X = the output of an MES plant in an industry divided by total industry sales

K = capital requirements, defined as the cost of fixed capital required to establish an MES plant

A = advertising intensity, defined as the ratio of industry advertising expenditures to industry sales

TABLE 5.3   **Bain's Ranking of 20 Manufacturing Industries According to the Estimated Height of the Aggregate Barrier to Entry**

A.   Industries with very high entry barriers:

Automobiles	Liquor
Cigarettes	Tractors
Fountain pens ("quality grade")	Typewriters

B.   Industries with substantial entry barriers:

Copper	Shoes (high-priced men's and specialties)
Farm machines (large, complex)	Soap
Petroleum refining	Steel

C.   Industries with moderate to low entry barriers:

Canned fruits and vegetables	Meat packing
Cement	Metal containers
Farm machinery (small, simple)	Rayon
Flour	Shoes (women's and low-priced men's)
Fountain pens (low-priced)	Tires and tubes
Gypsum products	

Source: Bain, Joe S., *Barriers to New Competition* (Cambridge: Harvard University Press, 1956), p. 170.

R = research and development intensity, defined as the ratio of industry R & D expenditures to industry sales

r = a measure of risk, calculated as the standard deviation of industry profit rates

C = a dummy variable included to measure the effects of high concentration. C is equal to 1 for industries assigned by Orr to the most highly concentrated class and 0 otherwise.

G = past rate of growth of industry output

S = industry sales

What are the predicted signs of the regression coefficients? As discussed above in the theoretical sections, the coefficients of the variables measuring barriers to entry, X, A, and K should be negative; higher barriers should discourage entry. The coefficients of the variables measuring incentives to enter, π_p and G, should be positive. The coefficient of r, the measure of risk, is expected to be negative; for any expected profit rate, the higher the risk, the less attractive entry becomes.

Orr's equation includes three additional explanatory variables: R, C, and S. A measure of R & D intensity is included because R & D intensity may be a structural barrier to entry. For one thing, potential entrants may not be able to afford the high initial capitalization associated with large research expenditures. Another possible explanation of R & D as a barrier to entry is economies of scale in the research process. Additionally, established firms may have accumulated patents and specialized knowledge that function as barriers to entry. For these reasons, Orr expected the estimated coefficient of R to be negative.*

Orr included C, the measure of high concentration, to reflect opportunities for collusion among incumbents. He expected the coefficient of C to be negative; the more highly concentrated the industry, the greater the opportunities for collusion among incumbents aimed at deterring entry. S, industry sales, was included as a control variable. X, A, and R all have industry sales in their denominators; including S as a separate explanatory variable allows an examination of the effects of these variables on entry independent of size.

Orr estimated his basic equations several times using different samples and definitions of the variables.† He consistently found capital requirements, advertising intensity, and high concentration to be significant barriers to entry, whereas research and development intensity and risk were estimated to be modest barriers to entry. Industry size was positively related to entry. Past profit rates and the past industry rate of growth were also positively related to entry, although the links were weaker and often not statistically significant at customary levels.

Since the publication of Orr's study, other economists have used econometrics to examine the determinants of entry.[40] Evidence is accumulating from different countries, and we now have more information about the robustness of various results. The main results to date are listed below.‡

1. High historical profit rates have generally been found to be positively related to entry.
2. There is strong empirical support for the link between market growth and entry. This link is found in studies using both net entry and gross entry and in both cross-section and industry-level studies.
3. Higher capital requirements are negatively related to entry; the more capital required to build a plant of efficient scale, the slower entry is. Because of lack of data, capital requirements is typically the only absolute cost barrier that has been used in empirical studies.
4. The evidence on scale economies is unclear and confusing. Some studies find no relationship between MES as a percentage of market size and gross entry; others do find such a relationship. The evidence on scale economies and net entry is similarly mixed, leading to the conclusion that "the empirical evidence about scale economies as a barrier to entry is not very supportive of economic theory."[41]

---

*The predicted effect of R & D intensity on entry is not unambiguous, however. New firms may be able to use a strategy of product innovation to establish a niche for themselves. (See Zoltan J. Acs and David B. Audretsch, *Innovation and Small Firms* [Cambridge: MIT Press, 1990]).

†Orr deleted the variable X from the estimating equation because of concerns about serious multicollinearity with log K and log S.

‡Studies differ in their measure of entry. Some use net entry, in which the number of existing firms in one period is compared with the number of existing firms in the previous period. This measure treats exits as negative entries, thereby forcing the structural determinants of entry and exit to be the same. Other studies use gross entry, simply counting the number of new firms. Some empirical results are sensitive to the definition of entry; others are not.

5. Multiplant operations by incumbent firms appears to act as a barrier to entry. This evidence is somewhat tentative, however, because few studies of the effects of multiplant operations on entry have been done.
6. Studies of the determinants of *gross* entry find that advertising slows entry. The evidence from studies of the determinants of *net* entry, however, is less clear.
7. The evidence on the connection between research and development intensity and entry is "confusing, perhaps even chaotic."[42] While some studies suggest that research and development intensity serves as a barrier to entry, others indicate that small firms may actually find it easier to enter more innovative industries by finding market niches.

 Exit

Economic theory tells us that exit also plays an important role in influencing market structure and performance. Firms that earn negative economic profits should be able to leave an industry. Doing so will make resources available for production of goods in other industries.

Considerably less work has been done on exit than on entry. As with entry, both barriers and incentives should affect the rate of exit from an industry.

BARRIERS TO EXIT

Any cost that a firm must incur to leave an industry is an **exit barrier**. Suppose workers' contracts stipulate that the employer must pay a month's wages if workers are fired even as a result of the firm leaving that particular market. These severance fees are an exit barrier.[43]

Exit barriers are generally thought of as some type of sunk costs. Remember that sunk costs can never be recovered; an asset whose cost is sunk cannot be resold. Sunk costs typically arise from investments in assets that are durable and specific to the firm or the product. Examples include a patent combined with complementary physical or human capital* and investments in advertising and marketing.

Economists hypothesize that exit should be slower from markets in which capital costs cannot easily be recovered than from markets in which assets are readily resold. Having committed funds to nonrecoverable assets, the incumbents are tied to their markets by their inability to divest. Firms with relatively large sunk capital costs will stay in an industry longer than firms with fixed costs that

---

*The complementary physical or human capital combines with the patent to create an asset whose value to the holder is greater than its value in the next best alternative. It is not profitable for other firms to pay the holder enough to part with the patent (Gilbert, *Handbook of Industrial Organization*, p. 522).

can be recovered in an attempt to generate sufficient returns from their investment. A good example of an industry with large sunk capital costs is the railroad industry. Because of the large amount sunk in rails, railroad companies have been slow to leave the industry even when they are losing money.

INCENTIVES TO EXIT

Incentives to exit from an industry can be viewed as another side of incentives to enter. Just as positive economic profits encourage entry, negative profits ought to lead to exit. Also, while a high rate of growth is an inducement to enter, a permanent decrease in demand may lead to exit. This reasoning suggests that variables measuring profits and market growth should be included in any regression equation concerning exit.

EMPIRICAL EVIDENCE ON EXIT

Relatively few studies of exit have been done.[44] These are the main results:

1. The evidence on the link between low profitability and exit is mixed. Single equation models of gross exit generally support the hypothesis that low profitability leads to exit. However, single equation models of net exit and simultaneous models of gross exit have not found a relationship between exit and profitability.
2. Evidence generally indicates that firms exit at a higher rate from slow growth industries than from industries with a faster rate of growth.
3. Tangible durable specific assets, such as investment in plant and equipment, seem to act as a barrier to exit. Some studies find that intangible durable specific assets, such as those associated with research and development and advertising, deter exit, whereas others find no relationship to exit.

The Interaction of Entry and Exit

Evidence on patterns of entry and exit across industries shows a high correlation between the two. Industries with high rates of entry tend to have high rates of exit, while those with relatively few entrants also have relatively few firms exiting. This suggests that entry barriers and exit barriers may be highly correlated.

At least two hypotheses predict a high correlation between entry barriers and exit barriers. First, common determinants may exist: something that creates an entry barrier may also create an exit barrier. In fact, Caves and Porter, two economists who were among the first to recognize the importance of exit barriers, stated, "Each source of entry barriers identified by Bain can also erect a barrier to exit by going firms."[45]

A very important factor common to both entry barriers and exit barriers is sunk costs. Because such assets have limited, if any, scrap value, sunk costs increase the losses associated with unsuccessful entry. This raises the barriers to entry into the industry by increasing the riskiness of entry.* As we saw earlier, sunk costs also create barriers to exit.

A second reason for the high correlation between entry and exit rates across industries is possible interdependencies between the two.[46] For one thing, new firms may push some established firms out of the industry. In this situation, entry causes exit so that industries with high rates of entry will tend to have high rates of exit as well. A second possibility is that barriers to exit actually *are* barriers to entry. As discussed above, sunk costs create barriers to exit for established firms. Therefore, investment in durable and specific assets by incumbent firms sends a signal to potential entrants that the incumbents intend to remain in the market. This signal is discouraging to potential entrants; there is little room for them in the industry. Thus, high exit barriers lead to low rates of exit and to low rates of entry.

Economists have only recently begun to examine the interaction between entry and exit barriers empirically.[47] A study by Shapiro and Khemani emphasizes the importance of taking into account interdependencies between entry and exit rates. Their results support the hypotheses that barriers to exit are barriers to entry and that much exiting is due to displacement of established firms by entrants. Rosenbaum and Lamont suggest that markets without sunk capital costs do have higher exit rates than markets with sunk capital costs.[48] Their study, however, does not find evidence that exit barriers act as entry barriers. While the two market phenomena of entry and exit are related, the nature of the relationship is still unclear.

Another Recent Theoretical Development: Contestable Markets

We have focused on entry and exit because of the important role they play in determining existing firms' ability to exercise market power. In 1982, Baumol, Panzar, and Willig advanced a new theoretical framework for thinking about entry and exit—the theory of contestable markets.[49] While the promises of the contestability revolution have somewhat exceeded the realities, the theory has earned a place in the literature and is well worth understanding.

The **contestable markets** hypothesis contends that potential competition may be more important than actual competition and that even a completely monopolized market may perform as if it were perfectly competitive in structure. When it was introduced, this theory represented a dramatic departure from the conventional wisdom of economists, and, therefore, it drew a great deal of interest and scrutiny.

---

*Gilbert points out that in a world of perfect foresight, potential entrants would be able to correctly calculate their profits after entry and would avoid entering unprofitable markets. In such a world, the direct cost of exit would be irrelevant. In the real world of imperfect foresight, however, "the cost of potential mistakes is likely to be a major factor in the decision to enter markets and in the availability of external financing" (Gilbert, *Handbook of Industrial Organization*, p. 521).

Like the theory of perfect competition, the theory of perfectly contestable markets begins with a set of three basic assumptions:

Assumption 1: Entry is free. Free entry means that incumbent firms have no inherent advantages vis-à-vis potential entrants. There are no cost advantages, no patents, and no product differentiation advantages. Entrants are on completely equal footing with established firms, even with an established monopolist.

Assumption 2: Entry is absolute. Absolute entry implies that if a potential entrant enters the market and charges a price below the incumbent's price, then the entrant will *completely* displace the incumbent. This is a very strong assumption because it implies that the incumbent has no time or ability to respond to entry.

Assumption 3: No sunk costs are associated with entry. The assumption of no sunk costs permits "hit and run" entry. Firms can enter a market, extract profits for a period of time, and then withdraw with zero sunk cost losses. It is important to note that this assumption does not eliminate *fixed* costs but only *sunk* costs.

Consider the implications of these three assumptions. Suppose that a perfectly contestable market is also a natural monopoly; suppose also that potential entrants exist. Such a situation is depicted in Figure 5.5. What price must the monopolist charge? If it charges the monopoly price P_M and earns a positive economic profit, then the potential entrant will have an incentive to enter the market and charge a price below P_M, because *by assumption* it can enter with identical costs (assumption 1), displace the monopolist (assumption 2), and leave with no sunk cost losses (assumption 3). The only price that the monopolist can sustain is P_c = AC, the price at which the AC curve intersects the demand curve. A price equal to average cost is the only *sustainable* price because any higher price attracts entry, whereas any lower price results in economic losses.

The implications of the theory are remarkably strong. To achieve a zero-profit result, all that is required is the existence of *one* potential entrant. In this model potential competition is more important than actual competition, and even a natural monopolist may earn zero economic profits. The originators of the theory recognized that any movement away from the three basic assumptions would result in dramatically different results. If sunk costs were greater than zero, for example, then hit-and-run entry would be impossible and incumbents could earn excess profits without attracting entry.

Baumol and colleagues pointed to the airline industry, which had recently been deregulated, as an example of a perfectly contestable market. This choice made some sense in 1982 because there had been a great wave of entry into the industry in the years 1979–1981. According to the proponents of the theory of contestability, entry into the airline industry required little more than a pilot and the leasing of an old plane. The firm could enter whatever market happened to yield the highest profit at the moment. In December, for example, the plane could fly from New York to Miami. If a World Series were being played between the Yankees and the Dodgers, the plane could simply fly back and forth between New York and Los Angeles. In this market, hit-and-run entry could truly evolve

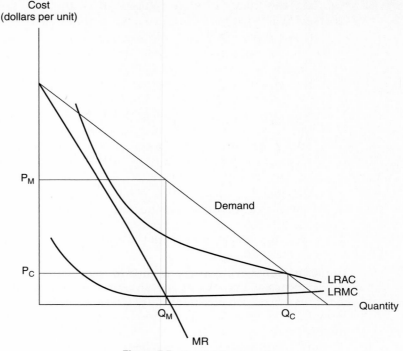

Figure 5.5 A natural monopoly.

into a highly computerized art form. Any carrier charging a price above average cost would be displaced and new airlines would rule the skies. If Baumol and colleagues had been right, we would all be flying on PeoplExpress and Midway instead of American and United.

Is the airline industry a good example of a contestable market? Consider the assumptions of a perfectly contestable market. Assumption 1 contends that entry is free in the sense that potential entrants and incumbents face identical costs. It is extremely unlikely that assumption 1 holds in the airline industry because potential entrants are likely to have difficulty obtaining gate slots for their planes. Also, they will be forced to spend significant amounts on advertising to penetrate any new market. Assumption 2 claims that entry is absolute and that a low-priced entrant will displace a high-priced incumbent. The assumption of complete displacement is highly questionable in any market, and is certainly not true in the airline industry, in which incumbents always have sufficient advance notice of any impending entry to permit them to respond with competitive price reductions. Assumption 3 contends that there are no sunk costs. This assumption is refuted by the necessity of advertising to enter a new market, and advertising certainly establishes sunk costs for any entrant. Thus none of the assumptions appear to be valid in the airline industry; therefore, it is unlikely that the industry would behave in a manner consistent with the theory of contestable markets.

A significant amount of empirical evidence now suggests that the airline industry is not perfectly contestable. Some of the evidence is anecdotal. The major airlines, for example, did not roll over and disappear when low-price carriers such as PeoplExpress, Southwest, and Air West entered the industry. There was clearly no absolute displacement of the major carriers.

Better evidence is provided by a number of good statistical studies. In one study, Call and Keeler used multiple regression analysis to examine the effects of several variables on airline fares, using data on 89 city pairs.[50] According to the contestable markets hypothesis, *actual* entry should have no effect on fares because potential entry should constrain fares to be equal to average costs. Similarly, the contestable markets hypothesis implies that concentration should have no significant effect on fares because, even in a monopolized market, fares should be forced down to average costs.

Call and Keeler's test of the contestable markets hypothesis revolves around the significance of the coefficients on three independent variables: a measure of market concentration and two measures of entry. Their results show that all three independent variables have significant effects on the cheapest available fare. Higher concentration results in significantly *higher* fares, while entry by either trunk or nontrunk carriers results in significantly *lower* fares. These results strongly suggest that concentration and entry have a significant impact on fares, yet in a *perfectly* contestable market neither concentration nor *actual* entry should have any impact on fares. These results, therefore, strongly refute the argument that the airline industry is perfectly contestable.

In another study that was highly critical of the contestable markets hypothesis, Moore found that the number of airline carriers on a route had a significant effect on fares in 1983.[51] In particular Moore found that routes with five or more carriers had much lower fares than routes with fewer than five competitors. Once again, such a result runs contrary to the contestable markets hypothesis.

Although the airline industry appears not to be a contestable market, the theory has had a major impact on the industry. The contestable markets hypothesis provided a rationale for the Reagan administration not to be concerned with concentration in the airline industry because, according to the theory, even a monopolized airline market would have to price at average cost. The contestable market hypothesis with regard to the airline industry, therefore, was consistent with a policy that permitted virtually all mergers in the industry and resulted in higher market concentration.

It should be noted that experimental economists have been able to simulate perfectly contestable markets and achieve the predicted results. But one of the major tests of any theory has always been its ability to predict and explain real-world phenomena, and according to this test, the contestable markets hypothesis has not fared very well.[52] It is possible that the theory may ultimately find its greatest use in the field of international trade, where it might be used to explain the impact of potential foreign competition on domestic markets. Also, just as perfect competition serves as a benchmark even though no real-world industries are truly perfectly competitive, contestability can serve as a useful theoretical benchmark when thinking about a multiproduct environment.

SUMMARY

1. Entry and exit conditions are important determinants of existing firms' market power. Both barriers and incentives affect entry into and exit from an industry.

2. Data on entry and exit patterns show a high rate of turnover among firms in manufacturing industries; both the entering and exiting firms are considerably smaller than existing firms, on average. Disaggregation of the data shows a considerable variation in entry and exit patterns across industries, although the correlation between average entry and exit rates is high.

3. We examined structural barriers to entry, conditions facing a firm over which it has no control. The four categories of structural barriers to entry are: (1) economies of scale; (2) absolute cost advantages; (3) capital costs; and (4) product differentiation.

4. Economies of scale can act as a barrier to entry if an industry has room for only a small number of firms, each of which is producing at the minimum efficient scale. If incumbent firms act as a perfect cartel and choose to hold output constant at pre-entry levels even after new firms enter the industry, entry may well drive price below average cost.

5. Economists have used three techniques to estimate economies of scale: statistical cost analysis, survivor studies, and engineering analysis.

6. Empirical evidence suggests that most industries in the United States can support a fairly large number of MES firms. In many cases actual concentration is higher than required by economies of scale.

7. A number of factors can create an absolute cost advantage for existing firms. Among these are control of a crucial input, access to investment funds at a lower interest rate than that facing potential entrants, superior production technologies, and the ability to pay less for scarce inputs such as raw materials or personnel.

8. Captial costs can create a barrier to entry in industries with large minimum efficient scales if new firms have to pay a higher interest rate on borrowed funds than established firms.

9. Advertising can create an advantage for incumbents through three channels: (1) creating an absolute cost advantage; (2) economies of scale; and (3) increasing the capital costs of entry.

10. Entry decisions depend on incentives as well as barriers. Two incentives of particular note are expected profitability and market growth.

11. Both barriers and incentives affect the rate of exit from, as well as the rate of entry into, an industry. Exit barriers are generally thought of as some type of sunk cost. Profits and market growth influence exit as well as entry.

12. Throughout the 1980s economists explored the implications of a new theoretical framework for thinking about entry and exit: contestable markets. This hypothesis contends that potential competition may be more important than actual competition and that even a completely monopolized market may perform as if it were perfectly competitive.

KEY TERMS

absolute cost advantage

contestable market

economies of scope

engineering studies

exit barrier

minimum efficient scale

statistical cost analysis

strategic barriers to entry

structural barriers to entry

survivor test

warranted concentration ratio

DISCUSSION QUESTIONS

1. Discuss the difference between Bain's definition of barriers to entry and Stigler's definition. Would each of the following factors be a barrier to entry using Bain's definition? Using Stigler's? Explain your reasoning.
   a. economies of scale
   b. a brand name
   c. exclusive ownership of a key input

2. Explain how an increase in the market demand for a product can reduce the importance of economies of scale as a barrier to entry.

3. In thinking about economies of scale as an entry barrier, Bain assumed that incumbent firms would act as a perfect cartel and that they would hold output constant at pre-entry levels even after entry. Do you think these assumptions are reasonable? Why or why not?

4. Explain the idea of the survivor test. Does this seem like a reasonable way to estimate economies of scale? Explain your reasoning.

5. Why is the steepness of the average cost curve at output levels less than the MES relevant when thinking about economies of scale as a barrier to entry?

6. Suppose an economist compares the interest rates charged to established firms and the interest rates charged to new firms and finds that established firms pay a lower rate. He concludes that this is evidence of imperfections in the loan market. Do you agree with him? Explain your reasoning.

7. Explain why the question of whether the effects of advertising carry over from one period to the next is important for determining whether advertising creates a barrier to entry. Do you think the effects of advertising last over time? Can you think of particularly memorable advertising campaigns?

8. Why might firms look at the trend in profits over recent years in deciding whether to enter an industry?

9. Explain why exit is likely to be affected by sunk costs. Can you think of industries other than the railroad industry in which large sunk costs might have slowed down exit even though firms are losing money?

10. In many ways the airline industry looks like a good example of a contestable market. Explain why. Other characteristics of this industry, however, make

the assumptions of contestability seem less applicable. Consider each of the following features and explain how they might contradict the assumptions of the contestability theory:

a. Part of an airline's capital is invested in terminal facilities.

b. Many people prefer to fly on a specific airline, particularly if they are members of a frequent flyer club.

c. Airports like O'Hare in Chicago and National in Washington, D.C., are operating very close to capacity.

d. In the period of deregulation, airlines have changed the way they organize their flights, developing hub-and-spoke designs.

NOTES

1. Timothy Dunne, Mark J. Roberts, and Larry Samuelson, "Patterns of Firm Entry and Exit in U.S. Manufacturing Industries," *Rand Journal of Economics* 19 (Winter 1988): 495–515.
2. Joe S. Bain, *Barriers to New Competition* (Cambridge: Harvard University Press, 1956), p. 3.
3. George J. Stigler, "Barriers to Entry, Economies of Scale and Firm Size," Chapter 6 in *The Organization of Industry* (Homewood, Illinois: Richard D. Irwin, 1968).
4. Stigler, *op cit.*, p. 67.
5. C. von Weizsacker, "A Welfare Analysis of Barriers to Entry," *Bell Journal of Economics* 11 (1980): 400.
6. Richard J. Gilbert, "Mobility Barriers and the Value of Incumbency," in R. Schmalensee and R. Willig (eds.), *Handbook of Industrial Organization* (New York: North Holland, 1989), p. 478.
7. Some early studies emphasized behavioral foundations more than Bain did. References include A.G. Papandreou and J.T. Wheeler, *Competition and Its Regulation* (Englewood Cliffs: Prentice-Hall, 1954), Chapter 12, and H.R. Edwards, "Price Formation in Manufacturing Industry and Excess Capacity," *Oxford Economic Papers* 7 (February 1955): 94–118.
8. See, for example, Ronald R. Braeutigam, Andrew F. Daughety, and Mark A. Turnquist, "The Estimation of a Hybrid Cost Function for a Railroad Firm," *Review of Economics and Statistics* 64 (August 1982): 394–404; Jeffrey A. Clark, "Estimation of Economies of Scale in Banking Using a Generalized Functional Form," *Journal of Money, Credit and Banking* 16 (February 1984): 53–68; Douglas W. Caves, L.R. Christensen, and M.W. Tretheway, "Economies of Density versus Economies of Scale: Why Trunk and Local Service Airline Costs Differ," *Rand Journal of Economics* 15 (Winter 1984): 471–489; and Merrile Sing, "Are Combination Gas and Electric Utilities Multi-product Monopolies?" *Review of Economics and Statistics* 69 (August 1987): 392–398.
9. George J. Stigler, "The Economies of Scale," *Journal of Law & Economics* 1 (October 1958): 54–71.
10. For examples, see T.R. Saving, "Estimation of Optimum Size of Plant by the Survivor Technique," *Quarterly Journal of Economics* 75 (November 1961): 569–607; Leonard W. Weiss, "The Survival Technique and the Extent of Suboptimal Capacity," *Journal of Political Economy* 72 (June 1964): 246–261; R.D. Rees, "Optimum Plant Size in United Kingdom Industries: Some Survivors Estimates," *Economica* 40 (November 1973): 393–401; and Seth W. Norton and Will Norton, Jr., "Economies of Scale and the New Technology of Daily Newspapers: A Survivor Analysis," *Quarterly Review of Economics and Business* 26 (1986): 66–83.
11. James E. Hibdon and Michael J. Mueller, "Economies of Scale in Petroleum Refining, 1847–1984: A Survivor Principle-Time Series Analysis," *Review of Industrial Organization* 5 (1990): 25–44.
12. Hibdon and Mueller, *op. cit.*, p. 36.
13. See William G. Shepherd, "What Does the Survivor Technique Show About Economies of Scale?" *Southern Economic Journal* 34 (July 1967): 113–122.
14. The pioneering study was done by Joe S. Bain. His results, covering 20 industries in the early 1950s, are reported in *Barriers to New Competition* (Cambridge, MA: Harvard University Press, 1956). The other engi-

neering studies estimate plant economies of scale as of the late 1960s and early 1970s. See C.F. Pratten, *Economies of Scale in Manufacturing Industry* (Cambridge, England: Cambridge University Press, 1971); F.M. Scherer, Alan Beckenstein, Erich Kaufer, and R.D. Murphy, *The Economics of Multi-Plant Operation: An International Comparison Study* (Cambridge, MA: Harvard University Press, 1975); and Leonard W. Weiss, "Optimal Plant Size and the Extent of Suboptimal Capacity," in Robert T. Masson and P.D. Qualls (eds.), *Essays on Industrial Organization in Honor of Joe S. Bain* (Cambridge, MA: Ballinger, 1975).

15. F.M. Scherer, "Economies of Scale and Industrial Concentration," in Harvey J. Goldschmid, H. Michael Mann, and J. Fred Weston (eds.), *Industrial Concentration: The New Learning* (Boston: Little, Brown, 1974), p. 28.

16. F.M. Scherer et al., *The Economics of Multi-Plant Operation*, p. 339; Scherer and Ross, *Industrial Market Structure and Economic Performance* (Boston: Houghton Mifflin, 1990), pp. 116–141.

17. John S. McGee, "Efficiency and Economies of Size," in Goldschmid et al., *op. cit.*, pp. 55–97.

18. *Ibid.*, p. 93.

19. See William J. Baumol, John C. Panzar, and Robert D. Willig, *Contestable Markets and the Theory of Industry Structure* (New York: Harcourt Brace Jovanovich, 1982) for an extensive discussion of multiproduct firms.

20. Elizabeth E. Bailey, and Ann F. Friedlaender, "Market Structure and Multiproduct Industries," *Journal of Economic Literature* 20 (1982): 1024–1048; Baumol, Panzar, and Willig, *op. cit.*; John C. Panzar and Robert D. Willig, "Economies of Scale in Multi-Output Production," *Quarterly Journal of Economics* 91 (1977): 481–493.

21. This discussion is drawn from Bailey and Friedlaender, pp. 1026–1028.

22. Ann F. Friedlaender, Clifford Winston and Kung Wang, "Costs, Technology, and Productivity in the U.S. Automobile Industry," *The Bell Journal of Economics* 14 (1983): 2.

23. *United States v. Aluminum Company of America*, 148 U.S. 416 (1945); for nickel—Robert D. Cairns, "Changing Structure in the World Nickel Industry," *Antitrust Bulletin* (Fall 1984): 561–575; for tobacco—*American Tobacco Co. et al. v. United States*, 328 U.S. 781 (1946).

24. Scherer et al., *Multi-Plant Operations*, pp. 284–287; Marc R. Reinganum and Janet K.

Smith, "Investor Preference for Large Firms: New Evidence on Economies of Size," *Journal of Industrial Economics* 32 (December 1983): 213–227.

25. G. William Schwert, "Size and Stock Returns, and Other Empirical Regularities," *Journal of Financial Economics* 12 (June 1983): 3–12; Marc R. Reinganum and Janet K. Smith, "Investor Preference for Large Firms: New Evidence on Economies of Size," *Journal of Industrial Economics* 32 (December 1983): 221–225; and K.C. Chan, Nai-fu Chen, and David A. Hsieh, "An Exploratory Investigation of the Firm Size Effect," *Journal of Financial Economics* 14 (September 1985): 451–471.

26. References include F.R. Edwards, "Concentration in Banking and Its Effect on Business Loan Rates," *Review of Economics and Statistics* 46 (August 1964): 294–300, and Paul A. Meyer, "Price Discrimination, Regional Loan Rates, and the Structure of the Banking Industry," *Journal of Finance* (March 1967): 37–48.

27. William S. Comanor and Thomas A. Wilson, *Advertising and Market Power* (Cambridge: Harvard University Press, 1974), Chapters 3 and 4; Comanor and Wilson, "Advertising and Competition: A Survey," *Journal of Economic Literature* 17 (June 1979): 453–476.

28. References include Jean J. Lambin, *Advertising, Competition and Market Conduct in Oligopoly over Time* (Amsterdam: North-Holland Publishing Company, 1976); and Darral G. Clarke, "Econometric Measurement of the Duration of Advertising Effect on Sales," *Journal of Marketing Research* 13 (November 1976): 345–357.

29. Clarke, *op. cit.*, p. 355.

30. Julian L. Simon, *Issues in the Economics of Advertising* (Urbana: University of Illinois Press, 1974), p. 15, and Michael E. Porter, "Interbrand Choice, Media Mix and Market Performance," *American Economic Review* 66 (May 1976): 402.

31. Porter, *op. cit.*, p. 403.

32. Comanor and Wilson, "Advertising, Market Structure and Performance," *Review of Economics and Statistics* 49 (November 1967): 426.

33. Richard Highfield and Robert Smiley, "New Business Starts and Economic Activity," *International Journal of Industrial Organization* 5 (1987): 51–66.

34. Paul A. Geroski, Richard J. Gilbert and Alexis Jacquemin, *Barriers to Entry and Strategic Competition* (Chur, Switzerland: Harwood Academic Publishers, 1990).

35. The discussion in this paragraph is based

on John J. Siegfried and Laurie Beth Evans, "Empirical Studies of Entry and Exit: A Survey of the Evidence," *Review of Industrial Organization* 9 (April 1994): 127.

36. This discussion and the examples are taken from Paul Geroski, Richard J. Gilbert, and Alexis Jacquemin, *Barriers to Entry and Strategic Competition* (Chur, Switzerland: Harwood Academic Publishers, 1990), p. 68.

37. Joe S. Bain, *Barriers to New Competition* (Cambridge, MA: Harvard University Press, 1956). Two other early studies were H. Michael Mann, "Seller Concentration, Barriers to Entry, and Rates of Return in Thirty Industries, 1950–1960," *Review of Economics and Statistics* 48 (August 1966): 296–307; and Edwin Mansfield, "Entry, Gibrat's Law, Innovation and Growth of Firms," *American Economic Review* 52 (December 1962): 1023–1050.

38. Fahri Karakaya and Michael J. Stahl, "Barriers to Entry and Market Entry Decisions in Consumer and Industrial Goods Markets," *Journal of Marketing* (April 1989): 80–91.

39. Dale Orr, "The Determinants of Entry: A Study of the Canadian Manufacturing Industries," *The Review of Economics and Statistics* 56 (February 1974): 58–65.

40. See John J. Siegfried and Laurie Beth Evans, "Empirical Studies of Entry and Exit: A Survey of the Evidence," *Review of Industrial Organization* 9 (April 1994): 121–155, for an excellent survey of the empirical evidence from more than 70 empirical studies of entry and exit.

41. Siegfried and Evans, *op. cit.*, p. 134.

42. *Ibid*, p. 142.

43. The discussion in this paragraph and this example are based on Gilbert, *Supra* note 6, p. 520.

44. The first careful empirical study of exit behavior is Richard E. Caves and Michael E. Porter, "Barriers to Exit," in P. David Qualls and Robert Masson (eds.), *Essays on Industrial Organization in Honor of Joe S. Bain* (Cambridge: Ballinger, 1976). Other references include Larry L. Duetsch, "An Examination of Industry Exit Patterns," *Review of Industrial Organization* 1 (1984): 60–68; James M. MacDonald, "Entry and Exit on the Competitive Fringe," *Southern Economic Journal* 52 (1986): 640–652; Timothy

Dunne and Mark J. Roberts, "Variation in Producer Turnover Across U.S. Manufacturing Industries," in P.A. Geroski and J. Schwalback (eds.), *Entry and Market Contestability* (Oxford: Basil Blackwell, 1991), pp. 187–203; and John J. Siegfried and Laurie Beth Evans, "Entry and Exit in United States Manufacturing Industries from 1977 to 1982," in David W. Audretsch and John J. Siegfried (eds.), *Empirical Studies in Industrial Organization: Essays in Honor of Leonard W. Weiss* (Dordrecht: Kluwer Academic Publishers, 1992).

45. Caves and Porter, *Supra* note 44, p. 44.

46. This paragraph is based on the discussion in Daniel Shapiro and R.S. Khemani, "The Determinants of Entry and Exit Reconsidered," *International Journal of Industrial Organization* (March 1987): 16.

47. Shapiro and Khemani, "Entry and Exit Determinants Reconsidered," *op. cit.*, pp. 15–26; David I. Rosenbaum and Fabian Lamort, "Entry, Barriers, Exit, and Sunk Costs: An Analysis," *Applied Economics* 24 (1992): 297–304.

48. Rosenbaum and Lamont, *op. cit.*

49. W.J. Baumol, J.C. Panzar and R.D. Willig, *Contestable Markets and the Theory of Industrial Structure* (San Diego: Harcourt Brace Jovanovich, 1982).

50. G.D. Call and T.E. Keeler, "Airline Deregulation Fares and Market Behavior: Some Empirical Evidence," in A. Daugherty (ed.), *Analytical Studies in Transport Economics* (New York: Cambridge University Press, 1985), pp. 222–247.

51. T.G. Moore, "US Airline Deregulation," *Journal of Law and Economics* 29 (April 1986): 1; for further evidence on the contestability hypothesis and the airline industry, see S.H. Baker, and J.B. Pratt, "Experience as a Barrier to Contestability in Airline Markets," *Review of Economics and Statistics* 71 (May 1989): 352; and Margaret A. Peteraf, "Sunk Costs, Contestability and Airline Monopoly Power," *Review of Industrial Organization* 10 (1995): 289–306.

52. Criticisms have also been raised concerning the theory of contestability. See, for example, Robert D. Cairns, "Asymmetry of Information and Contestability Theory," *Review of Industrial Organization* 9 (1994): 99–107.

PART II

MODERN INDUSTRIAL ORGANIZATION: GAME THEORY AND STRATEGIC BEHAVIOR

Chapter 6

Game Theory: A Framework for Understanding Oligopolistic Behavior

In the next few chapters a number of models of oligopolistic behavior are introduced. These models attempt to explain pricing in oligopolistic industries. Trying to predict oligopolistic price or nonprice competition presents many difficult problems for economic theorists. In the past these models often appeared to have little in common, and this section of an industrial organization course sometimes seemed liked a series of unrelated and highly speculative models of behavior. Recently the application of game theory to models of oligopoly behavior has established a basic framework for understanding this section of the course. In this chapter we introduce some of the basic game theoretic approaches used to examine oligopoly behavior.[1] In the next few chapters it will become clear why game theory provides a semblance of glue for holding the different models of oligopoly behavior together.

For more than 100 years one point has been apparent to economists: oligopolists recognize their interdependencies. General Motors understands that its actions affect Ford, Chrysler, Toyota, Nissan, and all other automobile manufacturers. When the number of competitors is relatively small, each firm realizes that any significant move on its part is likely to result in countering moves by its competitors. In this sense oligopolistic competition can be viewed as a "game," in which one move results in a counter-move by competitors. The illustrative games presented in this chapter are played by duopolists. As shown in later chapters, however, the implications of most of the results are true even when the number of players is greater than two.

What Is Game Theory?

Game theory is the study of how interdependent decision makers make choices. Game theory can be used to provide insight into many types of decision making, from political decisions such as voting to sports decisions such as whether a tennis player serves to the forehand or backhand side. In the last two decades game theory has been used by economists to analyze a wide variety of economic interactions. In industrial organization the primary concern is the interactions between competing oligopolists, and game theory provides a useful framework to understand these interactions.

A game must include players, actions, information, strategies, payoffs, outcomes, and equilibria. Together the *players*, *actions*, and *outcomes* define the rules of the game. The following simple definitions will be helpful as we proceed with the text:

1. The players are the decision makers. In most of our games the players will be two or more oligopolists, or a monopolist and a potential entrant.
2. The actions include all of the possible moves that a player can make.
3. Information is modeled by defining how much each player knows at each point in the game.
4. Strategies are rules telling each player which action to choose at each point in the game.
5. Payoffs usually consist of the profits or expected profits the players receive after all of the players have picked strategies and the game has been played out.
6. The outcome of the game is a set of interesting results the modeler selects from the values of actions, payoffs, and other variables after the game has been completed.
7. An equilibrium is a strategy combination that consists of the best strategy (for example, the long-run profit-maximizing strategy) for each player in the game.

Additional definitions of terms will be introduced as needed in the games that follow.

Simple Zero-Sum Games[2]

Consider the following simple game that was actually played by ice cream truck driver Don Waldman on July 4, 1968, and repeated on July 4, 1969. On those two holidays, Waldman was driving an ice cream truck in a New Jersey suburb of Philadelphia that held an annual Fourth of July parade. Unfortunately for Waldman, the suburb also had one other ice cream truck. The two drivers had to decide where to park during the parade. The parade route was about one-half mile long, and the trucks were free to park anywhere along the route. Where did the trucks locate?

Consider three possible locations, the beginning, middle, or end of the route.

Table 6.1 presents the possible sales payoffs for Waldman and the infamous "Other Truck." If both locate at the same point, the trucks split sales 50-50. But if one locates at the middle while the other locates at the beginning or end, the truck in the middle gets 75 percent of total sales. Both drivers faced identical choices, and Waldman reasoned as follows:

> If the other truck locates at the beginning of the parade, it is better for me to locate in the middle and gain 75 percent. If the other truck locates in the middle, it is still better for me to locate in the middle and gain a 50-50 split. Finally, if the other truck locates at the end of the parade, I should still locate in the middle. No matter what the other truck does, I should locate in the middle.

In this game, *middle* is Waldman's **dominant strategy**. A dominant strategy is a strategy that outperforms any other strategy *no matter what strategy an opponent selects*. Waldman of course decided to park in the middle, where he found the other truck already parked. The Other Truck had reasoned exactly as Waldman and played its dominant strategy–middle.

Looking at Table 6.1, one might ask why the trucks immediately selected middle-middle as the solution instead of beginning-beginning, end-end, beginning-end, or end-beginning. Closer inspection reveals that only middle-middle is a stable solution to the game. Suppose because of an early morning traffic jam, both trucks were initially located at the beginning. The split is 50-50, but if Waldman believes that Other Truck will remain at the beginning of the parade, then Waldman should move to the middle and gain a 75-25 split. Other Truck should reason exactly the same way, so there is no stability to the solution beginning-beginning. Even though the result in terms of sales split is identical at beginning-beginning and middle-middle, only middle-middle is stable.

Middle-middle has one unique characteristic compared with any of the other eight cells in the payoff matrix. It is the only one of the game's cells where both players are doing the best they can *given the choice of their opponent*. Such a solution is called a **Nash equilibrium** after mathematician John Nash, who first came up with the idea.[3] The concept of a Nash equilibrium is one of the most important concepts to understand about the application of game theory to economic behavior. Although all dominant solutions are Nash equilibria, some games without a dominant solution can have more than one Nash equilibrium.

TABLE 6.1 **Sales of Ice Cream (% Waldman Sales, % "Other Truck" Sales)**

		"Other Truck" Location		
		Beginning	**Middle**	**End**
Waldman Location	**Beginning**	50, 50	25, 75	50, 50
	Middle	75, 25	50, 50	75, 25
	End	50, 50	25, 75	50, 50

The game depicted by Table 6.1 has another important characteristic: in each and every cell the combined sales of the two trucks add up to 100 percent. It follows logically that for every 1 percent increase in sales for Waldman there will be a 1 percent reduction in sales for Other Truck. Such a game, in which one player's gain is always matched by another player's loss, is called a **zero-sum game**.

One dominant solution to all zero-sum games is obtained by using the so-called **minimax strategy**. If Waldman plays a strategy that minimizes the maximum possible outcome for Other Truck, Waldman will be playing his dominant strategy. Returning to Table 6.1, Waldman should surmise that if he parks at either the beginning or end, Other Truck will play middle and gain 75 percent. If Waldman selects middle, Other Truck will play middle and gain 50 percent. Waldman's minimax strategy is to play middle, which minimizes Other Truck's maximum possible outcome at 50 percent. Viewed from Other Truck's perspective, the minimax strategy is to maximize the minimum possible outcome for each possible play. Because the minimum possible result of playing either beginning or end is 25 percent, and the minimum possible result of playing middle is 50 percent, Other Truck will play middle.

The Information Structure of Games

In the ice cream truck example, each player knew all of the information in Table 6.1; *in addition*, each player knew that the other player also knew all of the information in Table 6.1. In this case information is referred to as common knowledge.

There are four other useful ways of categorizing the information structure of a game. In a game with **perfect information**, each player knows *every* move that has been made by the other players *before* taking any action. Given this definition, all games in which the players move *simultaneously* are games of imperfect information because the players do not know the simultaneous move of the other player. The Waldman ice cream truck game is an example of a game with imperfect information.

Many games require a *nonplayer* to take *random* actions at some point in the game. For example, in some games this nonplayer randomly determines at the beginning of the game whether one of the players will always take the same action (e.g., an established firm might *always* fight new firms) or vary its actions (e.g., an established firm might *sometimes* fight new firms and *sometimes* accommodate new firms). Game theorists refer to a nonplayer who takes such random actions as nature.

If a game includes nature, but nature does *not* move first, or nature's first move is observed by *all* players, the game is of **complete information**. Furthermore, if nature *never* moves after any other player moves, then the game is of **certain information**.

Finally, if all players have exactly the same information when each player moves, the game is said to be of **symmetric information**. If some players know different information than other players, then the game is of **asymmetric information**.

Prisoner's Dilemma Games[4]

All zero-sum games have fairly straightforward solutions. What happens, however, when we move into the realm of non–zero sum games?

Oligopoly games of collusion are typically non–zero sum games. In non–zero sum games, the total payoff in each cell varies. Consider a collusive agreement between two duopolists, General Electric and Westinghouse, to keep the price of turbine generators at the high joint profit–maximizing level. Table 6.2 represents a possible profit matrix for such a game. Note that the combined profits vary from cell to cell, from a minimum of $160 million to a maximum of $200 million. If both firms abide by the high price agreement, they each earn $100 million. If they both break the agreement, they each earn only $80 million. If only one chisels, the chiseler earns $140 million, leaving the high price firm with only $25 million. The game is of imperfect information because GE and Westinghouse *simultaneously* select prices. This game is also a **static game** because both players move simultaneously. *Static games* are distinguished from **dynamic games,** in which players take turns moving.

Start by considering whether there is a dominant strategy to this game. If GE prices high, then Westinghouse should price low and earn $140 million. If GE prices low, Westinghouse should still price low and earn $80 million. *No matter what strategy GE adopts*, Westinghouse should price low. Low price is a *dominant* strategy for Westinghouse. Furthermore, because the matrix is perfectly symmetric, GE's dominant strategy is also low price. Both firms should price low and earn $80 million. Yet something seems amiss with this result. They could both be better off if only they would agree to play high price.

The basic form of this game is known as the **prisoner's dilemma.** Chapter 9 explores several possible strategies to try to solve the prisoner's dilemma, but first let's consider why this game is called the prisoner's dilemma. Suppose two members of the mob, Big Boy and Mumbles, have just been arrested for drug dealing. The district attorney knows that she needs a confession from at least one of them to get a strong conviction and stiff sentence. Police detective Tracy puts them in separate rooms for interrogation, where both are offered the same deal. If either confesses and turns state's evidence, he will receive a lighter sentence. Of course, if both confess there is no need to use either of them in court, and they will receive a somewhat smaller break in return for a confession.

TABLE 6.2   **Profits (General Electric, Westinghouse)**

		Westinghouse Price	
		High Price	**Low Price**
GE Price	**High Price**	100, 100	25, 140
	Low Price	140, 25	80, 80

TABLE 6.3   Sentences (Big Boy, Mumbles)

		Mumbles' Action	
		Confess	**Don't Confess**
Big Boy's action	**Confess**	6 years, 6 years	1 year, 10 years
	Don't confess	10 years, 1 year	3 years, 3 years

The game matrix is represented by Table 6.3. Both Big Boy and Mumbles have a dominant strategy. No matter what the other does, both are better off if they confess. If Mumbles confesses, Big Boy reduces his sentence by four years by also confessing. If Mumbles stays quiet, Big Boy reduces his sentence by two years by confessing. Clearly Big Boy should confess, and so should Mumbles. Given this payoff matrix, confession is a dominant strategy. This is the classic form of the prisoner's dilemma.

Realizing this problem, the mob will work hard to find a solution to the dilemma. One solution might be to change the matrix so that it is known with virtual certainty that all "squealers" will be killed. This "slight" alteration in the matrix changes Table 6.3 into Table 6.4 and obviously changes the outcome. The dominant solution is now to play *don't confess*. The death threat actually reduces both Big Boy's and Mumbles's sentences.

Repeated Games[5]

The classic prisoner's dilemma game is played only once, but most oligopoly games are played repeatedly. IBM and Apple compete not only in the current period, but in many future periods as well. The repeated nature of oligopoly games makes it possible for a player's current action to affect future outcomes. If GE and Westinghouse competed in the turbine market in only *one* period and the payoff matrix was the one depicted in Table 6.2, then each firm has a powerful incentive to play *low price*. In a one-period game, no matter what GE does, it makes sense for Westinghouse to play *low price*, and vice-versa.

TABLE 6.4   Sentences (Big Boy, Mumbles)

		Mumbles' Action	
		Confess	**Don't Confess**
Big Boy's Action	**Confess**	Death, death	Death, 10 years
	Don't Confess	10 years, death	3 years, 3 years

Suppose GE and Westinghouse expect to compete in this market for a *finite* number of periods. Perhaps Westinghouse and GE anticipate that they will sell their turbine operations in ten years, so they expect to compete for another forty quarters. What should they do in each quarter for the next ten years? In a **repeated game** like this one, a simple one-period *simultaneous* move game is repeated over and over again. In each additional round, the players know the *previous* actions undertaken by all other players. Repeated games of this form are referred to as games of *almost perfect* information. Because the moves are simultaneous, the game must be of *imperfect information.*

Consider GE's strategy in the last quarter, the 40th, which occurs in ten years. In the 40th quarter, GE has nothing to fear regarding the future playing of the game, and therefore, in the last period (the 40th quarter), GE should play its dominant strategy—low price. This is in its best interest in the last period, no matter what Westinghouse does. Westinghouse, of course, does the same thing, so the 40th quarter results in a payoff of *low price, low price*, or $80 million.

Now what should GE do in the 39th quarter? Because the result of the 40th quarter is known, GE's action in the 39th quarter will not affect the 40th quarter outcome, and GE should play the 39th quarter as if it were the last quarter. This means it should play its dominant strategy in the 39th quarter—low price. Westinghouse does the same, and the 39th quarter results in an equilibrium of *low price, low price*. But now the 38th quarter becomes the last, and the actions undertaken in the 38th quarter will have no effect on the outcome in the 39th quarter. The equilibrium in the 38th quarter, therefore, must also be *low price, low price*. By simply continuing to work backward through time, it is obvious that the equilibrium play in *every period* is the dominant strategy in the last period—low price, low price. This will be true for any *finite* game: because there is no incentive to play *high price* in the last round, there will be no incentive to play *high price* in any earlier round.

To complicate things more, it is important to realize that most games played by oligopolists are *infinite* games. GE and Westinghouse probably expect to play the turbine generator game forever. In any infinite game, there is no known last round, and players can undertake early actions in the hopes of affecting the future strategy of their competitors. In an infinite game, GE may believe that an early play of *high price* on its part may encourage Westinghouse to play *high price* in the future. As we will see in Chapter 8, the optimal strategy in this infinite game may be very different from the optimal strategy in a finite game.

Games of Mixed Strategies[6]

So far all the games presented have resulted in one Nash equilibrium. Some games, however, fail to produce even one Nash equilibrium. Take the game depicted by the matrix in Table 6.5. McDonald's and Burger King engage in a game, but no matter what their current action, at least one of them has an incentive to change tactics in the next round of this infinite game. If the current position is McDonald's—low price, Burger King—heavy advertising, then McDonald's has an incentive to move to *heavy advertising*. But then in the cell *heavy advertising, heavy*

TABLE 6.5	Payoff Matrix (McDonald's Profits, Burger King's Profits)

		Burger King's Action		
		Low Price	Status Quo	Heavy Advertising
McDonald's Action	Low Price	60, 35	65, 20	55, 45
	Status Quo	40, 40	60, 40	45, 55
	Heavy Advertising	55, 50	60, 30	60, 40

advertising, Burger King has an incentive to play *low price*. Unfortunately, once the play is McDonald's—heavy advertising, Burger King—low price, then McDonald's has an incentive to play *low price* as well, but then Burger King has an incentive to play *heavy advertising* and we are right back where we started. As an exercise, prove to yourself that none of the status quo cells result in a stable equilibrium either, and that even if the two firms begin at *status quo, status quo*, things will quickly move toward alternating in a clockwise manner between the four corner cells.

In Table 6.5, *status quo* is a **dominated strategy**. A dominated strategy is a strategy that is *always* worse than some other strategy. *Status quo* can always be beaten by some other strategy. It is helpful to recognize dominated strategies and realize that they are not viable options. As such, dominated strategies can be eliminated as possible solutions to any game. If this is done, Table 6.5 can be transformed into Table 6.6. Even with *status quo* eliminated, there is still no simple solution to the game.

What should Ronald McDonald and the Burger King do? The answer is to play a **mixed strategy**. In an optimal mixed strategy, each player *randomly* selects its actions with given probabilities that maximize its expected payoff *given the randomly selected strategy being played by its opponent*. Although it is well beyond the mathematical rigor of this book, it can be proved that an optimal set of probabilities always exists to solve such problems.[7] For the matrix presented in Table

TABLE 6.6	Payoff Matrix with the Elimination of Dominated Strategy—Status Quo (McDonald's Profits, Burger King's Profits)

		Burger King's Action	
		Low Price	Heavy Advertising
McDonald's Action	Low Price	60, 35	55, 45
	Heavy Advertising	55, 50	60, 40

6.6, the optimal strategy for Burger King is to play *low price* 50 percent of the time and *heavy advertising* 50 percent of the time. For McDonald's the optimal strategy is also to play each strategy 50 percent of the time.*

To understand the remainder of this text, it is not important whether you understand the calculus in the footnote. It is important, however, to understand that one of the characteristics of all mixed strategy equilibria is that once the equilibrium is obtained, both players are indifferent between playing their equilibrium strategy and any other strategy. In Table 6.6, notice that *if McDonald's plays its optimal mixed strategy of 50 percent low price and 50 percent heavy advertising*, then Burger King's expected profits are $42.5 million *no matter what strategy Burger King selects*. You can check this result for yourself by observing that Burger King's expected profits are $42.5 million if it plays its own optimal strategy of a 50-50 split, or if it plays low price 100 percent of the time, or if it plays heavy advertising 100 percent of the time, or if it plays any other strategy.

This characteristic of optimal mixed strategies may at first seem strange, but it actually makes a great deal of intuitive sense if the optimal mixed strategy is envisioned as the strategy that makes your opponent's selection of a strategy *irrelevant* to its outcome. By playing the optimal mixed strategy, you have placed your opponent in a weak position where it simply does not matter what it does. In other words, once Burger King selects the strategy *low price* 50 percent of the time, *heavy advertising* 50 percent of the time, McDonald's will earn the same expected payoff no matter what strategy it selects, and vice-versa for Burger King.

---

*Using calculus, the solution to the game represented in Table 6.6 is obtained in the following manner: In the analysis, π represents profits, and ρ represents probability. For example, ρ_{LM} represents the probability that McDonald's plays "Low Price," and ρ_{HABK} represents the probability that Burger King plays "Heavy Advertising." The problem for both McDonald's and Burger King is to maximize their expected value of profits.

For McDonald's the problem is to maximize expected profits, $E(\pi)$, where:

$$E(\pi) = \rho_{LM}[60\rho_{LBK} + 55(1 - \rho_{LBK})] + (1 - \rho_{LM})[55\rho_{LBK} + 60(1 - \rho_{LBK})].$$

After some algebraic manipulation:

$$E(\pi) = 10\rho_{LM}\rho_{LBK} - 5\rho_{LM} - 5\rho_{LBK} + 60.$$

Assuming the existence of an interior solution, profit maximization requires:

$$\frac{\partial E(\pi)}{\partial \rho_{LM}} = 10\rho_{LBK} - 5 = 0 \text{ or } \rho_{LBK} = \frac{1}{2} \text{ and } \rho_{HABK} = \left(1 - \frac{1}{2}\right) = \frac{1}{2}.$$

For Burger King the problem is to maximize expected profits, $E(\pi)$, where:

$$E(\pi) = \rho_{LBK}[35\rho_{LM} + 50(1 - \rho_{LM})] + (1 - \rho_{LBK})[45\rho_{LM} + 40(1 - \rho_{LM})].$$

After some algebraic manipulation:

$$E(\pi) = -20\rho_{LBK}\rho_{LM} + 10\rho_{LBK} + 5\rho_{LM} + 40.$$

Assuming the existence of an interior solution, profit maximization requires:

$$\frac{\partial E(\pi)}{\partial \rho_{LBK}} = -20\rho_{LM} + 10 = 0 \text{ or } \rho_{LM} = \frac{1}{2} \text{ and } \rho_{HABK} = \left(1 - \frac{1}{2}\right) = \frac{1}{2}.$$

The 50-50 percent mixed strategy equilibrium is called a mixed strategy Nash equilibrium. A mixed strategy Nash equilibrium is inherently unstable because both players have little incentive to maintain the equilibrium.

◢ *Sequential Games*[8]

So far all our games have been *static games of imperfect information* in which both players move simultaneously. Many oligopoly games, however, are sequential, in which Firm 1 moves, then Firm 2 responds, then Firm 1 responds to Firm 2's response, and so on. If one player moves first, then it would be misleading to represent the game in matrix form because that would camouflage the fact that one player knows the other player's choice before making a move. Because the next player to move knows the previous move of its competitor, sequential games of this type are games of *perfect information*. Sequential games are known as dynamic games and are represented by **game trees**. The game tree representation of the game is known as the **extensive form of a game**. Game theorists distinguish the *extensive form* of a game from the simpler strategic form of a game.* In its *strategic form*, a game is represented by a simple profit matrix such as Table 6.7.

To illustrate why it is important to represent sequential games in their *extensive form*, consider Table 6.7 and Figure 6.1. Initially, both Table 6.7 and Figure 6.1 may appear to be representing the same game, but the outcomes may be quite different. If the game is represented in its *strategic form* as a simultaneous move game such as Table 6.7, then there are two Nash equilibria: *Top, Left* and *Bottom, Right*.

Now consider the extensive form of the same game as shown in Figure 6.1. In Figure 6.1, Firm B has been given the first move. Firm B must choose either *Right* or *Left*. As Dixit and Nalebuff noted, the first rule of game theory is to "look ahead and reason back."[9] Suppose Firm B does just that. Firm B knows that a choice of *Left* will result in a profit of $1 million no matter what Firm A does. However, a

---

*The *strategic form* of the game was originally known as the *normal form* of the game, but the term "normal form" is rarely used today.

TABLE 6.7   **Payoff Matrix (Firm A's Profit, Firm B's Profit)**

		Firms B's Action	
		Left	Right
Firm A's Action	**Top**	10, 1	0, −2
	Bottom	10, 1	4, 4

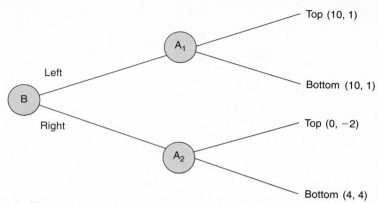

Figure 6.1 The extensive form of the game in Table 6.7 (Firm A's profits, Firm B's profits).

choice of *Right* means that the only sensible thing for Firm A to do is play *Bottom* because obviously, given a choice between earning $0 or $4 million, Firm A will select $4 million. Firm B knows that a play of *Right* will result in a profit of $4 million, and a play of *Left* results in a profit of only $1 million. The choice for Firm B is clear—play *Right*! Once Firm B has played *Right*, Firm A will play *Bottom* and also earn $4 million. In the extensive form of the game there is only one equilibrium—(*Bottom, Right*).

But wait a minute. Why should Firm A have to settle for just $4 million, when it could earn $10 million *if* Firm B would just play *Left*? Can't Firm A *threaten* to play *Top* if Firm B plays *Right*? Of course, Firm A can threaten to play *Top* if B plays *Right*, but is the threat *credible*? After all, once Firm B selects *Right*, A's choice is either earn $0 or earn $4 million. Given those choices, a rational firm would select $4 million.

Could Firm A ever manage to convince Firm B that it would play *Top* if B played *Right*? Surely there are ways to make this threat credible. Firm A could hire an impartial agent, perhaps a lawyer or a firm in another industry, and sign a contract that stated: if Firm B ever plays *Right*, my agent will make my move for me and play *Top*. By giving up the option of making the choice for itself, Firm A might convince Firm B that a play of *Right* will result in a payoff of −$2 million.

The game depicted by Figure 6.1 can easily be related to a game of potential entry. Consider Firm B as a potential entrant and Firm A as an established monopolist. If Left is *Stay Out*, Right is *Enter*, Top is *respond aggressively if entry occurs*, and Bottom is *maintain price at the current level*, the game becomes easy to reinterpret.

In Figure 6.2, we have made all of the changes in the game tree. Once this is done, the game becomes an entry choice for Firm B, followed by a response choice for Firm A. Given the preceding analysis, the equilibrium in this game is for Firm B to enter and Firm A to maintain its current price. In the real world, many a Firm A has attempted to change this game tree by making Firm B believe

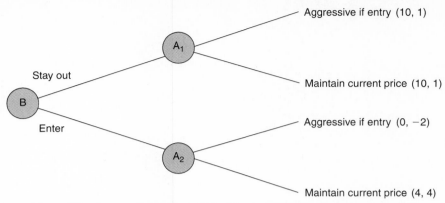

Figure 6.2 A game of entry (established firm's profit, potential entrant's profit).

that it would actually choose *aggressive if entry*. In Chapters 10 through 12 we consider some possible methods that Firm A might adopt to convince Firm B of its serious intention to play *aggressive if entry*.

SUMMARY

1. Game theory is the study of how interdependent decision makers make choices.

2. A game must include players, actions, information, strategies, payoffs, outcomes, and equilibria.

3. In simple zero-sum games the minimax strategy is a dominant solution to the game.

4. A Nash equilibrium exists if all the players are doing the best they can given the choices of their opponents.

5. It is important to understand the information structure of a game. In a game of perfect information each player knows every move that has been made by the other players before taking any action. In games of complete information, nature does not move first or nature's first move is observed by all the players. In a game of certain information, nature never moves after another player moves. In a game of symmetric information all players have exactly the same information when each moves.

6. The dominant solution to the classic prisoner's dilemma game results in a nonoptimal solution for the players.

7. In a game of mixed strategy there is no Nash equilibrium. Furthermore, in the mixed strategy equilibrium, both players are indifferent between playing their mixed strategy equilibrium and any other strategy.

8. In sequential games, the players take turns moving instead of moving simultaneously.

KEY TERMS

asymmetric information

certain information

complete information

dominant strategy

dominated strategy

dynamic game

extensive form of a game

game theory

game trees

minimax strategy

mixed strategy games

Nash equilibrium

perfect information

prisoner's dilemma game

repeated games

static game

symmetric information

zero-sum game

DISCUSSION QUESTIONS

1. Are all dominant strategy equilibria also Nash equilibria? Are all Nash equilibria also dominant strategy equilibria?

2. Can you suggest a business strategy that is equivalent to the death threat strategy used by organized crime to prevent squealing?

3. Suppose you are playing a game and your opponent is *not* playing her Nash equilibrium strategy. Should you play your Nash equilibrium strategy?

4. It was noted in the text that mixed strategy equilibria are inherently unstable. Explain why.

PROBLEMS

1. Suppose that in the Waldman ice cream truck example with a 1-mile parade route, the local police had forced Waldman to park $\frac{1}{4}$ mile from the beginning of the parade route and Other Truck to park $\frac{1}{4}$ mile from the end of the route. How would sales have been split in this case? Is this a Nash equilibrium? Is society better or worse off with this forced result?

2. Suppose that a game has the following extensive form:

A Game of Entry
(Firm A's Profit, Firm B's Profit)

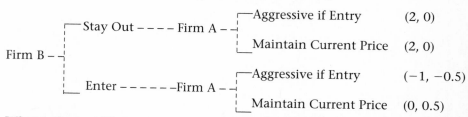

What is the equilibrium in the game? Can Firm A undertake an action to prevent this outcome?

3. Consider the following payoff matrix for Firm A and Firm B. Firm A's profits are shown first, followed by Firm B's profits.

		Firm B's Action	
		High Price	**Low Price**
Firm A's Action	**High Price**	40, 30	30, 35
	Low Price	35, 25	32, 20

Is there a dominant strategy in this game? Is there a Nash equilibrium in this game? What strategy would the firms adopt in this case?

REFERENCES

1. For an excellent basic introduction to game theory, see Avinash Dixit and Barry Nalebuff, *Thinking Strategically* (New York: Norton, 1991). For the early and seminal work, see John von Neumann and Oskar Morgenstern, *Theory of Games and Economic Behavior* (Princeton, NJ: Princeton University Press, 1944); see also Thomas C. Schelling, *The Strategy of Conflict* (Cambridge: Harvard University Press, 1960). For more advanced treatments directed at economics, see Martin Shubik, *Game Theory in the Social Sciences* (Cambridge: MIT Press, 1984); James W. Friedman, *Oligopoly and the Theory of Games* (Amsterdam: North-Holland, 1977); and R. Duncan Luce and Howard Raiffa, *Games and Decisions* (New York: John Wiley and Sons, 1957). For a recent summary of the field, see Jean Tirole, *The Theory of Industrial Organization* (Cambridge: MIT Press, 1988), especially chapter 11; and Robert Gibbons, *Game Theory for Applied Economists* (Princeton, NJ: Princeton University Press, 1992). See also Morton Davis, *Game Theory: A Nontechnical Introduction* (New York, Basic Books, 1983); and Eric Rasmusen, *Games and Information* (Oxford: Basil Blackwell, 1989).

2. For a good, simple treatment of zero-sum games, see J.D. Williams, *The Complete Strategist* (New York: McGraw-Hill, 1966).

3. John Nash, "Noncooperative Games," *Annals of Mathematics* 54 (September 1951): 286–295. The middle-middle solution was first identified by Hotelling. See Harold Hotelling, "Stability in Competition," *Economic Journal* 39 (1929): 41–57.

4. The prisoner's dilemma is usually attributed to R. Duncan Luce and Howard Raiffa, *Games and Decisions* (New York: John Wiley and Sons, 1957), p. 94. For an easy to follow treatment, see Dixit and Nalebuff, *supra* note 1, chapter 4, pp. 89–118. For more on the prisoner's dilemma, see Robert Axelrod, *The Evolution of Cooperation* (New York: Basic Books, 1984).

5. For a basic explanation of a repeated game, see Dixit and Nalebuff, *supra* note 1, pp. 95–118; and Gibbons, *supra* note 1, pp. 83–99. See also, Friedman, *supra* note 1; Axelrod, *supra* note 4; Richard Selten, "The Chain Store Paradox," *Theory and Decision* (April 1978): 127–159; Drew Fudenberg and Eric Maskin, "The Folk Theorem in Repeated Games with Discounting or with Incomplete Information," *Econometrica* (May 1986): 533–554; and Drew Fudenberg and Jean Tirole, "Game Theory for Industrial Organization: Introduction and Overview," in Richard Schmalensee and Robert Willig (eds.), *Handbook of Industrial Organization* (Amsterdam: North Holland, 1989).

6. For a basic explanation of mixed strategy equilibria, see Rasmusen, *supra* note 1, chapter 3, pp. 69–82. See also Dixit and Nalebuff, *supra* note 1, chapter 7, pp. 168–198; and Tirole, *supra* note 1, pp. 423–425.

7. Gibbons, *supra* note 1, pp. 29–33.

8. See Dixit and Nalebuff, *supra* note 1, chapter 5, pp. 119–141. Also Tirole, *supra* note 1, pp. 439–441; and Gibbons, *supra* note 1, pp. 55–82.

9. Dixit and Nalebuff, *supra* note 1, p. 34.

The Development of Oligopoly Theory

In this chapter we begin our consideration of oligopoly theory with the introduction of four important models developed during the nineteenth and twentieth centuries. These models were originally derived without the use of game theory and, as a result, sometimes seemed to be based on highly questionable assumptions. The application of game theory to oligopoly modeling has made it possible to obtain many of the theoretical results using what are generally regarded as more reasonable assumptions.

The chapter is divided into two main sections. The first deals with quantity-based models and the second with price-based models.

Models Based on Quantity Determination

THE COURNOT MODEL

Augustin Cournot made the first attempt at formal modeling of oligopoly behavior in 1838.[1] Cournot considered the case of a duopoly market with two identical firms. The firms face identical costs and there is no product differentiation. Under these conditions, price is a simple function of the total quantity produced by the two firms.

To make things more concrete, assume the following linear *industry* demand curve:

$$P = 100 - Q$$

where P is price and Q is total industry output. Assume further that both firms face identical constant marginal cost and average cost equal to 10 (i.e., $MC = AC = 10$), and that each firm believes, or conjectures, that its competitor will always maintain its current output.*

The assumption of output maintenance was critical to Cournot's result. Suppose Firm 2 observes that Firm 1 is currently producing $q_1 = 45$, the industry

---

*Models of the type presented in this chapter are often called models of *conjectural variations*.

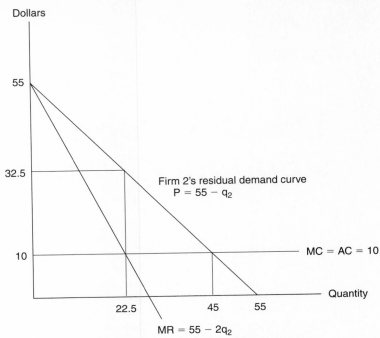

Figure 7.1 Firm 2's Cournot equilibrium when $q_1 = 45$.

joint profit-maximizing level of output, and price is \$55. What output should Firm 2 produce? Recall that the industry's demand curve is $P = 100 - Q$. If Firm 2 assumes that Firm 1 produces 45 units, then the demand curve faced by Firm 2 will be $P = 55 - q_2$. Firm 2's demand curve is called a **residual demand curve**, because it is derived by assuming that Firm 2 faces a demand curve that is simply left over, or residual, after Firm 1 has chosen its output.

To better understand the concept of a residual demand curve, consider what happens to price if Firm 1 produces $q_1 = 45$ and Firm 2 begins to produce any output greater than zero. If Firm 2 produces one unit, total industry output equals 46 and $P = 54$. Therefore, one point on Firm 2's residual demand curve is ($q_2 = 1$, $P = 54$). What if Firm 2 sells five units? Then $Q = 50$, and $P = 50$, so a second point on Firm 2's residual demand curve is ($q_2 = 5$, $P = 50$). Note that for each unit Firm 2 produces, the price declines by one additional dollar below \$55. The residual demand curve is, therefore, $P = 55 - q_2$.

Figure 7.1 depicts the situation from Firm 2's perspective. With MC = 10, recalling again that the MR curve bisects the linear demand curve, Firm 2 will maximize profit by producing where MR $= 55 - 2q_2 = 10 =$ MC, so $q_2 = 22.5$. Total industry output is now $Q = q_1 + q_2 = 45 + 22.5 = 67.5$, so $P = 32.5$.

Now it is Firm 1's turn to respond to Firm 2's output. If Firm 1 assumes that Firm 2 will maintain an output of 22.5, what is its profit-maximizing output? Figure 7.2 shows the situation from Firm 1's perspective. Assuming that q_2 is con-

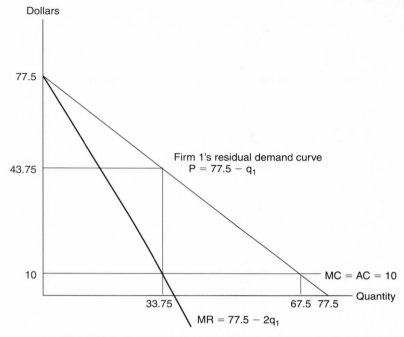

Figure 7.2 Firm 1's Cournot equilibrium when $q_2 = 22.5$.

stant at 22.5, Firm 1's residual demand curve will be $P = 77.5 - q_1$, and its profit-maximizing output will be 33.75 units. Total industry output will be $22.5 + 33.75 = 56.25$, and $P = 43.75$.

Now Firm 2 discovers that it was wrong. Firm 1 did not maintain output at 45. What should Firm 2 do? You might be tempted to think that Firm 2 should give up its obviously false assumption that Firm 1 will maintain output. According to Cournot, however, Firm 2 will now assume that Firm 1 will maintain output at 33.75. As shown in Figure 7.3, Firm 2's residual demand curve becomes $P = 66.25 - q_2$. Firm 2 will equate its new MR curve to MC $= 10$ and produce 28.125 units. Industry output is now $28.125 + 33.75 = 61.875$, and $P = 38.125$.

The story is still not over. Now Firm 1's assumption that $q_2 = 22.5$ has been violated, and Firm 1 must respond by changing output yet again. As an exercise, prove to yourself that Firm 1's next response will be to reduce its output to 30.94 units. This will result in yet another response by Firm 2.

When does all of this end? Only when both firms face identical residual demand curves, and therefore, both produce the same output. In Figures 7.1 to 7.3 the residual demand curves have been converging, and they eventually converge completely when Firm 1 faces a residual demand of $P = 70 - q_1$, and Firm 2 faces a residual demand of $P = 70 - q_2$. This equilibrium is shown in Figure 7.4. Only when each firm produces 30 units will each firm's assumption regarding the

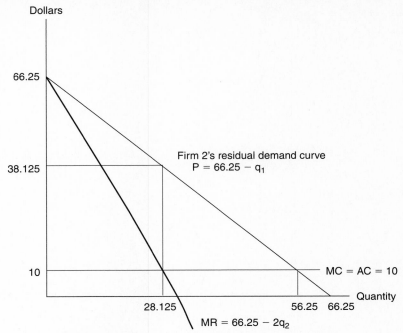

Figure 7.3   Firm 2's Cournot equilibrium when q_1 = 33.75.

other's output be correct. In equilibrium total industry output is 60 and P = 40. This is the Cournot equilibrium.

Several important characteristics are associated with the Cournot equilibrium. Note that the equilibrium output is between the joint profit-maximizing output of 45 and the perfectly competitive output of 90.* In fact, with linear demand and constant marginal costs, the Cournot equilibrium quantity with two firms is precisely equal to two thirds of the competitive equilibrium quantity.

An important and useful concept associated with the Cournot model is that of a **reaction function**.[2] To derive Firm 1's reaction function, begin with Cournot's major assumption—Firm 1 assumes that the output of Firm 2 will remain constant. Given this assumption, there exists an optimal output response for Firm 1 associated with any *given* output produced by Firm 2, and vice-versa. The functional relationship between q_1 and q_2 may be written as:

$$q_1 = f(q_2)$$

This function is firm 1's *reaction function*.

---

*It is possible to determine the profit-maximizing quantity by recalling the "twice as steep rule" for MR from Chapter 2. For demand curve P = 100 − Q, MR = 100 − 2Q, and the industry's profit maximizing output is where MR = 100 − 2Q = 10 = MC. Solving for Q, Q = 90/2 = 45. With Q = 45, the profit-maximizing price is P = 100 − 45 = 55.

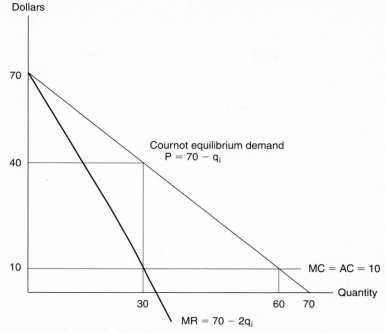

Figure 7.4   Final Cournot equilibrium when $q_1 = q_2 = 30$.

We can use calculus to show that, given our demand and cost conditions, Firm 1's reaction function is:*

$$q_1 = f(q_2) = \frac{90 - q_2}{2} = 45 - \tfrac{1}{2}q_2 \qquad [7.1]$$

---

*To maximize profits, Firm 1 must set MR = MC for any given level of Firm 2's output. Total revenue for Firm 1, TR_1, can be derived as follows:

$$TR_1 = q_1 P = q_1 (100 - q_1 - q_2)$$

or

$$TR_1 = 100q_1 - q_1^2 - q_1q_2$$

Marginal revenue, MR_1, is simply the partial derivative of TR_1:

$$MR_1 = \frac{\partial TR_1}{\partial q_1} = 100 - 2q_1 - q_2$$

Because MC = 10, we set $MR_1 = 10$ and obtain:

$$100 - 2q_1 - q_2 = 10$$

or

$$q_1 = \frac{90 - q_2}{2} = 45 - \tfrac{1}{2}q_2$$

Without calculus, the result can be obtained by recalling from Chapter 2 that for a linear demand curve the marginal revenue curve has the same intercept but twice the slope of the demand curve. For *industry* demand curve $P = 100 - q_1 - q_2$, Firm 1's residual demand curve can be identified by noting that for any given level of Firm 2's output, q_2, the quantity $(100 - q_2)$ is a constant. It follows that for any given q_2, Firm 1's demand curve is simply:

$$p_1 = (100 - q_2) - q_1 \qquad [7.2]$$

Because Equation 7.2 is a linear demand curve, with intercept $(100 - q_2)$ and slope -1, the associated marginal revenue curve is:

$$MR_1 = (100 - q_2) - 2q_1$$

To obtain Firm 1's reaction function, set MR = MC for profit maximization, so:

$$MR_1 = 100 - q_2 - 2q_1 = 10 = MC \qquad [7.3]$$

Solving for q_1, Firm 1's reaction function is:

$$q_1 = 45 - \tfrac{1}{2}q_2 \qquad [7.4]$$

Because Firm 2 faces identical demand and cost conditions, Firm 2's reaction function is:

$$q_2 = 45 - \tfrac{1}{2}q_1 \qquad [7.5]$$

Figure 7.5 shows both reaction functions on the same graph. The Cournot equilibrium occurs at the intersection of the two reaction functions because only at that point are both firms' assumptions concerning the output of the other correct. When each firm produces 30 units, neither firm has an incentive to change output, and therefore, the assumption that the other will maintain output is correct.

In Cournot's original model, no other output combination could be sustained. Suppose Firm 2 produced 40 units. Then Firm 1 should produce at point A in Figure 7.5 on its reaction function, and produce $q_1 = 45 - (40/2) = 25$ units. But if Firm 1 produced 25 units, then Firm 2 should operate at point B on its best response curve and produce $q_2 = 45 - (25/2) = 32.5$ units. But that would result in a response by Firm 1, which would result in a response by Firm 2, and so on. Only when each produces the Cournot equilibrium quantity is a stable equilibrium achieved.

The Cournot-Nash Equilibrium

The Cournot equilibrium is based on the questionable assumption of output maintenance by competitors. The Cournot equilibrium, however, is also a Nash equilibrium in a simple two-player game. The Cournot-Nash game is a *simultaneous move*, *quantity choice* game with *homogeneous products*. Because it is a simultaneous move game, it is a game of *imperfect information*. Assuming that industry

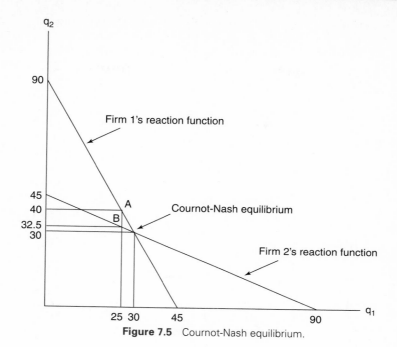

Figure 7.5 Cournot-Nash equilibrium.

demand is P = 100 − Q, and that MC = AC = 10 for both firms, each firms' profits will be:

$$\Pi_1 = TR_1 - TC_1 = Pq_1 - 10q_1 \tag{7.6A}$$

$$\Pi_2 = TR_2 - TC_2 = Pq_2 - 10q_2 \tag{7.6B}$$

where Π_1 and Π_2 represent Firm 1's and Firm 2's profits, respectively, TR represents total revenue, TC represents total costs, and q_1 and q_2 represent Firm 1's and Firm 2's outputs, respectively. Substituting P = 100 − q_1 − q_2, the industry demand curve, into the firms' profit equations 7.6A and 7.6B, we obtain:*

$$\Pi_1 = (90 - q_2)q_1 - q_1^2 \tag{7.7A}$$

$$\Pi_2 = (90 - q_1)q_2 - q_2^2 \tag{7.7B}$$

---

*The algebra is as follows:
Substituting P = 100 − q_1 − q_2 into 7.6A yields:

$$\Pi_1 = Pq_1 - 10q_1 = (100 - q_1 - q_2)\,q_1 - 10q_1$$
$$= 100q_1 - q_1^2 - q_1q_2 - 10q_1$$
$$= (90 - q_2)\,q_1 - q_1^2$$

Substituting P = 100 − q_1 − q_2 into 7.6B yields an analogous result.

Once the profit functions are known, it is possible to express all of the possible profit payoffs in the form of a game matrix like the matrices used in Chapter 6. In Table 7.1, Firm 1's profits are given in the bottom of each cell, and Firm 2's profits are given in the top. An "L" has been placed in any cell for which total output is greater than 90 because both firms would sustain economic losses if price dropped below 10, the average cost. Table 7.1 obviously does not show all of the possible profit payoffs because the firms could produce an infinite number of other output combinations. The table does, however, provide enough information to allow for an understanding of the game.

To begin, examine Table 7.1 and try to answer the following question: Does a Nash equilibrium exist? Recall from Chapter 6 that a Nash equilibrium exists if there is a cell where both players are doing the best they can *given the choice of their opponent*. In the context of the game in Table 7.1, a Nash equilibrium exists if neither firm has an incentive to change *its quantity* as long as the other firm maintains *its quantity* at its current level. Table 7.1 shows that there is one, and only one, Nash equilibrium, where $q_1 = q_2 = 30$. If both firms produce 30, then a unilateral move to produce more or less than 30 *always* reduces profits. If Firm 2 unilaterally moved to produce 20, for example, its profits would decline from 900 to 800. If Firm 1 unilaterally moved to produce 40, its profits would decline from 900 to 800.

Does the Nash equilibrium maximize joint profits? If the firms arrive at the Nash equilibrium, joint profits are 1800. Other cells, however, result in larger joint profits. If each firm produces 20, for example, combined profits increase to 2000.

It is possible to determine the profit-maximizing quantity by recalling the "twice as steep rule" for MR from Chapter 2. For demand curve $P = 100 - Q$ in Figure 7.6, $MR = 100 - 2Q$, and the industry's profit-maximizing output equals 45. With $Q = 45$, the profit-maximizing price is 55.

To maximize total industry profits, the two firms must combine to produce $Q = 45$. Note that in Table 7.1, regardless of how output is distributed between the two firms, if the two combine to produce 45 units of output, then total industry profits will be maximized at 2025. If the two combine to produce 45 units of output, however, the combination will *not* be a Nash equilibrium. Each firm could, for example, produce 22.5 units and earn profits of 1012.5. But as Table 7.1 indicates, if each firm produced 22.5 units, they would each have an incentive to increase output to 35 units and earn a profit of 1137.50. Alternatively, if a total output of 45 units was produced with Firm 1 producing 35 units and Firm 2 producing 10 units, then Firm 1 would have an incentive to increase its output to 40 to earn a profit of 1600, and Firm 2 would have an incentive to increase its output to 27.5 units to increase its profit to 756.23.

Because the Cournot equilibrium is also a Nash equilibrium, the equilibrium has come to be known as a **Cournot-Nash equilibrium**. The Cournot equilibrium and the Nash equilibrium are identical because both occur at the point at which the two reaction functions in Figure 7.5 intersect. The Cournot equilibrium occurs at that point because only there are both firms' output maintenance assumptions concerning the other correct. The Nash equilibrium occurs at that point because it is the only output combination in which both players are doing

TABLE 7.1   Cournot-Nash Profit Payoffs (Firm 2's Profits on Top, Firm 1's Profits on Bottom)

Each cell is shown as **Firm 2's profit / Firm 1's profit**.

$q_1 \downarrow$ \ $q_2 \rightarrow$	0	10	20	22.5	25	27.5	30	35	40	50	60	70	80	90
0	0 / 0	800 / 0	1400 / 0	1518.75 / 0	1625 / 0	1718.75 / 0	1800 / 0	1925 / 0	2000 / 0	2000 / 0	1800 / 0	1400 / 0	800 / 0	0 / 0
10	0 / 800	700 / 700	1200 / 600	1293.25 / 575	1375 / 550	1443.73 / 525	1500 / 500	1575 / 450	1600 / 400	1500 / 300	1200 / 200	700 / 100	0 / 0	
15	0 / 1125	650 / 975	1100 / 825	1181.25 / 787.5	1250 / 750	1306.23 / 712.5	1350 / 675	1400 / 600	1400 / 525	1250 / 375	900 / 225	350 / 75		
20	0 / 1400	600 / 1200	1000 / 1000	1068.25 / 950	1125 / 900	1168.73 / 850	1200 / 800	1225 / 700	1200 / 600	1000 / 400	600 / 200	0 / 0		
22.5	0 / 1518.75	575 / 1293.25	950 / 1068.25	1012.25 / 1012.25	1062.5 / 956.25	1099.98 / 900.25	1125 / 843.25	1137.50 / 731.25	1100 / 618.25	875 / 393.25	450 / 168.25			
25	0 / 1625	550 / 1375	900 / 1125	956.25 / 1062.5	1000 / 1000	1031.23 / 937.5	1050 / 875	1050 / 750	1000 / 625	750 / 375	300 / 125			
30	0 / 1800	500 / 1500	800 / 1200	843.25 / 1125	875 / 1050	893.73 / 975	900 / 900	875 / 750	800 / 600	500 / 300	0 / 0			
35	0 / 1925	450 / 1575	700 / 1225	731.25 / 1137.5	750 / 1050	756.23 / 962.5	750 / 875	700 / 700	600 / 525	250 / 175				
40	0 / 2000	400 / 1600	600 / 1200	618.25 / 1100	625 / 1000	618.73 / 900	600 / 800	525 / 600	400 / 400	0 / 0				
45	0 / 2025	350 / 1575	500 / 1125	506.25 / 1012.5	500 / 900	481.23 / 787.5	450 / 675	350 / 450	200 / 225					
50	0 / 2000	300 / 1500	400 / 1000	393.25 / 875	375 / 750	343.73 / 625	300 / 500	175 / 250	0 / 0					
55	0 / 1925	250 / 1375	300 / 825	281.25 / 687.5	250 / 550	206.23 / 412.5	150 / 275	0 / 0						
60	0 / 1800	200 / 1200	200 / 600	168.25 / 450	125 / 300	68.73 / 150	0 / 0							
65	0 / 1625	150 / 975	100 / 325	56.25 / 162.5	0 / 0									
70	0 / 1400	100 / 700	0 / 0											
75	0 / 1125	50 / 375	0 / 0											
80	0 / 800	0 / 0												
90	0 / 0													

the best they can given the choice of the other. The result is the same, but the Nash assumptions are much more reasonable than the Cournot assumptions and therefore provide a more solid theoretical basis for the equilibrium.

COURNOT-NASH MODEL WITH MORE THAN TWO FIRMS[3]

We have developed the Cournot-Nash equilibrium for a duopoly, but the result can be generalized to any number of identical firms. Assuming N *identical* firms, each firm faces an identical reaction function. An easy method of identifying the Cournot-Nash equilibrium in this case is to calculate a representative ith firm's reaction function.* Because all N firms are identical, the equilibrium for each is symmetric, so:

$$q_i = \frac{Q}{N} \text{ or } Q = Nq_i.$$

Firm i's *residual demand curve* can then be written as:

$$P = (100 - Q) = 100 - Nq_i$$

or

$$P = [100 - (N - 1)\, q_j] - q_i$$

where q_j is the output of any firm other than the ith firm.

Using the "twice as steep" rule and remembering that firm i views q_j as constant, Firm 1's marginal revenue curve is:

$$MR_i = (100 - (N - 1)q_j) - 2q_i.$$

---

*Using calculus the analysis can be simplified. The ith firm wishes to maximize profits as follows:

$$\Pi_i = TR_i - TC_i = Pq_i - 10q_i.$$

The first-order condition for profit maximization is:

$$\frac{d\Pi_i}{dq_i} = P\frac{dq_i}{dq_i} + q_i\frac{dP}{dq_i} - \frac{d(10q_i)}{dq_i} = 0.$$

Because $\dfrac{dP_i}{dq_i} = (-1)$, we have:

$$\frac{d\Pi_i}{dq_i} = P + q_i\,(-1) - 10 = (100 - Nq_i) - q_i - 10 = 0$$

or:

$$90 - (N + 1)\, q_i = 0,$$

so:

$$q_i = \frac{90}{(N + 1)}.$$

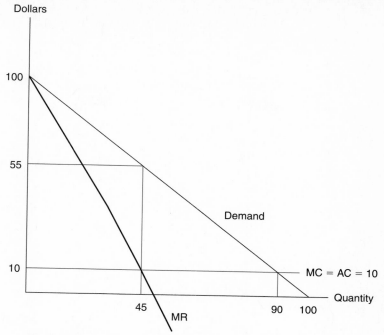

Figure 7.6 Joint profit maximization with constant marginal costs.

Setting MR = MC = 10 for profit maximization yields Firm i's reaction function:

$$MR_i = (100 - (N - 1)q_j) - 2q_i = 10 = MC.$$

This can be rewritten as:

$$q_i = 45 - \frac{(N - 1)}{2} q_j. \qquad [7.8]$$

Multiplying equation 7.8 by 2 yields:

$$2q_i = 90 - (N - 1)q_j.$$

Recognizing that $q_i = q_j$ in equilibrium and solving for q_i yields:*

$$q_i = \frac{90}{N + 1}. \qquad [7.9]$$

---

*The algebra is:

$$2q_i + (N - 1)\, q_i = 90$$

$$(N + 1)\, q_i = 90$$

$$q_i = \frac{90}{N + 1}.$$

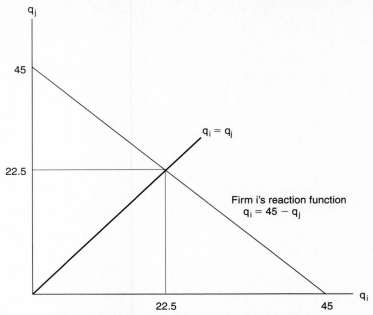

Figure 7.7   Cournot-Nash equilibrium with three firms.

From equation 7.9, total output Q will be:

$$Q = Nq_i = N\frac{90}{(N + 1)} = \frac{N}{(N + 1)}90.$$ [7.10]

Equation 7.10 has several significant implications. As the number of firms in a Cournot industry increases, total output continuously approaches the competitive output of 90. In our example, a monopolist (N = 1) would produce the profit-maximizing output of 45; duopolists (N = 2) would produce Q = 60 or two thirds of the competitive output; three firms would produce Q = 67.5 or three fourths of the competitive output; and for N "very large," Q approaches 90, the competitive output. There is something intuitively appealing about this result.

The equilibrium output for the ith firm could also be identified graphically using the ith firm's reaction function. Because of symmetry, $q_i = q_j$, for all values of i and j. In Figure 7.7, the reaction function for firm i in an industry with *three* firms is identified from equation 7.8 and symmetry as:

$$q_i = 45 - q_j.$$

Equilibrium is attained where the reaction function and the 45° line (where $q_i = q_j$) intersect. As noted above, in the case with three firms, each would produce 22.5 units for a total industry output of 67.5 units.

EMPIRICAL EVIDENCE OF COURNOT-NASH BEHAVIOR

Empirical evidence on the likelihood of Cournot-Nash behavior is difficult to obtain because it requires showing that oligopolists select prices between the competitive price and the joint profit-maximizing price. Because of this difficulty, economists have used experimental games to try to determine the likelihood of the Cournot-Nash outcome. Typically these games are played by college students who receive information concerning their profit payoffs after making an output decision. The student participants are allowed to keep some of the profits they earn so there is a strong incentive to do well. In one experiment run by Fouraker and Siegel, 16 pairs of "student duopolists" played a game for 25 rounds.[4] In their experiment, the Cournot-Nash solution was the most common outcome, occurring in 7 of the 16 games, compared with five competitive outcomes, three joint profit-maximizing outcomes, and one outcome between the Cournot-Nash and joint profit-maximizing outcome. The mean outcome was also the Cournot-Nash outcome. When the game was played by three students instead of two, the competitive outcome became the most common. In a more recent experiment, Holt found that the Cournot-Nash result was the most common outcome under a variety of different game structures.[5] A survey of experimental results by Plott found the Cournot-Nash outcome to be fairly common.[6]

One case study by Iwata concluded that in the Japanese flat-glass industry, which was dominated by two firms (Asahi and Nippon), firms produced outputs that were between the Cournot-Nash and joint profit-maximizing outputs.[7] Iwata could not reject the possibility of Cournot-Nash behavior. In addition, Brander and Zhang found evidence that the pricing behavior of American Airlines and United Airlines between 1984 and 1988 most closely resembled the Cournot-Nash model's predictions.[8] Overall, empirical evidence suggests that the Cournot-Nash equilibrium is more than a theoretical construction.

THE STACKELBERG MODEL[9]

The Cournot-Nash model is a one-period simultaneous move game. The Stackelberg model considers what would happen if the Cournot model is viewed as a two-stage *sequential game* in which one firm, the **Stackelberg leader**, moves first. According to the model, developed by Heinrich Von Stackelberg in 1934, the Stackelberg leader moves first in anticipation of the follower's move in the next period.

Suppose Firm 1 is the Stackelberg leader, and demand and cost conditions are once again:

$$P = 100 - Q.$$

$$MC = AC = 10.$$

The follower's reaction function, Firm 2's reaction function, has been calculated above, and is given by equation 7.5:

$$q_2 = 45 - \tfrac{1}{2} q_1. \qquad\qquad [7.11]$$

The Stackelberg leader recognizes that *after* it sets output, the follower will respond by selecting its best output according to its reaction function 7.11 above. The leader then calculates its profit-maximizing output as follows.*

Substituting $q_2 = 45 - \frac{1}{2} q_1$ from Equation 7.11 into the leader's demand curve yields:

$$p_1 = (100 - q_2) - q_1 = (100 - (45 - \frac{1}{2} q_1)) - q_1 = 55 - \frac{1}{2} q_1.$$

The "twice as steep rule" implies that for Firm 1, the Stackelberg leader:

$$MR_1 = 55 - q_1.$$

To maximize profits, set $MR_1 = MC$:

$$MR_1 = 55 - q_1 = 10$$

or:

$$q_1 = 45.$$

To obtain the follower's output, substitute $q_1 = 45$ into Firm 2's reaction function 7.11:

$$q_2 = 45 - \frac{1}{2} q_1 = 45 - \frac{1}{2} 45 = 22.5.$$

In Figure 7.8, the Stackelberg equilibrium is identified as point A. Note that point A is on Firm 2's reaction function, but it is *not* on the Stackelberg leader's reaction function. In the Stackelberg model the leader selects the point on the *follower's* reaction function that maximizes the *leader's* profits.

Some insight into the Stackelberg equilibrium can be illustrated with the help of the simplified payoff matrix in Table 7.2. Although it is impossible to identify all, or even most, of the possible payoffs in a matrix, Table 7.2 identifies the important points for the Stackelberg leader to recognize.

To obtain the Stackelberg equilibrium from Table 7.2, begin by identifying the points that are on Firm 2's reaction function. Then select the point on Firm

---

*Using calculus:

$$TR_1 = Pq_1 = [100 - (45 - \frac{1}{2} q_1) - q_1] q_1 = 55q_1 - \frac{1}{2} q_1^2$$

then

$$MR_1 = \frac{dTR_1}{dq_1} = 55 - q_1.$$

Setting $MR = MC$,

$$55 - q_1 = 10 \text{ or } q_1 = 45.$$

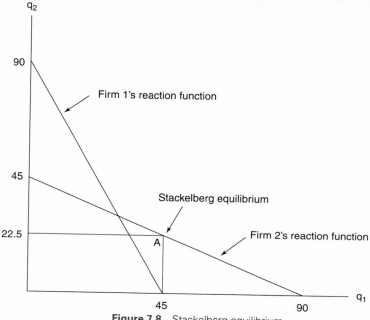

Figure 7.8   Stackelberg equilibrium.

2's reaction function that yields the largest profits for the Stackelberg leader, as follows:

Leader's output	*Firm 2's response*	*Leader's profits*
20	35	700
22.5	33.75	759.38
25	32.5	875
30	30	900
35	27.5	962.5
40	25	1000
45	22.5	1012.5
50	20	1000
60	15	900

The Stackelberg leader concludes that it should produce $q_1 = 45$ because Firm 2 will then produce $q_2 = 22.5$, and the leader will earn a profit of 1012.5, which is larger than any other possible profit on Firm 2's reaction function.

The Stackelberg equilibrium makes sense if there is a clear leader and follower.[10] In our example, however, both firms are identical, and it is not obvious why one firm should be the leader and the other the follower. If Firm 2 believes that it is the true Stackelberg leader, it will reason exactly as Firm 1 above and also

TABLE 7.2   Stackelberg Profit Payoffs (Follower's Profits on Top, Stackelberg Leader's Profits on Bottom)

$q_1 \downarrow$ \ $q_2 \rightarrow$	15	20	22.5	25	27.5	30	32.5	33.75	35	37.5	45
20	825 / 1100	1000 / 1000	1068.25 / 950	1125 / 900	1168.73 / 850	1200 / 800	1218.75 / 750	1223.43 / 725	1225 / 700	1218.75 / 650	1125 / 500
22.5	787.5 / 1181.25	950 / 1068.25	1012.5 / 1012.5	1062.5 / 956.25	1100 / 900.25	1125 / 843.25	1137.5 / 787.5	1139.06 / 759.38	1137.5 / 731.25	1125 / 675	1012.5 / 506.25
25	750 / 1250	900 / 1125	956.25 / 1062.5	1000 / 1000	1031.23 / 937.5	1050 / 875	1056.25 / 812.5	1054.69 / 781.25	1050 / 750	1031.23 / 687.5	900 / 500
30	675 / 1350	800 / 1200	843.25 / 1125	875 / 1050	893.73 / 975	900 / 900	893.75 / 825	885.94 / 787.5	875 / 750	843.75 / 675	675 / 450
35	600 / 1400	700 / 1225	731.25 / 1137.5	750 / 1050	756.23 / 962.5	750 / 875	731.25 / 787.5	717.19 / 743.75	700 / 700	656.25 / 612.5	450 / 350
40	525 / 1400	600 / 1200	618.25 / 1100	625 / 1000	618.73 / 900	600 / 800	568.75 / 700	548.44 / 650	525 / 600	468.75 / 500	225 / 200
45	450 / 1350	500 / 1125	506.25 / 1012.5	500 / 900	481.23 / 787.5	450 / 675	406.25 / 562.5	379.69 / 506.25	350 / 450	281.25 / 337.5	0 / 0
50	375 / 1250	400 / 1000	393.25 / 875	375 / 750	343.73 / 625	300 / 500	243.75 / 375	210.93 / 312.5	175 / 250	93.75 / 125	L
60	225 / 900	200 / 600	168.25 / 450	125 / 300	68.73 / 150	0 / 0	L	L	L	L	L

produce $q_2 = 45$, in which case, as indicated in Table 7.2, industry output will be $Q = 90$, and each firm's profits will be zero.

Given the assumptions of the Stackelberg game, if one of the firms has an advantage over the other, it would seem reasonable to assume that the firm with the advantage would be the Stackelberg leader. Suppose, for example, all conditions remain the same *except* that Firm 1 faces MC = AC = 10, while Firm 2 faces MC = AC = 20. Under this assumption, it is reasonable to expect Firm 1, the low-cost firm, to be the Stackelberg leader. If Firm 2's marginal costs are 20, its reaction function becomes:*

$$q_2 = 40 - \tfrac{1}{2} q_1. \tag{7.12}$$

Firm 1 calculates its profit-maximizing output as follows. Substituting for q_2 from Equation 7.12 yields:

$$p_1 = (100 - q_2) - q_1 = (100 - (40 - \tfrac{1}{2}q_1)) - q_1 = 60 - \tfrac{1}{2}q_1.$$

Using the "twice as steep" rule:

$$MR_1 = 60 - q_1.$$

To maximize profits, set $MR_1 = MC$:

$$MR_1 = 60 - q_1 = 10.$$

or:

$$q_1 = 50.$$

To obtain Firm 2's output, substitute $q_1 = 50$ into Firm 2's reaction function:

$$q_2 = 40 - \tfrac{1}{2} q_1 = 40 - \tfrac{1}{2} 50 = 15.$$

---

*For a given level of Firm 1's output, q_1, we know that Firm 2's marginal revenue is:
$$MR_2 = (100 - q_1) - 2q_2.$$
To obtain Firm 2's reaction function, set MR = MC = 20, or:
$$MR_2 = (100 - q_1) - 2q_2 = 20 = MC.$$
Solving for q_2 yields Firm 2's reaction function:
$$q_2 = 40 - \tfrac{1}{2} q_1.$$
Using calculus:
$$TR_2 = Pq_2 = (100 - q_1 - q_2) q_2 = 100 q_2 - q_1 q_2 - q_2^2$$
$$MR_2 = \frac{\partial TR_2}{\partial q_2} = 100 - q_1 - 2q_2^2$$
for profit maximization MR = MC, or:
$$MR_2 = 100 - q_1 - 2q_2 = 20 = MC \quad \text{or} \quad q_2 = 40 - \tfrac{1}{2} q_1.$$

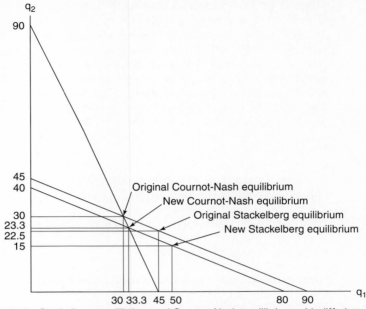

Figure 7.9   Stackelberg equilibrium and Cournot-Nash equilibrium with differing costs.

The introduction of a cost advantage for Firm 1 makes it the obvious Stackelberg leader and increases the ratio q_1:q_2 from 2:1 to 3.33:1.

Graphically, the increase in Firm 2's marginal cost from 10 to 20 shifts its reaction function as shown in Figure 7.9. Note that in Figure 7.9, the Cournot-Nash equilibrium has shifted from $q_1 = q_2 = 30$ (in the case of equal marginal costs of 10) to $q_1 = 33.3$ and $q_2 = 23.3$ (in the case of differing marginal costs).* The Stackelberg equilibrium has shifted from $q_1 = 45$ and $q_2 = 22.5$ to $q_1 = 50$ and $q_2 = 15$.

At least one empirical case study has found evidence suggesting the real-world use of Stackelberg quantity leadership. Gollop and Roberts studied the United States coffee-roasting industry in 1972 and concluded that the largest firm may have acted as a Stackelberg quantity leader.[11] They rejected the hypothesis that all firms in the industry adopted Cournot behavioral assumptions. In the

---

*The Cournot equilibrium is calculated by substituting Firm 2's reaction function into Firm 1's reaction function to yield:

$$q_1 = 45 - \tfrac{1}{2}\left(40 - \tfrac{1}{2}q_1\right)$$

or

$$q_1 = 45 - 20 + \tfrac{1}{4}q_1 \Rightarrow \tfrac{3}{4}q_1 = 25 \Rightarrow q_1 = 33.3.$$

With $q_1 = 33.3$,

$$q_2 = 40 - \tfrac{1}{2}q_1 = 40 - \tfrac{1}{2}(33.3) = 23.3.$$

study firms were grouped into three sizes: (1) the largest firm; (2) the next five largest firms (medium-sized firms); and (3) the remaining smaller firms. They found that both the medium-sized and the small firms made Cournot assumptions about the small firms; that is, both the medium and small firms assumed that the small firms would maintain their current output in the face of output expansion by medium or small competitors. The largest firm, however, appeared to assume that medium-sized firms would *reduce* output in response to an output expansion by the largest firm and that small firms would *expand* output in response to an output expansion by the largest firm. Only the largest firm, therefore, anticipated that *all firms* would change their outputs in response to a change in its output. This can be interpreted as evidence that the largest firm acted as a Stackelberg quantity leader.

Models Based on Price Determination

THE BERTRAND MODEL[12]

In 1883, Joseph Bertrand criticized Cournot's result by showing that if firms assumed that all other firms hold their *prices* constant, Cournot's logic results in an entirely different outcome.

Consider our Cournot duopoly example with a homogeneous product. If Firm 1 assumes that Firm 2 will maintain price at its current level, p_2, then Firm 1's demand curve is dependent on the relationship between p_1 and p_2. If $p_1 > p_2$, Firm 2 captures the entire market, and $q_1 = 0$. If $p_1 < p_2$, Firm 1 captures the entire demand, and $q_1 = 100 - p_1$. Finally, if $p_1 = p_2$, the two firms split the market, in which case each firm obtains half of the total industry demand curve, $P = 100 - Q$, and Firm 1's demand curve is:

$$p_1 = 100 - 2q_1. \qquad [7.13]$$

Solving 7.13 for q_1 yields:

$$q_1 = 50 - \tfrac{1}{2} p_1 \text{ for } p_1 = p_2.$$

Firm 1's demand curve, therefore, can be identified as:

$$q_1 = \begin{bmatrix} 0 & \text{if} & p_1 > p_2 \\ 50 - \tfrac{1}{2} p_1 & \text{if} & p_1 = p_2. \\ 100 - p_1 & \text{if} & p_1 < p_2 \end{bmatrix} \qquad [7.14]$$

The Bertrand model is driven by the assumption that one of the firms can capture the entire market if it charges a lower price than its competitor. Given this assumption, if Firm 1 charges a price *ever so slightly less* than p_2, it will virtually double its output and profits. This implies that if $p_1 = p_2 - \epsilon$, with ϵ representing a number that is *infinitesimally* greater than 0, Firm 1 captures the entire market. Of course, if $p_2 = p_1 - \epsilon$, then Firm 2 captures the entire market.

Given these assumptions, any price greater than MC, or $P > 10$ in our example, will result in a price cut by one firm that will result in a price cut by the other

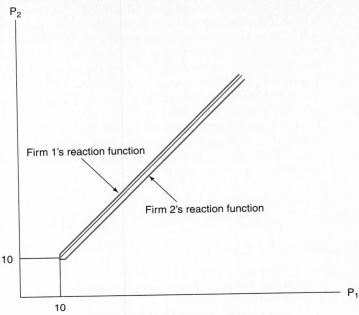

Figure 7.10   Bertrand equilibrium.

that will result in a price cut by the other, and so on. The only possible equilibrium occurs where price equals MC because only then will neither firm have an incentive to reduce price.

In the Bertrand model firms set prices, not quantities, and therefore, the reaction functions must be expressed in terms of price. Firm 1's reaction function is:

$$p_1 = f(p_2).$$

Figure 7.10 identifies the reaction functions for the Bertrand model, given our usual assumptions that the industry demand curve is $P = 100 - Q$ and $MC = AC = 10$. Firm 1's reaction function goes through the point (10,10) but is not identified for prices below 10 because a price cut below 10 would result in economic losses; price would be below average cost. For all $p_2 > 10$, Firm 1 charges a price $p_1 = p_2 - \epsilon$; therefore, for $p_2 > 10$, Firm 1's reaction function lies a distance ϵ to the *left* of the 45° line.* By analogous reasoning, Firm 2's reaction function lies a distance ϵ to the right of the 45° line. For $P > 10$, the two reaction functions will be parallel to each other and also parallel to the 45° line where $p_1 = p_2$. The Nash equilibrium occurs at the intersection point, (10,10), because this is the only point at which both firms are doing the best they can given the choice of their competitor.

---

*Because ϵ is *infinitesimally* greater than zero, it is impossible to draw the reaction functions a distance ϵ from the 45° line where $P_1 = P_2$. In Figure 7.10, the two reactions functions are drawn "very close" to the 45° line, but you should try to imagine that the distance shown is $\epsilon > 0$ and that the reaction functions almost overlap with the 45° line.

The Bertrand model is easy to interpret as a one-period simultaneous move game. Both firms reason: "If I set price at any p > 10, then my opponent will set price at p − ϵ, and I will sell nothing. But if I set price at p = 10, then I either capture the entire market or split the market 50-50. I should therefore set price equal to 10."

Although the implications of the Cournot model seem plausible, the implications of the Bertrand model may at first seem a bit bizarre. In a Bertrand duopoly, price falls to MC, the perfectly competitive price, and there is allocative efficiency. We will not go through the formal analysis, but this extreme result can be made much more reasonable by introducing some product differentiation into the Bertrand model, which we do in Chapter 13.[13] The introduction of product differentiation eliminates the highly implausible "all or nothing" nature of the model and results in an equilibrium price greater than marginal cost.

The results of some experimental games support the Bertrand equilibrium. Fouraker and Siegel found that when student players selected prices rather than quantities and were given Bertrand-type profit payoffs, three-player games almost always resulted in the Bertrand outcome.[14] The Bertrand result was also common with two players as long as the players did not have perfect price information about their competitor's price.

Recent pricing behavior in the airline industry has been consistent with Bertrand price behavior. American Airlines in particular has followed a policy of pricing near marginal cost on routes on which it faces competition.[15] The major carriers' rationale for this behavior is consistent with the Bertrand model's assumptions. Each of the major carriers fears that if its fares are even slightly higher than the competition, it will lose virtually its entire market share. Other strategic aspects of pricing in the airline industry are discussed in detail in Chapter 10.

DOMINANT FIRM PRICE LEADERSHIP MODEL[16]

Suppose a market consists of one dominant firm that controls a large percentage of total industry output and a significant number of relatively small "fringe" firms. This model differs from the Stackelberg model because there are a large number of relatively small fringe competitors, whereas in the Stackelberg model there are two large duopolists. In such a market, it makes sense to assume that the dominant firm will set the industry price and the fringe firms will take that price as given. In other words, the fringe firms behave exactly like perfectly competitive firms in the sense that they are price takers and maximize their profits by equating price to marginal cost.

The dominant firm price leadership model can be explained by example. In Figure 7.11, the industry demand curve D is $P = 100 - Q$ (in Figure 7.11, the industry demand curve is red for $100 \leq P \leq 25$ and black for $0 \leq P < 25$), the fringe's supply curve S_f is $P = 25 + 2q_f$, and the dominant firm's marginal cost curve is $MC_d = 25 + (1/3)q_d$. To obtain the dominant firm's residual demand curve, subtract the fringe supply curve from the total demand curve at every price greater than $P = 25$. For example, if $P = 75$, total *industry* quantity demanded would equal 25 units, and the fringe would supply the entire industry demand of 25. If $P = 75$, therefore, the residual demand for the dominant firm would be zero. If $P =$

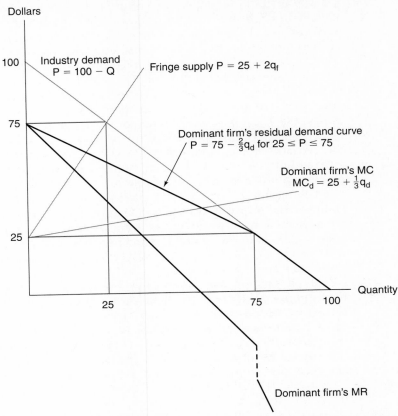

Figure 7.11 Derivation of the dominant firm's residual demand curve in the dominant firm price leadership model.

25, total industry quantity demanded would equal 75 units, and the fringe would supply zero. The residual demand for the dominant firm would then be 75 units. Similar calculations can be done to obtain the dominant firm's residual demand for any price between 25 and 75.* Such calculations yield the black linear residual demand curve that passes through the two points (0, 75) and (75, 25).

---

*For any price, to obtain the dominant firm's *residual demand,* it is necessary to subtract q_f from the total quantity demanded Q.

We have $P = 100 - Q$, so $Q = 100 - P$. In addition:

$$P = 25 + 2q_f \quad \text{or} \quad q_f = \tfrac{1}{2}P - 12.5.$$

Because $q_d = Q - q_f$,

$$q_d = (100 - P) - \left(\tfrac{1}{2}P - 12.5\right) = 112.5 - \tfrac{3}{2}P.$$

Solving for P yields:

$$P = 75 - \tfrac{2}{3}q_d.$$

The equation of this demand curve is:

$$P = 75 - \tfrac{2}{3} q_d \text{ for } 25 \leq P \leq 75.$$

By the "twice as steep rule," marginal revenue is:

$$MR_d = 75 - \tfrac{4}{3} q_d \text{ for } 25 \leq P \leq 75.$$

For prices between 0 and 25, the dominant firm's demand curve is identical to the industry demand curve and equals $P = 100 - q_d$. The dominant firm's residual demand curve, therefore, has a kink at $q_d = 75$, and the MR_d curve has a gap at $q_d = 75$. The residual demand curve and the MR_d curve are drawn in black in Figure 7.11.

Once the residual demand curve of the dominant firm is identified, the profit-maximizing output for the dominant firm can be calculated as shown in Figure 7.12. Recall that the marginal cost curve for the dominant firm is:

$$MC_d = 25 + \tfrac{1}{3} q_d.$$

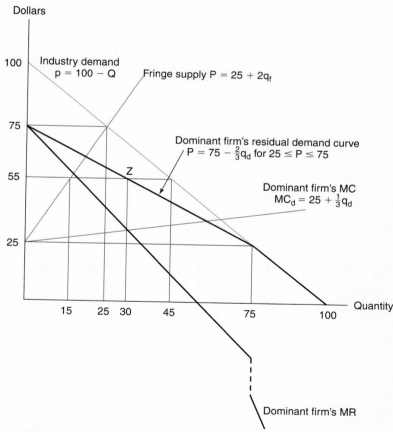

Figure 7.12 Equilibrium in the dominant firm price leadership model.

In Figure 7.12, to maximize profits, the dominant firm equates MC_d to MR_d and produces 30 units.* To obtain price, go up vertically to point Z on the dominant firm's residual demand curve and P = \$55.00.

Once price is known, the fringe firms act as perfectly competitive price takers and supply the quantity at which the fringe supply curve intersects the horizontal line P = \$55.00. In this case, $q_f = 15$.† Total industry output is simply the sum of the dominant firm's output and the fringe's output, or Q = 30 + 15 = 45.

One of the major implications of the dominant firm price leadership model is that the dominant firm's market share declines continuously over time. Worcester explained this tendency using the following dynamic model.[17] If the competitive fringe firms earn above normal economic profits, there will be an incentive for the fringe supply to increase over time as new firms enter and existing fringe firms expand output. As a result, the residual demand for the dominant firm will shift to the left (decrease), and the dominant firm's relative share of output will decline.

Suppose in our previous example profits existed for the competitive fringe, inducing new firms to enter the industry. Figure 7.13 shows what would happen if the number of fringe firms doubled. The fringe's supply curve would then double so that S_f would be P = $25 + q_f$. To obtain the dominant firm's new residual demand curve, subtract the fringe supply curve from the total demand curve at every price greater than P = 25. In Figure 7.13, if P = 62.5, total *industry* quantity demanded would equal 37.5 units, and the fringe would supply the entire industry demand of 37.5. If P = 62.5, therefore, the residual demand for the dominant firm would be zero. As in Figures 7.11 and 7.12, if P = 25, total industry quantity demanded would equal 75 units, and the fringe would supply zero. The residual demand for the dominant firm would then be 75 units. For prices between 25 and 62.5, the dominant firm's demand curve is a linear demand curve that passes through the two points (0, 62.5) and (75, 25). The equation of this curve is:

$$P = 62.5 - \tfrac{1}{2} q_d \text{ for } 25 \leq P \leq 62.5.$$

By the "twice as steep rule," marginal revenue is:

$$MR_d = 62.5 - q_d.$$

Just as in Figure 7.11, for prices between 0 and 25, the dominant firm's demand curve is identical to the industry demand curve and equals P = $100 - q_d$. The dominant firm's demand curve, therefore, has a kink at $q_d = 75$, and the MR_d curve has a gap at $q_d = 75$.

---

* $$MR_d = 75 - \tfrac{4}{3} q_d = 25 + \tfrac{1}{3} q_d = MC_d.$$

Solving for q_d yields $q_d = 30$.

†The competitive fringe firms set P = 55.00 equal to S_f or:

$$P = 55 = 25 + 2q_f = S_f$$

Solving for q_f yields $q_f = 15$.

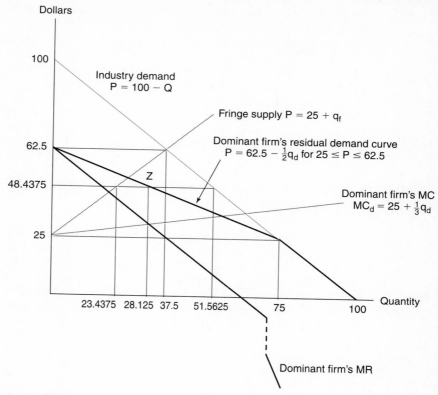

Figure 7.13 Equilibrium with an increased fringe supply in the dominant firm price leadership model.

Recall that the marginal cost curve for the dominant firm is:

$$MC_d = 25 + \tfrac{1}{3}q_d.$$

To maximize profits, the dominant firm equates MC_d to MR_d and produces 28.125 units.* To obtain price go up vertically in Figure 7.13 to point Z on the dominant firm's residual demand curve and $P = \$48.4375$.

Once price is known, the fringe firms act as perfectly competitive price takers and supply the quantity at which the fringe supply curve intersects the horizontal line $P = \$48.4375$. In this case, $q_f = 23.4375$.† Total industry output is the sum

---

*
$$MR_d = 62.5 - q_d = 25 + q_d = MC_d.$$
$$\text{Solving for } q_d \text{ yields } q_d = 28.125.$$

†The competititve fringe firms set $P = 48.4375$ equal to S_f or:
$$P = 48.4375 = 25 + q_f = S_f.$$
$$\text{Solving for } q_f \text{ yields } q_f = 23.4375.$$

of the dominant firm's output and the fringe's output, or $Q_l = 28.125 + 23.4375 = 51.5625$.

Because of the expansion of the competitive fringe, the dominant firm's market share has declined from 66.7 percent (30/45) to 54.5 percent (28.125/51.5625). After this expansion, if the competitive fringe is still earning excess profits, the dominant firm's share will continue to decline.

The dominant firm is remarkably passive in this model. This passivity is often cited as one of the major weaknesses of the model. As we will see in Chapters 10 through 12, a dominant firm can adopt certain strategies to help to maintain its market power in the face of potential entry.

Empirical Evidence of the Decline of Dominant Firm Price Leaders

Some empirical evidence suggests that dominant firms' market shares often decline substantially over time. At the turn of the century, US Steel appeared to behave as a classic dominant firm price leader. In 1902 US Steel held a 65 percent market share and priced its products at a level that induced entry and capacity expansion by fringe firms. As a result, US Steel found its market share decline to 50 percent in 1920.[18] In the low-volume segment of the copier industry, Xerox behaved as a classic dominant firm price leader.[19] Xerox set high profit-maximizing prices in this sector and conceded market share to its smaller rivals.

Few examples of dominant firm price leadership resulting in a decline in market share are more dramatic than the case of the Reynolds International Pen Corporation, which invented an improved ball-point pen that operated on gravity. Reynolds began selling the pens in 1945.[20] Initially the pens cost approximately 80 cents each to produce and Gimbel's department stores sold them for $12.50. Gimbel's sold 10,000 pens the first day they went on sale. By early 1946, Reynolds was producing 30,000 pens a day and earning large economic profits. But Reynolds's high prices encouraged the competitive fringe to enter. By Christmas 1946, many firms were in the industry and prices had fallen as low as 88 cents. By 1948 prices had declined further to 39 cents, and by 1951 they declined still further to as low as 19 cents. By then Reynolds was long gone from the industry. Reynolds came and went quickly, but for one brief, shining moment it was a dominant firm price leader and earned very large economic profits. This example points out clearly the risks associated with dominant firm price leadership. By being completely passive toward its competitors, Reynolds found itself booted out of the market in just a few years.

Other examples of dominant firm price leaders have included International Harvester in farm equipment, Goodyear in tires, RCA in color televisions, General Electric in appliances, and IBM in mainframe computers.[21] Most of these firms have lost significant market share to competitors as a result of a high price policy with little concern for the entry or expansion of competitors. Chapters 10 through 12 explore the reasons why these dominant firms elected to sacrifice market share to competitors, as well as what types of strategic decisions might have prevented their loss of market share.

SUMMARY

1. In this chapter four important oligopoly models were analyzed: the Cournot-Nash model, the Stackelberg model, the Bertrand model, and the dominant firm price leadership model. Each model was built on different assumptions and resulted in different equilibrium outcomes.

2. The Cournot-Nash model is based on the assumption that a firm's competitors maintain their current outputs. The model results in an equilibrium quantity that is greater than the monopoly quantity but less than the competitive quantity.

3. In the Stackelberg model, the leader assumes that the follower will respond to the leader's quantity decision by producing on its reaction function. The leader selects a quantity that maximizes profits given the follower's decision to remain on its reaction curve.

4. In the Bertrand model, firms take their competitors' prices, rather than quantities, as fixed. In the absence of product differentiation, the Bertrand model results in a price equal to marginal cost.

5. In the dominant firm price leadership model, the dominant firm sets the industry price subject to the supply of the competitive fringe of firms. If the competitive fringe earns positive economic profits, there is a tendency for the fringe to expand and the dominant firm's market share to decline over time.

6. Empirical evidence and experimental games suggest that some industries behave according to each of the models analyzed in this chapter. In particular there are quite a few examples of dominant firms declining just as predicted by the dominant firm price leadership model.

KEY TERMS

Bertrand model

Cournot-Nash equilibrium

dominant firm price leadership model

reaction function

residual demand curve

Stackelberg leader

Stackelberg model

DISCUSSION QUESTIONS

1. For any given demand and cost conditions, could a Stackelberg leader in a duopoly ever earn *lower* profits than it would earn with a standard Cournot-Nash equilibrium?

2. From the standpoint of allocative efficiency, compare the Cournot-Nash, Stackelberg, and Bertrand equilibriums.

3. The results expressed in the Bertrand model are often referred to as the "Bertrand Paradox." Why do you think this result is considered a paradox?

4. Under certain conditions the Cournot-Nash and Bertrand equilibriums are identical. One of these conditions has to do with the number of firms in the industry. What is this condition?
5. In the dominant firm price leadership model, the dominant firm is extremely passive toward its competitors. Why might firms with dominant market shares permit competitors to continually chip away at their market shares?

PROBLEMS

1. Consider the general case of two firms each facing a demand curve $P = a - bq$ and a marginal cost c, where a, b, and c are positive constants. What is the Cournot equilibrium output for each firm in this general case?
2. Suppose an oligopoly consists of three identical firms. Industry demand is $P = 100 - 2Q$ and $MC = AC = 20$. What is the Cournot-Nash equilibrium output in this industry for each firm?
3. Suppose Firm 1 is a Stackelberg leader in a duopoly, and industry demand and cost conditions are:

$$P = 60 - 2(q_1 + q_2)$$

$$MC_1 = 10 \text{ and } MC_2 = 20.$$

What are the Stackelberg equilibrium quantities? What is the Stackelberg equilibrium price?
4. Two duopolists face the following *industry* demand curve:

$$P = f(Q) = \frac{1,000}{Q}.$$

$MC = AC = 20$ for each firm. What is the Bertrand equilibrium output for each firm? What is total output in the Bertrand equilibrium?
5. Suppose in the context of international competition, the dominant firm in an industry is a foreign firm and the domestic firms make up the competitive fringe. Would a *per unit* tariff (a tax on imported goods), placed only on the foreign firm's sales in the domestic market, improve welfare in the domestic market? Explain, using a graph(s) and the concepts of consumer and producer surplus.

REFERENCES

1. Augustin Cournot, *Recherches sur les principes mathematiques de la theorie des richesses* (Paris: M. Riviere & Cie., 1938). Translated in *Researches into the Mathematical Principles of Wealth*, (New York: A.M. Kelly, 1960).
2. The concept was introduced by Arthur L. Bowley, *The Mathematical Groundwork of Economics* (Oxford: Oxford University Press, 1924).
3. See William Novshek, "Cournot Equilibrium with Free Entry," *Review of Economic Studies* (April 1980): 473–86; and Jean Tirole, *The Theory of Industrial Organization* (Cambridge, MA: MIT Press, 1988), pp. 218–21.

4. Lawrence Fouraker and Signey Siegel, *Bargaining Behavior* (New York: McGraw-Hill, 1963).

5. Charles A. Holt Jr., "An Experimental Test of the Consistent-Conjectures Hypothesis," *American Economic Review* 75 (June 1985): 314–25.

6. Charles R. Plott, "Industrial Organization Theory and Experimental Economics," *Journal of Economic Literature* 20 (December 1982): 1485–1527.

7. Gyoichi Iwata, "Measurement of Conjectural Variations in Oligopoly," *Econometrica* 42 (September 1974): 947–66.

8. James A. Brander and Anming Zhang, "Dynamic Oligopoly Behavior in the Airline Industry," *International Journal of Industrial Organization* 11 (September 1993): 407–35.

9. The original work was in Heinrich von Stackelberg, *Marktform und Gleichgewicht* (Vienna: Springer, 1934).

10. Anderson and Engers have argued that the sequential nature of the Stackelberg result makes it a more likely outcome than the Cournot-Nash result. See Simon P. Anderson and Maxim Engers, "Stackelberg versus Cournot Oligopoly Equilibrium," *International Journal of Industrial Organization* 10 (March 1992): 127–35.

11. Frank M. Gollop and Mark J. Roberts, "Firm Interdependence in Oligopolistic Markets," *Journal of Econometrics* 10 (1979): 313–31.

12. Bertrand's model was developed in a critical review of Cournot published 45 years after the original article in Joseph Bertrand, book review of "Recherches sur les Principes Mathematiques de la Theorie des Richesses," *Journal de Savants* 67 (1883): 499–508.

13. For a fairly simple treatment of the introduction of product differentiation into the Bertrand model, see Eric Rasmusen, *Games and Information: An Introduction to Game Theory* (Oxford: Basil Blackwell, 1989), pp. 267-9.

14. Lawrence Fouraker and Signey Siegel, *supra* note 4.

15. "The Airline Mess," *Business Week* (July 6, 1992): 50–5.

16. This model is sometimes referred to as the Forchheimer Model because it was derived in Karl Forchheimer, "Theoretisches zum unvollstandegen Monopole," *Schmollers Jahrbuch* (1908): 1–12; A.J. Nichol, *Partial Monopoly and Price Leadership* (Philadelphia: Smith-Edwards, 1930). See also Dean A. Worcester, "Why Dominant Firms Decline," *Journal of Political Economy* 65 (August 1957): 338–47.

17. Worcester, *ibid.*

18. See *United States* v. *United States Steel Corporation* 251 US 417 (1920).

19. Erwin A. Blackstone, "Limit Pricing and Entry in the Copying Machine Industry," *Quarterly Review of Economics and Business* 12 (Winter 1972): 57–65.

20. Thomas Whiteside, "Where Are They Now?" *New Yorker* (February 17, 1951): 39–58.

21. For evidence of the decline of each of these price leaders, see Richard T. Pascale, "Perspectives on Strategy: The Real Story Behind Honda's Success," *California Management Review* 26 (1984): 47–72.

Chapter 8

Collusion: The Great Prisoner's Dilemma

Few topics in industrial organization have attracted the attention of economists more than collusion. Models of overt and tacit collusion have abounded since Adam Smith declared:[1]

> People of the same trade seldom meet together, even for merriment and diversion, but the conversation ends in a conspiracy against the public, or in some contrivance to raise prices.

Intuitively one of the best methods for solving the prisoner's dilemma should be **overt collusion**, in which a group of competitors sit down to discuss and set price. As we discuss in detail in Chapters 18 and 19, one tremendous mitigating circumstance against the effective use of overt or **explicit collusion** in the United States is that it is illegal. Of course, so is running a red light, drug possession, and prostitution; and overt price fixing, despite its illegality, has been tried from time to time with varying degrees of success. Because overt collusion is illegal in the United States, most efforts to fix prices are tacit rather than overt or explicit. **Tacit collusion** results when different firms set identical prices without ever meeting to discuss prices because of a "meeting of the minds," whereby competitors recognize that it is in all their best interests to avoid price competition.

Recently, economists have recognized that because of the **prisoner's dilemma**, it is often difficult to maintain collusive agreements for very long.[2] Yet, exceptions occur. In the past, successful collusion existed for years and even decades in some industries, including steel, cement, glucose, oil, electrical equipment, and tobacco. Why do some attempts to fix prices work, and others fail miserably? In an effort to answer this question, this chapter explores the major theoretical approaches to collusion. Empirical evidence is presented in Chapter 9. We begin with a return to the prisoner's dilemma model of Chapter 6.

The Prisoner's Dilemma Revisited

In Chapter 6, the prisoner's dilemma was introduced. It was shown that in any finite prisoner's dilemma game, like the one depicted in Table 6.2, the players will

TABLE 8.1	Profits (General Electric, Westinghouse)		

| | | Westinghouse Action | |
		Collude	Defect
GE Action	Collude	100,100	25,120
	Defect	120, 25	80, 80

always play the dominant strategy of low price, low price. Table 6.2 is basically reproduced here as Table 8.1, except that the two options have been changed from High Price, Low Price to Collude, Defect.

In this chapter we use the term **perfect collusion** to indicate that the firms are producing the joint profit-maximizing output. Table 8.1 shows that if General Electric and Westinghouse are able to perfectly collude, they each earn a profit of 100, but if they each defect (i.e., charge a low price), they each earn 80. If only one defects, it earns 120, whereas the other firm earns 25. The dilemma for both firms is how to remain at the perfectly collusive result when each has an incentive to cheat.

Suppose General Electric and Westinghouse believe the game represented by Table 8.1 will go on forever, that is, the game is an **infinite game.** This is not an unreasonable assumption for modern corporations that anticipate survival for many years into the future. In an infinite game, firms can adopt strategies today to affect future outcomes. What strategies enable firms to achieve the joint profit-maximizing result? Consider the necessary characteristics of a solution to the dilemma. The firms must establish an environment in which each believes the other will stick to the collusive high-price policy. Intuitively, any solution to the dilemma has to be characterized by: (1) an ability to detect cheating and (2) an ability to punish cheaters. In the absence of these two conditions, firms will have such a strong incentive to defect that the result will almost certainly be the dominant strategy of Defect, Defect.

Recall from our discussion of the Mumbles-Big Boy example in Chapter 6 that an effective solution to the dilemma for the mob is to ensure that all squealers will be killed. This solution to the Mumbles-Big Boy game has both characteristics. The mob can identify the squealer (cheater) by observing the trial or the pretrial plea bargaining, and the mob has the ability to enact swift punishment. The death threat is extremely effective.

Short of a death threat, are there strategies that will enable firms to reach the cooperative solution? In an attempt to find the best solution to the prisoner's dilemma, political scientist Robert Axelrod invited world-renown game theorists to try to solve the dilemma.[3] In Axelrod's first competition, 14 theorists submitted computer programs. Each program was run a total of 15 times: once in head-to-head competition against each of the other 13 programs, once against a random computer-generated choice, and once against itself. The entrants knew that

TABLE 8.2   **Profits (Jensen, Waldman)**

		Waldman Action	
		Collude	**Defect**
Jensen Action	**Collude**	100,100	25,120
	Defect	120, 25	80, 80

the game would last 200 rounds. The winner of Axelrod's tournament was Anatol Rapoport, who used a relatively simple strategy known as **tit-for-tat.***

A tit-for-tat player adopts the following strategy:

1. Start off in the first round cooperating.
2. In every subsequent round, adopt your opponent's strategy in the previous round (e.g., in round N, adopt your opponent's strategy in round N-1).

Despite the fact that tit-for-tat *never* beat any of the other 13 strategies in head-to-head competition, it still won the overall contest! How? By piling up relatively good showings against every other strategy.

To understand how tit-for-tat works, consider the following Jensen-Waldman Mini Tournament, where Jensen plays tit-for-tat and Waldman plays the dominant strategy. As in the Axelrod tournament, the strategies will be pitted against each other and then they will be pitted against an opponent playing the same strategy. The game will be played according to the payoffs in Table 8.2. Begin with Jensen playing tit-for-tat against Waldman playing the dominant strategy. Waldman, of course, will defect in every round. We know that Waldman must win the head-to-head competition because the dominant strategy always beats or ties against any other strategy (it ties against another dominant strategy player). Based on the information in Table 8.2, we consider what happens in such a game, but first it is necessary to explain two important economic concepts: present value and discounting.

PRESENT VALUE AND DISCOUNTING

Before explaining the Jensen-Waldman Mini Tournament, we note that in repeated games players want to maximize *long-run,* not short-run, profits. Understanding long-run profit maximization requires understanding the economic concepts of **present value** and **discounting.** Because X dollars invested today at an interest rate i would increase in value to $X(1 + i)$ dollars in one year,

---

*It is interesting to note that Axelrod later ran his tournament with one slight modification. Instead of knowing that the game would last 200 rounds, there was a probability equal to 0.00346 that the game would end on any given round. Once again Rapoport and tit-for-tat won. Eric Rasmusen, *Games and Information: An Introduction to Game Theory,* (Oxford UK: Basil Blackwell, 1989), p. 120.

$X(1 + i)(1 + i) = X(1 + i)^2$ in two years, and $X(1 + i)^t$ in t years, the present value of $X(1 + i)^t$ dollars received t years from today is X dollars.* By similar reasoning, the promise to pay X dollars t years from today has a present value of:†

$$present\ value = \frac{X}{(1 + i)^t}$$

Let π_j represent a typical firm's profits in time period j, and $(1 + i)$ represent the rate at which the firm is willing to trade future for present income. The "i" in the term $(1 + i)$ is referred to as the firm's **discount rate**. π_{pv} represents the firm's **present value of profits** in the following equation:

$$\pi_{pv} = \frac{\pi_1}{(1 + i)} + \frac{\pi_2}{(1 + i)^2} + \frac{\pi_3}{(1 + i)^3} + ... + \frac{\pi_n}{(1 + i)^n} \qquad [8.1]$$

or:

$$\pi_{pv} = \sum_{j=1}^{n} \frac{\pi_j}{(1 + i)^j}$$

The maximization of long-run profits implies the maximization of π_{pv}. From equation 8.1 it is apparent that the maximization of long-run profits depends not only on the flow of economic profits, π_j, but also, and critically, on the discount rate i. Firms with short-time horizons will have high discount rates and will want to earn high profits in early periods even if it means sacrificing future profits, and firms with longer time horizons and lower discount rates will want to sacrifice current profits to earn higher profits in the future.‡ Assuming n goes to infinity and π_j is constant for all values of j, it is easy to prove that:§

---

*If X = $100 and i = 10%, then the present value of $110 received in one year is $100 because it is necessary to invest $100 today to receive $110 in one year. Similarly the present value of $121 received in two years is $100 today.

†At an interest rate of 10 percent, the promise to pay $100 in one year has a present value of $90.91 because:

$$present\ value\ of\ \$100\ received\ in\ one\ year = \frac{100}{(1.1)} = 90.909090.$$

‡For example, a firm owned by an individual nearing retirement with no heirs might have a very high discount rate.

§This result can be obtained by using simple algebra as follows:

$$\pi_{pv} = \frac{\pi_j}{(1 + i)} + \frac{\pi_j}{(1 + i)^2} + ... + \frac{\pi_j}{(1 + i)^n}$$

$$\pi_{pv} = \frac{1}{(1 + i)} \left[\pi_j + \frac{\pi_j}{(1 + i)} + \frac{\pi_j}{(1 + i)^2} + ... + \frac{\pi_j}{(1 + i)^n} \right]$$

$$\pi_{pv} = \frac{1}{(1 + i)} (\pi_j + \pi_{pv})$$

$$\pi_{pv} (1 + i) = \pi_j + \pi_{pv}$$

$$\pi_{pv} = \frac{\pi_j}{i}$$

$$\pi_{pv} = \sum_{j=1}^{n} \frac{\pi_j}{(1 + i)^j} = \frac{\pi_j}{i}.$$

Assuming, for simplicity, that Jensen and Waldman value a dollar earned to-day as equivalent to a dollar earned any time in the future, the discount rate is $i = 0$. Later in this chapter this simplifying assumption is eliminated.

A round-by-round depiction of the Jensen versus Waldman game would look as follows:

Round	Jensen Strategy (Profits) Plays Tit-for-Tat	Waldman Strategy (Profits) Plays Dominant Strategy
1	Collude (25)	Defect (120)
2	Defect (80)	Defect (80)
3	Defect (80)	Defect (80)
⋮	⋮ ⋮	⋮ ⋮
200	Defect (80)	Defect (80)
Total Profits:	Jensen = 15,945	Waldman = 16,040

In the first round Jensen uses the tit-for-tat strategy and plays collude. Waldman plays the dominant strategy in the prisoner's dilemma game and de-fects. Waldman wins the first round and earns 120. Jensen loses the first round and earns 25. In round 2, Jensen plays Waldman's round 1 strategy and defects. Waldman continues to play the dominant strategy and defects. In round 2 they each earn 80. In every subsequent round they both defect and earn 80. The 200 round totals: Waldman—16,040, Jensen—15,945. Waldman has "won," but it is surely a Pyrrhic victory because if they had reached the perfectly collusive result, they each would have earned profits of 20,000 (100 × 200).

In the Axelrod tournament, each strategy was also pitted against itself. Consider a game in which Jensen plays tit-for-tat against another tit-for-tat player. A round-by-round tit-for-tat versus tit-for-tat game would look as follows:

Round	Jensen Plays Tit-for-Tat	Player 2 Plays Tit-for-Tat
1	Collude (100)	Collude (100)
2	Collude (100)	Collude (100)
3	Collude (100)	Collude (100)
⋮	⋮ ⋮	⋮ ⋮
200	Collude (100)	Collude (100)
Total Profits:	Jensen = 20,000	Player 2 = 20,000

In tit-for-tat versus tit-for-tat, defections never occur, and each player earns the maximum 20,000.

By contrast, consider a game in which Waldman plays against another domi-nant strategy player. Defections *always* occur, and each player earns only 16,000. A round-by-round Waldman dominant strategy versus another player's dominant strategy game would look as follows:

Round	Waldman *Plays Dominant Strategy*	Player 2 *Plays Dominant Strategy*
1	Defect (80)	Defect (80)
2	Defect (80)	Defect (80)
3	Defect (80)	Defect (80)
⋮	⋮ ⋮	⋮ ⋮
200	Defect (80)	Defect (80)
Total Profits:	Waldman = 16,000	Player 2 = 16,000

Even in our greatly simplified tournament, Jensen's tit-for-tat easily defeats Waldman's dominant strategy in combined profits as follows:

Combined Profits in the Two Games for Each Strategy

Jensen's Profits Using Tit-for-Tat

> Game 1—Jensen v. Waldman
>> Jensen's Profits—15,945
>> Waldman's Profits—16,040
> Game 2—Jensen v. Another Tit-for-Tat Player
>> Jensen's Profits — 20,000

> Jensen's Tit-for-Tat Combined Profits = 15,945 + 20,000 = 35,945.

Waldman's Profits using the Dominant Strategy

> Game 1—Waldman v. Jensen
>> Jensen's Profits—15,945
>> Waldman's Profits—16,040
> Game 2—Waldman v. Another Dominant Strategy Player
>> Waldman's Profits—16,000

> Waldman's Dominant Strategy Combined Profits =
> 16,040 + 16,000 = 32,040.

In the Jensen-Waldman Mini Tournament, Jensen playing tit-for-tat wins 35,945 to 32,040. However, in terms of wins and losses, Jensen had a record of zero wins, 1 loss, and 1 tie; and Waldman had a record of 1 win, zero losses, and 1 tie. In the real Axelrod tournament, tit-for-tat won in exactly the same manner, by doing reasonably well against every other strategy, despite losing seven of the 14 head-to-head competitions. Its overall record in the Axelrod Tournament was a weak zero wins, 7 losses and 7 ties; yet it won.[4]

Does tit-for-tat solve the prisoner's dilemma? Not really. It does not guarantee that the collusive price will be maintained in all, or even most, rounds, yet it won by exhibiting several important properties: it is relatively *nice* toward competitors; it *punishes* all defections; and it *forgives* defectors who return to the fold. Tit-for-tat is nice in the sense that it never initiates an aggressive action. It is aggressive in the sense that it punishes all aggressive moves, even first-time defections, and it is forgiving in that it rewards defectors who revert to cooperation by also reverting to cooperation.

According to Axelrod, the niceness characteristic was tit-for-tat's most important advantage.[5] Virtually all of the highly rated strategies submitted to Axelrod were nice. In fact, each of the top eight ranking strategies was nice in the sense that it was *never* the first to defect until very close to the end of the game. The nice entries did much better than the more aggressive entries in terms of average scores.[6]

One major lesson to be learned from the victory of tit-for-tat in Axelrod's tournament is the importance of being able to recognize and punish defectors. But it would be incorrect to generalize tit-for-tat's victory into an implication that oligopolists should simply adopt the tit-for-tat strategy in all circumstances. Tit-for-tat has some glaring weaknesses as a solution to the prisoner's dilemma. For one thing, in a single elimination tournament, such as the NCAA basketball tournament, tit-for-tat would be knocked out early. If our simple Jensen-Waldman tournament had been a single-elimination tournament, Jensen's tit-for-tat would have been defeated and eliminated by Waldman's dominant strategy in the first round. For another thing, in a game with *uncertain* and *incomplete* information where the nonplayer nature randomly enters the game once in a while and selects defect as the move to be played by one of the players, two Tit-for-Tat players competing against each other fare very poorly.*

To understand why two tit-for-tat players fare very poorly in such a game, consider a 200-round game played by General Electric and Westinghouse where nature randomly selects defect *once for each firm* between round 2 and round 10, but otherwise both firms always play tit-for-tat. Recall Table 8.1 shows the payoff matrix. The pattern in such a game would be:

Round	*GE Strategy (Profits)*	*Westinghouse Strategy (Profits)*
1	Collude (100)	Collude (100)
2	Collude (100)	Collude (100)
3	*Nature selects defect* (120)	Collude (25)
4	Collude (25)	Defect (120)
5	Defect (120)	Collude (25)
6	Collude (25)	Defect (120)
7	Defect (120)	Collude (25)
8	Collude (25)	Defect (120)
9	Defect (80)	*Nature selects defect* (80)

---

*Recall from Chapter 6 that many games require a nonplayer (nature) to take random actions at some point in a game. If a game includes nature, but nature does not move first, or nature's first move is observed by all players, the game is of *complete information*. Furthermore, if nature never moves after any other player moves, then the game is said to be of *certain information*. In the game being played here, nature moves after a move by another player, and nature's move is not observed by both players; therefore, the game is a game of incomplete and uncertain information.

Round	GE Strategy (Profits)	Westinghouse Strategy (Profits)
10	Defect (80)	Defect (80)
11	Defect (80)	Defect (80)
12	Defect (80)	Defect (80)
⋮	⋮ ⋮	⋮ ⋮
200	Defect (80)	Defect (80)
Total Profits:	15,995	15,995

In this game with incomplete and uncertain information, either firm would earn higher profits by playing the dominant strategy and earning either 16,040 if its opponent played tit-for-tat or 16,000 if its opponent played the dominant strategy.

If both firms behaved even more nicely and played tit-for-*two*-tats, however, they would have fared much better. Suppose that General Electric and Westinghouse play tit-for-two-tats, with nature randomly selecting defect once for each firm between round 2 and round 10. Such a game would have the following pattern:

Round	GE Strategy (Profits)	Westinghouse Strategy (Profits)
1	Collude (100)	Collude (100)
2	Collude (100)	Collude (100)
3	*Nature selects defect* (120)	Collude (25)
4	Collude (100)	Collude (100)
5	Collude (100)	Collude (100)
6	Collude (100)	Collude (100)
7	Collude (100)	Collude (100)
8	Collude (100)	Collude (100)
9	Collude (25)	*Nature selects defect* (120)
10	Collude (100)	Collude (100)
11	Collude (100)	Collude (100)
12	Collude (100)	Collude (100)
⋮	⋮ ⋮	⋮ ⋮
200	Collude (100)	Collude (100)
Total Profits:	19,945	19,945

Thus if General Electric and Westinghouse are just a bit nicer and allow for one unpunished defection, their profits increase from 15,995 to 19,945, an increase of 24.7 percent. The decision to play the more aggressive tit-for-tat strategy would cost each firm a great deal of profit. In Axelrod's first tournament, a strategy of tit-for-two-tats would have won.[6]

Just as nature randomly selects defect in the above games and this random defection can destroy effective collusion, in the real world of oligopolistic competition a price reduction or defection can be misinterpreted by competitors as an aggressive act, leading to a large decline in price unless competitors behave nicely.

◢ A Real World Example of "Nice" Behavior in Response to Random or "Accidental" Defections

AUTOMOBILES[7]

After World War II, General Motors was the dominant firm in the automobile market. Until the late 1970s, the automobile manufacturers announced price changes once each year when the new models were introduced in the fall. The general pricing policy was for Ford and Chrysler to match General Motors' percentage price increases. Sometimes, however, Ford or Chrysler would introduce their new car models before General Motors introduced its new cars. In those years Ford and Chrysler would try to guess how large GM's price increases would be and announce their price increases accordingly. If they guessed "too high," Ford and Chrysler would lower their prices to match GM's price increases. This is not surprising because Ford and Chrysler had to be competitive with the industry leader.

In 1956, 1970, and 1974, however, Ford and Chrysler introduced their new cars first and guessed "too low"—GM later announced higher price increases. Ford and Chrysler clearly preferred lower price increases than GM in 1956, 1970, and 1974, and Ford and Chrysler could have used those lower prices to gain market share at GM's expense. Instead, in each of those three years, Ford and Chrysler behaved "nicely" and revised their price increases upward to match GM's increases. By behaving nicely, Ford and Chrysler were able to maintain industry pricing stability and avoid a potential downward price spiral.

◢ Another Strategy for Maintaining Effective Collusion: Trigger Price Strategies[8]

In Chapter 7 the Bertrand equilibrium in a finite game played by two firms, Firm 1 and Firm 2, was identified as $P = MC$. Recall the basic conditions of the Bertrand game in Chapter 7: Firm 1 and Firm 2 produce a homogeneous product; industry demand is $P = 100 - Q$, and $MC = AC = 10$ for both firms. If the firms could solve the prisoner's dilemma and engage in perfect collusion, the joint profit-maximizing quantity of 45 would be produced and price would equal 55. However, given Bertrand behavioral assumptions, $Q = 90$ and $P = 10$.

Now consider an infinitely repeated version of this game played with both firms following the behavioral rules listed:

1. Start by cooperating and charging the joint profit-maximizing price P = 55.
2. Continue to charge the joint profit-maximizing price P = 55 *unless* the other player lowers price below P = 55, in which case charge the Bertrand equilibrium price P = 10 forever.

The strategy in this game is referred to as a **trigger price strategy** because even a single deviation from cooperation ends cooperation forever. Because of the swift and aggressive punishment associated with defecting in this game, this strategy is also often called the **grim strategy.**

What is the equilibrium in the grim strategy game? If the two firms engage in perfect collusion, P = 55, $q_1 = q_2 = 22.5$, and $\pi = Q (P - AC) = 22.5 (55 - 10) = 1012.50$ for each firm. In this case the firms share the industry's jointly maximized profit of 2025. Using the results of the discussion of present value and discounting earlier in this chapter, we find that if both firms cooperate forever beginning at time t = 0, the present value of profits for each is:

$$\pi_{pv}^{collude} = \sum_{t=0}^{\infty} \frac{1012.50}{(1+i)^t} = 1012.50 + \sum_{t=1}^{\infty} \frac{1012.50}{(1+i)^t}$$

$$= 1012.50 + 1012.50 \left(\frac{1}{(1+i)} + \frac{1}{(1+i)^2} + \frac{1}{(1+i)^3} + \ldots \right) = 1012.50 + \frac{1012.50}{i}.$$

Suppose Firm 1 decides to defect in period t = 0 and charge a price P = 55 − ϵ. The price P is *infinitesimally* less than 55. Firm 1 would then capture the *entire* market (remember the product is homogeneous) in period t = 0, and Firm 1 would earn an amount *infinitesimally* less than 2025. By the grim strategy, however, in every subsequent round P = 10 and economic profits are zero because P = 10 = AC. The present value of Firm 1's profits would then be:

$$\pi_{pv}^{defect} = 2025 - \epsilon + \sum_{t=1}^{\infty} 0 = 2025 - \epsilon.$$

Should Firm 1 cooperate? It makes sense to cooperate as long as the following condition is met:

$$\pi_{pv}^{collude} > \pi_{pv}^{defect}$$

or if

$$1012.50 + \frac{1012.50}{i} \geq 2025 \Rightarrow i \leq 1.$$

A discount rate i > 1 (or a discount rate above 100 percent) would imply that Firm 1 cares little about future profits and is willing to sacrifice more than $200 dollars in profits next year in return for just $100 in profits this year. Such a high discount rate, although not impossible, is quite improbable in the world of modern corporations. In the real world, firms' discount rates will typically be much less than 1 because firms place considerable value on future profits as well as on current profits. Economists typically assume a discount rate in the range of 5 percent to 10 percent (0.05–0.10) as being reasonable. A discount rate of 10 percent implies that the firm is willing to sacrifice $110 dollars in profits next year in return for $100 in profits this year.

As long as i ≤ 1, the equilibrium in the grim strategy game is for both firms to *always* charge the perfectly collusive price P = 55 and share maximum joint profits in each period. Intuitively, the reason for this result is that if a firm charges a price below the monopoly price in any period it gains *all* of the monopoly profits in that period, but for one period only; then the price cutter earns economic profits equal to zero forever. In this game even a small price cut triggers a punitive response that lowers price to marginal cost, and therefore the collusive result holds for all periods.*

Collusive Agreements as Viewed by One Firm in a Cartel

Suppose a cartel consists of many firms. How will any one firm view its best alternative given the choices of the other firms? Consider a hypothetical firm, the "MidEast Corporation." Suppose, in Figure 8.1, the cartel price has been set by an explicit agreement at P_o, the cartel's joint profit-maximizing price. If *all* cartel members *always* abide by the cartel price then MidEast's demand curve can be calculated as D_F, where D_F is called a **followship demand curve** because it assumes that MidEast is simply following the price of all other cartel members. The cartel's price, P_o, may or may not be the price for which $MR_F = MC$ for MidEast.

MidEast Corporation can consider two broad pricing options: (1) maintaining the price at P_o or (2) attempting to *secretly* reduce its price below P_o. If MidEast is able to secretly reduce its price relative to other cartel members, then it should be able to steal buyers away and move along its **non-followship demand curve**, D_{NF}, which is drawn under the assumption that MidEast alone changes price while all other firms price at P_o. D_{NF}, therefore, will be more elastic than D_F. For prices below P_o, D_{NF} is simply a *cheating on the cartel* demand curve. If MidEast decides to cheat, then profit maximization calls for an expansion of output to Q_{ch} and a lowering of price to P_{ch}.

Of course, if MidEast thinks it can cheat without being detected, why wouldn't every other cartel member think the same way? And if each and every member of the cartel believed that it could cheat without being detected, then each firm would lower price, and MidEast would move along its *followship demand curve* D_F. If every firm behaved exactly like MidEast and cut price to P_{ch}, then MidEast would operate on D_F and sell only Q_1 units. Because P_o represents the cartel's joint profit-maximizing price, industry profits must decline when the industry's price declines to P_{ch}.

---

*The grim strategy provided a formal game theoretic foundation for successful perfect collusion, but there is a problem with the result. If instead of the perfectly collusive price P = 55, the two firms began the game by charging any price between 10 and 55, and then adopted the grim strategy, the initial price would also be a valid equilibrium price. This result is known as the **Folk Theorem** because it was part of the oral tradition or "folk wisdom" among game theorists long before it was published.

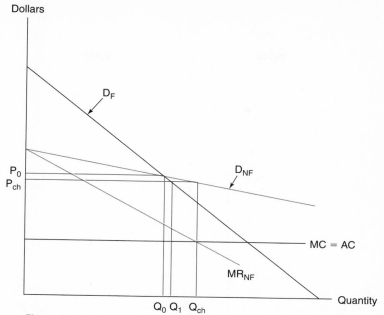

Figure 8.1 Followship and non-followship demand curves in a cartel.

The MidEast situation is simply another example of the prisoner's dilemma. A price reduction is a dominant solution for MidEast because it is MidEast's best option no matter what strategy is adopted by the other cartel members. If the other members maintain price at P_o, then MidEast should move along its non-followship demand curve and cut price to P_{ch}. On the other hand, if the other cartel members reduce price below P_o, then MidEast would experience a dramatic reduction in sales unless it matched the price reduction.

Previously we stated that "the cartel's price, P_o, may or may not be the price for which $MR_F = MC$ for MidEast." If P_o is the joint profit-maximizing price, shouldn't it be the price for which $MC = MR_F$ for MidEast and every other member? If all firms face identical costs of production and there is no significant product differentiation, then P_o should be the price for which $MC = MR_F$ for MidEast. If the firms have differing costs, however, or if product differentiation is significant, then P_o will be a compromise price that is unlikely to coincide with MidEast's desired profit-maximizing price.

Figures 8.2(a) through 8.2(c) depict a situation where duopolists have differing costs. Suppose that ABC Inc. is a low-cost producer and XYZ Inc. is a high-cost firm. In panel 8.2(a) industry demand is:

$$P = 100 - \tfrac{1}{2} Q = 100 - \tfrac{1}{2} (q_{ABC} + q_{XYZ}).$$

Therefore, by the *twice as steep rule*, marginal revenue is:

$$MR = 100 - (q_{ABC} + q_{XYZ}).$$

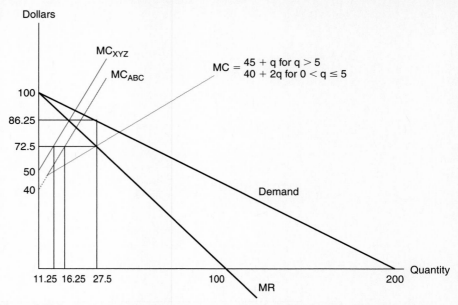

Figure 8.2(a) The joint profit-maximizing price in a duopoly where the firms have different costs.

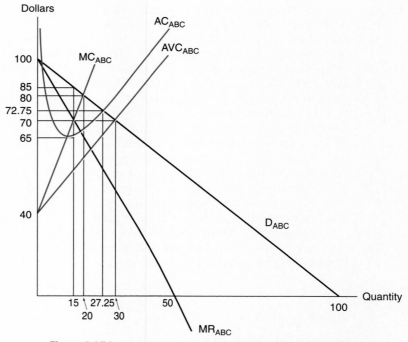

Figure 8.2(b) Profit-maximizing price for the low-cost firm ABC.

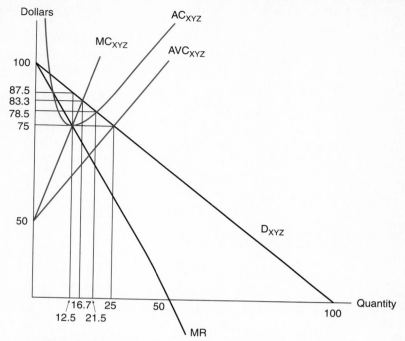

Figure 8.2(c) Profit-maximizing price for the high-cost firm XYZ.

Assume there is no product differentiation, and therefore, if the firms charge the same price, they split the demand curve. In panels 8.2(b) and 8.2(c), the equal shares demand curves are drawn as:

$$p_{ABC} = 100 - q_{ABC} \text{ and } p_{XYZ} = 100 - q_{XYZ}.$$

By the *twice as steep rule,* the firms' equal shares marginal revenue curves are:

$$mr_{ABC} = 100 - 2q_{ABC} \text{ and } mr_{XYZ} = 100 - 2q_{XYZ}.$$

In Figures 8.2(b) and 8.2(c), the firms have the following cost curves:

$$FC = 150$$

$$mc_{ABC} = 40 + 2q_{ABC} \text{ and } mc_{XYZ} = 50 + 2q_{XYZ}.$$

Equating mc and mr in panels (b) and (c) yields the following preferred profit-maximizing quantity and price for ABC and XYZ, respectively:

$$q_{ABC} = 15 \text{ and } p_{ABC} = 85.00$$

$$q_{XYZ} = 12.5 \text{ and } p_{XYZ} = 87.50$$

Not surprisingly, the high-cost firm, XYZ, prefers a price that is higher than that of the low-cost producer ABC. Furthermore, note that the two firms have different marginal costs at their preferred profit-maximizing quantities, with $mc_{ABC} = 70$ and $mc_{XYZ} = 75$. Because joint profit maximization requires that the marginal cost of production be equal for both firms, this outcome is clearly not the joint profit-maximizing result.

How do these preferred prices compare with the joint profit-maximizing price? To determine the joint profit-maximizing price, the *industry* marginal cost curve must be equated to the *industry* marginal revenue curve. This is done in panel (a). Notice that the industry marginal cost curve is derived by adding the two individual marginal cost curves *horizontally*, not vertically, to yield:*

$$MC = 40 + 2Q \text{ for } 0 < Q \leq 5$$

$$MC = 45 + Q \text{ for } Q > 5.$$

For joint profit maximization:

$$MC = 45 + Q = 100 - Q = MR.$$

Solving for Q yields $Q = 27.5$, and substituting back into the demand curve yields $P = 100 - 0.5(27.5) = 86.25$.

The joint profit-maximizing price is a compromise between the preferred prices of the two firms. This creates a serious problem for the firms in their attempt to arrive at a price agreement regardless of whether the agreement is explicit or tacit.

Another serious barrier to achieving joint profit maximization with differing costs is that it requires significant differences in the outputs of the two firms. With joint profit maximization, total industry output is 27.5 units, but the division of output between ABC and XYZ would have to ensure that the marginal cost of each firm was *equal.* In this example, each firm's marginal cost would have to equal the industry's marginal cost of 72.50 in panel (a). To maximize industry profits XYZ would be forced to reduce its output to 11.25 units compared with

---

*For marginal costs between 40 and 50, only the low-cost firm ABC's marginal cost curve is relevant, so for industry outputs between 0 and 5 the marginal cost curve is simply $MC = 40 + 2Q$.

For marginal costs greater than 50, the industry's marginal cost curve is derived by adding the *quantities* for any given marginal cost as follows:

$$mc_{ABC} = 40 + 2 q_{ABC} \quad \text{or} \quad q_{ABC} = \tfrac{1}{2} mc - 20.$$

$$mc_{XYZ} = 50 + 2 q_{ABC} \quad \text{or} \quad q_{XYZ} = \tfrac{1}{2} mc - 25.$$

$$Q = q_{ABC} + q_{XYZ} = \tfrac{1}{2} mc - 20 + \tfrac{1}{2} mc - 25 = mc - 45$$

or

$$mc = 45 + Q.$$

16.25 units for ABC.* Unless the two firms can figure out a way to share profits more equitably, it is doubtful XYZ would go along with such a result.

Why doesn't ABC simply announce its desired low price, 85.00, and force XYZ to go along? Although this might seem like an easy solution, it presents serious potential problems for ABC. If XYZ wants to show its displeasure with P = 85.00, it might start a price war. XYZ has latitude to lower price, because it could reduce price to marginal cost, P = 83.3, and still earn positive economic profits because its price would be above average total cost, even if ABC matched its price cut to 83.3. ABC, of course, could respond to XYZ's price cut by lowering its price to P = 80.00, cover its marginal cost, and earn positive economic profits, but such a move would be risky for a number of reasons. First, if ABC reduced price to 80.00, XYZ could still reduce price further. In fact, XYZ could reduce price to 78.50 and still cover its average total cost. If XYZ got really upset with ABC, XYZ could reduce its price considerably below 78.50, all the way down to 75 and still cover its *average variable cost* (AVC). Of course, the low-cost producer ABC could more than match any cuts by XYZ and could reduce price to 70 and still cover its AVC.

A price reduction by ABC below its AVC of 70, however, might result in legal trouble in the United States. As we discuss in detail in Chapters 18 and 21, the antitrust laws make it illegal to reduce prices in a effort to monopolize a market. Price reductions aimed at monopolizing a market are referred to as **predatory prices,** and a cut below AVC, which is below the firm's *shutdown price,* might be viewed as predatory and result in antitrust action.

Second, if ABC cuts price to marginal cost at 80.00, but XYZ cuts only to 83.3, then ABC will have a major price advantage and customers are likely to flock to ABC. As a result the assumption of an equal shares demand curve would no longer be valid, and ABC would be faced with a much more elastic *non-followship* demand curve. The problem for ABC might then be its inability to meet this additional demand with its existing capacity. Angry customers might willingly return to buy available supplies from XYZ, and ABC might end up losing much of its good will.

To summarize briefly, when firms face differing costs, it is much more difficult to agree on a price.

---

*To maximize joint profits each firm must produce the output for which mc = 72.50. For XYZ, this implies that:

$$mc_{XYZ} = 50 + 2q_{XYZ} = 72.50$$

or:

$$q_{XYZ} = 11.25.$$

For ABC, this implies that:

$$mc_{ABC} = 40 + 2q_{ABC} = 72.50$$

or:

$$q_{ABC} = 16.25.$$

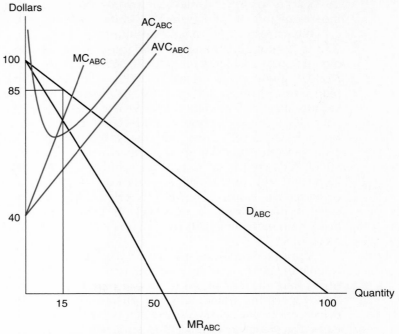

Figure 8.3(a) Profit-maximizing price for Firm ABC with a larger demand.

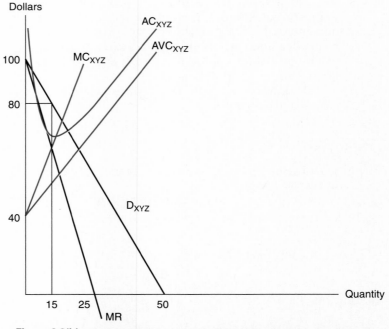

Figure 8.3(b) Profit-maximizing price for Firm XYZ with a smaller demand.

An analogous argument can be made for industries with significant product differentiation.[9] Suppose, for example, that ABC and XYZ have identical marginal costs, but because of product differentiation, ABC's demand is greater than XYZ's demand. Figures 8.3(a) and 8.3(b) show such a situation. In Figures 8.3(a) and 8.3(b), the following demand curves are drawn under the assumption that both firms charge an identical price:*

$$\text{ABC's demand curve: } p_{ABC} = 100 - q_{ABC}$$

$$\text{XYZ's demand curve: } p_{XYZ} = 100 - 2q_{XYZ}$$

Using the *twice as steep rule*, the marginal revenue curves are:

$$mr_{ABC} = 100 - 2q_{ABC}$$

$$mr_{XYZ} = 100 - 4q_{XYZ}$$

Suppose each firm's costs are:

$$FC = 150$$

$$mc = 40 + 2q$$

Equating mc and mr in Figures 8.3(a) and 8.3(b) yields the preferred profit-maximizing quantity and price for each firm. The profit-maximizing quantities and prices for ABC and XYZ are:

$$q_{ABC} = 15 \text{ and } p_{ABC} = 85.00$$

$$q_{XYZ} = 10 \text{ and } p_{XYZ} = 80.00$$

In this case ABC, with a larger demand, prefers the higher price. Once again, the firms will have to compromise if they are to reach any kind of price agreement.

Factors Affecting the Ease or Difficulty of Effective Collusion

Recall that effective collusion entails an ability to detect and punish cheaters. In addition to cost or demand differences, many other factors affect the ease or diffi-

---

*The assumption of identical prices in a market with product differentiation may seem highly unlikely. This assumption is used here in part to simplify the mathematical analysis. It is, however, plausible that firms *tacitly* agree to compete strictly on the basis of product differentiation and avoid price competition. For example, Ben and Jerry's and Häagen Dazs Ice Cream may recognize that competition based on product differentiation in the form of different flavors, different fat contents, and different social images may result in greater profits than competition based on price, because it is less likely to result in a breakdown in discipline.

culty of detecting cheating or punishing cheaters. Some other major factors are considered next.[10]

NUMBER OF FIRMS[11]

Generally speaking, as the number of firms increases reaching an agreement to fix price becomes harder because detecting cheating becomes more difficult. Strong theoretical and empirical evidence supports this view. When two or three firms are involved it is extremely unlikely that one firm can get away with a significant price reduction without being detected. Conversely, with fifty firms the likelihood of escaping detection is much greater.

Not only is detection easier with a smaller number of firms, but also the incentive to retaliate against price cutting is far greater. If one relatively small firm of fifty cheats, it is unlikely to have a major impact on the profits of the other forty-nine firms, and it may not be worth the profit sacrifice for the others to retaliate. However, cheating by one of three firms is very likely to make a major dent in the profits of the other two, resulting in a strong incentive for retaliation.

Empirical studies of the incidence of price fixing support both these general conclusions. Very few price fixing cases involve more than two dozen firms.

CONCENTRATION[12]

Concentration should also influence the likelihood of effective collusion. High concentration should make it easier for the leading firms to behave as price leaders with smaller firms simply following. Consider two industries, each with twenty firms. If the four-firm concentration ratio is 80 in industry 1, and 30 in industry 2, then the four dominant firms in industry 1 should be able to agree on price with less concern about the response of the competitive fringe of firms.

Empirical evidence supports a positive relationship between concentration and *effective* collusion. Hay and Kelly, for example, found that most stable cartels were formed in industries with a fairly high degree of concentration.[13]

RATE OF TECHNOLOGICAL CHANGE

A rapid rate of technological advance results in either new products or new, lower-cost methods of production. Frequent introduction of new products results in fluctuations in demand *among* firms, leading to the problems associated with differing demand curves. Constantly changing production processes leads to cost differences and their associated problems.

A contrast between two industries should help clarify this point. Reaching a price agreement in the computer industry is very difficult because technology changes both the product mix and the costs of production so rapidly. Any price agreement reached today is likely to be cheated on by the newest low-cost or new

product producer tomorrow. By contrast, in the gypsum board industry, technological change has proceeded at a snail's pace over the last eighty years, and few,
if any, differences exist between firms' production methods.* Therefore gypsum
board producers can relatively easily reach price-fixing agreements.

DEMAND GROWTH AND ELASTICITY[14]

The impact of the rate of growth in demand on the likelihood of effective collusion is ambiguous. In industries in which demand is stagnant or declining, firms
may sustain economic losses and turn to collusion in a desperate attempt to earn
a profit. Slow rates of demand growth, therefore, may be associated with higher
levels of collusion. However, declining demand may make it difficult to maintain
effective collusion. Such was the case throughout the 1950s in the electrical
equipment industry. Firms in the industry were quick to attempt to tighten up on
collusive agreements during recessions and were just as quick to break the agreements. OPEC has also tried hard to reach agreement during recessions, but, like
the electrical equipment manufacturers, OPEC has had difficulty maintaining
those agreements.

Things are a bit more clear-cut with regard to the relationship between the
elasticity of demand and collusion. The more inelastic the demand, the greater
the incentive to collude because it is easier to raise price without having to significantly reduce industry output. If demand is highly elastic, even the strongest cartels will struggle to increase price, because a price increase will result in a large reduction in industry output and require significant output reductions by all cartel
members.

FREQUENCY OF SALES[15]

In some industries, such as light bulbs and toiletries, the frequency of sales is very
rapid and orders come in at a smooth, consistent pace. In industries with a high
frequency of sales, the loss of an order or two creates few problems for any firm
and there is less need to turn to collusion to allocate market shares.

In other industries, such as commercial aircraft and electric turbines, the frequency of sales is slow and orders come in at a lumpy, inconsistent pace. In industries with a low frequency of sales, one order can keep a plant in operation for
months, sometimes even years. Consider, for example, the importance of defense
contracts in the aerospace industry or orders for multimillion dollar electric turbines in the electrical equipment industry. In the absence of collusion, such
lumpiness of orders often makes it difficult to avoid price wars as each firm battles to maintain its market share. To avoid destructive price competition, such industries often turn to price-fixing agreements.

Table 8.3 summarizes the major factors that affect the ease or difficulty of
reaching collusive agreements.

---

*Gypsum board is commonly known as *wallboard* and is used to build walls in most modern
homes.

TABLE 8.3   **Different Factors' Impacts on the Ease of Collusion**

Factors Facilitating Effective Collusion	Factors Hindering Effective Collusion
1. Identical costs for all firms	Differing costs between firms
2. No product differentiation	Significant product differentiation
3. Small number of firms	Large number of firms
4. High concentration	Low concentration
5. Slow rate of technological advance	Rapid rate of technological advance
6. Steady rate of demand growth	Slow rate of demand growth or declining demand
7. Low elasticity of demand	High elasticity of demand
8. Low frequency of sales	High frequency of sales

SUMMARY

1. Firms wish to collude to maximize long-run, not short-run, profits.
2. Solutions to the prisoner's dilemma require the ability to detect and punish cheaters. Effective solutions also appear to require that the leading firms exhibit some degree of *niceness* toward competitors.
3. A "tit-for-tat" strategy appears to be one possible solution to the prisoner's dilemma. Another possible solution is a trigger price strategy such as the "grim strategy."
4. Differences in costs and demand increase the difficulty of solving the prisoner's dilemma and often require elaborate schemes to solve the game theoretic problems associated with collusion.
5. Product differentiation, a large number of firms, low concentration, a rapid rate of technological advance, declining industry demand, a high elasticity of demand, and large frequency of sales all make effective collusion less likely.

KEY TERMS

discounting
discount rate
explicit collusion
Folk theorem
followship demand curve
grim strategy

infinite game
non-followship demand curve
overt collusion
perfect collusion
predatory prices
present value

prisoner's dilemma   tit-for-tat strategy

tacit collusion   trigger price strategy

DISCUSSION QUESTIONS

1. Is the chapter's assumption of a zero discount rate in the Waldman-Jensen Tournament reasonable? Explain.

2. If the Axelrod Tournament had been a single-elimination tournament (that is, losing once to an opponent results in elimination from the tournament), would there be a strategy that ensured you could never lose the tournament?

3. Suppose in a duopoly one firm produces with high fixed costs and low variable costs and the other firm produces with low fixed costs and high variable costs. Which firm would prefer a lower price? Will that firm be able to force the other firm to charge that lower price?

4. In which of the following industries would you expect price collusion to be easier to maintain?

   a. Steel or ready-to-eat cereals

   b. Hotels or crude oil production

   c. Glass containers or fast food

PROBLEMS

1. What is the present value of a promise to pay $1,000 in two years at a discount rate of 10 percent? What is the present value of a promise to pay $1,000 for the next 100 years at a discount rate of 10 percent? What would these values be if the discount rate were 5 percent? What would these values be if the discount rate were 20 percent?

2. What would the result of a competition between Jensen and Waldman have been if Jensen played the "grim strategy" and Waldman played "tit-for-tat"?

3. Suppose a duopoly faces an industry demand curve of $P = 100 - Q$. If the firms charge the same price, they share the demand so that they each face a demand curve:

$$P_i = 100 - 2q_i \text{ for } i = 1, 2$$

The firms, however, face the following different marginal costs:

$$mc_1 = 10 + 2q_1 \text{ and } mc_2 = 22 + 2q_2$$

   a. If both firms charge the same price, what is Firm 1's preferred price?

   b. If both firms charge the same price, what is Firm 2's preferred price?

   c. What is the joint profit maximizing price? How much output would each firm produce if they charged the joint profit maximizing price?

4. Would it be easy or difficult to maintain effective collusion if two duopolists faced the following profit matrix:

		Firm B's Action	
		High Price	**Low Price**
Firm A's Action	**High Price**	1,000, 150	700, 100
	Low Price	800, 50	500, 75

Does there appear to be a dominant firm in this industry? Does Firm A have a dominant solution to this game? Does Firm B have a dominant solution to this game?

REFERENCES

1. Adam Smith, *An Inquiry into the Nature and Causes of the Wealth of Nations* (New York: Modern Library Edition, 1937), p. 128.
2. See, for example, R. Preston McAfee and John McMillan, "Bidding Rings," *American Economic Review* 83 (June 1992): 579–99; and Jonathan Cave and Stephen W. Salant, "Cartel Quotas Under Majority Rule," *American Economic Review* 85 (March 1995): 82–102.
3. Robert Axelrod, *The Evolution of Cooperation* (New York: Basic Books, 1984).
4. Axelrod, *ibid.*, p. 194.
5. Axelrod, *ibid.*, p. 33.
6. Axelrod, *ibid.*, p. 33.
7. U.S. Senate, Committee on the Judiciary, Subcommittee on Antitrust and Monopoly, Report, *Administered Prices: Automobiles*, (Washington, DC: Government Printing Office, 1958), pp. 53–4 and 67–9; "Chrysler Increases Prices Again For '71, Following G.M. Pattern," *New York Times* (December 2, 1970): 35; and "Ford Motor Adds to Boost on '75 Models; Price Rise Will Near G.M.'s Almost 10%," *Wall Street Journal* (August 21, 1974): 3.
8. For an expanded discussion, see Jean Tirole, *The Theory of Industrial Organization*, (Cambridge, MA: MIT Press, 1988), pp. 245–7. See also James Friedman, "Noncooperative Equilibrium for Supergames," *Review of Economic Studies* 28 (1971): 1–12; James Friedman, *Oligopoly and the Theory of Games* (Amsterdam: North-Holland, 1977); D. Fudenberg and E. Maskin, "The Folk Theorem in Repeated Games with Discounting and
with Incomplete Information," *Econometrica* 54 (1986): 533–54; E. Green and R. Porter, "Noncooperative Collusion Under Imperfect Price Information," *Econometrica* 52 (1984): 87–100; R. Porter, "Optimal Cartel Trigger Price Strategies," *Journal of Economic Theory* 29 (1983): 313–38; and A. Rubinstein, "Equilibrium in Supergames with the Overtaking Criterion," *Journal of Economic Theory* 21 (1979): 1–9.
9. For game theory approaches to this issue, see Myong-Hun Chang, "The Effects of Product Differentiation on Collusive Pricing," *International Journal of Industrial Organization* 9 (September 1991): 543–69; Thomas W. Ross, "Cartel Stability and Product Differentiation," *International Journal of Industrial Organization* 10 (March 1992): 1–13; Jonas Hächner, "Collusive Pricing in Markets for Vertically Differentiated Products," *International Journal of Industrial Organization* 12 (June 1994): 155–77; and Philippe Jehiel, "Product Differentiation and Price Collusion," *International Journal of Industrial Organization* 10 (December 1992): 633–41.
10. Although these are the major factors, there are, of course, other possible factors. Scott has argued that increased product diversification makes it easier to maintain effective collusion. See John T. Scott, "Multimarket Contact among Diversified Oligopolists," *International Journal of Industrial Organization* 9 (June 1991): 225–38. Taking a different approach, Lambson has suggested that collusion is more difficult in markets where "aggregate efficiency (i.e., the ability

of firms to profitably produce at prices exceeding the Cournot price) is large relative to the level of demand." See Val Eugene Lambson, "Aggregate Efficiency, Market Demand, and the Sustainability of Collusion," *International Journal of Industrial Organization* 6 (June 1988): 263–71. In addition, Feinberg has pointed out that increases in imports should reduce the effectiveness of collusion. Robert M. Feinberg, "Imports as a Threat to Cartel Stability," *International Journal of Industrial Organization* 7 (June 1989): 281–88.

11. Almarin Phillips, *Market Structure, Organization and Performance* (Cambridge: Harvard University Press, 1962); Samuel M. Loescher, *Imperfect Collusion in the Cement Industry* (Cambridge: Harvard University Press, 1959); Jesse W. Markham, *Competition in the Rayon Industry* (Cambridge: Harvard University Press, 1952); James W. McKie, *Tin Cans and Tin Plate* (Cambridge: Harvard University Press, 1959); Edmund P. Learned and Catherine C. Ellsworth, *Gasoline Pricing in Ohio* (Boston: Harvard Business School Division of Research, 1959); and Oliver E. Williamson, "A Dynamic Theory of Interfirm Behavior," *Quarterly Journal of Economics* 79 (November 1965): 579–607.

12. George A. Hay and Daniel Kelley, "An Empirical Survey of Price Fixing Conspiracies," *Journal of Law & Economics* (April 1974): 13–38; Arthur G. Fraas and Douglas F. Greer, "Market Structure and Price Collusion: An Empirical Analysis," *Journal of Industrial Economics* (September 1977): 29–33.

13. G.A. Hay and D. Kelley, *supra* note 12, p. 26.

14. G.A. Hay and D. Kelley, *supra* note 12, p. 15; J.M. Clark, *Studies in the Economics of Overhead Costs* (Chicago: University of Chicago Press, 1923), pp. 434–50; L.G. Reynolds, "Cutthroat Competition," *American Economic Review* 30 (December 1940): 736–47; Samuel M. Loescher, *Imperfect Collusion in the Cement Industry* (Cambridge, MA: Harvard University Press, 1959), pp. 191–9; Almarin Phillips, *Market Structure, Organization and Performance* (Cambridge, MA: Harvard University Press, 1962), pp. 16–9 and 221–42; Ralph G.M. Sultan, *Pricing in the Electrical Oligopoly*, vol. 2 (Boston: Harvard Business School Division of Research, 1974), pp. 286–98; and Joseph L. Bower, *When Markets Quake: The Management Challenge of Restructuring Industry*, (Boston: Harvard Business School Press, 1986), Chapter 4.

15. Sidney L. Carroll, "The Market for Commercial Airliners," in R. Caves and M. Roberts (eds.), *Regulating the Product Quality and Variety* (Cambridge, MA: Ballinger, 1975), pp. 150, 163; John Newhouse, *The Sporty Game* (New York: Alfred A. Knopf, 1982); *Business Week* (May 8, 1989): 34–5; and *Business Week* (January 25, 1988): 38.

Chapter 9

Collusion in the Real World: Methods of Achieving Effective Collusion

Chapter 8 examined the topic of collusion theoretically. In this chapter, our attention turns toward real-world attempts to achieve effective collusion. As you read the chapter keep in mind the two overriding principles of successful collusion laid out in the previous chapter: the need to identify cheaters and the ability to punish them.

Recall the factors that affect the ease or difficulty of attaining effective collusion, including: (1) the number of firms; (2) concentration; (3) the degree of product differentiation; (4) demand growth and elasticity; (5) the frequency of sales; and (6) the rate of technological change. At the beginning of each industry example, these six factors are presented, and in the chapter summary we attempt to determine whether these factors appear important in these cases. The remaining sections of this chapter analyze several methods that have been tried to solve the prisoner's dilemma.

Attempted Methods of Achieving Effective Collusion

1. *Find a Large Firm to Act as the Industry's Dominant Firm Price Leader and Benefactor*

    a. **Oil Production—1973–1985**

        Characteristics of the Industry

        (1) Number of Firms—medium (12 members of the formal cartel)

        (2) Concentration[1]—moderate (% of proven reserves 1988); four-firm concentration ratio—50.9 (Saudi Arabia 19%, Iraq 11%, Iran 10.5%, Abu Dhabi 10.4%)

(3) Product Differentiation—low
(4) Demand Elasticity—inelastic
(5) Lumpiness of Orders—no
(6) Rate of Technological Advance—slow

Some of the best examples of overt price-fixing cartels have come from the annals of international commodity cartels, and no example is more famous, or infamous, than the international oil cartel, OPEC (The Organization of Petroleum Exporting Countries). In Chapter 8's hypothetical example of the MidEast Corporation, MidEast's alternatives closely approximated those faced by the smaller members of OPEC, as well as non-OPEC oil-producing countries such as Egypt, Great Britain, and Mexico, since OPEC gained economic power in the 1970s. Saudi Arabia has been the major player and leader of OPEC. From the viewpoint of the relatively small producers, an increase in output should have little effect on price and might result in greatly increased profits *so long as Saudi Arabia attempts to maintain the cartel's official price at a higher level.* If the Saudis hold price at the official high level, cartel members such as Kuwait, Venezuela, Algeria, Qatar, Gabon, and Ecuador have a strong incentive to increase production to increase revenues and profits.

Another problem for OPEC's stability has been the tendency for non-OPEC oil-producing countries to take the official OPEC price as a **parametric price** or a price that is *fixed* by economic conditions. In Figure 9.1 suppose the official OPEC price is P_{OPEC} and the marginal cost and average cost of producing oil for a non-OPEC oil producer such as Mexico are represented by the curves MC and AC. If Mexico believes that countries such as Canada and the United States would just as soon buy Mexican oil instead of OPEC oil at identical prices, then theory suggests that Mexico should take OPEC's price as given and maximize profits by producing the *competitive* output Q_1. Under these conditions there is little or no incentive for Mexico to restrict its output below the competitive output of Q_1. As a result, Mexico would gain market share at OPEC's expense.

This is precisely what happened almost continuously after OPEC gained its economic power in the mid-1970s, and especially after the fall of the Shah of Iran in 1979 sent oil markets into turmoil and pushed official OPEC prices up to $34 a barrel in 1981. From 1974 to 1985, OPEC's share of world production fell from 55 percent to 30 percent, and non-OPEC producers (including the United States) and producers from the communist and former communist states experienced an increase in their share from 45 percent to over 70 percent.[2]

The biggest loser from the relative decline in OPEC's market share was Saudi Arabia. To stabilize prices, Saudi Arabia was forced to significantly reduce its output from an average of 6.5 million barrels per day in 1982 to 5.1 million in 1983, 4.7 million in 1984, and 3.4 million in 1985. When output reached a rate of about 2 million barrels per day in the summer of 1985, Saudi Arabia reached the limit of its restraint on behalf of the cartel.[3] In late 1985 the Saudis decided to assert their always present economic power to control price. Once the Saudis decided to increase output to preserve their market share, instead of attempting to maintain a high price, industry prices plummeted to below $10 a barrel in 1986. At $10 a barrel the output of non-OPEC countries began to decline as marginal

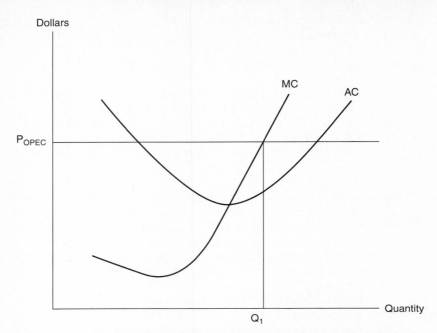

Figure 9.1   Profit maximization for a smaller member of OPEC.

wells were shut down.[4] When the price was eventually stabilized at approximately $18 a barrel in 1986–87, OPEC's share relative to non-OPEC countries once again began to increase.

In the early years of this scenario, Saudi Arabia did not play even a moderately aggressive strategy such as tit-for-tat, or even tit-for-two-tats. In fact, Saudi Arabia probably had no incentive to play tit-for-tat in response to "small" amounts of cheating. A hypothetical game matrix will help to explain why. Table 9.1 represents a possible game matrix for Saudi Arabia and Venezuela, which is used here to represent any small OPEC member. In Table 9.1 Saudi Arabia sets the price for the cartel—either high or low. Because Saudi Arabia produces so much more output than Venezuela, a decision to respond to a defection by cutting price actually results in a large reduction in Saudi Arabia's profits (from 9,000 to 7,000). In Table 9.1 the Saudis have a dominant strategy—set a high price. No matter what Venezuela does, the Saudis should keep the price high. Venezuela, of course, also has a dominant strategy—defect.

Table 9.1 suggests a possible solution to the prisoner's dilemma: find a large price leader that has a self-interest in keeping the price high *regardless* of the actions of the other cartel members. This requires an industry structure in which one firm is strongly dominant.

Not all economists believe OPEC has operated as a cartel. One alternative theory suggests that oil-producing states have set production to generate sufficient revenues to cover their oil investment requirements. According to this theory, producing states view prices as fixed, that is, set by competitive forces, and there-

TABLE 9.1   **Profits (Saudi Arabia, Venezuela)**

		Venezuela's Strategy	
		Cooperate	Defect
Saudi Arabia Strategy	**High Price**	10,000, 500	9,000, 1,000
	Low Price	8,000, 375	7,000, 450

fore, an increase in industry price permits a reduction in output to meet the country's investment requirements.[5] James Griffin attempted to test empirically whether the oil industry operated competitively or as a cartel.[6] His findings suggested that OPEC countries operated as a cartel, but that non-OPEC countries operated according to the competitive model. Overall, Griffin concluded that a "partial market-sharing cartel model dominates the competitive model."[7]

b. Steel—1901–1920

Characteristics of the Industry

(1) Number of Firms—medium (eight firms controlled most of the market)
(2) Concentration[8]—high (four-firm concentration ratio—74.2 in 1902)
(3) Product Differentiation—low
(4) Demand Elasticity—inelastic
(5) Lumpiness of Orders—yes
(6) Rate of Technological Advance—slow

Just as Saudi Arabia has played the role of dominant firm price leader for OPEC, United States Steel played that role in the steel industry at the turn of the century, with much the same consequences. In the 1890s, before the formation of the United States Steel Corporation, the steel industry was characterized by periods of aggressive price competition. In fact, as the corporation began to take shape in 1900, steel prices were declining.[9] US Steel was formed in 1901 through the consolidation of twelve major steel companies. At the time, US Steel accounted for over 65 percent of the industry's output. Although US Steel almost certainly had the power to force compliance with its pricing policies, it chose a different path. Instead of aggressively cutting price to eliminate its competitors, it cooperated with them.

US Steel cooperated through a variety of devices, including pools, associations, trade meetings, and, most infamously, from 1907 until 1911, the "Gary dinners," at which Judge Elbert Gary, President of US Steel, invited competitors to "dinner" for the more or less expressed purpose of fixing and stabilizing prices.[10] Because US Steel decided to set prices at a level that attracted entry, and because it refrained from predatory practices, its market share declined continuously after its formation, and by 1920 its share had declined to approximately 50 percent.[11]

US Steel continued to provide a price umbrella for its smaller competitors even after 1911 when the explicit collusion associated with the Gary dinners ended as a result of a government antitrust investigation. After 1911 US Steel became the recognized price leader and held that role for decades until its power was permanently eroded by foreign competition.

c. Plug-Compatible Computer Equipment—1969–1975
Characteristics of the Industry
   (1) Number of Firms—medium (IBM plus eleven other firms)
   (2) Concentration[12]—high initially, but declining (IBM's share varied from 100 percent in some equipment in 1969 to 25 percent in some areas in 1975)
   (3) Product Differentiation—low
   (4) Demand Elasticity—elastic
   (5) Lumpiness of Orders—no
   (6) Rate of Technological Advance—rapid

IBM's behavior in the plug-compatible computer equipment market in the late 1960s provides another example of a solution to the prisoner's dilemma through reliance on a dominant firm price leader.[13] At the time, IBM controlled approximately 75 percent of the mainframe computer market. Twenty-five years ago the computer industry was a complicated industry. A system consisted of a central processing unit (CPU), which acted like a brain, and a great deal of peripheral equipment that plugged into the CPU. Almost everyone who has worked on a computer has seen a good deal of peripheral equipment, including terminals, line printers, input and output tapes, disc drives, tape drives and so forth. In 1970 IBM and a few other firms, such as Digital Equipment and Honeywell, produced full systems, while many other smaller firms produced only peripheral equipment.

In the 1960s, the main IBM system was the System/360, which IBM priced according to a *value-of-service* pricing policy. Under a value-of-service policy, IBM priced hardware according to the value it supplied the consumer rather than the cost of producing it. A fast tape drive might cost only a little more to produce than a slow drive, but IBM charged much more for the fast drive. Although hardware was priced according to a value-of-service policy, software and support services were provided free of charge. Under this pricing scheme IBM charged prices well above manufacturing costs for hardware, including plug-compatible equipment, to cover the costs of the software and service it provided free, and IBM's profit margin was very high. This created a strong incentive for firms to enter the market for relatively *low-tech, low-cost* plug-compatible equipment such as tape and disk drives. Because of the significant incentive to enter, the number of plug-compatible peripheral equipment manufacturers increased from only three in 1966 to approximately 100 in 1972.[14] Telex, CalComp, Memorex, CDC, and Ampex all took advantage of this opportunity and were able to make significant inroads into IBM's plug-compatible market. IBM still controlled the vast percentage of new plug-compatible sales, presenting it with a dilemma similar to the one faced by Saudi Arabia: how to compete against the incursion of these new competitors without destroying IBM's profit base from the sale of its own equipment.

If IBM chose to slash prices, it would gain back market share, but it would dramatically reduce its own profits.

The erosion of IBM's market share continued well into 1970, at which time IBM decided to respond. Their strategy was to maintain relatively high prices on IBM's plug-compatibles for the system 360 so as not to sacrifice profits on the system 360, and, at the same time, to develop a new generation of mainframe computers, the system 370, which was designed to make it much more difficult to use non-IBM plug-compatible equipment. IBM also priced the plug-compatible disk drives on the 370 much lower than on the 360. In addition, IBM developed a term-lease plan that gave manufacturers a strong incentive to commit to IBM products for one or two years.

As a result of these actions, the plug-compatible manufacturers were forced to cut their prices and their profits, and market share declined significantly. For a number of years, however, IBM, like Saudi Arabia and US Steel, provided a price umbrella over the heads of its smaller plug-compatible competitors.

Dominant firm price leadership is generally only partially successful in solving the prisoner's dilemma. Because the system provides a tremendous incentive for new firms to enter and for smaller incumbent firms to expand output, downward pressure on price often ensues. Furthermore, even if cheating is easily detected, the dominant firm may have little incentive to punish price cutters.

2. Collusive Price Leadership

To solve the prisoner's dilemma, some method of communication between firms is crucial. One method is to overtly collude; another is to rely on a price leader or leaders to signal price changes, with the expectation that others will follow the leader. The ability of a price leader to force adherence depends critically on an industry's market structure. Chapter 7 developed a model of dominant firm price leadership in which one firm had a very large market share, generally over 60 percent, and a cost advantage over fringe firms that enabled it to set its price independently. The dominant firm price leadership model suggests that if the dominant firm price leader sets a high price, new firms enter, existing firms expand, and ultimately the dominant firm's market share declines. As shown in the previous section, this is precisely what happened to Saudi Arabia, US Steel, and IBM.

When a dominant firm price leader loses its dominant position, a different type of leadership often evolves—**collusive price leadership**. Collusive price leadership exists when a few large firms in a concentrated industry set price and expect that the price will be followed by others.[15] It is not important for the identity of the price leader to remain the same, but it is important that price changes be followed. In the rare instance when a change is not followed, the price leader will usually rescind the change, but if the leader fails to rescind, a price war may result in which all firms are big losers. Examples are easy to come by.

a. Steel 1911–1960
Characteristics of the Industry
(1) Number of Firms—medium (varied from eight to twelve important manufacturers)

(2) Concentration[16]—high; four-firm concentration ratio—approximately 60 throughout the period
(3) Product Differentiation—low
(4) Demand Elasticity—inelastic
(5) Lumpiness of Orders—yes
(6) Rate of Technological Advance—slow

With the end of the Gary dinners in 1911, US Steel became the tacit price leader in steel and held that role for decades. The steel industry's use of tacit price leadership provided price stability that was at least as effective as the explicit attempts to fix prices through the Gary dinners and provides evidence that tacit collusion can be as effective as explicit collusion.

From 1920 until the early 1960s, US Steel was the acknowledged price leader in the steel industry. As Adams and Mueller noted,[17]

> During the administered price era, steel prices were characterized by remarkable rigidity and uniformity. Price stability was obtained at the expense of instability in output and employment. Unless impelled by sharp increases in direct cost or dangerous sniping by rivals, U.S. Steel generally preferred to resist both price increases and decreases and to sacrifice stability "only when the decision [was] unavoidable."
>
> After World War II, this price policy was transformed into one of "upward rigidity," that is, a pattern of stairstep price increases at regular intervals. . . . With or without resort to the conspiratorial basing point system,* the integrated giants matched each other's prices with monotonous consistency. They maintained a lockstep price uniformity by punishing any major mill that showed deviationist tendencies.

As US Steel lost its dominant position, it remained the recognized price leader even in fields in which it held a clear minority market share. In 1957, for example, US Steel held only a 26.6 percent share of capacity for cold-rolled piling compared with Bethlehem's 72.2 percent, yet US Steel was the price leader.[18] Similarly, in the Northeast, National was the output leader in cold-rolled sheets, but it followed US Steel's prices without question.[19]

In 1958 something unprecedented occurred in the steel industry: US Steel failed to lead an industry-wide price increase.[20] On July 1, 1958, a large wage increase for steel workers went into effect. Wage increases traditionally meant that US Steel would increase prices. When US Steel failed to respond, Armco, with a mere 4.4 percent of industry ingot capacity, announced a price increase. Other firms, including US Steel, followed, and the price increase stuck. A new chapter in the history of price leadership in steel had begun. US Steel had relinquished its position as the only price leader. Thereafter, price changes were initiated by one of several firms, most commonly US Steel, Armco, Bethlehem, or Republic.[21]

The passing of the old system created new uncertainty and less pricing stability. This became clear in a 1968 episode. After US Steel undercut Bethlehem on a

---

*Basing point systems are explained in detail in section 5 of this chapter.

major order, Bethlehem retaliated with a 22 percent price decrease on hot-rolled sheets (from $113.50 to just $88.50 per ton).[22] The other majors, including US Steel, followed Bethlehem's retaliatory price cut; however, three weeks later, US Steel suddenly increased its price to $125.00 per ton. Nine days later, Bethlehem followed with an increase, but only to $117.00 per ton. When US Steel matched the $117.00 price, the brief price skirmish was over. In this instance, industry discipline had been brought about by Bethlehem's disciplinary price cut, and US Steel was actually the defector in this episode. As the once-mighty US Steel disappeared from the steel industry, Bethlehem assumed the major burden of price leadership.[23]

b. Lead-Based Antiknock Compounds—1974-1979[24]
Characteristics of the Industry
  (1) Number of Firms—small (four firms controlled the entire market)
  (2) Concentration—high; four-firm concentration ratio—100
  (3) Product Differentiation—low
  (4) Demand Elasticity—inelastic
  (5) Lumpiness of Orders—no
  (6) Rate of Technological Advance—moderate

In the days when most gasoline contained lead, only a few firms produced lead-based antiknock gasoline additives. From 1920 to 1948 Ethyl Corporation was the only American producer. In 1948 Du Pont entered, and in the early 1960s PPG Industries and Nalco Chemical entered. In 1974 Du Pont held a 36 percent market share, followed by Ethyl with 34 percent, PPG with 17.5 percent, and Nalco with 12.5 percent.[25]

From 1974 to 1979 there were twenty-four price changes in the industry.[26] In twenty of these cases all four changed price on the same day. In the other four cases, all four firms had identical prices a day or two apart. Such a high degree of price uniformity required a sophisticated form of price leadership. Leadership was characterized by: (1) at least thirty days advance notice of all price changes; (2) public press notices of all price changes; (3) a delivered price system that required buyers located in the same city to pay the same price (these systems are discussed in a later section); and (4) the use of *most favored customer clauses*, whereby if one buyer received a lower price, all buyers would receive the same reduced price. Price leadership was clearly established to ensure both detection of all price cuts and punishment of cheaters.

The thirty days advance notice of price changes gave competitors ample time to respond and also gave the initiator of any change time to rescind its decision if the change was not matched by the others. If, for example, Du Pont intended to raise its price on May 1, it would announce its intention by April 1. Of course, Du Pont could also announce an intended price change earlier. An announcement on March 28, for example, would give its competitors three days to either announce matching changes or do nothing. If they matched the change, the new price would go into effect on May 1. If they failed to match, Du Pont could simply rescind its announcement. All of this occurring in public, through the press, guarded against secret price cuts, as did the use of a delivered price system and most favored customer clauses.[27]

c. Cigarettes—1923–1941

Characteristics of the Industry

(1) Number of Firms—small (three firms had virtual control of the market)
(2) Concentration—high; three-firm concentration ratio—over 90
(3) Product Differentiation—high
(4) Demand Elasticity—inelastic
(5) Lumpiness of Orders—no
(6) Rate of Technological Advance—moderate

One of the most famous instances of price leadership occurred in the cigarette industry.[28] As a result of a 1911 antitrust decree, the American Tobacco Company's monopoly over cigarettes was destroyed, and more than a dozen new cigarette companies were established, including Liggett & Myers and R.J. Reynolds. For about a decade, the cigarette producers competed aggressively, but in the early 1920s price competition suddenly ceased. Between 1928 and 1941, prices were identical and there were only eight price changes, five increases and three decreases. All five price increases were announced first by Reynolds, with American and Liggett following immediately. Of the three price decreases, American led two and Reynolds one.

In June 1931, the Big 3, as American, Reynolds, and Liggett & Myers were known, controlled 90 percent of the cigarette market. During that month, because of the Depression, raw tobacco prices were at their lowest since 1905. In the midst of the greatest economic crisis the nation had ever seen, on June 23, 1931, Reynolds *raised* the net wholesale price of Camel cigarettes, its leading brand, from $5.64 to $6.04 per thousand. The same day, American and Liggett & Myers raised the price of their leading brands, Lucky Strikes and Chesterfield, respectively, to an identical $6.04.[29]

According to the president of Reynolds, the rationale for this action was "to express our own courage for the future and our own confidence in our industry."[30] In a perhaps more honest assessment, the president of American gave as his rationale "the opportunity of making some money."[31] Both presidents, however, greatly underestimated the cross-elasticity of demand between the leading premium brands that sold for 13 cents per pack and the lower-quality 10-cent brands. After the Big 3 increased their list prices, the 10-cent brands saw their market share increase from a mere 0.28 percent in June 1931 to 22.78 percent in November 1932. As a result, in January 1933, the Big 3 were forced to reduce the net price of their leading brands from $6.04 to $5.20 per thousand, and in February, they had to cut their price further to just $4.85 per thousand. It was estimated that at a price of $4.85 per thousand, Camels and Lucky Strikes were being sold at a loss. Despite these price cuts, the market share of the Big 3 was never again close to 90 percent.

The price increase of 1931 proved to be a monumental mistake. It led to the introduction of new brands and the establishment of new companies such as Brown and Williamson and Philip Morris, which would seriously challenge and, in some cases, actually displace the Big 3. Price leadership, however, survived. After World War II Reynolds and American remained the price leaders. In 1956 an attempt by Liggett & Myers to lead a price increase was rejected by the two leaders, and Liggett rescinded. Similarly, in 1965 Lorillard's effort to raise prices was rejected and rescinded. Finally, in the 1970s the establishment of Philip Morris's Marlboro brand as the worldwide sales leader seller enabled it to assert some leadership.[32]

Like dominant firm price leadership, collusive price leadership is generally only partly successful in solving the prisoner's dilemma. Problems arise because no single firm is capable of effectively disciplining its rivals. If, for example, the firms are of more or less equal size and economic power, it may be difficult to discipline any one of the major players that becomes a price maverick.

3. Barometric Price Leadership

Dominant firm and collusive price leadership have been used effectively to try to move price toward the joint profit-maximizing level. A third type of price leadership, **barometric price leadership**, has also been used in some industries. With barometric price leadership, the price leader tends to be a small, nondominant firm that acts, as the name implies, more or less as an indicator of change. The barometric leader is relatively small; it does not have the ability to discipline rivals or enforce its will on the industry. Instead, it leads through example. When demand or cost conditions warrant a price change, the barometric price leader is the first to move. The more dominant firms then choose to either follow or reject the lead. Like collusive price leadership, barometric price leadership is a less effective method of solving the prisoner's dilemma than dominant firm price leadership.

There is evidence of barometric price leadership in fields as diverse as gasoline, steel, cellophane, and electric turbines. The previously cited example of Armco, instead of US Steel, increasing steel prices in 1958 is an example of a barometric leader indicating that it was time for a change in an industry's pricing policy.[33]

a. Electric Turbines—1950–1960

Characteristics of the Industry
(1) Number of Firms—small (three firms had control of the market)
(2) Concentration—high; three-firm concentration ratio—100
(3) Product Differentiation—medium
(4) Demand Elasticity—inelastic
(5) Lumpiness of Orders—yes
(6) Rate of Technological Advance—moderate

In electric turbines, Westinghouse and Allis-Chalmers were the price leaders on actual *transactions prices* in the 1950s even though General Electric, with approximately a 60 percent market share, led changes in *book prices*.[34] Sultan has suggested that in this case General Electric acted as a buffer to prevent larger swings in price.[35] According to this theory, in a period of falling demand, General Electric would not reduce book prices but would permit Westinghouse and Allis-Chalmers to reduce transactions prices. Similarly, in a period of rising demand, General Electric would not increase book prices but would permit Westinghouse and Allis-Chalmers to increase transactions prices. General Electric's relative market share would then fall during recessions, but it would increase during expansions when General Electric's actual transactions prices would be below Westinghouse's and Allis-Chalmers' prices. Over the entire expansion-contraction business cycle, such a policy would result in stable prices and stable market shares.

b. Cellophane—1941–1957
Characteristics of the Industry
  (1) Number of Firms—small (three firms had control of the market)
  (2) Concentration—high; three-firm concentration ratio—100
  (3) Product Differentiation—low
  (4) Demand Elasticity—elastic
  (5) Lumpiness of Orders—no
  (6) Rate of Technological Advance—moderate

There is evidence of barometric price leadership in the cellophane industry, with Avisco leading price changes that were often not followed by Du Pont.[36] Avisco led most price changes in the cellophane industry despite Du Pont's dominant position.

c. Gasoline Retailing in Ohio—1950s
Characteristics of the Industry
  (1) Number of Firms—medium (ten important gasoline retailers controlled 65 percent of the market)
  (2) Concentration[37]—medium; four-firm concentration ratio—approximately 35
  (3) Product Differentiation—low
  (4) Demand Elasticity—inelastic
  (5) Lumpiness of Orders—no
  (6) Rate of Technological Advance—slow

Standard Oil of Ohio (SOHIO) was the barometric price leader in the retail gasoline market in Ohio even though it was relatively small compared with the large national chains with which it competed.[38]

An advantage of barometric leadership is that it prevents price changes by the leaders from being misinterpreted as aggressive strategic decisions. A barometric leader's price change is less likely to result in a breakdown in industry pricing discipline than a price change initiated by a major firm under collusive price leadership. Although barometric price leadership may at first appear to be an innocent method of reading market signals, it may also be symptomatic of an attempt to raise and stabilize price.

One of the major factors necessary to solve the prisoner's dilemma, an ability to discipline, is missing in cases of barometric price leadership. Barometric price leadership, therefore, may not be very effective.

4. Most Favored Customer Clauses and "Low-Price" Guarantees[39]
Two of the more counter-intuitive methods of getting around the prisoner's dilemma are to offer either a **low-price guarantee** or a **most favored customer**

clause. *Low-price guarantees* promise the customer that the seller "will not be undersold and will match or beat any competitor's price." Such guarantees are extremely common in retailing, as when Sears offers appliance buyers the guarantee that if the buyer finds the same appliance sold or advertised for a lower price at another store in the next 30 days, Sears will match the other store's price. *Most favored customer clauses* promise that if the seller charges any future buyer a lower price than current buyers, the current buyers can receive a reimbursement to cover the price difference. Sears also uses most favored customer clauses when it sells an appliance with the guarantee that if the appliance goes on sale at Sears in the next 30 days the buyer can receive a reimbursement to cover the difference in costs.

a. Electric Turbines—1963–1975[40]
Characteristics of the Industry
(1) Number of Firms—small (two firms, a duopoly)
(2) Concentration—high; two-firm concentration ratio—100
(3) Product Differentiation—medium
(4) Demand Elasticity—inelastic
(5) Lumpiness of Orders—yes
(6) Rate of Technological Advance—moderate

In Chapter 8 we used General Electric and Westinghouse as players in a hypothetical prisoner's dilemma game. Now consider the real-world battle between these two corporate giants. General Electric and Westinghouse compete in virtually every major segment of the electrical equipment industry. Throughout the 1950s, it was common practice for firms to fix prices through direct price-fixing agreements.[41] In 1960, however, the industry was caught red-handed breaking the antitrust laws, and the formal overt agreements fell apart as firms were fined and executives were sent to prison. Through a series of antitrust consent decrees the defendants were enjoined from entering into any further overt attempts to fix prices. One of the consent decrees, signed on October 1, 1960, required General Electric, Westinghouse, and Allis-Chalmers (the only three American producers of turbine generators) to set turbine prices independently and to publicly announce their prices.[42] As a result of the uncovering of the conspiracy and the consent decree, price competition developed in the turbine market between 1960 and 1963. In fact, competition became so intense that low prices and large discounts forced Allis-Chalmers out of the market in December 1962.[43] This left only two domestic producers, General Electric and Westinghouse.

In May 1963, General Electric introduced a new turbine pricing policy.[44] First, General Electric announced its intention of maintaining its book prices and eliminating all discounts. Second, General Electric published a revised price book that simplified the procedure for determining prices. To determine prices under the new system, buyers simply multiplied General Electric's book price by a published multiplier. For example, if General Electric announced a multiplier of 0.80, actual prices equaled 80 percent of book prices. The third component was a *price protection clause* whereby General Electric guaranteed that if it lowered *any* product's price below its list price to *any* buyer, it would retroactively grant the lower price to any buyer that had purchased the product during the previous six months. Furthermore, to guard against secret price reductions, General Electric opened its books to public inspection.

Within days of learning about General Electric's new pricing policy, Westinghouse began using the General Electric pricing system, even *using General Electric's price book to set its prices*! Nine months later, Westinghouse introduced its own price book but continued to follow General Electric's prices. As a result of these policies, after August 1964, the two firms charged identical prices on all turbine orders.

The system worked because it ensured detection of cheating and guaranteed punishment. Detection was ensured by the open books policy that allowed anyone to check on the price either charged to any buyer. Any price reduction, therefore, would immediately be detected. Punishment was ensured because if either firm reduced a price to *any* buyer, regardless of whether it was a General Electric buyer or a Westinghouse buyer, it would have to reduce its price to *all* buyers of that product over the previous six months. Any price cut by General Electric would therefore primarily hurt General Electric, not Westinghouse, and any price cut by Westinghouse would primarily hurt Westinghouse. The scheme was an excellent solution to the prisoner's dilemma, and it worked.

b. Electronics Retailing 1980–[45]
Characteristics of the Industry
(1) Number of Firms—large (thousands of electronics retailers in the metropolitan New York City area)
(2) Concentration—low
(3) Product Differentiation—medium
(4) Demand Elasticity—elastic
(5) Lumpiness of Orders—no
(6) Rate of Technological Advance—slow

Even in highly competitive industries, low-price guarantees can help maintain discipline. Have you ever wondered why so many major appliance dealers offer low-price guarantees? You know the guarantees: "We will not be undersold by anyone"; or "We match any competitor's lowest price." Customers who believe that such guarantees ensure the lowest possible price in a highly competitive market should think again.

Crazy Eddie was a large dealer of audio equipment in New York City. Anyone who used to watch New York City television probably knows the "crazy" Crazy Eddie commercials. Crazy Eddie claimed that his prices were "insane," because they would not be undersold. Newmark & Lewis, one of Crazy Eddie's largest competitors, also had a low-price guarantee. In fact, Newmark & Lewis promised to pay *double* the difference between its price and a competitor's lower price.

Suppose that both Crazy Eddie and Lewis & Newmark charged $1000 for a particular stereo component. One day Crazy Eddie gets "crazy" and cuts the price to $900. Will this attract customers to its store? Quite the contrary: the price cut actually drives customers to Newmark & Lewis, where they can now buy the component for $800 ($1000 minus twice the difference between Newmark & Lewis's price of $1,000 and Crazy Eddie's price of $900). Furthermore, as customers come in to get the $800 bargain, they act as informants against Crazy Eddie's price cut. Crazy Eddie's price cut is identified and punishment in the form of lost sales is immediate. As a result of the low-price guarantees, the only policy that makes sense is to maintain the price at $1000. Crazy Eddie could rant and rave about low prices all he wanted to on television because the more he did, the higher prices would be. He wasn't so crazy after all, although he did have to flee from the United States because of charges of embezzlement.

The use of most favored customer clauses is an effective method of solving the prisoner's dilemma. Cheating is easily detected by consumer-provided information, and punishment in the form of lost customers is swift.

5. Basing Point Pricing Systems

Under a **basing point pricing** system, or delivered price system, one or more geographic locations are established as basing points. Buyers are charged prices that include standard freight charges from the nearest basing point, even if the seller's manufacturing plant is located far from the basing point. Basing point systems are most common in industries characterized by high transportation costs relative to value, such as steel, cement, and lumber.

a. **Steel—1901–1948**
   Characteristics of the Industry
   (1) Number of Firms—medium (varied from eight to twelve important manufacturers)
   (2) Concentration—high; four-firm concentration ratio—approximately 60 throughout the period
   (3) Product Differentiation—low
   (4) Demand Elasticity—inelastic
   (5) Lumpiness of Orders—yes
   (6) Rate of Technological Advance—slow

The most famous basing point system was the steel industry's "Pittsburgh Plus" system.[46] From 1884 to 1924 Pittsburgh was the only basing point in the steel industry, and all steel shipments included a freight charge from Pittsburgh, even if the steel was shipped from Chicago or Birmingham. If a Chicago appliance manufacturer purchased steel from a Chicago steel mill, it paid for freight from Pittsburgh. No freight charges were actually incurred; the Chicago producer was able to pocket this **phantom freight**. If a Chicago mill sold steel to a Pittsburgh buyer, however, it would be forced to absorb the freight charges.

Consider the example illustrated in Figure 9.2. In 1920 the base price of steel purchased in Pittsburgh was $40 per ton. The curve ABC represents the actual basing point price of steel at various locations between Pittsburgh and Chicago, and the curve DBE represents the $40.00 per ton base price plus true freight costs from Chicago. A mill located in Chicago received phantom freight on all shipments between Chicago and location X_1, and it absorbed freight costs on all ship-

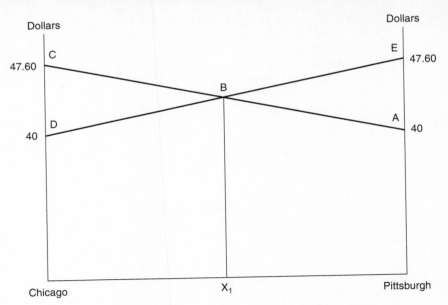

Figure 9.2 Phantom freight with a basing point pricing system.

ments between location X_1 and Pittsburgh. Only at location X_1 would a Chicago seller receive a price that covered actual freight charges. In 1920, transportation costs from Pittsburgh to Chicago were $7.60 per ton, so the Chicago price was $47.60. If a buyer in Chicago bought from a mill in Chicago, the price was $47.60, and the Chicago seller received $7.60 in phantom freight. If a buyer in Pittsburgh purchased from a Chicago mill, it would pay only $40.00 and the seller would incur $7.60 in freight absorption charges.

Basing point systems have two major advantages for oligopolists. First and foremost, prices are fixed for delivery anywhere in the country; the system is an excellent method for maintaining price discipline. Second, all firms do reasonably well under basing point systems. Firms located at a basing point can compete with producers located far from the basing point, and firms located far from the basing point obtain phantom freight on many shipments to cover their freight absorption on shipments close to the basing point.

A basing point system can easily be used as a method of tacit collusion to solve the prisoner's dilemma. The system establishes uniform prices in any location in the country. Furthermore, it discourages price chiseling because if chiselers are caught, the other members of the industry can establish a *punitive basing point* at the cheater's plant location, meaning that prices would be established at the punitive basing point at a level below the cheater's average cost. If a punitive basing point were established, the price cutter would sustain an economic loss on every sale and would eventually be forced to raise prices to accepted levels, to leave the market, or to sell out to a competitor. The punitive basing point would be successful in restoring price discipline because the price cheater would sustain economic losses on every sale, while its competitors would sustain losses only on sales in the price cutter's market.

The basing point system requires a method for setting the base price. In the steel industry that method was price leadership by US Steel. As discussed previously, in the early part of this century US Steel had the ability and incentive to unilaterally set the price of steel. The basing point system simply provided a way to minimize price cutting. The system worked well until the Great Depression drove capacity utilization rates under 20 percent and led to widespread price cutting.[47]

b. Southern Plywood—1963–1971[48]
Characteristics of the Industry
   (1) Number of Firms—medium (five firms charged with collusion, eight controlled the market)
   (2) Concentration[49]—high; four-firm concentration ratio—61
   (3) Product Differentiation—low
   (4) Demand Elasticity—inelastic
   (5) Lumpiness of Orders—no
   (6) Rate of Technological Advance—slow

In the 1970s the basing point system once again became a topic of interest because of the discovery of a delivered price system in the plywood industry. Until 1963 all the plywood produced in the United States came from the Northwest. A technological advance in the early 1960s, however, allowed builders to substitute southern pine for Northwestern Douglas fir. As a result the industry expanded rapidly into the South. The first Southern entrants, led by Georgia-Pacific in 1963, were also the leading producers of Northwestern Douglas fir. Spurred on by the large potential freight savings associated with Southern production, by 1969 there were 34 Southern plywood mills, producing about 21 percent of the nation's output.[50]

Georgia-Pacific initially priced its Southern plywood by using a basing point system based on shipment from Portland, Oregon. The Southern pine price was adjusted slightly downward, apparently to account for some perceived, as opposed to actual, product differentiation on the part of buyers, who continued to believe that Douglas fir was a superior wood. Additional firms entering the Southern market all used the same Oregon-based price system.

The basing point system was extremely functional. Beginning in 1958, two trade publications, *Crow's* and *Random Lengths*, had published plywood prices on a weekly basis. These weekly price lists were used as a basis for future price negotiations in the industry. The Southern manufacturers of plywood simply adopted the *Crow's* and *Random Lengths* prices and added freight charges from Portland, Oregon. This pricing system generated large phantom freight profits for the Southern producers.

It is not surprising that when the first Southern mill was established, Georgia-Pacific elected to charge a Portland-based price. Economic theory predicts that one Southern mill would have virtually no impact on price, and therefore, that mill would act as a perfectly competitive firm and take the Portland-based price as the competitive price. What is surprising is that as capacity in the South increased to roughly 30 percent of national output in 1973, 25 Southern producers operating 53 mills were *still* setting Portland-based prices.[51]

As noted previously, basing point systems can be effective methods of maintaining discipline only if a method exists to fix the basing point price. In the Southern plywood industry, two trade publications located thousands of miles away were the effective method of setting price.

Basing point systems have proved to be effective methods of solving the prisoner's dilemma. Cheating is easily detected, and punishment in the form of the adoption of a *punitive basing point* can be very quick and effective.

6. Trade and Professional Associations
a. Sugar—1927–1935
Characteristics of the Industry
(1) Number of Firms—medium (fifteen members)
(2) Concentration—medium (fifteen-firm concentration ratio—70 to 80)
(3) Product Differentiation—low
(4) Demand Elasticity—inelastic
(5) Lumpiness of Orders—no
(6) Rate of Technological Advance—slow

In the early part of the century most sugar was sold through independent brokers, who before the creation of the Sugar Institute had made it a common practice to grant discriminatory price concessions to buyers. These concessions often led to a general breakdown in price discipline. To eliminate this price discrimination, the Sugar Institute was established. The fifteen members produced 70 to 80 percent of the refined cane sugar in the United States. The Institute established a *code of ethics* that distinguished "ethical" from "unethical" types of behavior. The code required far more than the simple announcement of prices. Institute members agreed to refuse to deal with: (1) water carriers who refused to announce freight rates or who granted price concessions to any sugar refiner; (2) wholesalers who granted any price concessions; and (3) any trucker, broker, or warehouse owners who granted secret rebates.

The Sugar Institute sought to force compliance with its policies through an elaborate system of punishments.[52] The main objective was to require adherence to prices that were publicly announced and to eliminate all price discrimination. The Institute required brokers to sign a written contract stating that they would not grant discriminatory price concessions and that, if they did, they would have to pay a rebate to the refiner equal to the amount of the concession. Such a contract provided a strong enforcement mechanism against price cutting by brokers. As a further enforcement mechanism, members refused to deal with any broker who would not sign the agreement.

Evidence suggests that the Sugar Institute was somewhat successful in its efforts to stabilize price. Compared with raw sugar, the number and frequency of price changes declined for refined sugar after the establishment of the Institute's code of ethics. Furthermore, despite the existence of large excess capacity, price-cost margins and profits increased after the Sugar Institute's plan was implemented.[53]

b. Legal Services in Virginia—1970s
Characteristics of the Industry
(1) Number of Firms—large (thousands of lawyers in Virginia)
(2) Concentration—low (As noted in Chapter 4, service industries tend to have low levels of concentration; law is no exception.)
(3) Product Differentiation—medium
(4) Demand Elasticity—inelastic
(5) Lumpiness of Orders—yes
(6) Rate of Technological Advance—slow

In 1971, the Goldfarbs purchased a home in Fairfax County, Virginia. To secure a mortgage, they were required to obtain title insurance. The Goldfarbs contacted 36 lawyers and were told by each that the fee would be 1 percent of the value of the property.[54] They were also told that the Fairfax County Bar Association "suggested" this 1 percent fee to its members.

The reason for the identical pricing quickly became clear to the Goldfarbs: the 1 percent figure came right from the published list of minimum fees of the Virginia State Bar. The Virginia State Bar published a suggested minimum fee schedule in 1962 and a revised schedule, with higher fees, in 1969. The Bar Association even had a special "Committee on Economics of Law Practice" that recommended the fee schedules.

To enforce its suggested prices, the State Bar threatened to investigate any lawyer charging a lower fee (higher fees were considered ethical) and warned its members that the charging of lower fees "raises a presumption that such lawyer is guilty of misconduct."[55] A lawyer found guilty of misconduct was in very serious professional trouble because, according to the rules of the Virginia Supreme Court of Appeals, all lawyers were required to be members "in good standing" of the Virginia State Bar to practice law in Virginia.[56]

c. Engineering Services—1960s
Characteristics of the Industry
(1) Number of Firms—large (thousands of engineering firms throughout the United States)
(2) Concentration—low (As noted in Chapter 4, service industries tend to have low levels of concentration; engineering is no exception.)
(3) Product Differentiation—medium
(4) Demand Elasticity—inelastic
(5) Lumpiness of Orders—yes
(6) Rate of Technological Advance—slow

In July 1964, the National Society of Professional Engineers adopted a code of ethics that prohibited competitive bidding.[57] Under the code, engineers were prohibited from discussing fees until *after* a client had selected an engineer for a project. If a client demanded an advanced discussion of fees, the engineer was required to withdraw from the project. The policy was designed to eliminate all competitive bidding. Detection of cheating was accomplished by policing adherence through direct and indirect contacts with members and clients. The threat of punishment took the form of being thrown out of the society and disgraced in the eyes of one's peers.

The Society argued that such a restriction was necessary to protect the "public health, safety, and welfare."[58] According to this defense, competitive bidding would result in low-quality engineering work, which would result in collapsed buildings and bridges. Given what would happen to an engineering firm's reputation if one of its buildings collapsed, it is difficult to place much faith in this argument, however.

Trade and professional associations have had mixed results in their efforts to solve the prisoner's dilemma. Because there are often such a large number of firms, detecting cheating can be very difficult. In addition, punishment may not be effective. The Virginia Bar Association's plan was extremely effective in solving the prisoner's dilemma, however. In this case, cheating was easily detected because many fees, such as closing costs on a home, were public, and the threat of professional sanctions and a loss of the right to practice law made punishment effective.

7. Schemes to Divide Markets
a. Switchgear Assemblies* in the Electrical Equipment Industry—1950s
Characteristics of the Industry
(1) Number of Firms—small (five firms)
(2) Concentration—high; five-firm concentration ratio—just under 100
(3) Product Differentiation—medium
(4) Demand Elasticity—inelastic
(5) Lumpiness of Orders—yes
(6) Rate of Technological Advance—slow

As previously stated in the discussion of the electric turbine market, price fixing was rampant in the electrical equipment industry in the 1950s. The five major manufacturers of switchgear assemblies, General Electric, Westinghouse, Allis-Chalmers, I-T-E, and Federal Pacific, however, faced repeated cheating in their attempts to fix prices. Many methods were used to try to fix prices, but one was so unique and ingenious that it has received a great deal of attention. On November 9, 1958, the five manufacturers reached an agreement to divide the sealed bid market as follows: GE, 39 percent; Westinghouse, 35 percent; I-T-E, 11 percent; Allis-Chalmers, 8 percent; and Federal Pacific, 7 percent. A bit later, the five firms established the *phases of the moon* pricing system.[59]

The **phases of the moon system** contained not only a method to set price,

---

*According to Herling, "Switchgear assemblies control and protect electrical apparatus used in the generation, conversion, transmission, and distribution of electrical energy. They consist of switching and interrupting devices in combination with control, metering, protection, and regulating equipment and their associated interconnections and supporting structures." (John Herling, *The Great Price Conspiracy* [Washington, DC: Luce, 1962], p. 353.)

but also detection and enforcement mechanisms. Under the system, each company was awarded a target percentage of the switchgear market. Just as the phases of the moon rotate every week, the company in the low-bid position rotated on a periodic basis. For example, GE might occupy the low-bid position for three weeks, followed by Allis-Chalmers for a week. The firm in the low-bid position was supposed to submit the agreed-on low bid, and each of the other four firms knew exactly how much more they were supposed to bid. As a result, the purchasing agency would receive five different bids, thereby "proving" the existence of competition.

To try to enforce adherence, the conspirators met 25 times between November 1958 and November 1959. There was even a cloak-and-dagger atmosphere to the conspiracy. According to the testimony of Nye Spencer of I-T-E, for example, "It was considered discreet not to be too obvious, and to minimize telephone calls, to use plain envelopes if mailing material to each other, not to be seen together in traveling, and so forth."[60] At the meetings, a cumulative list of all sealed-bid transactions was presented and compared with the agreed-on quotas. If one firm was receiving "too much" business (or "too little"), adjustments would be made on future bids.[61]

The phases of the moon system is an excellent example of an attempt to fix prices by establishing quotas to divide the market. According to the following song that made its way around GE, it must have worked:[62]

> (To be sung to the tune of "Moonglow")

> It must have been Moonglow
> Way up in the blue
> It must have been Moonglow
> That brought that bid to you.

> I still hear them saying
> As they rigged the price
> The customer's paying
> Too much, but it's so nice!

> We've fixed the prices in the air
> All of our schemes sock the buyer everywhere

> If we play it cozy
> And build our cartel
> Our life will be rosy
> Who cares—and what the hell?

In addition to the phases of the moon system, the electrical manufacturers used other devices to establish quotas.[63] In the power switching equipment* market, fifteen companies established a *quadrants* system to divide the United

---

*According to Herling, "Power switching equipment is used for interrupting an electrical circuit or for isolating a portion of it when changing connections, replacing equipment, repairing a fault or breakdown, or when for other reasons a completely open circuit is desired." (John Herling, *The Great Price Conspiracy* [Washington, DC: Luce, 1962], p. 354.)

States. Four companies were assigned to each quadrant. These companies would meet and decide how to divide the market in their region. After the meetings, companies that were not present would be contacted for approval of the agreement.

By the time the government completed its investigation of the electrical equipment industry, twenty indictments covering twenty-two product groups had been handed down. Every indictment resulted in a plea of either guilty or *nolo contendere*.* Eventually seven executives spent thirty days each in jail, another two dozen received thirty-day or one-month suspended sentences, and fines totaling approximately $2,000,000 were imposed on firms and individuals.[64]

8. Patent Cartels
a. Glass Containers—1924–1945[65]
Characteristics of the Industry
(1) Number of Firms—small (twelve firms)
(2) Concentration—high; four-firm concentration ratio in 1947—63; 12-firm concentration ratio in 1938—94
(3) Product Differentiation—low
(4) Demand Elasticity—inelastic
(5) Lumpiness of Orders—no
(6) Rate of Technological Advance—slow

Patents sometimes provide a wonderful opportunity to create effective cartels that last well beyond the life of the patents. This is precisely what occurred in the glass container industry from 1924 to 1945.

A bit of history is useful. At the turn of the century, glass making was still done primarily by hand. However, in 1904 Owens-Illinois developed the first fully automated suction process machine for producing glass containers. When Owens refused to license its revolutionary machine, many glass container manufacturers were threatened with extinction. Unfortunately for Owens, a competing machine was developed that used the suspended gob feeding process. Hartford-Fairmont (the predecessor of Hartford-Empire) acquired the basic gob process patents and improved on them. At the same time, The Empire Machine Company, which was controlled by Corning Glass, owned certain gob process patent applications that interfered with Hartford-Fairmont's patents. In 1916 Hartford-Fairmont and Empire granted each other exclusive cross-licenses on their gob patents. Further negotiations led to the consolidation of the two firms as the Hartford-Empire Company on October 6, 1922.

Throughout this period Owens-Illinois also held gob process patents that were in conflict with Hartford's patent claims. On April 9, 1924, Owens and Hartford-Empire settled their conflicting patent claims. Under the agreement:

---

*A plea of *nolo contendere* means that while the indicted party does not admit to guilt, it chooses not to contest the charges. It is a very common plea in antitrust cases.

(1) Owens granted Hartford an exclusive license on its patents, and Hartford granted Owens a nonexclusive license to make machines under Hartford's patents; (2) Owens received half of all Hartford's royalties over $600,000 per year; and (3) Owens received a veto over any attempt by Hartford to grant a license to any company that used any of Owens' patents. The agreement also prevented Owens from entering the pressed and blown glass field, which was reserved for Corning Glass, and left Owens in complete control of its original suction process patents.

After reaching this settlement with Owens, Hartford-Empire attempted to purchase all of the existing patents on gob feeder equipment. By 1938, Hartford had acquired over 600 glass manufacturing patents.[66] Once its patent control was complete, Hartford allocated each glass manufacturer a strict production quota on each specific type of glass container.

In 1931 Hartford's control was enhanced by the establishment of the "statistical committee" of the Glass Container Association. In consultation with the major glass manufacturers, the statistical committee assigned quotas to the Association's members and through the use of patent infringement suits was aggressive in its efforts to enforce the quotas.[67] As a result of these complex agreements, in 1938 94 percent of all glass containers were produced on machines using one or more of Hartford-Empire's patents.[68]

The use of *patent pooling* by Hartford enabled the glass container manufacturers to solve the prisoner's dilemma by simply having Hartford negotiate and set quotas. Cheating was easily detected, and the threat of punishment in the form of a lower quota on one or more glass container items was always present.

b. Gypsum Board 1929–1948[69]
Characteristics of the Industry
   (1) Number of Firms—small (eight firms)
   (2) Concentration—high (The top firm, US Gypsum, controlled 55% and the eight-firm concentration ratio was over 90.)
   (3) Product Differentiation—low
   (4) Demand Elasticity—inelastic
   (5) Lumpiness of Orders—no
   (6) Rate of Technological Advance—slow

Another classic example of patent pooling is found in the gypsum board industry. Since its organization in 1901 United States Gypsum has been the dominant firm in the gypsum products market. In 1939, US Gypsum controlled 55 percent of the wallboard market, and the eight-firm concentration ratio was over 90.[70] US Gypsum's control was built primarily on one patent, the Utzman patent, for producing wallboard with closed edges. Until 1912, wallboard had been produced by sandwiching a gypsum core between two pieces of paper. Utzman's idea was to enclose the edges of the gypsum core with a paper cover so that the edges would be much less likely to crumble. Essentially, Utzman received a patent for the idea of covering the entire gypsum core (including the edges) with paper instead of enclosing just the two sides. It's hard to believe that such a minor technological advance could result in US Gypsum's domination of an industry for a quarter century, but it did.

Between 1917 and 1929 US Gypsum followed an aggressive policy of filing infringement suits against any firm that came close to infringing on the Utzman patent. The courts upheld one of these infringement suits in 1921, and shortly thereafter US Gypsum began settling suits out of court by licensing competitors to produce wallboard under the Utzman patent at prices fixed by US Gypsum. As a result virtually all wallboard with closed edges was produced under the Utzman patent by 1929.

When the Utzman patent expired in 1929, US Gypsum met with each of its licensees to work out a new set of patent agreements based on a new US Gypsum patent for producing *bubble board*, a new type of wallboard produced by introducing a soap foam into the wallboard mixture. Bubble board was supposedly a lighter and lower-cost product that could increase the industry's profits. On June 6, 1929, two months before the Utzman patent expired, US Gypsum and its licensees met in Chicago to discuss a new licensing agreement. What emerged was an agreement signed on August 6, 1929, the exact day the Utzman patent expired, that expanded US Gypsum's patent control into a full-blown cartel. Each licensee agreed to pay a royalty on "all plaster board and gypsum wallboard of every kind" whether or not made by patented processes. The agreement covered fifty patents and seven patent applications, and was to run until the most junior patent expired. As it turned out, two bubble board patents were granted in 1937, so the agreements were to run until 1954. Through these agreements US Gypsum was able to fix the minimum price on all wallboard products.

Technically the agreement gave US Gypsum only the power to fix minimum prices, but in reality the agreements fixed prices. US Gypsum issued a series of bulletins that detailed both prices and terms of sale. The bulletins adopted a basing point system and, to prevent competition through product differentiation, specified standard wallboard shapes and sizes. Furthermore, the licenses prohibited the granting of long-term credit, consignment sales, and the delivery of wallboard directly to building sites.

To prevent cheating, US Gypsum set up a subsidiary, Board Survey, Inc., to check complaints that a licensee had violated the agreement. It was common practice for Board Survey to send letters to licensees requesting explanations for alleged violations and to audit a licensee's books to check that price concessions were not being made on non–gypsum board products as a cover for negotiated secret price concessions. Frequent meetings were also held to explain provisions of the bulletins that were unclear.

Evidence suggests that the agreements resulted in increased gypsum board prices after 1929, and letters written by the licensees to US Gypsum indicated that the major objective of the agreement was to raise and stabilize wallboard prices.

An analysis of the glass container and gypsum board industries suggests that patents can be used not only as a spur for technological advance, but also as a spur for collusion. Patent cartels have proved to be effective methods of solving the prisoner's dilemma. Cheating is easily detected, and punishment in the form of patent infringement suits may be swift and effective.

How Successful are the Solutions?

EXCESS CAPACITY PROBLEMS

One of the ironies of a successful solution to the prisoner's dilemma is that it almost invariably sows the seeds for the future demise of effective collusion.[71] Suppose an industry engages in a form of effective explicit or tacit collusion, and prices and profits rise. The increase in profits encourages the entry of new firms and the expansion of capacity by existing firms. Often, this entry and capacity expansion results in serious excess capacity problems that put great strains on any attempt to maintain discipline. It makes little difference whether the capacity expansion is by firms that join the collusive agreements or not.

Considerable evidence indicates that excess capacity has been a recurring theme in many cartels, especially during recessions.[72] In recent years, for example, OPEC has been plagued by such problems. OPEC's success in the 1970s and early 1980s resulted in capacity expansion both within and outside of OPEC. Because the smaller producers had a great incentive to expand output, world capacity increased dramatically. Between 1973 and 1986, crude oil production in Western Europe (North Sea oil) increased from 139 million to 1,395 million barrels per year, an increase of *1,256 percent*.[73] During the same period output increased by 1,800 percent in communist nations, and by 360 percent in Asia.[74] To maintain prices, Middle Eastern members of OPEC were forced to reduce their output from 7,745 million barrels in 1973 to just 4,639 million barrels in 1986.[75] In an attempt to stabilize prices, by the mid-1980s the Saudis were producing only 2.5 million barrels a day, well below their OPEC quota of over 4 million barrels per day.[76] This implied that the more successful Saudi Arabia was in stabilizing price, the greater was the development of excess capacity and the greater were the cartel's future problems.

The basing point system in the cement industry also provides evidence of the effect of collusion on capacity. The first apparent use of a basing point system in cement occurred in 1901. In 1902 the American Portland Cement Association was established as the industry's trade association, and by 1908 the Association's "Trade Relations Committee" had established a policy that "all prices quoted for portland cement shall be the prices for delivery at the point required by the purchaser."[77] By 1915 the basing point system was firmly entrenched on a national basis.

As indicated in Table 9.2, the cement industry experienced chronic excess capacity before the Supreme Court struck down the basing point system in 1948 and much less excess capacity thereafter. Table 9.2 indicates that capacity utilization rates fell below 80 percent for thirteen consecutive years between 1929 and 1941, and then again from 1943 until 1946. Declining demand during the Great Depression certainly was the major cause of the excess capacity problem. However, more than demand factors appears to have been involved. According to Loescher, "On top of the capacity idled by the depression there existed an estimated 60,000,000 barrels of practical capacity idled by excessive building—or about 25 percent of the average practical capacity of the period 1931 to 1935."[78]

Evidence indicates that during the height of explicit collusion in the electric

TABLE 9.2   **Practical Capacity and Production of Cement in the United States, 1909–1964 (in millions of barrels per year)**

Year	Practical Capacity	Production	% Cap.	Year	Practical Capacity	Production	% Cap.
1909	84.2	65.0	77.2	1937	229.7	116.2	50.6
1910	87.9	76.6	87.1	1938	230.1	105.4	45.8
1911	101.2	78.5	77.6	1939	230.5	121.9	52.9
1912	99.8	82.4	82.6	1940	228.4	129.8	56.8
1913	104.3	92.1	88.3	1941	222.2	163.6	73.6
1914	104.3	88.2	84.6	1942	223.4	182.1	81.5

Basing point system in full force

Year	Practical Capacity	Production	% Cap.	Year	Practical Capacity	Production	% Cap.
1915	116.8	85.9	73.5	1943	217.0	132.4	61.0
1916	120.6	91.5	75.9	1944	215.0	89.9	41.8
1917	123.1	92.8	75.4	1945	215.9	101.3	46.9
1918	123.1	71.1	57.4	1946	215.8	162.3	75.2
1919	120.7	80.8	66.9	1947	221.9	184.6	83.2
1920	131.8	100.0	75.9	1948	226.5	203.0	89.6

Basing point system ends

Year	Practical Capacity	Production	% Cap.	Year	Practical Capacity	Production	% Cap.
1921	129.1	98.8	76.1	1949	231.1	207.5	89.8
1922	131.6	114.8	87.2	1950	249.7	228.8	93.2
1923	145.7	137.5	94.4	1951	251.9	241.8	96.8
1924	157.6	149.4	94.8	1952	251.9	245.2	97.3
1925	174.2	161.6	92.8	1953	258.7	260.5	100.7
1926	193.8	164.5	84.9	1954	264.9	268.7	101.4
1927	204.4	173.2	84.7	1955	280.4	293.3	104.6
1928	219.3	176.3	80.4	1956	314.5	316.4	100.6
1929	233.0	170.6	73.2	1957	342.4	298.4	87.1
1930	243.0	161.1	66.3	1958	362.5	311.5	85.9
1931	244.6	125.4	51.3	1959	378.4	339.1	89.6
1932	244.2	76.7	31.4	1960	389.6	319.0	81.9
1933	242.4	63.7	26.3	1961	398.4	324.1	81.4
1934	236.4	77.7	32.5	1962	422.0	336.5	79.7
1935	235.7	76.7	32.5	1963	429.8	352.5	82.0
1936	230.0	112.6	49.0	1964	431.5	368.6	85.4

Sources: Samuel M. Loescher, *Imperfect Competition in the Cement Industry* (Cambridge: Harvard University Press, 1959), pp. 168–9; and *Federal Trade Commission Report on Mergers and Vertical Integration in the Cement Industry* (Washington: U.S. Government Printing Office, 1966), p. 55.

turbine market GE, Westinghouse, and Allis-Chalmers were all expanding capacity at a rate that exceeded any possible demand increases.[79] Capacity expansion was encouraged because the turbine producers often used the existence of large amounts of excess capacity as a bargaining chip at meetings designed to divide the market.

ENCROACHMENT OF SUBSTITUTE PRODUCTS

Any successful attempt to fix price also encourages the development and marketing of substitute products, resulting in a much more elastic demand curve in the long run than the short run. Substitutes have been a continuing problem for OPEC. The dramatic price increases of the mid-1970s led many consumers to shift to wood for heating and many utilities to switch to coal for electricity generation. Furthermore, it encouraged the production of more energy-efficient automobiles, homes, and factories. As a result, world oil consumption declined by about 32.5 percent from 1975 to 1986.[80]

A similar pattern emerged in the steel industry. Between 1947 and 1967 the relative price of steel increased compared with plastic, aluminum, cement, and glass. During the same twenty-year period, domestic steel production increased by just 35 percent compared with increases of 1900 percent for plastic, 500 percent for aluminum, and 100 percent for both cement and glass.[81]

SUMMARY

1. Table 9.3 summarizes the major themes running through this chapter. This is by no means a scientifically controlled sample, but the cases do represent many of the classic attempts to solve the prisoner's dilemma. A few points are striking. First, in thirteen of nineteen cases concentration was high and in only three cases was it low.

2. In two of the three cases in which concentration was low, a professional association was required to try to solve the dilemma in a more elaborate manner.

3. Product differentiation was low in eleven cases and high in only two. As our theoretical analysis in Chapter 8 suggested, solutions to the dilemma appear to be much easier when dealing with an essentially homogeneous product.

4. The rate of technological advance was slow in twelve cases and rapid in only one, suggesting that it is difficult to reach agreements in industries characterized by rapid product or process changes.

5. In sixteen of the nineteen cases demand was inelastic.

6. Table 9.3 suggests that solutions to the prisoner's dilemma will be more effective in industries with moderate to high concentration, relatively few firms, little product differentiation, a relatively slow rate of technological growth, and an inelastic demand.

7. As theorized in Chapter 8, all successful collusion appears to require a method of detecting cheaters and a threat of effective punishment.

TABLE 9.3   Summary of Industry Attempts to Solve the Prisoner's Dilemma

	Number of Firms	Concen-tration	Product Differen-tiation	Demand Elasticity	Lumpi-ness of Orders	Rate of Technological Advance
Large firm						
OPEC	Medium	Medium	Low	Inelastic	No	Slow
Steel, early	Medium	High	Low	Inelastic	Yes	Slow
IBM	Small	High	High	Elastic	No	Rapid
Most Favored						
Turbines	Small	High	Medium	Inelastic	Yes	Moderate
Stereo Eq	Large	Low	Medium	Elastic	No	Slow
Trade associations						
Sugar	Medium	Medium	Low	Inelastic	No	Slow
Legal services	Large	Low	Medium	Inelastic	Yes	Slow
Engineers	Large	Low	Medium	Inelastic	Yes	Slow
Divide markets						
Switchgear	Small	High	Medium	Inelastic	Yes	Moderate
Patents						
Glass containers	Small	High	Low	Inelastic	No	Slow
Gypsum board	Small	High	Low	Inelastic	No	Slow
Basing point						
Steel, 1884–1948	Medium	High	Low	Inelastic	Yes	Slow
Plywood	Medium	High	Low	Inelastic	No	Slow
Price leadership						
Steel, 1911–	Medium	High	Low	Inelastic	Yes	Slow
Anti-knock	Small	High	Low	Inelastic	No	Moderate
Cigarettes	Small	High	High	Inelastic	No	Moderate
Cellophane	Small	High	Low	Elastic	No	Moderate
Retail gasoline	Medium	Medium	Low	Inelastic	No	Slow
Turbines	Small	High	Medium	Inelastic	Yes	Moderate

KEY TERMS

barometric price leadership
basing point pricing system
collusive price leadership
low-price guarantee

most favored customer clause
parametric price
phantom freight
phases of the moon system

DISCUSSION QUESTIONS

1. What is the likely impact of successful collusion on the amount of excess capacity in an industry? Explain.
2. In all three cases discussed in the chapter in which a large firm acted as the industry's dominant firm price leader and benefactor, the leader's market dominance eventually declined. Suggest a theoretical reason as to why this happened in each of these cases.
3. What is the difference between collusive and barometric price leadership? Is it always easy to distinguish between the two?
4. Is it possible for a cartel to set a price that maximizes short-run profits but is "too high"? Explain.
5. Can you identify an industry in your geographic area in which all the firms use a low-price guarantee? Do prices in that industry appear to vary much from store to store?
6. How does the use of a basing point pricing system result in suboptimal economic performance? Which buyers are hurt by a basing point pricing system? Why do you think *single* basing point systems were generally unstable and most industries ultimately adopted *multiple* basing point systems?
7. Would an industry with only three firms be expected to use a trade association to fix prices? Would an industry with 1000 firms use a trade association to fix prices?
8. What facts about an industry's pricing behavior might lead you to suspect that the firms were fixing prices?
9. Why is there typically so much cheating in cartels?
10. Would you suspect that price fixing agreements would become more or less stable over time?
11. Would you be surprised to learn that in many antitrust price-fixing cases the defendants argue that the agreements were broken far more than they were maintained? Does this mean that these agreements had no negative impacts on economic performance?

REFERENCES

1. American Petroleum Institute, *Basic Petroleum Data Handbook*, Vol. VIII, No. 1 (January 1988).
2. Stephen Martin, "The Petroleum Industry," in Walter Adams (ed.), *The Structure of American Industry*, 8th edition (New York: MacMillan, 1990), p. 50.
3. "Saudi Arabia Plays High-Stakes Game," *New York Times* (January 24, 1986): D1; "Belt-Tightening by Saudis," *New York Times*, (January 28, 1986): D1; "Why the Saudis Keep Talking the Price of Oil Down," *Business Week* (March 17, 1986): 52; and "OPEC Panel to Tackle Pricing," *New York Times* (November 14, 1986): D1.
4. Martin, *supra* note 2, p. 50.
5. See Jacque Cremer and D. Salehi-Isfahani, "A Competitive Theory of the Oil Market: What Does OPEC Really Do?" Working Paper, No. 80–4 mimeo, University of Pennsylvania, 1980; Ali Ezzati, "Future OPEC Price and Production Strategies as Affected by Its Capacity to Absorb Oil Revenues," *European Economic Review* 8 (August 1976): 107–38; and David Teece, "OPEC Behavior: An Alternative View," in J.M. Griffin, *OPEC Behavior and World Oil Prices* (London: Allen & Unwin, 1982).
6. James M. Griffin, "OPEC Behavior: A Test of Alternative Hypotheses," *American Eco-*

nomic Review (December 1985): 954–63.

7. *Ibid.*, p. 962.

8. Walter Adams and Hans Mueller, "The Steel Industry," in Walter Adams (ed.), *The Structure of American Industry,* 8th edition (New York: MacMillan, 1990), p. 76.

9. Don E. Waldman, *The Economics of Antitrust: Cases and Analysis* (Boston: Little Brown and Company, 1986), p. 49.

10. *Ibid.*

11. *Ibid.*

12. See *California Computer Products, Inc. et al.* v. *International Business Machines Corporation, 613 F.2d 727* (1979).

13. Richard T. DeLamarter, *Big Blue: IBM's Use and Abuse of Power* (New York: Dodd Mead, 1986); and Gerald W. Brock, *The U.S. Computer Industry* (Cambridge: Ballinger, 1975).

14. Don E. Waldman, *supra* note 9, p. 63.

15. For a somewhat different explanation based on a classic model see V. Bhaskar, "The Kinked Demand Curve," *International Journal of Industrial Organization* 6 (September 1988): 373–84.

16. Walter Adams and Hans Mueller, *supra* note 8, p. 76.

17. *Ibid.*, p. 84.

18. Walter Adams, "The Steel Industry," in Walter Adams (ed.), *The Structure of American Industry,* 4th edition (New York: MacMillan, 1971), p. 94.

19. *Ibid.*

20. Leonard W. Weiss, *Case Studies in American Industry,* (New York: John Wiley and Sons, 1980), pp. 191–2.

21. *Ibid.*, p. 192.

22. "Bethlehem Cuts Major Prices 22%," *New York Times* (November 5, 1968): 67; "Steel Industry Hit By Major Price Cut," *Business Week* (November 9, 1968): 35; "U.S. Steel Moves to End Price War," *New York Times* (November 28, 1968): 75; "New Split Opens in Steel Pricing," *New York Times* (December 7, 1968): 73; "Revolution in Steel Pricing?" *Business Week* (December 14, 1968): 41; "Bethlehem Steel Cuts Steel Sheet List," *New York Times* (February 5, 1969): 47; and "Steel Heads Up Again," *Business Week* (February 8, 1969): 27.

23. "Dr. Bethlehem's New Formula," *Business Week* (November 15, 1969): 39 "A Hold on Steel Prices," *Business Week* (November 4, 1972): 33; and "Bethlehem, National Lift Prices," *New York Times* (August 9, 1986): A29.

24. See George A. Hay, "Practices that Facilitate Cooperation: The Ethyl Case," in J.E. Kwoka and Lawrence A. White (eds.), *The Antitrust Revolution* (Glenview, IL: Scott Foresman, 1989), pp. 183–207.

25. *Ibid.*, pp. 204–5.

26. *Ibid.*, p. 195.

27. *Ibid.*, pp. 193–7.

28. *American Tobacco Company* v. *United States,* 328 US 781 (1946).

29. Richard B. Tennant, "The Cigarette Industry," in Walter Adams (ed.), *The Structure of American Industry,* 4th edition (New York: MacMillan, 1971), p. 225.

30. *American Tobacco Company* v. *United States,* 328 US 781 (1946), p. 805.

31. *Ibid.*

32. "Marketing Observer," *Business Week* (February 24, 1973): 48.

33. Weiss, *supra* note 20.

34. Ralph G.M. Sultan, *Pricing in the Electrical Oligopoly,* vol. I (Boston: Harvard Business School Division of Research, 1974), pp. 213–4.

35. Sultan, *ibid.*, vol. II, pp. 234–5.

36. A.D.H. Kaplan, Joel B. Dirlam, and Robert Lanzillotti, *Pricing in Big Business: A Case Approach* (Washington: Brookings Institution, 1958), pp. 100–3.

37. The actual figure was 36.8 percent in the Midwestern market in 1966. See Thomas G. Moore, "The Petroleum Industry," in Walter Adams (ed.), *The Structure of American Industry,* 4th edition (New York: MacMillan, 1971), p. 127.

38. Edmund P. Learned and Catherine C. Ellsworth, *Gasoline Pricing in Ohio* (Boston: Harvard Business School Division of Research, 1959), pp. 23–5 and 106–7; and A.D.H. Kaplan, Joel B. Dirlam, and Robert Lanzillotti, *Pricing in Big Business: A Case Approach* (Washington: Brookings Institution, 1958), pp. 100–3.

39. See also David Besanko and Thomas P. Lyon, "Equilibrium Incentives for Most-Favored Customer Clauses in an Oligopolistic Industry," *International Journal of Industrial Organization* 11 (September 1993): 347–67.

40. Waldman, *supra* note 9, pp. 155–7.

41. See Ralph G.M. Sultan, *Pricing in the Electrical Oligopoly*, vol. I (Boston: Harvard Business School Division of Research, 1974).

42. Waldman, *supra* note 9.

43. Waldman, *supra* note 9; and Don E. Waldman, "The Inefficiencies of 'Unsuccessful' Pricing Fixing Agreements," *Antitrust Bulletin* (Spring 1988): 67–93.

44. Waldman, *supra* note 9.

45. This section is adapted from Avinash Dixit and Barry Nalebuff, *Thinking Strategically* (New York: Norton, 1991), pp. 102–5.

46. James W. McKie, *Tin Cans and Tin Plate* (Cambridge: Harvard University Press, 1959), pp. 66–71.

47. Walter Adams, *supra* note 18, p. 73.
48. *In the Matter of Boise Cascade Corporation et al.* 91 FTC 1 (1978); and Samuel M. Loescher, "Economic Collusion, Civil Conspiracy, and Treble Damages Deterrents with Southern Plywood," *Quarterly Review of Economics and Business* 20 (Winter 1980): 6–35.
49. The 61 percent figure is for 1971, *In the Matter of Boise Cascade Corporation et al.* 91 FTC 1 (1978).
50. Loescher, *supra* note 48, p. 14.
51. *Ibid.*
52. *Sugar Institute* v. *United States* 297 US 553 (1936), p. 587.
53. *Ibid.*, p. 583.
54. *Goldfarb* v. *Virginia State Bar* 421 US 773 (1975).
55. *Ibid.*, p. 778.
56. *Ibid.*, p. 776.
57. *National Society of Professional Engineers* v. *United States*, 435 US 679 (1978), p. 684.
58. *Ibid.*, p. 686.
59. John Herling, *The Great Price Conspiracy* (Washington: Luce, 1962), p. 70.
60. Herling, *ibid.*, p. 109.
61. *Ibid.*, p. 71.
62. J.G. Fuller, *The Gentleman Conspirators* (New York: Grove, 1962), p. 66.
63. Herling, *op cit.*, p. 88.
64. *Ibid.*, pp. 335–51.
65. *Hartford-Empire Company* v. *United States* 323 US 386 (1945); and Waldman, *supra* note 9, pp. 217–22.
66. Waldman, *ibid.*, p. 218.
67. *Hartford-Empire* v. *United States* 323 US 386 (1945), p. 400.
68. Waldman, *supra* note 9, p. 218.
69. *United States* v. *United States Gypsum Company* 333 US 3664 (1948); and Waldman, *supra* note 9, pp. 222–5.
70. Waldman, *supra* note 9, p. 222.
71. See Margaret E. Slade, "Cheating on Collusive Agreements," *International Journal of Industrial Organization* 8 (December 1990): 519–43; and Chaim Fershtman, "Disadvantageous Semicollusion," *International Journal of Industrial Organization* 12 (June 1994): 141–54.
72. Don E. Waldman, "The Inefficiencies of 'Unsuccessful' Pricing Fixing Agreements," *Antitrust Bulletin* (Spring 1988): 67–93.
73. Stephen Martin, "The Petroleum Industry," in Walter Adams (ed.), *The Structure of American Industry,* 8th edition (New York: MacMillan, 1992), p. 51.
74. *Ibid.*
75. *Ibid.*
76. *Ibid.*, p. 62.
77. Samuel M. Loescher, *Imperfect Competition in the Cement Industry* (Cambridge: Harvard University Press, 1959), pp. 95–6.
78. Loescher, *ibid.*, p. 181.
79. Waldman, *supra* note 72, pp. 85–92.
80. American Petroleum Institute, *Basic Petroleum Data Book,* vol. 8, 1988.
81. Adams, *supra* note 18, p. 99.

Chapter 10

Oligopoly Behavior: Entry and Pricing to Deter Entry

The preceding two chapters suggested that because of the prisoner's dilemma, oligopolists often have difficulty coordinating their behavior. Also, following a strict short-run profit-maximizing strategy is likely to result in the entry of new firms or the capacity expansion of smaller established firms, not to mention the loss of market share to close substitute products. This is precisely what happened in the steel, oil, and computer plug-compatibles markets. Conversely, Alcoa in aluminum and Inco (International Nickel) in nickel managed to maintain their monopolies for more than fifty years. Can a pricing strategy be identified that enables some firms to maintain their market power over long periods? We begin by reviewing one of the earliest major models of dynamic behavior, the limit pricing model, and then proceed to analyze the possible use of predatory pricing.

Limit Pricing

LIMIT PRICING WITH A COST ADVANTAGE FOR THE INCUMBENT FIRM

Limit pricing theory begins with the logical assumption that rational firms should maximize *long-run*, not short-run, profits.[1] Recall from Chapter 8 that maximizing long-run profits requires maximizing π_{pv}, the present value of profits.

Suppose that a dominant firm, or incumbent, wishes to maximize π_{pv}. Further assume that the incumbent has a cost advantage over potential entrants, perhaps because of an important patent, so that in Figure 10.1 the dominant firm faces demand curve $P = 110 - Q$ and has marginal and average cost curves $MC_d = AC_d = 10$, but a potential entrant faces higher costs, $MC_e = AC_e = 20$. Now consider a simple model in which the incumbent has a choice between the following policies:

1. Charging the profit-maximizing price $P_M = 60$, selling $Q_M = 50$, earning an economic profit of 2500 [$Q(P - AC) = 50(60 - 10) = 2500$], and attracting entry; or

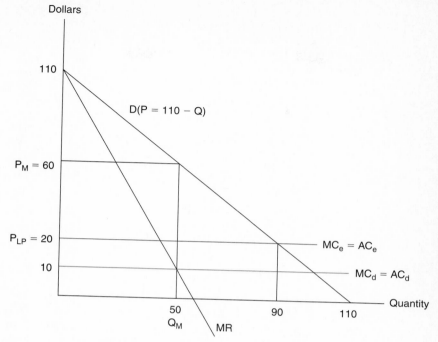

Figure 10.1 Limit pricing with a cost advantage.

2. Charging a price P_{LP} infinitesimally less than 20, that is, $P_{LP} = 20 - \epsilon$, selling a quantity infinitesimally greater than 90, $Q = 90 + \epsilon$, earning an economic profit just under 900 [$Q(P - AC) = 90(20 - 10) = 900$], and preventing all entry.

P_{LP} is called the **limit price** and may be thought of as the highest possible price that prevents all entry.

In the original limit pricing models, one critical assumption was that the incumbent would maintain its output even after entry occurred.[2] Of course, in the real world the incumbent might expand, contract, or maintain its output in the face of entry. The assumption of post-entry output maintenance is highly questionable, but for the time being we will use it.

Using Figure 10.1, consider the implications of this output maintenance assumption. An incumbent maintains its output at $Q = 50$ unless it switches to a limit pricing policy. Suppose that in each time period t, the incumbent either (1) continues to produce $Q = 50$ or (2) switches to a limit pricing policy of $P = 20 - \epsilon$. Further assume that for each period during which price exceeds the limit price, new entrants will produce and sell ten *additional* units in the next period. In other words, if the incumbent produces $Q_d = 50$ in t = 0, then entrants will produce $Q_e = 10$ in t = 1, and if the incumbent produces $Q = 50$ in t = 0 and t = 1, then entrants will produce ten units in period t = 1 and twenty units in period t = 2, and so on.

T A B L E   1 0 . 1 **Dollar Profits Associated with Switching to the Limit Price at Different Times**

Time of Switch to Limit Price	Profits at t = 1	Profits at t = 2	Profits at t = 3	Profits at t = 4	Profits at t = 5 . . . t = n
t = 0	900[1]	900	900	900	900
t = 1	2,500[2]	800	800	800	800
t = 2	2,500	2,000[3]	700	700	700
t = 3	2,500	2,000	1,500[4]	600	600
t = 4	2,500	2,000	1,500	1,000[5]	500

[1]$\pi = Q(P - AC) = 90(20 - 10) = 900$
[2]$\pi = Q(P - AC) = 50(60 - 10) = 2500$
[3]$\pi = Q(P - AC) = 50(50 - 10) = 2000$
[4]$\pi = Q(P - AC) = 50(40 - 10) = 1500$
[5]$\pi = Q(P - AC) = 50(30 - 10) = 1000$

Table 10.1 shows how the incumbent's dollar profits would be affected by switching to a limit pricing policy at any time between t = 0 and t = 4. The table indicates that a limit pricing policy results in higher future profits in exchange for lower near-term profits. Given the profit information in Table 10.1, it is possible to calculate the present value of profits associated with a switch to the limit price at times t = 0, 1, 2, 3, 4 as follows:

1. Switch to limit price at t = 0

$$\pi_{pv} = \frac{900}{(1 + i)} + \frac{900}{(1 + i)^2} + \frac{900}{(1 + i)^3} + \cdots + \frac{900}{(1 + i)^n}$$

or

$$\pi_{pv} = \frac{900}{i}.$$

2. Switch to limit price at t = 1

$$\pi_{pv} = \frac{2,500}{(1 + i)} + \frac{800}{(1 + i)^2} + \frac{800}{(1 + i)^3} + \cdots + \frac{800}{(1 + i)^n}$$

$$= \frac{2,500}{(1 + i)} + \frac{800}{i} - \frac{800}{(1 + i)}.$$

3. Switch to limit price at t = 2

$$\pi_{pv} = \frac{2,500}{(1 + i)} + \frac{2,000}{(1 + i)^2} + \frac{700}{(1 + i)^3} + \cdots + \frac{700}{(1 + i)^n}$$

$$p = \frac{2,500}{(1 + i)} + \frac{2,000}{(1 + i)^2} + \frac{700}{i} - \frac{700}{(i + 1)} - \frac{700}{(1 + i)^2}.$$

4. Switch to limit price at t = 3

$$\pi_{pv} = \frac{2{,}500}{(1+i)} + \frac{2{,}000}{(1+i)^2} + \frac{1{,}500}{(1+i)^3} + \frac{600}{(1+i)^4} + \cdots + \frac{600}{(1+i)^n}$$

$$= \frac{2{,}500}{(1+i)} + \frac{2{,}000}{(1+i)^2} + \frac{1{,}500}{(1+i)^3} + \frac{600}{i} - \frac{600}{(1+i)} - \frac{600}{(1+i)^2} - \frac{600}{(1+i)^3}.$$

5. Switch to limit price at t = 4

$$\pi_{pv} = \frac{2{,}500}{(1+i)} + \frac{2{,}000}{(1+i)^2} + \frac{1{,}500}{(1+i)^3} + \frac{1{,}000}{(1+i)^4} + \frac{500}{(1+i)^5} + \cdots + \frac{500}{(1+i)^n}$$

$$= \frac{2{,}500}{(1+i)} + \frac{2{,}000}{(1+i)^2} + \frac{1{,}500}{(1+i)^3} + \frac{1{,}000}{(1+i)^4} + \frac{500}{i} - \frac{500}{(1+i)} - \frac{500}{(1+i)^2} - \frac{500}{(1+i)^3} - \frac{500}{(1+i)^4}.$$

Table 10.2 uses these equations to calculate the present value of the incumbent's profits for different discount rates i and different times t for switching to a limit pricing policy. In Table 10.2 the optimal times for switching are indicated by printing the profits associated with those switches in bold type. At a discount rate of 5 percent, the optimal time to switch is t = 0, while at a discount rate of 15 percent, the optimal time is t = 3.

The optimal time to switch to the limit price is a function of a number of factors, including the size of the incumbent's cost advantage and the discount rate. The lower the discount rate, the more valuable are future profits and the earlier the incumbent will switch to a limit pricing policy.

One major criticism of the original limit pricing model was its assumption of output maintenance after entry occurred.[3] Such an assumption contradicts short-run profit maximization, which requires the incumbent to reduce its output in response to entry. Using a *residual demand curve*, introduced in Chapter 7, we can calculate the profit-maximizing post-entry quantity for the incumbent in Figure 10.1. For each ten units produced by entrants, the incumbent's residual demand

TABLE 10.2 **The Present Value of Profits Associated with Switching to the Limit Price at Different Times for Different Discount Rates i**

Discount Rate	Switch to Limit Price at t = 0	Switch to Limit Price at t = 1	Switch to Limit Price at t = 2	Switch to Limit Price at t = 3	Switch to Limit Price at t = 4
i = 5%	**18,000**	17,619	16,893	15,857	14,540
i = 7%	12,857	**13,017**	12,818	12,305	11,520
i = 10%	9,000	9,545	**9,711**	9,560	9,151
i = 15%	6,000	6,812	7,215	**7,303**	7,150

curve shifts down by 10. If entrants produce ten units, for example, the incumbent's residual demand curve becomes

$$P = 100 - Q.$$

If entrants produce twenty units, the incumbent's residual demand curve becomes

$$P = 90 - Q.$$

Once the post-entry demand curve is identified, the incumbent's new short-run profit-maximizing output can be calculated. In Figure 10.2, for example, if entrants produce ten units, the incumbent's short-run profit-maximizing output is Q = 45, not Q = 50. In other words, once entry occurs, to maximize short-run profits the incumbent should reduce its output below fifty units and lower its price to $55. Similarly, if entrants produce twenty units, the incumbent's short-run profit-maximizing output would be Q = 40.

Although short-run profit maximization calls for a post-entry restriction in the incumbent's output, another possible logical strategy is for the incumbent to expand its output in response to entry and reduce price below 20. If the incumbent were willing to lower price to 15, for example, any entrant would sustain an economic loss, and therefore no entry would occur. With P = 15, the incumbent,

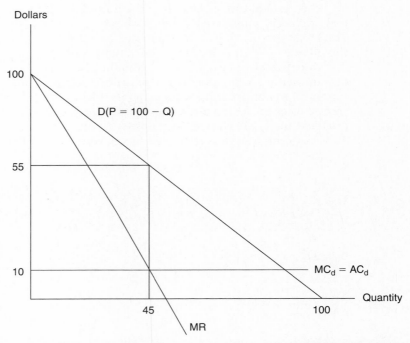

Figure 10.2   The incumbent's profit-maximizing output and price after entry by one firm.

however, would continue to earn an economic profit of 475.* A post-entry policy of either reducing output or expanding output almost always makes more sense than maintaining output.

LIMIT PRICING IN THE ABSENCE OF A COST ADVANTAGE FOR THE INCUMBENT FIRM

Suppose that in our previous example, potential entrants could also produce with $MC = AC = 10$. The limit price would therefore equal 10. The changes that would occur in Tables 10.1 and 10.2 are identified in Tables 10.3 and 10.4. In Table 10.3 the major change is that profits fall to zero as soon as the incumbent adopts a

---

*Note that with $P = 15$, $\pi = Q(P - AC) = 95(15 - 10) = 475$.

TABLE 10.3 **Profits Associated with Switching to the Limit Price at Different Times**

Time of Switch to Limit Price	Profits at $t = 1$	Profits at $t = 2$	Profits at $t = 3$	Profits at $t = 4$	Profits at $t = 5 \ldots t = n$
$t = 0$	0^1	0	0	0	0
$t = 1$	$2{,}500^2$	0	0	0	0
$t = 2$	2,500	$2{,}000^3$	0	0	0
$t = 3$	2,500	2,000	$1{,}500^4$	0	0
$t = 4$	2,500	2,000	1,500	$1{,}000^5$	0

[1] Since the limit price is 10, $\pi = Q (P - AC) = 100 (10 - 10) = 0$
[2] $\pi = Q (P - AC) = 50 (60 - 10) = 2500$
[3] $\pi = Q (P - AC) = 50 (50 - 10) = 2000$
[4] $\pi = Q (P - AC) = 50 (40 - 10) = 1500$
[5] $\pi = Q (P - AC) = 50 (30 - 10) = 1000$

TABLE 10.4 **The Present Value of Profits Associated with Switching to the Limit Price at Different Times for Different Discount Rates i**

Discount Rate	Switch to Limit Price at $t = 0$	Switch to Limit Price at $t = 1$	Switch to Limit Price at $t = 2$	Switch to Limit Price at $t = 3$	Switch to Limit Price at $t = 4$
$i = 5\%$	0	2,381	4,195	5,491	**6,313**
$i = 7\%$	0	2,336	4,083	5,307	**6,070**
$i = 10\%$	0	2,273	3,926	5,053	**5,736**
$i = 15\%$	0	2,174	3,686	4,672	**5,244**

limit pricing policy. This of course provides no incentive to limit price, and, as Table 10.4 indicates, the incumbent would always put off limit pricing as long as there was some remaining positive economic profit to be earned. The incumbent would be better off simply maintaining output at Q = 50 and earning some economic profits for as long as possible.

Tables 10.3 and 10.4 might be misinterpreted to mean that limit pricing would always be irrational in the absence of a cost advantage for the incumbent. The results in Tables 10.3 and 10.4, however, follow from the fact that with MC = AC = 10, there are no economies of scale in production. If economies of scale exist, a limit pricing policy may make sense even in the absence of a cost advantage for the incumbent.

In Figure 10.3(a), significant economies of scale exist, and we assume that the incumbent and potential entrants face identical costs. Suppose that an incumbent produces with long-run average costs represented by the hypothetical curve LRAC* and potential entrants face no cost disadvantage and are capable of producing with identical long-run average costs LRAC.

The total industry demand curve is given by P = 100 − 1.25Q, and the residual demand curve faced by a potential entrant will depend on the price charged by the incumbent. Given the cost curves in Figure 10.3(a), if the incumbent max-

---

*The numbers associated with the cost curves in Figures 10(a)–10(c) are strictly hypothetical and are not associated with any real industry.

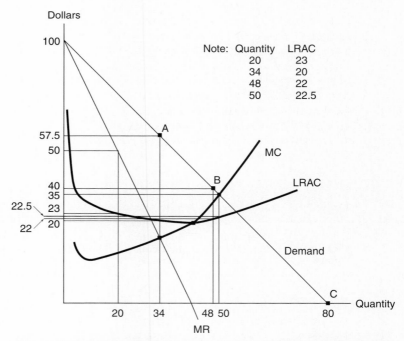

Figure 10.3(a)   Limit pricing with economies of scale and no cost advantage.

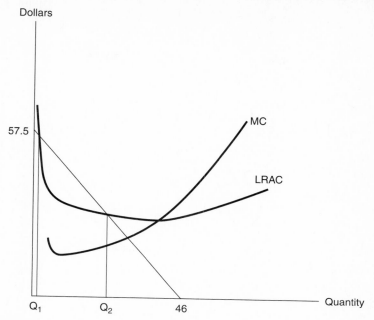

Figure 10.3(b) Potential entrant's residual demand curve and costs if the incumbent sets price equal to 57.5.

imizes short-run profits, it will sell a quantity of 34 at a price of $57.50 and earn profits of $1,275.* The residual demand curve faced by a potential entrant will then be the line segment AC in Figure 10.3(a), or P = 57.50 − 1.25q.

In Figure 10.3(b), this residual demand curve has been drawn in relation to the curve LRAC. Notice that the potential entrant could enter profitably because the demand curve is above the LRAC for all outputs between Q_1 and Q_2.† What is the limit price in this case? Assuming once again that the incumbent will maintain output after entry, the incumbent must lower its price sufficiently to ensure that the potential entrant's residual demand curve lies everywhere below the average cost curve LRAC. If the incumbent lowers price to P = 40 in Figure 10.3(a), the residual demand curve faced by potential entrants will be the line segment BC, or P = 40 − 1.25q. In Figure 10.3(c), the residual demand curve P = 40 − 1.25q is drawn in relation to the curve LRAC. Notice that the LRAC curve is just tangent to the residual demand curve at q = 10. Any price that is infinitesimally less than 40 will shift the potential entrant's residual demand curve to the left in Figure 10.3(c) and deter entry. It would thus be possible for the incumbent to prevent entry by limit pricing at P = 40 − ϵ, even in the absence of a cost advantage.

---

*Profits = Q(P − AC) = 34(57.50 − 20) = 1,275.
†If the demand curve were below the LRAC in Figure 10.3(b), then profitable entry would be impossible even if the incumbent maximized short-run profits. Under these circumstances entry would be *blockaded* by the existence of significant economies of scale.

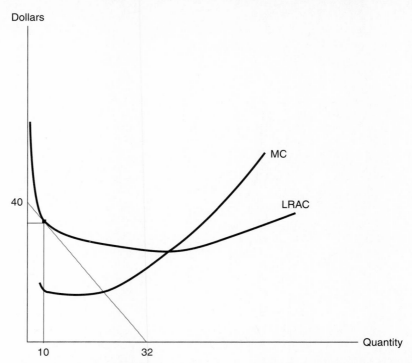

Figure 10.3(c)   Potential entrant's residual demand curve and costs if the incumbent sets price equal to 40.

THE CRITIQUE OF GAME THEORISTS

Game theorists have sharply criticized the basic limit pricing result. To understand their criticism, we begin by illustrating the situation depicted in Figure 10.3(c) as a sequential game similar to the game presented in Figure 6.2. Figure 10.4 shows a sequential game associated with the market conditions in Figures 10.3(a) and 10.3(c). Recalling from Chapter 6 that sequential games must be solved *backwards*, we find only one solution to the game in Figure 10.4. Assuming that both firms have the same information, a potential entrant would reason as follows:

1. If I stay out, I earn zero.
2. If I enter and the incumbent produces the limit price quantity $48 + \epsilon$, I sustain an economic loss and the incumbent earns $264 - \epsilon$.
3. If I enter and the incumbent shares the market and maximizes joint profits, we each earn 540.*

---

*An alternative assumption would be that the two firms arrive at a Cournot-Nash equilibrium, in which each firm earns less than 540 but more than 264. This assumption would not change the implications of the game.

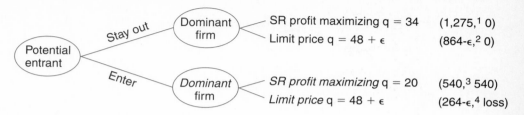

$^1 \pi = q(P - AC) = 34(57.5 - 20) = 1275$

$^2 \pi = q(P - AC) = 48(40 - 22) - \epsilon = 864 - \epsilon$

^{3} If the incumbent firm shares the market the two firms split the demand curve, so each faces a demand curve of $P = 100 - 2.5q$. Therefore, profit maximization requires that $MR = 100 - 5q = MC$. In figure 10.3(a), profit maximization requires $q = 20$ and $p = 50$, so:

$$\pi = q(P - AC) = 20(50 - 23) = 540$$

^{4} If entry occurs the entrant produces $q = 10$ and the incumbent produces $q = 48 + \epsilon$, therefore, total $Q = 58 + \epsilon$ and $P = 100 - 1.25(58 - \epsilon) = 27.5 - \epsilon$. It follows that:

$$\pi = q(P - AC) = 48(27.5 - 22) - \epsilon = 264 - \epsilon$$

Figure 10.4 A game of entry (dominant firm's profit, potential entrant's profit).

4. If I enter, the incumbent has a choice between sharing the market and earning 540 or producing $48 + \epsilon$ and earning $264 - \epsilon$. *Given these choices, the incumbent's only rational choice is to share the market.*
5. I will enter and earn 540, which is much better than staying out and earning 0.

The game has only one solution: the entrant will enter and the incumbent will share the market. Any other threatened response is simply not credible.[4] But suppose that, for some unexplained reason, the potential entrant elects not to enter. The game is reduced to a choice for the incumbent of either (1) maximizing short-run profits or (2) limit pricing. A quick examination of Figure 10.4 reveals that the incumbent has only one rational choice. If entry does not occur, the choice is either earn 1275 or earn $864 - \epsilon$. Given this choice, the incumbent would choose the 1275 and maximize short-run profits. A limit pricing policy is not believable. It reduces the incumbent's profits this period and does not credibly deter entry next period because the entrant knows that the incumbent will share the market after entry occurs. The problem with the original limit pricing model is obvious: there simply is no reason for the entrant to stay out even if the incumbent charges the limit price.

If the entrant faces higher costs than the incumbent, a limit pricing strategy still makes no game theoretic sense. Consider the example depicted in Figure 10.1. If we relax the output maintenance assumption, Figure 10.1 can be translated into the game tree in Figure 10.5. In Figure 10.5 it is assumed, as it was in Figure 10.1, that if entry occurs, the entrants produce ten units of output. If the incumbent can respond to entry by either increasing, decreasing, or maintaining output, the limit pricing option is a weak one. What good does it do to charge the limit price before entry? If the entrant stays out, the choices are to earn either

[1] $\pi = q(P - AC) = 50(60 - 10) = 2500$
[2] $\pi = q(P - AC) = 90(20 - 10) - \epsilon = 900 - \epsilon$
[3] Based on figure 10.2, the dominant firm's profits would be:

$$\pi_d = q_d(P - AC) = 45(55 - 10) = 2025$$

and the entrant's profits would be:

$$\pi_e = q_e(P - AC) = 10(55 - 20) = 350$$

[4] Based on Figure 10.2, the dominant firm's profits would be:

$$\pi_d = q_d(P - AC) = 50(50 - 10) = 2000$$

and the entrant's profits would be:

$$\pi_e = q_e(P - AC) = 10(50 - 20) = 300$$

[5] See footnote 2.

Figure 10.5   A game of entry (dominant firm's profit, potential entrant's profit).

2500 or $900 - \epsilon$. Only the 2500 choice makes sense. The real challenge for the incumbent in Figure 10.5 is to convince the potential entrant that it will choose the aggressive response to entry with a payoff of ($900 - \epsilon$, Loss). Making the aggressive response credible is not easy because it requires the incumbent to convince the potential entrant that it will pass up the dominant solution of earning 2025 in favor of earning $900 - \epsilon$.

So far, game theory suggests that limit pricing is not a reasonable competitive strategy. Milgrom and Roberts have shown, however, that under certain reasonable game assumptions limit pricing might be a rational strategic choice.[5] The Milgrom and Roberts model is presented in detail in Chapter 12.[6]

Empirical Evidence of Limit Pricing

Empirical evidence on limit pricing comes from a number of case studies and a few statistical studies. The case study approach attempts to identify industries in which firms have maintained dominant positions and yet earned only normal or even below-normal profits, or industries in which large increases in output have not been associated with increased net earning. Of course, finding a dominant firm with below-normal profits does not prove the existence of limit pricing because such an outcome could occur for many other reasons. For example, demand could be low, many close substitutes could exist, or costs could be high. But some case studies reveal strong circumstantial evidence suggesting the use of limit pricing.

DU PONT IN CELLOPHANE[7]—From 1924 to 1947 Du Pont held a virtual monopoly in the United States cellophane industry. Significant economies of scale existed in the industry, and Du Pont realized early on the advantages of moving down the average cost curve before competitors had entered. As a result, Du Pont followed a policy of continually lowering price. Prices declined by 84.8 percent between 1924 and 1940, from $2.51 per pound to just $0.38 per pound.[8]

During the industry's early years demand increased rapidly, and entrants might have been able to penetrate the market if Du Pont had maintained high prices. But by continually reducing its cellophane prices, Du Pont established control before new firms had an opportunity to enter. Potential entrants undoubtedly realized that large-scale entry required either a post-entry reduction in Du Pont's output or a dramatic post-entry industry-wide price reduction. Du Pont's pricing between 1924 and 1940 was consistent with that of a firm attempting to deter entry. To maintain its dominant market position, Du Pont was apparently willing to accept lower prices and reduced profits on cellophane.

UNITED SHOE MACHINERY[9]—Until the mid-1950s United Shoe Machinery Corporation (USM) controlled the market for virtually all shoe machinery in the United States, with a national market share between 85 and 90 percent. United Shoe has been called the classic example of a "good trust." United's rental rates were reasonable and uniform, its rate of return on invested capital was typically normal or below normal, the machines performed well, service was provided free, and the cost of shoe machinery averaged less than 2 percent of the wholesale price of shoes.

Despite USM's good behavior, in an antitrust case the government complained that its power resulted from its marketing conduct, and in a 1954 decision the Supreme Court ruled that United had monopolized the industry. As part of the decree the Court ordered that in ten years the case would be reviewed to determine whether the industry had become more competitive.

A comparison of United Shoe's pricing policies before and after the 1954 Supreme Court decision provides some evidence of limit pricing behavior.[10] The Court's decision gave USM an incentive to raise prices and reap high short-run profits rather than keep prices down to deter entry. USM surely knew that if its market share remained around 90 percent, the government would demand a stronger structural remedy in ten years. It seems reasonable that USM would end whatever pricing restraint it may have been practicing. Because high prices and profits would help attract entrants, the worse USM's pricing policies became for its buyers, the better those policies might appear to the courts in ten years.

In the two years following the decree, USM's prices and profits rose dramatically. In 1954 United's net income was only $7.2 million, and its rate of return on equity was a modest 8.2 percent.[11] In 1955, however, net income soared to a company record of $18.9 million, and USM's rate of return reached an all-time high of 18.3 percent.[12] This tremendous leap resulted in part from windfall revenues generated from the sale of many machines that had been leased before 1955, but much of the jump also resulted from large increases in the rental rate for United's machinery.

As USM hiked prices, new firms entered the industry. The appearance of fifty-six new firms in the ten years after the Supreme Court's decree suggests that

USM's high-price policy was effective in attracting entrants or, put differently, that USM's early policy of keeping prices relatively low was effective in deterring entry.[13]

GENERAL FOODS—In a study of the pricing policies of twenty major industries, Kaplan, Dirlam, and Lanzillotti found evidence that General Foods placed a greater emphasis on long-term than short-term profits.[14] On specialty items such as Minute Rice, Postum, Sanka, Jell-O, and Birds Eye frozen foods, management realized that it was unwise to set high profit margins that would shorten the lives of these products as specialty items. While recognizing the ability to set high margins on these brands, General Foods' management also understood that "a high price [would] restrict the volume and that it [would] speed up the process of developing competition."[15]

Kaplan and colleagues found that General Foods took potential competition into account in all of its pricing decisions. A former chairman of the board of directors at General Foods told the researchers that the strategy objective was aimed at a "stable franchise."[16] In other words, General Foods kept prices well below the short-run profit-maximizing level, realizing full well that any gain associated with higher prices would be more than offset by subsequent losses to new competitors.

XEROX[17]—Blackstone has suggested that Xerox engaged in a complex pricing strategy that included elements of limit pricing during the early years of its dominance in the copier industry. When Xerox introduced its plain paper copiers in 1959, it had no significant cost advantage over Electrofax coated paper technology in the low-volume segment of the industry and therefore decided to price its low-volume copiers at the short-run profit-maximizing level. High profits encouraged at least twenty-five firms to enter the low-volume segment of the industry between 1961 and 1967.[18] In the medium-volume segment, however, Xerox had a modest cost advantage and elected to price below the profit-maximizing level but above the strict limit price. In this segment, ten firms entered, and Xerox recognized that it would eventually give up a considerable amount of market share to competitors. Finally, in the high-volume segment, where Xerox enjoyed a significant cost advantage, it priced close to the limit price, and only three firms entered.[19]

Statistical Tests

It is difficult to test the limit pricing model using a large data set because it is statistically impossible to identify the actual limit price or the actual profit-maximizing price in an industry. Masson and Shaanan, however, have made two good efforts to test statistically the limit pricing hypothesis.[20] They tested for which of the following three competing limit pricing theories most accurately predicted firms' pricing behavior:

> *Theory 1*[21]—Firms charge either the short-run profit-maximizing price or the strict limit price. In this model, when entry barriers are high, firms charge the limit price; when entry barriers are low, firms charge the profit-maximizing price.

Theory 2[22]—If no entry barriers exist, the incumbent charges the high short-run profit-maximizing price and permits entry. As entry barriers rise, the incumbent's optimal price declines. When entry barriers reach a critical level, B*, the optimal price exactly equals the strict limit price, and no entry occurs. As barriers continue to increase beyond B*, the optimal price and the limit price remain equal to each other and rise in lockstep together (obviously, the limit price rises as entry barriers rise) until the optimal price and the limit price return to the short-run profit-maximizing price for very high entry barriers.

Theory 3[23]—The optimal price is always above the limit price but converges toward the limit price for very high entry barriers. In this model some entry is permitted, but the incumbent controls the rate of entry by varying the difference between the actual price and the limit price.

Masson and Shaanan first studied a sample of thirty-seven American manufacturing industries to determine which, if any, of these theories was consistent with observed pricing behavior.[24] Their 1982 results strongly supported theory 3 and rejected both theory 1 and theory 2.

One implication of Masson and Shaanan's 1982 results was that few firms charge either the strict limit price or the strict short-run profit-maximizing price. Instead, prices tend to lie between the two extremes, thereby encouraging some entry but discouraging a flood of entry. This finding is consistent with the theoretical belief that strict limit pricing rarely makes economic sense and with Blackstone's earlier observed pricing by Xerox in the 1960s.

In 1987 Masson and Shaanan replicated their previous study using a sample of forty-three Canadian manufacturing industries.[25] The statistical results of this follow-up study were less robust than those of their 1982 study but were still consistent with theory 3.

Predatory Pricing

As noted, one possible strategy for an incumbent is to maintain a short-run profit-maximizing strategy until entry occurs and then to expand output aggressively and cut price. Figure 10.4 presented the case of an incumbent with no cost advantage. Figure 10.6 reproduces Figure 10.4 with one change: instead of a limit pricing strategy, we include a predatory strategy of expanding output to the level at which P = MC to drive entrants from the market. What would happen if an incumbent played the predatory strategy in response to *every* entry? It seems likely that potential entrants would eventually get the message and assume that the incumbent would respond aggressively to all entry, and, as a result, all potential entrants would stay out. By establishing a reputation for being tough *early*, the incumbent would prevent *later* entry. Such a result depends critically on the information available to the incumbent and potential entrants.

The game in Figure 10.6 has been extensively analyzed by economists and can be viewed as a sequential game with a fixed number of rounds.[26] First consider the game if it is played with an information structure that is *perfect, cer-*

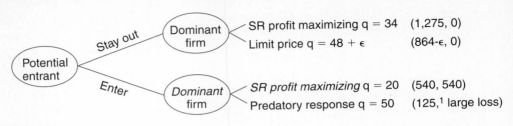

---

[1] If entry occurs the entrant produces q = 10 and the incumbent produces q = 50; therefore, total Q = 60 and P = 100 − 1.25(60) = 25. It follows that:

$$\pi_d = q(P - AC) = 50(25 - 22.5) = 125$$

Figure 10.6   A game of entry (dominant firm's profit, potential entrant's profit).

tain, complete, and *symmetric.* Assume there are N markets that must be entered sequentially from market N to market 1. The game is being played backwards with the Nth market entered first and the first market entered last.[27] A potential entrant into market N-1 (the second market entered) has observed either the reaction of the incumbent to entry in market N (the first market entered) or the lack of entry into market N. A potential entrant into market 1 has observed the reactions of the incumbent to entry or the lack of entry in markets N through 2.

Suppose the payoff matrix in each round is identical and is given by the matrix in Figure 10.6. In market 1, the *last* market, the incumbent has no incentive to adopt the predatory response. An aggressive response has no "tough reputation effect" on any future markets because there are no future markets. The incumbent therefore will share market 1 and earn a profit of 540. The potential entrant into market 1 knows this and enters market 1. The potential entrant into market 2 also knows that the incumbent will share market 1 and therefore knows that the incumbent has no incentive to establish a tough reputation in market 1 by responding aggressively to entry in market 2. In a sense market 2 now becomes the last market in the game, and the incumbent will share market 2, so entry occurs in market 2. Regardless of the number of markets, by similar backwards induction to the Nth market (the first market entered), the incumbent will *never* have an incentive to behave aggressively, and it will accommodate entry in *every* market. In this model entry occurs in all N markets and the incumbent always shares the market. Selten first identified this result and called it the **chain store paradox.**[28] It is easy to understand why Selten described this as a paradox because even with a large number of markets, the implication is that entry will be accommodated in each and every market, a result that seems counterintuitive.

Now let's change the game's information structure. In the new game information is *imperfect, certain, incomplete,* and *asymmetric.* Suppose *nature* first selects the incumbent to be either (1) *strong,* in which case the firm enjoys being predatory and is always predatory, or (2) *weak,* in which case the incumbent will be predatory in one market only if it believes it will increase its profits in future mar-

Always predatory	Play mixed strategy	Always accommodate

N X Y 1

Figure 10.7 Response of "weak" incumbent to entry in markets N through 1.

kets to compensate for its predatory response.[29] Only the incumbent knows if it is strong or weak. Potential entrants gain some information from observing the behavior of the incumbent, but initially potential entrants do not know whether they are facing a strong or weak incumbent. Such a game is a game of *incomplete information* because nature moves *first*, and it is a game of *asymmetric information* because one player, the incumbent, has more information than the other player, the potential entrant.

Consider a game with 200 markets and the above information structure. By behaving aggressively in early markets, a weak incumbent may prevent entry in other markets by fooling potential entrants into thinking that it is strong. A weak incumbent therefore may increase its present value of profits by being aggressive. Although it is technically somewhat difficult to develop the solution to this predatory pricing game with asymmetric information, the equilibrium result is intuitively appealing and fairly easy to explain. As we show in the appendix the equilibrium has the following characteristics:

1. In early markets such as the first 150 markets in a 200-market game, entry will *not* occur because both *strong* and *weak* firms will adopt a predatory response to all entry. This occurs because in early markets even a *weak* firm has a great incentive to build up a reputation as a *strong* firm. If, for example, entry occurred in the third market and was not met with a predatory response, then all future potential entrants would know that the incumbent was *weak*, and by the chain store paradox, there would be no deterrent to entering the fourth through two hundredth markets.

2. As the number of markets approaches 200, a *weak* incumbent has little incentive to continue to put forward a facade as a *strong* firm, and the incumbent will share the market.

3. Between the early and late markets, the incumbent plays a mixed strategy of predatory pricing in the *nth* market with a probability of μ_n and sharing the market with a probability of $(1 - \mu_n)$, where μ_n *generally* diminishes in later rounds.* Of course, if the incumbent actually shares even *one* market, then the incumbent is identified as *weak*, and by the logic of the chain-store paradox the incumbent will accommodate all future entry.

Figure 10.7 shows this basic result. In markets from N through X, a *weak* incumbent will always behave aggressively. In markets Y through 1, a *weak* incumbent will always accommodate entry. In markets X through Y, however, the in-

---

*The Kreps and Wilson model presented in the appendix explains the derivation of μ_n.

cumbent adopts a mixed strategy and is indifferent between predation and sharing.

Perhaps the most important implication of the asymmetric information model of predatory behavior is that as N becomes very large, even a small probability that an incumbent is strong may deter entry.[30] The appendix provides a detailed explanation of this model of predatory pricing, which was developed by David Kreps and Robert Wilson.[31]

◢ Empirical Evidence: Predatory Pricing and Building a Tough Reputation

EARLY EXAMPLES: STANDARD OIL AND AMERICAN TOBACCO

Historians consider Standard Oil of New Jersey the classic predatory firm.[32] In the first half of the twentieth century, historians and economists reported that John D. Rockefeller forced many competitors out of the oil refining business by lowering price below average cost. In a 1959 article, however, John McGee provided evidence that Standard Oil rarely resorted to predatory behavior but, instead, tended to purchase its competitors on what might be deemed reasonable terms.[33] All of Standard's actions, however, seemed aimed at one objective: maintaining control over the oil refining business in the United States. It managed to maintain a 90 percent market share for a long time by acquiring more than 100 competitors; controlling the major oil pipelines, which permitted it to restrict oil supplies to its competitors; obtaining freight rebates from railroads not only on its own shipments but also on its competitors' shipments; and using some degree of localized price cutting to drive its most stubborn competitors from the market.

Although Standard Oil received most of the historical attention around the turn of the century, American Tobacco was a more aggressive monopolist.[34] Before 1890, five companies dominated the cigarette segment of the tobacco industry: W. Duke, Allen and Ginter, Kinney Tobacco, W.S. Kimball, and Goodwin. These firms accounted for 95 percent of domestic cigarette production. In January 1890 the five merged to form the American Tobacco Company with James B. Duke as the dominant force behind the consolidation. One of the corporation's first actions was to close Goodwin, one of its own members. This move was just the beginning of a series of aggressive acquisitions followed by aggressive dismantlings.

American's attempt to gain control of the plug tobacco market is typical of its behavior.[35] Plug tobacco is chewing tobacco that is pressed into a round container. In 1893 American approached several plug manufacturers to suggest possible mergers. When the plug producers refused, American embarked on a five-year effort to force them out of the market by selling plug tobacco at prices below average total costs. Between 1893 and 1898, American lost more than $4 million in the plug market but succeeded in gaining control over the major plug producers.

Its aggressive behavior did not stop in 1898; in 1899 alone, it acquired and shut down thirty competitors.*

American Tobacco used a variety of aggressive techniques, including predatory pricing, massive advertising campaigns, and the creation of "fighting brands" that were sold below cost. During the so-called plug-war of 1895 to 1898, competition centered on one fighting brand appropriately named Battle Axe. Before the war Battle Axe was a small and relatively unimportant brand. In 1891 Battle Axe sold for 50 cents per pound, but in 1895 American reduced the price to 13 cents, which did not cover average costs.[36] As a result of the plug-war, American Tobacco earned a profit of 56 percent on sales in 1899, and it had captured more than 90 percent of the market.[37]

There is little doubt that Standard Oil to some extent, and American Tobacco to a far greater extent, engaged in predatory pricing to create a tough reputation and intimidate competitors. Several more recent cases suggest that the practice continues.

REALEMON[38]

Borden's ReaLemon brand has historically dominated the market for reconstituted lemon juice. ReaLemon held a 92 percent national market share in 1970. Golden Crown Citrus Corporation began marketing lemon juice in the Midwest in 1969 and in 1970 expanded into several eastern states.

When Golden Crown became a serious threat to ReaLemon's national market share, Borden responded aggressively, particularly to Golden Crown's inroads into the northeastern market. Borden adopted a policy of providing much larger promotional allowances to buyers in the Northeast than in the rest of the country. Legitimate promotional allowances are given to buyers to help to cover their actual costs of marketing the product. The 1971 Borden Marketing Plan for ReaLemon spelled out its strategy to maintain market share as follows:[39]

> In those markets where competition has been making inroads, tentative plans are to increase the size of the [promotional] allowances to as much as $1.20 per case, or 10 [cents] per bottle. . . . In general terms, competitive activity exists in the Eastern half of the United States and for the Western half promotional allowances will be limited to a range of 60 to 70 cents per case.

---

*According to Malcolm Burns, American Tobacco's predatory pricing strategy enabled it to purchase competitors at significantly reduced prices. Burns hypothesized that as the number of American Tobacco's predatory pricing episodes increased, American was able to acquire competitors at increasingly lower prices. Burns tested this theory by identifying seven predatory pricing episodes between 1891 and 1906 and then analyzing data for the complete set of forty-three firms acquired by American Tobacco during that fifteen-year period. Burns's regression results suggest that, as a direct consequence of its predatory pricing policy, American was able to obtain an average 25 percent price discount when it acquired a competitor. See Malcolm R. Burns, "Predatory Pricing and the Acquisition Cost of Competitors," *Journal of Political Economy* 94 (1986): 266–96.

The heaviest promotional activities were undertaken in Philadelphia and Buffalo. As a result of these allowances, retail prices of the most popular quart size of ReaLemon, which typically ranged between 69 and 79 cents, declined to between 39 and 49 cents.[40] Furthermore, because ReaLemon enjoyed a premium brand image, competitors such as Golden Crown were forced to sell their lemon juice at prices 10 to 15 cents per quart lower than that of ReaLemon.[41] If ReaLemon sold for 39 cents per quart, therefore, Golden Crown would sell at 29 cents per quart, or just $3.48 per 12 quart case. Because Golden Crown's estimated costs were approximately $4.00 per case, it was impossible for Golden Crown to compete with a 39 cent price of ReaLemon.[42] Partly as a result of Borden's price reductions, Golden Crown suffered a net loss of approximately $500,000 in the year ending October 1973 and sold its lemon juice operations to a Seven-Up subsidiary in 1974.[43]

The ReaLemon case can be viewed as one of establishing a tough reputation in the Northeast to slow down or prevent Golden Crown and others from attempting to enter other regions of the country.

MAXWELL HOUSE COFFEE[44]

In 1970 General Foods held approximately a 43 percent national market share for non-instant coffee. A majority of that share was held by Maxwell House, and General Foods was the only national distributor of ground coffee. Procter and Gamble's Folgers brand, the leading brand in the West, was not sold in the East. But in 1971 Procter and Gamble began to market Folgers in the East by selling in a few test markets, including Cleveland, Pittsburgh, Philadelphia, and Syracuse. In each of these markets the Maxwell House brand commanded the lead, with a market share two to five times larger than the second-ranking brand.

In response to Folgers' entry, General Foods slashed the price of Maxwell House in the four test markets. Evidence suggested that Maxwell House was sold at prices below marginal and average variable costs. In the late winter of 1974, for example, Maxwell House was sold for $2.095 per three-pound can in Pittsburgh, whereas the price of a three-pound can of unroasted green coffee beans was $2.10.[45]

According to Hilke and Nelson, General Foods' aggressive actions had the effect of making Procter and Gamble believe that General Foods would respond aggressively to entry into any eastern market.[46] As a result, Folgers eastern expansion lagged, and General Foods earned higher profits in the eastern market for several additional years.

AIRLINES

Until the late 1970s airline fares in the United States were regulated by the Civil Aeronautics Board (CAB). Deregulation of the industry resulted in the entry of many new airline carriers, among them Midway, People Express, and Southwest. These new airlines had significantly lower costs than established carriers, such as American, United, and Delta, and initially were able to gain a substantial market share on many routes.

Table 10.5 suggests the dramatic impact of entry on fares. In each of the four comparison cases, fares decreased considerably on routes on which entry occurred, and fares increased by more than 50 percent on routes without entry.

TABLE 10.5 **Comparative Airline Fares in Markets Entered by People Express and Southwest**

Market	Distance	1980 Fare	1984 Fare	Percent Change
New York-Buffalo (People Express)	282	$48	$36	−25%
Boston-Philadelphia	281	$52	$79	53%
New York-Norfolk (People Express)	284	$48	$32	−30%
Chicago-Columbus	284	$48	$98	103%
Dallas-Little Rock (Southwest)	303	$59	$49	−17%
Atlanta-Mobile	303	$56	$87	56%
El Paso-Phoenix (Southwest)	346	$74	$44	−41%
St. Louis-Tulsa	351	$60	$110	83%

Source: Daniel P. Kaplan, "The Changing Airline Industry," in Leonard W. Weiss and Michael W. Klass (eds.), *Regulatory Reform: What Actually Happened* (Boston: Little, Brown, 1986), p. 59.

Table 10.5 suggests that deregulation had the anticipated positive effect of reducing fares. Hidden behind these fare figures, however, is another story: the aggressive use of selective predatory pricing by established carriers in markets entered by new airlines.

To understand why Table 10.5 suggests the use of predatory tactics, consider this list of new jet carriers that entered the industry between 1979 and 1984 after deregulation:[47]

1. Midway (entered 1979)
2. New York Air (1980)
3. People Express (1981)
4. Muse (1981)
5. Jet America (1982)
6. Pacific Express (1982)
7. Northeastern (1982)
8. Pacific East (1982)
9. American International (1982)
10. Hawaii Express (1982)
11. Air One (1983)
12. Sunworld (1983)
13. America West (1983)
14. Frontier Horizon (1984)
15. Florida Express (1984)
16. Air Atlanta (1984)

In reaction to these entrants, the established carriers, led by American Airlines, followed a practice of aggressive price cutting. In virtually every market in which a major carrier faced competition from a new carrier, the established firm responded by slashing prices to match or undercut the entrant's fares.

A classic example is Northwest's response to the entry of People Express into the Minneapolis–St. Paul market in June 1984.[48] People Express entered the Newark-to-Minneapolis market with fares of $99 weekdays and $79 weekends and evenings. People Express was a low-cost, low-service operation that charged for amenities such as meals and baggage handling. In June 1984 Northwest's standard economy fare between Minneapolis and each of the three New York airports was $263, and the lowest highly restrictive fare available was $149. Following the entry of People Express, Northwest slashed its unrestricted fares to $95 weekdays and $75 weekends and evenings. Because Northwest flew to all three New York airports and its fares included meals, wider seats, and baggage handling, these fare reductions represented a significant undercutting of People Express fares. People Express responded by further reducing its fares to $79 and $59, but Northwest met those fares as well.

The Northwest–People Express scenario was repeated in many markets, and partly as a result, very few of the new airlines survived. Of the sixteen entrants listed above, only America West was still flying in 1993.

The aggressive response of the established airlines to new entry in the 1980s is consistent with a predation strategy. In response to every entry, the established airlines responded with aggressive price cuts and gave the impression that they were *strong* firms (even if they were in fact weak) that would respond aggressively to all entry.

SUMMARY

1. Firms wish to maximize long-run not short-run profits.
2. The theory of limit pricing suggests that firms may charge lower short-run prices to restrict future entry.
3. Game theorists have criticized basic limit pricing theory because of its lack of a credible threat of retaliation in the face of entry. Instead they have concentrated on extending the limit pricing model so that limit pricing results in a credible threat of retaliation.
4. Empirical evidence suggests that firms may utilize limit pricing.
5. As an alternative to limit pricing, firms may charge profit-maximizing prices before entry and respond to entry by using predatory pricing policies.
6. In a game with *perfect*, *certain*, *complete*, and *symmetric* information predatory pricing is irrational because of Selten's chain-store paradox.
7. In a game with *imperfect*, *certain*, *incomplete*, and *asymmetric* information, it may be rational for "weak" incumbents to engage in predatory pricing to fool potential entrants into believing that the incumbent is "strong."
8. Empirical evidence suggests that firms sometimes engage in predatory pricing to build a tough reputation.

KEY TERMS

chain-store paradox	present value of profits
credible threat	strong incumbent
limit pricing	weak incumbent
predatory pricing	

DISCUSSION QUESTIONS

1. In an industry with no cost advantage for incumbent firms, would limit pricing become more or less viable as economies of scale become more significant? Explain, using a graph or graphs.

2. Does limit pricing improve allocative efficiency?

3. An economist estimates that one monopolist prices where the elasticity of demand equals 1.5 and another monopolist prices where the elasticity of demand equals 0.5. Which monopolist is more likely to be limit pricing? Why?

4. Suppose you suspected that a firm was engaged in predatory pricing tactics. What evidence might convince you that the firm was in fact behaving in a predatory manner?

PROBLEMS

1. Suppose that the industry demand curve is given by

$$P = 200 - Q$$

and the incumbent firm faces the following total cost function:

$$TC_I = 50q_I$$

and potential entrants face the following cost function:

$$TC_E = 60q_E$$

   a. What is the limit price in this market?
   b. If the incumbent charged its profit-maximizing price, what would its profits equal?
   c. If the incumbent charged the limit price, what would its profits equal?

2. Let the rate of entry be a function of the differential between the incumbent's price and the limit price, so that:

$$E = \lambda [P_A - P_{LP}]$$

where E is the rate of entry, λ is a positive constant that measures the speed of entry, P_A is the actual price, and P_{LP} is the limit price. If λ is very small (approaches zero), do you think that limit pricing would be an attractive strategy for the incumbent? If λ is very large (approaches infinity), do you think that limit pricing would be an attractive strategy for the incumbent? What values of λ would result in a high likelihood of limit pricing? What factors might affect your answer?

3. You will need a calculator and some patience to do this problem. Work it through step by step. Recalculate Table 10.1 assuming that for each period during which price exceeds the limit price of 20, new entrants will produce and sell 20 additional units in the next period. In other words, if the incumbent produces $Q_d = 50$ in $t = 0$, then entrants will produce $Q_e = 20$ in $t = 1$, and if the incumbent produces $Q = 50$ in $t = 0$ and $t = 1$, then entrants will produce 20 units in period $t = 1$ and 40 units in period $t = 2$, and so on.

   Next recalculate Table 10.2 for discount rates of 10 percent and 15 percent.

   Does the increase in output by entrants change the optimal time to switch to a limit pricing policy?

4. Suppose that in a predatory pricing game with imperfect, certain, incomplete, and asymmetric information, the probability that the incumbent is strong in period $n + 1$ is ρ_{n+1}. Suppose that $\rho_{n+1} = 0.25$. If entry occurs in period $n + 1$ and the incumbent accommodates entry, what would be the value of ρ_n?

5. **For those who read the appendix:**

   a. Suppose that in the Kreps and Wilson model the values of N, a, b, and δ are:

      $$N = 10; \ a = 2; \ b = 1/2; \ \text{and} \ \delta = 1/4.$$

      The only change in these values from the example in the appendix is that $\delta = 1/4$ instead of $\delta = 1/10$; that is, there is a higher initial probability that the incumbent is strong. What changes would occur in this game compared with the game played out in Table 10.6? Provide an intuitive explanation for this change.

   b. Suppose that in the Kreps and Wilson model the values of N, a, b, and δ are:

      $$N = 10; \ a = 2; \ b = 1/4; \ \text{and} \ \delta = 1/10.$$

   The only change in these values from the example in the appendix is that $b = 1/4$ instead of $b = 1/2$; that is, the entrant's profits are smaller if the incumbent does not fight entry. What changes would occur in this game compared with the game played out in Table 10.6 (page 258)? Provide an intuitive explanation for this change.

REFERENCES

1. See J.S. Bain, *Barriers to New Competition* (Cambridge, MA: Harvard University Press, 1956); P. Sylos-Labini, *Oligopoly and Technical Progress* (Cambridge, MA: Harvard University Press, 1962); and F. Modigliani, "Developments on the Oligopoly Front," *Journal of Political Economy* 66 (June 1958): 215–32.

2. See Bain, *supra* note 1; Sylos-Labini, *supra* note 1; and Modigliani, *supra* note 1.

3. Darius W. Gaskins, Jr., "Dynamic Limit Pricing: Optimal Pricing Under Threat of Entry," *Journal of Economic Theory* 3 (September 1971): 306–22; N.J. Ireland, "Concentration and the Growth of Market Demand," *Journal of Economic Theory* 5 (October 1972): 303–5; Kenneth L. Judd and Bruce C. Peterson, "Dynamic Limit Pricing: A Reformulation," *Review of Industrial Organization* 2 (1985): 160–77.

4. See Thomas C. Schelling, *The Strategy of Conflict* (Cambridge, MA: Harvard University Press, 1960), Chapter 5; and Eric Rasmusen, *Games and Information: An Introduction to Game Theory* (Oxford, England: Basil Blackwell, 1989), pp. 85–7.

5. P. Milgrom and J. Roberts, "Limit Pricing and Entry Under Incomplete Information an Equilibrium Analysis," *Econometrica* 50 (March 1982): 443–60.

6. See the presentation in Chapter 12, which is adapted from Jean Tirole, *The Theory of Industrial Organization* (Cambridge, MA: MIT Press, 1988), pp. 368–72.

7. Don E. Waldman, "The Du Pont Cellophane Case Revisited: An Analysis of the Indirect Effects of Antitrust Policy on Market Structure and Economic Performance," *Antitrust Bulletin* (Winter 1980): 805–30. See also *United States* v. *E. I. du Pont de Nemours,* 351 US 377 (1956).

8. Waldman, *op cit.,* p. 818.

9. Don E. Waldman, *Antitrust Action and Market Structure* (Lexington, MA: D.C. Heath, 1978), pp. 40–9. See also *United States* v. *United Shoe Machinery Corporation,* 347 US 521 (1954) and 391 US 244 (1968).

10. Waldman, *ibid.,* pp. 47–9.

11. *Ibid.,* p. 48.

12. *Ibid.*

13. *Ibid.,* p. 49.

14. A.D.H. Kaplan, Joel B. Dirlam, and Robert F. Lanzillotti, *Pricing in Big Business: A Case Approach* (Washington: Brookings Institution, 1958), pp. 214–7.

15. *Ibid.,* p. 216.

16. *Ibid.*

17. The following is taken from Erwin A. Blackstone, "Limit Pricing and Entry in the Copying Machine Industry," *Quarterly Review of Economics and Business* 12 (Winter 1972): 57–65.

18. *Ibid.,* p. 60.

19. *Ibid.,* p. 61.

20. Robert T. Masson and Joseph Shaanan, "Stochastic-Dynamic Limit Pricing: An Empirical Test," *Review of Economics and Statistics* 64 (August 1982): 413–22; and Masson and Shaanan, "Optimal Oligopoly Pricing and the Threat of Entry," *International Journal of Industrial Organization* 5 (September 1987): 323–39. For a statistical test suggesting the possible use of limit pricing in the airline industry, see Margaret A. Peteraf and Randal Reed, "Pricing and Performance in Monopoly Airline Markets," *Journal of Law and Economics* 37 (April 1994): 193–214.

21. This is the model based on Bain's assumptions, Bain, *op cit.*

22. This is the model based on Gaskins, *supra* note 3.

23. This model is based on Morton I. Kamien and Nancy L. Schwartz, "Limit Pricing and Uncertain Entry," *Econometrica* 39 (May 1971): 441–54; and David P. Baron, "Limit Pricing, Potential Entry, and Barriers to Entry," *American Economic Review* 63 (September 1973): 666–74.

24. Robert T. Masson and Joseph Shaanan, "Stochastic-Dynamic Limit Pricing: An Empirical Test," *Review of Economics and Statistics* 64 (August 1982): 413–22

25. Robert T. Masson and Joseph Shaanan, "Optimal Oligopoly Pricing and the Threat of Entry," *International Journal of Industrial Organization* 5 (September 1987): 323–39.

26. See Richard Selten, "The Chain Store Paradox," *Theory and Decision* 9 (1978): 127–59; David Kreps and Robert Wilson, "Reputation and Imperfect Information," *Journal of Economic Theory* 27 (August 1982): 253–79; Paul Milgrom and John Roberts, "Predation, Reputation, and Entry Deterrence," *Journal of Economic Theory* 27 (August 1982): 280–312; Joseph E. Harrington Jr., "Collusion and Predation Under (Almost) Free Entry," *International Journal of Industrial Organization* 7 (September 1989): 381–401; and R. David Simpson, "Signaling in an Infinitely Repeated Cournot Game with Output Restrictions," *International Journal of Industrial Organization* 9 (September 1991): 365–88.

27. The following is adopted from Selten, *supra* note 26.

28. Selten, *supra* note 26.

29. Kreps and Wilson, *supra* note 26; Eric Rasmusen, *Games and Information: An Introduction to Game Theory* (Oxford, England: Basil Blackwell, 1989), pp. 285–8.

30. Kreps and Wilson, *supra* note 26.

31. Kreps and Wilson, *supra* note 26.

32. Alan Nevins, *Study in Power: John D. Rockefeller* (New York: Scribner's, 1953). Also *Standard Oil Company of New Jersey* v. *United States,* 221 US 1 (1911).

33. John S. McGee, "Predatory Price Cutting: The Standard Oil (N.J.) Case," *Journal of Law & Economics* 1 (October 1958): 137–69.

34. *United States* v. *American Tobacco Company,* 221 US 106 (1911).

35. Don E. Waldman, *The Economics of Antitrust: Cases and Analysis* (Boston: Little, Brown, 1986), pp. 47–8.

36. Malcolm R. Burns, "Outside Intervention in Incumbentic Price Warfare: The Case of the "Plug War" and the Union Tobacco Company," *Business History Review* 56 (Spring 1982): 38.

37. Waldman, *supra* note 35, p. 47.

38. A series of decisions in this case went all the way up to the Supreme Court; see primarily *In the Matter of Borden, Inc.,* 92 FTC 669 (1978). Also see 102 FTC 1147 (1983) and 461 US 940 (1983). For analysis see Richard Schmalensee, "On the Use of Economic

Models in Antitrust: The ReaLemon Case," *University of Pennsylvania Law Review* (April 1979): 994–1050; Clement G. Krouse, "Brand Name as a Barrier to Entry: The ReaLemon Case," *Southern Economic Journal* 51 (October 1984): 495–502; and David I. Rosenbaum, "Predatory Pricing and the Reconstituted Lemon Juice Industry," *Journal of Economic Issues* 21 (March 1987): 237–56.

39. *In the Matter of Borden, Inc.,* 92 FTC 669 (1978), p. 722.
40. *Ibid.,* p. 737.
41. *Ibid.,* p. 755.
42. *Ibid.*
43. *Ibid.,* p. 801.
44. The following analysis is taken from John C. Hilke and Philip B. Nelson, "Strategic Behavior and Attempted Monopolization: The Coffee (General Foods) Case," in John E. Kwoka Jr. and Lawrence J. White (eds.),

The Antitrust Revolution (Glenview, IL: Scott, Foresman and Company, 1989), pp. 208–40. See also *In the Matter of General Foods Corp.,* 103 FTC 204 (1984); and Philip B. Nelson and John C. Hilke, "Retail Featuring as a Strategic Entry or Mobility Barrier in Manufacturing," *International Journal of Industrial Organization* 9 (December 1991): 533–44.

45. Hilke and Nelson, *supra* note 44.
46. *Ibid.,* p. 224.
47. Daniel P. Kaplan, "The Changing Airline Industry," in Leonard W. Weiss and Michael W. Klass (eds.), *Regulatory Reform: What Actually Happened* (Boston: Little, Brown and Company, 1986), p. 58.
48. Alfred E. Kahn, "Thinking About Predation—A Personal Diary," *Review of Industrial Organization* 6 (1991): 141.

Appendix

DETAILS OF THE KREPS AND WILSON PREDATORY PRICING MODEL

Figure 10.8 presents the payoffs for the incumbent and the potential entrant in each round of the Kreps and Wilson predatory pricing game. In the Kreps and Wilson game, information is *imperfect, certain, incomplete,* and *asymmetric.* Nature first selects the incumbent to be either (1) *strong,* in which case the firm enjoys being predatory and is always predatory, or (2) *weak,* in which case the incumbent will be predatory in one market only if it believes it will increase its profits in future markets to compensate for its predatory response. ρ_n represents the potential entrant's subjective probability in round n that the incumbent is strong. In each additional round the potential entrant must reestimate the value of ρ based

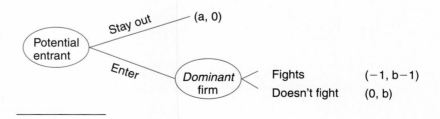

Where a > 1 and 0 < b < 1

Figure 10.8 A game of entry with a strong dominant firm (dominant firm's profit, potential entrant's profit).

on past beliefs and observed behavior. If the incumbent behaves aggressively and fights entry in any round, it *may* increase the value of ρ in later rounds. However, if the incumbent accommodates entry in *any* round, ρ decreases to *zero* in the next round because future potential entrants know that the incumbent is weak. The game is played sequentially from round N (the *first* round entered) through round 1 (the *last* round entered).

Let's consider the rules of the game as defined by Kreps and Wilson, beginning with their definition of the function ρ_n. Define ρ_n as follows:

1. In the Nth market, the *first* market subject to potential entry, set $\rho_n = \delta > 0$. This implies that, at the beginning of the game, the potential entrant believes that there is some positive probability that the incumbent will fight entry.
2. If there is no entry in round n + 1, then $\rho_n = \rho_{n+1}$.
3. If there is entry in round n + 1, this entry is fought, and $\rho_{n+1} > 0$, then ρ_n equals the maximum of b^n or ρ_{n+1}, where b comes from Figure 10.8 and represents the entrant's profits if the incumbent does *not* fight entry. Note that $0 < b < 1$.* Fighting entry in round n + 1 therefore can increase ρ_n in the next round of the game.

4. If there is entry in round n + 1 and either this entry is not fought or $\rho_{n+1} = 0$, then $\rho_n = 0$. This follows because accommodation to entry in any round reveals to *all* future potential entrants that the incumbent is a weak firm.

Given this definition of the function ρ_n, Kreps and Wilson created strategies for both players in terms of ρ_n. The following strategies define one possible set of strategies laid out by Kreps and Wilson:

Incumbent's Strategy

1. If the incumbent is *strong*, it *always* fights entry.
2. If the incumbent is *weak* and entry occurs in round n, then:
   a. If n = 1 (that is, the game is in the *last* round), the incumbent does not fight.
   b. If n > 1 and $\rho_n \geq b^{n-1}$, the incumbent fights. (Note that in each additional round, b^{n-1} gets *larger* because $0 < b < 1$, and therefore if ρ_n remains constant from round to round, a weak incumbent is less likely to fight in each additional round of the game.)
   c. If n > 1 and $\rho_n < b^{n-1}$, the incumbent plays a mixed strategy and fights with probability μ_n, where:

$$\mu_n = \frac{(1 - b^{n-1})\, \rho_n}{(1 - \rho_n)\, b^{n-1}},$$

and does not fight with probability $(1 - \mu_n)$. Notice that if $\rho_n = 0$, then $\mu_1 = 0$; and if $\rho_n = b^{n-1}$, then $\mu_n = 1$.

---

*The fact that the value of b is represented by a fraction does not imply that the potential profits associated with successful entry are small, because b can be measured in billions or trillions of dollars.

Potential Entrants' Strategies

1. If $\rho_n > b^n$, the potential entrant stays out.
2. If $\rho_n < b^n$, the potential entrant enters. (Note that in each additional round b^n gets *larger* because $0 < b < 1$, and therefore if ρ_n remains constant from round to round, the potential entrant is more likely to enter in each additional round of the game.)
3. If $\rho_n = b^n$, the potential entrant plays a mixed strategy of staying out with probability $\theta_n = 1/a$ and entering with probability $(1 - \theta_n) = 1 - (1/a)$. (Recall from Figure 10.8 that $a > 1$ is the profit earned by the incumbent if entry does *not* occur. Increases in the incumbent's potential profits therefore increase the probability that the potential entrant will enter; that is, higher industry profits make entry more likely.)

We now have sufficient information to play the game for given values of N (the total number of rounds), a (the incumbent's profits in the absence of entry), b (the entrants' profits if the incumbent does not fight), and δ (the potential entrants' initial subjective probability that the incumbent is strong).

Consider the game associated with the following values:

$$N = 10; a = 2, b = 1/2; \text{ and } \delta = 1/10.$$

TABLE 10.6 Kreps and Wilson Predatory Pricing Game

Round	ρ^n	b^n	b^{n-1}	Monopolist's Action	Potential Entrant's Action
10	1/10	1/1024	1/512	Fight	Stay Out
9	1/10	1/512	1/256	Fight	Stay Out
8	1/10	1/256	1/128	Fight	Stay Out
7	1/10	1/128	1/64	Fight	Stay Out
6	1/10	1/64	1/32	Fight	Stay Out
5	1/10	1/32	1/16	Fight	Stay Out
4	1/10	1/16	1/8	Mixed Strategy with: $\mu_4 = 7/9$ $(1 - \mu_4) = 2/9$	Stay Out
3	1/10	1/8	1/4	Mixed Strategy with: $\mu_3 = 1/3$ $(1 - \mu_3) = 2/3$	Enter
2 if entry was fought in round 3	1/4	1/4	1/2	Mixed Strategy with: $\mu_2 = 1/3$ $(1 - \mu_2) = 2/3$	Mixed Strategy with: $\theta_2 = 1/2$ $(1 - \theta_2) = 1/2$
2 if entry was not fought in round 3	0	1/4	1/2	Not Fight	Enter
1	0	1/2	1	Not Fight	Enter

This game would play out according to Table 10.6. Round 10 is played first. In round 10, $\rho_{10} = \delta = 1/10$; that is, the potential entrant assumes that there is a 10 percent probability that the incumbent is strong and will always fight. Because b = 1/2, $b^{10} = (1/2)^{10} = 1/1024$ and $b^9 = (1/2)^9 = 1/512$. Because $\rho_{10} > b^9$ [(1/10)>(1/512)], then by incumbent strategy 2(b), the incumbent would fight entry; and because $\rho_{10} > b^{10}$ [(1/10)>(1/1024)], by potential entrants' strategy 1, the potential entrant stays out. The same conditions hold for rounds 9, 8, 7, 6, and 5.

In round 4, $\rho_4 < b^3$ [(1/10)<(1/8)], and therefore by incumbent strategy 2(c), the incumbent plays a mixed strategy of fighting entry with probability 7/9 ($\mu_4 = 7/9$) and not fighting with probability 2/9 [$(1 - \mu_4) = 2/9$].* Entry, however, will not occur, because $\rho_4 > b^4$ [(1/10) > (1/16)].

In round 3, however, $\rho_3 < b^3$ [(1/10)<(1/8)], and by the potential entrant's strategy 2, the firm will enter. There is a 1/3 probability (that is, $\mu_3 = 1/3$) that the incumbent will fight entry in round 3, and a 2/3 probability [that is, $(1 - \mu_3) = 2/3$] that entry will not be fought.†

The outcome in round 2 now depends critically on whether entry was fought in round 3. If entry was *not* fought, the incumbent is revealed to be weak so $\rho_2 = 0$, entry will occur in round 2, and the incumbent will not fight. If entry was fought in round 3, however, then ρ_2 equals the maximum of $b^2 = 1/4$ or $\rho_3 = 1/10$; in this case the maximum is $\rho_2 = 1/4$. By fighting entry in round 3, the incumbent has greatly *increased* the potential entrant's assessment of the probability that the

---

*From the incumbent's strategy 2(c), we have:

$$\mu_4 = \frac{(1 - b^{n-1})\rho_n}{(1 - \rho_n)b^{n-1}}$$

$$= \frac{\left(1 - \frac{1}{8}\right)\frac{1}{10}}{\left(1 - \frac{1}{10}\right)\frac{1}{8}} = \frac{\frac{7}{8}\frac{1}{10}}{\frac{9}{10}\frac{1}{8}}$$

$$= \frac{\frac{7}{80}}{\frac{9}{80}} = \frac{7}{9}.$$

It follows that $(1 - \mu_4) = 1 - \frac{7}{9} = \frac{2}{9}$.

†From the incumbent's strategy 2(c), we have:

$$\mu_3 = \frac{(1 - b^{n-1})\rho_n}{(1 - \rho_n)b^{n-1}}$$

$$= \frac{\left(1 - \frac{1}{4}\right)\frac{1}{10}}{\left(1 - \frac{1}{10}\right)\frac{1}{4}} = \frac{\frac{3}{4}\frac{1}{10}}{\frac{9}{10}\frac{1}{4}}$$

$$= \frac{\frac{3}{40}}{\frac{9}{40}} = \frac{1}{3}.$$

It follows that $(1 - \mu_3) = 1 - \frac{1}{3} = \frac{2}{3}$.

incumbent will fight entry in round 2. If entry was fought in round 3, then because $\rho_2 = b^2 [(1/4) = (1/4)]$ by potential entrants' strategy 3, the potential entrant will play a mixed strategy in round 2 and enter with a probability of $\theta_2 = 1/a = 1/2$ and stay out with a probability of $(1 - \theta_2) = [1 - (1/a)] = 1/2$. Fighting in round 3 therefore may deter entry in round 2.

In round 1, of course, there is no credible threat of fighting, and therefore entry occurs and a weak incumbent does not fight.

Generalizing the Kreps and Wilson model, in a game with N rounds and asymmetric information, a *weak* incumbent may be able to prevent entry in later markets by behaving aggressively in early markets. As noted earlier in this chapter, the equilibrium has the following characteristics:

1. In early rounds (here, rounds 10, 9, 8, 7, 6, and 5), entry will not occur because both strong and weak incumbents will fight all entry. This occurs because in early markets even a weak incumbent has a great incentive to establish a reputation as a strong firm. In our example, if entry occurred in round 9 and was *not* met with a predatory response, then all future potential entrants would know that the incumbent was weak, and there would be no deterrent to entering markets 8 through 1.
2. As the number of markets approaches n = 1, a weak incumbent has little incentive to continue to put forward a facade as a strong firm, and the incumbent will not fight entry.
3. Somewhere between the early and late rounds, the incumbent plays a mixed strategy of fighting in the nth market with a probability of μ_n and sharing the market with a probability of $1 - \mu_n$, where μ_n generally diminishes as n moves toward the last market where n = 1. Of course, if the incumbent does not fight in any round, then the incumbent is identified as weak, and by the logic of the chain-store paradox, the incumbent will accommodate all future entry.

We saw this result in Figure 10.7. In rounds N through X (here markets 10 to 5), a weak incumbent will always behave aggressively. In markets Y through 1 (here only market 1), a weak incumbent will always accommodate entry. In markets X through Y (here markets 4 to 2), the incumbent adopts a mixed strategy.

The most important implication of Kreps and Wilson's asymmetric information model of predatory behavior is that as N becomes very large, the size of δ needed to deter entry becomes small.* In Table 10.6, for example, $\delta = 1/100$ would deter entry in rounds 10, 9, and 8. Therefore, even a very small probability that an incumbent is strong may deter entry.

---

*David Kreps and Robert Wilson, "Reputation and Imperfect Information," *Journal of Economic Theory* (August 1982): 253–79.

Chapter 11

Oligopoly Behavior: Entry and Nonpricing Strategies to Deter Entry

In Chapter 10 we asked the question: Can dominant firms or effective cartels engage in pricing behavior to prevent their loss of market power in the long run? We suggested that limit pricing or predatory pricing can delay or prevent a loss of market share. This chapter extends the analysis to consider nonpricing strategies that can delay or prevent entry. Nonpricing strategies may be preferable to pricing strategies from a legal and economic standpoint. From a legal viewpoint, nonpricing strategies are less likely to raise antitrust concerns, and from an economic standpoint they are less likely to be misinterpreted by competitors as aggressive acts.

This chapter includes an examination of the empirical evidence regarding which strategies are most commonly used by dominant firms.

Excess Capacity[1]

Consider an incumbent firm with the cost advantage depicted in Figure 11.1. Assume that all fixed costs are *sunk costs* so that once the firm selects a level of capacity, it must maintain that *minimum* level of capacity and cannot reduce its capacity by selling off a portion of its capacity to recover some of its fixed costs. The curve $LRMC_i = LRAC_i$ represents the long-run marginal and average costs for the incumbent, and the curve $LRMC_e = LRAC_e$ represents the long-run marginal and average costs for a potential entrant. Like all long-run average cost curves, these curves are *envelope curves* of all the possible short-run average cost curves. Figure 11.1 shows two short-run marginal and two short-run average cost curves for the incumbent. $SRAC_1$ is the optimal short-run average cost curve for producing Q_1 units of output, and $SRAC_2$ is the optimal short-run average cost curve for pro-

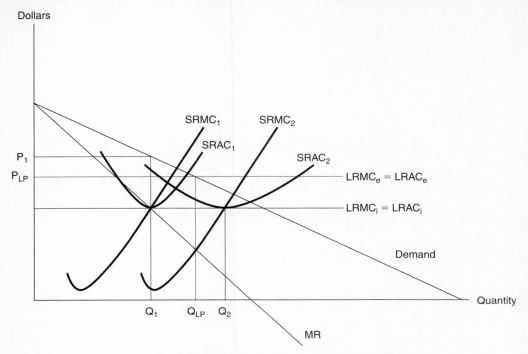

Figure 11.1   Excess capacity as a deterrent to entry.

ducing Q_2 units of output. If the incumbent intends to produce Q_1 units, it should build the capacity associated with $SRAC_1$, whereas if it intends to produce Q_2 units of output it should build the capacity associated with $SRAC_2$.

  If the incumbent wishes to maximize profits, it should equate $LRMC_i$ to MR, sell Q_1 units at a price of P_1, and produce with the technology associated with the short-run cost curves $SRMC_1$ and $SRAC_1$. This strategy maximizes profits, but does nothing to deter entry because the incumbent has no incentive to price at the limit price. Given $SRAC_1$, setting price equal to the limit price P_{LP} would result in significant losses for the incumbent because $P_{LP} < SRAC_1$ for an output of Q_{LP}. If the incumbent has short-run average costs of $SRAC_1$ no credible entry deterrent exists, and entry will almost certainly occur.

  As an alternative strategy, the incumbent could build excess capacity associated with the cost curves $SRMC_2$ and $SRAC_2$. The short-run profit-maximizing quantity would then be Q_{LP} with a price equal to the limit price, P_{LP}. Entry would shift the incumbent's residual demand curve to the left; the incumbent's short-run profit-maximizing response to entry would be to lower price *below* the limit price of P_{LP}. The options for a potential entrant would be either: (1) stay out and earn zero or (2) enter and be assured of an economic loss. Excess capacity precommits the incumbent to price below P_{LP} in the face of entry. Given these options, potential entrants would stay out and the incumbent would maintain its dominant position.

Although excess capacity can create a credible entry deterrent, it also results in a large profit sacrifice for the incumbent. The incumbent must accept reduced profits year after year because of the extra costs associated with excess capacity. If the incumbent has a very low discount rate, this might be an attractive strategy; otherwise, it will be a very unattractive strategy.

In its landmark 1945 *Alcoa* antitrust decision, a majority of the second circuit court of appeals ruled that Alcoa had built excess capacity to deter entry into the aluminum refining industry. According to Judge Hand:[2]

> It was not inevitable that [Alcoa] should always anticipate increases in the demand for ingot and be prepared to supply them. Nothing compelled it to keep doubling and redoubling its capacity before others entered the field. It insists that it never excluded competitors; but we can think of no more effective exclusion than progressively to embrace each new opportunity as it opened, and face every newcomer with new capacity already geared into a great organization, having the advantage of experience, trade connections and the elite of personnel.

Raising Rivals' Costs[3]

Incumbent firms also may attempt to deter entry by raising the costs of entry. Consider the game tree in Figure 11.2, which reproduces Figure 10.5. In the limit pricing model in Chapter 10 there was no credible threat to entry in this game, and the only solution was for the entrant to enter and the incumbent to share the

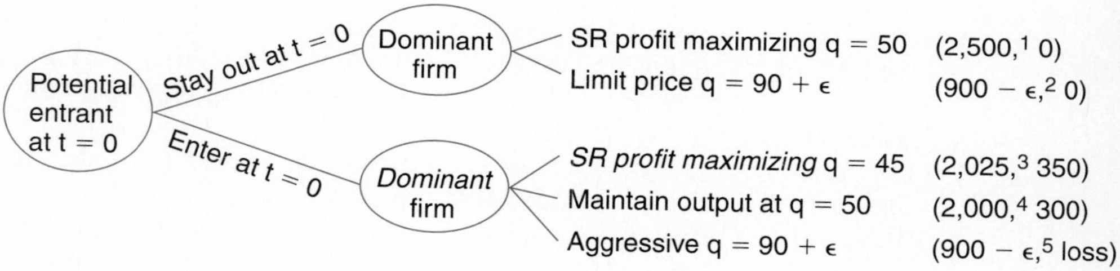

$$^1 \; \pi = q(P - AC) = 50(60 - 10) = 2500$$
$$^2 \; \pi = q(P - AC) = 90(20 - 10) - \epsilon = 900 - \epsilon$$

[3] Based on Figure 10.2, the dominant firm's profits would be:

$$\pi_d = q_d(P - AC) = 45(55 - 10) = 2025$$

and the entrant's profits would be:

$$\pi_e = q_e(P - AC) = 10(55 - 20) = 350$$

[4] Based on Figure 10.2, the dominant firm's profits would be:

$$\pi_d = q_d(P - AC) = 50(50 - 10) = 2000$$

and the entrant's profits would be:

$$\pi_e = q_e(P - AC) = 10(50 - 20) = 300$$

[5] See footnote 2.

Figure 11.2 A game of entry (dominant firm's profit, potential entrant's profit).

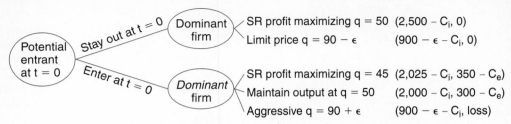

Figure 11.3   A game of entry (dominant firm's profit, potential entrant's profit).

market. But what happens if the incumbent can undertake a strategic action that raises the potential entrant's costs by C_e so that the form of the game changes into the game tree depicted in Figure 11.3? Because the action may also be costly to the incumbent, C_i represents the costs of the action to the incumbent.

Assume that the incumbent succeeds in raising both its costs and the potential entrant's costs by 400. Under this action, $C_i = C_e = 400$, and Figure 11.4 shows the new game tree. Because the entrant now sustains an economic loss no matter what action the incumbent takes in response to entry, entry will not occur. The only solution to the game is for the entrant to stay out and the incumbent to earn maximum profits of 2100.

A number of methods of raising rivals' costs have been suggested. One is to lobby the government to impose an increase in costs.[4] The incumbent might lobby for a licensing fee to enter the industry. In Figure 11.3 an "optimal" fee from the incumbent's standpoint would be a fee greater than 350 imposed on any new firm while exempting existing firms. A fee greater than 350 would prevent entry. If a fee of 400 was imposed on all firms, the profit matrix would look like Figure 11.4, and entry would be prevented. A realistic case might be the imposition of mandatory pollution control devices that impose a fixed cost on both the incumbent and entrants.

Increased advertising is often suggested as a method of raising rivals' costs.[5] Because advertising affects both the demand and costs for the incumbent, it can have either a positive or negative effect on profits; analysis quickly becomes complicated. Intuitively, however, the incumbent's advertising should create brand loyalty and a more inelastic demand for the incumbent's product. These factors would limit the likelihood of a net negative effect of advertising on the incumbent's profits. Significantly increased advertising by the incumbent could force

Figure 11.4   A game of entry (dominant firm's profit, potential entrant's profit).

Figure 11.5 A game of entry (dominant firm's profit, potential entrant's profit).

late entrants to spend at least matching funds on advertising. By advertising before entry the incumbent gains a **first-mover advantage** over latecomers, and heavy advertising by the incumbent may create an asymmetry between the incumbent and potential entrants.*

Such a hypothetical asymmetry is depicted in Figure 11.5. Here we assume that additional advertising expenditures increase costs *more* than revenues, and this difference between the *negative* effect on costs and the *positive* effect on revenues is referred to as the *net advertising cost* associated with additional advertising. In Figure 11.5 it is assumed that for every $1 in increased net advertising cost to the incumbent, C_i, the entrant would face a $2 increase in *net* advertising cost C_e, so $C_e = 2C_i$. In Figure 11.5 the incumbent has increased its net advertising costs by 176 to deter entry (with $C_e = 352$). Again there is only one solution to this game: no entry and short-run profit maximization by the incumbent. At a 10 percent discount rate, the use of advertising to deter entry in Figure 11.5 results in $\pi_{pv} = 23{,}240$.†

EMPIRICAL EVIDENCE ON RAISING RIVALS' COSTS THROUGH ADVERTISING AND FIRST MOVER ADVANTAGES

The first mover advantages associated with advertising have been important, effective methods of maintaining market share in many industries.

Canned Soups

A comparison of the history of the canned soup industry in the United States and Britain provides a particularly interesting test of the first mover theory.[6] In the United States, Campbell's first entered the soup market in 1869 and adopted a strategy of heavy advertising and low prices. Heinz was a late entrant and, despite heavy advertising, was unable to make a significant dent in Campbell's domination. At one time, Heinz's promotional costs exceeded 33 percent of its sales revenues, yet it could not gain a major market share. In 1986, Campbell's still held a huge 82 percent share.[7]

---

*The theory of first mover advantagers is considered in detail in Chapter 13.
†The present value is calculated as follows:

$$\Pi_{pv} = \frac{2{,}324}{.10} = 23{,}240.$$

By comparison, in Great Britain, Heinz entered first and Campbell's second. The scenario played out exactly the same way, only with Heinz the leader. Heinz entered the British market in 1930 with ready-to-eat canned soups, as opposed to Campbell's condensed soups, and used heavy advertising to establish its market dominance. Campbell's entered the market in the 1950s with a full line of condensed soups. Heinz's initial reaction was to offer its own line of premium-priced condensed soups, but Heinz quickly switched to a low-price policy on condensed soups. The low-price strategy apparently led British consumers to view condensed soup as a poor-quality alternative to ready-to-eat soups, and Heinz was able to force Campbell's into the role of a minor player in the British market. In the mid-1980s Heinz held a 58 percent market share compared with Campbell's 12 percent.[8]

In the United States Heinz has been relegated to being a producer of private label soup, whereas in Britain, Campbell's was forced into an identical private label status. In the United States Campbell's forced Heinz out of the premium brand market, and in Britain Heinz forced Campbell's out. The advantages of the first mover are striking in this example.

Soft Drinks

One more or less given in the soft drink industry in the United States is that every few years Pepsi will launch a major advertising campaign aimed at taking away Coke's leadership. Sometimes these campaigns gain early success, but eventually Coke always seems to maintain its position. Much of Coke's advantage appears to stem from its first mover advantage of a century ago. With a distinctive bottle and heavy advertising, Coca-Cola established its early leadership in the first two decades of this century.

In 1966, Coke held a 33.4 percent share compared with Pepsi's 20.4 percent.[9] Despite a highly successful advertising campaign built around the "Pepsi Generation," Pepsi's market share fell to 19.8 percent in 1972, compared with Coke's 34.7 percent. Pepsi then launched another major advertising campaign based on consumers taking "the Pepsi Challenge" (a taste test). In 1975, however, Coke continued to maintain a 35.3 percent to 21.2 percent market share lead.

In the 1980s Coke feared some slippage in its market dominance and introduced "New Coke" in 1985. "New Coke" bombed with consumers but resulted in the reintroduction of "Coca-Cola Classic," which proved to be a great success. Ironically Coke's marketing mistake improved its market position, as it continued to dominate the market with "Coca-Cola Classic." In 1985 Coke continued to lead the industry with a 37.4 percent market share, and Pepsi continued to follow with a 28.9 percent share.[10]

Consumer Batteries

In 1986 Duracell and Eveready dominated the consumer battery market with a combined 80 percent market share.[11] When corporate giant Kodak attempted to enter the industry, both incumbents responded with expensive advertising campaigns. Eveready boasted that toys powered with its batteries "keep on going and going and going." Duracell relied on powerful athletes to show how "tough" its batteries were. Big and powerful Kodak tried but was unable to appreciably penetrate the market. Other factors besides advertising clearly were at work here; for example, shelf space was difficult for Kodak to obtain, and Duracell and Eveready also reduced prices. Nevertheless, there is little doubt that the significant increases in advertising impeded Kodak's entry.*

Learning By Doing

As output increases certain production processes result in lower costs because experience gained through the actual production process results in lower direct labor costs.[12] A good example is the purchase of a set of outdoor chairs that come in boxes completely unassembled. The buyer reads the assembly instructions only to discover that the writer had difficulty explaining things in English. The instructions boldly state that "any child can assemble a chair in less than 30 minutes"; however, two hours into the assembly of the first chair, it still resembles a bunch of unassembled plastic pieces and hardware. Finally, four hours after beginning the process, the first chair is assembled. The consumer now understands many, but not all, of the errors made in assembling the first chair, and the second chair requires a mere two hours to put together. The third chair is finished in one hour, and the fourth is ready for use in just 45 minutes. This is an example of **learning by doing**.

Imagine the same process on a grand scale in the aircraft industry. To assemble just a few prototypes of a new plane requires a huge investment of time and resources, but later prototypes require less and less time. Eventually, through experience, copies of the model can be produced at relatively low cost.

When learning by doing is important, early entrants into the market may be able to maintain a large market share and increase their present value of profits by strategically producing significantly larger outputs early on than would be justified by short-run profit-maximizing behavior. By producing large quantities in early periods, the first firms into the market can significantly reduce their costs later. A new firm attempting to enter the market later will face a significant cost disadvantage because it will not yet have moved down its *learning curve*. In markets characterized by significant learning by doing, entry is likely to be difficult.

An illustration of a simple learning curve is:†

$$AC(q) = 10 + \frac{100}{2^{\lambda q}}, \qquad [11.1]$$

---

*In addition to the above cases, several statistical studies have suggested that first mover advantages are extremely important. For example, Robinson found that, compared with late entrants, first movers had market shares that were 23.6 percentage points higher in consumer goods markets and 17.2 percentage points higher in industrial goods markets. See William T. Robinson, "Sources of Market Pioneer Advantages: The Case of Industrial Goods," *Journal of Marketing Research* (February 1988): 87–94.

†Generally the learning curve can be thought of as:

$$AC(q) = m_0 + c_0 e^{-\lambda q},$$

where m_0 represents the minimum possible average cost, e is the base of the natural logarithmic function such that $\ln e = 1$ (e is a *transcendental number* where $e = 2.718\ldots$), and c_0 represents the cost disadvantage of a firm that produces zero units of output.

where AC(q) represents the average unit cost of production for a cumulative output of q and λ is a constant measuring the rate at which unit costs decline with volume, or the *speed of learning*. According to equation 11.1, if $\lambda = 1.5$ and $q \rightarrow \infty$ (i.e., if cumulative output approached infinity), the second term on the right-hand side would approach zero, and minimum average costs of 10 would be achieved. On the other extreme, if $\lambda = 1.5$ and if $q = 0$, then $2^{1.5q} = 1$ and average unit costs would be at the maximum of 110.

Consider the impact of the learning curve on competitive behavior. If λ is very large, average costs approach 10 very quickly for all firms and the industry will behave competitively, just as if it had constant long-run average costs of 10. When λ is very small, average costs will remain stuck around 110 for all firms, and the industry will reach a competitive equilibrium with long-run average costs of 110. It is for intermediate values of λ that the outcomes become interesting.

Figure 11.6 shows how the average cost curve in equation 11.1 is related to λ. The larger the value of λ, the more quickly average costs decline to 10. For intermediate values of λ, early entrants can create a type of absolute cost entry barrier by expanding output beyond the short-run profit-maximizing output. By producing large outputs, the first firm or firms into the market are protected from some, if not all, future potential entrants and will maintain higher long-run average

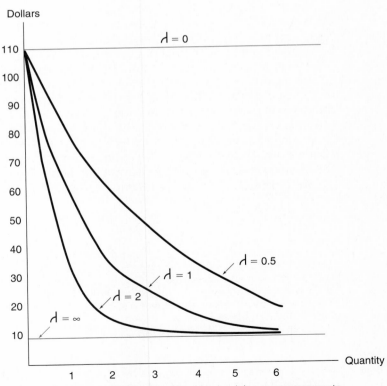

Figure 11.6 The impact of learning by doing on average costs.

market shares. Models based on the existence of learning by doing have suggested that, in markets with a moderate rate of learning, entry ceases with only a few firms (usually three or four).[13]

Learning by doing can be viewed as an investment in cost reduction. The early entrant is willing to invest in large current outputs to reduce its future costs, even if this investment significantly reduces current profits. Process-oriented research and development (R&D) expenditures may also be viewed as an investment in cost reduction. Existing firms invest in process R&D to lower future costs and gain an advantage over potential entrants. R&D is discussed at length in Chapter 14.

EMPIRICAL EVIDENCE ON LEARNING BY DOING

In industries characterized by steep learning curves, early entrants can prevent future entry by moving down the learning curve. In such industries the first mover advantage can create a permanently concentrated market. The phenomenon was first identified in the aircraft industry but has since been noted in many other markets.

Commercial Aircraft

The *learning curve* was first identified in the aircraft industry during World War II when it was discovered that with each 100 percent increase in *cumulative* output direct labor costs in hours declined by 20 percent.[14] In other words, the fourth plane required only 80 percent of the labor hours needed to produce the second plane; the twentieth plane required 80 percent of the labor hours needed to produce the tenth plane; the hundredth plane required 80 percent of the labor hours needed to produce the fiftieth plane; and so forth.

During World War I the aircraft industry expanded tremendously because of military production, but only after the war did the commercial industry become important. In the 1930s four manufacturers dominated the market: Boeing, Douglas, Lockheed, and Curtiss-Wright. When Douglas developed the DC-3, it was the best commercial aircraft available and Douglas came to dominate the market. As Table 11.1 indicates, from 1937 through 1941 Douglas held a huge market share that ranged from 85 to 98 percent.

During World War II, the commercial aircraft industry effectively ceased to exist as all productive capability was turned toward the military. Lockheed, for example, was a small factor in the commercial industry before the war. Given the government's insatiable demand for planes, a few new firms became major government suppliers during the war. Chief among these were Convair and Martin. During the war, the government required cross-licensing of patent designs, and as a result, when the war ended Lockheed, Convair, and Martin had all become viable competitors for Douglas. In the absence of the war, it is likely that Douglas would have continued to move down its learning curve and would have remained the dominant firm.

From 1948 to 1955, five producers—Douglas, Boeing, Lockheed, Convair, and Martin—jockeyed for industry leadership. Given the importance of large production runs to lower costs, it is not surprising that price competition was intense

TABLE 11.1 **Douglas's Control of the Commercial Aircraft Industry, 1936–1941**

Year	Total Aircraft Manufactured	Douglas DC-3	Douglas's Market Share (%)
1936	42	29	69
1937	54	47	87
1938	24	21	88
1939	41	40	98
1940	112	95	85
1941	36	35	97

Source: David C. Mowery and Nathan Rosenberg, "The Commercial Aircraft Industry," in Richard R. Nelson (ed.), *Government and Technical Progress: A Cross-Industry Analysis* (New York: Pergamon Press, 1982), 107.

in the postwar period.[15] In 1958 the industry underwent its next major technological breakthrough when Boeing introduced the 707 and Douglas introduced the DC-8. Competition now centered on which of these firms could expand production and move down its learning curve more quickly. As a result both firms engaged in aggressive price cutting to obtain sales. The three other firms more or less dropped out of the market, and eventually, as Table 11.2 indicates, Boeing came to dominate the industry.

Boeing continued to control the market, and in 1967 Douglas was forced to merge with McDonnell, a firm that produced a military product line, to form McDonnell-Douglas.[16] Shortly thereafter, aggressive price competition between McDonnell-Douglas and Lockheed in the market for wide-body jets left Lockheed on the verge of financial collapse. Only a $250 million government loan guarantee averted Lockheed's bankruptcy.[17]

The history of competition in the commercial aircraft industry is consistent with the strategic use of the learning curve. The key to success is to be the first firm to introduce a major technologically superior plane and to price it low enough to take advantage of the learning curve. This strategy was the key to both Douglas's early success and Boeing's later success. More recently Boeing has been locked in a battle with the European Airbus to maintain its leadership position.*

Automobiles

From 1909 until 1926, Ford followed a strategy of lowering the price of its Model T to take advantage of the learning curve. In 1908, when the Model T was first introduced at a price of $950, the least expensive Ford was priced at $850. Henry Ford was determined to dramatically increase output and cut price even without knowing what his future costs would be, so he announced his plans to eventually sell cars for $400.[18] As it turned out, Ford was able to sell the Model T for just $355 in 1921 and for $290 in 1925.[19]

---

*The Boeing–Airbus battle is discussed in detail in Chapter 23.

TABLE 11.2 **Market Shares in the Commercial Aircraft Industry, 1947–1965**

Year	Douglas	Boeing	Convair	Lockheed	Martin
1947	74.3%	0.0%	0.0%	17.1%	8.6%
1948	21.7	0.0	60.0	5.2	13.0
1949	1.7	17.2	48.3	32.8	0.0
1950	9.8	0.0	11.8	60.8	17.6
1951	47.6	0.0	0.0	23.8	28.6
1952	14.9	0.0	16.2	16.2	52.7
1953	29.1	0.0	58.3	9.4	3.1
1954	66.7	0.0	24.0	9.3	0.0
1955	38.2	0.0	3.6	43.6	0.0
1956	40.0	0.0	15.2	8.0	0.0
1957	67.0	0.0	12.8	18.4	0.0
1958	59.8	0.0	0.0	14.6	0.0
1959	10.8	30.1	0.0	57.8	0.0
1960	39.2	35.1	14.4	11.3	0.0
1961	9.6	45.6	19.2	12.0	0.0
1962	12.1	51.5	31.8	0.0	0.0
1963	8.7	69.6	21.7	0.0	0.0
1964	6.7	91.6	1.7	0.0	0.0
1965	12.6	78.5	0.0	0.0	0.0

Source: David C. Mowery and Nathan Rosenberg, "The Commercial Aircraft Industry," in Richard R. Nelson (ed.), *Government and Technical Progress: A Cross-Industry Analysis* (New York: Pergamon Press, 1982), 111.

As Ford lowered the price of the Model T, its sales and market share increased dramatically. Table 11.3 shows that its sales increased by *12,358 percent* between 1909 and 1925 compared with an increase for the remaining firms in the industry of just 1900 percent. Furthermore, Ford's profits continued to increase as it moved down the learning curve. In 1909 it took 21 days to build a Model T, by 1913 it took 14 days, and by 1921 it required just 4 days from beginning to end of the production process.[20] During this period the labor hours required to build a Model T declined by 60 percent.[21]

The Achilles heel in Ford's strategy turned out to be that the Model T's design remained essentially unchanged for eighteen years. When General Motors began producing heavier cars with closed bodies and much greater comfort, Ford was slow to respond. As a result, Ford's market share declined from 40 percent in 1925 to 10 percent in 1927. As Alfred Sloan, the person who created the strategy that catapulted GM into the leadership position, stated:[22]

> Mr. Ford . . . had frozen his policy in the Model T, . . . preeminently an open-car design. With its light chassis, it was unsuited to the heavier closed body, and so in less than two years the closed body made the already obsolescing design of the Model T noncompetitive as an engineering design. . . .

TABLE 11.3 **Sales of the Model T, 1909–1925**

Year	Price of Model T Ford	Total Ford Sales	Total Industry Sales	Ford Market Share	Ford Profits ($mil)
1909	$950	12,000	124,000	9.7%	na
1911	690	40,000	199,000	20.1	$21
1913	550	182,000	462,000	39.4	75
1915	440	342,000	896,000	38.2	74
1917	450	741,000	1,746,000	42.4	51
1919	525	664,000	1,658,000	40.0	140
1921	355	845,000	1,518,000	55.7	125
1923	295	1,669,000	3,625,000	46.0	193
1925	290	1,495,000	3,735,000	40.0	219

Source: Lawrence J. White, "The Automobile Industry," in Walter Adams, *The Structure of American Industry,* 5th edition (New York: MacMillan, 1977), p. 173; and William J. Abernathy and Kenneth Wayne, "Limits of the Learning Curve," *Harvard Business Review* (Sept/Oct 1974): 114.

The story of Ford's rise and fall in the automobile industry is remarkably similar to Douglas's rise and fall in the aircraft industry. In both cases, an early technological leader maintained its dominance by reducing price in advance of cost reductions and moving down the learning curve, only to be overtaken by later technological developments. In recent years this same scenario played itself out in the semiconductor market.

Semiconductors

The semiconductor industry is a high-tech industry in which the learning curve has long been recognized as important. New products are priced very close to manufacturing costs to take advantage of the learning curve, and the first firm into a new product line tends to gain a significant cost advantage. In 1976 Motorola executive Robert R. Heikes described the competitive environment as follows:[23]

> The frightening thing in this business is that if you're not first—or a fast second or third—you're in trouble. . . . If you come in a year late, you'd better have a much improved version or a new process that permits you to make the product more cheaply.

One example of the importance of the learning curve in the semiconductor industry is Intel's 1971 introduction of the 1024-bit random access memory (RAM) integrated circuit. The Intel 1024-bit RAM was initially priced at $28.00 per unit; by April 1974 the price had declined to between $3.00 and $4.00 per unit.[24] The learning curve has forced firms to price for market share and to anticipate dramatic cost reductions as output increases.

Product Proliferation

Product proliferation refers to the strategic decision to preempt potential entrants by creating brands to fill every available product niche. Have you ever wondered why, for example, there are so many different varieties of cereal, almost all produced by Kellogg's, General Mills, or General Foods (Post) or so many different varieties of beer, most produced by Busch or Miller? Economists theorize that by filling many different niches in the market for cereal or beer, the incumbents are able to prevent potential entrants from gaining even a small foothold in the industry.[25]

Because even a simple game theoretic analysis of this strategy can become complicated, a detailed examination is presented in advanced topics Chapter 12. The intuition behind the product proliferation model presented in Chapter 12 is best understood from the viewpoint of a dominant incumbent such as Kellogg's or Budweiser. Essentially the optimal strategy for the dominant firm is to enter a new niche (such as "sugar-frosted grape-flavored corn flakes") just before it is profitable for a potential entrant to enter that niche. By entering at precisely that moment, the dominant incumbent is able to preempt entry and earn greater long-run profits than it would earn if it permitted entry.

Suppose, for example, that a potential entrant into the sugar-frosted grape-flavored corn flakes market knows that if it does not enter the grape-flavored corn flakes market by time $t = 10$, Kellogg's will find it profitable to enter at $t = 10$ and thereby freeze the potential entrant out of the market. The potential entrant must therefore try to preempt Kellogg's by entering at some time earlier than $t = 10$, say $t = 10 - \epsilon$. Knowing this, Kellogg's must try to preempt the potential entrant by entering at an even earlier time, perhaps $t = 10 - 2\epsilon$. Of course, such a game regresses backward to a point at which Kellogg's enters the market just infinitesimally before it is profitable for the entrant to enter at all. This is the only solution to the game. Kellogg's enters before it is profitable for the potential entrant to enter and preempts the potential entrant from the grape-flavored corn flakes market. In this manner, Kellogg's maintains its monopoly.

EMPIRICAL EVIDENCE ON THE USE OF PRODUCT PROLIFERATION

It does not take an economist to detect industries that appear full of products in every niche. Commonly cited examples include the ready-to-eat cereal, beer, safety razor, canned soup, and laundry detergent markets.

Ready-to-Eat Cereals

The ready-to-eat (RTE) cereal market is the most commonly used example of product proliferation. In this industry, the six leading manufacturers (Kellogg's, General Mills, General Foods [Post], Quaker, Nabisco, and Ralston) increased the number of brands from twenty-six in 1950 to eighty in 1973.[26] During that twenty-three-year period, eighty-four new brands were introduced, but thirty did not survive.[27]

The rate of introduction increased somewhat over time as follows:[28]

Period	New Brands Introduced
1950–55	8
1956–60	15
1961–65	22
1966–70	19
1971–73	20

The new brands typically took market share away from older, established brands. Corn flakes, which accounted for 33 percent of sales in 1940, accounted for only 10.8 percent in 1972, and only 6.8 percent in 1982. Furthermore, the average market share per RTE cereal brand declined from 4 percent in 1950 to just 1.3 percent in 1972.[29]

Between 1950 and 1972, Kellogg's introduced twenty-four new brands, General Mills introduced thirty-four, and General Foods introduced twenty-one.[30] Most of these new brands achieved only small market shares. In fact, only seven new brands ever achieved market shares exceeding 2 percent.*

The only attempt by new competitors to enter the RTE cereal market occurred in the early 1970s.[31] One niche that had previously gone unfilled was the "natural cereal" niche. Natural cereals or granolas were generally sold only in health food stores. In the 1970s, Pet, Pillsbury, and Colgate all entered, with some initial success. Pet's Heartland cereal reached almost a 2 percent market share in 1974.[32] The initial success of the intruders led to a response by the major firms. In 1973 Quaker responded first with the introduction of Quaker 100% Natural Cereal. General Mills followed with Nature Valley and Kellogg's with Country Morning. As a result, Heartland's sales plummeted to just 0.1 percent in 1980, and Pillsbury and Colgate left the market. In the long run only Quaker 100% Natural Cereal has left a lasting mark on the industry.[33]

One complicating factor in the cereal industry is that launching a new cereal brand requires huge advertising expenditures. It is possible, therefore, that Kellogg's was able to maintain its dominant share because of lower advertising expenditures per dollar of sales, which resulted in a first-mover advantage.[34] Table 11.4 indicates that Kellogg's had consistently lower advertising costs than its two major competitors.

---

*The seven brands introduced between 1950 and 1972 that achieved at least a 2 percent market share were: Kellogg's Frosted Flakes (peak market share of 6.3 percent in 1971); Kellogg's Special K (4.1 percent in 1971); General Foods' Post Alpha Bits (2.7 percent in 1959); General Mills' Total (2.6 percent in 1967); Quaker Cap'n Crunch (2.4 percent in 1965); Quaker Life (2.0 percent in 1966); and General Mills' Jets (2.1 percent in 1955). *Federal Trade Commission* v. *Kellogg et al.,* Docket No. 8883, 99 FTC Reporter 8 (1982), §589.

TABLE 11.4 **RTE Cereal Advertising to Sales Ratio, 1958–1972**

Year	Kellogg	General Mills	General Foods
1958	14.57%	18.47%	16.09%
1959	17.23	22.56	15.92
1960	16.26	17.43	14.81
1961	15.42	20.15	13.49
1962	15.21	18.43	14.71
1963	15.19	20.57	15.30
1964	15.23	20.19	16.99
1965	16.61	22.38	18.62
1966	15.72	19.81	20.98
1967	15.56	20.69	22.09
1968	12.08	17.25	18.43
1969	12.09	16.05	15.39
1970	10.60	13.23	16.34
1971	9.74	12.72	14.67
1972	9.39	14.76	13.78
15-year averages	14.06%	18.31%	16.50%

Source: *Federal Trade Commission* v. *Kellogg et al.,* Docket No. 8883, 99 *FTC Reporter* 8 (1982), 430.

In 1982, Kellogg's continued to lead the industry with a 39 percent share followed by General Mills with 21 percent, General Foods with 16 percent, and Quaker Oats with 9 percent.[35] One reasonable interpretation of the evidence is that Kellogg's initially relied on a first mover advantage to establish its dominance in the basic brands such as Corn Flakes and Rice Krispies, and later used a brand proliferation strategy to maintain its dominant position.[36] In recent years Campbell's appears to be following a similar strategy in soups.[37]

Campbell's Canned Soups and Other Products

We noted earlier that Campbell's established its dominance in the American canned soup market through a policy of heavy advertising. Recently, however, that policy has been augmented by a *product proliferation* strategy. Campbell's is now trying to fill not only every national soup niche, but regional niches as well. In Texas and California, for example, Campbell's makes a spicier nacho cheese soup than it does anywhere else.[38] In 1987, it marketed a Creole soup in Southern markets and a red-bean soup in some Hispanic markets.

Campbell's is creating new brands not only in soups these days. It introduced more than 400 new products in the five-year period between 1981 and 1985.[39] In some cases it introduced entirely new product lines, in an attempt to fill a variety of niches at once. Examples include a full line of Prego spaghetti sauces and Le Menu frozen dinners.

Statistical Evidence on Product Proliferation

Statistical evidence on the use of product proliferation is limited. In one important study, however, John Connor investigated the use of the strategy in the food products industry.[40] Connor used data in *Advertising Age* magazine to identify all new brands in the food products industry for the years 1977 and 1978. The sample included 419 new products introduced into 102 product classes. New products and new flavor varieties were included, but new package sizes and designs were excluded. The ten most active product lines were:[41]

Product Category	*New Products 1977 and 1978*
1. Nonalcoholic beverages and mixes	70
2. Alcoholic beverages	49
3. Pet foods	39
4. Flour mixes and baking ingredients	38
5. Frozen foods	30
6. Candy and chewing gum	27
7. Canned fruits, vegetables, and specials	26
8. Breakfast cereals	24
9. Tobacco products	23
10. Dehydrated vegetables and soup mixes	20

Of the 419 new products, 59 percent were marketed by the top fifty food or tobacco firms and 70 percent came from the top 200 firms.[42]

Connor also tested a number of hypotheses using regression analysis. One regression result of particular interest was:[43]

$$\text{NEWPROD} = -26.60 + 0.37^b \text{ CR4} - 0.003^b \text{ CR4SQ}$$
$$(2.17) \qquad (-2.01)$$

$$+ 0.96^a \text{ ADS} + 2.16^a \text{ SIZE} + 0.13^a \text{ PACKCOST}$$
$$(3.36) \qquad (4.50) \qquad (4.38)$$

$$R^2 = .45,$$

where NEWPROD is the number of new products introduced in the product category; CR4 is the four-firm concentration ratio; CR4SQ is the square of the four-firm concentration ratio;* ADS is the advertising to sales ratio of the top four firms in the product category; SIZE is the wholesale shipments value; and PACK-COST is percentage of production costs incurred for packaging materials. An "a" superscript indicates the coefficient is statistically significant at the 1 percent level and a "b" superscript indicates the coefficient is statistically significant at the 5 percent level. The t-statistics are in parentheses. Connor used many other independent variables, such as research and development intensity and the rate of growth of demand, but none were statistically significant.

Connor's regression result suggests that product proliferation is in fact more common in concentrated industries. The negative effect of CR4SQ suggests that, for small values of concentration, the relationship between the number of new products and concentration is positive, but for larger values of concentration the relationship between the number of new products and concentration is negative.[†] This suggests that when concentration becomes large either all product niches have already been filled or product proliferation is less necessary to protect the leading firms' market shares. The advertising to sales ratio, ADS, is used as a proxy for product differentiation and is significantly positive. Greater product differentiation does indeed result in greater product proliferation, holding other things

---

*The use of the square of concentration tests whether a *linear* or *nonlinear* relationship exists between concentration and the number of new products introduced. Consider for example the following hypothetical regression result:

$$y = 12 + 2x - \frac{1}{4}x^2,$$

Which graphs as:

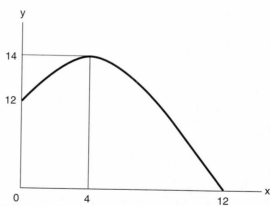

Figure F11.1 Graph of the nonlinear relationship $y = 12 + 2x - \frac{1}{4}x^2$.

This graph shows that the relationship between the dependent variable y and the independent variable x is nonlinear because of the significant *negative* coefficient on the squared term. For values of x < 4 the relationship between y and x is *positive*, but for values of x > 4 the relationship is *negative*.

[†]See the previous footnote.

equal.* The statistical significance of SIZE suggests that in industries with larger demands there is "room" for more product proliferation. Finally, the PACKCOST variable may be interpreted as a proxy for the ease with which brands can be physically differentiated from each other through the use of packaging. Connor concluded by noting that:[44]

> The results reported here for the food-manufacturing industries provide empirical support for the market structure-conduct linkage suggested by [the product proliferation] model. Product proliferation is one of several forms of business conduct open to firms in oligopolistic industries with differentiated products, but it appears to be a widespread strategy in the food industries.

A significant amount of empirical evidence suggests the use of product proliferation as an entry-deterring strategy. Based on the theoretical and empirical evidence, it seems fair to conclude that the combination of heavy advertising and product proliferation can significantly reduce the rate of entry into an industry.

Empirical Evidence on the Use of Price and Nonprice Strategies to Deter Entry

Chapters 10 and 11 suggested a number of strategic methods of maintaining long-run market dominance, including:

1. Limit pricing
2. Establishing a "tough" reputation (the threat of predatory pricing)
3. Creating excess capacity
4. Raising rivals' costs (e.g., advertising costs)
5. Utilizing learning by doing
6. Product proliferation (filling product niches)

Robert Smiley devised a business questionnaire to examine how often each method of deterrence was used. Smiley's results were based on 294 responses from product managers of major corporations.[45] The product managers were asked to rate on a scale from 1 to 5 the degree to which different entry-deterring strategies were used in their product markets. Smiley's results are shown in Table 11.5.[46]

The most striking finding was that the strategic use of advertising and product proliferation was common in both new and existing product markets. For both new and existing product lines, 78 percent of respondents claimed that advertising was used at least occasionally to deter entry. Limit pricing and excess capacity appeared to be the least used strategies, but even these were used in a substantial number of markets. For example, 36 percent of the new product respondents and 53 percent of existing product respondents reported at least occasional use of limit

---

*This study, and others like it, have been severely criticized by some economists because of the use of advertising to proxy product differentiation, and the resulting conclusion that increased advertising and increased product differentiation *cause* increased product proliferation. This ignores the distinct and at least as likely possibility that increased product proliferation *causes* increased advertising and increased product differentiation. Given that important caveat, the results of the regression are presented as Connor reported them.

TABLE 11.5 **Smiley's Entry Deterrence Strategy Study, Frequency of Use of Different Strategies**

	New Products				
	Frequently	Occ./Freq.	Occasionally	Never/Occ.	Never
1. Excess capacity	6%	16%	20%	22%	36%
2. Advertising	32	30	16	17	5
3. R&D strategies	31	25	15	12	17
4. Tough reputation	10	17	27	24	23
5. Limit pricing to prevent all entry	2	4	17	34	44
6. Limit pricing to "slow" rate of entry	3	8	21	33	35
7. Use learning-by-doing	9	17	29	27	18

	Existing Products				
	Frequently	Occ./Freq.	Occasionally	Never/Occ.	Never
1. Excess capacity	7%	14%	17%	32%	30%
2. Advertising	24	28	26	14	7
3. R&D strategies	11	20	16	31	23
4. Tough reputation	8	19	22	31	21
5. Limit pricing to prevent all entry	7	15	21	32	25
6. Limit pricing to "slow" rate of entry	6	14	21	32	27
7. Product proliferation-filling niches	26	31	22	14	6
8. Hide profits	31	28	20	10	12

Source: Robert Smiley, "Empirical Evidence on Strategic Entry Deterrence," *International Journal of Industrial Organization* 6 (1980): 172.

pricing.[47] Smiley also reported that 54 percent of new product respondents and 58 percent of existing product respondents reported frequent use of at least one strategy and that 89 percent of new product and 98 percent of existing product respondents reported at least occasional use of some strategy.[48]

Respondents were also asked the following open-ended question, "Have you observed any other activities that appear to be designed primarily to prevent or slow entry?" In order of frequency of response, respondents noted the following strategies:[49]

1. Sign long-term contracts with customers, middlemen, or wholesalers.
2. Have product specifications or controlling regulations designed so that only your product qualifies.

3. React aggressively when a new entrant is in the promotion stage, especially with wholesalers and retailers, thereby denying them reliable information about their new product's steady-state profitability.
4. Keep products or processes secret as long as possible.
5. Make preemptive purchases of all available raw materials or supplies.
6. Make early sales to critical buyers–opinion leaders.
7. Announce the product long before it is ready.

Smiley's study suggests that entry deterrence should be of more than theoretical interest to economists. In fact, fully 54 percent of respondents rated entry deterrence as "at least as important" as other strategic marketing and production decisions in the "grand scheme of things."[50]

One final point with regard to Smiley's study is worth noting. Modern industrial organization is sometimes criticized because different theoretical models that, on the surface, appear to be quite similar yield dramatically different results. For example, compare the outcome in the basic Cournot quantity game with the outcome in the basic Bertrand price game in Chapter 7. The Smiley study provides evidence that in the real world firms use many different methods to deter entry, and at least two of these methods appear on the surface to be diametrically opposed: keeping products or processes secret as long as possible, and announcing the product long before it is ready. Both of these strategies were used by real-world firms to achieve the same end. Here is an example of an empirical survey supporting the proliferation of theory in industrial organization. In the real world slightly different circumstances result in very different strategies, and so it is in theory as well.

SUMMARY

1. Game theorists have concentrated on models that result in credible threats of retaliation. These models suggest that there are several ways of credibly deterring entry, including predatory pricing, the building of excess capacity, raising rivals' costs, product proliferation, and first mover advantages associated with the learning curve.
2. Excess capacity can create a credible entry deterrent, but it may result in large profit sacrifices for the incumbent.
3. A number of methods of raising rivals' costs have been suggested. One is to lobby the government to impose an increase in costs. Another is to increase advertising to force competitors to advertise more.
4. If learning by doing is important, early entrants into the market may be able to maintain a large market share and increase their present value of profits by strategically producing significantly larger outputs early on than would be justified by short-run profit-maximizing behavior.
5. By filling many different niches in the market, incumbents may be able to prevent potential entrants from gaining even a small foothold in an industry. This practice is called *product proliferation*.

> 6. Empirical evidence suggests that firms use many different types of entry-deterrence strategies. The most common strategies appear to be heavy advertising, product proliferation, and investment in research and development. Far fewer firms use limit pricing or the building of excess capacity.

KEY TERMS

excess capacity

first-mover advantage

learning by doing

product proliferation

raising rivals' costs

DISCUSSION QUESTIONS

1. As a firm's discount rate *increases,* is it more or less likely to build excess capacity to deter entry? Explain.

2. The Federal Aviation Administration (FAA) sets safety standards for commercial airlines in the United States. Would you expect the major carriers, such as American Airlines and United Airlines, to fight the FAA's attempts to require costly additional safety features on commercial aircraft? Explain your reasoning.

3. Can you identify a case of learning by doing in your life experience? Was the speed of learning slow or fast?

4. Identify three markets in which product proliferation appears to be important. Would you categorize concentration in these markets as low, moderate, or high? What does this suggest about the effect of product proliferation?

5. Sometimes a dominant firm fails to fill an important niche in an industry before a competitor does. Can you identify a dominant firm that lost considerable market share because it failed to fill an important market niche?

6. Based on Smiley's findings, which strategies appear to be most commonly used by firms to deter entry? What strategies are least commonly employed? Are these findings consistent with the theory presented in Chapters 10 and 11?

PROBLEMS

1. In Fig. 11.1, the incumbent produces output with a SRAC curve that minimizes cost at Q_2. Why doesn't the incumbent produce with a SRAC curve that minimizes cost at Q_{LP}?

2. Consider the following extensive form of a game of entry. The numbers in parentheses represent the dominant firm's profits and the potential entrant's profits, respectively.

```
                          Dominant    ┌──SR Profit Maximizing      (2,500, 0)
          ┌─ Stay Out ────Firm────────┤
          │   at t = 0               └──Limit Price                (450, 0)
Potential │
Entrant───┤
at t = 0  │
          │                Dominant    ┌──SR Profit Maximizing      (1,000, 500)
          └─ Enter ────────Firm────────┤
              at t = 0                  │
                                        │
                                       └──Aggressive                (450, Loss)
```

What is the current solution to this game?

Suppose the dominant firm knows that for every dollar it spends on net advertising costs, an entrant would have to spend 2 dollars to maintain its relative market position. How much would the incumbent have to spend on advertising to prevent entry? What would be the solution to this new game?

3. Suppose q represents cumulative firm output and λ is a positive constant measuring the speed of learning. Long-run average costs are:

$$\text{LRAC}(q) = 50 + \frac{100}{10^{\lambda q}}$$

   a. If $\lambda = 0$ what would be the long-run equilibrium price in this industry?

   b. If $\lambda = \infty$ what would be the long-run equilibrium price in this industry?

   c. Would you anticipate that there would be more firms in this industry if $\lambda = 0$ or if $\lambda = 1$? Explain.

REFERENCES

1. For an early treatment see John T. Wenders, "Excess Capacity as a Barrier to Entry," *Journal of Industrial Economics* 20 (November 1971): 14–9; John T. Wenders, "Collusion and Entry," *Journal of Political Economy* 79 (Nov/Dec 1971): 1258–77. For later treatments see A. Michael Spence, "Entry Capacity, Investment and Oligopoly Pricing," *Bell Journal of Economics* 8 (Autumn 1977): 534–44; Avinash Dixit, "A Model of Duopoly Suggesting a Theory of Entry Barriers," *Bell Journal of Economics* 10 (Spring 1979): 20–32; Jeremy Bulow, John Geanakoplos, and Paul Klemperer, "Holding Idle Capacity to Deter Entry," *Economic Journal* 95 (March 1985): 178–82; Marius Schwartz and Michael Baumann, "Entry-Deterrence Externalities and Relative Firm Size," *International Journal of Industrial Organization* 6 (June 1988): 181–97; David I. Rosenbaum "An Empirical Test of the Effect of Excess Capacity in Price Setting, Capacity-Constrained Supergames," *International Journal of Industrial Organization* 7 (June 1989): 231–41; Pankaj Ghemawat, "The Snowball Effect," *International Journal of Industrial Organization* 8 (September 1990): 335–51; Elizabeth A. Hall, "An Analysis of Preemptive Behavior in the Titanium Dioxide Industry," *International Journal of Industrial Organization* 8 (September 1990): 469–84; and Beth Allen, "Ca-

pacity Precommitment as an Entry Barrier for Price-Setting Firms," *International Journal of Industrial Organization* 11 (March 1993): 63–72. For conclusions that run against conventional wisdom see Jean-Pierre Benoît and Vijay Krishna, "Entry Deterrence and Dynamic Competition," *International Journal of Industrial Organization* 9 (December 1991): 477–95; and A.M. McGahan, "The Effect of Incomplete Information about Demand on Preemption," *International Journal of Industrial Organization* 11 (September 1993): 327–46.

2. *United States* v. *Aluminum Company of America,* 148 F.2d 416 (1945).

3. See Thomas G. Krattenmaker and Steven C. Salop, "Anticompetitive Exclusion: Raising Rivals' Costs to Achieve Power Over Price," *Yale Law Journal* 96 (1986): 209–93; Steven C. Salop and David T. Scheffman, "Cost-Raising Strategies," *Journal of Industrial Economics* 36 (1987): 19–34; Scott M. Fuess, Jr., and Mark A. Lowenstein, "On Strategic Cost Increases in a Duopoly," *International Journal of Industrial Organization* 9 (June 1991): 389–95.

4. For an example taken from the United States margarine market see John Sutton, *Sunk Costs and Market Structure* (Cambridge, MA: MIT Press, 1991) pp. 213–4.

5. John Cubbin, "Advertising and the Theory of Entry Barriers," *Economica* 48 (April 1981): 289–98; Richard Schmalensee, "Product Differentiation Advantages of Pioneering Brands," *American Economic Review* 72 (June 1982): 349–65; and A. Michael Spence, "Notes on Advertising, Economies of Scale, and Entry Barriers," *Quarterly Journal of Economics* 56 (November 1980): 472–5.

6. Sutton, *op.cit.,* pp. 207–9.

7. *Ibid.,* p. 209.

8. *Ibid.,* p. 210.

9. The market shares in this section are taken from Sutton, *ibid.,* p. 220.

10. Lawrence J. White, "Applications of the Merger Guidelines: The Proposed Merger of Coca-Cola and Dr. Pepper," in John E. Kwoka, Jr. and Lawrence J. White (eds.), *The Antitrust Revolution* (Glenview, IL: Scott, Foresman and Company, 1989), p. 82.

11. See "Battery Makers See Surge in Competition," *The Wall Street Journal* (November 30, 1987): 8; and *The Wall Street Journal* (April 10, 1990): B1 and B5.

12. For explanations of the theory see Jack Hirshleifer, "The Firm's Cost Function: A Successful Reconstruction?" *Journal of*

Business 35 (July 1962): 235–55; Kenneth J. Arrow, "The Economic Implications of Learning by Doing," *Review of Economic Studies* 29 (April 1962): 155–73; L.E. Preston and E.C. Keachie, "Cost Functions and Progress Functions: An Integration," *American Economic Review* 54 (March 1964): 100–6; Sherwin Rosen, "Learning by Experience as Joint Production," *Quarterly Journal of Economics* 86 (August 1972): 366–82; Karl F. Habermeier, "The Learning Curve and Competition: A Stochastic Model of Duopolistic Rivalry," *International Journal of Industrial Organization* 10 (September 1992): 369–92; and Clement G. Krouse, "Market Rivalry and Learning-by-Doing," *International Journal of Industrial Organization* 12 (December 1994): 437–56

13. A. Michael Spence, "The Learning Curve and Competition," *Bell Journal of Economics* 12 (Spring 1981): 62.

14. Frank J. Andress, "The Learning Curve as a Production Tool," *Harvard Business Review* 32 (Jan/Feb 1954): 87–8.

15. David C. Mowery and Nathan Rosenberg, "The Commercial Aircraft Industry," in Richard R. Nelson (ed.), *Government and Technical Progress: A Cross-Industry Analysis* (New York: Pergamon Press, 1982), pp. 109–13.

16. *Ibid.,* p. 113.

17. *Ibid.*

18. William J. Abernathy and Kenneth Wayne, "Limits of the Learning Curve," *Harvard Business Review* 52 (Sept/Oct 1974): 112.

19. Lawrence J. White, "The Automobile Industry," in Walter Adams (ed.), *The Structure of American Industry* (New York: MacMillan, 1977), p. 173.

20. William J. Abernathy and Kenneth Wayne, *op.cit.,* p. 113.

21. *Ibid.*

22. *Ibid.,* p. 114.

23. "New Leaders in Semiconductors," *Business Week* (March 1, 1976): 43.

24. "The Complexities of Electronics Pricing," *Business Week* (April 6, 1974): 44–5.

25. See Richard Schmalensee, "Entry Deterrence in the Ready-to-Eat Breakfast Cereal Industry," *Bell Journal of Economics* 9 (1978): 305–27; Bruce L. Benson, "Increasing Product Variety and Rising Prices," *Review of Industrial Organization* 5 (1990): 31–52; Chong Ju Choi and Carlo Scarpa, "Credible Spatial Preemption Through Reputation Extension," *International Journal of Industrial Organization* 10 (September 1992): 439–47; and Ruth S. Raubitschek, "Hitting the Jackpot: Product Proliferation

by Multiproduct Firms Under Uncertainty," *International Journal of Industrial Organization* 6 (December 1988): 469–88.

26. *Federal Trade Commission* v. *Kellogg et al.,* Docket No. 8883, 99 FTC Reporter 8 (1982) §581.
27. *Ibid.*
28. *Ibid.*
29. *Federal Trade Commission* v. *Kellogg et al.,* Docket No. 8883, 99 FTC Reporter 8 (1982), §582; and F.M. Scherer, "The Breakfast Cereal Industry," in Walter Adams (ed.), *The Structure of American Industry,* 7th Edition (New York: MacMillan, 1986), p. 178.
30. *Federal Trade Commission* v. *Kellogg et al.,* Docket No. 8883, 99 FTC Reporter 8 (1982), §585.
31. F.M. Scherer, "The Breakfast Cereal Industry," in Walter Adams, *The Structure of American Industry,* 7th edition (New York: MacMillan, 1986), pp. 181–2.
32. *Ibid.,* p. 182.
33. *Ibid.*
34. Sutton, *op.cit.,* pp. 235-6.
35. F.M. Scherer, *supra* note 31, p. 176.
36. Sutton, *op.cit.,* Chapter 10, pp. 227–47.
37. "Marketing's New Look: Campbell Leads a Revolution in the Way Consumer Products Are Sold," *Business Week* (January 26, 1987): 64–9.
38. *Ibid.,* p. 64.
39. *Ibid.,* p. 67.
40. John M. Connor, "Food Product Proliferation: A Market Structure Analysis," *American Journal of Agricultural Economics* 63 (November 1981): 607–17.
41. *Ibid.,* p. 613.
42. *Ibid.*
43. *Ibid.,* p. 614.
44. *Ibid.,* p. 615.
45. Robert Smiley, "Empirical Evidence on Strategic Entry Deterrence," *International Journal of Industrial Organization* 6 (1980): 170.
46. Note in Table 11.5 that "hiding profits" was cited by many respondents as an entry-deterring strategy. For an explanation of this strategy see Nils-Henrik Mørch von der Fehr, "How Entry Threats Induce Slack," *International Journal of Industrial Organization* 10 (June 1992): 231–49.
47. Smiley, *op.cit.,* p. 174.
48. *Ibid.,* p. 174.
49. *Ibid.,* pp. 174–5.
50. *Ibid.,* p.177.

Chapter 12

Advanced Games of Strategic Deterrence: Extensions of the Limit Pricing and Product Proliferation Models

The preceding two chapters explored the basic theory of strategic deterrence and introduced the limit pricing and product proliferation models. In this chapter we expand those two models to gain a more detailed understanding of precisely how economists have developed models of strategic deterrence. Students interested in exploring game theory in more detail will find this chapter particularly helpful. The analysis here does not require advanced mathematical knowledge beyond that required in the rest of the text, but to understand this chapter, it is necessary to first read Chapters 10 and 11.

Limit Pricing Revisited, or Can Limit Pricing Theory Be Saved?

Chapter 10 showed that in models with symmetric information, predatory pricing is not a reasonable strategy. It also revealed that in the presence of asymmetric information, predatory pricing might be a viable strategy. Milgrom and Roberts have demonstrated that with asymmetric information, **limit pricing** might also be a reasonable strategic decision.[1] The information structure in the Milgrom and Roberts model presented below is *imperfect*, certain, *asymmetric*, and *incomplete*.

Figure 12.1 shows Firm 1 as an established monopolist with demand curve $P = 100 - Q$ and either high costs of production HAC = HMC = 25 or low costs of production LAC = LMC = 10.[2] Nature moves first and chooses the monopolist

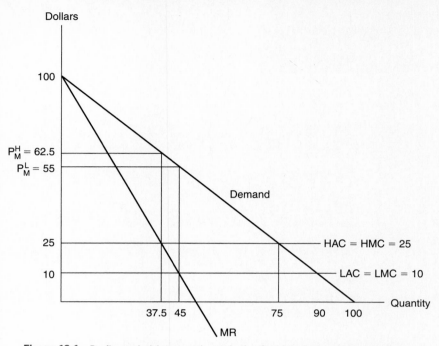

Figure 12.1   Profit-maximizing quantity and price for high-cost and low-cost firms.

to be either high-cost or low-cost. The probability that the monopolist is a high-cost producer (HAC = HMC = 25) is ρ_H, and the probability that the monopolist is a low-cost producer (LAC = LMC = 10) is $(1 - \rho_H)$. Based on Figure 12.1, a high-cost producer maximizes short-run first period profits by charging $P_M^H = 62.50$, and a low-cost producer maximizes short-run first period profits by charging $P_M^L = 55$. The model is a two-period model, and only the monopolist knows whether it is a high- or low-cost producer in period 1.

Firm 2 is a potential entrant, and before entering it has no knowledge concerning whether the monopolist is a high-cost or low-cost producer. If Firm 2 enters in period 2, however, it learns about the monopolist's costs immediately. Assume that Firm 2 produces output with the following costs:

$$TC_2 = 550 + 25q_2.$$

Therefore, Firm 2's marginal costs are 25 and its fixed costs are 550. Further assume that Firm 2 has an incentive to enter if, and only if, the monopolist is a high-cost producer, that is:

$$\pi_2^H > 0 > \pi_2^L,$$

where π_2^H represents Firm 2's profits in period 2 after entry if the monopolist is a high-cost producer, and π_2^L represents Firm 2's profits in period 2 after entry if the monopolist is a low-cost producer. With complete information, the potential entrant would enter only if the monopolist is a high-cost producer.

To maintain its monopoly, Firm 1 needs to convince the potential entrant that it is a low-cost monopolist, regardless of whether it actually is a low-cost producer. The problem for the monopolist is that it cannot directly inform the potential entrant that it is a low-cost firm, even if it is, until after the potential entrant enters the market.* The monopolist, however, may send a signal to the potential entrant that it is a low-cost producer by charging a low price.

The two types of equilibria in the Milgrom and Roberts model are a **separating equilibrium** and a **pooling equilibrium**. Under a separating equilibrium, high-cost and low-cost monopolists charge different prices in period 1, and therefore, the monopolist's price in period 1 fully reveals whether it is a high- or low-cost producer. Under a pooling equilibrium, high-cost and low-cost monopolists charge the same price in period 1, and therefore, the potential entrant learns nothing about the monopolist's costs unless it enters.

We will analyze the more complex separating equilibrium first. In Figure 12.1 the market demand curve in each period was identified as $P = 100 - Q$. In the absence of a threat of entry, a high-cost monopolist would maximize profits by charging $P_M^H = 62.50$, and a low-cost monopolist would maximize profits by charging $P_M^L = 55$.

The following analysis assumes that if entry occurs, the monopolist and potential entrant reach a Cournot-Nash equilibrium. If entry occurs and the monopolist is a high-cost firm, then the Cournot-Nash equilibrium in period 2 yields $q_1 = q_2 = 25$, total output $Q = 50$, and $P = 50$.† If the monopolist is a low-cost producer, then with entry in period 2, $q_1 = 35$, $q_2 = 20$, total quantity $Q = 55$, and $P = 45$.‡ The entrant's profits depend critically on whether the monopolist is a high-cost or low-cost firm. If the monopolist is a high-cost producer, then Firm 2's profits in period 2 would be:

---

*Any attempt by the monopolist to inform the potential entrant directly that it is a low-cost firm would simply not be believed because a rational potential entrant would know that a high-cost monopolist would have a tremendous incentive to lie about its costs.

†Recall from Chapter 7 that because both firms produce with $MC = 25$, the Cournot-Nash equilibrium quantity is two-thirds of the competitive quantity. With $MC = 25$, the competitive quantity is 75 and the Cournot-Nash total quantity equals 50.

‡Recall from Chapter 7 that the monopolist's reaction curve is derived as follows:

$$MR_1 = (100 - q_2) - 2q_1 = 10 = MC_1.$$

Solving for q_1 yields:

$$q_1 = 45 - \frac{1}{2}q_2.$$

With higher marginal cost of 25, the entrant's reaction curve is:

$$MR_2 = (100 - q_1) - 2q_2 = 25 = MC_2.$$

Solving for q_2 yields:

$$q_2 = 37.5 - \frac{1}{2}q_1.$$

The two reactions functions intersect where $q_1 = 35$ and $q_2 = 20$.

$$\pi_2^H = TR_2 - TC_2 = q_2P - (550 + 25q_2)$$
$$= 25(50) - [550 + 25(25)] = 1250 - 550 - 625 = 75 > 0 .$$

If the monopolist is a low-cost producer, then Firm 2's profits in period 2 would be:

$$\pi_2^L = TR_2 - TC_2 = q_2P - (550 + 25q_2)$$
$$= 20(45) - [550 + 25(20)] = 900 - 550 - 500 = -150 < 0 .$$

Because $\pi_2^H > 0 > \pi_2^L$, the decision to enter depends critically on the potential entrant's beliefs concerning ρ_H, the probability that the monopolist is a high-cost producer. Under complete information, the potential entrant would enter if the monopolist were a high-cost firm and stay out if the monopolist were a low-cost firm.

Suppose that we define P* as a price that will definitely deter entry. What would be the characteristics of P*? P* must be low enough that a high-cost monopolist would *never* reduce its price to P* to deter entry. In other words, a high-cost monopolist might charge a price P > P* in an attempt to send a false signal to the potential entrant that the monopolist was a low-cost firm, but it would never set a price P = P*.

We will show that no rational high-cost monopolist would ever lower its price to P* = 35, but that a high-cost monopolist might lower its price to 36. Consider P* = 35 and Q = 65. A price of P* = 35 in the first period would deter entry and result in the profit-maximizing price of 62.50 in the second period. Assume that the monopolist has a 10 percent discount rate. If Π_1^M and Π_2^M represent the monopolist's profits in periods 1 and 2, then a first period price of 35 would result in the following total profits for a high-cost monopolist:

$$\Pi = \Pi_1^M + \Pi_2^M = 65\,(35 - 25) + \frac{37.5\,(62.5 - 25)}{1.1}$$
$$= 650 + 1278.41 = 1928.41$$

Instead of charging P = 35, the high-cost monopolist could charge $P_M^H = 62.5$ in the first period, permit entry, charge the Cournot-Nash price P = 50 in the second period, and earn total profits:

$$\Pi = \Pi_1^M + \Pi_2^M = 37.5\,(62.5 - 25) + \frac{25\,(50 - 25)}{1.1}$$
$$= 1406.25 + 568.18 = 1974.43.$$

Because 1974.43 > 1928.41, the high-cost monopolist with a 10 percent discount rate would maximize short-run profits and permit entry rather than charging a price of 35 to deter entry. *No high-cost monopolist would, therefore, ever lower price to 35.*

A price of 36 yields a different conclusion. If the high-cost monopolist set P = 36 and successfully deterred entry, then total profits would be:

$$\Pi = \Pi_1^M + \Pi_2^M = 64\,(36 - 25) + \frac{37.5\,(62.5 - 25)}{1.1}$$
$$= 704 + 1278.41 = 1982.41.$$

Because 1982.41 > 1974.43, a high-cost monopolist might rationally charge a price of P = 36 to deter entry. Potential entrants know that it would be rational for the high-cost monopolist to try to deter entry by charging a price of 36. Therefore, potential entrants may not be deterred by a price of 36; they might believe that the monopolist is a high-cost firm *pretending* to be a low-cost firm.

What should the high-cost monopolist do? Because a price P* = 35 yields less profit than $P_M^H = 62.5$ and because a price P = 36 may not deter entry, the high-cost monopolist maximizes short-run profits and permits entry. The high-cost firm *does not engage in limit pricing*.

But what if the monopolist is a low-cost producer? If it charges $P_M^L = 55$, the potential entrant might think it was a high-cost producer trying to fool the potential entrant into thinking it is a low-cost producer. If the low-cost monopolist charges P* = 35, then the potential entrant knows with certainty that it is a low-cost producer because no rational high-cost producer would ever charge a price of 35. If the low-cost monopolist charges P* = 35, it will deter entry. This will be a rational strategy for the low-cost monopolist as long as the low-cost monopolist's profits are higher charging P* = 35 in the first period and deterring entry compared with charging $P_M^L = 55$ and permitting entry.

Consider the low-cost monopolist's profits under the two alternative pricing strategies. If the low-cost monopolist limit prices at P* = 35 in period 1, it deters entry and charges its profit-maximizing price, P = 55, in period 2. Its profits are:

$$\Pi = \Pi_1^M + \Pi_2^M = 65 \, (35 - 10) + \frac{45 \, (55 - 10)}{1.1}$$

$$= 1625 + 1840.91 = 3465.91.$$

If the low-cost monopolist charges $P_M^L = 55$ in period 1 and permits entry, it charges the Cournot-Nash price, P = 45, in period 2, and its profits are:

$$\Pi = \Pi_1^M + \Pi_2^M = 45 \, (55 - 10) + \frac{35 \, (45 - 10)}{1.1}$$

$$= 2025 + 1113.63 = 3138.63.$$

The low-cost monopolist earns larger profits by setting P = P* = 35, the limit price.

To summarize, in a separating equilibrium, a high-cost monopolist charges its monopoly price ($P_M^H = 62.50$ in Figure 12.1) and allows entry. A low-cost monopolist, however, charges a price P* that is below its preferred monopoly price of P_M^L, because if a low-cost monopolist charged a price of P_M^L, the potential entrant might believe that the low-cost monopolist was really a high-cost monopolist sending a false signal. In the separating equilibrium, therefore, the low-cost monopolist charges a limit price to avoid being mistaken for a high-cost firm.

In the separating equilibrium, the monopolist's price fully reveals its costs to the potential entrant because if $P = P_M^H$ the monopolist is revealed to be high-cost, whereas if P = P* the monopolist is revealed to be low-cost. With a separating equilibrium: if $P = P_M^H$, entry occurs; and if P = P* entry is deterred.

The analysis of a pooling equilibrium is much simpler. In a pooling equilibrium, both high-cost and low-cost monopolists charge the low-cost monopolist's preferred price of P_M^L. The existence of a pooling equilibrium requires that:

$$\rho_H \pi_2^H + (1 - \rho_H) \, \pi_2^L < 0, \qquad\qquad [12.1]$$

which simply states that if the potential entrant is left guessing about the monopolist's true costs, it will not enter because its expected profits will be negative.* If inequality 12.1 is not satisfied, there is no pooling equilibrium, and only a separating equilibrium can exist. If this condition is satisfied, the monopolist has a great incentive to keep the potential entrant in the dark regarding its true costs. If high-cost and low-cost monopolists charge the low-cost monopolist's short-run profit-maximizing price, P_M^L, then a potential entrant will not learn anything about the monopolist's costs and the potential entrant will have to base its profit expectations on inequality 12.1 and stay out. With a pooling equilibrium, the low-cost monopolist charges its preferred price $P = P_M^L$, whereas a high-cost monopolist engages in limit pricing, by setting $P = P_M^L$, and as a result all entry is deterred.

Milgrom and Roberts's results suggest that in a model with *asymmetric* information, limit pricing *may* occur; however, the model does not suggest that limit pricing *will* occur. Furthermore, according to Milgrom and Roberts, both high-cost and low-cost monopolists may engage in limit pricing.

Product Proliferation Revisited

The game theoretic analysis of **product proliferation** can become complicated, but it is possible to present the basic model in a fairly simple framework.[3] The product proliferation game is often presented as a **location game**, in which firms choose between different locations for their plants.[4] In fact, we can begin by returning briefly to the first game presented in Chapter 6—the ice cream truck game. Recall that the solution to the ice cream truck game was for both firms to locate in the middle of the parade route. Now consider a similar example.

The product proliferation game is one of common knowledge with perfect, certain, symmetric, and complete information. In Figure 12.2, suppose that a monopolist produced only corn flakes with no sugar but that consumers are spread

---

*In our numerical example, if:

$$\rho_H = 0.50,$$

$$\pi_2^L = -150, \text{ and } \pi_2^H = 75,$$

$$\text{then } \rho_H \pi_2^H + (1 - \rho_H) \, \pi_2^L = 37.5 - 75 = -37.5 < 0;$$

then the potential entrant's expected post-entry profit would be negative, and the potential entrant would stay out.

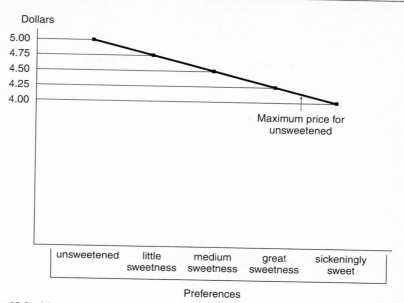

Figure 12.2   Maximum price for a box of unsweetened corn flakes by consumer preferences.

out with **uniform density** over the five preferences in Figure 12.2. U*niform density* simply means that consumers are equally spaced over the preferences. Suppose there are ten consumers: two consumers prefer unsweetened corn flakes, two consumers prefer a little sweetness, two consumers prefer medium sweetness, two consumers prefer great sweetness, and two consumers prefer sickeningly sweet corn flakes.* For a perfectly sweet box of cereal, each consumer will pay a price of $5. But for *each* step away from perfection, the maximum price the consumer is willing to pay declines by $0.25. Figure 12.2 shows the maximum price that each consumer would be willing to pay for a box of unsweetened corn flakes. In Figure 12.2, the consumer located at sickeningly sweet will pay only $4.00 for an unsweetened box, and the consumer in the middle would pay $4.50 for a box.

Suppose that at time t = 1, a monopolist, hypothetically called the "Big K" Corporation, produces only unsweetened corn flakes at a marginal cost of $1.00 per box (MC = $1.00). For simplification, further assume that the only alternative to producing unsweetened corn flakes is to produce sickeningly sweet corn flakes, also at MC = $1.00, and that at any moment another plant can be built to produce only sickeningly sweet corn flakes at a fixed cost of $60.00.

Consider the profit possibilities for monopolist Big K. If it continues to produce only unsweetened corn flakes, and maximizes profits by selling one box to

---

*If six of the ten consumers preferred "medium sweetness" and only one consumer preferred each of the other four alternatives, then consumers would be spread out with *non-uniform density* over the five preferences.

each consumer at its profit-maximizing price of $4.00, its flow of profits, ignoring fixed costs, in each period would be:*

$$\pi_{un} = PQ - Q(MC) = 4.00(10) - 10(1.00) = 30.00,$$

where π_{un} represents Big K's profit if it produces only unsweetened corn flakes. If Big K's discount rate is 10 percent, and assuming constant demand, Big K's present value of profits is:

$$\pi_{pv}^{un} = \frac{30.00}{.10} = 300.00.$$

Now suppose that at t = 1, Big K builds a second plant to produce sickeningly sweet corn flakes at a fixed cost of $60.00. Because of product differentiation, its new profit-maximizing price will increase to $4.50.† Four consumers, those preferring no sweetness and a little sweetness, will buy unsweetened corn flakes. Four consumers, those preferring great sweetness and sickeningly sweet, will buy sickeningly sweet corn flakes. And two consumers, those preferring medium sweetness, will be indifferent between the two types at a price of $4.50. Assume that the two consumers preferring medium sweetness divide randomly, with one buying unsweetened and the other buying sickeningly sweet corn flakes. Big K will then sell one box to each of the ten consumers, and in each period its flow of profits, again ignoring fixed costs, would be:

$$\pi_{unss} = 4.50(10) - 10(1.00) = 35.00,$$

---

*Big K's profit-maximizing price is $4.00 because the marginal revenue curve is as follows:

Quantity	*Price*	*Marginal Revenue*
2	$5.00	—
4	$4.75	$4.50
6	$4.50	$4.00
8	$4.25	$3.50
10	$4.00	$3.00

Because the marginal cost is $1.00 per box, profit maximization requires expanding output to ten units and selling all units at the same price of $4.00.

†A price of $4.50 now maximizes profits because any price above $4.50 would prevent the medium sweetness consumers from buying corn flakes, whereas a price below $4.50 would not increase total sales. The demand curve for both types of corn flakes is:

Quantity	*Price*	*Marginal Revenue*
4	$5.00	—
8	$4.75	$4.50
10	$4.50	$3.50

Because marginal revenue is above marginal cost of $1.00 per box, Big K should set price to $4.50 and produce ten boxes of corn flakes.

where π_{unss} represents Big K's profits if it produces both types of corn flakes. Assuming again a discount rate of 10 percent and constant demand, and recognizing the fixed cost of $60.00 to build the second plant, Big K's present value of profits with two plants would be:

$$\pi_{pv}^{unss} = \frac{35.00}{.10} - \frac{60}{1.1} = 350.00 - 54.5 = 295.50.$$

If there is no threat of entry, Big K maximizes its present value of profits by producing *only* unsweetened corn flakes because $\pi_{pv}^{un} = 300.00 > 295.50 = \pi_{pv}^{unss}$.

Given this monopoly market, is there a current threat of entry? Consider the options for a potential entrant, hypothetically called "Big G" Corporation. Big G can build a plant for $60.00 to produce sickeningly sweet corn flakes with MC = $1.00 and compete with Big K. Suppose that if Big G produces sickeningly sweet corn flakes, Big K and Big G compete through price and product differentiation. Figure 12.3 shows the maximum price each consumer would be willing to pay for each type of corn flakes. The little sweetness consumers would pay a maximum of $4.75 for unsweetened but only $4.25 for sickeningly sweet corn flakes. The little sweetness consumers therefore would be willing to pay a premium of $0.50 a box for unsweetened corn flakes compared with sickeningly sweet corn flakes. If Big K were to charge $1.50 for unsweetened corn flakes, then Big G would have to charge $0.99 to attract the little sweetness customers. However, because a price of $0.99 is below marginal cost of $1.00, Big G would not be willing to reduce price to $0.99. Big K could thus protect its little sweetness and unsweetened markets

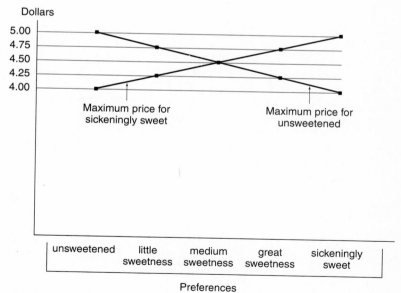

Figure 12.3   Maximum price for a box of corn flakes by consumer preferences and sweetness of cereal.

from Big G by charging a price of $1.50. Similarly, the great sweetness consumer would be willing to pay Big G a premium of $0.50 more for a box of sickeningly sweet corn flakes compared with unsweetened corn flakes. If Big G were to charge $1.50 for sickeningly sweet corn flakes, then Big K would have to charge $0.99 to attract the great sweetness customers. However, because a price of $0.99 is below marginal cost of $1.00, Big K would not be willing to reduce price to $0.99. Big G could, therefore, protect its great sweetness and sickeningly sweet markets from Big K by charging a price of $1.50. The medium sweetness consumers would pay a maximum of $4.50 for either box and no premium for either brand.

With two firms, the price will settle at $1.50 per box, with five consumers purchasing each type of corn flakes. The price of $1.50 prevents Big G from being able to take the little sweetness consumers away from Big K, because Big G would have to reduce price to $0.99 (below marginal cost) to induce the little sweetness consumers to purchase sickeningly sweet corn flakes. Similarly, the price of $1.50 prevents Big K from being able to take the great sweetness consumers away from Big G, because Big K would have to reduce price to $0.99 to induce the great sweetness consumers to purchase unsweetened corn flakes. At a price of $1.50, it is assumed that the medium sweetness consumers divide equally between the two brands.

If Big G enters at t = 1 and price declines to $1.50, Big G's flow of profits will be:

$$\pi_G = PQ - Q(MC) = 1.5(5) - 5(1.00) = 2.50.$$

With constant demand, fixed costs of $60.00, and a 10 percent discount rate, Big G's present value of profits would be:

$$\pi_{pv}^{G} = \frac{2.50}{.10} - \frac{60.00}{1.1} = 25.00 - 54.50 = -29.50 < 0.$$

Because Big G's present value of profits is negative, it would *not* enter. Big K would remain a monopolist and produce only unsweetened corn flakes; its present value of profits would be 300.00.

Now relax one assumption. Suppose that at time T_{3d} the density of the demand function suddenly triples, so that there are exactly six consumers of every type instead of two. To simplify the discussion, we will define the time T_{3d} as t = 1. This implies that the present period is t < 1. To simplify further, suppose that this is the only time that demand will ever increase. If the demand density triples and Big G produces sickeningly sweet corn flakes at t = T_{3d} = 1, its flow of profits after T_{3d} would exactly triple to:

$$\pi_{G3d} = PQ - Q(MC) = 1.50(15) - 15(1.00) = 22.50 - 15.00 = 7.50.$$

With a 10 percent discount rate, Big G's present value of profits would be:

$$\pi_{pv}^{G3d} = \frac{7.50}{.10} - \frac{60}{1.1} = 75 - 54.5 = 20.50. \qquad [12.2]$$

Entry is now profitable. In the absence of any strategic move by Big K, Big G would enter at time t = T_{3d} = 1, earn present value profits equal to $20.50, and split the market with Big K. As noted previously, Big G's entry would reduce price to $1.50, so that Big K's profits would also decline to a flow of $7.50 (3 × 2.50) per period.

Can Big K do anything to prevent such an outcome? Consider the following strategic move: Big K could preempt Big G by moving to produce sickeningly sweet corn flakes first.[5] If Big G has not entered at t = 1, consider Big K's options at that time when demand triples. At time t = T_{3d} = 1, Big K could either continue to produce only unsweetened corn flakes or produce both types. If Big K is still a monopolist, its new profit flows if demand density tripled would also triple to:

$$\pi_{un} = 90.00 \text{ and } \pi_{unss} = 105.00.$$

The present value of Big K's profits if Big K produced only unsweetened corn flakes beginning at time t = t_0 < 1 would become:

$$\pi_{pv}^{un} = \sum_{t=t_0}^{0} \frac{30}{(1.1)^t} + \sum_{t=1}^{\infty} \frac{90}{(1.1)^t}. \qquad [12.3]$$

If Big K entered the sickeningly sweet corn flakes market at time t = T_{3d} = 1 and produced both types of corn flakes, the present value of Big K's profits would be:*

$$\pi_{pv}^{unss} = \sum_{t=t_0}^{0} \frac{30.00}{(1.1)^t} + \sum_{t=1}^{\infty} \frac{105.00}{(1.1)^t} - \frac{60.00}{(1.1)^T}. \qquad [12.4]$$

Because the first terms in equations 12.3 and 12.4 are identical, to compare the two equations, it is necessary to compare only the last term in 12.3 with the last two terms in 12.4, which yields the following:

$$\sum_{t=1}^{\infty} \frac{105}{(1.1)^t} - \frac{60}{(1.1)^1} = 1050 - 54.5 = 995.5 > \sum_{t=1}^{\infty} \frac{90}{(1.1)^t} = 900.$$

Therefore, $\pi_{unss}^{pv} > \pi_{un}^{pv}$, and it now makes sense for Big K to produce *both* types of corn flakes.

Now the game becomes interesting. In the absence of entry by the other firm, each firm would choose to produce sickeningly sweet corn flakes at t = T_{3d} = 1. However, once one firm produces sickeningly sweet corn flakes, the other firm has no incentive to produce them because if both produced sickeningly sweet corn flakes, competition would drive price to marginal cost of $1.00 for consumers with preferences at medium sweetness, great sweetness, and sickeningly sweet, and the second firm to enter would not recover its fixed costs. In other

---

*The first term on the right-hand side of Eq. 12.4 represents Big K's profits if it produces only unsweetened corn flakes beginning at time t = t_0 before demand triples. The second and third terms represent Big K's profits if it enters the sickeningly sweet market at time t = 1 when demand triples.

words, there is room for only one profitable producer of sickeningly sweet corn flakes, and the first firm in will prevent the other firm from entering.

The key to solving the "who will enter when" game is to recognize that there *must* exist some time $t < 1 = T_{3d}$ at which the potential entrant is indifferent between entering and not entering the market for sickeningly sweet corn flakes. If $t_G < 1$ is the time of Big G's entry into the sickeningly sweet corn flakes market, then the present value of profits for Big G is given by:

$$\pi_{pv}^G = \sum_{t=t_G}^{0} \frac{2.50}{(1.1)^t} + \sum_{t=1}^{\infty} \frac{7.50}{(1.1)^t} - \frac{60.00}{(1.1)^{t_G}}$$

$$= \sum_{t=t_G}^{0} \frac{2.50}{(1.1)^t} + 75.00 - \frac{60.00}{(1.1)^{t_G}}.$$

On a computer a straightforward calculation shows that for $t_G = -4$, $\pi_G^{pv} = 2.41$; for $t_G = -5$, $\pi_G^{pv} = -2.34$.*

In Figure 12.4, the present values of profits associated with Big G's entry at any time t are identified as curve π_{pv}^G. Notice that at some critical time $t^* < 1$, $\pi_{pv}^G = 0$, and Big G is indifferent between entering and not entering.

Figure 12.4 identifies two other curves. These curves represent Big K's possible present values of profits. The higher curve, π_{KF}, represents Big K's profits if it enters the market for sickeningly sweet corn flakes first; the lower curve, π_{KNE}, represents Big K's profits if Big G enters the sickeningly sweet corn flakes market first, in which case Big K does *not* enter the sickeningly sweet market. The present value of Big K's profits if it enters the sickeningly sweet market first at $t = t_K$ is given by:†

$$\pi_{KF} = \sum_{t=t_{un}}^{t_K-1} \frac{30.00}{(1.1)^t} + \sum_{t=t_K}^{0} \frac{35.00}{(1.1)^t} + \sum_{t=1}^{\infty} \frac{105.00}{(1.1)^t} - \frac{60.00}{(1.1)^{t_K}}, \qquad [12.5]$$

---

*The calculations are as follows:

$$\pi_G = \sum_{t=t_G}^{0} \frac{2.50}{(1.1)^t} + \sum_{t=1}^{\infty} \frac{7.50}{(1.1)^t} - \frac{60}{(1.1)^{t_G}}$$

$$= \sum_{t=t_G}^{0} \frac{2.50}{(1.1)^t} + 75.00 - \frac{60}{(1.1)^{t_G}};$$

for $t_G = -4$, $\pi_{pv}^G = 15.26 + 75.00 - 87.85 = 2.41$,

and for $t_G = -5$, $\pi_{pv}^G = 19.29 + 75.00 - 96.63 = -2.34$.

Of course, similar calculations could be done for any value of t_G.

†The first term on the right-hand side of equation 12.5 represents Big K's profits if it produces only unsweetened corn flakes beginning from time $t = t_{un}$ until time $t = t_K - 1$. The second and fourth terms represent Big K's profits if it produces *both* types of corn flakes from time $t = t_K$ until time $t = 0$. The third term represents Big K's profits if it continues to produce both types of corn flakes after demand triples at $t = 1$.

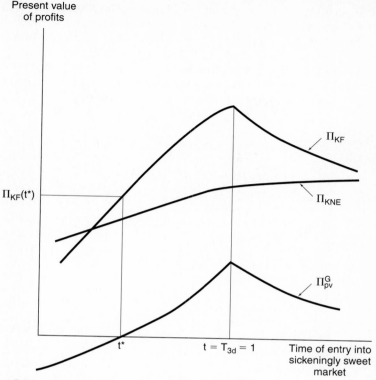

Figure 12.4 Present value of Big G's and Big K's profits by time of first entry into sickeningly sweet market.

where t_{un} represents the time at which Big K entered the unsweetened corn flakes market. If Big G enters the sickeningly sweet market first at $t = t_K$, Big K stays out of the sickeningly sweet market, and Big K's profits are given by:

$$\pi_{KNE} = \sum_{t=t_{un}}^{t_K-1} \frac{30.00}{(1.1)^t} + \sum_{t=t_K}^{0} \frac{2.50}{(1.1)^t} + \sum_{t=1}^{\infty} \frac{7.50}{(1.1)^t}.$$ [12.6]

Comparing the right sides of equations 12.5 and 12.6, notice that for *any given time of entry* t_K, the first terms are equal, but the second and third terms are much larger in equation 12.5 than in equation 12.6. Therefore, unless the negative fourth term (which represents the discounted fixed costs of entering the sickeningly sweet market) in equation 12.5 is very large, $\pi_{KF} > \pi_{KNE}$. This implies that in virtually all circumstances, Big K will prefer entering the sickeningly sweet corn flakes market first.

Given the curves in Figure 12.4, consider the game from Big G's standpoint. Big G knows that if it does not enter at $t = T_{3d} = 1$, Big K will. Therefore, Big G must try to preempt Big K by entering at some time earlier than $t = T_{3d} = 1$; let's call it t = 1 − ε. Understanding this, Big K must try to preempt Big G by entering at some time earlier, perhaps t = 1 − 2ε. Of course, the game regresses to the point at which Big K enters the market for sickeningly sweet corn flakes just infinitesimally before t*. This is the only solution to the game. Big K enters before the increase in demand and in time to preempt Big G. In Figure 12.4, Big K's profits after entry will be $\pi_{KF}(t^*)$, and Big G will be prevented from entering. In this way Big K maintains its monopoly.

SUMMARY

1. By assuming asymmetric information, it is possible to show that limit pricing may be a rational and profitable strategy. Furthermore, both high- and low-cost firms may engage in limit pricing.

2. With regard to product proliferation, filling up market niches before a potential competitor enters may enable a dominant firm to maintain market power for a long time. The product proliferation model helps to explain the rapid expansion of product lines that occurs in many consumer products, such as cereal, beer, and cigarettes.

KEY TERMS

limit pricing	product proliferation
location game	separating equilibrium
pooling equilibrium	uniform density

DISCUSSION QUESTIONS

1. What is the difference in the information structure in the Milgrom and Roberts limit pricing model compared with the limit pricing model presented in Chapter 10? How does this difference in the information structure affect the outcomes in the two games?

2. Explain the difference between a pooling and a separating equilibrium. In which equilibrium does a high-cost firm limit price?

3. What is the information structure in the product proliferation game?

4. In the product proliferation game, if the demand for all types of cereals continued to increase, would you expect that eventually the incumbent would produce little sweetness, medium sweetness, and great sweetness corn flakes? Why?

PROBLEMS

1. (You will need a calculator for this problem.) Consider the model of product proliferation presented in this chapter. If the fixed costs of producing sickeningly sweet corn flakes were 100 instead of 60, would product proliferation

still be a rational strategy? If so, would the monopolist enter the sickeningly sweet market earlier, later or at the same time as that depicted in Figure 12.4?

If the fixed costs of producing sickeningly sweet corn flakes were $55 instead of $60, would product proliferation still be a rational strategy? If so, would the monopolist enter the sickeningly sweet market earlier, later, or at the same time as depicted in Figure 12.4?

2. (You will need a calculator for this problem.) Consider the Milgrom and Roberts limit pricing model. Suppose the probability that an incumbent is a high-cost producer is $\rho_H = 0.75$. If an incumbent is a high-cost firm, an entrant would earn a profit of 75 on entry, but if an incumbent is a low-cost firm, an entrant would lose 300 on entry. Does a pooling equilibrium exist in this case? Would a high-cost firm limit price in this case?

3. (You will need a calculator for this problem.) Consider the following two-period model. Suppose an established monopolist with demand curve $P = 100 - Q$ is either a high-cost producer with HAC = HMC = 25 or a low-cost producer with LAC = LMC = 10. The probability that the monopolist is a high-cost producer (HAC = HMC = 25) is $\rho_H = 0.75$, and the probability that the monopolist is a low-cost producer (LAC = LMC = 10) is $(1 - \rho_H) = 0.25$. Only the monopolist knows whether it is a high-cost or low-cost producer. Nature moves first and chooses the monopolist to be either high-cost or low-cost. If an incumbent is a high-cost firm, an entrant would earn a profit of 75 on entry, but if an incumbent is a low-cost firm, an entrant would lose 300 on entry. Assume the monopolist's discount rate equals 10 percent.
   a. Would a high-cost monopolist limit price in period 1?
   b. Would a low-cost monopolist limit price in period 1?
   c. What would be the total profits earned by a high-cost monopolist in the two periods?
   d. What would be the total profits earned by a low-cost monopolist in the two periods?

REFERENCES

1. P. Milgrom and J. Roberts, "Limit Pricing and Entry Under Incomplete Information an Equilibrium Analysis," *Econometrica* 50 (March 1982): 443–60. For a different theoretical justification of the possible existence of limit pricing, see Luis C. Corchón and Félix Marcos, "Entry, Stackelberg Equilibrium and Reasonable Conjectures," *International Journal of Industrial Organization* 6 (December 1988): 509–15.
2. The following presentation is adapted from Jean Tirole, *The Theory of Industrial Organization* (Cambridge, MA: MIT Press, 1988), pp. 368–72.
3. The following analysis is based on Jean Tirole, *The Theory of Industrial Organization* (Cambridge, MA: MIT Press, 1988), pp. 346–9.
4. The seminal paper was by Harold Hotelling, "Stability in Competition," *Economic Journal* 39 (March 1929): 41–57. See also Donald A. Hay, "Sequential Entry and Entry-Deterring Strategies in Spatial Competition," *Oxford Economic Papers* (July 1976): 240–57.
5. Tirole, *supra* note 3.

PART III

BUSINESS PRACTICES

Chapter 13

Product Differentiation and Advertising

Product differentiation and advertising have been recurring topics throughout this text. Chapter 2 presented the model of monopolistic competition, in which product differentiation gave monopolistically competitive firms some degree of market power. Chapter 5 identified product differentiation and advertising as determinants of market structure. Recall that product differentiation and advertising are associated with possible advantages for incumbent firms. These advantages include increased economies of scale, possible cost advantages for incumbents, and an increase in the capital barrier to entry. Chapters 11 and 12 developed the model of product proliferation and showed that incumbents might use product proliferation to strategically prevent entry. This chapter expands on our previous analysis and emphasizes the impact of product differentiation and advertising on economic welfare.

Forms of Product Differentiation

The objective of product differentiation is to increase profits by increasing demand and decreasing the price elasticity of demand. Sellers attempt to differentiate their products in many ways. Common forms of differentiation include location, service, physical characteristics, and subjective image differences.

Here is an example of location differentiation:[1] In Utica, New York, one national franchiser has two identical soft yogurt stands located in different malls. One stand is in a relatively upscale mall on the south side of the city and is usually busy. The other stand is located in a low-quality mall on the north side of the city and rarely seems to be crowded. One franchise appears to be a success while the other flounders. Such examples are common and support the adage that business success depends first and foremost on "location, location, location." Professional sports franchises are another good example of the importance of location. Franchises in big television markets are generally worth more than franchises in smaller markets.[2]

In addition to location, products are differentiated by service. Some firms offer high-quality service, usually at a high price. Others offer little or no service at

303

low prices. If a consumer purchases a computer from a local computer store and something goes wrong, the dealer may send a representative to fix the problem. If a consumer purchases the same computer from a discount warehouse such as Sam's Club or BJ's and she has a problem, she may be on her own with an 800 telephone number as her only source of help. Many consumers are willing to pay a price for better service. Sears has dominated the market for major household appliances, not because the company sells better washers, dryers and refrigerators, but because "Sears Services What It Sells." IBM's market power in computers from 1960 to 1985 was also built on the company's reputation for solving its customers' problems quickly and efficiently.

A third form of differentiation is based on physical characteristics. Water-based paints are different from oil-based paints. Wool suits are different from polyester suits. Fresh-squeezed orange juice is different from Hi-C fruit drink with 10 percent fruit juice. Because consumers value variety and because they have different tastes, it is not surprising that firms attempt to pry consumers away from their current products by offering physically differentiated products.

Finally, product differentiation is often based on efforts to create subjective image differences between products. A famous example is Clorox bleach. Clorox is fundamentally the same product as any other liquid bleach, yet Clorox has been able to create a premium image that has enabled it to consistently sell for higher prices than competitive products.[3] Cigarette advertising is infamous for attempting to create an image for a product that brings financial and sexual success when, in fact, all of the objective evidence suggests the contrary. McDonald's has long used Ronald McDonald to create an image as a great place to take young children, by ignoring the quality and price of the food and emphasizing the battle between Ronald McDonald and the Hamburglar.

Economists distinguish between two broad categories of product differentiation based on the attributes or characteristics of products: **horizontal differentiation** and **vertical differentiation**. *Horizontal differentiation* refers to differences between brands based on different product characteristics but not on different overall quality. Horizontal differentiation is common in the fast-food industry. A McDonald's Quarter Pounder is somewhat different from a Burger King Whopper or a Wendy's Single, but the overall quality of the three burgers is similar. By comparison, *vertical differentiation* refers to differences in the actual quality of two brands. Ben & Jerry's ice cream and Häagen Dazs ice cream have a higher fat content than Breyers ice cream, which has a higher fat content than the typical store brand of ice cream. A Lexus is a higher-quality car than a Taurus. However, differences between similar models, such as a Toyota Camry and a Ford Taurus, represent horizontal differentiation.

Theoretical Analysis of Product Differentiation

THE POTENTIAL IMPACT OF PRODUCT DIFFERENTIATION ON PRICE: THE BERTRAND MODEL REVISITED

In Chapter 7 we derived the Bertrand equilibrium in a model with a homogeneous product. Recall that the equilibrium resulted in price equal to marginal cost. As a first theoretical step toward analyzing the possible impact of product differentiation on price, we analyze a Bertrand model with a *differentiated product.*

Suppose that, because of brand loyalty, two Bertrand firms face the following symmetric demand curves:

$$q_1 = 96 - 2p_1 + p_2 \qquad\qquad [13.1A]$$

$$q_2 = 96 - 2p_2 + p_1 \qquad\qquad [13.1B]$$

where $q_1, q_2, \geq 0$ and $p_1, p_2 \leq 48$.

The restriction that $q_1, q_2 \geq 0$ prevents quantities from becoming negative, and the restriction that $p_1, p_2 \leq 48$ prevents output from becoming infinite as an opponent's price increases. Eq. 13.1A shows that Firm 1's demand is an inverse function of p_1 and a *positive* function of p_2. Notice that even if $p_1 > p_2$, Firm 1 still has a positive quantity demanded. For example, even if the price of Ben & Jerry's ice cream is greater than the price of Häagen Dazs, some consumers will select Ben & Jerry's. Furthermore, in Eq. 13.1A, an increase in p_2 results in an increase in q_1; that is, an increase in the price of Häagen Dazs will increase the quantity demanded of Ben & Jerry's.

Assume MC = 12, so that in the absence of product differentiation, the Bertrand equilibrium price would equal MC of 12. Using calculus, it is fairly simple to derive Firm 1's reaction function $p_1 = f(p_2)$ as:*

$$p_1 = 30 + \frac{1}{4}p_2. \qquad\qquad [13.2]$$

---

*To obtain marginal revenue for Firm 1 begin by solving Eq. 13.1A for p_1 and proceed as follows:

$$2p_1 = 96 + p_2 - q_1 \Rightarrow p_1 = 48 + \frac{1}{2}p_2 - \frac{1}{2}q_1$$

$$TR_1 = p_1 q_1 = \left[48 + \frac{1}{2}p_2 - \frac{1}{2}q_1\right] q_1 = 48q_1 + \frac{1}{2}p_2 q_1 - \frac{1}{2}q_1$$

$$MR_1 = \frac{\partial TR_1}{\partial q_1} = 48 + \frac{1}{2}p_2 - q_1.$$

To find the reaction function, set $MR_1 = MC = 12$:

$$MR_1 = 48 + \frac{1}{2}p_2 - q_1 = 12 = MC.$$

Solving for q_1 yields:

$$q_1 = 36 + \frac{1}{2}p_2.$$

Substituting $q_1 = 96 - 2p_1 + p_2$ into the above equation and solving for p_1 yields the reaction function:

$$q_1 = 36 + \frac{1}{2}p_2 = 96 - 2p_1 + p_2 \Rightarrow 2p_1 = (96 - 36) + p_2 - \frac{1}{2}p_2 \Rightarrow 2p_1 = 60 + \frac{1}{2}p_2$$

or

$$p_1 = 30 + \frac{1}{4}p_2.$$

The reaction function shown in Eq. 13.2 can also be derived by using the twice as steep rule. In the following derivation of Firm 1's reaction function, remember that the function $p_1 = f(p_2)$ is in terms of prices, not quantities, and Firm 1 assumes p_2 is constant throughout. First solve Eq. 13.1A for p_1:

$$2p_1 = 96 + p_2 - q_1 \Rightarrow p_1 = (48 + \tfrac{1}{2}p_2) - \tfrac{1}{2}q_1.$$

Because p_2 is assumed to be constant, by the twice as steep rule MR_1 is:

$$MR_1 = (48 + \tfrac{1}{2}p_2) - q_1.$$

Profit maximization requires MC = MR, so:

$$MR_1 = (48 + \tfrac{1}{2}p_2) - q_1 = 12 = MC$$

or

$$q_1 = 36 + \tfrac{1}{2}p_2. \qquad [13.3]$$

To obtain the reaction function in terms of *prices*, that is, $p_1 = f(p_2)$, substitute $q_1 = 96 - 2p_1 + p_2$ from Eq. 13.1A into 13.3, which yields:

$$96 - 2p_1 + p_2 = 36 + \tfrac{1}{2}p_2 \Rightarrow 2p_1 = 60 + p_2 - \tfrac{1}{2}p_2$$

or

$$p_1 = 30 + \tfrac{1}{4}p_2. \qquad [13.4]$$

By analogous reasoning, Firm 2's reaction function is:

$$p_2 = 30 + \tfrac{1}{4}p_1. \qquad [13.5]$$

At the Nash equilibrium, $p_1 = p_2$. Substituting $p_2 = 30 + \tfrac{1}{4}p_1$ from Eq. 13.5 into Eq. 13.4 and solving for p_1 yields the Nash equilibrium:

$$p_1 = 30 + \tfrac{1}{4}(30 + \tfrac{1}{4}p_1) = 37.5 + \tfrac{1}{16}p_1$$

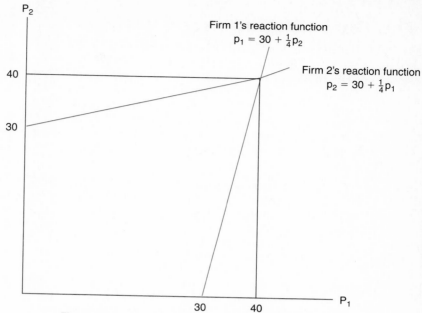

Figure 13.1   Bertrand equilibrium with product differentiation.

or

$$\frac{15}{16}p_1 = 37.5$$

or

$$p_1 = 40.$$

By analogous reasoning, $p_2 = 40$.

Figure 13.1 shows the two reaction functions and the Nash equilibrium. The Bertrand equilibrium with product differentiation yields a price of 40. In the absence of product differentiation, the Bertrand equilibrium is $p_1 = p_2 = MC = 12$. The introduction of product differentiation has resulted in a dramatically *increased* price.

That increased product differentiation can result in higher prices does *not* imply that increased product differentiation lowers social welfare, because in return for higher prices consumers receive increased variety. The next section addresses the theoretical impact of increased product differentiation on social welfare.

The Optimal Amount of Variety: Monopolistic Competition Revisited[4]

The model of monopolistic competition was presented in Chapter 2. Recall that in long-run equilibrium each firm earns a normal economic profit and produces output on the downward sloping portion of its average cost curve. Figure 2.15 is reproduced here as Figure 13.2. Panel A in Figure 13.2 depicts the short-run equilibrium for a firm, and panel B depicts the long-run equilibrium.

In concluding our discussion of monopolistic competition in Chapter 2, we noted:[5]

> Economists have identified two sources of inefficiency in a monopolistically competitive market. First, at the firm's profit-maximizing choice of output in both the short and long run, price is greater than marginal cost. Therefore, as in a monopoly, there is a deadweight loss in a monopolistically competitive market. Second, note from Figure [13.2] that in equilibrium the firm does not operate at the minimum of its average cost curve. This situation, in which the monopolistically competitive firm produces a smaller output level than that which minimizes average cost, is often described as "excess capacity." If fewer firms were in the industry, each could operate at a larger scale and a lower average cost. Note, however, that consumers undoubtedly value the opportunity to choose among a variety of products with different characteristics. The "variety" benefits of product differentiation should be considered in addition to the costs of the inefficiencies in formulating public policy.

We now examine the social benefits of variety in a monopolistically competitive industry. Initially assume that only one firm is in the industry and this firm is in short-run equilibrium as shown in panel A of Figure 13.2. This firm is the "founding father" firm of the industry, like McDonald's in the fast-food industry. As additional firms enter the industry, the demand curve for the first firm shifts to the left and its profits decline until, in long-run equilibrium, economic profits are zero. In long-run equilibrium, all firms earn zero economic profits as depicted in panel B of Figure 13.2.

As each additional firm enters the industry, profits per firm decline, so there is a *negative* relationship between the number of firms in the industry and the profits earned by each firm. This relationship is shown by the function $\pi(n)$ in Figure 13.3, where n is the number of firms in the industry. The long-run equilibrium number of firms is n_{eq} where $\pi(n_{eq}) = 0$. In long-run equilibrium, economic profits equal zero for each firm.

Is n_{eq} the socially optimal number of firms? The optimal number of firms must maximize total industry surplus, which equals the sum of consumer surplus and total producer profits.* Total profits are calculated by multiplying the number of firms, n, by the profits per firm, $\pi(n)$. Figure 13.4 shows the total profits function, $n \times \pi(n)$.

---

*We simplify the analysis by assuming that the equilibrium number of firms has no impact on the producer surplus of input suppliers, so that the firms' profits measure the producer surplus.

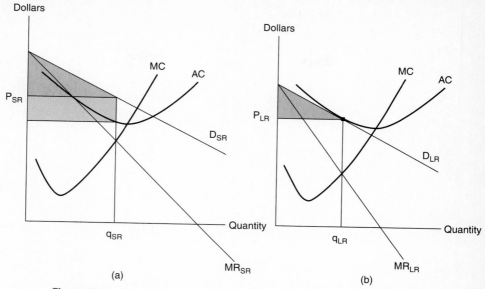

Figure 13.2   Short-run and long-run equilibrium under monopolistic competition.

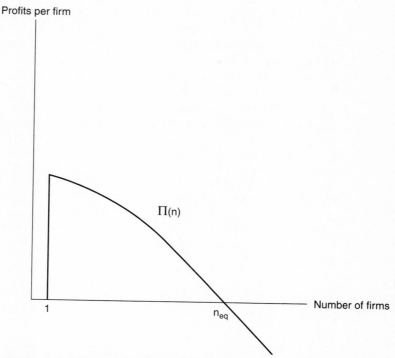

Figure 13.3   Relationship between the number of firms in the industry and firm profits under monopolistic competition.

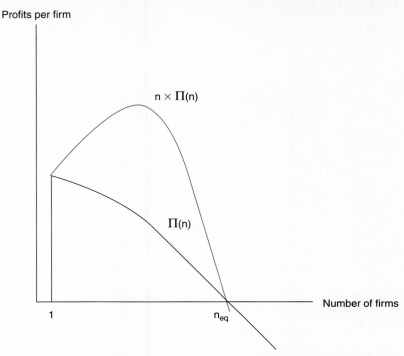

Figure 13.4   Relationship between the number of firms in the industry and total industry profits under monopolistic competition.

Total consumer surplus, CS, is also a function of the number of firms, CS(n). In Figure 13.2, consumer surplus with one firm is equal to the gray triangle in panel A, and consumer surplus per firm with n_{eq} firms is equal to the gray triangle in panel B. With n_{eq} firms in panel B total consumer surplus would equal [n_{eq} × (area of the gray triangle)]. Generally, total consumer surplus increases with an increase in the number of firms for two reasons: (1) entry causes total industry output to increase and prices to decline and (2) new firms increase variety and increase the likelihood that a particular consumer will find a product that exactly matches his or her tastes. Figure 13.5 shows CS(n) as a positively sloped curve.*

To determine total surplus we add the total producer profits and total consumer surplus so:

$$\text{Total Surplus } (n) = [n \times \pi(n)] + CS\ (n).$$

---

*It is unlikely, but conceivable, that CS(n) could decrease with increases in n if increased variety enables each firm to cater very closely to the demands of a select group of consumers, thereby enabling firms to dramatically increase prices as variety increases. In our analysis we ignore this possibility.

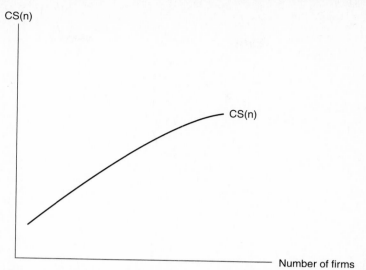

Figure 13.5   Consumer surplus as a function of the number of firms with monopolistic competition.

In Figure 13.6, the total surplus curve is derived from the sum of the $[n \times \pi(n)]$ curve in Figure 13.4 and the CS (n) curve in Figure 13.5. The socially optimal number of firms is n*. Only with n* firms does the industry maximize total surplus.

In Figure 13.6 the optimal number of firms n* is less than the equilibrium number of firms n_{eq}. In this case, the monopolistically competitive industry will have too many firms and provide too large a variety of goods; therefore, product differentiation is excessive.

This result, however, is not the only possibility. In Figure 13.7 a different monopolistically competitive industry is shown, where n* > n_{eq} and the industry provides too little variety. There is, therefore, too little product differentiation in the industry represented in Figure 13.7. It is, of course, theoretically possible to construct an industry where n* = n_{eq}. It follows that in a monopolistically competitive industry, product differentiation may be greater than, less than, or equal to the socially optimal level of product differentiation.

The source of this ambiguity lies in the difference between the *private* benefits and the *social* benefits associated with entry. As long as there is some positive economic profit associated with entry, additional firms will enter the industry. Entry, however, reduces the profits of each of the incumbent firms. The total change in profits for society resulting from entry is, therefore, always less than the private profit of the entering firm, so that from a social viewpoint, the firm has "too much" incentive to enter. This profit effect tends to result in too many firms and too much product differentiation.

Conversely, entry results in an *increase* in consumer surplus, but the entrant ignores this increase in consumer surplus and considers only the increase in profit associated with entry. This consumer surplus effect tends to result in too few firms and too little product differentiation.

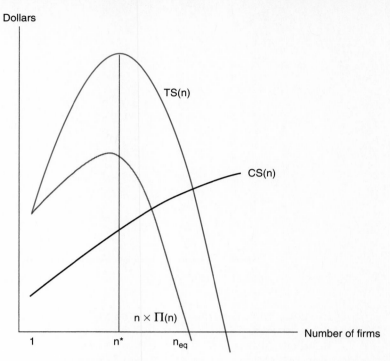

Figure 13.6   A monopolistically competitive industry with too many firms and too much product differentiation.

The profit effect and the consumer surplus effect work in opposite directions, and therefore, the net effect depends on which effect is dominant. In Figure 13.6, the profit effect is dominant and there is too much product differentiation, whereas in Figure 13.7, the consumer surplus effect is dominant and there is too little product differentiation. Only if the two effects are exactly equal will the socially optimal level of product differentiation be achieved.

THE WALDMAN ICE CREAM TRUCK REVISITED: AN EXAMPLE OF INEFFICIENT PRODUCT DIFFERENTIATION

One of the most common methods of differentiation is by geographic location. Recall the Waldman ice cream truck example presented in Chapter 6, in which both Waldman and "Other Truck" located at the middle of the parade route. Middle was a dominant strategy in that simple zero-sum game. Here we ask the question: Was the equilibrium outcome in that game (middle-middle) a socially optimal outcome?

Hotelling first addressed this type of question in 1929.[6] Suppose that a market consists of a 10-mile stretch of road and 100 consumers are distributed uniformly over that 10-mile stretch at one-tenth-of-a mile intervals beginning at the 0.05-mile mark and ending at the 9.95 mile mark. Figure 13.8 shows the 10-mile

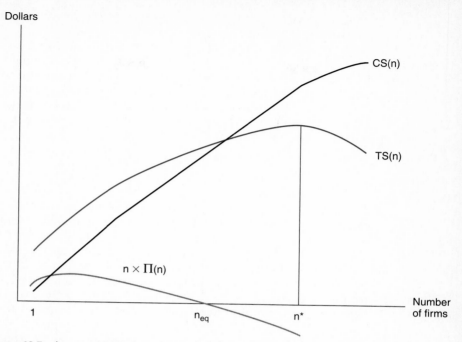

Figure 13.7 A monopolistically competitive industry with too few firms and too little product differentiation.

stretch of road starting with the 0-mile mark on the left and ending with the 10-mile mark on the right. If two duopolists, Waldman and Jensen, sell a homogeneous product at the same price, a consumer will select her seller strictly on the basis of which firm is closer, and therefore, which firm minimizes the consumer's transportation costs. Using the logic of the Waldman ice cream truck example from Chapter 6, both firms will locate at the middle of the road right at the 5-mile mark, and the two firms will divide sales and profits equally, with fifty consumers purchasing from each. The 5-mile mark is a Nash equilibrium because if either firm moved even slightly away from the middle, the firm that remained at the middle would capture a greater share of the market. If Jensen moved 1 mile to the left to the 4-mile mark, leaving Waldman alone in the middle, Waldman would capture all fifty of the consumers located to the right of the 5-mile mark *plus* the consumers located at the 4.95-, 4.85-, 4.75-, 4.65 and 4.55-mile marks.

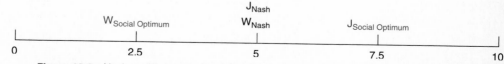

Figure 13.8 Nash equilibrium and social optimum for the ice cream truck Waldman-Jensen game.

Waldman would capture fifty-five consumers, leaving Jensen with only forty-five consumers.

With Waldman and Jensen each located at the 5-mile mark, a Nash equilibrium has been reached, but is "middle-middle" the optimal choice of locations from the standpoint of society? Society wishes to maximize consumer welfare by minimizing total transportation costs. Suppose transportation costs equal $1 per mile. With both firms located at the 5-mile mark, the average distance of a consumer from a seller is 2.5 miles, so the total transportation costs for the 100 consumers would equal

$$2.5 \times 100 \times \$1 = \$250.^*$$

What locations would minimize transportation costs? Suppose Waldman located at the 2.5-mile mark and Jensen located at the 7.5-mile mark. Waldman would now sell to the fifty consumers located between the 0.05- and 4.95- mile marks, and Jensen would sell to the fifty consumers located between the 5.05- and 9.95-mile marks. Each firm would still sell to fifty consumers, but consumers would travel an average of only 1.25 miles.† In fact, the farthest any consumer would travel would be 2.5 miles, which is equal to the average distance traveled with the Nash equilibrium outcome. Total transportation costs for the 100 consumers would equal $1.25 \times 100 \times \$1 = \$125$. By moving to the 2.5- and 7.5-mile marks, Waldman and Jensen would reduce society's transportation costs by 50 percent with no profit sacrifice to either firm. Clearly, in this example, the Nash equilibrium yields too little product differentiation.

This analysis can be generalized to consider other types of product differentiation besides location. For example, before the widespread introduction of cable TV and satellite TV into the broadcasting industry, most sections of the country received at most three network stations (ABC, CBS, and NBC), and many rural areas received only two stations. If an area received only two stations, both stations would have an incentive to provide very similar "middle-of-the-road" programming with some combination of the same type of shows: some news, some daytime soap operas, prime time comedies and dramas, some sports, and some local programming. If either of the two networks in a rural area had tried to move to-

---

*There are several ways to calculate the average distance traveled by consumers. One could calculate the total miles traveled by all consumers and then divide by 100, as follows:

$$\text{Average Miles Traveled} = \frac{2\,(0.05 + 0.15 + 0.25 + \ldots + 4.95)}{100} = \frac{250}{100} = 2.5.$$

Using calculus and recognizing that the functional relationship between consumers and miles traveled for the fifty consumers on each side of the 5-mile mark is:

$$\text{Miles Traveled by the xth consumer} = 0.1x \text{ for } 1 \le x \le 50.$$

The average miles traveled by the fifty consumers located between the 5- and 10-mile marks is:

$$\text{Average Miles Traveled} = \frac{\int_0^{50} \frac{x}{10}\,dx}{50} = \frac{125}{50} = 2.5.$$

†See the previous footnote for details on how to calculate the average miles traveled per customer.

ward a more specialized format such as all news (CNN), all sports (ESPN), or more intellectual programming (A&E), that station would have lost more viewers than it gained. Therefore, viewers with more extreme tastes, such as current CNN, ESPN, or A&E viewers, were left highly dissatisfied with both stations. The opening up of competition in the industry has resulted in far greater opportunities for those with more extreme tastes.

The Social Benefits and Costs of Advertising

We have shown that product differentiation often has a positive social impact. Good locations are good for the economy because they minimize the costs of obtaining goods and services and therefore increase consumer welfare. Similarly, given a choice between good and bad service, many consumers willingly pay a premium to receive good service. The premium price that many consumers willingly pay to eat Ben & Jerry's or Häagen-Dazs ice cream instead of lower-quality brands also has social value.[7]

The most controversial aspect of product differentiation is advertising aimed at creating subjective differences between products. These images may border on being fraudulent. Cars and cigarettes do not make one sexy and virile; beer consumption often leads to tragic consequences; and, sadly, students have killed each other over a pair of athletic shoes that may be of no higher quality than an inexpensive pair. These examples have resulted in a call from some to limit or even ban persuasive advertising. Recently, the Federal Trade Commission proposed a ban on the use of Joe Camel to sell cigarettes. Much of the remainder of this chapter concerns the social benefits and costs of advertising.

THE SOCIAL BENEFITS OF ADVERTISING

We begin by distinguishing between **informational** and **persuasive advertising**. Informational advertising provides consumers with truthful information about price, location, or quality. Most newspaper, magazine, and direct mail advertising is informational. Newspapers in particular are full of advertisements emphasizing price. Grocery stores contend that they are the "low price leader." Department stores announce major sales. Automobile dealers advertise rebates and low-cost credit. These are examples of procompetitive informational advertising. In 1994, newspaper advertising accounted for 23.1 percent of total advertising expenditures in the United States, magazine advertising accounted for 5.4 percent, and direct mail advertising accounted for 19.7 percent.[8] These three media accounted for almost half of all advertising expenditures, and most of that advertising provided valuable information.

Empirical evidence suggests that advertising about price, referred to as *price advertising,* results in lower prices. Two separate studies found that eyeglass prices were significantly lower in markets that permitted optometrists to advertise than in markets that prohibited advertising.[9] Similarly, prescription drug prices are lower in states that permit price advertising.[10] Porter found that local newspaper advertising has a procompetitive effect by reducing the profits of convenience goods advertised in newspapers.[11] Arterburn and Woodbury found that magazine advertising tended to increase the level of price competition for **shopping goods** such as furniture and appliances.[12] Shopping goods are relatively expensive goods that are purchased intermittently, such as appliances, automobiles, and televisions. Shopping goods are distinguished from **convenience goods**, which are relatively inexpensive items that are purchased on a regular basis, such as soft drinks, cigarettes, and gasoline.

Product differentiation puts pressure on manufacturers to produce high-quality products.[13] Even the simple act of placing a trademark on a product provides some guarantee that the manufacturer believes in the quality of the product and will stand behind it. In the absence of trademark identification, consumers would not know who produced a product and there would be less incentive for producers to maintain quality.

Advertising may help manufacturers take advantage of economies of scale in production and distribution. In 1990 General Motors sold its first Saturn automobile. GM began advertising the introduction of Saturn well in advance of the production of the first car. If GM had been prevented from advertising, it is doubtful it could have sold enough cars to take advantage of production economies of scale.[14] The Saturn example suggests that advertising may encourage increased investment in research and development by helping manufacturers to rapidly inform consumers of new products and to find a large pool of potential first-time buyers.

Advertising provides a social benefit by subsidizing the mass media. Most of the revenues received by newspapers, magazines, radio, and television are from advertising.[15] Imagine what the Sunday *New York Times* would cost without advertising revenues. The price would be prohibitive to most consumers. In fact, there would not be a Sunday *New York Times* without advertising. Finally, advertising is an entertaining art form, and some of it is quite good. The best, or worst, advertising often becomes part of modern culture. Walter Mondale adapted a Wendy's advertising campaign to be the cornerstone of his 1984 Presidential campaign when, in reference to economic policy, he asked Ronald Reagan, "Where's the Beef?" The NFL Super Bowl has even turned into a Super Bowl for commercials.

THE SOCIAL COSTS OF ADVERTISING

In 1994 over $148 billion was spent on advertising in the United States.[16] This is almost six times more than federal, state, and local governments spent on Aid to Families with Dependent Children in 1992.[17] Table 13.1 lists the 100 leading advertisers in the United States in 1993. Procter & Gamble spent almost $2.4 billion in 1993 to advertise its soaps, detergents, and food products. The same year Philip Morris spent over $1.8 billion, and General Motors spent over $1.5 billion. The opportunity cost of these advertising expenditures is large and raises questions about whether much of this $148 billion would have been better spent on AIDS research, health care, education, or new infrastructure.

Few economists argue that informational advertising creates serious economic waste. The complaints center on persuasive advertising. Persuasive advertising is designed to create a subjective positive reaction to a product. Much of

TABLE 13.1 **100 Leading National Advertisers 1993 (in millions of dollars)**

1. Procter & Gamble`	2,397.5	51. Quaker Oats	246.5
2. Philip Morris	1,844.3	52. News Corp.	243.5
3. General Motors	1,539.2	53. Schering-Plough	233.1
4. Sears	1,310.7	54. Mazda	228.0
5. Pepsico	1,038.9	55. Tandy	223.1
6. Ford	958.3	56. Federated Dept. Stores	223.0
7. AT&T	812.1	57. US Dairy Farmers	215.1
8. Nestle	793.7	58. S. C. Johnson	209.9
9. Johnson & Johnson	762.5	59. General Electric	204.8
10. Chrysler	761.6	60. Mattel	201.1
11. Warner-Lambert	751.0	61. Joh. A. Benckiser GmBH	199.2
12. Unilever	738.2	62. Clorox	198.3
13. McDonald's	736.6	63. Coors	197.8
14. Time Warner	695.1	64. ITT	196.2
15. Toyota	690.4	65. Helene Curtis	192.6
16. Walt Disney	675.7	66. Paramount	185.3
17. Grand Metropolitan	652.9	67. ConAgra	183.2
18. Kellogg	627.1	68. Ciba-Geigy	182.7
19. Kodak	624.7	69. IBM	171.8
20. Sony	589.0	70. Citicorp	169.8
21. J.C. Penney	585.2	71. Broadway Stores	169.5
22. General Mills	569.2	72. Wendy's	168.3
23. K-Mart	558.2	73. Gillette	167.2
24. Anheuser-Busch	520.5	74. Goodyear	163.1
25. American Home Prod.	501.6	75. Roll International	160.1
26. RJR Nabisco	499.4	76. Philips	158.3
27. Nissan	413.1	77. Campbell Soup	150.1
28. May Stores	403.6	78. Upjohn	146.5
29. Matsushita Electric	385.1	79. Bayer AG	145.3
30. Ralston Purina	372.8	80. Wrigley	144.9
31. Hershey	366.3	81. American Stores	143.0
32. Honda	354.4	82. American Brands	142.7
33. Coca-Cola	341.3	83. Marriott	132.6
34. Mars	337.6	84. AMR Corp.	131.3
35. American Express	324.8	85. CPC International	129.4
36. Heinz	318.9	86. Apple	129.1
37. Circuit City	308.5	87. Seagram	126.8
38. U.S. Government	304.4	88. Dr. Pepper/7-Up	125.5
39. Sara Lee	299.7	89. Dow Chemical	125.1
40. MCI	297.4	90. Loews	124.5
41. Colgate-Palmolive	287.4	91. Visa	122.5
42. Nike	281.4	92. Kimberly-Clark	119.8
43. Macy's	280.5	93. U.S. Shoe Corp.	118.8
44. Hasbro	277.3	94. Imasco	117.6
45. SmithKline Beecham	269.7	95. B.A.T. Industries	116.9
46. Dayton Hudson	266.7	96. Daimler-Benz	116.6
47. Sprint	264.8	97. Bally Manufacturing	115.1
48. Wal-Mart	251.9	98. Pfizer	114.9
49. Bristol-Myers	250.2	99. Mitsubishi	113.4
50. Levi Strauss	248.9	100. Delta Air lines	113.1

Source: Advertising Age (September 28, 1994), p. 1

the advertising on television is persuasive.[18] Beautiful people drive fast, good-looking automobiles. Kids love the experience of going to McDonald's. Bud Light defeats Bud (or vice versa) in the Bud Bowl. Beer drinkers proclaim "life is good." People who wear Calvin Klein jeans look like models. The list of commercials aimed at creating subjective image differences is endless. Many of these advertisements are entertaining but provide relatively little information. Conversely, many television commercials mix information with persuasion, as when McDonald's advertised it was introducing the Arch Deluxe hamburger "aimed at adults," or when General Mills advertised that it was reducing prices on all of its cereals. Furthermore, all advertisements add some information by announcing that the product is available to consumers.

Persuasive advertising may provide valuable information about the quality of **experience goods**. *Experience goods* are those whose qualities can be identified only through trial *after buying the good*. Common examples include consumer nondurable convenience goods such as beer, toothpaste, soap, toiletries, and cereal and consumer durable goods including household appliances such as refrigerators and washing machines. Experience goods are distinguished from **search goods**, whose qualities can be judged before purchase through prepurchase testing. Search goods include fresh fruits and vegetables, which can be squeezed and smelled to test for freshness; fresh meats, which can be viewed; shoes, which can be tried on; and sofas and chairs, which can be sat on.

Consider two producers of toothpaste. Both toothpastes contain fluoride and have the American Dental Association seal of approval, but the high-quality toothpaste tastes wonderful, and the low-quality toothpaste tastes horrible. The costs of production are equal for both products. Toothpaste is an experience good, so consumers cannot determine quality (taste) unless they buy the toothpaste.

Which firm has a greater incentive to advertise?[19] The horrible-tasting toothpaste producer can induce consumers to buy its product once, but few will buy a second time. The wonderful-tasting toothpaste producer, however, can depend on many repeat purchases. The producer of the high-quality toothpaste has a much greater incentive to advertise because advertising will result not only in initial purchases but in repeat purchases. The low-quality toothpaste manufacturer has little incentive to advertise because advertising will result in initial purchases but few repeat purchases. Large advertising expenditures by the high-quality toothpaste manufacturer signal consumers that it produces a high-quality product, because only high-quality producers would advertise extensively. The low-quality producer would realize that consumers will not buy its toothpaste a second time regardless of their advertising expenditures, and therefore, the low-quality manufacturer would not waste resources on useless advertising.

According to this theory, Philip Morris initially spent a huge amount to advertise Miller Lite beer because Philip Morris knew that Lite was a high-quality product that consumers would be willing to buy again. If Philip Morris had thought that Lite beer was a low-quality product, it would not have wasted its scarce advertising resources on a known "loser." Viewed from a different angle, when Coca-Cola realized most consumers considered New Coke to be of lower quality than Coca-Cola Classic, the company quickly stopped advertising its "low-quality" New Coke and dramatically increased its advertising of "high-quality" Coca-Cola Classic. This advertising strategy signaled consumers that the company believed in the high quality of Coca-Cola Classic but had little faith in the quality of New Coke. It is not surprising, therefore, that in the long run only Coca-Cola Classic survived nationally.

Although the social benefits of persuasive advertising may be hard to identify, the private benefits are obvious. Persuasive advertising may increase market power and economic profits. The social costs of persuasive advertising, therefore, may be substantial.

Advertising and Market Structure

THE DORFMAN-STEINER MODEL[20]

One of the earlier models of the relationship between market structure and advertising was developed by Dorfman and Steiner. They consider a monopolist characterized by the following demand function:

$$Q = Q(P,A),$$

where Q represents the quantity demanded, P represents price, and A represents advertising expenditures. The monopolist wishes to maximize profits represented by Π as follows:

$$\Pi = TR - TC = P \cdot Q - C(Q) - A = P \cdot Q(P, A) - C(Q(P, A)) - A, \quad [13.6]$$

where $TC = C(Q) + A = C(Q(P,A)) + A$.

In the Dorfman-Steiner model, only Q is a function of A, whereas P is independent of the level of advertising expenditures A. Two conditions are necessary for profit maximization in Eq. 13.6. First, the monopolist must equate marginal revenue to marginal cost. Recall from Chapter 2 that the MR = MC condition implies:

$$\frac{P - MC}{P} = \frac{1}{|e_D|}, \quad [13.7]$$

where e_D is the price elasticity of demand.

Second, the monopolist must equate the marginal revenue associated with an increase in advertising expenditures, $\Delta TR/\Delta A$, to the marginal cost of the additional advertising expenditures $\Delta TC/\Delta A$. Because Dorfman and Steiner assumed $\Delta P/\Delta A = 0$, this condition can be written as:

$$MR = \frac{\Delta TR}{\Delta A} = P\frac{\Delta Q}{\Delta A} = MC = \frac{\Delta C}{\Delta Q}\frac{\Delta Q}{\Delta A} + \frac{\Delta A}{\Delta A} = \frac{\Delta TC}{\Delta A}. \quad [13.8]$$

Some algebraic manipulation of Eq. 13.8 yields the Dorfman-Steiner result:*

$$\frac{A}{PQ} = \frac{e_A}{|e_D|} = \left(\frac{P - MC}{P}\right)e_A.$$
[13.9]

Eq. 13.9 states that the advertising to sales ratio, A/PQ, is directly related to the price-cost margin, (P − MC)/P; inversely related to the price elasticity of demand, $|e_D|$; and directly related to the advertising elasticity of demand, e_A. The advertising elasticity of demand, e_A, is the percent change in the quantity demanded divided by the percent change in advertising expenditures. Industries in which advertising expenditures have a large impact on sales have high advertising elasticities of demand. For example, RCA and Hughes Electronics introduced the DSS 18-inch satellite TV dish with a tremendous advertising blitz, and the response from consumers was phenomenal.[21] In this case, therefore, the advertising elasticity of demand was very large. Eq. 13.9 creates a theoretical link between market structure and advertising because $1/|e_D|$ is the Lerner Index of market power as discussed in Chapter 2. If the monopolist faces competition from substitute products, e_D is large, its price-cost margin is low, and the advertising sales ratio will be small. As e_D decreases, the price-cost margin increases, and the advertising to sales ratio increases.

The basic Dorfman-Steiner model for monopoly suggests a positive link between market power and advertising: as the Lerner Index of market power increases, so does the advertising to sales ratio. The Dorfman-Steiner model, however, is a model of *monopoly* behavior, not a model of *oligopoly* behavior, and therefore, its implications are limited.

We now extend the model to cases of oligopoly.

---

*The algebra is as follows. Equation 13.8 can be written as:

$$P\frac{\Delta Q}{\Delta A} = \frac{\Delta C}{\Delta Q}\frac{\Delta Q}{\Delta A} + 1.$$

First multiply each side by ΔA to yield:

$$P\Delta Q = \frac{\Delta C}{\Delta Q}\Delta Q + \Delta A.$$

The term ΔC/ΔQ is simply MC, so we have:

$$(P - MC)\,\Delta Q = \Delta A.$$

Next multiply each side of the equation by:

$$\frac{A}{PQ\Delta A},$$

which yields:

$$\left(\frac{P - MC}{P}\right)\frac{\Delta Q}{\Delta A}\frac{A}{Q} = \frac{A\Delta A}{PQ\Delta A} = \frac{A}{PQ}.$$

Because $\frac{\Delta Q}{\Delta A}\frac{A}{Q}$ is the advertising elasticity of demand,

it follows that:

$$\frac{A}{PQ} = \left(\frac{P - MC}{P}\right)e_A = \frac{e_A}{|e_D|}.$$

ADVERTISING AND OLIGOPOLY BEHAVIOR

Consider the Dorfman-Steiner model in the case of duopoly with two identical firms. Firm 1's output is represented by q_1, its advertising expenditures are represented by A_1, and its market share is represented by $m_1 = (q_1/Q)$, where $Q = q_1 + q_2$. To simplify the analysis, we initially assume Cournot behavior with regard to advertising expenditures; that is, both firms assume their rival will maintain its current level of advertising. The advertising elasticity of demand for Firm 1 is denoted by e_{A1} and is equal to:*

$$e_{A1} = \left(\frac{A_1}{Q} \frac{\Delta Q}{\Delta A_1} \right) + \left(\frac{A_1}{m_1} \frac{\Delta m_1}{\Delta A_1} \right), \qquad\qquad [13.10]$$

where m_1, refers to the market share of Firm 1.

The two terms on the right-hand side of Eq. 13.10 represent the two effects of an increase in advertising. The first term is the *industry output effect*. Firm 1's increased advertising increases the demand for the generic industry product, not just its own brand. If Coke increases its advertising, consumers will purchase more soft drinks of all types, including Pepsi, 7-Up, Dr. Pepper, and store brands.

---

*The intuitive interpretation of this result is explained in the next paragraph. The technical derivation using calculus is:

$$\Pi = P \cdot q_1 - C(q_1) - A_1 = P \cdot q_1 \, (P, A_1) - C \, (q_1 \, (P, A_1)) - A_1.$$

To maximize profit, take the derivative with respect to A_1 and set it equal to zero:

$$\frac{d\pi}{dA_1} = P \frac{\partial q_1}{\partial A_1} - \frac{\partial C}{\partial q_1} \frac{\partial q_1}{\partial A_1} - \frac{\partial A_1}{\partial A_1} = (P - MC) \frac{\partial q_1}{\partial A_1} - \frac{\partial A_1}{\partial A_1} = 0.$$

Now substitute the following relationship:

$$q_1 = \frac{q_1}{Q} Q = m_1 Q$$

to yield:

$$\frac{d\pi}{dA_1} = (P - MC) \frac{\partial (m_1 Q)}{\partial A_1} - 1 = 0,$$

recognizing that:

$$\frac{\partial (m_1 Q)}{\partial A_1} = m_1 \frac{\partial Q}{\partial A_1} + Q \frac{\partial m_1}{\partial A_1}$$

for profit maximization, we obtain:

$$\frac{d\pi}{dA_1} = (P - MC) \left[m_1 \frac{\partial Q}{\partial A_1} + Q \frac{\partial m_1}{\partial A_1} \right] = 1,$$

or multiplying both sides by $\frac{A_1}{P q_1}$:

$$\frac{A_1}{P q_1} = \left(\frac{P - MC}{P} \right) \left[m_1 \frac{\partial Q}{\partial A_1} + Q \frac{\partial m_1}{\partial A_1} \right] \left(\frac{A_1}{q_1} \right)$$

$$\frac{A_1}{P q_1} = \left(\frac{P - MC}{P} \right) \left[\frac{m_1 A_1}{q_1} \frac{\partial Q}{\partial A_1} + \frac{\frac{A_1}{q_1} \frac{\partial m_1}{\partial A_1}}{Q} \right]$$

or

$$\frac{A_1}{P q_1} = \left(\frac{P - MC}{P} \right) \left[\frac{A_1}{Q} \frac{\partial Q}{\partial A_1} + \frac{A_1}{m_1} \frac{\partial m_1}{\partial A_1} \right]$$

The second term on the right side represents the *market share effect.* If Coke increases its advertising, its market share will increase relative to Pepsi, 7-Up, Dr. Pepper, and store brands.*

An example may help to clarify Eq. 13.10. If initially $Q = 1000$ and $q_1 = 500$, then $m_1 = .50$. Suppose Firm 1 increases its advertising by 1 percent, industry output increases by 1 percent to $Q' = 1010$ and Firm 1's market share increases by 2 percent to $m'_1 = .51$. According to Eq. 13.10, the advertising elasticity of demand for Firm 1 is $e_{Ai} = 1 + 2 = 3$. Firm 1's new output is $m'_1Q' = (.51) 1010 = 515$. The percentage change in q_1 is 3 percent.† As predicted by Eq. 13.10, a 1 percent increase in advertising expenditures results in a 3 percent increase in q_1.

Substituting e_{A1} from Eq. 13.10 into Eq. 13.9 yields:‡

$$\frac{A_1}{PQ_1} = \left(\frac{P-MC}{P}\right)e_{A1} = \left(\frac{P-MC}{P}\right)\left[\left(\frac{A_1}{Q}\frac{\Delta Q}{\Delta A_1}\right) + \left(\frac{A_1}{m_1}\frac{\Delta m_1}{\Delta A_1}\right)\right]. \qquad [13.11]$$

Eq. 13.11 suggests that oligopolists have an additional incentive to advertise. Not only does advertising increase the total demand for the product, Q, but it increases Firm 1's market share, m_1.

A comparison of Eqs. 13.9 and 13.11 suggests that for any given price-cost margin, the advertising to sales ratio will be larger in oligopoly than in monopoly because the advertising elasticity of demand, e_A, is larger under oligopoly than under monopoly. Intuitively, an increase in advertising does not change the monopolist's 100 percent market share, and this reduces the monopolist incentive to advertise.

One implication of Eq. 13.11 is that firms in competitive environments that face highly elastic demand curves with low price-cost margins will advertise very little. In fact, as the price-cost margin approaches zero, the advertising to sales ratio also approaches zero. This helps explain why individual farmers rarely advertise their wheat, milk, or oranges. Advertising in this case makes economic sense only if the farmers advertise collectively through organizations such as the American Dairy Council or the Florida Orange Growers.

There is a potential problem with the formulation of Eqs. 13.10 and 13.11. Suppose the Cournot assumption concerning advertising is wrong, and Firm 2 chooses to increase its advertising in response to Firm 1's increased advertising. Eq. 13.10 would then have to reflect the impact of Firm 2's increased advertising on total industry output and on Firm 1's market share. The new formulation would be:

$$e_{A1} = \left[\frac{(A_1 + A_2)}{(q_1 + q_2)}\frac{\Delta(q_1 + q_2)}{\Delta(A_1 + A_2)}\right]\frac{A_1}{A_1 + A_2} + \left(\frac{A_1}{m_1}\frac{\Delta m_1}{\Delta A_1}\right) + \left(\frac{A_2}{m_1}\frac{\Delta m_1}{\Delta A_2}\right)\left(\frac{A_1}{A_2}\frac{\Delta A_2}{\Delta A_1}\right). \qquad [13.12]$$

---

*Remember that assuming Cournot behavior regarding advertising, the other firm maintains its level of advertising expenditures. We will relax this assumption shortly.

†The percentage change in q_1 is:

$$\frac{\Delta q_1}{q_1} \times 100 = \frac{15}{500} \times 100 = 3\%.$$

‡See the footnote on page 321 for the derivation of this result using calculus.

Eq. 13.12 looks formidable, but it is simply the sum of three straightforward terms. The first term represents the industry output effect and must be positive. It incorporates the elasticity of industry output with respect to a change in total industry advertising expenditures (the term in brackets) and Firm 1's share of industry advertising.* The second term is identical to the second term in Eq. 13.10 and is the *market share effect* of Firm 1's advertising on Firm 1's market share. This term must be greater than or equal to zero. The additional third term reflects the impact of Firm 2's increased advertising on Firm 1's market share. The third term typically would be less than or equal to zero because $(\Delta m_1/\Delta A_2) \leq 0$ and $(\Delta A_2/\Delta A_1)$ would usually be greater than zero. In theory, however, $(\Delta A_2/\Delta A_1)$ could be negative if Firm 2 received so much benefit from an increase in Firm 1's advertising that it decided to reduce its own advertising in response.

Which formulation of e_{A1}, Eq. 13.10 with Cournot behavior or Eq. 13.12, is closer to reality? We know that under duopoly the prisoner's dilemma makes retaliation in response to price reductions fairly certain, but a response to a new advertising campaign is much more problematic. Price cuts can be matched immediately, whereas a new advertising campaign takes time to devise and implement. When Miller Lite commercials hit the television airwaves, it took quite some time for competitors to respond effectively, and much of Miller's increased market share has remained in place for decades. Until competitors come up with an effective advertising response, the firm that moves first with a successful campaign may significantly increase its market share.

Advertising campaigns, however, are inherently unpredictable. Optimistic firms tend to overestimate the positive second term in Eq. 13.12 and underestimate the negative third term. If the negative third term in Eq. 13.12 is underestimated or ignored, firms will have a tendency to advertise beyond their profit-maximizing level of advertising.

The possibility of excessive advertising beyond the profit-maximizing level can also be explained by the prisoner's dilemma. Figure 13.9 depicts a possible payoff matrix for high and low levels of advertising. This game has a dominant solution. Regardless of the competitor's choice, it always pays to choose a high level of advertising expenditures, and each firm will earn an economic profit of $100 million. If the two could manage to solve the dilemma, they would reduce their advertising expenditures to a low level and earn a profit of $120 million each. Overspending on advertising costs each firm $20 million in profits.

Evidence suggests that oligopolists often engage in excessive advertising of the type suggested by Figure 13.9. One of the most frequently studied examples is cigarette advertising. When antitrust policy broke up the American Tobacco Company and turned the industry into an oligopoly, advertising expenditures increased from $4.3 in 1910 to $13.8 million in 1913.[22] In the 1950s the introduction of king-sized cigarettes caused a sharp escalation in advertising expenditures.[23] More recently the ban on television and then radio advertising in the 1960s and 1970s resulted in a simultaneous decrease in advertising expenditures

---

*An alternative formulation weights the term in brackets by Firm 1's share of industry output.

	Firm 2 high advertising expenditures	Firm 2 low advertising expenditures
Firm 1 high advertising expenditures	100, 100	130, 80
Firm 1 low advertising expenditures	80, 130	120, 120

Figure 13.9   Oligopolistic advertising and the prisoner's dilemma (Firm 1's profits in $million, Firm 2's profits in $million).

and increase in profits. This evidence suggests that cigarette advertising has often gone beyond the joint profit-maximizing level.[24]

In a detailed econometric study of advertising in European markets, Lambin found that many industries appeared to advertise beyond the joint profit-maximizing level. These included the gasoline, coffee, yogurt, insecticide, deodorant, detergent, and soft drink industries.[25] Netter found similar results for a sample of American industries.[26]

To summarize the main conclusions concerning advertising to this point:

1. Firms with little market power have low price-cost margins and should have low advertising to sales ratios.
2. As a firm's price-cost margin increases, so should its advertising to sales ratio.
3. *Ceteris paribus,* oligopolists will have larger advertising to sales ratios than monopolists or competitive firms.
4. Oligopolists may tend to engage in excessive advertising.

Figure 13.10 summarizes the expected relationship between market power and advertising expenditures. The relationship is nonlinear. The advertising to sales ratio increases with increases in the concentration ratio up to level CR* and decreases with increases in concentration beyond that level. Notice that the monopolist's advertising is significantly greater than the perfectly competitive level of advertising.

So far we have concentrated on the relationship between market structure and product differentiation by emphasizing a theoretical link suggesting that increased concentration causes increased product differentiation; that is, increased market power causes increased advertising. The link between market structure and product differentiation, however, may run in the opposite direction, with increased product differentiation causing increased concentration.[27] The discussion of product proliferation in Chapters 11 and 12 suggested such a linkage, as did the discussion of raising rivals' costs through advertising in Chapter 11. We now consider this alternative view of the relationship between product differentiation and market structure.

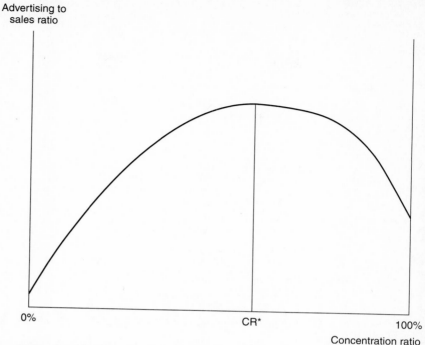

Figure 13.10 A nonlinear relationship between concentration and the advertising to sales ratio.

THE PRODUCT DIFFERENTIATION ADVANTAGES OF FIRST MOVERS

Consider the market for a newly introduced experience good, hypothetically called a *zerbit*. Recall that experience goods are goods whose qualities can only be identified through trial after buying the good. Examples include beer, toothpaste, soap, toiletries, cereal, refrigerators, and washing machines.

The first mover into the zerbit market faces a problem because consumers are initially uninformed about zerbits. Consumers, therefore, risk being disappointed if they purchase a zerbit for the first time. In Figure 13.11, if all consumers were fully informed about zerbits the demand would be:

$$P = 100 - Q.$$

Before their introduction, however, all consumers are uninformed about zerbits and risk buying a zerbit and disliking it. Uninformed consumers will be willing to pay less for zerbits than informed consumers, so the demand for zerbits before introduction is less than $P = 100 - Q$. Assume the demand for zerbits if all consumers are uniformed is:[28]

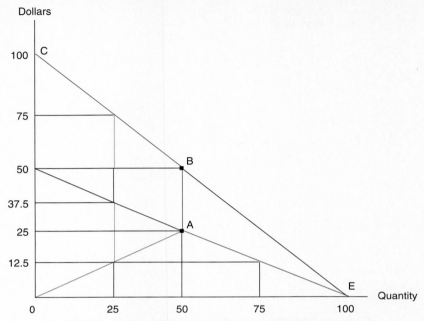

Figure 13.11   The demand curve for a first mover in the zerbit market.

$$P = (100 - Q)(1 - \tau),$$

where τ represents the risk-cost factor of trying zerbits for the first time. τ measures the risks associated with wasting money on the purchase of a good that the consumer might dislike. The risk-cost factor τ is larger the larger the probability of a bad consumption experience. In addition, τ is larger with less frequent repeat purchases because with infrequent repeat purchases the consumer is "stuck" with a bad decision for a long time. For example, τ is larger for a washing machine than a box of cereal because a mistake in buying a box of cereal can be corrected in a matter of days, whereas a bad washing machine can cause the consumer problems for years.

If $\tau = 0.5$, then the introductory demand for zerbits is:

$$P = (100 - Q)(1 - 0.5) = 50 - \frac{1}{2}Q.$$

Figure 13.11 depicts both demand curves. At the time of introduction the first mover faces the lower demand curve, $P = 50 - \frac{1}{2}Q$. Suppose that the first mover decides to introduce zerbits at a low introductory price of $P = 25$ and sells fifty units. After the introductory offer ends, demand increases to $P = 100 - Q$ for the fifty consumers who are completely informed, and the first mover monopolist can increase price to P = 50 and continue to sell fifty zerbits. After introduction, the new demand curve for the first mover is depicted in Figure 13.11 as the red kinky line CBAE, which is composed of part of the informed and part of the uninformed demand curves.

Even if Firm 2 develops a zerbit that is actually identical to the first mover's zerbits, it faces a different demand curve than line CBAE because consumers cannot be certain that Firm 2's zerbits are actually identical to Firm 1's zerbits. To derive Firm 2's demand curve, it is necessary to separate consumers into two groups. Group 1 consists of informed consumers who are already "hooked" on the first mover's zerbits. Each of these consumers, except the fiftieth consumer, receives consumer surplus greater than zero from the consumption of zerbits. Consider the consumer who buys the twenty-fifth zerbit: that consumer's reservation price is 75 while the price is 50, so for the consumer of the twenty-fifth zerbit, consumer surplus equals 25 (75 − 50). What is the highest price this consumer would pay to try Firm 2's zerbits? Assume group 1 consumers would pay a maximum price to try Firm 2's zerbits of:

$$P = (100 - Q)(1 - \tau) - S,$$

where S represents the amount of current consumer surplus the consumer receives from the consumption of the first mover's zerbits. Consumer surplus enters into the consumer's decision because the consumer risks sacrificing this consumer surplus if he or she tries Firm 2's zerbits and does not like them. For the consumer of the twenty-fifth zerbit in Figure 13.11, S = 25, and therefore, the maximum price this consumer would be willing to pay to try Firm 2's zerbits is:

$$P = (100 - Q)(1 - \tau) - S = (100 - 25)(1 - 0.5) - 25 = 75(0.5) - 25 = 12.5.$$

This creates a large **first-mover advantage** because the twenty-fifth consumer would rather continue to pay 50 for the first mover's zerbits rather than try Firm 2's zerbits at a price greater than 12.5. The consumer of the fiftieth unit receives no consumer surplus and would try Firm 2's zerbits at a price of P = (100 − 50)(0.5) − 0 = 25, and the consumer of the tenth unit receives consumer surplus equal to 40 (90 − 50) and would try Firm 2's zerbits at a price of P = (100 − 10)(0.5) − 40 = 5. In Figure 13.11, the line 0A traces out the maximum price that each group 1 consumer would pay to try Firm 2's zerbits.

Group 2 consumers have never tried zerbits because the first mover's introductory price of 25 was above the reservation price that they were willing to pay to try zerbits. Group 2 consumers lie on the section of the uninformed consumer demand curve depicted by AE. To induce these consumers to try its zerbits, Firm 2 must charge a price below 25.

If the first mover continues to charge P = 50, Firm 2 will have to charge a price below 25 to sell any zerbits.[29] Firm 2's demand curve in Figure 13.12 is derived by taking the horizontal difference between the upward sloping line seg-

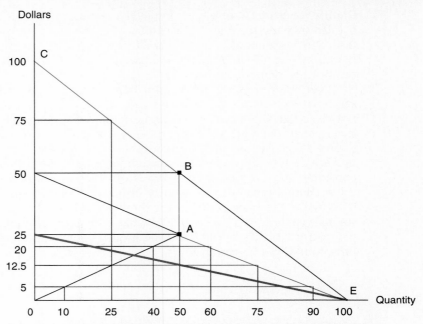

Figure 13.12   Derivation of Firm 2's demand curve in the zerbit market.

ment 0A and the downward sloping red line segment AE. Consider the following points on the demand curve for Firm 2's zerbits:

Firm 2's Price	(1) Quantity on Line AE in Figure 13.12	(2) Quantity on Line OA in Figure 13.12	(1) Minus (2) Firm's 2 Quantity Demanded
25	50	50	0
20	60	40	20
15	70	30	40
12.5	75	25	50
10	80	20	60
5	90	10	80
0	100	0	100

Firm 2's introductory demand curve is:

$$P_2 = 25 - \frac{1}{4}q_2.$$

Firm 2's demand curve is identified as the heavy black line in Figure 13.12.

This lower demand curve places Firm 2 at a tremendous disadvantage vis-à-vis the first mover. While the first mover sells at a price of 50, Firm 2 will have to sell at a price below 25. For example, recall the consumer of the twenty-fifth zerbit. This consumer would have tried the first mover's zerbits at a price of 37.5 but will try Firm 2's zerbits only at a price below 12.5. To capture consumers with high reservation prices, Firm 2 must charge a very low price.

If there are significant sunk costs associated with entry, Firm 2 may find it impossible to enter and earn a profit. Suppose, for example, that the marginal cost of producing zerbits is constant and equal to 10, and sunk costs are 400. If Firm 2 enters at its profit-maximizing introductory price of 17.5, it sells thirty zerbits, and profits would be:*

$$\Pi = PQ - mcQ - \text{Sunk Costs} = (17.5)(30) - (10)(30) - 400 = -175.$$

Under these cost conditions, Firm 2 cannot enter and earn a profit. However, the first mover has already paid its sunk costs and earns a profit of:

$$\Pi = PQ - mcQ = 50(50) - 10(50) = 2,000$$

In response to entry, the first mover is capable of responding aggressively and lowering price below 50 while still earning a substantial economic profit. This serves as an additional deterrent to entry.

Empirical evidence of the success of first movers is particularly strong in the pharmaceuticals industry. Several studies have found that first movers in this industry retain a large advantage over late entrants, even when the first mover's price remains well above the entrant's price. Masson and Steiner found that retailers paid far more for leading branded drugs than the competitive generic drugs of late entrants.[30] For a sample of twenty-nine drugs, Hurwitz and Caves found that the price of branded leaders was more than twice the price of latecomer generic equivalents.[31] In the Hurwitz and Caves study, the market leaders continued to dominate, despite selling at much higher prices. In addition, the leaders' market shares were positively related to their investment in sales promotion, including advertising.

There are many other documented cases of first movers maintaining dominant shares despite selling at higher prices than late entrants.[32] Some of the well-documented cases were discussed in earlier chapters, including Clorox liquid bleach, ReaLemon reconstituted lemon juice, Campbell's soups in the United States, Heinz soups in Great Britain, and Coca-Cola soft drinks.

---

*From the twice as steep rule,

$$MR = 25 - \frac{1}{2}Q.$$

For profit maximization, MR = MC:
$$25 - \frac{1}{2}Q = 10 \text{ or } Q = 30.$$

▗ *Advertising as a Barrier to Entry*

Recall from Chapter 5 that there may be an *absolute cost advantage* for incumbent firms associated with the *cumulative* effects of advertising. Because advertising generally has an effect on future as well as current demand, it must be viewed as an investment rather than a current expenditure. Successful advertising campaigns have impacts far into the future. Miller Lite's "tastes great, less filling" campaign ended many years ago, yet the impact of that campaign continues into the present. If the impact of advertising is cumulative, entrants have to overcome not only current advertising efforts but also the impact of past campaigns by established firms. If a new cola manufacturer wishes to compete with Coke and Pepsi, it will have to spend far more on advertising in its first few years than the combined amounts spent by Coca-Cola and Pepsico. The cumulative impact of advertising provides a powerful advantage for successful first movers.

Figure 13.13 shows the possible advertising advantage for first movers. Two **advertising response functions** are drawn in Figure 13.13. An advertising response function is $Q = f(A)$, where Q is sales and A is number of advertising messages. The entrant's advertising response function is first horizontal, then rises at an increasing rate, then rises at a decreasing rate, and finally decreases. This assumes a threshold level of advertising messages, AM_1 in Figure 13.13, that the entrant must exceed to have any impact on sales.* Once the threshold level is

---

*Figure 13.13 is based on the assumption that consumers must be saturated with some minimum level of advertising to learn about the existence of the good and be enticed into a trial.

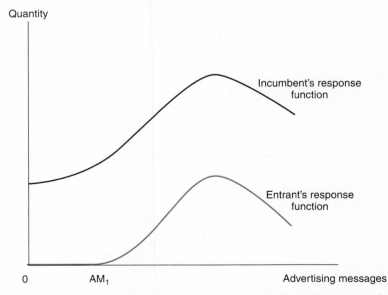

Figure 13.13   Comparison of an incumbent's and an entrant's advertising response function.

reached, the marginal impact of additional advertising messages increases, then the marginal impact decreases, and finally the marginal impact becomes *negative* as consumers become tired of the advertising campaign and respond with a negative backlash. An incumbent firm has no threshold level of advertising because the cumulative effect of previous advertising campaigns ensures that current advertising has an immediate impact on sales. Because the impact of previous advertising has not been completely depreciated, the incumbent firm will have a higher level of sales for any given level of advertising expenditures. This results in lower average advertising expenditures for incumbents than for established firms.

The threshold level of advertising expenditures for entrants is a sunk cost associated with entry and creates an entry barrier because incumbent firms have paid this sunk cost in the past. If the threshold level of advertising is large, the sunk costs of entry will rise significantly and the capital barrier to entry will increase. High sunk costs result in a more or less permanent advantage for first movers over late entrants. The ability of Miller Lite to maintain a large market share in the face of a great deal of entry into the light beer market may be viewed in part as a result of Miller's first mover advantage. Even a financially strong entrant may find it difficult to overcome the sunk costs of entry. Kodak learned this lesson when it attempted to enter the consumer battery industry.[33]

Strategic Advantages of Heavily Advertised Brands

Established brands have an ability to respond aggressively to entry by expanding advertising. Recall from Chapter 10 that given asymmetric information, firms might attempt to preempt future entry by cutting price in response to current entry. In markets dominated by heavily advertised brands, established firms may respond to entry by aggressively expanding advertising.

Several examples of aggressive advertising responses to entry have been documented. At the turn of the century when the American Tobacco Company was threatened with a loss of market share to Turkish tobacco brands, it responded by introducing its own Turkish tobacco brands and increasing its advertising expenditures from 0.5 percent to 20.3 percent of sales.[34] When Procter & Gamble introduced a new decaffeinated coffee, "High Point," in 1980, General Foods increased the advertising of its dominant brand "Sanka" by more than 700 percent to $90 million a year.[35] Minute Maid and Tropicana also responded aggressively to Procter & Gamble's entry into the ready-made orange juice market in 1983.[36]

Cubbin and Domberger found that for a sample of forty-two British firms in eighteen consumer goods industries, dominant firms were much more likely to respond to entry with a large increase in advertising.[37] Significant retaliation occurred in 61 percent of the markets (11 of 18) and by 38 percent of established firms (16 of 42).

These examples of the strategic use of advertising in response to entry are consistent with the findings of Smiley reported in Chapter 11 that advertising is the most commonly used method of entry deterrence.

◢ *Product Differentiation and Increased Competition*

To this point the emphasis of this chapter has been on how product differentiation and advertising result in increased market power. Product differentiation and advertising, however, may result in lower levels of market power. We have already noted that informational advertising is likely to have a procompetitive impact. In addition, numerous case studies show that advertising can lead to a *decrease* in concentration. Advertising may be the only effective method of entering some markets. RCA and Hughes Electronics entered the direct satellite television market with the DSS system through the use of a massive advertising campaign. The small satellite dishes provided new competition to cable systems and large satellite dish systems. Market penetration for the DSS system would undoubtedly have been far lower in the absence of a huge advertising campaign.[38] In the fast-food industry, the entry of Wendy's and Subway on a national level was made possible through extensive advertising campaigns. Advertising also helped Japanese automobile manufacturers enter the United States market on a large scale in the 1960s and 1970s. The recent success of Saturn in the automobile market has also been heavily dependent on advertising. Finally, advertising enabled Pepsi to slowly chip away at Coke's dominant market share. Pepsi's share increased from 10 percent in 1940 to 31 percent in 1987.[39] Pepsi's major market share gains have come during periods when Pepsi's advertising to sales ratio was higher than Coke's.

◢ *Advertising and Welfare*

Informational advertising lowers prices and increases welfare. There is little debate among economists concerning informational advertising and welfare.[40] The welfare debate concerns persuasive advertising. Some economists believe persuasive advertising reduces welfare, whereas others believe the effect is ambiguous.

One of the most influential models in this debate was developed by Dixit and Norman.[41] Figure 13.14 illustrates their argument for the monopoly case. Let A represent the monopolist's initial level of advertising and A* represents an increased level of advertising. The increased advertising causes an increase in demand from D(A) to D(A*). Marginal cost, excluding advertising, is MC, and p, Q, p*, and Q* represent the profit-maximizing levels of price and output given A and A*, respectively. Dixit and Norman note that two different welfare standards can be applied: one is based on the lower demand curve D(A), and the other is based on the higher demand curve D(A*).

CASE I: D(A) AS THE WELFARE STANDARD

First consider the change in welfare based on the lower demand curve D(A) as the welfare standard. Advertising results in an increase in consumption of Q* − Q, and this increase in consumption causes an increase in social surplus equal to area DEGF, or the red shaded area in Figure 13.14. The change in welfare is there-

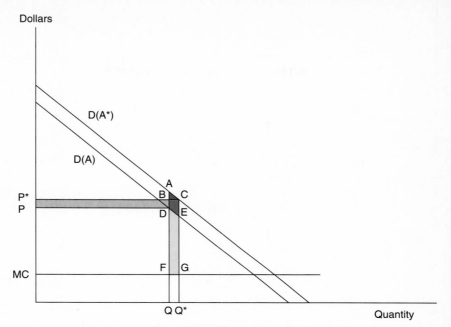

Figure 13.14 The welfare effects of increased advertising.

fore the red shaded area *minus* the increased cost of advertising (A* − A). (Note that the increased cost of advertising [A* − A] is not shown in Figure 13.14.)

CASE II: D(A*) AS THE WELFARE STANDARD

Now consider the change in welfare based on the higher demand curve D(A*) as the welfare standard. An increase in consumption of Q* − Q causes an increase in social surplus equal to area ACGF or the sum of the dark gray and red solid and shaded areas. The change in welfare is therefore the dark gray and red solid and shaded areas *minus* the increased cost of advertising (A* − A), which is not shown in Figure 13.14. For small changes in advertising, the dark gray and solid red areas, area ACED, will be very small relative to the red shaded area, area DEGF, and therefore, the red shaded area, area DEGF, *minus* (A* − A) is a close approximation of the change in welfare associated with a small change in advertising.

Regardless of the standard being used, in Figure 13.14 the red shaded area minus (A* − A) is a good approximation of the change in welfare associated with a small change in advertising.

An alternative approximation of this area and of the welfare change is:

$$\Delta W = (\text{light gray} + \text{solid red} + \text{red shaded area}) - (\text{light gray area}) - (A^* - A) \qquad [13.13]$$

The (light gray + solid red + red shaded area) − (A* − A), however, is simply the change in profits, $\Delta \pi$, associated with an increase in advertising from A to A*. Eq. 13.13, therefore, can be expressed as:

$$\Delta W = \Delta \pi - (\text{light gray area}) = \Delta \pi - Q(\Delta p). \qquad [13.14]$$

Dividing both sides of Eq. 13.14 by ΔA, the change in welfare associated with a change in advertising can then be identified as:

$$\frac{\Delta W}{\Delta A} = \frac{\Delta \pi}{\Delta A} - Q\frac{\Delta P}{\Delta A}. \qquad [13.15]$$

The term $\Delta \Pi/\Delta A$ is the marginal profit associated with a change in advertising expenditures. Profit maximization requires that: the monopolist continue to increase advertising as long as $\Delta \Pi/\Delta A > 0$, and therefore, for the *last* dollar spent on advertising, $\Delta \Pi/\Delta A = 0$. Using this fact, we see that profit maximization requires that for a small change in advertising:

$$\frac{\Delta W}{\Delta A} = \frac{\Delta \pi}{\Delta A} - Q\frac{\Delta P}{\Delta A} = 0 - Q\frac{\Delta P}{\Delta A} < 0. \qquad (13.16)$$

The implication of Eq. 13.16 is that for a profit-maximizing monopolist, a slight *decrease* in advertising must *increase* welfare. From a social standpoint the monopolist's advertising is excessive.

In regard to the Dixit and Norman welfare analysis, Fisher and McGowan argued that it is generally improper to compare welfare on the basis of just one of the two demand curves because advertising changes consumers' preferences, and therefore, the consumers' utility, given demand curve D(A), cannot be compared with the consumers' utility given demand curve D(A*).[42]

Empirical Evidence

Advertising and product differentiation, in theory, can have a positive or negative impact on prices, profits, and welfare. Informative advertising tends to have a positive impact, whereas persuasive advertising tends to have a negative impact. Economists have conducted a vast array of empirical studies to test the relationship among advertising, market structure, and profits. To distinguish between informative and persuasive advertising, most studies have classified goods into different categories based on their characteristics and the way they are marketed.

Recall that experience goods include consumer nondurable convenience goods such as beer, toothpaste, soap, toiletries, and cereal. Search goods include fruits and vegetables, shoes, and sofas and chairs. Theory suggests that much of the advertising associated with experience goods is persuasive, and much of the advertising associated with search goods is informational.

Another important distinction is between manufacturers' advertising and retailers' advertising. Manufacturers' advertising tends to emphasize persuasion and the importance of brand loyalty, whereas retailers' advertising is more likely to emphasize lower prices. A great deal of manufacturers' advertising is through television and radio, whereas most retailers' advertising appears in the print media. Given these characteristics, manufacturers' advertising is more likely to have anticompetitive effects, and retailers' advertising is more likely to have a positive impact.

Empirical attempts to identify the nature of the relationship between advertising and market power are plagued by one serious problem: the direction of the relationship is uncertain. Advertising may erect an entry barrier that enables firms to earn high profits. However, high profits may enable firms to spend large amounts on advertising. Statistical investigations of the relationship between profits and advertising, therefore, may suffer from **simultaneity bias**. The studies noted below generally assume that causation runs *from* advertising *to* profitability; that is, advertising erects an entry barrier that enables firms to earn high profits. It is important to recognize, however, that the direction of causation *from* profitability *to* advertising is equally plausible. Many of the studies apply statistical techniques aimed at correcting for this problem.* Given this important caveat, we proceed to the current state of empirical evidence.

Empirical evidence has generally been consistent with expectations.[43] First, a large number of statistical studies in manufacturing industries have attempted to explain the determinants of profitability by using advertising as one of a group of independent variables. Table 13.2 summarizes the results of these studies. Twenty-five of the thirty-three studies showed some evidence of a positive and statistically significant relationship between profits and advertising. In ten studies the advertising variable was statistically insignificant in at least some portion of the study, whereas in two studies the sign of the advertising variable was indeterminate because the sign was sometimes positive and sometimes negative. Table 13.2 suggests that advertising is likely to exert a positive influence on profits in manufacturing industries.

The studies in Table 13.2 examined the relationship between profits and advertising; other studies have analyzed the link between prices and advertising. The National Commission on Food Marketing found, for example, that advertised brands consistently sold at higher prices than non-advertised distributors' brands.[44] On average, prices were 21 percent higher for the advertised brands. Similarly, Morris found that advertised brands of instant coffee, margarine, and toothpaste were sold at much higher prices than distributors' brands in Britain.[45] For a sample of 133 processed food products, Wills and W. F. Mueller found a strong relationship between advertising outlays and prices.[46] Overall there is an impressive body of evidence that on average manufacturers' advertising results in higher profits and prices.

With regard to retailing, the evidence is much more limited, but several studies provide valuable insight. The empirical evidence concerning the relationship between retailers' advertising and profits leads to a very different conclusion than the evidence with regard to manufacturers' advertising. Much of this evidence was presented earlier in this chapter. Recall that eyeglass prices were significantly lower in markets that permitted optometrists to advertise than in markets that prohibited advertising, and prescription drug prices were lower in states that permitted price advertising.[47] Furthermore, local newspaper advertising reduced the

---

*The technique uses a simultaneous system of equations to estimate the relationship between profits and advertising.

TABLE 13.2 **Summary of Studies of the Relationship Between Profits and Advertising in Manufacturing Industries**

Author(s)—Year of Study	Relationship Between Profits and Advertising			
	Positive (+)	Negative (-)	Not Significant (e)	Indeterminate (?)
B. Imel and P. Helmberger—1971			e	
L. Esposito and F. Esposito—1971	+[1]			
W. Shephard—1972	+[2]			
J. Vernon and R. Nouse—1973	+			
K. Boyer—1974	+			
M. Porter—1974	+[3]		e[4]	
P. Nelson—1975				?
R. Caves, J. Khalilzadeh-Shirazi, M. Porter—1975	+			
J. Dalton and J. Penn—1976	+			
A. Strickland and L. Weiss—1976	+[5]		e[6]	
R. Stonebraker—1976	+			
P. Hart and E. Morgan—1977	+			
J. Carter—1977	+			
S. Nickell and D. Metcalf—1978	+			
T. Hitris—1978			e	
H. Grabowski and D. Mueller—1978			e[7]	
M. Porter—1979			e	

[1]For consumer goods. [4]For nonconvenience goods. [6]For consumer goods.

[2]For consumer goods. [5]For producer goods. [7]Pharmaceuticals industry only.

[3]For convenience goods.

Sources: B. Imel and P. Helmberger, "Estimation of Structure-Profit Relationships with Application to the Food Processing Sector," *American Economic Review* 61 (1971): 614–27; L. Esposito and F. Esposito, "Foreign Competition and Domestic Industry Profitability," *Review of Economics and Statistics* 53 (1971): 343–53; W. G. Shepherd, "The Elements of Market Structure," *Review of Economics and Statistics* 54 (1972): 25–37; J. M. Vernon and R. E. Nourse, "Profit Rates and Market Structure in Advertising Intensive Firms," *Journal of Industrial Economics* 22 (1973): 1–20; Kenneth D. Boyer, "Informative and Goodwill Advertising," *Review of Economics and Statistics* 56 (November 1974): 541–8; Michael E. Porter, "Consumer Behavior, Retailer Power and Market Performance in Consumer Goods Industries," *Review of Economics and Statistics* 56 (November 1974): 429; Philip Nelson, "The Economic Consequences of Advertising," *Journal of Business* (April 1975): 237; Richard E. Caves, J. Khalilzadeh-Shirazi and M. E. Porter, "Scale Economies in Statistical Analyses of Market Power," *Review of Economics and Statistics* (May 1975): 133–40; J. A. Dalton and D. W. Penn, "The Concentration-Profitability Relationship: Is There a Critical Concentration Ratio?" *Journal of Industrial Economics* 25 (1977): 133–42; Allyn D. Strickland and Leonard W. Weiss, "Advertising, Concentration, and Price-Cost Margins," *Journal of Political Economy* (October 1976): 1109–21; John Carter, "In Search of Synergy: A Structure-Performance Test," *Review of Economics and Statistics* 59 (1977): 279–89; R. J. Stonebraker, "Corporate Profits and the Risk of Entry," *Review of Economics and Statistics* 58 (1976): 33–9; P. Hart and E. Morgan, "Market Structure and Economic Performance in the United Kingdom," *Journal of Industrial Economics* 25 (1977): 177–93; S. Nickell and D. Metcalf, "Monopolistic Industries and Monopoly Profits or, Are Kellogg's Cornflakes Overpriced," *Economic Journal* 88 (1978): 254–68; T. Hitiris, "Effective Protection and Economic Performance in UK Manufacturing Industry, 1963 and 1968,"

Author(s)—Year of Study	Relationship Between Profits and Advertising			
	Positive (+)	Negative (-)	Not Significant (e)	Indeterminate (?)
S. Martin—1979	+			
T. Nakao—1979	+			
S. Martin—1979	+			
P. Geroski—1981	+			
T. Nagle—1981			e	
P. Geroski—1982	+			
R. Bradburd, R. Caves—1982				?
D. Ravenscraft—1983	+			
V. Gupta—1983	+			
R. Clarke—1984			e	
M. Salinger—1984	+			
J. Borthwell, T. Cooley and T. Hall—1984	+			
R. Connoly, M. Hirschey—1984			e	
J. Kwoka and D. Ravenscraft—1986	+			
W. Shepherd—1986	+			
I. Domowitz, R. Hubbard, and B. Peterson—1986	+			

Economic Journal 88 (1978): 107–20; H. G. Grabowski and D. C. Mueller, "Industrial Research and Development, Intangible Capital Stocks, and Firm Profit Rates," *Bell Journal of Economics* 9 (1978): 328–43; M. E. Porter, "The Structure Within Industries and Companies' Performance," *Review of Economics and Statistics* 61 (1979): 214–27; Stephen Martin, "Entry Barriers, Concentration and Profits," *Southern Economic Journal* 46 (1979): 471–88; T. Nakao, "Profit Rates and Market Shares of Leading Industrial Firms in Japan," *Journal of Industrial Economics* 27 (1979): 371–83; Stephen Martin, "Advertising, Concentration and Profitability: The Simultaneity Problem," *Bell Journal of Economics* (Autumn 1979): 639–47; P. Geroski, "Specification and Testing the Profits-Concentration Relationship: Some Experiments for the UK," *Economica* 48 (1981): 279–88; T. T. Nagle, "Do Advertising-Profitability Studies Really Show that Advertising Creates a Barrier to Entry," *Journal of Law and Economics* 24 (1981): 333–50; P. A. Geroski, "Simultaneous-Equation Models of the Structure-Performance Paradigm," *European Economic Review* 19 (1982): 145–58; R. M. Bradburd and R. E. Caves, "A Closer Look at the Effect of Market Growth on Industries' Profits," *Review of Economics and Statistics* 64 (1982): 635–45; David Ravenscraft, "Structure-Profits Relationships in Line of Business and Industry Level," *Review of Economics and Statistics* 65 (1983): 22–31; V. Gupta, "A Simultaneous Determination of Structure, Conduct and Performance in Canadian Manufacturing," *Oxford Economic Papers* 35 (1983): 281–301; R. Clarke, "Profit Margins and Market Concentration in UK Manufacturing Industry: 1970–6," *Applied Economics* 16 (1984): 57–71; Michael Salinger, "Tobin's q, Unionization and the Concentration-Profits Relationship," *Rand Journal of Economics* (Summer 1984): 159–70; James L. Bothwell, Thomas F. Cooley, and Thomas E. Hall, "A New View of the Market Structure-Performance Debate," *Journal of Industrial Economics* (June 1984): 397–417; John E. Kwoka, Jr. and David J. Ravenscraft, "Cooperation vs. Rivalry: Price-Cost Margins by Line of Business," *Economica* (August 1986): 351–63; William G. Shepherd, "Tobin's q and the Structure-Conduct-Performance Relationship: Comment," *American Economic Review* (December 1986): 1205–10; and Ian Domowitz, R. Glenn Hubbard, and Bruce C. Peterson, "The Intertemporal Stability of the Concentration-Margins Relationship," *Journal of Industrial Economics* (September 1986): 13–33.

profits of convenience goods, and magazine advertising tended to increase the level of price competition for shopping goods such as furniture and appliances.[48] Furthermore, although Boyer found a significant positive relationship between advertising and profits for manufacturing industries, he also found that for retailing there is a significant negative relationship between advertising and profits.[49] Overall, it appears that in retailing, advertising exerts a negative effect on profits.

SUMMARY

1. A reexamination of the Bertrand model with product differentiation suggests that product differentiation can result in higher prices.

2. Monopolistic competition and oligopoly may result in either too much or too little product differentiation.

3. Product differentiation and advertising can have either a positive or a negative economic impact. Informational advertising, particularly price advertising, tends to have a positive impact, whereas persuasive advertising often has a negative impact.

4. Theory suggests that advertising intensity should be highest in oligopoly, lowest in highly competitive markets, and somewhere in between in monopolized markets. Furthermore, advertising in oligopoly may exceed the socially optimal level. Persuasive advertising in particular is likely to exceed the social optimum.

5. The first-mover advantage associated with the introduction of a new product may result in persistent market power. If significant sunk costs are also associated with entering the market, entrants will have great difficulty competing effectively against first movers.

6. Product proliferation may be used strategically to preempt entry and maintain market power. Increased advertising expenditures can be used to raise rivals' costs and deter entry.

7. Empirical evidence supports the position that advertising can have positive or negative effects. Generally, positive effects are associated with retailing and search goods, and negative effects are associated with manufacturing and experience goods. There are, however, many exceptions to this general rule.

KEY TERMS

advertising response function	informational advertising
convenience goods	persuasive advertising
Dorfman-Steiner model	search goods
experience goods	shopping goods
first-mover advantage	simultaneity bias
horizontal product differentiation	vertical product differentiation

DISCUSSION QUESTIONS

1. In what type of market structure would you expect the most product differentiation: perfect competition, oligopoly, or monopoly? Why?

2. You are to argue in a debate on the topic, "advertising is a waste of society's resources." Which side of the argument would you prefer to argue: pro or con? Why?

3. In 1964 the United States banned television advertising of cigarettes. Is it possible that the television advertising ban increased the cigarette industry's profits? Explain.

4. Suppose society decided to place an "excess advertising tax" on advertising above 5 percent of a firm's gross sales. Do you believe such a tax would improve economic efficiency? Would firms such as Coca-Cola and Pepsico fight such a tax? Should they fight such a tax?

5. Which market structure is likely to result in the most advertising: perfect competition, oligopoly, or monopoly? Why?

6. Are oligopolists likely to advertise at the joint profit maximizing level? Explain why or why not.

7. Does empirical evidence suggest that advertising is a barrier to entry? Why or why not?

PROBLEMS

1. (You need a calculator to answer this problem.) In the Bertrand Model with product differentiation, suppose that the two Bertrand firms face the following symmetric demand curves:

$$q_1 = 96 - 2p_1 + \frac{1}{2}p_2$$

$$q_2 = 96 - 2p_2 + \frac{1}{2}p_1$$

where $q_1, q_2, \geq 0$ and $p_1, p_2 \leq 48$

   a. Is product differentiation more or less significant in this example than in the example given in the text in Eqs. 13.1A and 13.1B? Why?
   b. Given your answer to part (a), would you expect the equilibrium price to be higher or lower than the equilibrium price of 40 given Eqs. 13.1A and 13.1B?
   c. Find the Bertrand equilibrium.

2. The Waldman Ice Cream truck example used two trucks. The Nash equilibrium in the absence of collusion was for the two firms to locate at the middle. Interestingly, if there were three trucks competing instead of two, no Nash

equilibrium exists. Instead, there is only a mixed strategy equilibrium. Why is there no pure strategy equilibrium with three trucks? [Hint: Try positioning the trucks anywhere along the route. Why does at least one truck always have an incentive to move?]

3. (You need a calculator to answer this problem.) In a monopolistically competitive industry, total profits π are a function of the number of firms n as follows:

$$\pi = \pi(n) = 10 - \frac{1}{10}n$$

Furthermore, consumer surplus CS is a function of n where:

$$CS(n) = \sqrt{n}$$

   a. In long-run equilibrium how many firms will exist in this industry?
   b. In long-run equilibrium what is the sum of profit plus consumer surplus? Is this the socially optimal level of product differentiation? [Hint: What happens to the value of $\pi(n) + CS(n)$ for values of n slightly smaller and slightly larger than the value of n that answers part (a)?]
   c. (optional using calculus) What is the optimal number of firms in this industry? [Hint: For what value of n is $\pi(n) + CS(n)$ maximized?]

4. (You need a calculator to answer this question.) In the first-mover model of the zerbit industry presented in this chapter, suppose the risk-cost factor τ increased from 0.5 to 0.75.

   a. What would be the new introductory demand curve for zerbits?
   b. If the first mover introduced zerbits at a price P = 12.5, what would be the new demand curve faced by the first mover?
   c. Derive the demand curve for a second-mover firm. What is the highest price at which the second mover can sell any zerbits?
   d. Has the increase in the risk-cost factor τ made entry more difficult?

REFERENCES

1. For a theoretical discussion see André de Palma, Robin Lindsey, Balder von Hohenbalken, and Douglas S. West, "Spatial Price and Variety Competition in an Urban Retail Market: A Nested Logit Analysis," *International Journal of Industrial Organization* 12 (September 1994): 331–57. For empirical evidence see Richard J. Claycombe and Tamara E. Mahan, "Spatial Aspects of Retail Market Structure Beef Pricing Revisited," *International Journal of Industrial Organization* 11 (June 1993): 283–91.
2. *Financial World* (May 10, 1994), p. 1
3. F. M. Scherer, *Industrial Market Structure and Economic Performance* (Chicago: Rand-McNally, 1980), p. 381–2.

4. The results obtained in the section draw on Avinash K. Dixit and Joseph E. Stiglitz, "Monopolistic Competition and Optimum Product Diversity," *American Economic Review* 67 (1977): 297–308; and Michael A. Spence, "Product Selection, Fixed Costs, and Monopolistic Competition," *The Review of Economic Studies* 43 (1976): 217–36. For different approaches see John S. Pettingill, "Monopolistic Competition and Optimum Product Diversity: Comment," *American Economic Review* 69 (1979): 957–60; and Roger W. Koenker and Martin K. Perry, "Product Differentiation, Monopolistic Competition, and Public Policy," *The Bell Journal of Economics* 12 (1981): 217–31.

5. Chapter 2 *Supra,* p. 41.
6. Harold Hotelling, "Stability in Competition," *Economic Journal* 39(1929): 41–57.
7. Products such as Ben & Jerry's and Häagen-Dazs are often priced high on introduction to signal to consumers that the product is of high quality. See Kyle Bagwell and Michael H. Riordan, "High and Declining Prices Signal Product Quality," *American Economic Review* 81 (March 1991): 134–239.
8. *Statistical Abstract of the United States 1995* (Washington: U.S. Bureau of the Census, 1995), p. 584.
9. John E. Kwoka, Jr., "Advertising and Price and Quality of Optometric Services," *American Economic Review* (March 1984): 211–6; Lee Benham, "The Effect of Advertising on the Price of Eyeglasses," *Journal of Law and Economics* 15 (October 1972): 337–52. See also John R. Schroeter, Scott L. Smith, and Steven R. Cox, "Advertising and Competition in Routine Legal Services Markets," *Journal of Industrial Economics* 36 (September 1987): 49–60; and Amihai Glazer, "Advertising, Information, and Prices—A Case Study," *Economic Inquiry* 19 (October 1981): 661–71.
10. John F. Cady, "An Estimate of the Price Effects of Restrictions on Drug Price Advertising," *Economic Inquiry* (December 1976): 493–510.
11. Michael E. Porter, "Interbrand Choice, Media Mix and Market Performance," *American Economic Review* (May 1976): 398–406.
12. Alfred Arterburn and John Woodbury, "Advertising, Price Competition, and Market Structure," *Southern Economic Journal* (January 1981): 763–75.
13. See Makoto Mizuno, "Does Advertising Mislead Consumers to Buy Low-Quality Products," *International Journal of Industrial Organization* 8 (December 1990):545–58.
14. "Saturn Reaches Critical Marketing Strategy Phase," *Automotive News* (March 12, 1990): 32.
15. U.S. Bureau of the Census, *Statistical Abstract of the United States: 1979* (Washington, DC: Government Printing Office, 1979). Unfortunately there are no comparable data for later years.
16. *Statistical Abstract of the United States 1995* (Washington: U.S. Bureau of the Census, 1995), p. 584.
17. *Statistical Abstract of the United States 1995,* (Washington: U.S. Bureau of the Census, 1995), p. 377.
18. For more on which products are likely to be advertised on television, see Michael R. Butler, "The Diffusion of Television Advertising," *Review of Industrial Organization* 6 (1991): 283–90.
19. See Phillip Nelson, "Advertising and Information," *Journal of Political Economy* 81 (1970): 729–54; Paul Milgrom and J. Roberts, "Price and Advertising Signals of Product Quality," *Journal of Political Economy* 94 (1986): 796–821; Richard Kihlstrom and Michael Riordin, "Advertising as a Signal," *Journal of Political Economy* 92 (1984): 427–50; and Richard Schmalensee, "A Model of Advertising and Product Quality," *Journal of Political Economy* 86 (1978): 485–503.
20. Robert Dorfman and Peter O. Steiner, "Optimal Advertising and Optimal Quality," *American Economic Review* 44 (December 1954): 826–36.
21. "Sharp, Thompson Switch on $20 M Campaigns," *Advertising Age* (August 28, 1995): 30; "DBS Business Flying High; Direct Broadcasting Satellites; Telemedia Week," *Broadcasting & Cable* 125 (January 9, 1995): 55; and "Ads that Work: Advertising Campaigns that Introduced a Product, Introduced a City and Introduced a Product to a City," *Indiana Business Magazine* (April 1996).
22. Neil Borden, *The Economic Effects of Advertising* (Chicago: Irwin, 1942), pp. 212–6.
23. Lester G. Telser, "Advertising and Cigarettes," *Journal of Law and Economics* 70 (October 1962): 494–8; and Henry G. Grabowski and Dennis C. Mueller, "Imitative Advertising in the Cigarette Industry," *Antitrust Bulletin* 16, (Summer 1971): 257–92.
24. M.A. Alemson, "Advertising and the Nature of Competition in Oligopoly Over Time," *Economic Journal* 80 (June 1970): 293; Henry G. Grabowski and Dennis C. Mueller, "Imitative Advertising in the Cigarette Industry," *Antitrust Bulletin* 16 (Summer 1971): 257–92. See also James L. Hamilton, "The Demand for Cigarettes, Advertising, the Health Scare, and the Cigarette Advertising Ban," *Review of Economics and Statistics* 54 (November 1972): 401–11; Eugene M. Lewit, Douglas Coate, and Michael Grossman, "The Effects of Government Regulation on Teenage Smoking," *Journal of Law and Economics* 24 (December 1981): 545–75; and Lynne Schneider, Benjamin Klein, and Kevin Murphy, "Government Regulation of Cigarette Health Information," *Journal of Law and Economics* 24 (December, 1981): 576–612.
25. Jean Jacques Lambin, *Advertising, Competition, and Market Conduct in Oligopoly over*

Time (Amsterdam: North-Holland, 1976).

26. Jeffrey M. Netter, "Excessive Advertising: An Empirical Analysis," *Journal of Law and Economics* 30 (June 1982):361–73.

27. Bagwell and Ramey have argued that incumbent firms may under-advertise to deter entry if they wish to signal uninformed potential entrants that demand is low. See Kyle Bagwell and Garey Ramey, "Advertising and Pricing to Deter or Accommodate Entry when Demand is Unknown," *International Journal of Industrial Organization* 8 (March 1990): 93–113.

28. Richard Schmalensee, "Product Differentiation Advantages of Pioneering Brands," *American Economic Review* 72 (June, 1982): 349–65.

29. The first mover may want to discriminate in price between new and repeat customers. See Thomas J. Hoerger, "Two-part Pricing for Experience Goods in the Presence of Adverse Selection," *International Journal of Industrial Organization* 11 (December 1993): 451–74.

30. Alison Masson and Robert L. Steiner, *Generic Substitution and Prescription Drug Prices*, Federal Trade Commission staff report (Washington: U.S. Government Printing Office, October 1985). Jung has suggested that entry into the prescription drug industry may result in higher prices being charged by the leading brands because after entry the leading brands mostly have very loyal buyers with highly inelastic demands. See Chao-Shun Jung, "On Monopoly Power in a Differentiated Product Industry," *Review of Industrial Organization* 9 (August 1994): 425–33.

31. Mark A. Hurwitz and Richard E. Caves, "Persuasion or Information? Promotion and the Shares of Brand Name and Generic Pharmaceuticals," *Journal of Law and Economics* 31 (October 1988): 299–320.

32. For additional empirical evidence see William T. Robinson, Gurumurthy Kalyanaram, and Glen L. Urban, "First-Mover Advantages from Pioneering New Markets: A Survey of Empirical Evidence," *Review of Industrial Organization* 9 (February 1994): 1–23.

33. "Battery Power; Kodak Readies New Charge," *Advertising Age* (September 7, 1987); and "Kodak Draws 10% Share of Supermarket Batteries Sales," *Supermarket News* (April 6, 1987).

34. See also Douglas F. Greer, "Some Case Study Evidence on the Advertising-Concentration Relationship," *Antitrust Bulletin* (Summer 1973): 307–32. For additional evidence of strategic use of advertising in the cigarette industry see Barry J. Seldon and Khosroe Doroodian, "Does Purely Predatory Advertising Exist?" *Review of Industrial Organization* 5 (1990): 45–70.

35. *Business Week* (January 26, 1981): 65.

36. *Business Week* (October 31, 1983): 50; *Business Week* (January 23, 1989): 38; and *The Wall Street Journal* (August 17, 1984): 14.

37. John Cubbin and Simon Domberger, "Advertising and Post-Entry Oligopoly Behavior," *Journal of Industrial Economics* (December 1988): 123–40.

38. "Sharp, Thompson Switch on $20 M Campaigns," *Advertising Age* (August 28, 1995): 30; "DBS Business Flying High; Direct Broadcasting Satellites; Telemedia Week," *Broadcasting & Cable* 125 (January 9, 1995): 55; and "Ads that Work: Advertising Campaigns that Introduced a Product, Introduced a City and Introduced a Product to a City," *Indiana Business Magazine* (April 1996).

39. Greer, *Industrial Organization and Public Policy* (New York: Macmillan, 1992), p. 492.

40. Little debate does not mean no debate. Stegeman has argued that informational advertising in a competitive market may result in either too little or too much advertising compared with the socially optimal amount. See Mark Stegeman, "Advertising in Competitive Markets," *American Economic Review* 81 (March 1991): 210–23. See also Michael Meurer and Dale O. Stahl II, "Informative Advertising and Product Match," *International Journal of Industrial Organization* 12 (March 1994): 1–19.

41. Avinash Dixit and Victor Norman, "Advertising and Welfare," *Bell Journal of Economics* 9 (1978): 1–17.

42. Franklin M. Fisher and John J. McGowan, "Advertising and Welfare: Comment," *The Bell Journal of Economics* 10 (1979): 726–7.

43. For other empirical evidence see Frances F. Esposito, Louis Esposito, and William V. Hogan, "Inter Industry Differences in Advertising in U.S. Manufacturing: 1963–1977," *Review of Industrial Organization* 5, (1990): 53–80; Takeo Nakao, "Market Share, Advertising, R&D, and Profitability: An Empirical Analysis of Leading Industrial Firms in Japan,"*Review of Industrial Organization* 8 (June 1993): 315–28.

44. National Commission on Food Marketing, *Special Studies in Food Marketing*, Technical Study 10 (Washington: The Commission, 1966), pp. 66, 70–71.

45. David Morris, "Some Aspects of Large-Scale Advertising," *Journal of Industrial Economics* (December 1975): 119–30.

46. Robert L. Wills and Willard F. Mueller, "Brand Pricing and Advertising," *Southern Economic Journal* (October 1989): 383–95.

47. John E. Kwoka, Jr., "Advertising and Price and Quality of Optometric Services," *American Economic Review* (March 1984) 211–6; Lee Benham, "The Effect of Advertising on the Price of Eyeglasses," *Journal of Law and Economics* 15 (October 1972): 337–52. See also John R. Schroeter, Scott L. Smith, and Steven R. Cox, "Advertising and Competition in Routine Legal Services Markets," *Journal of Industrial Economics* 36 (September 1987): 49–60; Amihai Glazer, "Advertising, Information, and Prices—A Case Study," *Economic Inquiry* 19 (October 1981): 661–71; and John F. Cady, "An Estimate of the Price Effects of Restrictions on Drug Price Advertising," *Economic Inquiry* (December 1976): 493–510.

48. Michael E. Porter, "Interbrand Choice, Media Mix and Market Performance," *American Economic Review* (May 1976): 398–406; and Alfred Arterburn and John Woodbury, "Advertising, Price Competition, and Market Structure," *Southern Economic Journal* (January 1981): 763–75.

49. Kenneth D. Boyer, "Informative and Goodwill Advertising," *Review of Economics and Statistics* 56 (November 1974): 541–8.

Chapter 14

Technological Change and Research and Development

The importance of technological change is stressed throughout this text. In Chapter 1 we wrote, "Most economists recognize that even if an industry achieves static efficiency its performance may be poor if it fails to invest in research and development at an optimal rate." In this chapter we analyze the theoretical and empirical work in the area of technological change and research and development (R&D), with an emphasis on trying to ascertain whether a relationship exists between market structure and the rate of technological advance. The objective is to determine whether there is an ideal market structure that results in an optimal rate of technological advance. We also examine the United States patent system to determine its impact on the rate of technological advance.

In one of the most influential economic treatises written in this century, Joseph Schumpeter first emphasized the primary importance of dynamic efficiency. We begin with a discussion of Schumpeter's argument. Much of the remaining debate centers on whether Schumpeter was right or wrong.

Schumpeter and the Process of "Creative Destruction"

In 1942, Joseph Schumpeter's *Capitalism, Socialism, and Democracy* was published.[1] The book mainly examined Marxism and socialism and asked the question: "Can capitalism survive?" To this, Schumpeter answered, "No. I do not think it can."[2] Schumpeter theorized that capitalism would eventually collapse from the weight of its own success. One of the linchpins of his argument was a belief that capital would increasingly be concentrated in a few large-scale, technologically advanced firms.

Because of the historical importance of Schumpeter's hypothesis, we present a rather lengthy excerpt from *Capitalism, Socialism, and Democracy*. The following passages have had a continuing impact on economic thought for more than half a century. Schumpeter wrote:

> The essential point to grasp is that in dealing with capitalism we are dealing with an evolutionary process. . . .
>
> Capitalism . . . is by nature a form or method of economic change and not only never is but never can be stationary. . . . The fundamental impulse that sets and keeps the capitalist engine in motion comes from the new consumers' goods, the new methods of production or transportation, the new markets, the new forms of industrial organization that capitalist enterprise creates. . . .
>
> The opening up of new markets, foreign or domestic, and the organizational development from the craft shop and factory to such concerns as U.S. Steel illustrate the same process of industrial mutation — if I may use that biological term — that incessantly revolutionizes the economic structure *from within*, incessantly destroying the old one, incessantly creating a new one. This process of Creative Destruction is the essential fact about capitalism. It is what capitalism consists in and what every capitalist concern has got to live in. This fact bears upon our problem in two ways.
>
> First, because we are dealing with a process whose every element takes considerable time in revealing its true features and ultimate effects, there is no point in appraising the performance of that process *ex visu* of a given point in time; we must judge its performance over time, as it unfolds through decades or centuries. A system — any system, economic or other — that at *every* given point of time fully utilizes its possibilities to the best advantage may yet in the long run be inferior to a system that does so at *no* given point of time, because the latter's failure to do so may be a condition for the level or speed of long-run performance. . . .
>
> The first thing to go is the traditional conception of the *modus operandi* of competition. Economists are at long last emerging from the stage in which price competition was all they saw. As soon as quality competition and sales effort are admitted into the sacred precincts of theory, the price variable is ousted from its dominant position. . . . [I]n capitalist reality as distinguished from its textbook picture, it is not that kind of competition which counts but the competition from the new commodity, the new technology, the new source of supply, the new type of organization (the largest-scale unit of control for instance)—competition which commands a decisive cost or quality advantage and which strikes not at the margins of the profits and the outputs of the existing firms but at their foundations and their very lives. . . .
>
> In the case of retail trade the competition that matters arises not from additional shops of the same type, but from the department store, the chain store, the mail-order house and the supermarket which are bound to destroy those pyramids sooner or later. . . .

Having argued that capitalism is driven by *dynamic efficiency*, not *static efficiency*, Schumpeter went on to argue the type of market structure necessary to achieve dynamic efficiency:

> [T]here are superior methods available to the monopolist which either are not available at all to a crowd of competitors or are not available to them so readily: for there are advantages which, though not strictly unattainable on

the competitive level of enterprise, are as a matter of fact secured only on the monopoly level, for instance, because monopolization may increase the sphere of influence of the better, and decrease the sphere of influence of the inferior, brains, or because the monopoly enjoys a disproportionately higher financial standing. . . .

There cannot be any reasonable doubt that under the conditions of our epoch such superiority is as a matter of fact the outstanding feature of the typical large-scale unit of control, though mere size is neither necessary nor sufficient for it. These units not only arise in the process of creative destruction and function in a way entirely different from the static schema, but in many cases of decisive importance they provide the necessary form for the achievement. They largely create what they exploit. Hence the usual conclusion about their influence on long-run output would be invalid even if they were genuine monopolies in the technical sense of the term. . . .

Thus it is not sufficient to argue that because perfect competition is impossible under modern industrial conditions — or because it always has been impossible — the large-scale establishment or unit of control must be accepted as a necessary evil inseparable from the economic progress which it is prevented from sabotaging by the forces inherent in its productive apparatus. What we have got to accept is that it has come to be the most powerful engine of that progress and in particular of the long-run expansion of total output not only in spite of, but to a considerable extent through, this strategy which looks so restrictive when viewed in the individual case and from the individual point of time. In this respect, perfect competition is not only impossible but inferior, and has no title to being set up as a model of ideal efficiency.

The implications of Schumpeter's thesis were revolutionary. Perfect competition was not the ideal market structure, but instead large-scale firms with monopoly power became the superior market structure. Creative destruction drove a capitalist economy forward in the long run, and large-scale monopolists engaged in research and development led to creative destruction. In the neoclassical world, perfect competition and an increasing capital-labor ratio ensured long-run growth. In the Schumpeterian world large firms with monopoly power ensured long-run growth.

The theory of **creative destruction** raised the following questions: How important is technological change to long-run growth? Do most technological changes originate in large-scale monopoly enterprises? Is monopoly the ideal market structure for dynamic efficiency? Do successful large-scale monopolists inevitably grow to control larger and larger percentages of capital?

In a seminal article Robert Solow addressed the question of how important technological change is to long-run growth.[3] Examining the 105 percent increase in output of nonfarm labor between 1909 and 1949, Solow found that 87.5 percent of the increase resulted from technological change, whereas only 12.5 percent resulted from an increase in the use of capital relative to labor. Given Solow's findings, it is hard to argue with one of Schumpeter's main points: technological change drives an economy forward.[4]

The Process of Technological Change

Before proceeding, it is important to distinguish between the different stages of development of a new commercial product or process. Many major technological changes begin with **basic research**, which is research aimed at gaining knowledge for its own sake. The research scientist in a major university laboratory working on quantum physics is engaged in basic research. **Applied research** is aimed at obtaining knowledge with the objective of using that knowledge for commercial purposes. The chemist working on AIDS in a pharmaceutical company's laboratory is doing applied research. The lines between basic and applied research, however, often become blurred. The chemist, for example, may in the course of his or her applied research make a basic research discovery concerning how the immune system works to fight disease. Successful applied research results in **invention** or the discovery of an idea that "should" work. In the invention stage the idea passes through its first rough tests, which indicate that it will indeed work. Invention is an important step in the process of technological development, but it is only a preliminary step. The next stage in the process is **innovation**, which is the first commercial application of the invention. Innovation requires refinement of the invention to "get the bugs out" and develop a marketable product. Large R & D labs spend much time on innovation. Finally, **diffusion** is the stage at which the innovation comes into common use.

Although all of these stages of development are important, this chapter is primarily concerned with invention, innovation, and diffusion. Private firms are primarily engaged in these three stages of technological development. Most basic research, however, is carried out at academic and nonprofit institutions (56 percent of total basic research spending in 1985) and by the government (24 percent of spending in 1985).[5]

The Relationship Between Market Structure, Firm Size, and Technological Advance

Schumpeter argued that from the standpoint of dynamic efficiency, monopoly is superior to perfect competition. This argument spurred economists to examine the issue both theoretically and empirically. We begin with the theory.

The following model was developed by Arrow.[6] Suppose two markets have identical demands of $P = 100 - Q$. Industry 1 is a monopoly and Industry 2 is perfectly competitive. Figure 14.1 analyzes the impact of a cost reduction by the monopolist. Initially $MC = AC = 30$ and the profit-maximizing monopolist sets $Q = 35$ and $P = 65$. Profits are represented by π_M, and:

$$\pi_M = Q(P - AC) = 35(65 - 30) = 1225.$$

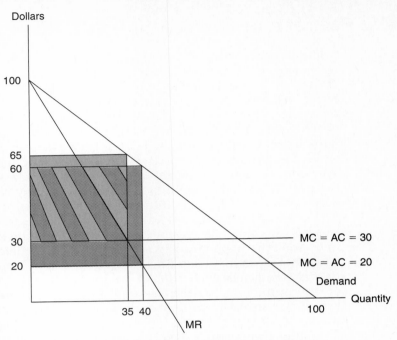

Figure 14.1   Cost reduction by a monopolist.

Suppose a monopolist's innovation produced a cost-saving device that reduced its MC from 30 to 20. The monopolist's new profits would be π'_M, where:

$$\pi'_M = Q'(P' - AC') = 40(60 - 20) = 1600.$$

Profits increase by 375 as a result of the cost-saving device. Notice in Figure 14.1
that consumer surplus also increases because P declines to 60 and Q increases to 40.

Figure 14.2 analyzes the impact of the same cost-saving innovation introduced in a perfectly competitive industry. Initially MC = AC = 30 and the perfectly competitive industry sets Q = 70 and P = 30. Because of perfect competition, profits equal zero, or $\pi_C = 0$, where:

$$\pi_C = Q(P - AC) = 70(30 - 30) = 0.$$

Suppose one firm produced a patented cost-saving innovation that reduced
MC from 30 to 20. In a perfectly competitive market, if the innovating firm tried
to raise price above 30 it would be unable to sell *any* output. Its best option,
therefore, is to license the patent for a royalty of 10 per unit of output. The industry's MC continues to equal 30 (including the royalty payment of 10 per unit),

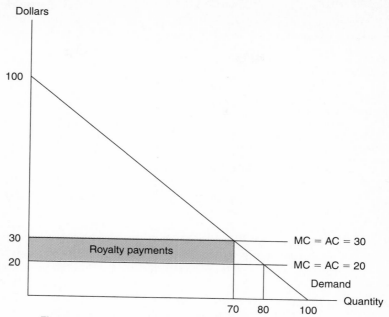

Figure 14.2   Cost reduction in a perfectly competitive industry.

and the industry price continues to equal 30. In Figure 14.2, the patent holder's royalties would be 700 (10Q = 700). The innovator earns an economic rent of 700 as a result of the introduction of the cost saving device. Notice that consumer surplus does not change because P still equals 30. The entire 700 economic rent accrues to the patent holder. The innovator in the perfectly competitive industry earns almost twice as much (700 compared to 375) from the new innovation as the monopolist. Therefore, a perfectly competitive firm has a greater economic incentive to develop the cost-saving device. Arrow's conclusion runs contrary to the Schumpeterian view.

What drives Arrow's result? Because the monopolist restricts output compared with the perfectly competitive industry, the monopolist applies the new device to far fewer units than the perfectly competitive industry[7] (40 units in Figure 14.1 compared to 70 units in Figure 14.2).

THE IMPACT OF OLIGOPOLY

So far our analysis has centered on whether monopoly or perfect competition is more likely to result in a rapid rate of technological advance. As usual, the introduction of oligopoly makes the analysis more realistic and more complicated. Intuitively, investments in research and development aimed at improvements in technology require both an incentive and an ability to invest. Table 14.1 summarizes the incentive and ability to invest in research and development under perfect competition, oligopoly, and monopoly. Under perfect competition economic profits are normal, and there is little ability to invest in R & D. Few individual

TABLE 14.1 **Incentives to Invest in Research and Development**

	Ability	Incentive
Perfect competition	Low, profits = 0	Moderate
Oligopoly	Moderate, profits ≥ 0	High
Monopoly	High, profits > 0	Low to moderate

farmers, for example, have the time or funds necessary to invest in fertilizer or pesticide research and development. In a monopoly, profits may be greater than zero for long periods, giving the monopolist the ability to invest large sums in R&D. A good example is AT&T's ability to establish Bell Labs when it was a regulated monopoly. In terms of ability, oligopoly lies somewhere in between. Depending on the level of effective competition, oligopolists may or may not have profits available to invest in R&D. Examples of oligopoly industries that have earned excess profits for long periods include computer equipment, automobiles, electronics, cereals, cigarettes, beer, photographic equipment, electric turbines, and aircraft. High profits in these industries can be channeled into R&D.

With regard to incentives, the monopolist has a low to moderate incentive to develop new technologies. Because the monopolist has a 100 percent market share and is protected from competition, it will have little concern about either losing its market share to rivals or gaining market share at its rivals' expense. The monopolist, therefore, will have limited concern about the time at which it introduces a new technological advance. AT&T, for example, continued to supply only black dial telephones for many years beyond the technical necessity of doing so. As long as its monopoly was protected, AT&T would earn few additional profits by offering consumers touch-tone phones in designer colors. Furthermore, because it had no competitors in telephone equipment in its protected markets, AT&T had no reason to worry about competitors gaining market share by introducing color touch-tone phones. However, according to Arrow's model, the monopolist earns additional profits from an innovation, and therefore, it still has some incentive to invest in R&D.

In Arrow's model the perfectly competitive firm has a powerful incentive to invest in R&D. One problem not accounted for in Arrow's model is that diffusion is often rapid in perfectly competitive markets, and profits decline quickly to normal. In retailing, for example, any new technological advance is rapidly duplicated by competitors. The introduction of the supermarket quickly made the small food store obsolete. Similarly, discount stores have virtually eliminated the independent pharmacist and clothing store from America. Because of rapid diffusion in competitive markets, innovation results in lower profits than in less competitive markets, and therefore, there is less ability to invest in R&D in highly competitive markets.

Table 14.1 shows that a perfectly competitive firm has the incentive but limited ability to invest in R&D, and a monopolist has the ability but limited incentive to invest in R&D. An oligopolist has both the ability and the incentive to invest in R&D. Oligopolists have an incentive to invest because they gain vis-à-vis rivals by being the first to develop a new product or process. Monopolists have nothing to gain vis-à-vis existing rivals, whereas perfectly competitive firms realize that imitation by rivals will be very rapid. The expected moderate rate of imitation in oligopoly gives the oligopolist the largest incentive to invest in R&D. For example, when Miller Beer introduced Miller Lite, it initially obtained a large market share from competitors, and competitors only slowly regained their market shares. Similarly when small tobacco companies introduced king-size cigarettes in the 1950s, they gained a large market share at the expense of the leading firms, who were never able to recapture their entire market.

Scherer developed a formal model relating the rate of technological advance to market structure.[8] The model compares the present value of costs and benefits associated with a new technological advance under different market structures. Consider the time-cost trade-off associated with a new technological advance. The present value of the cost of development can be identified as:

$$C_{pv} = C_0 + \frac{C_1}{1 + r} + \frac{C_2}{(1 + r)^2} + \frac{C_3}{(1 + r)^3} + \ldots + \frac{C_n}{(1 + r)^n}, \quad [14.1]$$

where C_{pv} represents the present value of the costs of development, C_i represents the costs of development in time period i, and r represents the firm's discount rate.

If the firm aims at a rapid rate of technological advance, early values such as C_0 and C_1 will be very large because rapid technological advance requires the use of multiple paths of experimentation. The firm aiming at an early technological breakthrough typically proceeds down many scientific avenues at once hoping that one or more will pay off. Rapid technological advance also may require moving on to the next development step before the previous step has been perfected. This too raises costs. Consider, for example, the biological and medical battle against AIDS. If society were truly committed to finding a vaccine or a cure for AIDS in the next three years, huge resources would have to be devoted to AIDS research. These resources would have to come from other areas of medical research, such as heart disease, cancer, and kidney disease. The opportunity cost of transferring resources to AIDS research would be very high because it would mean more deaths from heart disease, cancer, and kidney disease. In Eq. 14.1, the values for C_0, C_1, C_2, and C_3 would be extremely large compared with a path that has a time horizon measured in decades. The present AIDS research strategy is to invest less in early years, perfect small steps (e.g., AZT), and then move on to the next small step. Given the current strategy, the values of C_0, C_1, C_2, and C_3 are relatively low and costs are spread over many years.

The AIDS example suggests that to speed up the rate of technological advance, most of the costs of development must be *front loaded;* that is, most of the costs will be in early periods with high present values. As a project is stretched out over time, the present value of development declines because future costs are discounted and, therefore, add less to the present value of costs. In Eq. 14.1 the present value C_{pv}, therefore, will be much higher if the time of development is short rather than long. In Figure 14.3, the cost curve C_{pv} shows the present value of the costs of development for any given time. The curve C_{pv} is downward sloping to

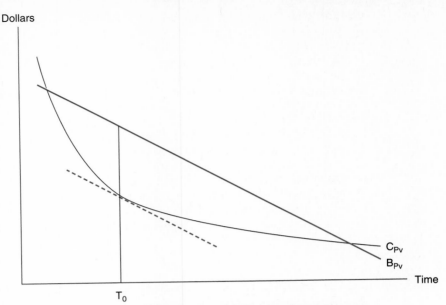

Figure 14.3   The optimal time for technological development.

indicate that the present value of the cost of development decreases as the time of development is lengthened.

Now consider the benefits to the firm of speeding up the rate of technological development:

$$B_{pv} = B_0 + \frac{B_1}{1 + r} + \frac{B_2}{(1 + r)^2} + \frac{B_3}{(1 + r)^3} + \dots + \frac{B_n}{(1 + r)^n},$$ [14.2]

where B_{pv} represents the present value of the benefits of development, B_i represents the benefits of development in time period i, and r represents the firm's discount rate.

A more rapid rate of technological advance results in a higher present value of benefits for several reasons. First, if the introduction comes late most of the benefits will be highly discounted and contribute less to B_{pv}. Early introduction allows the firm to earn benefits when they are most valuable in terms of present value. Second, later development reduces the first-mover advantage for the innovator. Consider AIDS research again. A drug company that introduces a new AIDS drug today will immediately tap into large potential economic benefits. Significant delays in introduction greatly reduce the gains available and greatly increase the probability that another company will introduce a close substitute drug first, which could permanently reduce demand for the innovation.

In Eq. 14.2 the present value B_{pv}, therefore, will decrease as the time of development is lengthened. In Figure 14.3, the curve B_{pv} represents the present value of the benefits of development for any period. The curve is downward sloping to

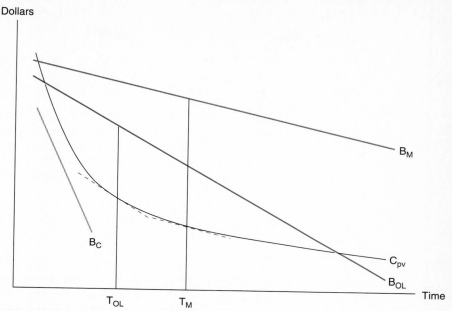

Figure 14.4   Relationship between market structure and the time of technological advance.

indicate that the present value of benefits increases as the time of development is shortened.

The optimal development time occurs when benefits exceed costs by the largest amount, or when the marginal benefit of reducing the time of development equals the marginal cost of reducing the time of development. Graphically, this occurs where the slope of the benefit curve equals the slope of the cost curve, or at time T_0 in Figure 14.3.

How would the model be affected by market structure? It is reasonable to assume that the cost function is independent of changes in market structure because it is primarily a function of technological knowledge and inputs.* The benefit function, however, should vary with changes in market structure. Figure 14.4 shows three different benefit curves. The curve B_M represents the present value of benefits for a pure monopolist. The curve B_M is drawn as the highest and flattest curve. Regardless of the time of development, the monopolist gains the most because it has the largest market share and the lowest threat of imitation. Therefore, B_M is always above the other curves. The curve B_M is the flattest curve because the monopolist faces the lowest threat of imitation. The monopolist, therefore, gets to keep most of its gains regardless of when it introduces the innovation.

---

*Technically, the cost function is independent of market structure only if there are no R&D *spillovers* across firms, that is, if Firm A's technological advance does not lower Firm B's cost of technological advance. Otherwise, a change in market structure that affects Firm A's rate of technological advance could have an impact on Firm B's costs of technological advance.

The curve B_C represents the present value of benefits for a perfectly competitive firm. The curve B_C is the lowest of the three benefit curves because the perfectly competitive firm has the smallest market share and the greatest threat of imitation and, therefore, gains the least from the introduction of a new innovation regardless of the time of introduction. The curve B_C slopes rapidly downward because a delay in introduction increases the probability that another firm will imitate the innovation.

Finally, the curve B_{OL} represents the present value of benefits for an oligopolist. The curve lies between the other two curves because the oligopolist has a larger market share than the competitive firm but a smaller market share than the monopolist, and it faces an intermediate threat of imitation. The intermediate threat of retaliation results in a slope that is between the other two benefits curves.

Figure 14.4 shows that innovation will not take place with perfect competition because the present value of benefits is always less than the present value of costs. The monopolist introduces the innovation at time T_M and the oligopolist introduces at time T_{OL}. The most rapid rate of technological advance occurs with oligopoly. Of course, it is possible that higher costs could prevent the oligopolist from introducing the innovation. Figure 14.5 shows a situation in which only the monopolist would introduce the innovation. It is also possible that, with lower costs, the perfectly competitive firm would introduce the innovation first. Such a situation is depicted in Figure 14.6. Scherer's analysis suggests, however, that under a wide variety of cost and benefits conditions, oligopoly will result in the most rapid rate of technological advance.

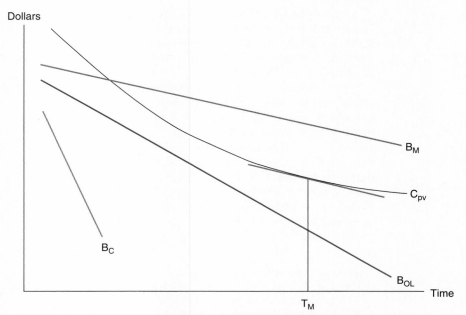

Figure 14.5   Higher costs result in technological advance only with monopoly.

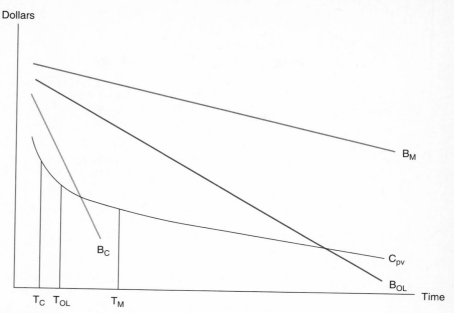

Figure 14.6 Lower costs result in rapid technological advance in a perfectly competitive industry.

DOMINANT FIRMS AS FAST-SECOND INNOVATORS

Consider an industry with one dominant firm and one small firm. In Figure 14.7, the benefit curve B_D is the dominant firm's benefit curve, assuming that the smaller firm has not innovated, and the red curve B_S is the small firm's benefit curve, assuming that the dominant firm has yet to innovate.

Which firm will innovate first? In the absence of innovation by either firm, the optimal time for the small firm to innovate is T_S, and the optimal time for the dominant firm to innovate is T_D. Innovation will be undertaken first by the small firm at time $T = T_S$. As soon as the small firm innovates, however, the dominant firm's benefit function shifts down, to B'_D, and the dominant firm's optimal time to innovate is dramatically speeded up to T'_D. Once the small firm innovates, the dominant firm has a strong incentive to imitate rapidly to avoid any further erosion in its market share. In this *fast second* case, the small firm innovates first, but the dominant firm is quick to respond and thereby limits the small firm's inroads.

Examples of **fast-second innovators** are common. Wilkinson introduced stainless steel shaving blades in the 1960s, but Gillette quickly caught up. Sperry Rand introduced the first mainframe computers, but IBM's fast second came to dominate the industry. Similarly, Apple led the way in personal computers in the late 1970s, but IBM took over in the 1980s, although its dominance did not last long. AT&T played the role of the fast second in the development of both microwave relay systems and communication satellites. Kellogg, General Mills, and Quaker Oats lost market share to new granola manufacturers such as Pet and Car-

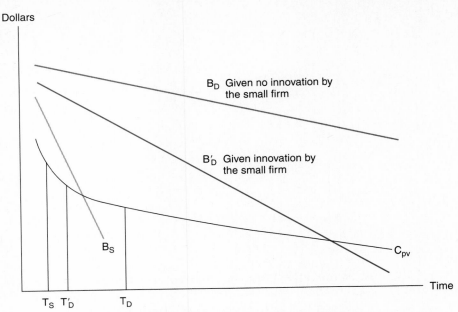

Figure 14.7 The dominant firm as a fast-second innovator.

nation in the 1970s but quickly regained control, with Quaker Natural Cereal the ultimate winner in this market. Boeing briefly lost technological leadership to the European Airbus consortium, then bounced back as the world's leading aircraft manufacturer. Finally, Snapple's introduction of a line of fruit juice drinks led to a successful response by Coca-Cola with its Frutopia line of juice drinks.

A CONTRIBUTION OF GAME THEORY

The impact of rapid imitation on the rate of innovation, which is very important in the Scherer model, has been addressed through the use of a simple game theoretic model.[9] The game assumes that duopolists face *constant returns to scale* (a horizontal LRAC) and engage in *Bertrand pricing*. An innovator firm incurs R&D costs equal to 1, and innovation is immediately imitated at zero cost, so that if Firm A innovates first, Firm B immediately and costlessly imitates. Furthermore, Bertrand competition always drives price down to marginal cost and average cost. Table 14.2 shows the payoff matrix. If Firm A is the innovator and Firm B is the imitator, then Firm A incurs costs equal to its R&D expenditures and its profits equal -1. By symmetry, if Firm B is the innovator and Firm A is the imitator, then Firm B sustains an economic loss equal to -1. If both innovate, they each sustain an economic loss equal to -1. There is a dominant solution to the game: both firms *imitate* and the innovation is never developed. Rapid imitation and competitive Bertrand pricing eliminate the innovation altogether.

Suppose that, instead of Bertrand pricing, Firm A and Firm B collude to charge the joint profit maximizing price. Once again the cost of innovation equals 1 and imitation is costless. The new payoff matrix is shown in Table 14.3.

TABLE 14.2 Innovation Game with Costless Imitation and Bertrand Pricing (Firm A's Profits, Firm B's Profits)

		Firm B's Action	
		Innovate	Imitate
Firm A's Action	Innovate	−1, −1	−1, 0
	Imitate	0, −1	0, 0

If both innovate, each firm earns a profit of 2. If one firm innovates and the other imitates, the innovator earns a profit of 2, but the imitator earns a profit of 3. The imitator earns a higher profit because it avoids the cost of innovation. If both imitate, each earns a profit equal to 1. The game has two Nash equilibria (innovate, imitate) and (imitate, innovate) and a mixed strategy equilibrium in which each firm plays innovate half the time and imitate the other half of the time.* Recall from Chapter 6 that if each firm plays its optimal mixed strategy, its opponent earns the same profits regardless of its strategy. Given the payoff matrix in Table 14.3, if Firm A plays its optimal mixed strategy of innovate 50 percent of the time and imitate 50 percent of the time, Firm B's expected profits equal 2 regardless of Firm B's strategy.

The problem with the mixed strategy equilibrium is that it results in an inefficient outcome 50 percent of the time. With each firm playing innovate 50 percent of the time and imitate 50 percent of the time, there is a 25 percent probability that the result will be (imitate, imitate) and a 25 percent probability that the result will be (innovate, innovate). Both outcomes are inefficient because (imitate, imitate) results in no technological advance, and (innovate, innovate) results in a total innovation cost of 2 when society could produce the same innovation for a total cost of 1 with either an (innovate, imitate) or an (imitate, innovate) outcome.

To prevent the (imitate, imitate) outcome in Table 14.3, the government can grant an exclusive license or a patent to the innovator. We examine the impact of patents on the game in the appendix on patent races.

---

*Using calculus, to obtain the mixed strategy equilibrium maximize expected profits $E(\pi_i)$. Let ρ equal the probability that Firm A innovates and $(1 - \rho)$ equal the probability that Firm A imitates, and let τ equal the probability that Firm B innovates and $(1 - \tau)$ equal the probability that Firm B imitates. Firm A's expected profits are:

$$E(\Pi_A) = \rho[2\tau + 2(1 - \tau)] + (1 - \rho)[3\tau + (1)(1 - \tau)]$$

$$= 2\rho\tau + 2\rho(1 - \tau) + 3(1 - \rho)\tau + (1 - \rho)(1 - \tau)$$

$$= \rho + 2\tau - 2\rho\tau + 1.$$

To maximize profits, differentiate $E(\Pi_A)$ with respect to ρ to obtain:

$$\frac{\partial E(\Pi_A)}{\partial \rho} = 1 - 2\tau = 0 \text{ or } \tau = 0.5 \text{ and } (1 - \tau) = 0.5.$$

Because of symmetry, by analogous calculations, the optimal mixed strategy requires $\rho = 0.5$ and $(1 - \rho) = 0.5$.

TABLE 14.3 Innovation Game with Costless Imitation and Collusive Pricing (Firm A's Profits, Firm B's Profits)

		Firm B's Action	
		Innovate	Imitate
Firm A's Action	Innovate	2, 2	2, 3
	Imitate	3, 2	1, 1

THE IMPACT OF FIRM SIZE

Recall that Schumpeter not only extolled the virtues of monopoly, but he also extolled the advantages of the "large-scale unit of control." Schumpeter argued that large firms drove the process of creative destruction. John Kenneth Galbraith expanded on Schumpeter's argument in the 1950s and suggested that large firms were the major force behind modern technological advance:[10]

> A benign Providence . . . has made the modern industry of a few large firms an almost perfect instrument for inducing technical change. . . . There is no more pleasant fiction than that technical change is the product of the matchless ingenuity of the small man forced by competition to employ his wits to better his neighbour. Unhappily, it is a fiction. Technical development has long since become the preserve of the scientist and the engineer. Most of the cheap and simple inventions have, to put it bluntly, been made.

Both Schumpeter and Galbraith argued that technological leaps and bounds are driven almost exclusively by large firms. Subsequent theorists suggested, however, that the relationship between firm size and technological advance is far more complex than Schumpeter and Galbraith hypothesized. First, consider the arguments in favor of large firms. Large firms have greater resources to invest in R&D than smaller firms, and given the large costs of establishing a modern R&D laboratory, only large firms can set them up. Second, economies of scale are associated with R&D. Large firms can more easily afford to purchase highly specialized equipment, such as high-powered electron microscopes and supercomputers. Large, diversified firms can also employ scientists and specialists in many fields to cross-fertilize each other's projects. For example, if a team working on one project runs into a problem beyond their expertise, that team can receive immediate help from other teams within the firm. Third, large firms can spread risk over many projects, thereby reducing the overall risk associated with R&D. By contrast, in a small firm a failed high-cost research and development project can cause the demise of the firm. Fourth, large firms are often highly diversified, and a technological advance in one area may be useful in another. Finally, large firms may have longer time horizons that enable them to persevere with expensive long-term R&D projects.

At first glance, these points represent an impressive array of arguments in favor of bigness. There are, however, a similar array of arguments in favor of smaller firms. Perhaps the most powerful argument against the large corporation is the tendency for large firms to become bureaucratically inefficient. Successful large corporations often become complacent and refuse to approve new projects or approve them far too slowly.

Consider the experience of IBM in the personal computer market. At the top of the IBM management structure in the 1970s and 1980s was the Management Committee (MC) in Armonk, New York, that consisted of three to six members and which historically decided all matters, even trivial ones. Until 1989, for example, the MC sat in judgment on everything from what a product looked like to whether a salesperson could grant a reduced price to keep a customer.[11] IBM's managerial system was slow, cumbersome, and not suited to the fast-paced personal computer industry of the 1980s. Furthermore, the decision makers typically had only limited technical insight into the personal computer industry, because the CEOs and other top managers were generally drawn from the ranks of the sales department, not from technical areas.

Many of IBM's recent problems have resulted from management's failure to recognize that the personal computer would one day be something more than a home toy. To IBM's senior management in the 1970s and early 1980s the future was still in mainframes and minicomputers for commercial use. According to one member of the MC, "The general attitude was that you don't have big problems in small markets, and we thought the personal computer was a very small market."[12] In 1985, for example, Don Estridge, the original mastermind of the IBM PC operation, wanted to produce a new line of PCs based on Intel's fast 80386 microprocessor. Estridge theorized that the way to fight the PC clones was to destroy them by producing much faster and better PCs. The MC, fearing that faster PCs would threaten IBM's mainframe business, which still was the basis for most of IBM's revenues, refused to approve Estridge's plan.

By the 1980s, the MC had become so conservative that it refused to take even moderate risks of damaging or making obsolete some of IBM's product lines. According to Carroll:[13]

> The senior executives, all ex-salesmen, preferred the less disruptive approach that was more conventional around IBM and that had helped it wring such extraordinary profits out of the mainframe business. The executives wanted to milk the existing product line as long as possible. After all, all the expensive work that goes into designing PCs had already been paid for. So why not just sit back and keep producing PCs that cost IBM about half what customers would pay? Only when IBM couldn't delay any longer would it pay to design and bring out products using new technology.

As late as the mid-1980s, IBM's management had completely missed the coming personal computer revolution. Bill Gates, one of the cofounders of Microsoft, however, had seen the future a full decade earlier. In a 1995 interview Gates noted that:[14]

> [In the mid 1970s] microprocessors were instantly attractive to [Paul Allen and me] because you could build something for a fraction of the cost of conventional electronics. . . .
>
> I remember, from the very beginning, we wondered, "What would it mean for DEC once microcomputers were powerful and cheap enough?

What would it mean for IBM?" To us it seemed that they were screwed to-morrow. We were saying, "God, how come these guys aren't stunned? How come they're not just amazed and scared?". . . The notion was fairly clear to us that computers were going to be a big, big personal tool.

The IBM example appears to undermine the argument that only large firms are willing to take on risky R&D efforts. Any IBM forward movement on a re-search project required approval at many managerial levels. By comparison, at Microsoft and other small computer hardware and software companies, the deci-sion to move forward on a project rested in the hands of a few creative leaders such as Bill Gates.

Computer technology has also reduced the advantages associated with economies of scale as more and more R&D projects are contracted out to inde-pendent R&D companies. It may still be true that one small firm cannot purchase "specialized equipment such as wind tunnels, supercomputers, and differential scanning calorimeters," but independent R&D firms working for many small firms and spreading their costs among many projects can purchase such equip-ment. These independent R&D companies can also employ specialists in many R&D areas.

With regard to the relationship between firm size and technological advance and between market structure and innovation, theory can take us just so far, and it is necessary to examine the empirical evidence.

Empirical Evidence

Schumpeter's writings and subsequent theoretical work generated an extensive body of empirical work, most of which looked at two hypotheses. The first is that inventive activity increases more than proportionately with firm size. The second is that there is a positive relationship between inventive activity and market con-centration. As a result of the focus on these two hypotheses, until recently rela-tively little work had been done on other determinants of inventive activity.* In this section we review the empirical literature.[15]

MEASUREMENT ISSUES

Measurement issues are particularly difficult in empirical investigations of inno-vation and technical change. Increases in knowledge clearly contribute to tech-nological progress, yet we do not know how to measure "knowledge." How can innovations from different industries be compared? Should the measure of inven-tive activity somehow take the value of a discovery into account? All these issues

---

*Cohen and Levin note that focusing on the two hypotheses has actually worked against gaining an understanding of the fundamental determinants and economic consequences of technologi-cal progress, something that Schumpeter was interested in fostering. See Wesley M. Cohen and Richard C. Levin, "Empirical Studies of Innovation and Market Structure," in Richard Schmalensee and Robert D. Willig (eds.), *Handbook of Industrial Organization* (Amsterdam: North-Holland, 1989).

remain unsolved problems, although economists have used a variety of measures of inventive activity in their studies.[16]

The two general classes of measures of innovation are outputs and inputs. Fewer studies use measures of outputs than of inputs. This is so because of the many problems associated with counting innovations, especially across industries. Some studies have counted significant innovations for specific industries. In an early study, Mansfield constructed data for the steel, petroleum refining, and bituminous coal industries.[17] Innovation in the pharmaceutical industry has been widely studied, in part because of the availability of annual firm-specific data on the number of new chemical entities.[18] Other studies have looked at significant innovations in the semiconductor industry.[19]

The most common measure of innovative outputs across industries is a count of patents.[20] Patent data has the advantage of being widely available. However, problems are associated with using counts of patents to measure innovative output. The economic value of patents varies widely; a few patents are highly important and valuable, but many are never used commercially. Also, the propensity to patent varies greatly across industries. In some industries, firms tend to keep discoveries secret rather than patenting them and thereby revealing information to competitors. If a patent count is used to measure innovative output, then an industry with a low propensity to patent will look less innovative than one with a high propensity to patent.[21]

Most studies of innovation, especially the earlier studies, use data on inputs. Expenditures on R&D or the number of R&D personnel are the most commonly used measures of innovative inputs. These measures also have problems. Because of accounting rules, expenditures on R&D include the total amount spent in a given year on equipment, even for equipment that will last several years. Thus, R&D expenditures will be overstated in the year a piece of durable equipment is purchased and understated in the subsequent years. Also, because what is counted as R&D expenditures varies considerably across firms, it is hard to know how comparable the figures are. Although counts of R&D personnel do not suffer from these problems, they measure only part of the resources devoted to research by a firm.

A final measurement issue concerns the basic definition of inventive activity or technical change. We have noted that there are different stages of technical change. The first stage is invention, which is the initial insight or idea and the rough working out of that idea. The next stage is innovation, and the final stage is diffusion, or the spreading of an innovation into widespread use. The importance of these different stages for empirical work is that variables that affect one stage of research do not necessarily affect another. Unfortunately, data disaggregated by stage of research activity are not usually available. Researchers must often assume, therefore, that the same determinants apply across all stages of inventive activity.

TESTING SCHUMPETER'S HYPOTHESES

A large number of studies have investigated the relationship between firm size and innovation. Rather than surveying this huge literature in detail, we discuss a few studies, summarize the stylized facts, and consider some methodological problems.* Within this section, we divide our examination of the evidence into two parts: (1) the relationship between firm size and inventive *effort*, or inputs; and (2) the relationship between firm size and inventive *output*.

FIRM SIZE AND INVENTIVE EFFORT

Several early studies examined the relationship between firm size and R&D intensity, typically measured as the ratio of either R&D expenditures or R&D employment to firm size. Comanor, for example, regressed the log of R&D expenditures on firm size using 1955 and 1960 data for 387 firms in 21 groups.[†22] He found evidence of, at most, a very weak positive association between R&D intensity and firm size. Other early studies found similar results.

In two 1965 studies, Scherer criticized both the data and the specification of the estimated regressions in earlier studies.[23] He noted that the samples were biased because only firms with sizable research programs were included. Also, he argued that the specifications used had assumed a linear relationship and that such a specification might not be appropriate. The results of Scherer's studies, in which he employed a larger sample and estimated a nonlinear specification, showed that R&D employment increased more than proportionately with firm size among the smaller firms in his sample but more slowly among the larger firms. In fact, Scherer found that the relationship between R&D employment and firm size might even be *negative* among the very largest firms in some industries. Scherer noted, however, that in some industries, such as chemicals, automobiles, and steel, R&D intensity appeared to increase with firm size.

Scherer's findings were more or less confirmed by other studies, and his results became the consensus opinion in the mid-1970s and early 1980s. In the words of a review article published in 1975:

> Thus, it seems that with the possible exception of the chemical industry, there is hardly any support for the hypothesis that the intensity of innovational effort increases with firm size. [A previous review] concluded that innovational effort tends to increase more than proportionately with firm size up to some point that varies from industry to industry. For still larger firms, innovation intensity appears to be constant or decreasing with size. Subsequent investigations are consistent with and tend to reinforce that generalization.[24]

More recent work using more disaggregated data sets has shaken this consensus view. Scherer himself contributed to the questioning of the earlier consensus.[25] He used data from the Federal Trade Commission's Line of Business surveys, a data set that reports information on manufacturing companies

---

*For comprehensive literature surveys of empirical literature concerning the two Schumpeterian hypotheses, see M.I. Kamien and N.L. Schwartz, *Market Structure and Innovation* (Cambridge: Cambridge University Press, 1982), and W.L. Baldwin and J.T. Scott, *Market Structure and Technological Change* (Chichester: Harwood, 1987).

†Comanor chose the log of R&D intensity rather than R&D intensity as the dependent variable because R&D intensity must, by definition, be non-negative. See W.S. Comanor, "Market Structure, Product Differentiation, and Industrial Research," *Quarterly Journal of Economics* 81 (November, 1967): 639–57.

disaggregated by individual lines of business. For example, consider the activities of General Motors. Recall from Chapter 4 that the standard government SIC data report all of GM's activities in the fields of gas turbines, diesel locomotives, buses, and missile guidance systems under the broad heading "motor vehicles and equipments." Line of business data reports these activities under their correct subheadings. Scherer studied *business units* such as GM's unit that manufactures diesel locomotives, and found that for 40 of 196 business units in his sample, R&D intensity increased with business unit size; for most of the remaining lines of business (140 of 196), Scherer's results indicated *no size effect* on R&D intensity.

Another study using the Line of Business data emphasized the need to control for industry effects and to make a distinction between the size of the firm and the size of the business unit.[26] After taking these factors into account, Cohen and colleagues found no effect of size, either of the firm or of the business unit, on R&D intensity. They did find evidence of a threshold effect in the decision to undertake R&D: the likelihood of a business unit engaging in R&D increased as the size of the business unit increased.* Cohen and co-workers also noted that the size variables explained less than 1 percent of the total variance of R&D intensity and that the magnitude of the effect was very small. Other evidence, however, indicates that R&D intensity is higher among small and large firms than among intermediate-sized firms.[27]

What can we conclude about the relationship between firm size and R&D intensity from the available evidence? The evidence is inconclusive and sometimes contradictory. However, there is certainly no strong support for the claim that R&D intensity increases more than proportionately with firm size.

FIRM SIZE AND INVENTIVE OUTPUT

Fewer studies have examined the relationship of size to inventive output than of size to inventive inputs. As mentioned earlier, measuring inventive output is particularly difficult. Most studies use patents as a measure of inventive output.

The relatively early evidence about outputs from studies measured at the firm level, rather than at the line of business level, was generally consistent with that about inputs. Given that R&D expenditures and patents are highly correlated, this is not surprising. In their 1975 survey, Kamien and Schwartz summarized the available evidence on innovational output as follows:

> . . . the conclusion about the effect of size on innovational effort tends to be supported and reflected in evidence on size and innovational output. Beyond some magnitude, size does not appear especially conducive to either innovational effort or output in either this country or in European countries where studies have been conducted. However, patterns differ by industry. It seems noteworthy that the chemical industry is cited as an exception both for the United States and abroad.[28]

---

*Another study also found evidence of a threshold in terms of the decision to engage in R&D along with no effect of firm size beyond that threshold. See Albert N. Link, Terry G. Seaks, and Sabrina R. Woodbery, "Firm Size and R&D Spending: Testing for Functional Form," *Southern Economic Journal* 54 (April 1988): 1027–38.

More recent results support this. Using the Line of Business data, Scherer found that the number of patents increased more than proportionately with size for only 14 of 124, or 11 percent, of the business units. For most industries, 91 of 124, R&D performance as measured by patent counts increased proportionately with size.* Neutrality with regard to the effects of size is the norm.

REMAINING QUESTIONS

Some evidence indicates that the inventive process is far too complicated to be described by firm-specific variables such as size. Jewkes, Sawers, and Stillerman compiled a collection of case histories of important inventions of the twentieth century.[29] They described complex interactions of firms in which, for example, large firms sometimes acquire smaller firms to bring an invention to market. It is worth quoting their conclusion about size: "It may well be that there is no optimum size of firm but merely an optimal pattern for any industry, such a distribution of firms by size, character and outlook as to guarantee the most effective gathering together and commercially perfecting of the flow of new ideas."[30] To gain a better understanding of the inventive process, economists need to consider the type of interactions described by Jewkes, Sawers, and Stillerman more fully.

MARKET STRUCTURE AND INVENTIVE ACTIVITY

In a very early study, Maclaurin compared two rankings of thirteen U.S. industries: (1) by important innovations from 1925 to 1950; and (2) by the extent of monopolization.[31]† He found that *some* degree of monopoly power is necessary for technological progress, but that it is not sufficient. Other factors, including ease of entry, entrepreneurial leadership, and the underlying engineering or scientific base, seemed to be much more important.

Maclaurin's results have stood up reasonably well over time. Most studies that look at the relationship between market concentration and industry R&D/sales ratios have found a positive relationship, both for the United States and for other industrialized nations.[32]

A number of studies have examined the specification of the relationship between market concentration and R&D intensity, testing for nonlinearities. Early evidence suggested that the relationship might take the nonlinear form of an "inverted-U," in which R&D intensity increases with concentration at first but then decreases as concentration levels increase still further.‡ Using 1960 data on R&D employment as a percent of total employment, Scherer found a peak in R&D intensity at four-firm concentration levels between 50 and 55.[33] He also found evidence of a threshold: industries with four-firm concentration ratios below 15 appeared to do almost no research and development.

---

*For the remaining nineteen industries, there was a disadvantage associated with being large.

†Each ranking was subjective. The ranking by important innovations was based on factors such as the number of patents issued and the presence or absence of a separate research department. The monopolization ranking took into account size of industry price leaders and ease of entry.

‡Recall from Chapter 2 that many economic relationships tend to be nonlinear; see Chapter 2, *Supra*, pp. 46–47.

The inverted-U hypothesis has been tested further using more disaggregated data. Simple tests that regress R&D intensity against the concentration ratio and the square of the concentration ratio support the inverted-U hypothesis. Levin, Cohen, and Mowery found a peak R&D/sales ratio at a four-firm concentration ratio of 52.[34] Similarly, Scott found a peak in R&D intensity at a four-firm concentration ratio of 64.[35]

As long ago as Maclaurin's study, however, economists recognized the importance of industry-specific factors. Including additional explanatory variables to account for some of these factors weakens the empirical support for the inverted-U hypothesis. Examples include indices, based on survey results, that measure the relevance of various scientific fields to specific industries' R&D efforts and the importance of contributions from outside an industry to that industry's technological progress.[36] These indices reflect differences in **technological opportunity** or the inherent interindustry differences in ability to make major technological progress. Some industries, such as the computer or the drug industry, have many scientific opportunities to make progress, whereas others, like the brick industry or the glass bottle industry, have far fewer scientific opportunities. Other indices measure **appropriability**, or the ability of a firm to maintain exclusive control over its technology without seeing that technology lost to competitors. Examples include indices assessing the strength of patents, secrecy, and lead times. Including such measures reduces the statistical significance of the coefficient of market concentration.

In addition to possible problems caused by omitted variables, investigations of the relationship between market concentration and inventive activity may suffer from *simultaneity bias*. The regressions considered thus far have assumed that the direction of causation runs *from* concentration *to* R&D. Some economists have suggested, however, that the causation may also run in the opposite direction, with a rapid rate of innovation leading to concentration.[37] If this is the case, econometric techniques that take this simultaneity into account should be employed in empirical work.

Some studies have attempted to correct for the potential simultaneity between innovation and concentration.[38] Two tentative conclusions emerge from this work. First, econometric tests find evidence of simultaneity, rejecting the hypothesis that the causal connection between market structure and R&D runs only in one direction. Second, techniques that take the simultaneity into account do not seem to change the coefficient of the concentration variable in the equation explaining R&D intensity.

SUMMARY OF EMPIRICAL WORK ON THE SCHUMPETERIAN HYPOTHESES

Although some stylized facts have emerged from the empirical work on the relationships between firm size and inventive activity and between market structure and inventive activity, the results are not particularly robust. Omitting important variables can bias the estimated coefficients and lead a researcher to draw incorrect conclusions about the relationship of interest. Results seem to be sensitive to industry conditions, making it necessary to think about the fundamental determinants of inventive activity. Economists have recently turned their attention to such fundamental determinants, focusing on three categories: market demand, technological opportunity, and appropriability conditions. Historical literature and case studies make the importance of these factors evident, yet much work remains to be done and little is known at present.*

The Economics of the Patent System

A United States patent is a seventeen-year legal monopoly grant that is awarded to inventors in exchange for their agreement to disclose their inventions to the public. A valid patent gives an inventor monopoly power to decide on the use, transfer, or withholding of an innovation. The awarding of a patent has an admirable objective, the dissemination of technological knowledge that might otherwise be kept secret, but the patent grant may be abused and come in direct conflict with another economic goal, the reduction of monopoly power.

Patents exist for one economic purpose—to increase the rate of technological advance. Without question, some major technological breakthroughs would never have been developed, or would have been developed much later, in the absence of patent protection. Economic theory suggests, however, that patent protection may not increase the rate of technological advance. In fact, theory suggests that in some cases patent protection *decreases* the rate of technological advance.[39]

To understand the potential dilemma associated with the current system, consider the following three possible scenarios.

SCENARIO 1

Suppose a weekend garage inventor, hypothetically named Mr. Tinker, is driven to invent, not by money, but by a fairly common character trait—curiosity. One day Mr. Tinker discovers a new method for cheaply harnessing solar energy. Although Mr. Tinker never gave any thought to the patent system as he worked on his invention every weekend, on realizing the importance of his discovery, he runs to a patent attorney, and a few years later receives a patent. He then turns the patent over to a large firm, hypothetically called International Solar Machines (ISM), and on the basis of Mr. Tinker's patent ISM develops a solar energy device, which it prices well above marginal and average cost. Over the next decade, other firms spend millions of dollars in an unsuccessful attempt to invent around the ISM patent. Finally, after seventeen years, the ISM patent is made public, but by then ISM is a virtual monopolist in the solar energy business. Furthermore, during the period of patent protection, ISM patented a number of minor technological advances based on Mr. Tinker's original patent, so that by the time the original patent expires, ISM is firmly entrenched as the leader in the solar energy field, and few firms will consider attempting to challenge ISM's dominance. Mr. Tinker, ISM's management, and ISM's stockholders have all made large fortunes, but the solar energy industry has performed in a very inefficient manner in terms of static

*See Cohen and Levin in *Handbook of Industrial Organization* (Amsterdam: North-Holland, 1989), pp. 1079–98 for a discussion of the work that has been done.

efficiency. Furthermore, to protect its investment in Tinker's original device, ISM withheld using some of its improvement patents for several years; therefore, ISM slowed the rate of technological advance on improvements to the Tinker patent. Society has benefited from Mr. Ticker's device but has also paid a price in the form of reduced static efficiency and a slow rate of technological improvement on the basic patent.

SCENARIO 2

Now consider an alternate scenario to the Mr. Tinker story, one without a patent system. Mr. Tinker develops the same solar energy device, and takes the device to ISM. A member of the ISM development department likes the idea, and ISM proceeds with development. Because of a lack of patent protection, ISM decides to introduce the device as quickly as possible before its competitors learn about the existence of the invention (perhaps rumors of the device have already begun to circulate). ISM is first into the market and initially charges a high profit-maximizing price. Within twelve to twenty-four months, ISM and Mr. Tinker have made a large economic profit, and the first imitations of Mr. Tinker's invention appear on the market. After another twenty-four months many imitations are available, but to keep one step ahead of the competition, ISM and some of its competitors have already marketed more advanced devices based on the original Tinker technology. Within five years, the basic Tinker device is obsolete, and many companies are competing for a share of the solar energy harnessing market. Some firms make a profit, others sustain an economic loss and leave the market, but on average the industry is earning normal economic profits. Prices approximate marginal and average cost, and the industry is performing efficiently from a static standpoint. In this scenario, the lack of patent protection has actually increased the rate of technological advance, and the outcome is preferable to that of scenario 1 from both a static and dynamic perspective.

SCENARIO 3

Now consider another possible scenario in the absence of patent protection. Mr. Tinker develops the same solar energy device and approaches the development department at ISM. After careful consideration, the development department concludes that although the device is technologically sound, development would be too expensive, and therefore, without patent protection ISM could not expect to earn a profit. Mr. Tinker then approaches several other large high-technology firms, but each responds in the same negative manner. Finally, completely discouraged, Mr. Tinker gives up, and the device never becomes a commercial reality. Because of a lack of patent protection, society has lost all of the potential benefits associated with Mr. Tinker's device.

Economic uncertainty surrounding the patent system exists because it is impossible to determine how often the first scenario occurs, as opposed to how often the second or third scenarios *would* occur in the absence of patent protection. Scenario 2, without patent protection, is clearly preferable to scenario 1, with patent protection. However, scenario 1, with patent protection, is clearly preferable to scenario 3, without patent protection.

Another way to think about this dilemma is to recognize that some inventions and innovations are *patent dependent* and others are *not patent dependent*; that is, some technology would become available only with a patent system, but other technology would become available just as quickly, or even more quickly, without a patent system. Like many economic issues, the patent system involves trade-offs. Some inventions and innovations that are not patent dependent are protected to ensure that society receives the benefits of all patent-dependent inventions and innovations. Because the system involves social costs as well as social benefits, patent holders should not be granted unrestricted rights and privileges.

The impact of the patent system on development time can be analyzed using the framework of Figure 14.4. Figure 14.4 shows three benefits curves, one each for a monopolist, an oligopolist, and a perfectly competitive firm. Suppose we consider the impact of the patent system within such a framework. As the length of patent protection increases, the patent holder gains increasingly more monopoly power and the benefit curve moves higher and becomes flatter. Figure 14.8 reproduces Figure 14.4 except the benefit curves are labeled as B_0, B_7, and B_{17}, where the subscripts 0, 7, and 17 represent the length of patent protection in years. In Figure 14.8, no innovation takes place without patent protection (the B_0 case) because the present value of costs always exceeds the present value of benefits. Patent protection is necessary for innovation to occur, but the time of development is faster with a patent life of seven years rather than seventeen years. Of course, every case will be different, but it is possible that a seventeen-year patent length could slow down the rate of technological advance.

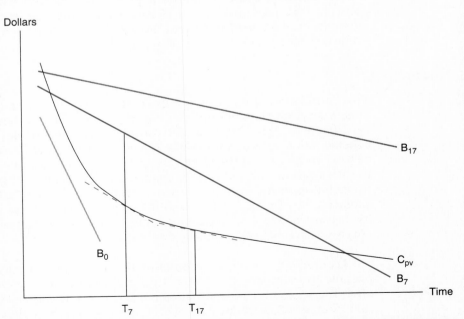

Figure 14.8 Relationship between the length of patent life and the rate of technological advance.

It is, of course, also possible that a patent life longer than seventeen years would be required to induce technological advance. If the cost curve is everywhere above the B_{17} curve, then a patent longer than seventeen years is required to obtain the benefits associated with the technological advance.

EMPIRICAL EVIDENCE ON THE IMPACT OF PATENTS

Patents induce inventions and innovation, but also increase monopoly power. The patent system *always* results in net social benefits for patent-dependent innovations. The patent system, however, *always* results in net social losses for nonpatent-dependent innovations because these innovations would be developed without the costs of granting monopoly power. There are a variety of reasons why many high-technology innovations would be developed without patents. First, many inventions and innovations result from human curiosity and genius. Such inventions are driven primarily by a need to understand. The development of fire and the wheel, for example, were certainly not driven by patents. Second, sufficient economic incentives for invention and innovation often result from first-mover advantages or an ability to move rapidly down a learning curve. Third, complementary investments in marketing and service can provide sufficient protection from competition for new inventions or innovations (e.g., IBM). Finally, secrecy may provide better protection against imitation than patents because with patent protection the new technology is made public, whereas with secrecy competitors are prevented from gaining insight into the new invention or innovation.

To try to determine the relative importance of patents compared with these other incentives, Levin and colleagues conducted a survey of 650 high-level R&D executives in 130 lines of business.[40] The R&D executives were asked to rate the importance of patents in protecting the competitive advantages of new processes or products on a scale from 1 = not at all effective to 7 = very effective. The executives were also asked to rate on the same scale the effectiveness of secrecy, lead time, learning curves, and sales or service effort.

Table 14.4 shows Levin and co-workers' major findings. The results were described by the authors as "striking."[41] For new processes, patent protection was the *least* effective method of protection. The executives rated lead time (a first-mover advantage) the most effective method of protecting a new process, followed by learning curve advantages, sales or service effort, and secrecy, respectively. Furthermore, 80 percent of the respondents rated patent effectiveness *below* a 4.0, whereas 80 percent rated lead time above a 4.3 and learning curve advantages above a 4.5. Even secrecy was considered far more effective than patents.

The findings for new products are only slightly more favorable toward patents. With regard to new products, patents were rated less effective than lead time, sales or service effort, and learning curve advantages, but more effective than secrecy. Still, only 20 percent of the executives rated patents above a 5. Compare this with the 80 percent who rated sales or service efforts above a 5.

Table 14.5 shows Levin and colleagues' results for the eighteen industries with ten or more respondents. Except in petroleum refining, patent effectiveness was consistently rated higher for new products than for new processes. Levin noted:[42]

> The data on these eighteen most heavily sampled industries help to establish the robustness of our conclusion about the limited effectiveness of patents as

TABLE 14.4 **Effectiveness of Alternative Means of Protecting Advantages of New or Improved Processes and Products**

Method of Appropriation	Overall Sample Means		Distribution of Industry Means[1]	
	Processes	Products	Processes	Products
Patents to prevent duplication	3.52	4.33	2.6–4.0	3.0–5.0
Patents to secure royalty income	3.31	3.75	2.3–4.0	2.7–4.8
Secrecy	4.31	3.57	3.3–5.0	2.7–4.1
Lead time	5.11	5.41	4.3–5.9	4.8–6.0
Moving quickly down the learning curve	5.02	5.09	4.5–5.7	4.4–5.8
Sales or service effort	4.55	5.59	3.7–5.5	5.0–6.1

Source: Richard C. Levin, Alvin K. Klevorick, Richard R. Nelson, and Sidney G. Winter, "Appropriating the Returns from Industrial Research and Development," *Brookings Papers on Economic Activity,* No. 3 (1987): 794.

Note. Range: 1 = not at all effective; 7 = very effective.

[1]From the upper bound of the lowest 20 percent to the lower bound of the highest 20 percent.

a means of appropriation. In none did a majority of respondents rate patents—either to prevent duplication or to secure royalty income—as more effective than the most highly rated of the other four means of appropriating returns from new processes, although in drugs and petroleum refining a majority regarded process patents as at least the equal of the most effective alternative mechanism of appropriation. In only one industry, drugs, were product patents regarded by a majority of respondents as strictly more effective than other means of appropriation.

The Levin and co-workers findings raise serious questions concerning the extent to which new process and product innovations are patent dependent. There are strong implications that most inventions and innovations would come into being without patent protection. Taking this implication one step farther, the authors noted, "The perceived ineffectiveness of patents in most industries raises the question of why firms use them."[43] Executives in the study noted two motives for patents having little to do with protecting innovations.[44] First, firms may obtain patents to measure the productivity of their R&D employees. Second, firms may obtain patents because some foreign governments require patent licensing as a condition of entry into their markets.

More evidence on patent dependency is supplied by Mansfield, who surveyed 100 R&D directors to try to ascertain what proportion of their companies' inventions produced between 1981 and 1983 were patent dependent. Mansfield's results are reported in Table 14.6. Of the twelve industry groups, the executives rated patents as completely unimportant in six industries. Only in pharmaceuticals were more than half the inventions patent dependent, and in only three in-

TABLE 14.5 **Effectiveness of Process and Product Patents in Industries with Ten or More Survey Respondents**

Industry	Process Patents		Product Patents	
	Mean	Standard Error	Mean	Standard Error
Pulp, paper, and paperboard	2.6	0.3	3.3	0.4
Cosmetics	2.9	0.3	4.1	0.4
Inorganic chemicals	4.6	0.4	5.2	0.3
Organic chemicals	4.1	0.3	6.1	0.2
Drugs	4.9	0.3	6.5	0.1
Plastic materials	4.6	0.3	5.4	0.3
Plastic products	3.2	0.3	4.9	0.3
Petroleum refining	4.9	0.4	4.3	0.4
Steel mill products	3.5	0.7	5.1	0.6
Pumps and pumping equipment	3.2	0.4	4.4	0.5
Motors, generators, and controls	2.7	0.3	3.5	0.5
Computers	3.3	0.4	3.4	0.4
Communication equipment	3.1	0.3	3.6	0.3
Semiconductors	3.2	0.4	4.5	0.4
Motor vehicles parts	3.7	0.4	4.5	0.4
Aircraft and parts	3.1	0.5	3.8	0.4
Measuring devices	3.6	0.3	3.9	0.3
Medical instruments	3.2	0.4	4.7	0.4
Full sample	3.5	0.06	4.3	0.07

Source: Richard C. Levin, Alvin K. Klevorick, Richard R. Nelson, and Sidney G. Winter, "Appropriating the Returns from Industrial Research and Development," *Brookings Papers on Economic Activity,* No. 3, (1987): 797.

dustries—pharmaceuticals, other chemicals, and petroleum—were 25 percent or more of the inventions patent dependent. Mansfield's results are consistent with Levin and colleagues' findings.

Levin and co-workers also surveyed the executives concerning the impact of patents on the cost and time requirements of imitation. The results are reported in Tables 14.7 and 14.8. Respondents reported that patents typically increased the costs of imitation and lengthened the time required to duplicate an innovation. These responses suggest that patents may significantly reduce the rate of imitation and thereby slow the rate of technological advance.

These survey findings imply that a relatively small percentage of inventions and innovations are patent dependent. To obtain the benefits associated with this small percentage of patent-dependent inventions and innovations, society pays a price in the form of higher monopoly profits and slower imitation. Is the price worth the benefits associated with patent-dependent inventions and innova-

TABLE 14.6 **Estimated Percentage of Patent-Dependent Inventions by Industry Group 1981–1983**

Industry Group	Percentage of Inventions Whose Existence Depends on Patent Protection
Pharmaceuticals	60
Other chemicals	38
Petroleum	25
Machinery	17
Fabricated metal products	12
Electrical equipment	11
Primary metals	1
Instruments	1
Office equipment	0
Motor vehicles	0
Rubber products	0
Textiles	0

Source: Edwin Mansfield, "Patents and Innovation," *Management Science* (February 1986): 175.

tions? No definitive answer is possible because the patent-dependent inventions and innovations may be the most valuable technological advances. For example, if technological advances in the pharmaceutical industry are heavily driven by patents, as Mansfield's findings suggest, then one of the greatest benefits of the patent system is saving lives, a benefit that surely should not be taken lightly. As Pakes and Simpson have noted:[45]

> . . . To take an extreme example, a finding that only 0.5 percent of a firm's inventions was dependent on patent protection would not mean that patent protection was unimportant to the firm if that same 0.5 percent accounted for 99.5 percent of the total returns to the firm's R&D program. . . .
> . . . Moreover, half of all the estimated value of patents rights accrues to between 5 and 10 percent of all patents.

All that can be safely concluded is that technological advance would continue even if the patent system was eliminated. Most inventions and innovations would still be developed and effectively protected by some combination of first-mover advantages, learning curves, sales or service efforts, or secrecy. Furthermore, elimination of the patent system would reduce the degree of monopoly power in the economy and increase the rate of imitation. Society, however, might be better or worse off as a result of such a dramatic policy change.

It is unclear from this discussion what policy changes, if any, are called for in the patent system. Proposed changes have included one or more of the following: (1) changing the number of years of protection either above or below seventeen

TABLE 14.7 Cost of Duplicating an Innovation as a Percentage of Innovator's Research & Development Cost, Frequency Distribution of Median Responses in 127 Lines of Business

Type of Innovation	Less than 25%	26%–50%	51%–75%	76%–100%	More than 100%	Timely Duplication Impossible
New process						
Major patented new process	1	5	19	66	26	10
Major unpatented new process	5	10	55	49	6	2
Typical patented new process	2	15	61	41	6	2
Typical unpatented new process	8	43	58	14	4	0
New product						
Major patented new product	1	2	17	63	30	12
Major unpatented new product	5	13	58	40	7	4
Typical patented new product	2	18	64	32	9	2
Typical unpatented new product	9	58	40	15	5	0

Source: Richard C. Levin, Alvin K. Klevorick, Richard R. Nelson, and Sidney G. Winter, "Appropriating the Returns from Industrial Research and Development," *Brookings Papers on Economic Activity*, No. 3 (1987): 809.

TABLE 14.8 **Time Required to Duplicate an Innovation Frequency Distribution of Median Responses in 129 Lines of Business**

Type of Innovation	Less than 6 Months	6 Months to 1 Year	1–3 Years	3–5 Years	More than 5 Years	Timely Duplication Impossible
New process						
Major patented new process	0	4	72	37	9	7
Major unpatented new process	2	20	84	17	2	4
Typical patented new process	0	40	73	13	0	3
Typical unpatented new process	8	66	47	6	1	1
New product						
Major patented new product	2	6	64	40	8	9
Major unpatented new product	3	22	89	12	1	2
Typical patented new product	5	39	72	6	4	3
Typical unpatented new product	18	67	39	4	1	0

Source: Richard C. Levin, Alvin K. Klevorick, Richard R. Nelson, and Sidney G. Winter, "Appropriating the Returns from Industrial Research and Development," *Brookings Papers on Economic Activity,* No. 3 (1987): 810.

years; (2) requiring compulsory licensing to all at "reasonable" royalties; (3) expanding the scope of patent protection to include new areas such as university research; (4) tightening the legal requirements to gain patent protection; or (5) speeding up the patent review process so that patents would be granted more quickly. In the last twenty years the legal changes adopted by Congress have moved in the direction of strengthening the value of a patent grant.

In 1980 Congress gave small businesses and universities exclusive patent rights to inventions and innovations developed with the help of federal funding. The 1980 law also reduced the likelihood that the federal courts would find a patent invalid. More recently Congress lengthened the life of drug patents that must receive approval from the Food and Drug Administration (FDA). Congress was addressing the problems associated with the lengthy review period for new drugs, a process that significantly reduces the effective life of most drug patents. Because many inventions and innovations in the drug industry are patent dependent, this extension probably makes economic sense.

SUMMARY

1. Schumpeter theorized that technological change came about in dramatic upheavals, which he termed the process of *creative destruction.*

2. For Schumpeter, perfect competition was not the ideal market structure; instead large-scale firms with monopoly power became the superior market structure. Creative destruction drove a capitalist economy forward in the long run, and large-scale monopolists engaged in research and development led to creative destruction.

3. Later theoretical work suggested that either perfect competition or oligopoly was likely to result in a more rapid rate of technological advance than was monopoly.

4. Oligopolists have both the ability and the incentive to invest in R&D. Traditional theories suggested that, under a wide variety of cost and benefit conditions, oligopoly results in the most rapid rate of technological advance.

5. Game theorists have suggested, however, that oligopolists may either underinvest or overinvest in R&D.

6. The theoretical relationship between firm size and technological advance is complex. Large firms may engage in greater research and development efforts because: (1) they have greater resources to invest in R&D; (2) large economies of scale may be associated with R&D; (3) large firms can spread risk over more projects; (4) large firms are often highly diversified and a technological advance in one area may be useful in another; and (5) large firms may have longer time horizons.

7. There are arguments in favor of smaller firms. The most powerful argument against the large corporation is the tendency for large firms to become bureaucratically inefficient.

8. Empirical studies of the relationship among firm size, market structure, and technological change are burdened by numerous methodological problems.

9. Few strong conclusions emerge from a thorough investigation of the available evidence. It appears, however, that no strong empirical support exists for Schumpeter's hypothesis that large firms in concentrated industries are best suited for rapid rates of technological change.

10. There is no support for the claim that R&D increases more than proportionally with increases in firm size. R&D output as measured by patents appears to increase proportionally with the size of the firm.

11. There is some empirical support for the hypothesis that oligopolists engage in more R&D effort than either competitive firms or monopolists. Recent work suggests, however, that rather than increased concentration leading to increased R&D expenditures, increased R&D expenditures may lead to increased concentration.

12. The relationship between concentration and R&D effort is not linear, but rather R&D efforts peak somewhere in the oligopoly range of market structures.

13. Although some stylized facts have emerged from the empirical work on the relationship between firm size and inventive activity and between market structure and inventive activity, the results are not particularly robust. Omitting important variables can bias the results and lead a researcher to draw incorrect conclusions about the relationship of interest.

14. Economists have recently turned their attention to fundamental determinants such as product market demand, technological opportunity, and appropriability conditions. Case studies make the importance of these factors clear.

15. The patent system sometimes increases the rate of technological advance, yet there are theoretical reasons for suspecting that the system also may slow down the rate of advance.

16. In the absence of patents, most inventions would still be made because sufficient economic incentives for invention and innovation often result from first-mover advantages or an ability to move rapidly down a learning curve. In some cases simple secrecy provides better protection against imitation than patents.

17. Several survey findings suggest that a relatively small percentage of inventions and innovations are patent dependent.

18. To obtain the benefits associated with this small percentage of patent-dependent inventions and innovations, society pays a price in the form of higher monopoly profits and slower imitation. Conversely, very important technological advances, for example, in the pharmaceuticals industry, may be heavily driven by patents and result in great benefits for society.

KEY TERMS

applied research

appropriability

basic research

creative destruction

diffusion

fast-second innovators

innovation

invention

patent race

technological opportunity

DISCUSSION QUESTIONS

1. Would Schumpeter be concerned if an industry were not producing the output for which price equaled marginal cost?

2. Give two examples of creative destruction.

3. Technological progress in agriculture has been remarkable in this century, yet individual farmers invest little in research and development. Why has the industry been able to attain such a high rate of technological advance?

4. What is the *simultaneity bias* in statistical work on the relationship between market concentration and R&D? Does empirical work support the existence of such a bias?

5. How is it possible for patents to slow the rate of technological advance?

6. One difficult question for policy makers has been whether to permit patent holders to license their patents with a price-fixing clause in the license. For example, if I hold a patent on widgets and license you to produce widgets, should I be permitted to fix the price of your widgets? Discuss the pros and cons of permitting price fixing in this case.

PROBLEMS

1. Using graphs, show how it is possible for an elimination of patent protection to increase the rate of technological advance. Show how it is also possible for the elimination of patent protection to slow down the rate of technological advance.

2. Suppose a monopolist faces a demand curve of $P = 50 - Q$. Currrently LRMC = LRAC = 25. If the monopolist has developed a cost-saving device that lowers its costs to LRMC = LRAC = 20, how much will profits increase after the introduction of the new technology?

   If this industry were perfectly competitive, how much could a patent holder earn on this technology?

   Does a monopolist or a patent holder in a perfectly competitive industry have a greater incentive to introduce this technology?

3. Suppose the payoff matrix for a game of innovation is as follows:

Firm A's Profits, Firm B's Profits

		Firm B's Action	
		Innovate	Imitate
Firm A's Action	Innovate	4,4	4,5
	Imitate	5,4	1,1

   a. Is there one Nash equilbrium in pure strategies in this game?
   b. Are there any Nash equilibria in this game?
   c. Show that if Firm A plays innovate with a probablity of 75 percent and imitate with a probability of 25 percent, Firm B earns the same profits regardless of what strategy Firm B selects. What does this suggest about Firm A's strategy of innovating with a probability of 75 percent?
   d. If both firms play innovate with a probablity of 75 percent and imitate with a probability of 25 percent, what is the probability of a non-optimal outcome in the sense that the industry will not maximize joint profits?

REFERENCES

1. Joseph A. Schumpeter, *Capitalism, Socialism, and Democracy* (New York: Harper & Brothers Publishers, 1942).
2. *Ibid.,* p. 61.
3. Robert M. Solow, "Technical Change and the Aggregate Production Function," *Review of Economics and Statistics* 39 (August 1957): 312–9.
4. For an updated confirmation of Solow's result see also Edward F. Denison, *Trends in American Economic Growth 1929–1982* (Washington: Brookings, 1985).
5. F.M. Scherer and David Ross, *Industrial Market Structure and Economic Performance* (Boston: Houghton Mifflin, 1990), p. 616.
6. Kenneth J. Arrow, "Economic Welfare and the Allocation of Resources for Invention," in National Bureau of Economic Research conference volume, *The Rate and Direction of Inventive Activity* (Princeton, NJ: Princeton University Press, 1962), pp. 609–25.
7. For a different approach and conclusion see Harold Demsetz, "Information and Efficiency: Another Viewpoint," *Journal of Law and Economics* 12 (April 1969): 1–22.
8. F.M. Scherer, *Innovation and Growth: Schumpeterian Perspectives* (Cambridge, MA: MIT Press, 1984), pp. 120–9.
9. For early contributions see Glenn C. Loury,"Market Structure and Innovation," *Quarterly Journal of Economics* 93 (August 1979): 395–410; and Tom Lee and Louis L. Wilde, "Market Structure and Innovation," *Quarterly Journal of Economics* 94: (1980): 429–36.
10. John Kenneth Galbraith, *American Capitalism* (Boston: Houghton Mifflin, 1956), p. 91.
11. Paul Carroll, *Big Blues: The Unmaking of IBM* (New York: Crown Publishers, 1993), p. 20.
12. *Ibid.,* p. 23.
13. *Ibid.,* p. 123.
14. "Bill Gates & Paul Allen Talk," *Fortune* (October 2, 1995): 70.
15. The organization and discussion in this section draws on that in Wesley M. Cohen and Richard C. Levin, "Empirical Studies of Innovation and Market Structure," in Richard Schmalensee and Robert D. Willig

(eds.), *Handbook of Industrial Organization* (Amsterdam: North-Holland, 1989), pp. 1060–107.

16. Zvi Griliches, "Issues in Assessing the Contribution of Research and Development to Productivity Growth," *Bell Journal of Economics* 10 (1979): 92–116.

17. Edwin Mansfield, "Size of Firm, Market Structure, and Innovation," *Journal of Political Economy* 71 (1963): 556–76.

18. For examples, see Martin N. Baily, "Research and Development Costs and Returns: The U.S. Pharmaceutical Industry," *Journal of Political Economy* 80 (1972): 70–85; H. Grabowski, J. Vernon, and L.G. Thomas, "Estimating the Effects of Regulation on Innovation: An International Comparative Analysis of the Pharmaceutical Industry," *Journal of Law and Economics* 21 (1978): 133–63; and Elizabeth J. Jensen, "Research Expenditures and the Discovery of New Drugs," *Journal of Industrial Economics* 36 (1987): 83–95.

19. J. Tilton, *International Diffusion of Technology: The Case of Semiconductors* (Washington, D.C.: Brookings Institution, 1971); and R.W. Wilson, P.K. Ashton, and T.P. Egan, *Innovation, Competition, and Government Policy in the Semiconductor Industry* (Lexington, MA: Lexington Books, 1980).

20. For early examples, see F.M. Scherer, "Firm Size, Market Structure, Opportunity, and the Output of Patented Inventions," *American Economic Review* 55 (1965): 1097–125 and H.G. Grabowski, "The Determinants of Industrial Research and Development: A Study of the Chemical, Drug, and Petroleum Industries," *Journal of Political Economy* 76 (1968): 292–306. More recent work includes J. Bound, C. Cummins, Z. Griliches, B.H. Hall, and A. Jaffe, "Who Does R&D and Who Patents?" in Z. Griliches (ed.), *R&D, Patents, and Productivity* (Chicago: University of Chicago Press for the National Bureau of Economic Research, 1984).

21. Z. Griliches, B. Hall, and A. Pakes, "The Value of Patents as Indicators of Inventive Activity," in P. Dasgupta and P. Stoneman (eds.), *Economic Policy and Technological Performance* (Cambridge: Cambridge University Press, 1987).

22. W.S. Comanor, "Market Structure, Product Differentiation, and Industrial Research," *Quarterly Journal of Economics* 81 (November 1967): 639–57.

23. F.M. Scherer, "Size of Firm, Oligopoly, and Research: A Comment," *Canadian Journal of Economics and Political Science* 31 (May 1965): 256–66; and F.M. Scherer, "Firm Size, Market Structure, Opportunity, and

the Output of Patented Inventions," *American Economic Review* 55 (December 1965): 1097–125.

24. Morton L. Kamien and Nancy L. Schwartz, "Market Structure and Innovation: A Survey," *Journal of Economic Literature* (March 1975): 1–37.

25. F.M. Scherer, "Technological Change and the Modern Corporation," in Betty Bock et al. (eds.), *The Impact of the Modern Corporation* (New York: Columbia University Press, 1984).

26. Wesley M. Cohen, Richard C. Levin, and David C. Mowery, "Firm Size and R&D Intensity: A Re-Examination," *Journal of Industrial Economics* 35 (June 1987): 543–65.

27. J. Bound, C. Cummins, Z. Griliches, B.H. Hall, and A. Jaffe, "Who Does R&D and Who Patents?" in Z. Griliches (ed.), *R&D, Patents, and Productivity* (Chicago: University of Chicago Press for the National Bureau of Economic Research, 1984).

28. Kamien and Schwartz, *supra* note 10, p. 19.

29. John Jewkes, David Sawers, and Richard Stillerman, *The Sources of Invention*, 2nd edition. (New York: W.W. Norton, 1969).

30. Jewkes, Sawers, and Stillerman, *ibid.*, p. 168.

31. W.R. Maclaurin, "Technological Progress in Some American Industries," *American Economic Review* 44 (May 1954): 178–89.

32. For a survey, see William L. Baldwin and John T. Scott, *Market Structure and Technological Change* (Chur: Harwood, 1987).

33. F.M. Scherer, "Market Structure and the Employment of Scientists and Engineers," *American Economic Review* 57 (1967): 524–31.

34. Richard C. Levin, Wesley M. Cohen, and David C. Mowery, "R&D, Appropriability, and Market Structure: New Evidence on Some Schumpeterian Hypotheses," *American Economic Review* 75 (May 1985): 20–4.

35. John T. Scott, "Firm versus Industry Variability in R&D Intensity," in Zvi Griliches (ed.), *R&D, Patents, and Productivity* (Chicago: University of Chicago Press, 1984), pp. 200–24.

36. See Levin et al., *supra* note 33.

37. Richard R. Nelson and Sidney G. Winter, "Forces Generating and Limiting Concentration Under Schumpeterian Competition," *Bell Journal of Economics* 9 (1978): 524–48; and Richard R. Nelson and Sidney G. Winter, "The Schumpeterian Tradeoff Revisited," *American Economic Review* 72 (1982): 114–32.

38. J.D. Howe and D.G. McFetridge, "The Determinants of R&D Expenditures," *Canadian Journal of Economics* 9 (1976): 57–61; R.A. Connolly and M. Hirschey, "R&D, Market Structure, and Profits: A Value-Based Ap-

proach," *Review of Economics and Statistics* 66 (1984): 682–6; Levin, Cohen, and Mowery, *op. cit.*; R.C. Levin and P.C. Reiss, "Tests of a Schumpeterian Model of R&D and Market Structure," in Z. Griliches (ed.), *R&D, Patents, and Productivity* (Chicago: University of Chicago Press for the National Bureau of Economic Research, 1984).

39. See William G. Shepherd and Clair Wilcox, *Public Policies Toward Business* (Homewood, IL: Irwin, 1979), p. 506; C.T. Taylor and Z.A. Silberston, *The Economics of the Patent System* (Cambridge, UK: Cambridge University Press, 1973); and W.D. Nordhaus, *Invention, Growth, and Welfare* (Cambridge, MA: MIT Press, 1969).

40. Richard C. Levin, Alvin K. Klevorick, Richard R. Nelson, and Sidney G. Winter, "Appropriating the Returns from Industrial Research and Development," *Brookings Papers on Economic Activity*, No. 3 (1987), pp. 783–820.

41. *Ibid.*, p. 794.

42. *Ibid.*, p. 796.

43. *Ibid.*, p. 798.

44. *Ibid.*, p. 798.

45. Ariel Pakes and Margaret Simpson, "Patent Renewal Date," in *Brookings Papers on Economic Activity: Microeconomics 1989* (Washington, D. C.: Brookings Institution, 1989), pp. 361–2.

Appendix

GAME THEORY AND PATENT RACES

Patents may solve the innovation-imitation game represented by the payoff matrix in Table 14.3 on page 358. Consider a simple **patent race** game in an oligopoly with three firms, Firm A, Firm B, and Firm C.* The government grants a patent monopoly to the first firm to innovate. Each firm simultaneously selects a level of R&D spending $x_i \geq 0$ for i = A,B,C.

The time of innovation, T, is a function of R&D spending. Innovation occurs at time $T(x_i)$ and $\Delta T/\Delta x_i < 0$.† Increased R&D spending, therefore, reduces the time of innovation. The present value of profits associated with the patent equals V > 0, and if two or three firms innovate at the same time, the firms share the profits V. The profit payoffs for Firm i are defined as follows:‡

$$\pi_i = V - x_i \text{ if } T(x_i) < T(x_j) \text{ for } j \neq i \text{ (Firm i receives the patent)}$$

$$\pi_i = \frac{V}{1+m} - x_i \text{ if } T(x_i) = T(x_j) \text{ (Firm i shares the patent with m = 1 or 2 other firms)}$$

$$\pi_i = -x_i \text{ if } T(x_i) > T(x_j) \text{ for some j (Firm i does not get the patent)}$$

Figure 14.9 depicts the payoffs for Firm A assuming V = 100, $x_B = 30$, and $x_C = 20$. If $x_A < 30$, Firm A does not get the patent and sustains a loss of $-x_A$. If $x_A > 30$, Firm A gets the patent and earns $100 - x_A$. If $x_A = 30$, Firm A and Firm B innovate simultaneously and share the profit of 100, so Firm A's net earnings then equal 20 (50 − 30).

There is no Nash equilibrium in this game because for any values of x_B and x_C less than V = 100, Firm A would maximize profits by spending $\epsilon > 0$ more on R&D than the max $\{x_B, x_C\}$. For example, given $x_B = 30$ and $x_C = 20$, Firm A should obtain the patent by spending $x_A = 30 + \epsilon$ on R&D. If either $x_B = 100$ or $x_C = 100$, then Firm A should spend $x_A = 0$ on R&D.

This game has many possible mixed strategy equilibria.§ Here we derive one of the possible mixed strategy equilibria. Recall that the game is symmetric. Let $M_i(x)$ represent the probability that Firm i chooses an R&D level less than or equal to x. If Firm B and Firm C play any mixed strategy equilibria, then Firm A is indifferent between any pure or mixed strategy it chooses. If Firm A plays a pure strategy consisting of $x_A = 0$ all of the time or if it plays a pure strategy consisting

---

*See Herve Moulin, *Game Theory for the Social Sciences* (New York: New York University Press, 1986). This patent race is presented in simple form in Eric Rasmusen, *Games and Information: An Introduction to Game Theory* (Oxford, UK: Basil Blackwell, 1989), pp. 294–300.
†Using calculus, dT/dx < 0.

‡The following two simplifying assumptions are built into the profit payoffs: the firms are risk neutral and have a zero discount rate.
§For proof that there is a continuum of mixed strategy equilibria in this game, see Michael Baye, Dan Kovenock, and Casper G. de Vries, "Rigging the Lobbying Process: An Application of the All Pay Auction," *American Economic Review*, 83 (March 1993): 289–94.

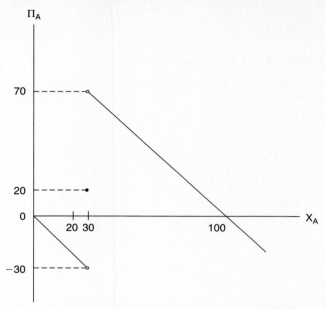

Figure 14.9   Patent race: Firm A's profits, Π_A, given $X_B = 30$ and $X_C = 20$.

of $x_A = 100$ all the time, its expected profits equal zero; therefore, any other mixed strategy equilibria for Firm A must have an expected profit equal to zero. Firm A's expected profit from any R&D spending x_A is the expected value of winning the patent minus the cost, x_A, of its R&D. The probability that Firm A wins the patent race equals the probability that Firm A spends more on R&D than either Firm B or Firm C. For Firm A to win the patent race, therefore, x_A must be greater than *both* x_B and x_C. The probability that Firm A spends more on R&D than either Firm B or Firm C equals the probability that $x_B < x_A$ *times* the probability that $x_C < x_A$, or $M_B(x_A)M_C(x_A)$*. Because any mixed strategy equilibrium for Firm A must have an expected profit of zero, it follows that:

$$V \cdot M_B(x_A)M_C(x_A) - x_A = 0. \tag{14.3}$$

Algebraic manipulation of equation 14.3 yields:

$$M_B(x_A)M_C(x_A) = \frac{x_A}{V}. \tag{14.4}$$

If all three firms select the same mixed strategy, then $M_B(x_A) = M_C(x_A)$, and:

---

*$M_B(x_A)$ represents the probability that Firm B spends *less* on R & D than does Firm A.

$$M(x_i) = \sqrt{\frac{x_i}{V}} \quad \text{for } 0 \leq x_i \leq V. \qquad [14.5]$$

Equation 14.5 represents one possible mixed strategy equilibrium.

What is of primary interest in the patent race game is that the expected profit for each firm equals *zero*. The entire potential profit of V is lost to *society* because the firms race to be the first to gain the patent, and in so doing spend too much on R&D. Innovation occurs earlier than it would with a monopolist, but the speeding up of the time of innovation is not worth the extra development costs to society.*

---

*A monopolist by comparison would maximize profits by setting $x = \epsilon$, where ϵ is infinitesimally greater than zero, and the monopolist would earn a profit of $V - \epsilon \cong V$. With monopoly and a zero discount rate, society would receive a net benefit approximately equal to V. The time of innovation, however, would be very slow because $\Delta T / \Delta x_i < 0$. With a patent race the probability that any of the three firms would spend less than ϵ on R&D is:

$$M(\epsilon) = \sqrt{\frac{\epsilon}{V}} \cong 0.$$

The probability that the monopolist would innovate faster than the three firms engaged in a patent race is virtually zero.

Chapter 15

Price Discrimination

Price discrimination exists when a firm charges either different consumers different prices for the same product supplied with identical costs or different consumers the same price even though the cost of supplying the good varies between consumers. More generally, price discrimination exists whenever the difference in prices between consumers is *not proportional* to the difference in costs. In other words, price discrimination exists whenever *the price-cost margin* varies between different consumers.

Consider some examples of price discrimination: Two airline passengers paying different fares for coach seats on the same flight; a lawyer charging the same fee for a will that requires 30 minutes of preparation time as a will that requires 8 hours of preparation time; or a department store offering a second pair of jeans at a price 50 percent lower than the first pair. However, two passengers paying different fares for coach seats on different days of the year (e.g., Thanksgiving Day and November 1) may not constitute price discrimination.

There are several important points to understand about price discrimination. Perhaps the most significant point is that discrimination can exist only if market power exists. If two sellers in a perfectly competitive market charge different prices for the same good, consumers will buy only from the lower-priced seller. Also, the existence of most price discrimination implies a lack of *Pareto efficiency;* because different consumers face different marginal rates of substitution, efficiency in exchange is not achieved.* In the discussion that follows it is important to realize that when price discrimination "improves" economic efficiency, it is usually in a second-best sense. In a first-best world all prices would equal marginal cost for all buyers and there would be no price discrimination.

---

*Recall that Pareto efficiency requires the marginal rate of substitution (MRS) to be equal for all consumers where:

$$\text{MRS} = \frac{\text{MU}_x}{\text{MU}_y} = \frac{P_x}{P_y}$$

If the price of good x is different for different buyers but the price of good y is the same, then the MRS varies across consumers and an exchange is possible that will benefit one consumer without hurting the other.

Price discrimination not only requires some degree of market power, but also an ability to separate demand into different groups, each with a different elasticity of demand. Examples include airline tickets purchased well in advance (more elastic) and those purchased on the day of departure (less elastic) and adult (less elastic) and child (more elastic) movie tickets.

Finally, effective price discrimination requires an ability to prevent the transfer of the good from one group to another. Consider, for instance, that although movie theaters discriminate in ticket prices between adults and children, they do not charge children lower popcorn prices because if they did, virtually all popcorn consumed by adults would be bought by children.

Types of Price Discrimination

Following Pigou, economists have identified three types of price discrimination — first, second, and third degree.[1] In **first-degree price discrimination**, which is often referred to as **perfect discrimination**, each consumer pays his or her reservation price for the good. Figure 15.1 shows a demand curve of $P = 10 - Q$ with a marginal cost of 2. In such a market first-degree discrimination would require the first unit of the good to be sold at a price of 9, the second unit at 8, the third at 7, and so on, until the eighth unit was sold at $P = MC = 2$. First-degree discrimination results in total revenue of 44 ($9 + 8 + 7 + 6 + 5 + 4 + 3 + 2 = 44$) on the

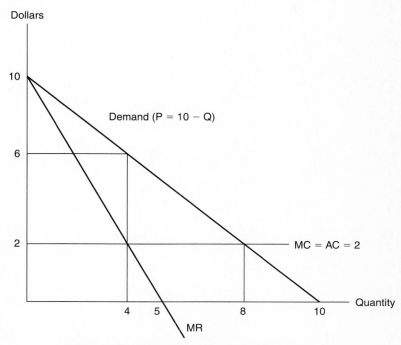

Figure 15.1 First-degree price discrimination.

sale of eight units. By comparison, if discrimination was impossible or illegal and the firm charged the profit-maximizing price of 6 and sold four units, total revenue would equal 24. First-degree discrimination increases total revenue from 24 to 44, but also doubles output from 4 to 8.

Under **second-degree discrimination** the discriminator offers all consumers the same price schedule, and then consumers *self-select* into the different price categories. Consumers pay different prices, but every consumer who buys within the same price category pays the same price. Common examples include airline price discrimination between those passengers who stay over a Saturday and those who do not, Pizza Hut charging $10 for a first large pizza but only $5 for the second large pizza, and quantity discounts given for bulk purchases of a good.

Figure 15.2 illustrates one common example of second-degree discrimination. The first two buyers pay 8, the next two pay 6, the next two pay 4, and the last two pay P = MC = 2. A total of eight units are sold, and total revenue is 40 (16 + 12 + 8 + 4). Firms use second-degree discrimination when they know different groups of consumers have different reservation prices, but the firms are unable to identify, or it is too costly to identify, each type of consumer separately.

Third-degree price discrimination is quite different and depends on the price discriminator's ability to effectively separate consumers into two or more groups according to their elasticities of demand. So long as the groups have different elasticities at any given price, it will make sense for the firm to practice

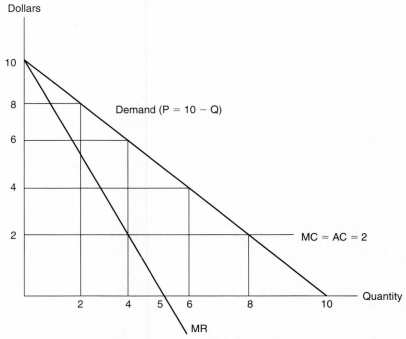

Figure 15.2   Second-degree price discrimination.

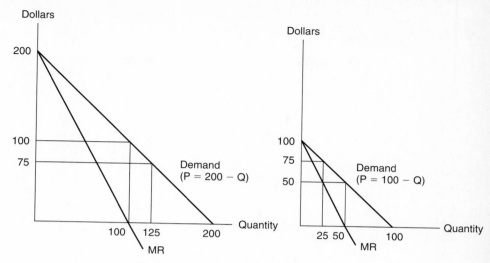

Figure 15.3 Third-degree price discrimination.

price discrimination. Consider Figure 15.3, where consumers in group 1 face a demand of $P = 200 - Q$ while consumers in group 2 face a demand of $P = 100 - Q$. Note that at any $P > 0$ the demand for group 1 consumers is more inelastic than the demand for group 2 consumers.* To simplify the analysis, assume marginal cost is zero. This is actually a reasonable assumption in some real-world examples of third-degree price discrimination. Consider a movie theater that charges higher prices for adults than children. If the movie theater is not full, the marginal cost of an additional patron, regardless of whether it is an adult or a child, is approximately zero. To maximize profits, which in the case of $MC = 0$ is identical to maximizing total revenue, the firm should set $MR = MC = 0$ and sell $q_1 = 100$ with $P_1 = 100$ for group 1, and $q_2 = 50$ with $P_2 = 50$ for group 2. The price in the less elastic market is twice the price in the more elastic market.

---

*Recall that for any linear demand curve, the elasticity of demand, e_D, equals one at the midpoint, $e_D > 1$ for the section above the midpoint, and $e_D < 1$ for the section below the midpoint. In Figure 15.3, this implies that for $P = 50$, $e_D < 1$ for group 1, but $e_D = 1$ for group 2. Similarly, for $P = 100$, $e_D = 1$ for group 1, but $e_D > 1$ for group 2. This also implies that for $50 < P < 100$; $e_D < 1$ for group 1, but $e_D > 1$ for group 2.

Another way to understand this point is to recognize that the elasticity of demand for a linear demand curve is defined as:

$$e_D = -\frac{\Delta Q}{\Delta P}\frac{P}{Q}$$

For the linear demand curves in Figure 15.3, $-(\Delta Q/\Delta P) = 1$, but for $100 < P < 0$, the ratio of P/Q is always larger for group 2 than for group 1. For $100 < P < 0$, therefore, e_D is always more elastic for group 2 than group 1.

Welfare Effects of Price Discrimination

To determine the welfare effects of price discrimination it is necessary to compare the total consumer surplus *plus* producer surplus with price discrimination with the total consumer surplus *plus* producer surplus without price discrimination. With *first-degree discrimination* in Figure 15.4, consumer surplus is zero but producer surplus is the entire triangle ABC. If a firm were legally required to charge one price to all buyers, then the profit-maximizing quantity would be 4 and price would be 6. With a one-price policy total consumer surplus would be the triangle AED and producer surplus would be the rectangle CDEF; there would also be a *welfare loss triangle* of EBF. First-degree price discrimination, therefore, improves welfare. In fact, in the case of first-degree discrimination, allocative efficiency is achieved because price equals marginal cost for the last unit purchased, and every consumer who is willing to pay a price greater than or equal to marginal cost receives the good.*

The welfare results of *second-degree discrimination* may be similar to those of first-degree discrimination. In Figure 15.4 the last two units are sold at a price equal to marginal cost so allocative efficiency is achieved. Consumer surplus is equal to the sum of the four shaded gray triangles, and producer surplus is equal to the sum of the three shaded red rectangles. Once again there is no deadweight loss, as there would be with a uniform price policy, and therefore, second-degree discrimination improves welfare.†

With many forms of second-degree discrimination, however, the welfare analysis is more complex. Consider second-degree discrimination in the airline industry. Airlines commonly charge different fares for different types of tickets; for example, airlines discriminate between vacation travelers who stay for a week or longer at their destination and business travelers who stay for one day. Suppose that "Get-You-There Air" charges two fares for its flights from New York to Los Angeles, an unrestricted roundtrip coach fare of $749 and a "vacation special" fare of $400 if you stay in Los Angeles for a minimum of two weeks. A business traveler is willing to pay a maximum of $800 for a round-trip ticket to fly to Los Angeles on Tuesday and return on Wednesday, but this business traveler is willing to pay a maximum of only $450 for a ticket with a minimum stay of two weeks. However, a vacation traveler is willing to pay a maximum of $400 for a ticket with a restriction of a two-week minimum stay and has no interest in staying for one day.

---

*Pareto efficiency is also achieved with first-degree discrimination because it is impossible to exchange the endowed units of the good in any way that helps one consumer without hurting another.

†Unlike first-degree discrimination, second-degree discrimination is not Pareto efficient because the differing marginal rates of substitution across consumers make it possible to redistribute the good in a way that will increase one consumer's utility without hurting another consumer. See H.E. Leland and R.A. Meyer, "Monopoly Pricing Structures with Imperfect Discrimination," *Bell Journal of Economics*, Autumn 1976, p. 457.

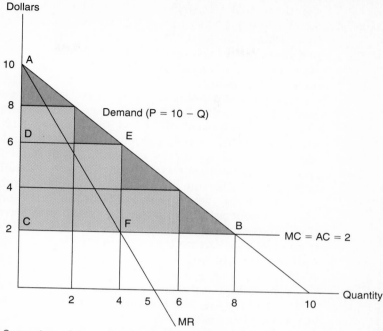

Figure 15.4 Comparison of the welfare loss in first-degree and second-degree price discrimination.

If Get-You-There-Air calculates that the marginal cost per passenger is $100 for the round-trip flight, then by charging $749 for an unrestricted ticket and $400 for a restricted ticket with a two-week minimum stay, "Get-You-There-Air" earns profit of $1,149 − $200 = $949. The business traveler obtains consumer surplus equal to $51, but the vacation traveler earns no consumer surplus. The total profits plus consumer surplus with price discrimination, therefore, equals $949 + $51 = $1,000.

If price discrimination were impossible or illegal, then the profit-maximizing strategy would be to charge one price of $800 for all passengers and earn a profit of $800 − $100 = $700.* Only the business traveler flies to Los Angeles by air; the vacation traveler stays home, drives, or takes the train. The total profits plus consumer surplus of $1000 with price discrimination is significantly greater than the total of $700 without price discrimination. Welfare is unambiguously improved by price discrimination in this case.

Second-degree discrimination, however, can reduce welfare compared with a uniform price policy. Suppose the preferences in the above example are changed

---

*A price of $800 yields a profit of $700, which is a larger profit than the airline earns by charging a price of $400, selling two tickets and earning $800 − $200 = $600.

slightly so that a business traveler is willing to pay a maximum of $800 for a round-trip ticket to fly to Los Angeles on Tuesday and return on Wednesday, but this business traveler is willing to pay a maximum of only $400 for a ticket with a minimum stay of two weeks. A vacation traveler is willing to pay a maximum of $650 for an unrestricted ticket but only $600 for a ticket with a two-week minimum stay restriction.

With discrimination, Get-You-There-Air charges $800 to the business traveler and $600 to the vacation traveler. There is zero consumer surplus and Get-You-There-Air's profit equals ($800 + $600) − $200 = $1200.

Without discrimination, Get-You-There-Air would charge $650 for an unrestricted fare, sell two tickets, and earn a profit of ($650 × 2) − $200 = $1100. In addition, the business traveler would receive consumer surplus equal to $800 − $650 = $150. The sum of profits *plus* consumer surplus would then equal $1100 + $150 = $1250, which is greater than the total profit plus consumer surplus of $1200 without price discrimination. In this case, second-degree price discrimination reduces welfare. The reason for this reduction in welfare is that the airline must reduce the fare for the vacation traveler from $650 to $600 to induce the vacation traveler to stay for two weeks, which is longer than the vacation traveler prefers.

Third-degree discrimination is by far the most common form of discrimination and, unfortunately, the form with the most complicated welfare implications. However, a few basic points concerning welfare can be made. Consider the case of linear demand curves with differing elasticities such as those in Figure 15.3. Recall that the discriminating firm would charge $P_1 = 100$ to consumers in group 1 and $P_2 = 50$ to consumers in group 2. Suppose that the firm was forced by law to charge a uniform price to all buyers. What price would the firm charge? The combined demand curve for the two groups is depicted in Figure 15.5. For $100 \leq P \leq 200$ only the demand for group 1 is relevant, so in that price range the combined demand is $P = 200 − Q$ and $MR = 200 − 2Q$. For $0 \leq P < 100$ both demands are relevant and the combined demand is the horizontal summation of the two group demands, or $P = 150 − \frac{1}{2}Q$ and $MR = 150 − Q$.* Because $MR = MC = 0$ for $Q = 150$, the profit-maximizing firm would produce $Q = 150$ and charge a price of 75 to all consumers. Consumers in group 1 would purchase 125 units at $P = 75$ and consumers in group 2 would purchase 25 units at $P = 75$.

---

*To understand why there is a discontinuity in the MR curve in Figure 15.5, consider the following numerical calculations:

Q	P	TR	MR
98	102	9,996	—
99	101	9,999	3
100	100	10,000	1
101	99.5	10,049.5	49.5
102	99	10,098	48.5

Note how the marginal revenue of the 101st unit, 49.5, is much greater than the marginal revenue of the 100th unit, 1.

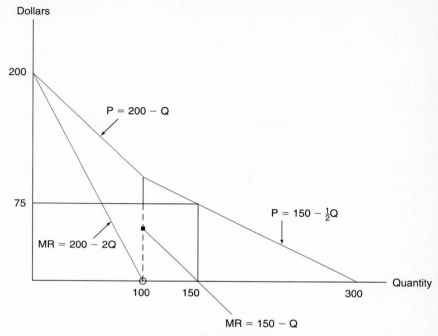

Figure 15.5 Profit maximization charging a uniform price with two different consumer groups.

Total output is the *same* both with and without price discrimination. This is a basic result of price discrimination with *linear* demand curves and constant marginal costs.[2] Regarding welfare, with MC = 0 total consumer plus producer surplus is the *entire area* under the demand curve. Table 15.1 compares welfare in the two cases. Consumer plus producer surplus is larger *without* discrimination, so

TABLE 15.1	Total Consumers' Plus Producers' Surplus With and Without Price Discrimination		
	Group 1	**Group 2**	**Total**
With price discrimination	15,000[1]	3,750	18,750
Without price discrimination	17,187.5	2,187.5	19,375
Differences	−2,187.5	1,562.5	−625

Note. The calculations require only the geometric formula for the area of a trapezoid, which is:

$$\text{AREA} = \frac{1}{2}h(b_1 + b_2),$$

where h is the height and b_1 and b_2 are the two bases of the trapezoid.

[1]The calculation is:

$$\text{Welfare} = 0.5 \times 100 \,(200 + 100) = 15,000$$

price discrimination *reduces* welfare. This is generally the result with linear demands. There is, however, a major exception: if one of the groups would be priced out of the market without price discrimination.*

Unfortunately, as soon as the assumption of linearity in the demand curves is eliminated, the welfare implications of third-degree price discrimination become complicated and ambiguous.[3] It is possible to show, however, that the change in welfare associated with price discrimination has both a minimum and maximum value (or a lower and upper bound).[4] This result is shown in the Appendix.

---

*If one group would only consume the good with discrimination, then discrimination increases welfare. Consider the previous example with the demand for group 2 changed to $P = 50 - Q$. The combined demand curve is then as follows:

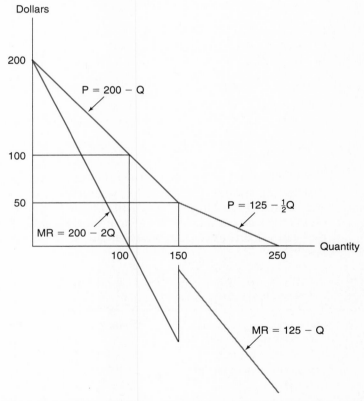

Figure F15.1 Profit maximization charging a uniform price with two different consumer groups when one group is priced out of the market.

In this case, the uniform price result would imply an output of 100, all going to group 1 consumers.

With price discrimination, total output would increase to 125 units with 100 sold to group 1 consumers and twenty-five sold at a price of 25 to group two consumers. In this case welfare is increased by discrimination.

The appendix also shows that a necessary but not sufficient condition for third-degree price discrimination to increase welfare is that the discrimination increases total output. Intuitively it may seem that any discrimination that increases total output should increase welfare, but this is not the case because third-degree price discrimination distorts the marginal rate of substitution between consumers, and that distortion always reduces welfare compared to a uniform price policy. If discrimination is to result in a net welfare increase, it must increase output enough to reduce the monopoly price distortion associated with a uniform price policy and more than offset the welfare loss associated with differing marginal rates of substitution.

Income Effects of Price Discrimination

The income effects of price discrimination are straightforward—producers as a group gain and consumers as a group lose. In fact, the producer's incentive to discriminate is a desire to increase profits. First-degree discrimination carries this to an extreme: all of the consumer surplus is transferred to producers.

Is this redistribution of income good or bad? The answer depends entirely on value judgments. Because price discrimination always increases profits, and because much of it is done by large corporations with market power, many believe that this redistribution is bad for society. If price discrimination generally redistributes income from consumers at large to stockholders and managers, it will generate some increase in the degree of inequality in society.

One often-cited example, however, suggests that redistributional effects may have net social benefits. Physicians are among the largest beneficiaries of price discrimination. Doctors routinely discriminate between high- and low-income patients or those with and without good insurance. Discrimination helps explain why doctors have such high incomes. Yet consider the case of a doctor in a small rural community facing the demand and cost situation depicted in Figure 15.6. Because the AC curve is always above the demand curve, no single fee would enable the physician to cover her costs. If she uses second-degree discrimination and charges a group of high-income patients F_H, a group of middle-income patients F_M, and her low-income patients F_L, then she will see a total of Q_3 patients and her average cost per patient will be C_{ALL}. The doctor will earn an excess profit of the light gray area F_HADC_{ALL} from her high-income patients and an excess profit of the red area BCED from her middle-income patients. These excess profits will offset her loss of the dark gray area EFHG from low-income patients. Only by discriminating is the doctor able to remain in the community. In this case many would argue that the redistributional impact of price discrimination is socially positive.

Effect on Competition

Price discrimination can have positive or negative effects on competition. Much depends on whether the discrimination is done by small fringe firms or large dominant firms, and whether it is sporadic or systematic. At one extreme, if discrimination is done by fringe firms in a sporadic attempt to gain additional sales,

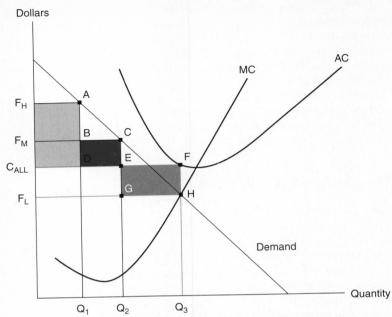

Figure 15.6   Price discrimination by a doctor in a small town.

then the impact is positive. Examples of price discrimination stimulating competition are easy to identify. A firm may temporarily cut its price in one geographic
area to find out if demand is elastic. If the firm discovers that demand is more
elastic than expected, the discrimination could result in a permanent across-the-
board price reduction. Supermarket chains may cut prices in some areas to induce
customers to try their stores. Such price cuts are often very deep: eggs may sell for
29 cents a dozen, or milk may sell for 49 cents a half-gallon. Such "loss-leaders"
enhance competition between stores. Haggling with a dealer over the price of a
new car is another example of price discrimination that increases competition.

The long-distance telecommunications industry provides a good recent example of sporadic price discrimination. MCI and Sprint seem to change their
price structures for each customer in an effort to pry business away from AT&T.
AT&T customers know that on any given day MCI might offer a cash bribe, a
month of free calls, or a rate reduction to call ten phone numbers of your choice
for a year if you will switch to MCI. Sprint, of course, is making the same type of
offers, and AT&T is trying to match both of them. As a result, many customers of
the same company pay different long-distance rates, and competition through
price discrimination drives the general rate schedule down.

Some price discrimination in the airline industry has also been procompetitive. The major carriers now use sophisticated computer reservation systems to
change fares by the hour. If a flight is overbooking, fares are increased, whereas
fares can be reduced on empty flights. The result is more competition and fewer
empty seats, both of which are positive economic outcomes.[5] It is important to
distinguish the airlines' price discrimination to control capacity utilization from

predatory fare reductions aimed at eliminating competition (see Chapter 10). It is also important to note that the computer reservation systems are biased in favor of booking on the major carriers, and therefore, the systems themselves may make it difficult for small airlines to compete with the majors.

The list of positive examples could go on, but the important point is clear: a good deal of price discrimination is procompetitive and should not be discouraged by public policy.

On the other extreme, systematic price discrimination by dominant firms can reduce competition by entrenching the positions of the dominant firm(s). Chapters 9 and 10 analyzed several examples of this type of price discrimination. In Chapter 9 the basing point pricing system was discussed as a method of solving the prisoners' dilemma. In addition to being a solution to the dilemma, basing point systems are excellent examples of anticompetitive price discrimination because different buyers face vastly different price-cost margins under the system. Figure 9.2 is reproduced here as Figure 15.7. Recall that the buyer in Chicago that purchased steel from a Chicago mill paid a price of $47.60 per ton while the buyer in Pittsburgh paid $40.00. The basing point system discriminated against buyers located close to a steel mill but far from a basing point. This discrimination was systematic and used by all the firms in the industry.

How could the basing point system used in the steel, cement, and plywood industries reduce competition? Consider two small appliance manufacturers, one located in Pittsburgh and the other in Chicago under the Pittsburgh-plus system. The appliance manufacturer located in Pittsburgh purchased one of its important inputs at a much lower price-cost margin than the firm located in Chicago, and as

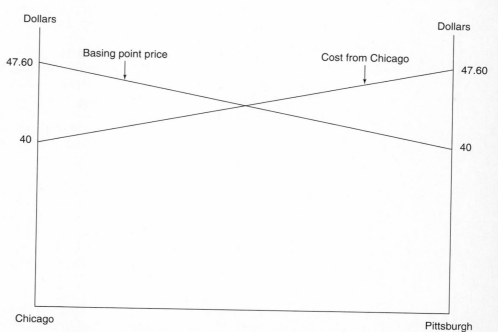

Figure 15.7 Price discrimination under the basing point pricing system.

a result the Chicago firm might have a difficult time competing with the Pittsburgh-based manufacturer. This is an example of price discrimination that reduces competition in the **secondary line market**, by reducing the level of competition between the buyers of the good.

Chapter 9 examined some of the most famous cases of price discrimination that hindered **primary line** competition. Primary line competition refers to competition between sellers in the market in which price discrimination is being practiced. The cases in Chapter 10 dealing with predatory pricing included Standard Oil, American Tobacco, ReaLemon, Maxwell House, and the airlines. In each case, a dominant firm(s) systematically practiced price discrimination against a particular competitor(s) in an attempt to reduce competition. For those who read the appendix to Chapter 10, recall that in the Kreps and Wilson model of predatory pricing the objective of a weak firm behaving like a strong firm was to prevent competition from emerging.

Another method of price discrimination with potentially negative effects is the use of **tie-in sales**. A tie-in exists when a firm with market power over good X requires its buyers to purchase another item, good Y, to obtain good X. In one famous case American Can and Continental Can both adopted a policy of leasing their can-closing machines for a minimum of five years with the further restriction that the lessee purchase all of its can requirements during the five-year period from its machinery supplier. Under no circumstances were machines offered for sale. These policies enabled the major can companies to increase their profits by practicing a form of price discrimination in the machinery market. Market power was the result of superior machines, not superior cans, yet the companies leased their machines at rentals below average cost. This was possible because can prices were kept substantially *above* average cost. The cans were used as a method of metering machine use. The more cans a firm used, the larger were the profits it paid to its can supplier. A purchaser of 1 million cans paid ten times more for the use of closing machinery than the user of 100,000 cans.

The tie-in in the can industry was a special case of price discrimination called a **two-part tariff**, which consists of a lump-sum payment (the machine rental) and a per-unit charge (the price of the cans). Common examples of two-part tariffs include the rental of a car for which there is a daily charge (the lump sum) and a mileage charge (the per-unit charge); the rental of a copier with a per-copy charge; and the entry fee into a theme park accompanied by an additional charge per attraction. In each case, the firm is charging large users a higher price than small users.

The tie-in arrangement in the can industry had several possible anticompetitive effects. Because American and Continental controlled the machinery market, it was extremely difficult for independent can manufacturers to find a market because the tie-in foreclosed most of the market for cans. **Foreclosure** occurs when downstream firms have difficulty obtaining inputs or when upstream firms have difficulty finding buyers.* In this case, because independent can manufacturers

---

*Examples include Alcoa's control of bauxite ore foreclosing competitors from the raw material needed to produce virgin aluminum, and American automobile producers being foreclosed from Japanese automobile dealers that are controlled by the major Japanese automobile manufacturers.

could not find buyers, the only way to enter the can market was to produce both cans and can-closing machinery. Forcing firms to enter two markets instead of one increased the capital barrier to entry. More important, large R&D expenditures were required to produce non-infringing can-closing machinery capable of competing with American's and Continental's equipment. This proved to be an almost impossible barrier, and American and Continental were able to control both markets.

Tie-in sales have been used in an attempt to extend market power in many industries. Before computers were invented, IBM tied cards to its tabulating machinery. Kodak used to tie film processing to its film. Major movie distributors used to tie good films ("Star Wars") with a group of bad films ("Ishtar", "Howard the Duck", etc.), forcing exhibitors to show the bad films to get the good ones. United Shoe Machinery tied shoe machinery supplies to its shoe machinery. And many franchisors tied (or bundled*) several products together for their franchisees. More recently Microsoft has been accused of tying its Windows 95 software with Microsoft Network, its on-line information service access software. Because tie-ins can have anticompetitive effects, they have been the focus of a good deal of antitrust attention. This is considered in Chapter 22.

Examples of Price Discrimination

Many different methods are used to price discriminate between buyers. Although it is impossible to identify all the methods, it is useful to identify the more common techniques.[6]

Consider the following two questions as you read each of the examples:

1. Does the discrimination improve allocative efficiency, that is, does it bring output closer to the point at which P = MC?
2. Does the discrimination have a positive, negative, or neutral effect on competition?

MAKE-THEM-PAY-FOR-THE-LABEL DISCRIMINATION

In the July 1993 issue of the Lands' End catalog, the company advertised:[7]

Our $23 Weathered Mesh vs. the $55 "designer" mesh:
Same fabric.
Same Mill.
Same features.
Less than half the price.

Some folks are slapping their animal emblem on essentially the same shirt as ours and charging $55 for it.

---

*Bundling refers to the practice of forcing buyers to purchase an entire group of products from one supplier. Examples have included computer manufacturers selling computers only with a package of pre-installed software programs and service contracts, fast-food companies requiring franchisees to purchase all of their required ingredients and paper products from the franchiser, and petroleum refiners requiring franchised service stations to purchase not only gasoline, but also tires, batteries, and other products from the refiner.

According to the Lands' End advertisement, the shirt manufacturer is discriminating by making buyers pay $32 for a small animal emblem. This type of discrimination is widespread in the clothing and food distribution industries. It is also used in the automobile industry, in which consumers pay $1000 or more extra for a Toyota Corolla compared to a GEO Prizm, or for a Nissan Quest compared to a Mercury Villager, even though the twin vehicles come off the same production line.

It can be argued that make-them-pay-for-the-label discrimination is not discrimination because consumers receiving the label gain status and prestige, which they are willing to pay extra to obtain. In one famous antitrust case discussed in Chapter 21, Borden argued that its Borden label evaporated milk was considered by consumers to be a different product from its physically identical private-label evaporated milk. The Supreme Court ruled, however, that the physical characteristics of the milk determined whether the product was the same, and not the label. The Supreme Court's interpretation may not make economic sense, as we will see in Chapter 21.

KEEP-THEM-IN-THEIR-ZONES DISCRIMINATION

Under a basing point system, all buyers at the same location pay the same price, but prices vary by location. Under a keep-them-in-their-zones system, all buyers at a given location pay an identical price for the good, which is equal to the F.O.B. price, and the manufacturer absorbs all freight costs.* Under an F.O.B. pricing system with freight absorption, for example, steel would have been sold for the same price per ton ($40 in our example in Figure 15.7) anywhere in the United States and the steel companies would have absorbed all freight charges.

The keep-them-in-their-zones system attempts to eliminate competition between distributors in different geographic areas by forcing the distributors to pay all freight charges for deliveries outside their geographic markets, making it difficult for them to compete in distant markets. The major advantage of the system for manufacturers is that it greatly reduces competition between distributors and thereby keeps the manufacturer's distributors satisfied.

Ironically, with a freight absorption system, all buyers pay the same price for the good but the system is highly discriminatory because each buyer faces a different price-cost margin. In this case, buyers located far away face a much lower price-cost margin.

DUMP-THE-SURPLUS DISCRIMINATION

For many years American firms have argued that foreign companies "dump" their surpluses in the United States at prices below their domestic prices. Japanese firms have long been accused of dumping products such as steel and televisions. Dumping might be viewed as predatory if the exported goods are sold at prices below marginal cost. But it is also possible that dumping is merely a rational form of price discrimination.

---

*F.O.B. stands for "free on board" and means that the manufacturer will load the good at its manufacturing facility for the F.O.B. price and the buyer is responsible for paying for freight.

Consider one famous dumping case, *Matsushita* v. *Zenith,* in which seven Japanese firms were accused of dumping televisions in the United States at predatory prices beginning in the 1950s and continuing until 1974.[8]* During the period under investigation, the Japanese firms were able to sell televisions in Japan under a protected Japanese cartel that ensured high prices and high profits. Once Japan's domestic demand was satisfied, the firms had excess capacity remaining and used this capacity to sell abroad at lower prices. This was certainly a rational and profitable form of price discrimination. In 1986 a slim 5–4 majority of the Supreme Court ruled the behavior was not predatory, but that interpretation has been subject to economic criticism.[9]

SORT-BY-TIME-VALUE DISCRIMINATION

In this common form of discrimination, manufacturers supply coupons or rebates to consumers willing to spend the extra time needed to clip the coupons or send in the rebate forms. Consumers with high opportunity costs of time will choose to pay the high price and avoid the coupons, and those with lower opportunity costs will use coupons.

Coupons might be considered either a type of promotional sales activity designed to attract new customers or a form of price discrimination. In one test of these competing hypotheses, Levedahl observed that the average full price of paper towels was significantly higher in markets offering coupons than in markets without coupons.[10] This finding supports the hypothesis that couponing is a form of price discrimination because if coupons were used primarily for promotional activities, then one would expect that the average full price of paper towels would be the same both with and without coupons.

CLEAR-THE-STOCK DISCRIMINATION

Filene's Basement in Boston is a classic example of clear-the-stock discrimination, which is common in retailing. Filene's sells at full price upstairs and then moves merchandise to the basement where it is continuously reduced in price until it is sold. All major retailers use clear-the-stock discrimination during sales to eliminate inventory and allow for the introduction of new stock.

KEEP-THEM-LOYAL DISCRIMINATION

Every major airline offers a frequent-flyer program that encourages passengers to use the same airline to build up mileage credit. Most airlines have expanded their programs so that mileage can be earned without flying at all. Airline credit cards, for example, allow customers to earn one frequent flyer mile for each dollar they charge on the account. This makes it possible to earn free tickets without ever flying, and in fact it is possible to fly all over the world without ever paying for a single ticket. Undoubtedly the greatest beneficiaries of frequent-flyer programs are

---

*The seven Japanese firms were Matsushita, Toshiba, Hitachi, Sharp, Sanyo, Sony, and Mitsubishi.

businesspeople who are the most frequent flyers. The total effect of the program is to greatly reduce effective ticket prices for frequent flyers.

Another example of keep-them-loyal discrimination is the Preferred Reader Club at chain bookstores that costs $10 per year and gives a 10 percent price reduction on all purchases. Some bookstores practice further discrimination by sending members a $5.00 certificate for each $100 worth of purchases.

Keep-them-loyal discrimination may have a substantial effect on competition. It has been argued that the programs have tied businesses to the few national airlines that fly to most major cities.[11]

SUMMARY

1. Price discrimination tends to be a complex economic issue. There are so many different types of discrimination with so many possible effects that it is difficult to make many generalizations.

2. Price discrimination requires some market power.

3. The three basic types of discrimination are first, second, and third degree.

4. First-degree price discrimination improves allocative efficiency and increases welfare.

5. With linear demand curves and linear marginal cost, third-degree discrimination has no effect on output but generally reduces welfare.

6. Price discrimination always redistributes income from consumers to producers.

7. Firms use many different types of price discrimination. All types increase profits.

8. Price discrimination may have either positive or negative effects on both competition and welfare; therefore, it is necessary to analyze the effects of price discrimination on a case-by-case basis.

9. Because many types of price discrimination increase total industry output, price discrimination often has a positive effect on welfare.

10. Price discrimination often results in a redistribution of income that makes value judgments inevitable in any analysis of the effects of price discrimination.

KEY TERMS

first-degree price discrimination	second-degree price discrimination
foreclosure	secondary line market
perfect discrimination	third-degree price discrimination
primary line market	tie-in sales
price discrimination	two-part tariff

DISCUSSION QUESTIONS

1. Consider the following examples of price discrimination. What type of price discrimination, first-degree, second-degree, or third-degree, does each represent?
   a. If you buy one pair of Levi jeans, you can buy a second pair at half price.
   b. Senior citizens receive a cup of coffee for $.25 at McDonald's, but everyone else pays $.59.
   c. Five tickets to the Super Bowl are auctioned to the highest bidders. The tickets sell for $12,000, $11,990, $11,980, $11,975, and $11,970, respectively.

2. Suppose Microsoft charges computer manufacturers a fixed fee to place MS-DOS and Windows on any of their computers up to 100,000 units per year per company. Is Microsoft practicing a form of price discrimination? Which firms benefit under this system?

   How could Microsoft's policy make it difficult for the manufacturers of competing operating systems to have their operating systems installed on new computers by computer manufacturers?

3. It is common for movie theaters to charge lower admissions for children than for adults, but the theaters do not charge children and adults different prices for popcorn and soft drinks. Can you explain why theaters do not discriminate in popcorn and soft drinks?

4. Name a company that practices each of the following types of price discrimination:
   a. make-them-pay-for-the-label discrimination
   b. sort-by-time-value discrimination
   c. keep-them-loyal discrimination

5. Does the use of first-degree price discrimination ensure that the allocatively efficient output will be produced? How about second-degree discrimination?

6. Suppose Eat-Em-Up Pie Company produces frozen pies in a small town in Montana. In Montana, Eat-Em-Up has a 75 percent market share, but its market share is zero outside the state. If a large national producer that produced pies in California and held a 50 percent national market share in the frozen pie market entered the Montana market and charged prices in Montana that were 50 percent below the prices charged in California, would this be an example of price discrimination? Could this policy have a negative effect on competition? What factors would you consider in answering this question? [Note: The real-world example of such a case is considered in Chapter 21.]

PROBLEMS

1. An airplane is about to leave the jetway and take off with 50 empty seats. The regular coach fare is $400 for a seat, and the marginal cost of carrying an extra

passenger is $30. Forty stand-by passengers are hoping to get on the flight. If ten of those seats can be filled for $200, twenty-five seats can be filled for $100, and forty seats can be filled at $40, what is the *socially optimal* fare to charge stand-by passengers waiting to fill those seats?

Suppose the profit-maximizing airline must charge all the stand-by passengers the same price. Should it charge $40, $100, or $200 per ticket? Would the socially optimal result be achieved?

2. Suppose a business traveler is willing to pay $1,000 to fly from New York City to Miami on an unrestricted ticket. The business traveler, however, is willing to pay $200 for a ticket with a two-week minimum stay. A vacation traveler is willing to pay $250 for a ticket with a two-week minimum stay and has no interest in buying a ticket to stay less than a two-week stay. If the marginal cost of the ticket is $100, what is the profit-maximizing pricing policy for the airline? What is total surplus?

What is the profit-maximizing pricing policy if the business traveler is willing to pay $1,000 to fly from New York City to Miami on an unrestricted ticket and $200 for a ticket with a two-week minimum stay, and the vacation traveler is willing to pay $250 for a ticket with a two-week minimum stay and $650 for an unrestricted ticket? What is total surplus?

3. Suppose the demand for tickets to the symphony for adults is $P_A = 100 - 2q_A$ and the demand for children is $P_C = 50 - 2q_C$. What is the profit-maximizing pricing policy for the symphony? How many adults and children attend the concert?

If price discrimination were illegal and the symphony had to charge the same ticket price to adults and children, what would be the price of a ticket? How many adults and children would attend the concert?

Which policy results in greater social welfare?

4. Suppose a monopolist sells to two consumers. Consumer 1's demand is $P_1 = 100 - q_1$, and consumer 2's demand is $P_2 = 50 - q_2$. Marginal cost equals 10. If the monopolist uses a two-part tariff, what will be the maximum fixed fee charged to each consumer? What is the price per unit? What are the monopolist's profits?

REFERENCES

1. A.C. Pigou, *The Economics of Welfare* (London: MacMillan, 1920), pp. 240–56.
2. This result was first identified by Joan Robinson. See Joan Robinson, *The Economics of Imperfect Competition* (London: Macmillan, 1933).
3. David A. Malueg, "Bounding the Welfare Effects of Third-Degree Price Discrimination," *American Economic Review* 83 (September 1993): 1011–21.
4. For a brief derivation see J. Tirole, *The Theory of Industrial Organization* (Cam-
bridge: MIT Press, 1988), pp. 137–39. See also H. Varian, "Price Discrimination and Social Welfare," *American Economic Review* 75: (1985): 870–5.
5. See Ian L. Gale and Thomas J. Holmes, "Advance-Purchase Discounts and Monopoly Allocation," *American Economic Review* 83 (March 1993): 135–46.
6. The categories identified below are those used by Fritz Machlup. See F. Machlup, "Characteristics and Types of Price Discrimination," in National Bureau of Eco-

nomic Research conference report, *Business Concentration and Price Policy* (Princeton: Princeton University Press, 1955).

7. Lands' End Direct Merchants Catalog (July 1993), 3–4.

8. The case can be followed along from one decision to another. See *Zenith Radio Corp. et al.* v. *Matsushita Electric Industrial Corp. Ltd. et al.* 515 F. Supp. 1100 (1981); *Zenith Radio Corp. et al.* v. *Matsushita Electric Industrial Corp. Ltd. et al.*, 723 F.2d 238 (1983); and *Matsushita Electric Industrial Corp. Ltd. et al.* v. *Zenith Radio Corp. et al.* 475 U.S. 574, (1986).

9. David Schwartzman, *The Japanese Television Cartel: A Study Based on* Matsushita v. Zenith (Ann Arbor, MI: University of Michigan Press, 1993).

10. J.W. Levedahl, "Marketing, Price Discrimination, and Welfare: Comment," *Southern Economic Journal* (January 1984): 56–70.

11. Alfred E. Kahn, "Surprises of Airline Deregulation," *American Economic Review* (May 1988): 316–22; and William G. Shepherd, "The Airline Industry," in Walter Adams (ed.), *The Structure of American Industry* (New York: MacMillan, 1990), pp. 217–43.

Appendix

THE WELFARE IMPLICATIONS OF PRICE DISCRIMINATION WITH NONLINEAR DEMAND

Consider Figure 15.8 in which panel (a) shows a nonlinear *elastic* demand and panel (b) shows a nonlinear *inelastic* demand. Marginal cost is constant and equal to zero. The optimal prices with discrimination are P_1 and P_2, respectively, and the optimal single price without discrimination is p*. The actual change in welfare, ΔW, with discrimination is identified graphically as follows:

$$\Delta W = \text{Gain} - \text{Loss} = (\text{Areas A} + \text{B}) - (\text{Areas X} + \text{Y}).$$

From Figure 15.8 it is clear that:

$$\Delta W \geq (\text{Area A}) - (\text{Areas X} + \text{Y} + \text{Z})$$

or

$$\Delta W \geq (P_1 - MC)\Delta q_1 + (P_2 - MC)\Delta q_2.$$

[Note that with discrimination $\Delta q_1 > 0$ and $\Delta q_2 < 0$.]
In the general case with n different markets:

$$\Delta W \geq \sum_{i=1}^{n} (P_i - MC) \Delta q_i. \qquad\qquad \text{[Ineq 15.1]}$$

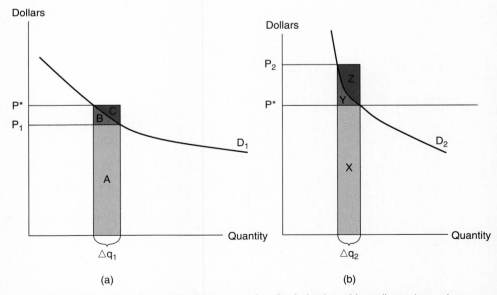

Figure 15.8 The welfare impact of third-degree price discrimination with nonlinear demand curves.

Ineq 15.1 establishes a *lower bound* for ΔW.

From Figure 15.8 it is also clear that:

$$\Delta W \le (\text{Areas A + B + C}) - (\text{Area X})$$

or

$$\Delta W \le (P^* - MC)\Delta q_1 + (P^* - MC)\Delta q_2.$$

In the general case with n different markets:

$$\Delta W \le (P^* - MC)\left(\sum_{i=1}^{n} \Delta q_i \right). \qquad \text{[Ineq 15.2]}$$

This establishes an *upper bound* for ΔW.

In the linear demand example given in Figures 15.3 and 15.5 note that $p_1 = 100$, $p_2 = 50$, $p^* = 75$, $\Delta q_1 = -25$, $\Delta q_2 = 25$, and MC = 0. By inequality 15.1 the lower bound for ΔW is:

$$\Delta W \ge (P_1 - MC)\Delta q_1 + (P_2 - MC)\Delta q_2.$$

or

$$\Delta W \ge (100 - 0)\,(-25) + (50 - 0)\,(25) = -2500 + 1250 = -1250,$$

and by inequality 15.2 the upper bound is:

$$\Delta W \le (75 - 0)\,(-25 + 25) = 0.$$

In the example in Figures 15.3 and 15.5 it follows that:

$$-1250 \le \Delta W \le 0.$$

The actual change in welfare for the example was calculated in Table 15.1 as -625, which, not surprisingly for linear demand, is right in the middle of the upper and lower bound.

An examination of inequality 15.2 reveals that any discrimination that results in a reduction in total output (i.e., $\Sigma \Delta q_i < 0$) *must* lower welfare. Furthermore, even if total output increases so that the upper-bound welfare change is positive, inequality 15.1 may result in a lower-bound welfare change that is negative, so welfare may still be reduced by price discrimination.

Chapter 16

Vertical Integration and Vertical Relationships

Chapter 3 explored the boundaries of the firm. Recall that firms often perform functions internally rather than using the market in an attempt to reduce transactions costs. It is important to bear in mind as you read this chapter that most vertical integration aimed at reducing transactions costs will have positive efficiency and welfare effects.

This chapter examines the theoretical effects of vertical integration and vertical relationships between independent firms, with an emphasis on the conduct and performance implications of vertical relationships. A balancing act is taking place in this chapter. In the first half of the chapter, we show that vertical integration and vertical relationships have a positive economic impact because they solve several potential economic problems. The second half of the chapter examines the potential problems associated with vertical integration and vertical relationships. This balancing act is a delicate one and should be taken seriously.

Vertical Relationships as a Solution to Economic Problems

THE PROBLEM OF DOUBLE MARGINALIZATION[1]

Consider the simplest possible vertical structure, in which an **upstream** wholesaler, perhaps a gasoline jobber, sells to a **downstream** retailer, say, a gasoline retailer, and the retailer simply turns around and sells the product to the final consumer. To simplify this model, it is common to assume that the transactions costs of transferring and delivering the good from one stage to another are zero. This implies that if a competitive gasoline retailer purchases a gallon of gasoline at a wholesale price P_W equal to $1.50, the retailer will sell the gallon to consumers at a retail price P_R equal to $1.50, that is, $P_W = MC_R = P_R = \$1.50$.

Any of the following situations is theoretically possible:

Case	Wholesaler is:	Retailer is:
A	Competitive	Competitive
B	Competitive	Monopolist
C	Monopolist	Competitive
D	Monopolist	Monopolist

Under which, if any, of these four competitive environments would vertical integration affect price and profits? In case A, both the wholesaler and retailer operate in perfectly competitive markets; price equals marginal cost everywhere, and vertical integration would have no impact on price.

Figure 16.1 depicts case B with a competitive wholesaler and a monopolist retailer. The downward sloping demand curve, D_R, and marginal revenue curve, MR_R, represent final retail consumer demand and marginal revenue, respectively. The MC_W curve represents the marginal cost of the product to the wholesalers (for example, the wholesalers' cost per gallon of gasoline). With case B the competitive wholesalers must charge a price equal to marginal cost, so $P_W = MC_W$. The monopolist retailer then takes that price as its marginal cost and charges the profit-maximizing price P_R to consumers. Note that P_R is the joint profit-maximizing price so that a profit-maximizing vertically integrated firm would also charge P_R. In this case the outcome is the same whether or not there is vertical integration.

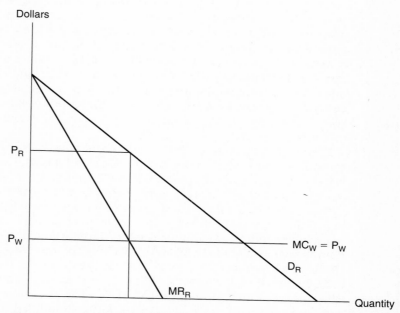

Figure 16.1 Vertical integration: competitive wholesalers, monopolist retailer.

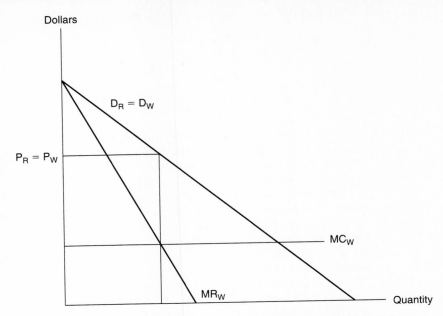

Figure 16.2   Vertical integration: monopolist wholesaler, competitive retailers.

Figure 16.2 depicts case C with a monopolist wholesaler and a competitive retailer. The downward sloping retailer demand curve, D_R, is also the demand curve D_W for the monopolist wholesaler, because the quantity along D_R represents the quantity of the good that retailers will sell at any given wholesale price. The marginal revenue curve for the monopolist wholesaler is therefore MR_W. The MC_W curve again represents the marginal cost of the product to the wholesaler. With case C the monopolist wholesaler sets $MC_W = MR_W$ and charges P_W. The wholesale price P_W becomes the competitive retailers' marginal cost, so $P_W = MC_R = P_R$. Once again, as in case B, P_R is the price that a profit-maximizing vertically integrated firm would charge. Thus, in case C, vertical integration again has no effect on output or price.

Now consider case D. Surely with monopoly in both vertical stages, vertical integration must have some effect on price, and it does. Consider Figure 16.3. The key distinction between Figure 16.3 and Figures 16.1 and 16.2 is that the *marginal revenue* curve of the retailer is now the *demand curve* for the wholesaler. The wholesaler knows that because the retailer will restrict output according to its marginal revenue curve MR_R, the wholesaler's demand at any given wholesale price will be indicated by the MR_R curve. If the wholesaler's demand is $D_W = MR_R$, then the wholesaler's marginal revenue curve becomes MR_W. The profit-maximizing wholesaler now sets $MC_W = MR_W$ and charges price P_W. The retailer then takes P_W as its marginal cost, sets $MC_R = MR_R$, and charges a price of P_R. The wholesaler earns an economic profit equal to P_WDFG. The retailer earns a profit of P_RBDP_W, and consumer surplus equals triangle ABP_R. Combined profits are equal to area P_RBFG.

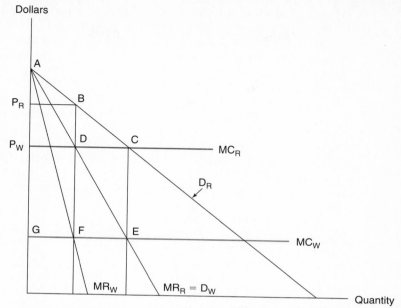

Figure 16.3   Vertical integration: monopolist wholesaler, monopolist retailer.

If the two monopolists vertically integrated, the firm would maximize profits by considering the internally evaluated marginal cost of the wholesale product to be MC_W, not P_W. As a result the integrated firm would charge a retail price of P_W, joint profits would be maximized at P_WCEG, and consumer surplus would equal triangle ACP_W. Vertical integration is better for the two monopolists because area P_WCEG is larger than area P_RBFG and better for consumers because area ACP_W is larger than area ABP_R. In this case, public policy should do everything possible to encourage vertical integration.

This conclusion is often associated with the Chicago school of economics, even though the model was developed by Joseph Spengler of Duke University.[2] Because of **double marginalization**, each successive stage of monopoly causes a greater price distortion compared with a vertically integrated firm. If the above logic is correct, then in cases A, B, and C, vertical integration has no welfare implications, and in case D, vertical integration increases output, lowers price, and improves economic welfare. Therefore, public policy should encourage as much vertical integration as possible where successive market power exists.

Alternative Methods of Achieving Joint Profit Maximization

The Spengler model provides a valuable framework for understanding why certain types of **vertical restraints** are common. *Vertical restraints* refer to a variety of methods used by manufacturers to limit the ways in which retailers can market their product. Two of the most common vertical restraints are **franchise fees**, whereby a manufacturer requires its retailers to pay a fixed fee for the right to sell the product, and **resale price maintenance agreements**, whereby the manufacturer sets a minimum or maximum retail price.[3] McDonald's, for example, requires its franchises to pay a franchise fee for the right to open a McDonald's restaurant. For many years Levi Strauss required the retailers of its jeans to abide by a resale price maintenance agreement that set a minimum permissible sale price for its jeans. Suppose that in the two-monopolists case in Figure 16.3 the wholesaler charges the retailer a price per unit equal to MC_W but also charges a fixed franchise fee equal to area P_WCEG. The retailer will then charge the joint profit-maximizing price of P_W but earn only a normal profit because the entire area P_WCEG is transferred to the wholesaler. The franchise fee eliminates the problem of "double marginalization" and improves welfare compared with successive stages of monopoly.

A resale price maintenance agreement could also improve welfare. Suppose the wholesaler sells the good to the retailer at some price between MC_W and P_W in Figure 16.3 and then sets a *maximum* retail price of P_W. Again the joint profit-maximizing result will be achieved. Profits will be divided according to the wholesale price. If the wholesale price is set close to MC_W, the retailer makes the bulk of the profit, whereas if the wholesale price is set close to P_W, the wholesaler makes most of the profit.

THE PROBLEM OF INSUFFICIENT PROMOTIONAL SERVICES[4]

In addition to simply carrying a selection of products, retailers provide pre-sale services to consumers. In fact, in some instances consumers select products primarily on the basis of the quality of pre-sale service. Stride Rite controls a large share of the "high-quality baby shoes" market because it is famous for having retailers who know how to fit baby shoes. Suppose that a monopolist wholesaler sells a product through a series of competitive independent retailers. The situation is like case C above with a monopoly at the wholesale level and a competitive retail market.

The demand for this product is a function not only of price but also of the pre-sale services provided by retailers. Demand can be represented as:

$$Q = D(P,S), \qquad [16.1]$$

where the quantity demanded, Q, increases with either a decrease in price, P, or an increase in pre-sale services per unit of output provided by retailers, S.

The situation is identical to that depicted in Figure 16.2. Competitive retailers have little or no incentive to supply services in this case because no matter what level of service they provide, competitive retailers will earn zero economic profit. In fact, if one retailer tried to provide greater pre-sale services, it would

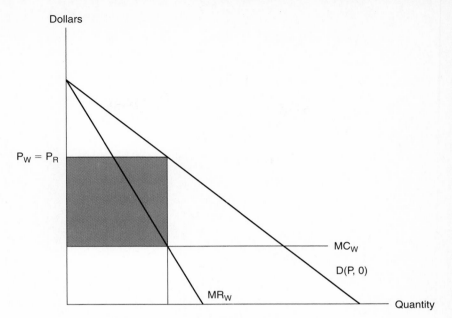

Figure 16.4 Wholesaler's profits if retailers provide no service.

have higher costs and be driven out of the market.* Suppose that initially all retailers provide no service, S = 0. The situation is shown in Figure 16.4, where Q = D(P,0) because S = 0. The monopolist wholesaler's profits are indicated by the shaded red area. This is clearly not an optimal situation for the monopolist because an increase in S shifts the demand curve to the right and increases the monopolist's profits by $(P_W - MC_W)\Delta Q$.

There must be some combination of price, call it P*, and services, call it S*, that maximizes the wholesaler's profits. In Figure 16.5 it is assumed that D(P,S*) is the demand curve that maximizes the wholesaler's profits. Suppose the monopolist wholesaler charged retailers a price $P_W > MC_W$, and in addition used a resale price maintenance agreement to require retailers to charge a price P*. If $P^* - P_W = S^*$, then the combination of a wholesale price P_W above marginal cost and a resale price maintenance (RPM) price set at a maximum price of P* would achieve the joint profit-maximizing result. That combination of policies forces the competitive retailers to provide services, S*, costing $(P^* - P_W)$ per unit of sales so that retail profits are driven down to zero.

To understand why the retailers have an incentive to provide services, consider the initial imposition of such a policy in place of a policy of charging price

---

*If one retailer tries to provide services of value to consumers and raises price to cover the costs of these services, then consumers can use the services and buy the good at a lower price from a "no-service," low-price retailer. This is an important case of **free riding** by the no-service retailers, who take advantage of the services provided by the high-service retailer but keep their prices low.

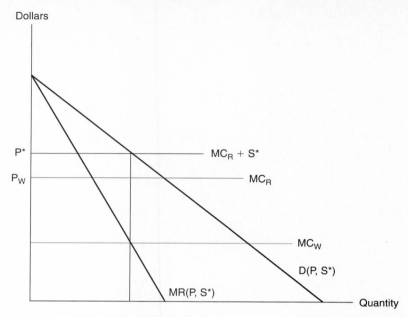

Figure 16.5   Wholesaler's profits if retailers provide the optimal level of service, S*.

P_W without RPM. Figure 16.5 shows that the imposition of RPM at price P* initially results in excess economic profits for the retailers because with no service (the initial situation) $P^* > P_W = MC_R$. The excess profits would encourage established and new retailers to compete by providing better service. The increased provision of services would increase demand and force incumbent competitive retailers to also provide services. In long-run equilibrium all retailers must provide the same level of services and earn zero economic profit.

Consider the welfare implication of the imposition of RPM. In Figure 16.6 combined consumer and producer surplus with no service equals areas B + C + E. With RPM consumer surplus equals areas A + B, producer surplus equals areas E + F, and areas C + D represent the cost of services provided by the retailers. RPM increases consumer surplus by area A, but decreases it by area C; producer surplus increases by area F. It follows that the net welfare effect is ambiguous because we do not know the size of areas A + F relative to area C; it will be different for every case. If (areas A + F) > (area C), then welfare increases; and if (areas A + F) < (area C), then welfare decreases.

In Figure 16.6 welfare increases because (A + F) > C. Although this is one possible outcome, Figure 16.7 shows an example in which welfare decreases because (A + F) < C. Bork has argued that Figure 16.6 is the more likely outcome; in his words, RPM is a "means of increasing distributive efficiency and should be permitted on grounds of efficient resource allocation."[5] Others have suggested, however, that Figure 16.7 is the more likely outcome because "demand is augmented more by extra service to those with low reservation prices than those who would buy the product even at much higher prices"; as a result, the demand

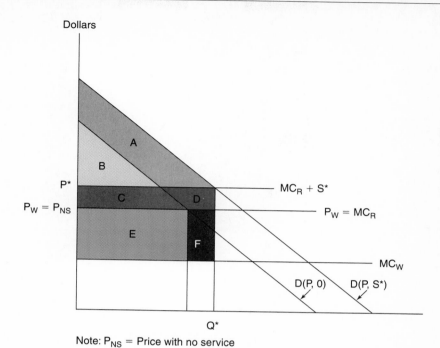

Figure 16.6   Positive welfare effect of resale price maintenance to induce service.

curve is likely to shift *upward* far less for consumers with *high* reservation prices than for consumers with low reservation prices, which is exactly what happens in Figure 16.7.[6] The only definite conclusion is that there is no conclusion: RPM agreements aimed at increasing pre-sale services may have either net positive or net negative welfare effects.

THE PROBLEM OF INPUT SUBSTITUTION[7]

In addition to solving the problems of double marginalization and insufficient promotional services, vertical integration and vertical restraints can solve problems associated with inefficient input substitution. Suppose that a monopolist produces good X, using only two inputs, input M and input C. Input M is produced by another monopolist, and input C is produced in a perfectly competitive market. Because the analysis is complex, it is left to an end-of chapter appendix to show that in the absence of vertical integration or vertical restraints, the monopolist producer of good X would use an inefficient combination of inputs, using "too much" of input C and "too little" of input M, to produce any given output of good X. Vertical integration or vertical restraints can solve this problem.[8]

Thus far most vertical integration and restraints appear to improve economic welfare. The analysis, however, has ignored the possible effects of vertical integration and vertical restraints on market structure and conduct. The next section considers these potential problems.

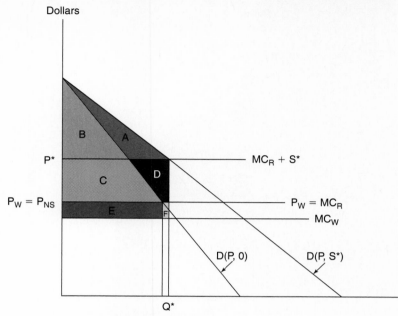

Note: P_{NS} = Price with no service

Figure 16.7   Negative welfare effect of resale price maintenance to induce service.

The Competitive Effects of Vertical Relationships

RESALE PRICE MAINTENANCE AGREEMENTS[9]

Previously, we showed that RPM agreements that fix *maximum* price levels are a possible welfare-improving method of dealing with the problem of double marginalization.* Recall from Figure 16.3 that if the wholesaler sells the good to the retailer at any price between MC_W and P_W and then requires the retailer to sell at a maximum price of P_W, the joint profit-maximizing result will be achieved, and welfare will be increased. In this case RPM is being used to set maximum resale prices, not minimum resale prices. There is little doubt that such maximum resale price fixing improves economic efficiency, even though in the United States the courts have generally frowned on the fixing of maximum prices as a violation of the antitrust laws.[10]

Maximum resale prices have been used in many industries, particularly those in which the product is not physically transformed as it moves from manufacturer to distributor to retailer.[11] Examples include television sets, refrigerators, au-

---

*The Appendix shows that RPM is also a possible welfare-improving method of dealing with the problem of input substitution.

tomobile tires, electric typewriters, newspapers, and stereo equipment.[12] Consider the example of a newspaper publisher with a local monopoly that gives each of its delivery workers an exclusive territory. Each delivery worker has a monopoly in her local territory and, in the absence of a maximum resale price, could exploit her monopoly power. This results in a classic potential double-marginalization problem. In terms of Figure 16.3, the delivery worker wants to set $P = P_R$. If the publisher sets a maximum resale price at P_W, the publisher earns greater profits and improves economic welfare.

Most RMP agreements require the setting of *minimum* rather than *maximum* resale prices. Many studies have shown that, except in rare cases, these RPM agreements result in higher retail prices and, therefore, lower sales for the manufacturer.[13] It is somewhat surprising that manufacturers would ever set minimum resale prices: once a manufacturer sets a product's wholesale price, it would normally be in the manufacturer's interest to increase sales by having the product sold at the lowest possible retail price. If RPM generally does not benefit manufacturers, why has it been so commonly used?

Four major arguments have been advanced to explain the adoption of RPM. First, RPM may be the result of collusion among retailers to keep prices high. According to this argument, the most important reason for RPM's popularity has been the desire of small retailers to compete with large discount stores. Historically, small retailers put pressure on Congress, and Congress responded by legalizing resale price maintenance with the passage of the **Miller-Tydings Act** in 1937. Second, resale price maintenance might make tacit collusion among manufacturers easier to maintain. Third, RPM might prevent retailers from selling high-quality products at low prices or as "loss leaders." According to this theory, if a high-quality product is consistently sold at a low price, consumers will begin to think of the product as a low-quality product, and this will hurt the manufacturer in the long run. Finally, RPM has been justified by the argument that some products require high-quality pre-sale service from retailers, and only RPM or vertical integration can ensure the provision of such services. We consider each of these arguments briefly.

Retailer Cartels

RPM agreements may result from collusion among retailers to keep prices high. Suppose, for example, that a group of competitive department stores and drug stores purchases perfume from perfume oligopolists. If the department and drug store owners meet at a trade convention and convince all of the perfume manufacturers to set minimum suggested retail prices, the price of perfume can be set above marginal cost.

In this example, RPM is being used by the department and drug stores as an effective method of solving the prisoner's dilemma. Price-cutting retailers can be easily identified and punished. Identification will surely be done by competing retailers, and punishment comes in the form of a cutoff of supplies to price cutters. If all the retailers and all the perfume oligopolists abide by the agreement, prices can be increased to the monopoly level and profits divided between the manufacturers and the retailers by charging a wholesale price between the marginal cost of producing the perfume and the profit-maximizing retail price. In this case the vertical restraint is nothing more than an effective method of collusion, and RPM reduces welfare.

One might wonder why the perfume oligopolists do not vertically integrate into retailing, charge the joint profit-maximizing retail price, and capture all of the monopoly profits for themselves. The problem with this solution is that it requires the development of a huge retailing network capable of covering the entire country just to sell perfume. This would be extremely costly, and it is hard to imagine any manufacturer setting up such a national network.

There is reason to believe that few such *retailer cartels* could earn excess profits in the long run. Entry into retailing is typically easy. Even if the RPM results in short-run excess profits, in the long run entry should reduce the retailers' profits by reducing each retailer's volume and increasing the costs of merchandising sales efforts aimed at gaining an advantage over competitors. This probably explains why evidence suggests that relatively few RPM agreements developed primarily because of retailer pressures applied to manufacturers.[14]

Facilitating Manufacturers' Cartels

Resale price maintenance might make it easier for manufacturers to maintain cartel prices. If retail prices are fixed, a manufacturer will have little incentive to reduce prices. Because the price reductions cannot be passed on to consumers, the cuts are likely to have a limited effect on the chiseler's market share.

Empirical evidence is not supportive of this theory. Overstreet found very few industries in which RPM was common and in which concentration was high enough to make a price-fixing conspiracy likely to survive.[15] Telser did find that the American light bulb industry may have used RPM to foster collusion in the early twentieth century, but there are few other documented cases.[16] Overall, facilitating manufacturers' collusion does not appear to explain many RPM agreements.

The Establishment of a High-Quality Image

Manufacturers have argued that RPM prevents retailers from damaging their products' images by selling them at low prices or as "loss leaders." Both Levi jeans and Izod alligator shirts may have been victims of this phenomenon when they moved away from RPM.[17] Levi Strauss was persuaded by the FTC to abandon RPM in 1977. Initially Levi's sales increased, but during the early 1980s it lost significant market share to designer jeans such as Gloria Vanderbilt, Ralph Lauren, and Calvin Klein. Similarly, Izod's image and appeal declined as the shirts became widely available.[18]

The welfare implications of the high-quality defense are difficult to assess. If I purchase an alligator shirt, it increases my utility. But if my purchase of an alligator shirt simultaneously decreases your utility, what are the net welfare implications of my purchase? Such circumstances call into question a basic conclusion about the efficiency of markets, because it no longer follows that increased consumption of a good increases consumer surplus. Furthermore, it is important to recognize other ways of dealing with this problem. The manufacturer could simply raise the price of the product, thereby creating an incentive for retailers to charge more. If, for example, Izod increases the price of alligator shirts, retailers almost certainly would charge higher prices. In conclusion, RPM seems like an awkward and indirect method of maintaining a high-quality image.

Ensure Dealer Pre-sale Services

RPM has been justified by the argument that some products require high-quality pre-sale service from the retailer, and only RPM can ensure such services.* It is certainly true that some products require high-quality pre-sale service from the retailer. For example, high-quality computer manufacturers might require high-quality pre-sale service from their dealers. By imposing RPM on their computer retailers, manufacturers could ensure that the dealers do not compete based on price but, instead, would compete by attempting to provide better service. In the absence of RPM, some computer dealers would provide good, but costly, service and charge high prices, and other dealers would provide little or no service and charge low prices. Consumers could then shop around at the high-priced, good-service dealers, but purchase their computers at the low-priced dealers. The low-priced dealers would then obtain a *free ride* on the services provided by the high-priced dealers, and over time, the high-priced, good-service dealers might be eliminated from the market.

The prevention of a significant **free rider problem** is the most convincing economic justification for RPM; however, relatively few goods actually require good pre-sale service. The argument may make sense for items such as automobiles, computers, audio and video equipment, and bicycles, for which in-store pre-sale services are important; it's difficult to believe that Levi's jeans, Izod shirts, Florsheim shoes, or Russell Stover candies, all items commonly sold under RPM, require the provision of good pre-sale service.

Despite the arguments that RPM rarely makes sense for manufacturers, firms continue to use RPM. The continued use of the practice suggests that benefits exist for at least some manufacturers. Perhaps there is a difference between the short-run and long-run effects of RPM. Elimination of RPM may result in short-run gains to manufacturers as more consumers purchase the good, but in the long run the elimination of RPM may result in a serious negative impact on the quality reputation of the good. Both Levi's jeans and Izod sportswear now have a much less posh reputation than they did under RPM pricing policies.[19]

One final point is that American retailing has become more competitive in the past two decades with the advent of large discount department stores, large outlet malls, and large retail chains such as The Gap and The Limited. With this changing market structure, the potential negative impacts of RPM have declined because manufacturers find it increasingly difficult to refuse to deal with stores in all of these various retail outlets.

---

*The argument does not hold much weight for postsale services, because a higher-quality service dealership should be able to charge higher prices for postsale service with little fear of losing significant business to low-quality dealerships.

In Chapter 22, the antitrust treatment of RPM is considered in detail. We delay the analysis of specific cases until then.

STRATEGIC USES OF VERTICAL INTEGRATION[20]

Recall from Chapter 11 that entry may be prevented if incumbents are able to raise their rivals' costs. Vertical integration and restraints may be used to raise rivals' costs in a number of ways. Under **exclusive dealing arrangements**, a retailer agrees to carry only one manufacturer's products. One argument in favor of exclusive dealing revolves around the provision of pre-sale services. In the absence of exclusive dealing, a manufacturer may supply a retailer with promotional services, such as advertising and employee training, that increase the flow of consumer traffic into the retail store only to have the retailer, who carries many brands, switch the consumer to a different brand. Classic examples of exclusive dealing include automobile dealerships, Electrolux dealers, and bicycle shops.

Now consider the potential negative effects of exclusive dealing. Under an exclusive dealing arrangement, a manufacturer with market power may be able to prevent entry while still charging a price above the potential entrant's average cost. Consider a monopolist who produces "ABC" brand widgets at MC = AC = 100 and sells the widgets at a wholesale price P = 125. Assume a potential entrant can produce a similar widget for the same MC = AC = 100. To enter effectively, the potential entrant must find dealers willing to take its product. If the monopolist makes it a clear and overtly stated policy that *any* dealer that accepts another firm's widgets will be immediately cut off from its supply of "ABC" widgets, entry can be deterred while the price of "ABC" widgets can be maintained at a level above average cost. To make the threat credible, any dealer that accepts competitors' widgets must be cut off quickly by the monopolist.

According to Comanor and Frech, this is exactly what happened in the United States market for silicone sealants in the 1970s.[21] Rhodia attempted to enter the sealants market by selling at a much lower price than the dominant firm, General Electric. GE controlled a 75 percent market share and sold its sealants through exclusive dealerships. When one of GE's largest dealers, C.R. Laurence, began to market Rhodia's sealants, GE responded immediately by dropping Laurence from its dealership list. As a result, no other GE dealers marketed Rhodia's sealants and further erosion of GE's market share was prevented.

Vertical integration also may be used strategically to raise the price of inputs for competitors. Suppose that a dominant manufacturer is vertically integrated into an important input and fringe manufacturers are not.[22] Because of economies of scale, the integrated manufacturer can produce the input at a lower cost than it can buy it from small unintegrated input manufacturers. The integrated manufacturer can then purchase enough of the input from independent suppliers to increase the price of the input. This will increase its rivals' costs because the unintegrated rivals must purchase the input from independent suppliers at a higher price.

In this scenario the integrated firm's average costs increase in proportion to its purchase of the input. If, for example, purchases by the integrated manufacturer increase the input price by $1.00 per unit, and the integrated manufacturer produces 75 percent of the input internally and purchases 25 percent from unintegrated input suppliers, the integrated manufacturer's average cost will increase by (0.25) × ($1.00) = $0.25. For the unintegrated fringe manufacturers, however, average costs would increase by the full $1.00 per unit, and the fringe supply would decrease.

Because this policy raises the integrated firm's costs, profits are reduced. The policy makes sense, therefore, only if the reduction in profits caused by the higher input cost is more than offset by an increase in profits that will result from a reduction in the supply of the fringe firms. As the fringe manufacturers reduce output, the integrated firm's output should increase, and this increase in output should result in increased profits. In this case the effect on welfare is unambiguously negative because both costs and price increase.

In other cases a vertically integrated dominant manufacturer of a final good and an important input may be able to strategically create a **price squeeze** on competitors by simultaneously increasing the price of the input and decreasing the price of the finished good. It has been argued, for example, that before 1930 Alcoa increased the price of aluminum ingots (the input) while simultaneously reducing the price of aluminum sheets and fabricated products.[23] Because Alcoa had a monopoly on ingots, this policy resulted in serious problems for unintegrated fabricators, such as Reynolds. Reynolds saw its input prices rising and its fabricated goods' prices falling. Alcoa was able to weather the reduction in profits on fabricated goods because its profits in the ingot market increased. Furthermore, observation of Alcoa's price-squeezing behavior would undoubtedly serve as a strategic reminder to any potential entrants into the fabricating business.

Alcoa's behavior also indicated that vertical integration can be used as an enabling device for price discrimination. In the 1930s and 1940s aluminum was used primarily to produce five manufactured goods: (1) iron and steel (aluminum was an important alloy); (2) cooking utensils; (3) electric cable; (4) automobile parts; and (5) aircraft. Because the availability of substitutes varied widely from one use to another, the elasticity of demand for aluminum varied as well. For example, the demand for aluminum in cooking utensils, for which many potential substitute inputs were available, was much more elastic than the demand for aluminum in aircraft, for which there were no good substitutes. Profit maximization required Alcoa to charge a higher price to aircraft manufacturers than to cooking utensil manufacturers. According to Perry, the demand for aluminum in cooking utensils, electric cable, and automobile parts was relatively elastic, and the demand for aluminum as an iron and steel alloy and in aircraft manufacturing was much more inelastic.[24]

In the absence of vertical integration, Alcoa would be forced to charge one price to all fabricators because otherwise one buyer could transfer the aluminum to another. If, for example, Alcoa attempted to charge aircraft manufacturers a higher price than utensil manufacturers for the same aluminum sheets, arbitrage would be possible between the aircraft and utensil manufacturers; the utensil manufacturer could purchase the aluminum at the low price and resell it to the aircraft manufacturer for a profit.

If Alcoa vertically integrated into utensils, however, it could increase the price to aircraft manufacturers without having to be concerned about the transfer of the good from one buyer to another. Perry has shown that in the early part of the twentieth century Alcoa behaved in just this manner.[25] Alcoa vertically integrated into the three markets with more elastic demands: cooking utensils, electric cables, and automobile parts. This enabled Alcoa to keep the prices it charged to the iron and steel and aircraft industries high. Vertical integration, therefore, enabled Alcoa to practice price discrimination.

RAISING THE CAPITAL BARRIER TO ENTRY

In the preceding section we observed that vertical integration can facilitate the use of certain types of strategic behavior to discourage entry. Recall from Chapter 5 that capital barriers present a formidable barrier to entry in the presence of imperfect capital markets. The existence of significant vertical integration may make it necessary to enter an industry at more than one vertical stage, thereby increasing capital barriers to entry. In aluminum, for example, Alcoa controlled much of the world's bauxite ore supply, the United States' ingot capacity, and a good deal of fabrication capacity. As a result, to compete effectively against Alcoa, it was probably necessary to enter more than one vertical stage of production. This increased the capital barrier to entry tremendously and made it impossible for all but a handful of firms to enter.

COLLUSION AND VERTICAL INTEGRATION

The relationship between vertical integration and the likelihood of effective collusion has troubled economists for many years.[26] Recall from Chapter 8 that two of the most significant factors affecting the probability of effective collusion are the number of firms and concentration. Increased vertical integration is likely to decrease the number of firms in a market and increase concentration. Consider Figure 16.8. In the absence of vertical integration, this industry is characterized by four upstream manufacturers and twenty downstream retailers. Collusion among the retailers will be difficult because twenty is a large number of firms and each firm controls a relatively small 5 percent of the market. Suppose that the manufacturers engage in a vertical merger blitz that transforms the industry struc-

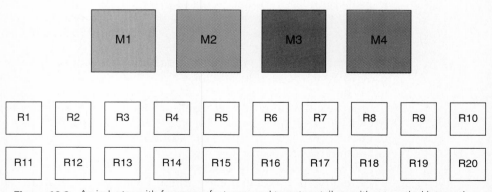

Figure 16.8   An industry with four manufacturers and twenty retailers without vertical integration.

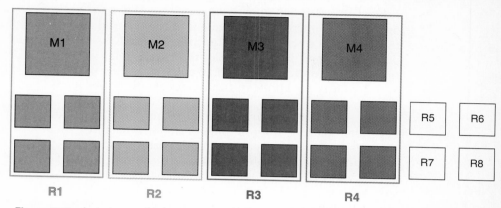

Figure 16.9 An industry with four manufacturers and twenty retailers and significant vertical integration.

ture into that in Figure 16.9. Now only eight retailers remain, and the four-firm concentration ratio has increased from 16 to 84. Given the structure of Figure 16.9 effective collusion is more likely to occur.

Vertical integration has been shown to help foster collusion in industries as diverse as textiles and pharmaceuticals.[27] Costello found that the key to suppressing price competition in the introduction of new antibiotics in the late 1940s and early 1950s was a combination of patent protection and forward vertical integration into packaging.[28] Telser has suggested that GE and Westinghouse marketed light bulbs only on consignment to eliminate any attempt by the retailers to bargain for better terms with manufacturers.[29] Further evidence is provided by Caves and Porter, who found that increased vertical integration resulted in greater stability of market shares in an industry.[30]

FORECLOSURE*

As noted previously, **foreclosure** occurs when downstream firms (such as retailers) have difficulty obtaining inputs or when upstream firms (such as manufacturers) have difficulty finding buyers for their products. The United States courts have emphasized foreclosure as the primary problem associated with vertical mergers. Economists, however, have been skeptical that foreclosure has much economic impact unless it increases the capital barrier to entry by virtually requiring an entrant to enter at multiple stages of production.[31] The courts have argued that foreclosure creates potential problems. For example, consider a series of vertical mergers that results in a shift in structure from the one in Figure 16.8 to the one in Figure 16.9. Such a change in structure may force potential entrants to enter both the manufacturing and retailing markets because of a fear of foreclosure. A potential entrant into the manufacturing stage in Figure 16.8 would have

---

*The major issues regarding foreclosure are examined in greater detail in later chapters dealing with public policy toward vertical mergers and other types of vertical restraints of trade. Here we simply introduce the concept.

twenty possible retail outlets. After the mergers, there are only eight retail outlets, only four of which are independent of the other manufacturers. If the integrated retailers carry only their manufacturer's brands, then the mergers foreclose the potential entrant from sixteen of the twenty retail outlets. The potential entrant may then be forced either to forgo entry altogether or to enter both vertical stages at once. Entry into both vertical stages greatly increases the capital barrier to entry.

The structure shown in Figure 16.9 also may foreclose the four remaining independent retailers from supplies of the manufactured good. This structure leaves the independents in a very precarious position at the mercy of the four integrated manufacturers for supplies. As a result, the independent retailers will probably abide by any demands made regarding vertical restraints, such as RPM or exclusive dealing, made by the manufacturers. The structure of Figure 16.9, therefore, also may make entry into the retailing sector far less likely than the structure of Figure 16.8.

It is important to understand that foreclosure is unlikely to have a major impact on pricing. The potential problem in Figure 16.8 is that there are only four manufacturers. This problem is no worse in Figure 16.9, in which there are still four manufacturers. It follows that except in extreme cases in which foreclosure is virtually complete and the capital barrier to entry is significantly increased, foreclosure is likely to cause few economic problems. As we will see in Chapter 22, however, this has not prevented the courts from using foreclosure as a primary reason for condemning vertical mergers.

SUMMARY

1. Most vertical integration reduces transactions costs.

2. Vertical integration and vertical relationships can solve several potential economic problems, including the problems of double marginalization, insufficient pre-sale service, and inefficient input substitution.

3. In the case of bilateral monopoly, double marginalization results in a higher price and lower welfare than a vertically integrated monopoly.

4. In the absence of vertical integration, downstream firms may attempt to free ride on the services provided by competitors. The use of resale price maintenance (RPM) may solve this free rider problem.

5. It has been suggested that RPM is used to facilitate collusion among either retailers or manufacturers, but little empirical evidence supports this theory.

6. Manufacturers may use RPM to maintain their products' high-quality images or to ensure that their retailers provide adequate services.

7. Vertical integration and vertical relationships can also be used strategically to increase entry barriers. Such practices include exclusive dealing arrangements and price squeezes.

8. Vertical integration may result in an increased capital barrier to entry if firms are forced to enter more than one vertical stage of an industry.

9. Some economists have suggested that vertical integration may be used to facilitate collusion or foreclose markets.

10. Because of the complexity of analyzing the impact of increased vertical integration, each case of increased vertical integration should be analyzed in detail to determine whether there is a positive or negative effect on economic efficiency.

11. It is safe to conclude that a great deal of existing vertical integration and many vertical relationships have either a positive or a neutral effect on welfare, but economists should guard against any negative welfare effects.

KEY TERMS

double marginalization	Miller-Tydings Act
downstream	price squeeze
exclusive dealing arrangements	resale price maintenance agreements
foreclosure	RPM
franchise fees	upstream
free rider problem	vertical restraints

DISCUSSION QUESTIONS

1. Why might Ralph Lauren refuse to allow retailers to sell its Polo clothing at discount prices?

2. Under what type(s) of market structure is the problem of double marginalization likely to arise? Suggest two solutions to this problem.

3. A manufacturer of shoes purchases a chain of shoe stores. The four-firm concentration ratio in both shoe manufacturing and shoe retailing is low. Would you expect any serious anticompetitive impacts of such a merger?

4. Cosmetics (e.g., Estee Lauder, Liz Claiborne) and certain name brand clothing (e.g., Liz Claiborne, Ralph Lauren) are commonly sold under RPM agreements. For which of these two product lines would you expect the provision of improved service to be a more valid justification for RPM? Why?

5. Can you suggest a good that you would be less likely to buy if it was not sold under suggested retail prices? What does this suggest about the relationship between your utility and the total number of units of this good that are sold?

6. A larger and larger percentage of American physicians are becoming employees of HMOs rather than being self-employed in their own practices. Might there be any anticompetitive effects if HMOs vertically integrated into hospital ownership? If most of America's largest hospitals were owned by HMOs, what do you think would happen to the number of self-employed physicians?

7. Microsoft is basically a monopolist in the production of computer operating systems for PCs, but it produces no computers. Why do you think Microsoft has not vertically integrated into manufacturing computers?

PROBLEMS

1. A franchisor is considering whether to charge a franchisee a royalty that is a percentage of the franchisee's profits or a royalty that is a percentage of a franchisee's total revenues. In terms of economic efficiency, does it matter which policy the franchisor adopts?

2. Consider a case of bilateral monopoly in which the demand for the final good is $P = 100 - Q$. The average and marginal cost of producing the monopolized input is LRAC = LRMC = 20. Calculate the total gain in consumer plus producer surplus if the two monopolists merged.

3. A monopolist manufacturer sells to competitive retailers. The competitive retailers currently provide no services for the manufacturer's good. Suppose the final consumer demand for the good at the retail level is $P = 100 - Q$ and the costs for the manufacturer of producing the good are represented by:

$$MC_W = AC_W = 20$$

Currently the monopolist sells the good to retailers at $P = 60$ and does not use RPM. If the manufacturer continues to sell the good to retailers at $P = 60$, but now uses RPM to set the minimum price at $P = 80$, demand increases to $P = 150 - Q$. In this case, does RPM improve economic welfare?

4. Consider a vertically integrated industry with a monopolist manufacturer and competitive retailers. The government is considering placing a per-unit tax of $1.00 on this good at either the manufacturing or retail levels. In terms of economic impact, does it matter whether the unit tax is placed on the manufacturer or the retailer?

REFERENCES

1. This result was first identified in Joseph J. Spengler, "Vertical Integration and Antitrust Policy," *Journal of Political Economy* 58 (August 1950): 347–52. This treatment is based on Jean Tirole, *The Theory of Industrial Organization* (Cambridge: MIT Press, 1988), pp. 174–81.
2. Spengler, *op cit.*
3. See Tirole, *supra,* note 1; Roger D. Blair and David L. Kaserman, "A Note on Incentive Incompatibility Under Franchising," *Review of Industrial Organization* 9 (June 1994): 323–30; Ester Gal-Or, "Optimal

Franchising in Oligopolistic Markets with Uncertain Demand," *International Journal of Industrial Organization* 9 (September 1991): 343–64; and Torsten Schmist, "An Analysis of Intrabrand Competition in the Franchise Industry, *Review of Industrial Organization* 9 (June 1994): 293–310.
4. This model is derived from Tirole, *supra* note 1, pp. 181–5. The original idea is based on Lester Telser, "Why Should Manufacturers Want Fair Trade?" *Journal of Law and Economics* 3 (1960): 86–105. See also G. Frank Mathewson and Ralph A. Winter,

"The Economic Theory of Vertical Restraints," *Rand Journal of Economics* 15 (1984): 27–38; Martin K. Perry and Robert H. Porter, "Can Resale Price Maintenance and Franchise Fees Correct Sub-optimal Levels of Retail Service?" *International Journal of Industrial Organization* 8 (March 1990): 115–41; and Howard P. Marvel and Stephen McCafferty, "Resale Price Maintenance and Quality Certification," *Rand Journal of Economics* 15 (1984): 346–59. For empirical evidence on the question see David W. Boyd, "The Choice Between Resale Price Maintenance and Exclusive Territories: Evidence from Litigation," *Review of Industrial Organization* 8 (December 1993): 755–63.

5. Robert H. Bork, "A Reply to Professors Gould and Yamey," *Yale Law Journal* (March 1967): 731; see also Robert H. Bork, "The Rule of Reason and the Per Se Concept: Price Fixing and Market Division," *Yale Law Journal* (January 1966): 402–3, 424; and Robert H. Bork, "Resale Price Maintenance and Consumer Welfare," *Yale Law Journal* (April 1968): 950–60.

6. F.M. Scherer, "The Economics of Vertical Restraints," *Antitrust Law Journal* 52 (1983): 700; and William S. Comanor, "Vertical Price Fixing and Market Restrictions and the New Antitrust Policy," *Harvard Law Review* 98 (March 1985): 990–8.

7. This section is based on John M. Vernon and Daniel A. Graham, "Profitability of Monopolization by Vertical Integration," *Journal of Political Economy* 79 (1971): 924–5. See also: Tirole, *supra* note 1, pp. 179–81; Roger D. Blair and David L. Kaserman, "Vertical Integration, Tying and Antitrust Policy," *American Economic Review* 68 (1978): 397–402; Richard Schmalensee, "A Note on the Theory of Vertical Integration," *Journal of Political Economy* 81 (1973): 442–9; Frederick R. Warren-Boulton, "Vertical Control with Variable Proportions," *Journal of Political Economy* 82 (1974): 783–802; Michael A. Salinger, "Vertical Mergers and Market Foreclosure," *Quarterly Journal of Economics* (1988): 345–56; and James L. Hamilton, "Input Substitutability and Vertical Integration," *Review of Industrial Organization* 7 (1992): 29–38.

8. Blair and Kaserman, *supra* note 7.

9. See the following for an excellent summary of the issues: Thomas R. Overstreet, *Resale Price Maintenance: Economic Theories and Empirical Evidence* (Washington: Federal Trade Commission Bureau of Economics staff report, November 1983). Also see Robert L. Steiner, "The Inverse Association Between the Margins of Manufacturers and Retailers," *Review of Industrial Organization* 8 (December 1993): 717–40.

10. See *Albrecht* v. *Herald Co.*, 390 US 145 (1968).

11. Roger D. Blair and David L. Kaserman, *Antitrust Economics* (Homewood, Ill.: Richard D. Irwin, 1985), pp. 342–7.

12. *Ibid.*, p. 342.

13. S.C. Hollander, in B.S. Yamey (ed.), *Resale Price Maintenance* (Chicago: Aldine, 1966), pp. 67–100; Marvin Frankel, "The Effects of Fair Trade: Fact and Fiction in the Statistical Findings," *Journal of Business* (July 1955); and J.F. Pickering, "The Abolition of Resale Price Maintenance in Great Britain," *Oxford Economic Papers* (March, 1975).

14. Thomas R. Overstreet, *Resale Price Maintenance: Economic Theories and Empirical Evidence* (Washington: FTC Bureau of Economics staff report, November 1983), pp. 13–9, 80, 140–4, 161–3; and Stanley I. Ornstein, "Resale Price Maintenance and Cartels," *Antitrust Bulletin* 30 (1985): 401–32.

15. Overstreet, *op cit.*, pp. 71–82.

16. Lester G. Telser, "Why Should Manufacturers Want Fair Trade?" *Journal of Law and Economics* 3 (October 1960): 86.

17. Robert L. Steiner, "Jeans: Vertical Restraints and Efficiency," in Larry L. Duetsch (ed.), *Industry Studies* (Englewood Cliffs, NJ: Prentice-Hall, 1993), pp. 182–205; and "Has Izod's Alligator Peaked?" *New York Times* (September 8, 1983): D1.

18. "Has Izod's Alligator Peaked?" *New York Times* (September 8, 1983): D1.

19. For an argument of how RPM worked to benefit Levi Strauss see Robert L. Steiner, "Jeans: Vertical Restraints and Efficiency," in Larry L. Duetsch (ed.), *Industry Studies* (Englewood Cliffs, N.J.: Prentice-Hall, 1993), pp. 182–205.

20. For a game theory model see Philippe Cyrenne, "Vertical Integration Versus Vertical Separation: An Equilibrium Model," *Review of Industrial Organization* 9 (June 1994): 311–22.

21. William S. Comanor and H.E. Frech III, "The Competitive Effects of Vertical Agreements," *American Economic Review* 75 (1985): 539–46.

22. This argument is based on Steven C. Salop and David T. Scheffman, "Cost-Raising Strategies," *Journal of Industrial Economics* 36 (1987): 19–34.

23. *United States* v. *Aluminum Company of America*, 148 F.2d 416 (1945).

24. Martin K. Perry, "Forward Integration by Alcoa: 1888-1930," *Journal of Industrial Economics* 29 (1980): 37–53.
25. *Ibid.*
26. See R.E. Caves and M.E. Porter, "Market Structure, Oligopoly, and Stability of Market Shares," *Journal of Industrial Economics* (June 1978): 289–313; and Ronald N. Johnson and Allen M. Parkman, "Vertical Mergers and Selective Price Cutting," *Review of Industrial Organization* 10 (October 1995): 533–40.
27. Irwin M. Stelzer, "The Cotton Textile Industry," in Walter Adams (ed.), *The Structure of American Industry* (New York: MacMillan, 1961), pp. 42–73; and Peter M. Costello, "The Tetracycline Conspiracy," *Antitrust Law & Economics Review* (Summer 1968): 13–44. See also Telser, *supra* note 4, pp. 96–104; M.G. Chazeau and Alfred E. Kahn, *Integration and Competition in the Petroleum Industry* (New Haven: Yale University Press, 1959), pp. 428–449; and Walter Adams and Joel Dirlam, "Steel Imports and Vertical Oligopoly Power," *American Economic Review* (September 1964): 626–55.
28. Peter M. Costello, "The Tetracycline Conspiracy," *Antitrust Law & Economics Review* (Summer 1968): 13–44.
29. Telser, *supra* note 4, pp. 96–104.
30. Caves and Porter, *supra* note 26.
31. There are exceptions, of course; see Roger D. Blair, James M. Fesmire, and Richard E. Romano, "A Note on Vertical Market Foreclosure," *Review of Industrial Organization* 5 (1990): 31–40.

Appendix

THE PROBLEM OF INPUT SUBSTITUTION

Suppose that a monopolist produces good X, using only two inputs, input M and input C. Input M is produced by a monopolist at marginal cost MC_M, and input C is produced in a perfectly competitive market at marginal cost MC_C. A vertically integrated firm that produced both inputs internally would maximize the following profits:

$$\Pi = TR - TC = P_X Q_X - (MC_M q_M + MC_C q_C)$$

It will be useful to define P_X^*, Q_X^*, q_M^*, and q_C^* as the price and quantities that maximize profits Π.

The profit-maximizing firm must minimize production costs $TC_X = (MC_M q_M + MC_C q_C)$. At this point it is necessary to recall some intermediate microeconomic theory. For any given production function the *marginal rate of technical substitution* (MRTS) is defined as the rate at which a firm can substitute one input for another input without changing output. Furthermore, the MRTS equals the slope of an isoquant at a point and firms *minimize their long-run costs* by equating the MRTS, given by the slope of an isoquant, to the ratio of input prices, given by the slope of the isocost lines. Given any production function $Q_X = f(q_M, q_C)$, cost minimization, therefore, requires that the vertically integrated firm equate the MRTS between inputs to the ratio of the input prices. In a perfectly competitive world with all prices equal to marginal cost, the ratio of input prices also equals the ratio of the marginal costs of the inputs. Summarizing the theory mathematically cost minimization requires:

$$MRTS = \frac{MP_M}{MP_C} = \frac{P_M}{P_C} = \frac{MC_M}{MC_C}, \qquad [16.2]$$

where MP_M represents the marginal product of input M, and MP_C represents the marginal product of input C. The *marginal product* of an input is the change in output associated with a small increase in the quantity of the input. The MP_M, for example, is the change in the quantity of good X (ΔQ_X) associated with a change in the quantity of input M (Δq_M), or $\Delta Q_X / \Delta q_M$.

Suppose the production function for good X, $Q_X = f(q_M, q_C)$, is as follows:*

$$Q_X = q_M^{\frac{1}{2}} q_C^{\frac{1}{2}}. \qquad [16.3]$$

---

*This production function is of the general form:

$$Q = Ax^\alpha y^\beta,$$

known as a Cobb-Douglas production function.

Further assume that $MC_M = MC_C = 1$. For production function 16.3, the cost-minimizing choice of inputs is defined by the following two equations:*

$$q_M = P_M^{-\frac{1}{2}} P_C^{\frac{1}{2}} Q_X \qquad\qquad [16.4]$$

$$q_C = P_C^{-\frac{1}{2}} P_M^{\frac{1}{2}} Q_X \qquad\qquad [16.5]$$

The vertically integrated firm would behave as though the input prices equaled marginal cost; that is, for the vertically integrated firm $P_M = MC_M = P_C = MC_C = 1$. Substituting $P_M = 1$ and $P_C = 1$ into Eqs. 16.4 and 16.5 yields:

$$q_M = 1^{-\frac{1}{2}} 1^{\frac{1}{2}} Q_X = Q_X \text{ and } q_C = 1^{-\frac{1}{2}} 1^{\frac{1}{2}} Q_X = Q_X.$$

Figure 16.10 shows the *isoquants*, which identify input combinations that yield equal outputs, for the production function given by Eq. 16.3 and for outputs $Q_X = 2$ and $Q_X = 4$. For $P_M = P_C = 1$, the equilibrium cost-minimizing combinations lie along the input expansion path $q_C = q_M$. The conditions for cost minimization imply that the vertically integrated firm would operate along the input expansion path OA utilizing the input combinations $q_M = q_C = Q_X$.

---

*Using calculus, the solution is derived by minimizing TC_X with respect to q_m and q_c as follows:

$$TC_X = P_M Q_M + P_C q_C \qquad (1)$$

subject to the condition that:

$$Q_X = q_M^{\frac{1}{2}} q_C^{\frac{1}{2}}. \qquad (2)$$

From (2):

$$q_C = \frac{Q_X^2}{q_M} = Q_X^2 q_M^{-1}. \qquad (3)$$

Substituting for q_C from (3) into (1):

$$TC_X = P_M Q_M + P_C Q_X^2 q_M^{-1}.$$

Minimizing with respect to q_m yields:

$$\frac{\partial TC_X}{\partial q_M} = P_M - P_C Q_X^2 q_M^{-2} = 0.$$

Solving for q_M:

$$q_M = \frac{\sqrt{P_C} Q_X}{\sqrt{P_M}} = P_M^{-\frac{1}{2}} P_C^{\frac{1}{2}} Q_X.$$

by analogous minimization with respect to q_c:

$$q_C = P_C^{-\frac{1}{2}} P_M^{\frac{1}{2}} Q_X.$$

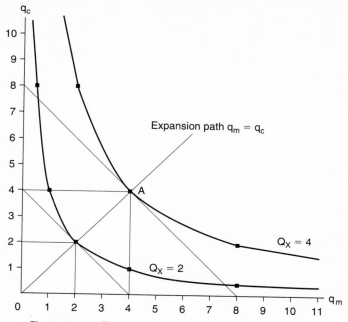

Figure 16.10 The socially optimal input expansion path OA.

Now consider the situation with three independent firms (one producing the final good and the other two producing the inputs). Would the monopolist manufacturer of X still operate along the expansion path $q_M = q_C$? Competition would ensure that $P_C = MC_C$. Profit maximization by the monopolist producer of input M, however, would ensure that $P_M > MC_M$. Assume that the monopolist input producer charges $P_M = 2$. From Eq. 16.4 and 16.5, with $P_M = 2$ and $P_C = 1$, the monopolist final good producer would now use input combinations:

$$q_M = 2^{-\frac{1}{2}} Q_X = \frac{Q_X}{\sqrt{2}}.$$

[16.6]

$$q_C = 2^{\frac{1}{2}} Q_X = \sqrt{2} Q_X.$$

[16.7]

In Figure 16.11 the profit-maximizing producer of good X would then operate along a steeper input expansion path OB with a slope equal to 2.* As a result,

---

*The slope of OB is 2 because from Eq. 16.6 and 16.7:

$$\frac{q_C}{q_M} = \frac{\sqrt{2} Q_X}{\dfrac{Q_X}{\sqrt{2}}} = \sqrt{2} \sqrt{2} = 2.$$

[16.8]

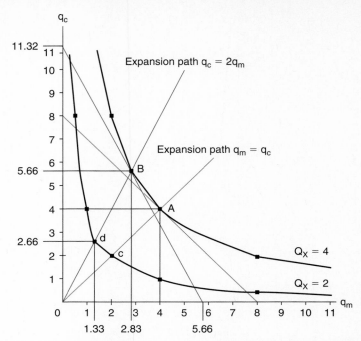

Figure 16.11 Comparison of the optimal input expansion path, OA with the non-optimal input expansion path, OB.

the social costs of producing any given output Q_X would be too high, and economic efficiency in production would not be achieved. In Figure 16.11, for example, at point A the minimum social cost of producing $Q_X = 4$ is $P_C q_C + P_M q_M = 1 \cdot 4 + 1 \cdot 4 = 8$. The nonintegrated producer of good X, however, would produce at point B with social costs of $P_C q_C + P_M q_M = 1(5.66) + 2(2.83) = 11.32$.* Furthermore, because the costs of producing any given Q_X are too high, the monopolist manufacturer restricts output below Q_X*, the profit-maximizing quantity, and welfare is unambiguously reduced compared with the vertically integrated case.

To eliminate the input substitution problem, the producer of good X need only integrate, perhaps through merger, with the producer of the monopolized input M. The integrated firm would then evaluate the cost of input M as $MC_M = 1$, and because $P_C = MC_C = 1$, the integrated firm would operate along the efficient input expansion path OA in Figure 16.11.

An alternative solution to the problem is for the producer of input M to use a

---

*Similarly, the minimum social cost of producing $Q_x = 2$ is 4 at point c, but the nonintegrated producer of X would produce at point d with social costs of 5.32.

tie combined with RPM to achieve the maximum profit. If the producer of input M purchases input C at $MC_C = 1$ and then ties the two products together for sale at prices such that:

$$\frac{P_M}{P_C} = \frac{MC_M}{MC_C} = 1,$$

the unintegrated monopolist manufacturer of good X will operate along input expansion path OA. Because the prices of the inputs will be greater than marginal cost, the monopolist producer of good X will want to charge a price greater than $P_X{}^*$. To guarantee that the profit-maximizing quantity $Q_X{}^*$ is produced, therefore, the input monopolist uses RPM to set the maximum retail price equal to $P_X{}^*$.

Chapter 17

Market Power and Performance: The Empirical Evidence

In the last several chapters we have been looking at the conduct of firms in oligopolistic industries, particularly with regard to pricing decisions. Among other issues, we have examined what determines firms' market power, that is, their ability to set price above marginal cost. As discussed in Chapter 2, pricing above marginal cost leads to a misallocation of resources. Price measures the value to society of an additional unit of output, and marginal cost measures the resource cost of producing that extra unit of output. If price is greater than marginal cost, then too little of the good is being produced from society's viewpoint.

Allocative inefficiency is a key reason for policy makers' concerns about market power. In the following chapters, we turn our attention to public policy toward industries. First, though, this chapter examines the available empirical evidence on the relationship between market power and efficiency. *Is* there a problem with market power?

Detecting market power and measuring its effects on performance have been the focus of much empirical work in industrial organization over many years. We will not attempt the nearly impossible task of comprehensively surveying the voluminous empirical work in the area. Instead, our goal is to help you understand both how economists approach the topic of market power and what stylized facts have emerged from their work.

Economists have used several different methodologies in their search for firms with market power. The most extensively used technique for many years was broad cross-section studies. This methodology underlies literally hundreds of empirical studies, and we begin our examination of the empirical evidence with this work. Along the way, we consider a variety of criticisms of cross-section studies. These criticisms fall into two broad categories: (1) concerns about data problems and measurement and (2) concerns about the methodology and the interpretation of results.

More recently, economists have turned to case studies in an attempt to avoid some problems associated with cross-section work. Case studies focus on market power in single industries or in closely related industries. Additionally, recognizing that cross-section and case studies tend to be largely static, some recent work has focused attention on dynamic issues. The last part of the chapter briefly examines the most recent approaches to the study of market power.

Structure-Conduct-Performance

As noted in Chapter 1, the structure-conduct-performance (SCP) paradigm, introduced in the late 1930s and 1940s, searches for a link between various elements of market structure and some measure of performance.[1] The traditional SCP approach hypothesized that certain elements of market structure increase the likelihood of collusive behavior and that collusive behavior results in higher prices and profits.* Because collusive behavior is not directly observable, however, SCP studies use evidence on the relationship between performance and various characteristics of market structure to make inferences about market power. If, for example, a researcher finds that higher concentration is associated with higher industry profits, the SCP explanation is that firms in highly concentrated industries are better able to collude, leading to higher prices and profits and allocative inefficiency.

The economists who developed and first used the SCP approach did not base it on formal oligopoly models such as those explored in Chapters 7 through 12. Yet these models can be used to develop a second interpretation of the standard regression estimated in SCP studies.† Assuming particular behavioral assumptions, a relationship between profits and some measure of industry concentration corresponds to a set of first-order conditions describing choice of price or output. Even though the relationship to be estimated is the same, collusion does not play an explicit role in this interpretation; prices are raised above marginal costs in an "apparently collusive" manner.[2]

Measurement Issues

Measurement issues are important in any SCP study. We first consider alternative measures of performance and then discuss the key structural variables.

---

*That a story of collusion underlies the SCP paradigm can be seen in Bain (1956, p. 191): "This predicted influence of the condition of entry on the size of price-cost margins and profits is clearly subject to the concomitant influence of the degree of seller concentration within the industry. Specifically, it is expected to be evidenced in a verifiable simple association of the condition of entry on profits *mainly as far as seller concentration throughout is high enough to support effective collusion* in industries with both high and medium entry barriers." [Emphasis added.]

†The standard SCP regression is discussed in detail later in this chapter.

MEASURES OF PERFORMANCE

Market power permits a firm to raise price above the competitive level. This suggests that a good way to measure market power might be to look directly at prices. Unfortunately, looking at prices makes sense only for a given product. To make comparisons across industries or even across firms that produce a variety of products, a common denominator is necessary.

One possible common denominator is costs. The Lerner index, defined in Chapter 2 as $\frac{P - MC}{P}$, is theoretically appealing because it directly measures the increase of price above marginal cost. The Lerner index, however, is difficult to estimate because data are lacking on firms' marginal costs. Four different measures have been used as a proxy for the Lerner index in SCP studies: **excess return on sales**, **profit rate**, **price-cost margin**, and **Tobin's q**. Not surprisingly, none of these measures is ideal.

Excess Return on Sales

Excess return on sales is the ratio of economic profits to sales revenue. Assuming that firms are in long-run equilibrium and are operating in the range of their production functions with constant returns to scale, the excess profit rate on sales $\left(\frac{TR - TC}{TR}\right)$ will, on average across all products produced by the firm, equal the Lerner index. To see this, begin with the Lerner index and recognize that if returns to scale are constant, $MC = AC$. Making this substitution and multiplying the index by $\frac{q}{q}$ yields $\frac{Pq - ACq}{Pq}$. Because AC equals $\frac{TC}{q}$, this is equal to $\frac{TR - TC}{TR}$, which is economic profits over sales.

Despite its theoretical appeal, few studies have used the excess profit rate on sales to measure performance. A difficulty arises in the calculation of economic, or excess, profits, which can be broken down into sales revenue minus noncapital costs minus depreciation minus annual capital costs. Theoretically, annual capital costs equal the total capital stock multiplied by the competitive cost per unit of capital, that is, the annual rental fees if capital were rented in a competitive market. Accounting data, however, do not report the competitive rate of return on capital; to measure the excess profit rate of return, a researcher must make a judgment about what the appropriate competitive rate of return is. For example, one study used 6 percent as the "normal" or competitive rate of return, arguing that this rate of return closely approximates the after-tax rate of return on equity over the long run in competitive industries.[3] Researchers who want to avoid the problem of estimating the competitive rate of return on capital turn to one of the other measures of performance.

Profit Rate

Many researchers use accounting profits as a measure of relative performance. These data are readily available from standard sources and do not require a judgment about the competitive rate of return. For purposes of comparison across firms, profits are divided by some base figure to yield a profit rate, or a rate of return. Earning positive economic profits is equivalent to earning a rate of return that is greater than the competitive rate of return. Suppose, for example, that a firm earns a 9 percent rate of return. If investment in a competitive industry yields a 6 percent rate of return, then 9 percent is an *excess* rate of return, and we can conclude that the firm is earning *positive* economic profits.

Most SCP studies have used the **rate of return on stockholders' equity after tax** to measure profitability. This is calculated as $\frac{\pi - T}{E}$, where π is profits, T is the tax on profits, and E is stockholders' equity. This measure is attractive because it corresponds with what individual investors are trying to maximize.* Also, competitive industries with the same risk will have the same rate of return on equity in the long run.†

A disadvantage of the rate of return on equity, however, is its sensitivity to variations in the debt/equity ratio across firms. Issuing both debt (bonds) and equity (stocks) results in two groups having claims on the assets of the firm, with debtholders getting paid before stockholders if a firm gets into financial trouble. The risk to stockholders of not getting paid increases as the debt/equity ratio increases. To compensate for the higher risk, stockholders will require a higher rate of return from a firm with a high ratio of debt to equity than from a firm with a low debt/equity ratio.

To reduce the problems associated with variations in the debt/equity ratio, some researchers use the **rate of return on assets after tax**. This is calculated as $\frac{\pi - T + I}{A}$, where π and T are as defined above, I is interest payments to debtholders, and A is total assets.‡ Although this measure differs from the rate of return on equity, the two profit rates are highly correlated.[4]

A serious problem with both the rate of return on equity and the rate of return on assets is that the numerator and denominator tend to move together. To see this, consider a firm that has some asset, such as a brand name or ownership of a scarce input, that gives it market power. If the firm that owns this asset is sold, the purchaser is likely to pay a higher price for the acquisition than it would pay if there were no market power. The higher price reflects the acquiring firm's expectations of earning positive economic profits. After the merger, therefore, the profit rate may appear to be competitive because the denominator, the value of equity or assets, has been written up to reflect the potential to earn positive economic profits. Even a firm that does not change hands may sometimes revalue an asset. In particular, a firm may write down the value of an asset that turns out to

---

*Note that investors care about the after-tax rate of return rather than the pre-tax rate of return. Firms in two different industries may have very different pre-tax rates of return but identical after-tax rates of return if they face different tax rates on their assets.

†Investors must be compensated for bearing risk: the higher the risk, the higher is the expected rate of return. Two competitive firms will have different rates of return, therefore, if they are pursuing projects with different degrees of risk. A firm is earning an excess rate of return if the actual rate of return is higher than the **risk-adjusted rate of return**, which is the return a competitive firm would earn if its projects carried the same level of risk as the firm being examined.

‡Interest payments must be added to the numerator because debtholders are paid interest; profits are paid to stockholders. Total assets measures the value of both equity and debt capital.

be less profitable than was expected. By increasing the equity of the more profitable firms and decreasing the equity of the less profitable firms, such revaluation tends to bias all firms toward equal profit rates.

Profit rates may be mismeasured because of problems with reported profits.[5] Although economic theory makes predictions about *economic* profits, reported profits are *accounting* profits. Using accounting data can lead to biased estimates of rates of return.

There are several key differences between economic profits and accounting profits. Theoretically, economic profits are revenues minus the opportunity costs of inputs. Reasonably good data exist on revenues, labor costs, and the costs of materials. However, accurately measuring the annual costs of long-lived assets such as plant and equipment, advertising, and research and development is difficult, if not impossible.

In calculating the annual capital costs of a firm, two problems arise with accounting data. First, capital should be valued at its **replacement cost**, which is the long-run cost of buying a capital asset of comparable quality. The rate of return calculated using replacement cost indicates whether entry or exit should occur. If the rate of return is greater than the competitive rate of return, then new capital should enter the industry. If the rate of return is less than the competitive rate of return, the industry should contract and capital should leave the industry.

Accounting data, however, use **book value**, which is calculated using the historical value of an asset. To illustrate the problem with this method, consider an asset that was inexpensive at the time of its purchase but whose price has increased significantly. In this case, the rate of return calculated using historical cost will be considerably greater than the rate of return using replacement cost, overestimating the profitability of investment in the industry.

A second problem with accounting data is the calculation of **depreciation**. Any durable asset, such as a machine, wears out over time; depreciation measures the decrease in economic value that occurs during the period the asset is used. Suppose, for example, that a landlord rents a building for $1500 per year and has to spend $300 per year to maintain the building. The $300 is depreciation, and the landlord's net annual rental is $1200. It is the return after depreciation has been deducted that matters to the landlord or, in general, to the investor.

Accountants calculate depreciation using one of several fixed formulas, such as **straight-line depreciation**. This method assumes that an asset lasts for some fixed period and decreases in value in equal increments over that fixed period. If, for example, a machine that costs $1000 is assumed to last for five years, the annual depreciation would be $200 for the first five years. If the machine happens to last more than five years, there would be no further depreciation.

Unfortunately, depreciation as calculated by an accounting formula does not necessarily correspond to the true decline in an asset's economic value. Using the reported rate of depreciation, therefore, may lead to a biased estimate of a firm's profitability.

Further problems with accounting data arise for expenditures on advertising and on research and development (R&D). Like expenditures on plant and equipment, money spent on advertising or on R&D may create effects that last over time. A successful advertising campaign in one year can affect demand in subsequent years if consumers remember the campaign. Similarly, R&D expenditures in one year can affect demand or costs in future years. A common accounting procedure is to deduct the entire costs of advertising or R&D in one year and then deduct nothing in subsequent years. If this practice is followed, the rate of return will be underestimated in the first year and overestimated in future years.

A final problem with accounting data arises from inflation. Researchers must be careful when comparing rates of return to ensure that all rates are either nominal rates, which include the effects of inflation, or real rates, which have been adjusted for inflation. To calculate a real rate of return, the increase in income due to the overall increase in prices must be subtracted from the total increase in the price of assets to find the actual increase in the value of assets.

Price-Cost Margins

Another measure of performance used in numerous industrial organization studies is the price-cost margin. The main advantage of using the price-cost margin rather than profit rates arises from the level of aggregation at which data are reported. Because profit rates are calculated from firm-specific data, reported profits for any diversified firm reflect profits from several industries.* Hence, it is difficult to match profits with industry-specific measures of structure, such as the concentration ratio. The price-cost margin, however, is calculated from data available in the *Census of Manufactures*. Census data are reported at the level of the individual plant, which is typically much less diversified than are firms.† Therefore, using *Census* data makes the fit between the measure of performance and the measures of structure much better.

Unfortunately, the same feature that makes census data attractive can also be seen as a drawback. Because each plant shares certain joint costs with other plants in the firm, researchers cannot use accounting profits to calculate rates of return. Instead they typically estimate a price-cost margin.[6]

To understand the rationale for using the price-cost margin as a measure of performance, start again with the Lerner index, $\frac{P - MC}{P}$. Because data on marginal costs are usually not available, economists often assume long-run constant returns to scale so that long-run average cost equals long-run marginal cost.[7] With this assumption, the Lerner index can be written as

$$\frac{P - v - (\rho + \delta)(K/Q)}{P} = \frac{PQ - vQ}{PQ} - (\rho + \delta)\frac{K}{PQ}, \qquad [17.1]$$

where v = variable cost per unit, δ = depreciation rate of capital, ρ = competitive rate of return, P = price, Q = output, and K = dollar value of capital employed. The first term on the right in equation 17.1, (total revenue − variable cost)/total revenue, is the price-cost margin. Under competitive conditions, price should

*Firm-specific data are often classified into industries using the primary industry method. In this method the entire accounting values of variables such as profits are assigned to a firm's primary industry—that industry in which its percentage of its total sales is the highest.
†Census data are reported at the four-digit industry level.

equal long-run average (and marginal) cost. This implies that the price-cost margin should on average equal the second term on the right of equation 17.1 if the industry is competitive. A common practice, therefore, is to use the price-cost margin as the dependent variable in a regression and to include the ratio of assets to sales as one of the independent variables. Equation 17.1 shows that this approach amounts to assuming that both the competitive rate of return and the rate of depreciation are the same for all industries in the sample, an assumption that may not be valid.

Researchers typically calculate variable costs as the cost of materials plus payroll. This calculation omits several possible variable costs, including advertising, central office expenses, taxes, and research and development.[8] Recognizing this problem, some researchers include industry aggregates for these factors as independent variables in their regression equations to control for their effects.

Tobin's q

Problems with accounting rates of return and price-cost margins have led many economists to measure profitability by *Tobin's q*, the ratio of the market value of a firm to the replacement value of its assets.[9] In a perfectly competitive industry in long-run equilibrium, the value of q would be 1; the market value of the firm would just equal what it would cost to rebuild it. If q is greater than 1, the market value of the firm is greater than its replacement cost. In this case, other firms would want to enter the industry, anticipating that the market value of their investment will be greater than its cost. Thus, in the absence of barriers to entry and exit, q will be driven to 1; it will persist above 1 if entry is barred.

Tobin's q has several advantages over rate of return measures.[10] The numerator of q, market value, reflects expected future profits, whereas accounting data reflect only past profits. Also, the market value of a firm depends partly on risk, so q incorporates an adjustment for risk.* In addition, q is much less sensitive to errors in measuring its components than are profits.†

Unfortunately, q is not without problems. Like rate of return measures, q reflects the operations of the entire firm, creating problems for diversified firms. Also, because accounting data are used to calculate the replacement cost, some of the objections to accounting rates of return also apply to estimates of q.‡

These problems involve the measurement of a firm's capital assets. The use by accountants of depreciation schedules that do not reflect true economic depreciation is a problem for calculation of q, as it was for calculation of accounting rates of return. Also, replacement costs should include the value of intangible as-

---

*Profit rates can be compared with an estimate of the risk-adjusted required rate of return. To do so, however, a specific asset pricing model has to be chosen. q is attractive because it contains the correct risk adjustment, regardless of the true asset pricing model.

†Suppose, for example, that revenues are 110 and costs are 100, giving profits of 10. If costs are measured with a 1 percent error, profits will be mismeasured by 10 percent. (Costs are mismeasured as 101, leading to an estimate of profits of 9.) By contrast, if a firm's capital stock is overestimated by 1 percent, q will be misestimated by only 1 percent.

‡For any publicly traded firm, market value, the numerator of q, is measured by the value of any securities the firm has issued, such as stocks and bonds.

sets resulting from expenditures on advertising and research and development. If a researcher ignores these intangible assets, the denominator of q will be too low, leading to an estimate of q that is greater than one even for competitive firms. In fact, one study estimated average Tobin's q over the period 1960 to 1976 for a sample of U.S. industries, finding a median value of q of 1.35.[11] This could indicate either that firms typically earn positive economic profits or that measurement errors biased q upwards. Without more information, it is not possible to distinguish one explanation from the other.

Correlations Among Measures of Performance

Before turning to measures of structure, it is worth pausing to look at how closely related one measure of performance is to another. A close relationship between two measures would suggest that the choice of which to use is not an important decision. If two measures are not closely related, however, empirical evidence for the link between structural variables and performance may depend on the choice of measure, and the researcher would have to decide whether one measure of profitability is theoretically more appealing than another.

A commonly used statistical measure of the strength of the relationship between two variables is the **correlation coefficient**, r. The correlation coefficient ranges from 1 to −1. If r equals 1, there is a perfect positively sloped linear relationship between the two variables: the value of one variable increases as the value of the other variable does. A correlation coefficient equal to −1 also indicates a perfect linear relationship; in this case the relationship is negative. If r equals 0, no relationship exists between the two variables.

Correlations among the accounting rates of return, such as the rate of return on equity and the rate of return on assets, are high. Liebowitz, for example, finds correlations between one rate of return and another almost always above 0.8.[12] Regression results are usually not sensitive to which measure of rate of return is chosen, so the choice is not critical.

The correlation of accounting rates of return with the price-cost margin, however, is lower. In fact, after calculating correlations among price-cost margins and other measures of profitability, Liebowitz concluded "None of the correlations seems high enough to warrant the conclusion that the census price-cost margin is a close substitute for non-census price-cost margins of any ilk or for other measures of profitability."[13] This low correlation of the price-cost margin with other measures of profitability thus makes the choice more critical. In light of this, Fisher's criticism of using the price-cost margin to infer monopoly power is important. He argues that it is an unreliable estimate of the Lerner index and that the measurement error associated with the price-cost margin can be large.[14] A large measurement error makes it hard to estimate relationships precisely; there is a lot of "noise" in the data. A more serious problem occurs if the measurement error is correlated, either positively or negatively, with the independent variables included in an SCP regression equation. A systematic relationship between the measurement error and the independent variables causes bias in the estimated coefficients. As a consequence, a statistical study may miss a true economic relationship or may report a spurious relationship. Fisher indeed shows that the measurement error is likely to be systematically related to the independent variables used in SCP regressions. His argument thus calls into question the results of studies that use the price-cost margin as the measure of performance.

What about the relationship between accounting rates of return and q? For the purpose of comparison, Salinger estimated regressions using both the rate of return on assets and q as the dependent variable.[15] He found that the results in the profitability regressions are significantly different from the results in the q regressions. Shepherd, however, notes that the profit rate and q are highly correlated with each other; he finds "similar patterns" in regressions using profit rates and those using q to measure profitability.[16] Further evidence on the reliability of alternative measures of profitability comes from a set of simulation experiments conducted by McFarland.*[17] McFarland's results suggest that, although measurement error exists both for estimates of q and for accounting rates of return, estimates of q are more closely related to the true value. The experiments also suggest that the measurement errors in both q and the rate of return may cause a bias in the estimated coefficients. Reassuringly, however, McFarland concluded that accounting measures of both q and the rate of return are useful measures of profitability, although they should be used with care.[18]

Summary of Measures of Profitability

We have covered a considerable amount of difficult ground, raising many questions about alternative measures of firm profitability. At this point it is reasonable to ask whether the flaws in accounting data are so serious that these data should not be used at all. This is the view of some economists.[19] Others, however, believe that the data can be used with caution.[20] We agree with those who believe that these data contain useful information, provided that researchers identify biases and correct for them whenever possible. At a minimum, if correcting for biases is not possible, the direction and likely magnitude of the bias should be considered in the interpretation of empirical results.

MEASURES OF MARKET STRUCTURE

A structure-conduct-performance study searches for a link between various elements of market structure and a measure of performance. In this section we consider the measures of structure commonly used in these studies. Fortunately, we already covered much of this material in earlier chapters.

Measures of Concentration

A key variable in most SCP studies is a measure of market concentration. As we saw in Chapter 4, there are several possible measures of market concentration. Ideally, oligopoly theory would indicate which measure of concentration is ap-

---

*These experiments were done using Monte Carlo methods. In these experiments, a universe of firms with known values of q and the rate of return is constructed, allowing the researcher to know "the truth." Then accounting estimates of the two measures of profitability are calculated and compared with the true values.

propriate.* Several authors have, in fact, used oligopoly theory to argue for a particular measure of concentration. In an early article, Stigler suggested using the Herfindahl-Hirschman index (HHI), arguing that it can be used to detect cheating on collusive agreements.[21] Cowling and Waterson also favored the HHI; they showed that if firms behave as Cournot oligopolists, the HHI is related to the weighted average of firms' price-cost margins.[22]

Under alternative behavioral assumptions, however, the concentration ratio is the appropriate measure. Thomas Saving modeled an industry consisting of a dominant group of firms and a competitive fringe. Using this model, profits of the industry and of the dominant firms increase with CR_n, the share of sales produced by the n dominant firms.[23] Unfortunately, therefore, theory does not give us an unambiguous choice of concentration ratio. Furthermore, given that some of the hypotheses of interest involve the effect of concentration on behavior, it is problematic to assume a particular model of behavior *ex ante*. Until theory can provide better guidance, it is advisable to view results that are sensitive to the choice of specification or of sample with some caution.[†]

Barriers to Entry

For a firm to maintain its price above the competitive level over time, there must be barriers to entry into the industry. Economists who have studied the determinants of market performance have, therefore, typically included some measure of entry barriers in their studies.

Chapter 5 discussed barriers to entry in detail. We saw which elements of market structure have been identified by economists as potential barriers, and we considered the methodologies used to measure barriers.

Some economists, beginning with Bain, used surveys in combination with publicly available evidence on specific industries to develop subjective estimates of the difficulty of entering those industries. Tables 5.2 and 5.3 gave examples of this kind of classification.

Many more economists have used proxies for entry barriers as independent variables in their regression equations. The variables included to measure entry barriers are similar to those used in the empirical studies of the determinants of

---

*In addition to choosing a measure of concentration, a researcher must also think about the definition of the market. As discussed in Chapter 4, markets as defined by the compilers of official statistics are often flawed. Many researchers accept the markets as given. Others try to correct for problems in market definition in various ways: dropping observations from the sample for which markets do not seem to be sensibly defined (Bain, 1951), adjusting published data for the existence of regional markets (W. G. Shepherd, *The Treatment of Market Power* [New York: Columbia University Press, 1974], or including the ratio of imports to domestic production to control for foreign competition (R. E. Caves, "International Trade and Industrial Organization: Problems, Solved and Unsolved," *European Economic Review* 28, [1985]: 377–95).

†Alternative measures of concentration tend to be highly correlated. However, the choice among even highly concentrated measures of concentration can affect the results. (See the discussion in Chapter 4 as well as Leo Sleuwaegen and Wim Dehandschutter, "The Critical Choice Between the Concentration Ratio and the *H*-index in Assessing Industry Performance," *Journal of Industrial Economics*, 35 [1986]: 193–8.)

entry discussed in Chapter 5. The commonly used measures of barriers to entry include:

1. Economies of scale: often approximated by the ratio of midpoint plant sales, the sales of the plant in the middle of the size distribution of plants, to total industry sales.

2. Capital requirements: typically measured by the estimated amount of capital required by a midpoint plant.

3. Product differentiation: Several measures of product differentiation have been used in SCP studies. The most common is advertising intensity, measured by the ratio of advertising expenditures to sales.

Some economists have estimated their regression equation separately for producer and consumer goods industries. As explained in Chapter 13, the argument for doing this is that advertising and other forms of product differentiation are expected to have less effect on concentration and on profitability in producer goods industries than in consumer goods industries, because buyers in producer goods industries tend to be large and well informed. This gives firms less room in producer goods industries than in consumer goods industries for persuasive advertising and for collusion that would increase profits.

Another way to allow the effect of concentration on profitability to differ across producer versus consumer goods industries is to include an interactive variable such as (CR4 × CONS) in the regression. This variable is the product of the four-firm concentration ratio and the percentage of industry sales going to consumer goods markets. Including this variable allows for a finer discrimination than the dichotomous choice of consumer versus producer goods industries does.

4. Research intensity: usually measured by the ratio of R&D expenditures to sales.*

Other Variables

Researchers have used a variety of additional explanatory variables in SCP studies. One is some measure of recent sales growth. This variable is included to control for the effects of disequilibrium.†

A second variable is the degree of unionization. This variable is included to test the hypothesis that a union may be able to capture at least some of the excess profits generated by product market power by bargaining for higher wages.

---

*As noted in the discussion of the determinants of entry in Chapter 5, research intensity might facilitate entry rather than serving as a barrier to entry. Empirical evidence is therefore necessary to determine the direction of the effect on profits.

†Note that there is no relationship between the degree of competition within an industry and short-run profits. In each of the four industry structures—perfect competition, monopolistic competition, oligopoly, and monopoly—short-run economic profits can be positive, zero, or negative, suggesting that a researcher should try to avoid disequilibrium periods when estimating an SCP study.

Early Structure-Conduct-Performance Studies

The first SCP empirical work primarily involved detailed case studies of individual industries.[24] These studies were extremely time-consuming and greatly limited by data constraints. Beginning with the work of Bain in the 1950s, economists employed an inter-industry, cross-section approach to examine the relationships among various measures of market structure, conduct, and performance.[25]

By today's standards, the empirical approach Bain used to test his hypotheses is simple. He gathered data on manufacturing industries and organized these data into groups according to a structural characteristic of interest, with the main focus on market concentration. After grouping the data, Bain compared average profit rates across groups to see if they differed. Bain's measure of profits for each industry was the average of the largest firms' (up to four per industry) accounting rate of return on stockholders' equity.*

Bain conducted two pioneering studies examining the relationship between profitability and market concentration. In these works Bain hypothesized that firms in highly concentrated industries were better able to collude, which led to increased prices and profits. In his first test of this hypothesis, Bain used data for forty-two manufacturing industries and divided his sample into two groups: those with an eight-firm concentration ratio above 70 percent and those with an eight-firm concentration ratio below 70 percent. As expected, Bain found that the more concentrated industries had higher average profit rates.

In his second study, Bain examined the simultaneous effect of market concentration and barriers to entry on profitability. He predicted that profits would be higher in concentrated industries with high barriers to entry than in concentrated industries with low barriers to entry. For this study, Bain used a sample of twenty manufacturing industries, noting that the amount of work needed to collect information about each industry imposed a "practical limitation" on the sample size.[26] His sample covered the periods 1936 to 1940 and 1947 to 1951.

Table 17.1 shows Bain's results, reporting the profit rate and four-firm concentration ratio for each industry organized by height of entry barriers. Bain found a statistically significant difference between the average profit rates of industries with *very high* entry barriers and those in the other categories.† Being in the substantial entry barriers category as opposed to the moderate to low entry barriers category, however, did not lead to a statistically significant difference in average profit rates. Although profit rates tended to increase with market concentration, Bain concluded that ". . . *seller concentration alone is not an adequate indicator of the probable incidence of extremes of excess profits and monopolistic output restriction.* The concurrent influence of the condition of entry should clearly be

---

*Bain used the average of the largest firms' profit rates because he hypothesized that concentration and entry barriers would primarily benefit the largest firms in an industry.

†Recall from Chapter 2 that a result is statistically significant if it is very unlikely to have occurred by chance.

TABLE 17.1 **Entry Barriers, Concentration, and Profit, 1947–1951: Results from Bain's Study**

Industry	CR4	Profit Rate (%)
Very high entry barriers		
Automobiles	90	23.9
Cigarettes	90	12.6
Typewriters	79	18.0
Liquor	75	18.6
Fountain pens	57	21.8
Average	78	19.0
Substantial entry barriers		
Copper	92	14.6
Gypsum products	85	15.4
Soap	79	15.8
Metal containers	78	10.7
Steel	45	11.2
Petroleum refining	37	12.9
Farm machines and tractors	36	13.4
Shoes (high-priced men's)	28	13.4
Average	60	13.4
Moderate to low entry barriers		
Rayon	78	18.0
Tires and tubes	77	12.7
Meat packing	41	5.1
Cement	30	14.3
Flour	29	10.1
Shoes	28	11.0
Canned fruits and vegetables	27	9.8
Average	44	11.6

Source: Joe S. Bain, *Barriers to New Competition* (Cambridge: Harvard University Press, 1956), p. 195.

taken into account."[27] This result is consistent with oligopoly models that predict that oligopolists may set price close to the competitive level if entry barriers are low.

Using Bain's methodology, Mann got similar results for data from 1950 to 1960.[28] In Mann's sample, profits were higher in more concentrated industries. The average rate of return for sample industries with eight-firm concentration ratios above 70 percent was 13.3 percent, whereas for industries in the less concentrated group, the average rate of return was only 9.0 percent. Like Bain, Mann found a distinct difference between the average profit rates for the very high entry barriers group and the other two entry barrier groups. Although there was also a profit rate difference between the substantial and the moderate to low barriers groups, it was less than half the difference between the average in the very high entry barriers group and that in the substantial entry barriers group.

Econometric Studies

Shortly after Mann's study was published, the empirical technique used to examine the structure-performance relationship changed, largely because of advances in computer technology. Economists began to estimate regressions, which allowed them to identify the effect of one variable on another variable while controlling for other influences. We turn now to a consideration of these studies, focusing first on the relationship between concentration and profitability.

CONCENTRATION AND PROFITABILITY: EVIDENCE FROM INDUSTRY-LEVEL STUDIES

Because they are published on a regular basis in the *Census of Manufactures*, industry-level data are easily available. Thus, many of the econometric studies of structure-performance relationships used large cross-section samples of manufacturing industries.

Collins and Preston

An early and influential industry-level study was published by Collins and Preston in 1969.[29] Their basic hypothesis was the same as Bain's: that, all other things equal, more highly concentrated industries should exhibit higher average profits. To test this hypothesis, Collins and Preston regressed the price-cost margin on the four-firm concentration ratio, the capital-sales ratio, and a measure of geographic dispersion.* Their sample consisted of data for 417 industries from the 1963 *Census of Manufactures*.

Table 17.2 shows Collins and Preston's regression results using the entire sample. The main coefficient of interest for testing the hypothesis that higher concentration facilitates collusion and thus higher profits is that of the four-firm concentration ratio. Table 17.2 shows that, as expected, the coefficient of concentration is positive and statistically significant, meaning that it is unlikely to occur by chance.†

---

*As discussed earlier, the capital-sales ratio is typically included in regressions using the price-cost margins because of the way these margins are calculated. An index of geographic dispersion is included to account for the fact, discussed in Chapter 4, that some geographic markets are primarily regional or local rather than national, as is assumed in the calculation of concentration ratios.

†The estimated coefficients of the capital-sales ratio and the index of geographic dispersion also have the expected signs and are statistically significant.

TABLE 17.2 **Collins and Preston's Results—Overall Sample**

PCM = 19.54 + 0.096[a]CR4 + 0.092[a]CSR − 0.029[b]DISP R^2 = 0.19

Abbreviations: PCM, price-cost margin; CR4, four-firm concentration ratio; CSR, capital-sales ratio; DISP, index of geographic dispersion.

[a]Significant at 1 percent level; such an estimate would occur only once in 100 times by chance, on average.

[b]Significant at 5 percent level; such an estimate would occur only five times in 100 by chance, on average.

Source: Norman R. Collins and Lee E. Preston, "Price-Cost Margins and Industry Structure," *Review of Economics and Statistics* (August 1969), p. 277.

Weiss

After the publication of Collins and Preston's study, economists used the same general methodology but included additional independent variables to control for factors other than concentration that affect profitability. One representative example is shown in Eq. 17.2, which is taken from a study by Weiss.[30]

$$PCM = 16.3 + 0.050\ CR4 - 0.029\ DISP + 0.119\ CAP/S \qquad [17.2]$$
$$ (2.08) \qquad (2.00) \qquad\quad (7.44)$$

$$+\ 1.30\ A/S - 1.90\ CAO + 0.023\ INV/S$$
$$(7.20) \qquad (0.42) \qquad\quad (0.169)$$

$$+\ 0.26\ GROW + 0.00083\ CONSxCR4$$
$$(2.90) \qquad\qquad (2.70)$$

$$+\ 0.095\ MID - 0.033\ PLANTCAP$$
$$(0.38) \qquad\quad (1.65)$$

$$N = 399,\ R^2 = 0.427$$

(t statistics of the estimated coefficients are shown in parentheses. A t statistic greater than 1.97 is statistically significant at a 5 percent level.)

where   PCM = price-cost margin; CR4 = the four-firm concentration ratio; DISP = an index of geographic dispersion (High values of DISP indicate low levels of dispersion of production. This variable is included to correct for poorly defined markets); CAP/S = the ratio of capital to sales; A/S = the ratio of advertising to sales; CAO = the ratio of central office employment to total employment (Like CAP/S, this variable is included because of the way price-cost margins are calculated); INV/S = the ratio of inventories to sales; GROW = past output growth; CONSxCR4 = the four-firm concentration ratio multiplied by the percentage of industry sales going to consumer goods markets; MID = the ratio of midpoint plant sales (the sales of the plant in the middle of the size distribution of plants) to total industry sales; and PLANTCAP = the estimated amount of capital required by a midpoint plant.

Summary of Industry-Level Results

Weiss's results are consistent with, and therefore a good example of, the cross–section industry-level studies of the determinants of profitability done in the 1960s and 1970s. Such studies usually found the estimated coefficient of concentration to be positive and statistically significant.*

Given the general robustness of the results of cross-section industry studies done in the 1960s and 1970s, most economists accepted the structure-conduct-performance hypothesis underlying these regressions. Higher levels of concentration were thought to facilitate collusion among firms, resulting in prices above marginal cost. This relationship appeared to be particularly strong in the presence of high barriers to entry.

Effects of Other Elements of Market Power on Profits

Many variables in addition to a measure of concentration have been included in cross-section SCP studies. Several of these are intended to measure barriers to entry.

Although Collins and Preston did not include any explanatory variables to measure barriers to entry, they did estimate their regression equation separately for consumer and producer goods industries. Table 17.3 reports Collins and Preston's results for the separate subsamples, which support the hypothesis that behavior differs in consumer and producer goods industries.

The estimated coefficient of concentration is much higher and its statistical significance is stronger for consumer than for producer goods industries. In consumer goods industries, increasing the concentration ratio by 10 percentage points (e.g., from 50 to 60 percent) would increase the average price-cost margin by 1.99 percent. In producer goods industries, however, the same increase in the concentration ratio would increase the average price-cost margin by only 0.3 percent.[†] As expected, concentration has a larger effect on profits in consumer goods industries, in which barriers to entry based on product differentiation are higher, than in producer goods industries.

---

*Hundreds of studies have examined the robustness of the industry-level structure-performance results, using different econometric techniques, samples, and explanatory variables. Worth mentioning are studies that examine the effects of competition from foreign suppliers. As theory suggests, imports as a percent of domestic sales are negatively associated with profitability: the ability of domestic firms to exercise market power is limited by competition from foreign firms.

†To give you an idea of how much of an increase this represents, the average price-cost margin in Collins and Preston's sample was .249.

TABLE 17.3	**Collins and Preston's Results—Consumer and Producer Goods Industries**

Consumer	PCM = 17.36 + 0.199[a]CR4 + 0.103 CSR − 0.022 DISP R^2 = 0.28
Producer	PCM = 19.48 + 0.033[b]CR4 + 0.133[a]CSR − 0.035[a]DISP R^2 = 0.26

Abbreviations: PCM, price-cost margin; CR4, four-firm concentration ratio; CSR, capital-sales ratio; DISP, index of geographic dispersion.

[a]Significant at 1 percent level; such an estimate would occur only once in 100 times by chance, on average.

[b]Significant at 10 percent level; such an estimate would occur only once in 10 times by chance, on average.

Source: Norman R. Collins and Lee E. Preston, "Price-Cost Margins and Industry Structure," *Review of Economics and Statistics* (August 1969), p. 277.

Other studies also found that the effect of concentration on profits is greater in consumer goods industries than in producer goods industries. One example is the study by Weiss reported earlier. The positive and statistically significant coefficient of the interaction variable CONSxCR4 in Eq. 17.2 shows that the effect of concentration increases as the percentage of industry sales going to consumer goods markets increases.

Evidence from studies that include advertising intensity as a measure of product differentiation support the hypothesis that consumer and producer goods industries are different. A result that emerges strongly from the available empirical work, much of which was reported in Chapter 13, is that advertising intensity is positively related to average industry profitability.[31] In producer goods industries, however, advertising intensity is negatively related to profitability.[32] Thus, advertising appears to act as a barrier to entry in consumer goods industries but not in producer goods industries.

The estimated coefficients of the variables measuring economies of scale and capital costs, such as MID and PLANTCAP in Weiss's study, tend to be positive in the industry-level studies. The statistical significance of variables such as MID and PLANTCAP tends to vary across studies; in Weiss's study, these variables are not statistically significant.

One explanation for this weak statistical significance is that measures of concentration and measures of scale-related barriers to entry are often highly correlated with each other. When two or more independent variables are highly correlated, estimating the independent effect of any one of them on the dependent variable is difficult. For example, the four-firm concentration ratio tends to increase as economies of scale increase; therefore, it is difficult to separate the effect of the four-firm concentration ratio on profitability from the effect of economies of scale on profitability.

Most evidence from cross-section studies indicates that research and development intensity has a positive effect on profitability. This effect is not as strong, however, when concentration is high. In fact, some evidence indicates that, at high levels of concentration, research intensity is negatively related to concentration.[33]

In considering the effect of factors other than concentration and entry barriers on profitability, the two most commonly included variables are a measure of past industry growth and of unionization. Almost all studies find that recent growth in revenue is positively related to profitability.[34] Unionization has a substantial negative effect on profitability in highly concentrated industries, reducing the price-cost margins by between 17 and 66 percent. The effect of unionization on profitability in unconcentrated industries is much smaller, decreasing price-cost margins between 0 and 13 percent.[35]

CONCEPTUAL PROBLEMS WITH SCP STUDIES

Even as many additional industry-level studies throughout the 1970s confirmed the general structure-performance results, criticisms were raised. Skeptics pointed out a number of conceptual problems and problems of interpretation with the studies, considered below.

Collusion Versus Efficiency

One important criticism concerns the interpretation of the observed statistical relationship between market concentration and profitability. Economists associated with the Chicago School, especially Harold Demsetz, noted that, rather than arising from collusion among leading firms, the statistical relationship between market concentration and profitability might be the result of efficiency.[36]

To understand the efficiency interpretation, suppose that there is in fact *no* relationship between concentration and firms' ability to increase price above marginal cost. Furthermore, suppose that more efficient firms earn both higher profits and a larger market share over time *as a result of* their superior efficiency. This would lead to a positive relationship between market share and profits at the firm level.

What is the connection between the supposed *true* relationship between market share and profits at the firm level and the *observed* relationship between concentration and profits at the industry level? The link is that: (1) high market shares, by definition, lead to high levels of industry concentration and (2) profits of large firms (assumed in this case to be the more profitable firms) receive more weight than profits of smaller firms in the calculation of the industry average level of profits. Therefore, more highly concentrated industries would, in fact, be associated with higher average profit levels, as shown repeatedly in the industry-level structure-performance studies.

Firm-Level Studies. One way to discriminate between the collusion hypothesis and the efficiency hypothesis is to include both concentration and market share in the same equation.[37] To do this, researchers must use a data set that enables them to measure the market share of individual firms. The results of one such study by Ravenscraft are:[38]

$$\text{PCM} = -22.3 + 0.183 \text{ S} - 0.022 \text{ CR4} + \text{other variables} \qquad [17.3]$$
$$(4.95)* \qquad (1.38)*$$

$$N = 3186, \text{ R}^2 = 0.208$$

---

*t-statistics

Eq. 17.3 shows that S, the measure of market share, is strongly and positively correlated with profitability. A firm with a higher market share will have a higher price-cost margin, all else being equal. Note from Eq. 17.3 that including market share in the estimated equation dramatically changes the estimated effect of concentration. The four-firm concentration ratio is now *negatively* associated with profitability, although its statistical significance is somewhat weak. Other firm-level studies using samples of firms from many industries have strongly supported both of Ravenscraft's results: (1) that market share is strongly correlated with profitability and (2) that the estimated coefficient of concentration is either negative or statistically insignificant.[39] Such studies suggest that the well-established connection between average industry profitability and concentration may not actually be a causal connection, but may instead be due to aggregating data from the firm to the industry level.

Can we conclude from the firm-level SCP studies that Demsetz's efficiency hypothesis has won the day? Perhaps not surprisingly, things are not that simple. Evidence from firm-level studies that focus on a specific manufacturing industry complicates the picture. If Demsetz's hypothesis is correct, the more efficient firms within an industry should be more profitable, and thus the positive relationship between market share and profitability should hold using an intra-industry as well as an inter-industry sample. This, however, is not the case. The link between profitability and market share *within* a particular manufacturing industry is not as strong as it is *across* industries, suggesting that the results of the firm-level inter-industry studies may be strongly influenced by a few unrepresentative industries.[40]

Large Versus Small Firms. Given that the evidence from firm-level studies does not definitely support either the collusion or the efficiency hypothesis, can other evidence help? Demsetz argued that evidence on the rates of return of large versus small firms could be used to distinguish between the collusion and the efficiency hypotheses.[41] He reasoned that collusion should benefit all firms in an industry; therefore, if concentration fosters collusion, both small and large firms in concentrated industries should earn higher rates of return. Conversely, if concentration is due to the greater efficiency of large firms, only the large firms in concentrated industries should earn higher rates of return.

Other economists have challenged the hypothesis that collusion ought to benefit *all* firms within a concentrated industry proportionately. Indeed, as noted earlier, Bain expected that concentration would primarily benefit the largest firms in an industry. He, and others, noted that small firms might have inefficiently small plants or smaller product-differentiation advantages than larger firms. The theoretical debate about what can be inferred from profit rate differentials across firms of different sizes continues.

The evidence on the relative rates of return of large versus small firms is also unclear. Some evidence indicates that the positive association between profits and concentration holds for large firms but not for small firms; other evidence shows no systematic differences by size.[42] In a study designed to test the effects of both the concentration and the efficiency explanations on the price-cost margins of firms of different sizes, Martin found support for both hypotheses.[43] His results indicated that increases in productivity increase the price-cost margin of firms in each size group, supporting the efficiency hypothesis. However, the price-cost margins of firms in each size group also increased with the market share of the four largest firms. This result suggests that concentration fosters collusion that benefits all firms in an industry.

Efficiency or Collusion: Summary. The results of tests intended to differentiate the efficiency hypothesis from the collusion hypothesis are, as one researcher said, "discouraging in a number of respects."[44] It seems likely that some complicated firm-specific intra-industry effects have not yet been explained by economic theory.

Assumption of Linearity

A second issue in SCP studies is the exact form of the relationship between concentration and profits. Most studies estimate a linear relationship like that shown in Figure 17.1(a). Some evidence suggests, however, that the relationship is nonlinear or discontinuous.[45] One example of a nonlinear relationship is shown in Figure 17.1(b). In this example, an increase in concentration has a greater effect on performance for intermediate levels of concentration than for either low or high levels. A linear approximation is appropriate if concentration ratios lie between CR_1 and CR_2 but not for very low or very high levels of concentration. As discussed in Chapter 2, assuming linearity when the true functional form is nonlinear may lead to biased estimates.

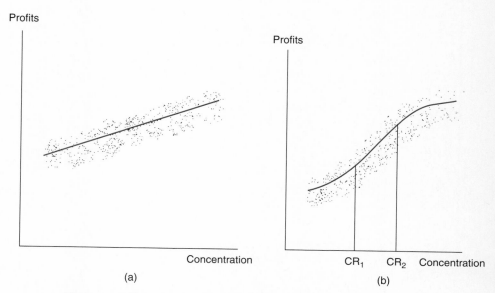

Figure 17.1 Two possible relationships between profits and concentration.

Variations over Time

Fairly recent evidence suggests that the relationship between concentration and profitability may not be stable over time. Domowitz, Hubbard, and Petersen constructed a database on price-cost margins in 284 manufacturing industries between 1958 and 1981.[46] This panel data set allowed them to focus on price-cost margins both across industries and over time.

Table 17.4 shows some of the results from Domowitz, Hubbard, and Petersen's study. This table replicates the basic regression estimated by Collins and

TABLE 17.4 Annual Price-Cost Margins-Concentration Regressions, 1958–1981

Year	Constant	CR4	K/Q	Adjusted R²
1958	.164(.010)	.100(.022)	.079(.017)	.18
1959	.168(.010)	.101(.022)	.100(.019)	.19
1960	.165(.011)	.102(.023)	.089(.019)	.17
1961	.163(.011)	.112(.024)	.077(.018)	.17
1962	.167(.011)	.116(.023)	.076(.018)	.17
1963	.174(.011)	.117(.023)	.080(.018)	.18
1964	.177(.011)	.115(.024)	.081(.019)	.16
1965	.175(.011)	.116(.023)	.096(.018)	.20
1966	.176(.011)	.116(.023)	.093(.018)	.19
1967	.187(.011)	.110(.023)	.076(.016)	.17
1968	.191(.012)	.106(.024)	.087(.017)	.17
1969	.194(.012)	.116(.024)	.068(.018)	.14
1970	.204(.012)	.099(.024)	.050(.017)	.10
1971	.207(.011)	.112(.025)	.038(.018)	.09
1972	.215(.012)	.092(.025)	.049(.018)	.08
1973	.212(.011)	.081(.024)	.079(.018)	.12
1974	.223(.011)	.050(.024)	.098(.021)	.10
1975	.218(.011)	.050(.025)	.071(.021)	.06
1976	.226(.012)	.063(.025)	.059(.023)	.05
1977	.236(.012)	.061(.025)	.042(.024)	.03
1978	.240(.012)	.066(.026)	.020(.024)	.03
1979	.240(.012)	.065(.025)	.042(.024)	.04
1980	.241(.013)	.059(.026)	.028(.025)	.02
1981	.247(.013)	.047(.026)	.021(.026)	.01

Note. Standard errors are in parentheses.

Abbreviations: CR4, four-firm concentration ratio; K/Q, capital-sales ratio.

Source: Ian Domowitz, Glenn R. Hubbard, and Bruce C. Petersen, "Business Cycles and the Relationship Between Concentration and Price-Cost Margins," *Rand Journal of Economics* (Spring 1986), Table 2.

Preston for each of the years in their sample. They found that the coefficient of CR4 initially increased, stabilized during the middle years of the 1960s, and then decreased throughout the remaining years of the sample. The statistical significance of this coefficient also falls from the late 1960s. The explanatory power of the regression, as indicated by the R^2, falls throughout the sample period; by the end of the period, the simple Collins and Preston model has almost no explanatory power.

Domowitz and colleagues explored possible reasons for the changes in the relationship between concentration and price-cost margins over time. Their evidence indicates that industry price-cost margins are sensitive to fluctuations in demand and that margins are more procyclical in concentrated than in unconcentrated industries. Failure to control for demand and business cycle effects therefore leads to biased estimates of the effects of concentration on price-cost margins. They also found some evidence that increased competition from imports reduced the effect of domestic market concentration on price-cost margins over time.

Endogeneity Problem

A final conceptual problem with SCP studies is the assumption that the structural variables are exogenous. The assumed chain of causation runs from market structure to market conduct to market performance. This assumption is clearly too simple: in the long run, conduct affects structure. Mergers affect concentration, the actions of established firms influence the attractiveness of entry, and innovation changes available technologies.

Thus, in the long run, almost all, if not all, structural variables are essentially endogenous. Treating these variables as exogenous can lead to biased estimates. Some authors have estimated models that treat at least some structural variables as endogenous.[47] Most of the studies that acknowledge and try to correct for the endogeneity have yielded estimates very similar to those of the simple SCP regressions. However, the similarity of results may be largely due to the particular methods used to control for the endogeneity.[48] At this point, the most that can confidently be said is that economists have recognized the problem of endogeneity but have not yet solved it definitively.

Prices and Concentration

Some economists have examined *price* rather than *profitability*. Before we briefly review this evidence, consider the relationship between profitability and price. Remember that resources are misallocated if the price of a good is not equal to the marginal cost of that good. We want to know, therefore, if there is a direct relationship between economic profits and pricing above marginal cost.

Consider first a firm in a perfectly competitive industry. Assuming profit-maximizing behavior, price will equal marginal cost. In the short run, economic profits can be positive, zero, or negative. In the long run, however, entry and exit will occur until economic profits are zero.

A monopolistically competitive firm differs from a perfectly competitive firm in that price is set above marginal costs. Thus, unlike a perfectly competitive industry, a monopolistically competitive industry does not produce the optimal quantity from society's viewpoint. Economic profits in the short run can be positive, zero, or negative, but again, because of entry or exit, long-run profits for a monopolistically competitive firm are zero.

Economic theory predicts that price will also be above marginal cost in oligopoly or monopoly. Short-run profits can again be postive, zero, or negative. In the long run, oligopoly or monopoly profits should be zero or positive, depending on the market demand and on the height of barriers to entry.

What do we learn from this brief summary of the predictions of economic theory? First, SCP studies should focus on long-run measures of performance rather than on short-run measures. Second, evidence that long-run profits equal zero does not imply that price equals marginal cost, as is evident from monopolistic competition. Long-run profits will be driven to zero if entry is easy, even if price is greater than marginal cost. Looking directly at price, therefore, is a theoretically attractive way to measure market power.*

Looking at price rather than profitability is also attractive because it avoids the serious accounting problems of profitability studies discussed earlier in this chapter. Finally, because the focus of price studies is a single industry, bias arising from omitted market-specific variables is of less concern than in cross-section profitability studies. The drawback of price studies, however, is that the data are less readily available.

One type of concentration-price study uses data from separate geographic markets in the same industry. Such studies have been done for a variety of markets, including life insurance, banking services, cement, air transportation, newspaper advertising, radio advertising, groceries, legal services, hospital services, beer, and railroads.[49] These studies all show strong evidence of a positive relationship between concentration and the level of price. Given that price-concentration studies have fewer problems than profitability-concentration studies, these robust results provide strong support for the concentration-collusion hypothesis.

A second type of concentration-price study uses time-series data to see how price changes as concentration changes. These studies also find a positive relationship between concentration and price. Some of this evidence comes from mergers or changes in regulation. An example is Xidex Corporation, a microfilm company. Xidex began the 1970s with a market share of 46 percent and then acquired two competitors, raising its market share to 55 percent as a result of the first acquisition and to 70 percent as a result of the second. An examination of Xidex's prices showed that, as a result of these acquisitions, price increased first by 11 percent and then by an additional 23 percent.[50] Another familiar example is long-distance telephone service. The entry of companies such as MCI and

---

*Positive long-run economic profits do, however, provide some information. They indicate that firms possess some degree of market power and that there are barriers to entry into that industry.

Sprint has reduced AT&T's market share and dramatically lowered the price of long-distance calls.

To summarize this brief discussion on price-concentration studies, "Our evidence that concentration is correlated with price is overwhelming."[51] This evidence strengthens the collusion hypothesis rather than the efficiency hypothesis.

Recent Work

Economists continue to use inter-industry studies to investigate the determinants of performance. In response to the criticisms of the SCP studies, however, industrial organization economists have turned to a new kind of empirical research. This approach, sometimes called the "new empirical industrial organization" (NEIO), attempts to use systematic statistical evidence in the study of single industries, rather than a cross-section of industries.

A review of the methodology of the NEIO studies is beyond the scope of this book. Instead, we briefly indicate the main ideas of these studies and summarize the results.[52]

The main ideas underlying the NEIO studies are:

1. Price-cost margins cannot be observed. A researcher, unable to *observe* a firm's marginal cost, can *infer* it from behavior or can use differences between closely related markets to identify the effects of changes in marginal cost. Alternatively, some NEIO studies measure market power without any measure of marginal cost at all.
2. Because of institutional details, industries are so individual that researchers cannot learn anything useful from broad cross-section studies of industries.
3. NEIO studies try to specify and estimate the behavioral equations by which firms set price and quantity.

To date, the evidence of NEIO studies is somewhat limited. The work has primarily focused on the measurement of market power rather than on its causes. Two general statements, however, can be made. The first is that several studies have found market power in some concentrated industries. Of course, this may be partly because an economist who develops a new method for detecting market power is likely to try it out first in those industries most likely to exhibit market power. The choice of industries has been guided by evidence from "old-fashioned" case studies or from prior knowledge of existing cartels.

The second general result of NEIO studies is that anticompetitive conduct is one important cause of high price-cost margins. Some studies find evidence of explicitly collusive behavior.[53]

The NEIO studies are appealing because they provide evidence that does not suffer from the criticisms of the SCP approach. The detail of the studies also makes rebuttal of alternative explanations possible, which is not true of SCP studies. Clearly, additional work on more industries needs to be done.

SUMMARY

1. Detecting market power and measuring its effects on performance have been the focus of much empirical work in industrial organization for many years.

2. The structure-conduct-performance paradigm, introduced in the 1930s and 1940s, hypothesizes that firm performance follows directly from industry structure. According to this paradigm, certain elements of market structure increase the likelihood of collusive behavior, leading to higher prices and profits. Oligopoly models can also be used to show, under certain behavioral assumptions, a link between industrial concentration and profitability.

3. Economists have used several measures of market power in their empirical work. Among these are the Lerner index, excess return on sales, profit rate, price-cost margin, and Tobin's q. Each of these measures has strengths and weaknesses.

4. Problems with several measures of profitability arise from the distinction between economic profits and accounting profits. Capital costs and expenditures on advertising and on research and development, in particular, are treated differently by accountants and by economists.

5. Measures of structure used in structure-conduct-performance studies commonly include measures of market concentration, economies of scale, capital requirements, product differentiation, and research intensity. Hundreds, if not thousands, of these studies have been done.

6. Studies using cross-section industry-level data typically found a strong, statistically significant relationship between market concentration and profitability. This relationship appeared to be particularly strong in the presence of high barriers to entry. Based on this evidence, the structure-conduct-performance paradigm was widely accepted by the early 1970s.

7. Even as additional industry-level studies throughout the 1970s confirmed the general structure-performance results, critics pointed out a number of conceptual problems and problems of interpretation.

8. One important criticism, raised by economists associated with the Chicago School, is that the statistical relationship between market share and profitability might be the result of efficiency rather than of collusion. According to this interpretation, high profits result from low costs rather than high prices, and market concentration is not the *cause* of collusion but the *result* of superior efficiency.

9. Economists have used firm-level data in an attempt to discriminate between the collusion hypothesis and the efficiency hypothesis. These studies suggest that the connection between average industry profitability and concentration may not actually be a causal connection, but may be caused by aggregating data from the firm to the industry level.

10. At this point, the results of the empirical research on concentration and profitability do not support one clear conclusion. Researchers have

learned to be cautious about inferring the existence of market power from market structure.

11. Some economists have examined the relationship between concentration and price, rather than profitability. Concentration-price studies using data from separate geographic markets in the same industry find strong evidence of a positive relationship between concentration and the level of price. Studies using time-series data also find evidence of this relationship.

12. Recent work, called the "new empirical industrial organization," argues that price-cost margins cannot be observed and that industries are so individual that researchers cannot learn anything useful from broad cross-section studies. This work focuses on a single industry and tries to estimate behavioral equation to make inferences about price and quantity.

KEY TERMS

book value

correlation coefficient

depreciation

excess return on sales

market power

price-cost margin

rate of return on stockholders' equity after tax

rate of return on assets after tax

replacement cost

risk-adjusted rate of return

Tobin's q

DISCUSSION QUESTIONS

1. To determine if a firm is earning positive economic profits, a researcher can compare the firm's rate of return to the competitive rate of return. If you were conducting such a study, how would you determine the competitive rate of return?

2. Explain why it is important to adjust rates of return for risk and how neglecting to make such an adjustment can affect the conclusions drawn from an examination of market power.

3. Think of an example of a firm that owns a scarce asset such as a brand name. Do you think this firm has market power? Now suppose that this firm is sold. Explain how the purchase is likely to affect the value of equity or assets. What effect does this have on the reported profits? Has the acquisition reduced the market power of the acquired firm?

4. Accountants use historical cost ("book value") to value a firm's physical capital stock; economists use replacement cost, writing the value of physical capital up or down to reflect its current market price. Discuss how this difference in the valuation of physical capital affects the measurement of market power.

5. Explain how an accountant's treatment of expenditures on advertising and research and development differs from an economist's treatment. What is the significance of this difference for estimating rates of return?

6. Explain what Tobin's q is and why values of q greater than 1 may indicate the existence of market power.

7. Economists have often looked at a sample of manufacturing industries to determine the relationship between an industry's profit rate and its structure.

   a. Based on the structure-conduct-performance paradigm, what is the expected relationship between profit and structure? Explain your answer.

   b. How do economists measure market power within a given industry? Briefly discuss the advantages and disadvantages of alternative measures of market power.

   c. Some economists have also included one or more measures of the height of entry barriers in their estimations. Explain the rationale for including measures of entry barriers.

   d. What features of an industry would you consider in deciding whether entry barriers are high or low? Why?

8. Why might a researcher studying the relationship of profit measures and concentration want to control for the degree of unionization in the study? What might the effect be of leaving this variable out of a regression equation?

9. Evaluate the validity of the following statement: The robust relationship between market concentration and the average profitability of an industry is strong support for the structure-conduct-performance paradigm.

10. Explain the rationale for including both market concentration and a firm's market share in a regression equation explaining profitability.

11. Explain how a firm can charge a price above marginal cost and yet earn zero economic profits.

REFERENCES

1. Early work includes Edward S. Mason, "Price and Production Policies of Large-Scale Enterprise," *American Economic Review* 29 (1939): 61–74; and Edward S. Mason, "The Current State of the Monopoly Problem in the United States," *Harvard Law Review* 62 (1949):1265–85.

2. The phrase "apparent collusion" is taken from J. Cubbin, "Apparent Collusion and Conjectural Variations in Differentiated Oligopoly," *International Journal of Industrial Organization* 2 (1983): 155–64, although others before him had derived relationships between measures of concentration and measures of profitability from

profit-maximizing behavior. See, for example, K. Cowling and M. Waterson, "Price-Cost Margins and Market Structure," *Economica* 43 (1976): 275–86.

3. P. David Qualls, "Concentration, Barriers to Entry, and Long Run Economic Profit Margins," *Journal of Industrial Economics* 20 (April 1972): 146–58.

4. Stanley J. Liebowitz, "What Do Census Price-Cost Margins Measure?" *Journal of Law and Economics* 25 (1982): 231–46.

5. For discussion of the problems associated with using accounting profits, see Franklin Fisher and John McGowan, "On the Misuse of Accounting Rates of Return to Infer

Monopoly Profits," *American Economic Review* 73 (March 1983): 82–97. They argue that the problems with accounting profits are so severe that using "accounting rates of return to make inferences about monopoly profits is a baseless procedure" (p. 89). For rebuttals, see William F. Long and David J. Ravenscraft, "The Misuse of Accounting Rates of Return: Comment," *American Economic Review* 74 (June 1984): 494–500; Stephen Martin, "The Misuse of Accounting Rates of Return: Comment," *American Economic Review* 74 (June 1984): 501–6; J.A. Kay and C.P. Mayer, "On the Application of Accounting Rates of Return," *Economic Journal* 96 (March 1986): 197-207; Henry McFarland, "Evaluating q as an Alternative to the Rate of Return in Measuring Profitability," *Review of Economics and Statistics* (November 1988): 614–22; and Stephen Martin, "The Measurement of Profitability and the Diagnosis of Market Power," *International Journal of Industrial Organization* 6 (September 1988): 301–21.

6. Pioneering use of price-cost margins in SCP studies was by Norman Collins and Lee E. Preston, "Price-Cost Margins and Industry Structure," *Review of Economics and Statistics* 51 (August 1969): 271–86; and *Concentration and Price-Cost Margins in Manufacturing Industries* (Berkeley: University of California Press, 1968).

7. Two studies that estimate marginal costs based on cost functions are Ann F. Friedlaender and Richard H. Spady, "A Derived Demand Function for Freight Transportation," *Review of Economics and Statistics* 62, (1980): 432-41; and Theodore E. Keeler, *Railroads, Freight, and Public Policy* (Washington, D.C.: Brookings Institution, 1983).

8. For criticisms of the price-cost margin as a measure of performance, see Stanley I. Ornstein, "Empirical Uses of the Price-Cost Margin," *Journal of Industrial Economics* 24 (December 1975): 105–17; S.J. Liebowitz, "What Do Census Price-Cost Margins Measure?" *Journal of Law and Economics* 25 (October 1982): 231–46; and Franklin M. Fisher, "On the Misuse of the Profit-Sales Ratio to Infer Monopoly Power," *Rand Journal of Economics* 18 (1987): 384–96.

9. See, for example, Stavros B. Thomadakis, "A Value-Based Test of Profitability and Market Structure," *Review of Economics and Statistics* 59 (1977): 179–85; Eric Lindenberg, and Stephen Ross, "Tobin's q Ratio and Industrial Organization," *Journal of Business* 54 (January 1981): 1-32; Michael A. Salinger, "Tobin's q, Unionization, and

the Concentration-Profits Relationship," *Rand Journal of Economics* 15 (Summer 1984): 159–70; Michael Smirlock, Thomas Gilligan, and William Marshall, "Tobin's q and the Structure-Performance Relationship," *American Economic Review* 74 (December 1984): 1051–60; and Steven Lustgarten and Stavros Thomadakis, "Mobility Barriers and Tobin's q," *Journal of Business* 60 (October 1987): 519–37.

10. See Michael A. Salinger, "Tobin's q, Unionization, and the Concentration-Profits Relationship," *Rand Journal of Economics* 15 (Summer 1984): 159–70; and Henry McFarland, "Evaluating q as an Alternative to the Rate of Return in Measuring Profitability," *Review of Economics and Statistics* 70 (November 1988): 614–22.

11. Eric Lindenberg, and Stephen Ross, "Tobin's q Ratio and Industrial Organization," *Journal of Business* 54 (January 1981): 1-32.

12. Liebowitz, *supra* note 8, p. 245

13. Liebowitz, *ibid.*, p. 241.

14. Franklin M. Fisher, "On the Misuse of the Profits-Sales Ratio to Infer Monopoly Power," *Rand Journal of Economics* 18 (Autumn 1987): 384–96.

15. Salinger, *supra* note 10, pp. 166–7.

16. William G. Shepherd, "Tobin's q and the Structure-Performance Relationship: Comment," *American Economic Review* 76 (December 1986): 1205-10. See also the reply by Smirlock, Gilligan, and Marshall in the same issue, pp. 1211–13.

17. Henry McFarland, "Evaluating q as an Alternative to the Rate of Return in Measuring Profitability," *Review of Economics and Statistics* 70 (November 1988): 614–22.

18. McFarland, *supra* note 10, pp. 621–22.

19. See Fisher and McGowan, *op. cit.*, Fisher, *op. cit.*, and George J. Benston, "The Validity of Profits-Structure Studies with Particular Reference to the FTC's Line of Business Data," *American Economic Review* 75 (March 1985): 37–67.

20. See William F. Long and David J. Ravenscraft, "The Misuse of Accounting Rates of Return: Comment," *American Economic Review* 74 (June 1984): 494–500; Stephen Martin, "The Misuse of Accounting Rates of Return: Comment," *American Economic Review* 74 (June 1984): 501–6; J. A. Kay and C. P. Mayer, "On the Application of Accounting Rates of Return," *Economic Journal* 96 (March 1986): 199-207; F. M. Scherer et al., "The Validity of Studies with Line of Business Data: Comment," *American Economic Review* 77 (March 1987): 205–17; and F. M. Scherer and David Ross, *Industrial Market Structure and Economic Per-*

formance, 3rd edition (Boston: Houghton Mifflin Company, 1990), pp. 421–22.

21. George J. Stigler, "A Theory of Oligopoly," *Journal of Political Economy* 72 (1964): 44–61.

22. Keith Cowling, and Michael Waterson, "Price-Cost Margins and Market Structure," *Economica* 43 (1976): 267–74.

23. Thomas Saving, "Concentration Ratios and the Degree of Monopoly," *International Economic Review* 11 (1970): 139–45.

24. An example is D.H. Wallace, *Market Control in the Aluminum Industry* (Cambridge, MA: Harvard University Press, 1937).

25. Joe S. Bain, "Relation of Profit Rate to Industry Concentration," *Quarterly Journal of Economics* 65 (1951): 293–324; Joe S. Bain, *Barriers to New Competition* (Cambridge: Harvard University Press, 1956).

26. Bain, *ibid.,* 1956, p. 44.

27. Bain, *ibid.,* 1956, p. 201.

28. Michael Mann, "Seller Concentration, Barriers to Entry, and Rates of Return in Thirty Industries, 1950–1960," *Review of Economics and Statistics* 48 (1966): 290–307.

29. Norman R. Collins and Lee E. Preston, "Price-Cost Margins and Industry Structure," *Review of Economics and Statistics* 51 (August 1969): 271–86.

30. Leonard W. Weiss, "The Concentration-Profits Relationship and Antitrust," in Harvey J. Goldschmid et al. (eds.), *Industrial Concentration: The New Learning* (Boston: Little, Brown, 1974), pp. 201–20 and updated in Scherer and Ross, *supra* note 20, p. 427.

31. W.S. Comanor and T.A. Wilson, "Advertising, Market Structure and Performance," *Review of Economics and Statistics* 49 (1967): 423–40; W. S. Comanor and T. A. Wilson, *Advertising and Market Power* (Cambridge: Harvard University Press, 1974); A. D. Strickland and L. W. Weiss, "Advertising, Concentration and Price-Cost Margins," *Journal of Political Economy* 84 (1976): 1109–21; S. Martin, "Advertising, Concentration and Profitability: The Simultaneity Problem," *Bell Journal of Economics* 10 (1979): 639–47; S. Martin, "Entry Barriers, Concentration and Profit," *Southern Economic Journal* 46 (1979): 471–88; J. L. Bothwell, T. F. Cooley, and T. E. Hall, "A New View of the Market Structure-Market Performance Debate," *Journal of Industrial Economics* 32 (1984): 397–417; I. Domowitz, R. G. Hubbard, and B. C. Petersen, "Business Cycles and the Relationship Between Concentration and Price-Cost Margins," *Rand Journal of Economics* 17 (1986): 1–17;

and I. Domowitz, R. G. Hubbard, and B. C. Petersen, "The Intertemporal Stability of the Concentration-Margins Relationship," *Journal of Industrial Economics* 35 (1986): 13–34.

32. R.M. Bradburd and R.E. Caves, "A Closer Look at the Effect of Market Growth on Industries' Profits," *Review of Economics and Statistics* 64 (1982): 635–45; and Domowitz et al. *supra* note 31, (1986) in *Rand*.

33. R.J. Stonebraker, "Corporate Profits and the Risk of Entry," *Review of Economics and Statistics* 58 (1976): 33–9; H.G. Grabowski and D.C. Mueller, "Industrial Research and Development, Intangible Capital Stocks, and Firm Profit Rates," *Bell Journal of Economics* 9 (1978): 328–43; R. A. Connolly and M. Hirschey, "R&D, Market Structure and Profits: A Value-Based Approach," *Review of Economics and Statistics* 66 (1984): 678–81; M. A. Salinger, "Tobin's *q*, Unionization and the Concentration-Profits Relationship," *Rand Journal of Economics* 15 (1984): 159–70; M. Hirschey, "Market Structure and Market Value," *Journal of Business* 58 (1985): 89–98.

34. A good example is Bothwell, Cooley, and Hall, *supra* note 31.

35. Richard B. Freeman and James L. Medoff, *What Do Unions Do?* (New York: Basic Books, 1984); Thomas Karier, "Unions and Monopoly Profits," *Review of Economics and Statistics* 67 (February 1985): pp. 34-42; and Paula B. Voos and Lawrence R. Mishel, "The Union Impact on Profits in the Supermarket Industry," *Review of Economics and Statistics* 68 (August 1986): 513–16.

36. This argument is advanced by, among others, Yale Brozen, "Concentration and Structural and Market Disequilibria," *Antitrust Bulletin* 16 (Summer 1971):244–8; Harold Demsetz, "Industry Structure, Market Rivalry, and Public Policy," *Journal of Law and Economics,* 16 (April 1973): 1–9; Demsetz, "Two Systems of Belief About Monopoly," in Harvey J. Goldschmid et al. (eds.), *Industrial Concentration: The New Learning* (Boston: Little, Brown, 1974), pp. 164–84; Richard B. Mancke, "Causes of Interfirm Profitability Differences: A New Interpretation of the Evidence," *Quarterly Journal of Economics* 88 (May 1974): 181–93; and Almarin Phillips, "A Critique of Empirical Studies of Relations Between Market Structure and Profitability," *Journal of Industrial Economics* (June 1976): 241–9.

37. An early advocate of this test was Leonard W. Weiss, "The Concentration-Profits Relationship and Antitrust," in Harvey J. Goldschmid et al. (eds.), *Industrial Concen-*

tration: The New Learning (Boston: Little, Brown, 1974).

38. David J. Ravenscraft, "Structure-Profit Relationships at the Line of Business and Industry Level," *Review of Economics and Statistics* 65 (February 1983): 22–31.

39. References include J.L. Bothwell, T.F. Cooley, and T.E. Hall, "A New View of the Market Structure-Market Performance Debate," *Journal of Industrial Economics* 32 (1984): 397–417; M. Smirlock, T. Gilligan, and W. Marshall, "Tobin's q and the Structure-Performance Relationship," *American Economic Review* 74 (1984): 1051–60; R. Schmalensee, "Do Markets Differ Much?" *American Economic Review* 75 (1985): 341–51; and D. Mueller, *Profits in the Long Run* (Cambridge: Cambridge University Press, 1986).

40. See Richard Schmalensee, "Inter-Industry Studies of Structure and Performance," in the *Handbook of Industrial Organization*, vol. 2, pp. 984–5.

41. Demsetz, "Two Systems of Belief about Monopoly," *supra* note 36, pp. 164–84.

42. M.E. Porter, "The Structure Within Industries and Companies' Performance," *Review of Economics and Statistics* 61 (May 1979): 214–27; R.T. Masson and J. Shaanan, "Stochastic-Dynamic Limit Pricing: An Empirical Test," *Review of Economics and Statistics* 64 (August 1982): pp. 413-22; M. Marcus, "Profitability and Size of Firm," *Review of Economics and Statistics* 61 (February 1969): 104–7; Louis Amato and Ronald P. Wilder, "The Effects of Firm Size on Profit Rates in U.S. Manufacturing," *Southern Economic Journal* 52 (July 1985): 181–90; and Louis Amato and Ronald P. Wilder, "Market Concentration, Efficiency, and Antitrust Policy: Demsetz Revisited," *Quarterly Journal of Business and Economics* 27 (1988): 3–19.

43. Stephen Martin, "Market Power and/or Efficiency?" *Review of Economics and Statistics* 70 (May 1988): 331–5.

44. Richard Schmalensee, "Collusion Versus Differential Efficiency: Testing Alternative Hypotheses," *Journal of Industrial Economics* 35 (June 1987): 420.

45. Studies examining the form of the concentration-profits relationship include Stephen A. Rhoades and Joe M. Cleaver, "The Nature of the Concentration-Price Cost Margin Relationship for 352 Manufacturing Industries: 1967," *Southern Economic Journal* 40 (June 1973): 90–102; J.A. Dalton and J.W. Penn, "The Concentration-Profitability Relationship: Is There a Critical Concentration Ratio?" *Journal of*

Industrial Economics 25 (1976): 133–42; Lawrence J. White, "Searching for the Critical Concentration Ratio: An Application of the 'Switching of Regimes' Technique," in S. Goldfeld and R. Quandt (eds.), *Studies in Non-Linear Estimation* (Cambridge, MA: Ballinger, 1976); J.E. Kwoka, Jr., "The Effect of Market Share Distribution on Industry Performance," *Review of Economics and Statistics* 59 (1979): 101–9; and R.M. Bradburd and A.M. Over, "Organization Costs, 'Sticky' Equilibria and Critical Levels of Concentration," *Review of Economics and Statistics* 64 (1982): 50–8.

46. Ian Domowitz, R. Glenn Hubbard, and Bruce C. Petersen, "Business Cycles and the Relationship Between Concentration and Price-Cost Margins," *Rand Journal of Economics* 17 (Spring 1986): 1-17.

47. Examples include W.S. Comanor and T.A. Wilson, *Advertising and Market Power* (Cambridge: Harvard University Press, 1974); A.D. Strickland and L.W. Weiss, "Advertising, Concentration and Price-Cost Margins," *Journal of Political Economy* 84 (1976): 1109–21; S. Martin, "Advertising, Concentration and Profitability: The Simultaneity Problem," *Bell Journal of Economics* 10 (1979): 639–47; P.A. Geroski, "Simultaneous Equations Models of the Structure-Performance Paradigm," *European Economic Review* 19 (1982): 145–58; and R.A. Connolly and M. Hirschey, "R&D, Market Structure and Profits: A Value-Based Approach," *Review of Economics and Statistics* 66 (1984): 678–81.

48. See Schmalensee in the *Handbook of Industrial Organization, supra* note 40, pp. 953–6.

49. An incomplete list of references includes J.D. Cummins, H.S. Denenberg, and W.C. Scheel, "Concentration in the U.S. Life Insurance Industry," *Journal of Risk and Insurance* 39 (June 1972): 177–99; R.A. Gilbert, "Bank Market Structure and Competition: A Survey," *Journal of Money, Credit and Banking* 16 (1984): 617–45; Roland H. Koller and L.W. Weiss, "Price Levels and Seller Concentration: The Case of Portland Cement," in L.W. Weiss (ed.), *Concentration and Price* (Cambridge, MA: MIT Press, 1989), pp. 17–40; E.E. Bailey, David R. Graham, and Daniel P. Kaplan, *Deregulating the Airlines* (Cambridge, MA: MIT Press, 1985), pp. 155–65; R.S. Thompson, "Structure and Conduct in Local Advertising Markets," *Journal of Industrial Economics* 33 (December 1984): 241–9; George J. Stigler, "A Theory of Oligopoly," *Journal of Political Economy* 72 (1964): 44–61; F.E. Geithman, H.P. Marvel, and L.W. Weiss, "Con-

centration, Price, and Critical Concentration Ratios," *Review of Economics and Statistics* 63 (1981): 346–53; Ronald W. Cotterill, "Market Power in the Retail Food Industry," *Review of Economics and Statistics* 68 (August 1986): 379–86; John R. Schroeter, Scott L. Smith, and Steven L. Cox, "Advertising and Competition in Routine Legal Service Markets: An Empirical Investigation," *Journal of Industrial Economics* (September 1987): 49–60; Monica Noether, "Competition Among Hospitals," *Journal of Health Economics* 7 (September 1988): 259–84; and James M. MacDonald, "Competition and Railroad Rates for the Shipment of Corn, Soybeans, and Wheat," *Rand Journal of Economics* 18 (Spring 1987): 151–63.

50. David M. Barton and Roger Sherman, "The Price and Profit Effects of Horizontal Merger: A Case Study," *Journal of Industrial Economics* 33 (December 1984): 165–77.

51. Weiss, *Concentration and Price* (Cambridge: MIT Press, 1989), p. 283.

52. This discussion draws on Timothy F. Bresnahan, "Empirical Studies of Industries with Market Power," in *Handbook of Industrial Organization*, pp. 1012–57.

53. R.H. Porter, "A Study of Cartel Stability: The Joint Executive Committee, 1880-1886," *Bell Journal of Economics* 14 (1983): 301–14; and T.F. Bresnahan, "Competition and Collusion in the American Automobile Oligopoly: The 1955 Price War," *Journal of Industrial Economics* 35 (June 1987): 457–82.

PART IV

PUBLIC POLICY AND INTERNATIONAL TRADE

Chapter 18

Antitrust: The Laws and Policy Toward Market Power

Throughout this book we have analyzed the potential problems associated with market power. In fact, if no problems were associated with increased market power there would be far less reason to study industrial organization as a subfield in economics. Chapter 17 investigated the empirical relationship between market power and efficiency. Here we turn our attention to the issue of government attempts to limit the negative effects of market power. In the United States these attempts have centered on two broad policies—antitrust and direct regulation. We begin with an analysis of the antitrust laws in general terms and how the laws have dealt with one major problem: monopoly power.

It is relatively easy to understand the political pressures that led to the passage of the **Sherman Act** in 1890.[1] Before the Civil War, the United States was mainly an agrarian society in which high transportation costs kept the geographic size of most industrial markets small. After the Civil War, the organization of American industry changed dramatically. The rapid growth of national markets in many products developed from a combination of (1) mass production, introduced by the industrial revolution, which resulted in significant economies of scale; (2) a national railroad system, which greatly increased the size of the geographic market for many products; (3) the development of modern capital markets that enabled firms to raise large amounts of capital in the equity market; and (4) the liberalization of the laws of incorporation in many states. With the growth of national markets, many small regional manufacturers faced competition for the first time. The larger national firms, which took advantage of economies of scale, were often able to invade local markets that were formerly insulated from competition and charge significantly lower prices. As the national producers captured a larger and larger share of many local markets, they threatened to eliminate many local producers.

During the 1888 national elections both the Democrats and the Republicans offered platform planks to fight the trusts, and immediately before the election

Republican Senator John Sherman introduced the first Senate antitrust bill. On July 2, 1890, President Harrison signed the measure, an act he probably thought would be little remembered by history.

The Content of the Antitrust Laws

The major provisions of the Sherman Act are Sections 1 and 2, which read in part:

Section 1: Every contract, combination in the form of a trust or otherwise, or conspiracy, in restraint of trade or commerce among the several states, or with foreign nations, is hereby declared to be illegal. Every person who shall make any such contract or engage in any such combination or conspiracy, shall be deemed guilty of a misdemeanor, and, on conviction thereof, shall be punished by fine not exceeding five thousand dollars, or by imprisonment not exceeding one year, or by both said punishments, in the discretion of the court. . . .

Section 2: Every person who shall monopolize, or attempt to monopolize, or combine or conspire with any other person or persons to monopolize any part of the trade or commerce among the several States, or with foreign nations, shall be deemed guilty of a misdemeanor. . . .

On a first reading, the Sherman Act sounds quite strong. Certain problems, with regard to the legal implications of the wording of the Act, arose soon after its passage, however. Section 1 made it illegal for competitors to combine to fix prices and created an incentive for firms to get around the law by *merging* with competitors. Paradoxically, therefore, the first major merger wave in the United States at the turn of the century was encouraged and fueled by the Sherman Act.

Another major problem developed from the somewhat ambiguous wording of Section 2. During the 1890s, Section 2 was completely ineffective in dealing with the monopolization problem. In 1911 two major decisions, the *Standard Oil* and *American Tobacco* rulings, provided both hope for enforcement and confusion with regard to what constituted a violation of Section 2. In its famous *Standard Oil* decision the Supreme Court ruled that only *unreasonable* attempts to monopolize violated the Sherman Act. This interpretation made only the verb "to monopolize" illegal, while permitting the noun "monopoly" to exist as long as the monopoly did not result from an aggressive attempt to monopolize. This precedent has come to be known as the **Rule of Reason**.

Partly as a result of the handing down of the Rule of Reason, and partly as a result of a lack of clarity in the wording of the Sherman Act with regard to certain types of specific business conduct, by 1912 there were calls for new legislation. What emerged in 1914 were two pieces of major antitrust legislation, the **Clayton Act** and the **Federal Trade Commission Act**.

The Clayton Act aimed to prevent certain specific types of business conduct. It contained the following four substantive sections:

Section 2 forbade price discrimination "where the effect of such discrimination may be to substantially lessen competition or tend to create a monopoly in any line of commerce." The section provided for three defenses: discrimination based on the quantity sold; the different costs of selling or transportation; or the need to meet a competitor's lower price. These defenses, particularly the quantity defense, turned out to be large loopholes in Section 2.

Section 3 forbade **tying contracts**, which forced a purchaser to buy good X to obtain good Y, and **exclusive dealing arrangements**, which forced a buyer to purchase its entire supply of a commodity from one seller.

Section 7 forbade the acquisition of the *stock* of another corporation if the acquisition would "restrain commerce in any section or community or tend to create a monopoly of any line of commerce." The section was directed at the merger wave that had developed after the passage of the Sherman Act, and was limited to horizontal mergers between direct competitors.

Section 8 forbade interlocking directorates between any two competing corporations. This prevented the same individual from sitting on the Boards of Directors of competing companies.

The **Federal Trade Commission Act** established the **Federal Trade Commission** (FTC) as an independent antitrust agency to enforce the Clayton Act. The FTC Act also contained one major substantive provision, Section 5, which reads in part:

> The commission is hereby empowered and directed to prevent persons, partnerships, or corporations, except banks, and common carriers subject to the Acts to regulate commerce, from using unfair methods of competition in commerce.

One can hardly imagine a broader mandate. "Unfair methods of competition" could include just about any business practice. Furthermore, many practices considered "unfair" by competitors may have a positive effect on competition. The FTC had little power in its early days. In fact, its only available remedy was to issue cease and desist orders.

The next major antitrust statute was the **Robinson-Patman Act** of 1936, which dealt with price discrimination. The Robinson-Patman Act amended Section 2 of the Clayton Act to include the following major provisions:

> *Section 2(a):* That it shall be unlawful for any person engaged in commerce, in the course of such commerce, either directly or indirectly, to discriminate in price between different purchasers of commodities of like grade and quality, . . . where the effect of such discrimination may be substantially to lessen competition or tend to create a monopoly in any line of commerce, or to injure, destroy or prevent competition with any person who either grants or knowingly receives the benefit of such discrimination, or with customers of either of them:
>
> PROVIDED, That nothing herein contained shall prevent differentials which make only due allowance for differences in the cost of manufacture, sale, or delivery resulting from the differing methods or quantities in which such commodities are to such purchasers sold or delivered.

Section 2(b): PROVIDED, HOWEVER, That nothing herein contained shall prevent a seller rebutting the *prima facie* case thus made by showing that his lower price or the furnishing of services or facilities to any purchaser or purchasers was made in good faith to meet an equally low price of a competitor, or the services or facilities by a competitor. . . .

Section 2(f): That it shall be unlawful for any person engaged in commerce, in the course of such commerce, knowingly to induce or receive a discrimination in price which is prohibited by this section.

The Robinson-Patman Act contained three additional sections that declared specific types of price discrimination illegal per se. An action is illegal per se if there is no acceptable legal justification for undertaking the action. In antitrust law most restraints of trade come under the Rule of Reason interpretation and can be justified by a "reasonableness" defense; a few actions, however, are illegal per se and cannot be justified as being "reasonable" restraints of trade. The sections of the Robinson-Patman Act pertaining to specific types of price discrimination attempted to close potential loopholes in the Act. *Section 2(c)* forbade the payment of any brokerage commission except for services actually rendered by an independent broker. This section was intended to prevent large grocery chains such as A&P from setting up their own brokerage agencies that would then "charge" their suppliers a brokerage "fee" for the act of transferring goods from A&P to A&P. *Section 2(d)* forbade a supplier from paying its buyers for promotional services, unless the payments were made available to all buyers on "proportionally equal terms." Finally, *Section 2(e)* forbade the supplier from providing promotional services to any buyer unless the services were made available to all buyers on "proportionally equal terms."

The Robinson-Patman Act is extremely controversial because it has often been used to protect individual competitors rather than the competitive process. The potential problems are easily seen in a careful reading of Section 2(a), which extended the Clayton Act's wording "where the effect of such discrimination may be substantially to lessen competition or tend to create a monopoly," to include the words "where the effect may be substantially . . . to injure, destroy, or prevent competition with any person. . . ." The addition of this last clause justified using the Robinson-Patman Act in cases in which price discrimination injured just one competitor, even if the discrimination actually increased effective competition and improved economic efficiency.

The final major amendment to the Clayton Act occurred in 1950 with the passage of the **Celler-Kefauver Act**. In 1926 the Supreme Court emasculated Section 7 of the Clayton Act when it ruled that corporations could legally avoid the law by acquiring the *assets* rather than the *stock* of another corporation. It wasn't until 1950 that this loophole was plugged. The Celler-Kefauver Act amended Section 7 of the Clayton Act to include mergers through asset as well as stock acquisition. The Celler-Kefauver Act also extended Section 7 to reach *vertical* and *conglomerate* mergers as well as horizontal mergers. With the passage of the Celler-Kefauver Act, Section 7 of the Clayton Act finally had some clout in dealing with anticompetitive mergers. It took thirty-six years, however, to plug this loophole.

◢ *Enforcement Procedures*

Antitrust enforcement typically begins with an action by either the Antitrust Division of the Justice Department or the Federal Trade Commission. Most cases are precipitated by either a complaint from a competitor or a report in the business press. Occasionally a case begins with a staff report from a government agency.

Once a Justice Department case is in the federal court system, it proceeds to trial and a decision in the District Court. Either side can appeal the District Court's decision to one of eleven Circuit Courts of Appeal. Once the Circuit Court rules, either side can appeal to the Supreme Court. The Supreme Court will hear the case (grant *certiorari*) if at least four justices agree that the legal issues warrant a hearing. Otherwise, the Supreme Court refuses to hear the case (*certiorari* denied) and the Circuit Court's decision stands. The entire process is typically long and drawn out with litigation periods averaging over five years, and some major cases lasting several decades.

The workings of the FTC are different from the Antitrust Division. The FTC is headed by five commissioners who are appointed by the President to serve seven-year terms. Although some Commissioners have been well trained in economics, many others have little understanding of economics because they are primarily political appointees. Initially an FTC case goes before an administrative law judge who works for the FTC. Based on a hearing that is very similar to a District Court trial, the administrative law judge makes a ruling. The judge's opinion can be appealed to the full commission by either the respondent or the FTC staff. The five-member commission hears the appeal and makes a decision, which only the respondent can appeal to the Circuit Court of Appeals. After the Circuit Court decision, either the FTC or the respondent can appeal to the Supreme Court.

Antitrust suits can also be filed by private parties. In fact, in most years private antitrust cases have greatly outnumbered government cases. In 1976, for example, 95.6 percent of all antitrust cases were filed by private parties.[2] Furthermore, for many firms the threat of a large private suit is much greater than the threat of a government action because private cases can result in treble damage awards that can dwarf the fines imposed in government cases.

REMEDIES

In the event of a government victory, there are several possible penalties or remedies. In criminal cases fines and jail sentences may be imposed. The original Sherman Act set a maximum fine of $5,000 per violation. This limit was increased to $50,000 in 1955, to $1,000,000 in 1974, and to $10,000,000 in 1992. The maximum imprisonment for a criminal violation was increased to three years in 1974. Recently the FTC has been given the power to impose a fine of $5,000 per day on any respondent who refuses to abide by an FTC order. To America's largest and most powerful corporations, these fines are likely to look insignificant. A $1,000,000 fine imposed on General Motors is likely to have about as much effect as a $5,000 fine imposed on H. Ross Perot or Donald Trump.

In civil cases, only remedies, not penalties, can be imposed. The distinction between a remedy and a penalty is purely semantic because many antitrust remedies provide more of a threat to violators than the maximum criminal penalties do. Civil remedies may include conduct or structural changes. In cases in which conduct is believed to be the major problem, injunctions are often issued forbidding a certain type of conduct, such as forbidding price discrimination or tying. Injunctions change future behavior without penalizing the defendant for past behavior.

In some extreme cases, the courts may adopt structural remedies. Structural remedies include divestiture, dissolution, and divorcement. These remedies have been used most commonly in merger cases. On a few occasions divestiture has been ordered in monopolization cases under Section 2 of the Sherman Act.

Policy Toward Monopolization

Monopoly power is often associated with *static* and *dynamic* inefficiencies, but monopoly power may be economically justified if it is based on economies of scale or necessary for invention and innovation. Policy makers, therefore, face the difficult task of trying to distinguish cases of justified monoply power from cases of unjustified monopoly power. Enforcement has ebbed and flowed with political trends: first fairly tight, then loose, then tight again, and recently loose once more. An understanding of antitrust policy, therefore, requires a historical as well as an economic perspective. We begin with an examination of early court interpretations and then show how that interpretation has changed over time.

EARLY CASES

NORTHERN SECURITIES CASE[3] (1904)—At the turn of the century two large railway systems monopolized the northwestern United States, the Great Northern Railway Company and the Northern Pacific Railway Company. In 1901 the Great Northern tried to gain control of the Northern Pacific through the creation of a holding company, The Northern Securities Company, which was established to acquire the stock of both the Great Northern and the Northern Pacific, but in 1904 the Supreme Court ordered the merger dissolved. There was no evidence in the *Northern Securities* case suggesting that the two firms had abused their market power or were aggressive toward competitors. The majority opinion was based on the simple *structural* principle that the combination had monopolized trade in the market "railroads in the northwestern United States." This precedent, however, was short lived.

STANDARD OIL OF NEW JERSEY CASE[4] (1911)—The *Standard Oil* case is unquestionably one of America's most famous legal cases. As discussed in Chapter 10, the case dealt with Standard's control of the oil refining industry during the last quarter of the nineteenth century. Recall that all of Standard Oil's actions seemed to be aimed at one objective: maintaining control over the oil refining business in the United States. Standard managed to maintain a 90 percent share for a long period by acquiring over 100 competitors through merger; controlling the major oil pipelines, which permitted it to cut off crude oil supplies from its competitors; obtaining freight rebates from railroads on not only its own shipments but its *competitors'* shipments as well; and, perhaps, using localized price cutting to drive its more stubborn competitors out of the market. In retrospect it appears that Standard rarely relied on predatory price cutting as a competitive weapon because it was less costly to buy out competitors by offering premium prices for their stock.[5]

The Supreme Court ruled unanimously against Standard Oil. In his landmark decision, Chief Justice White laid down his famous Rule of Reason doctrine, which declared that only unreasonable attempts to monopolize violated Section 2.

Chief Justice White emphasized Standard's intent and positive drive as being the key necessary to any conviction under Section 2. The significance of the *Standard Oil* decision from a legal and economic standpoint cannot be overstated. The decision firmly established the precedent that market power, in and of itself, is insufficient to condemn a firm under Section 2. Power must be combined with some effort to obtain and abuse that power. Standard Oil violated Section 2 not simply because it controlled 90 percent of the market, but because it went beyond the use of "normal methods of industrial development" to maintain control.

The Rule of Reason has resulted in cases that require proof of both the existence of market power and some effort to obtain that power through other than normal methods of business.

Immediately after the *Standard Oil* ruling, the Supreme Court handed down a companion decision in the *American Tobacco* case.[6] The points of law in the *American Tobacco* case were virtually identical to those in the *Standard Oil* case. Chapter 10 discussed the *American Tobacco* case as an illustration of a very aggressive "attempt to monopolize." Given American Tobacco's behavior, it is not surprising that the Court condemned its conduct and ruled against the Tobacco Trust.

After the *Standard Oil* and *American Tobacco* precedents, the government won several additional victories during the next decade. In 1920, however, the next major Supreme Court ruling took a different turn, greatly affecting subsequent antitrust policy.

US STEEL CASE[7] (1920)—The details of the *US Steel* case were discussed in Chapter 9. Recall that US Steel cooperated with its competitors through a variety of methods, such as pools, associations, trade meetings, and most famously (or infamously) through the Gary Dinners, at which Judge Elbert Gary, President of US Steel, invited competitors to "dinner" for the more or less expressed purpose of stabilizing and fixing prices.

By a 4–3 ruling, the Supreme Court acquitted US Steel and, in so doing, considerably weakened Section 2 for years to come. The four-Justice majority believed that US Steel could not control steel prices. The court reasoned that because US Steel had to conspire with its competitors to fix prices, it did not have monopoly power. This line of reasoning ignored the fact that if US Steel had chosen to discipline its competitors, it almost certainly could have maintained and even increased its market share.

Between 1920 and 1945 the *US Steel* precedent protected dominant firms that refrained from predatory actions from Section 2 attack. This policy changed abruptly, however, in 1945 with the handing down of the *Alcoa* decision.

THE ALCOA ERA

ALCOA CASE[8] (1945)—In 1937 the Justice Department charged the Aluminum Company of America (Alcoa) with monopolizing the aluminum ingot market. The District Court relied heavily on the *US Steel* precedent and dismissed the case, but the Justice Department appealed. The Supreme Court could not obtain a quorum of six justices to hear the case because four justices had previously been involved in the litigation of the case. As a result, the New York Court of Appeals served as the highest appeals court and under the leadership of Judge Learned Hand overturned the District Court ruling. Except for one aberrational case examined below, Judge Hand's ruling established the major precedent for Section 2 cases for the next twenty-five years.

The correct market definition was the first issue addressed by Judge Hand. The District Court had defined Alcoa's market share in 1937 as 33 percent by including secondary ingot (ingot produced from scrap aluminum) in the same market as primary ingot. Furthermore, the District Court had eliminated from the relevant market all ingots that Alcoa produced and then used in its vertically integrated fabrication operations. The Court of Appeals, however, ruled that because Alcoa produced virtually all primary aluminum, it indirectly controlled the secondary scrap market. According to the Court, Alcoa's market share was 90 percent of the relevant "primary aluminum ingot" market.

Once Judge Hand established that Alcoa had a 90 percent market share in 1937, he turned to the issue of Alcoa's intent. In keeping with typical judicial procedure, Judge Hand went to great lengths to make his ruling consistent with the *Standard Oil* Rule of Reason precedent. Yet in Alcoa there was little evidence of aggressive practices such as existed in the *Standard Oil* or *American Tobacco* cases. In fact, Alcoa's market power originated from a cost advantage associated with patents rather than predatory behavior. And its continued market domination resulted from high barriers to entry (especially economies of scale in the conversion of bauxite ore into aluminum oxide or alumina), vertical integration into all four stages of production, and a limit pricing policy that kept profits at moderate levels.

Judge Hand's decision greatly reduced the government's burden in Section 2 cases. Essentially Hand ruled that once the government had proved that Alcoa had a monopoly, the government had gone far enough, *unless* Alcoa could prove that the monopoly was "thrust upon it" because of the existence of large economies of scale or patents. Hand went on to state that "unchallenged economic power deadens initiative, discourages thrift and depresses energy; that immunity from competition is a narcotic, and rivalry is a stimulant, to industrial progress; that the spur of constant stress is necessary to counteract an inevitable disposition to let well enough alone."

The *Alcoa* decision seemed to reverse the *US Steel* precedent and set a new one: a monopolist with an overwhelming market share violated Section 2 unless that market power had been thrust on it and was virtually unavoidable.

UNITED SHOE MACHINERY CASE[9] (1954)—In 1954 the Supreme Court supported the *Alcoa* precedent in its *United Shoe Machinery* decision. United Shoe was a classic "good trust." Profits were normal, prices were uniform, its machines were reliable and efficient, service was provided free, and the cost of machinery was kept down to only 2 percent of the average wholesale price of shoes.

Despite United's good behavior, the Justice Department charged that its power resulted from an illegal long-term leasing policy. United refused to sell its machines but, instead, leased them for a minimum period of ten years. Lessees could return a machine before the expiration of a lease, but only if they paid a significant financial penalty. The ten-year leases created several problems for potential entrants. The leases eliminated competition from a second-hand market (such as exists in automobiles or business machines), increased the capital requirements for entry, and greatly limited the market available to potential entrants each year (to approximately one tenth of the total shoe machinery market).

The Supreme Court affirmed the decision of the District Court in favor of the Justice Department and in so doing endorsed the *Alcoa* precedent.

DU PONT CELLOPHANE CASE[10] (1956)—After the *Alcoa* and *United Shoe Machinery* decisions, the government appeared to have the advantage in Section 2 cases. In 1956, however, the Supreme Court acquitted Du Pont of a charge that it had monopolized the cellophane industry. Legally this case was an aberration during this period, but it is an excellent example of the tremendous importance of market definition in monopolization cases. The major issue was the definition of the relevant market. Du Pont admitted that in 1947 it controlled 75 percent of the cellophane market and received royalties on the remaining 25 percent. Du Pont contended, however, that cellophane competed so closely with all other "flexible wrapping materials" that all such materials should be included in the correct market definition. The Supreme Court accepted Du Pont's argument that cellophane was in the same market as waxed paper, glassine, parchment paper, sulfite paper, aluminum foil, and cellulose acetate, and its market share was, therefore, less than 20 percent. The *Du Pont* decision was an exception to a basically strict interpretation of Section 2 that followed the *Alcoa* decision.

GRINNELL CASE[11] (1966)—The last major Supreme Court decision during the "Alcoa era" is worth noting because it provides a sharp and fascinating contrast to the *Du Pont* decision. In the *Du Pont* case, the Supreme Court adopted a broad market definition that resulted in Du Pont's acquittal. In the *Grinnell* case, the Supreme Court selected the narrowest possible market definition and ruled in favor of the government.

The Justice Department's suit, filed in 1961, charged that Grinnell had monopolized the national market for "accredited central station protection services." According to this market definition Grinnell had approximately a 90 percent market share. "Accredited central station protection services" consisted of fire and burglary protection services that electronically connected the client's property to a central station and were accredited by Underwriters Laboratories (UL). Accreditation by UL generally was required for a protected property to qualify for discounts from insurance companies. If there was a fire or burglary at the property, an alarm would be set off at the central station, and an operator at the station would call the fire or police department. If a broad definition such as "all protection services and devices" was adopted, Grinnell had a small market share because "accredited central station protection services" competed with other protection services, such as watchmen, audible alarms, proprietary security systems, watchdogs, and protection services connected directly to police and fire departments.

The Supreme Court adopted the narrowest possible market definition, "accredited central station protection services," and ruled against Grinnell. Taken together, the *Du Pont* and *Grinnell* cases suggest that the courts can examine similar economic facts and arrive at very different legal conclusions. The two cases differed in one major respect. Unlike the *Du Pont* case, the Justice Department relied heavily on evidence of aggressive behavior as well as a large market share in the *Grinnell* case. The *Grinnell* decision, therefore, was consistent with the Rule of Reason, which requires aggressive behavior as well as monopoly power to find a firm guilty of violating Section 2.

RECENT TRENDS IN SECTION 2 CASES

The "Alcoa era" came to an end sometime in the mid-1970s. The Justice Department filed major suits against International Business Machines (IBM) in 1969 and American Telephone and Telegraph (AT&T) in 1974; however, a series of court and FTC decisions generally favoring fairly aggressive actions by dominant firms seems to have put an end, at least for the time being, to the approach of the *Alcoa* and *United Shoe* decisions. A few decisions are worth reviewing as examples of the more recent court interpretation.

TELEX V. IBM[12] (1975)—In the 1950s and 1960s the computer industry was a complicated one. A system consisted of a central processing unit (CPU), which acted like a "brain," and a great deal of peripheral equipment that plugged into the CPU. Peripheral equipment consisted of items such as terminals, line printers, card readers, input and output tapes, disc drives, and tape drives. IBM and a few other firms, such as Burroughs and Honeywell, produced full systems, and many other smaller firms, such as Telex, produced only peripheral equipment.

In the late 1960s, Telex and other peripheral manufacturers were offering IBM plug-compatible peripheral equipment at prices well below IBM's prices for comparable products. As a result, IBM lost a significant share of the market for IBM peripheral equipment. It responded by selectively and dramatically cutting the prices of certain peripheral equipment that competed directly with Telex's equipment; redesigning certain equipment so that it was much more difficult to connect Telex's equipment to IBM machines; announcing a "Fixed Term Leasing

Plan," which provided for an 8 percent price reduction for users signing a one-year lease on peripheral equipment, and a 16 percent price reduction for signers of a two-year lease; and announcing large price *increases* on IBM CPUs, allegedly to recoup revenues lost as a result of the other three actions.

As a result of these IBM responses, Telex was forced to cut its prices drastically. Despite IBM's price cuts, Telex increased its volume of business between 1970 and 1972, but its profits declined substantially.

Basing its decision primarily on the *Alcoa, United Shoe,* and *Grinnell* precedents, the District Court ruled in favor of Telex on most issues and awarded Telex $259.5 million in damages plus $12 million in attorney's fees. The Tenth Circuit Court of Appeals overturned the District Court's decision, arguing that IBM's actions were merely normal methods of competition.

The Appeals Court decision appeared to turn sharply away from a structural view of Section 2. In fact, this decision reads more like the 1920 *US Steel* decision than the *Alcoa* decision. There is little doubt that IBM's behavior was more aggressive than Alcoa's; yet the Court of Appeals chose to permit IBM's actions.

THE DU PONT TITANIUM DIOXIDE CASE[13] (1980)—Titanium dioxide is a whitening agent commonly used in paint and paper manufacturing. In the 1950s Du Pont had concentrated on using a chloride process to produce titanium dioxide, while all of its competitors had concentrated on a sulfate process. A worldwide shortage of raw materials during the 1970s caused a dramatic increase in the production costs of the sulfate process, and Du Pont suddenly found itself with a 25 percent cost advantage over its sulfate process–based rivals.

Recognizing its significant cost advantage, Du Pont embarked on a three-part growth strategy. First, it greatly expanded capacity. Second, it priced its titanium dioxide high enough to earn profits to finance its expansion but low enough to discourage expansion by its competitors. Third, Du Pont refused to license its low-cost chlorate process technology to competitors.

As a result of its strategy, Du Pont's market share increased from 30 percent in 1972 to 42 percent in 1977. At this point the Federal Trade Commission staff charged Du Pont with unfair and monopolistic practices and requested divestiture of two of Du Pont's titanium dioxide plants and royalty-free licensing of its technology.

In many respects, Du Pont's titanium dioxide strategy is similar to Alcoa's aluminum strategy; however, the Federal Trade Commission ruled unanimously in favor of Du Pont. The Commission declared that Du Pont's strategy was the result of a legally obtained cost advantage and that its pricing strategy had at all times earned a profit for Du Pont. The Commission stated, "the essence of the competitive process is to induce firms to become more efficient and to pass the benefits of the efficiency along to consumers. That process would be ill-served by using antitrust to block hard, aggressive competition that is solidly based on efficiencies and growth opportunities, even if monopoly is a possible result." Despite the fact that this decision appeared to move dramatically away from the *Alcoa* precedent, the Commission noted that it believed the ruling was "entirely consistent with the 'superior skill, foresight and industry' exception in *Alcoa.*" In any event, by 1988, Du Pont's market share had increased to 65 percent.

THE CEREAL CASE[14] (1981)—In 1972, the FTC attempted an original approach to the problem of market power. The Commission charged the major cereal producers with a *shared monopoly*. The FTC suit charged that the three leading producers, Kellogg's, General Mills, and General Foods (Post), had "tacitly colluded and cooperated to maintain and exercise monopoly power." Specifically, the complaint charged that all three had "reached an understanding" to avoid price competition and, instead, to channel their energies into practices that raised entry barriers. These practices included excessive advertising, product proliferation, the control of shelf space, and the elimination of some private-label brands.

The FTC relied heavily on two pieces of economic evidence: first, the high profitability of the cereal industry; and second, the complete lack of entry for decades despite high profits. On September 1, 1981, however, an administrative law judge recommended that the complaint be dismissed, and in January 1982, the FTC agreed to let the judge's decision stand.

AMERICAN TELEPHONE AND TELEGRAPH COMPANY (1982)—In 1974, the Justice Department filed a suit against the American Telephone and Telegraph Company (AT&T), the largest private corporation in the world. In 1981, AT&T had assets exceeding $130 billion and a market share of 83 percent of all telephones in the United States.

AT&T was a holding company that controlled twenty-two local distribution telephone companies, Bell Long Lines Division, Western Electric, and Bell Labs. Its control of the telecommunications industry was built on a combination of government regulation, vertical integration, and aggressive competitive practices.

The complaint charged that AT&T had monopolized the industry by adopting two major policies. First, AT&T had shut out independent equipment manufacturers from the AT&T markets by purchasing all of its equipment from AT&T's own equipment manufacturing arm, Western Electric. Second, AT&T had prevented competition by obstructing independent equipment and independent long-distance carriers from interconnecting with the AT&T system.

Originally the complaint suggested that AT&T be permitted to keep the twenty-two regulated local operating companies and be divested of Western Electric, Long Lines, and Bell Labs. On January 8, 1982, however, the Justice Department and AT&T signed a consent decree with just the opposite result. AT&T was permitted to keep Western Electric, Long Lines, and Bell Labs but agreed to divest its twenty-two local operating companies. Furthermore, AT&T was given permission to enter nonregulated markets. When the decree was carried out, it resulted in the largest divestiture in antitrust history, over $87 billion in assets. The impact of this decree is discussed in detail in Chapter 24.

ASPEN SKIING COMPANY CASE[15] (1985)—Nineteen years after the *Grinnell* case, the Supreme Court handed down its next Section 2 ruling. In 1967, Aspen Skiing Company (Aspen) gained control over three of the four ski areas in Aspen, Colorado, one of the nation's premier skiing areas. The fourth area was owned by Aspen Highlands Skiing Corporation (Highlands). From 1967 until 1978 the two companies worked in coordination to offer ski lift tickets that allowed skiers to ski all four areas during a week-long vacation. Revenues from these four-area ski tickets were divided based on usage at each area.

Aspen complained to Highlands for several years that it did not have faith in the accuracy of the monitoring system used to measure usage at each ski area. Then for the 1978–79 ski season, Aspen offered Highlands a take-it-or-leave-it fixed 12.5 percent of revenues from the sale of four-area tickets. This fixed percentage was below Highlands' historical usage figures, and Highlands rejected the offer. Aspen refused to consider any counteroffer from Highlands and eliminated the four-area tickets. However, Aspen continued to offer an attractive three-area pass that was good only at its three skiing resorts.

With the elimination of the four-area ticket, Highlands attempted to introduce its own version of a four-area ticket by issuing a product it called the "Adventure Pack," which consisted of three days of skiing at Highlands and three prepaid vouchers to ski at the three areas owned by Aspen. Although Highlands had prepaid for the vouchers, Aspen refused to accept them. Highlands was then forced to include American Express Traveler's Checks or money orders in its "Adventure Pack" to pay for skiing at Aspen's three areas. In response to the Traveler's Check offer, Aspen increased the price of a one-day lift ticket to $22, "thereby making it unprofitable . . . to market [the] Adventure Pack."

Aspen's policies had a devastating financial impact on Highlands, which saw its share of ski lift ticket revenues decline from 20.5 percent in 1976–77 to 15.7 percent in 1977–78, 13.1 percent in 1978–79, 12.5 percent in 1979–80, and 11 percent in 1980–81. Furthermore, Highlands' revenues from other ski services such as equipment rentals, schools, and restaurant facilities suffered similar declines.

A District Court jury awarded Highlands $2.5 million in actual damages and $7.5 million in treble damages plus court costs and attorney's fees. The Court of Appeals affirmed, ruling that the all-area ticket was an "essential facility" that Aspen had an obligation to market jointly with Highlands.

The Supreme Court also ruled in favor of Highlands. The Court noted that "the record in this case comfortably supports an inference that the monopolist made a deliberate effort to discourage its customers from doing business with its smaller rival. . . . The refusal to accept the Adventure Pack coupons in exchange for daily tickets was apparently motivated entirely by a decision to avoid providing any benefit to Highlands even though accepting the coupons would have entailed no cost to [Aspen] itself, would have provided it with immediate benefits, and would have satisfied its potential customers."

The *Aspen* case indicates that Section 2 cases can still succeed if the following two elements of the case are proved: "(1) the possession of monopoly power in a relevant market, and (2) the willful acquisition, maintenance, or use of that power by anticompetitive or exclusionary means or for anticompetitive or exclusionary purposes." This is a strong burden of proof for any plaintiff to sustain, but it is not an impossible one.

SPECTRUM SPORTS, INC. V. MCQUILLAN[16] (1993)—The *Aspen* case showed the importance of proving the existence of monopoly power in a relevant market to sustain a ruling against a defendant in a Section 2 case. In the 1993 *Spectrum Sports* case the Supreme Court reaffirmed the primacy of starting from a position of monopoly power in a relevant market. Sorbothane is a patented elastic polymer that has excellent shock-absorbing qualities and is used in a variety of medical, athletic, and equestrian products. Readers may be familiar with sorbothane inserts for athletic footwear.

BTR Inc. owned the patent rights to sorbothane in the United States and Britain. Through subsidiaries in the United States, in 1981 BTR established five regional distributorships for sorbothane in the United States. Shirley and Larry McQuillan received the exclusive distribution rights for sorbothane in the Southwest. The McQuillans were primarily interested in sorbothane because they were designing a horseshoe pad using the product. Spectrum Sports was selected as the distributor for another region.

In January 1982, BTR transferred responsibility for selling its medical products from the five regional distributors to one national distributor. Three months later, BTR informed the McQuillans that they would have to give up their athletic shoe insert distributorship if they wished to maintain their equestrian products distributorship. The McQuillans refused. In the fall of 1982, BTR appointed a national distributor for equestrian products, and shortly thereafter BTR began marketing a sorbothane horseshoe pad that was "allegedly indistinguishable from the one designed by [the McQuillans]." When BTR established Spectrum Sports Inc. as the national distributor of sorbothane athletic shoe inserts, the McQuillans attempted to acquire sorbothane directly from BTR in Britain, but BTR in Britain refused to sell them any of the product. The McQuillans were then forced to close their sorbothane business.

A District Court jury ruled for the McQuillans and the Ninth Circuit Court of Appeals affirmed. The Court of Appeals noted, however, that "the jury had found that [BTR] had violated [Section] 2 without specifying whether they had monopolized, attempted to monopolize, or conspired to monopolize" a relevant market.

The Supreme Court reversed and remanded the case to the lower court. The Supreme Court ruled that to prove "an attempt to monopolize" under Section 2 it is necessary to prove "(1) that the defendant has engaged in predatory or anticompetitive conduct with (2) a specific intent to monopolize and (3) a dangerous probability of achieving monopoly power." Proof of a Section 2 violation, therefore, requires a careful consideration of the definition of the relevant market and the defendant's realistic ability to "lessen or destroy competition in that market."

SUMMARY

1. The antitrust laws developed in response to the industrial revolution, which resulted in significant economies of scale and greatly increased the size of the geographic market for many products. The laws were also spurred by the development of modern capital markets that enabled firms to raise large amounts of capital in the equity market and the liberalization of the laws of incorporation in many states.

2. The Sherman Act was signed into law in 1890. Section 1 banned "restraints of trade" such as price fixing, and Section 2 banned "attempts to monopolize." Monopoly per se was not a violation of the Sherman Act.

3. In 1911, Chief Justice White laid down the Rule of Reason precedent in the *Standard Oil* decision. The Rule of Reason declared that only unreasonable attempts to monopolize violated the Sherman Act.

4. In 1914 the Clayton Act and Federal Trade Commission Act were signed into law. The Clayton Act outlawed specific types of economic behavior, such as tying agreements and price discrimination. The Federal Trade Commission established an independent commission to prevent "unfair methods of competition."

5. In 1936 the Robinson-Patman Act was passed to tighten the loopholes in the Clayton Act with regard to price discrimination.

6. In 1950 the Celler-Kefauver Act closed a major loophole in Section 7 of the Clayton Act that had permitted firms to acquire a firm's assets instead of its stock to avoid violating the law.

7. The interpretation of Section 2 in the courts has gone through a complete cycle, from the behavioral interpretation of the *Standard Oil* decision to the structural interpretation of the *Alcoa* decision, and then back again to a behavioral interpretation in recent rulings.

8. Currently the courts appear to be taking a position that is reminiscent of earlier cases such as the 1920 *US Steel* decision.

9. Violation of Section 2 of the Sherman Act requires proof of monopoly power in some well-defined market and evidence of an intent to monopolize that market. The mere existence of monopoly power is not sufficient to establish a violation of the law.

10. It is impossible to predict whether this interpretation is permanent. A historical perspective would suggest that the courts' position might change again someday.

11. As things stand today dominant firms can adopt fairly aggressive policies with relatively little fear from the antitrust laws.

KEY TERMS

Celler-Kefauver Act

Clayton Act

exclusive dealing agreements

Federal Trade Commission

Federal Trade Commission Act

Robinson-Patman Act

Rule of Reason

Sherman Act

tying contracts

DISCUSSION QUESTIONS

1. The antitrust laws have rarely worked exactly as Congress intended. Describe two specific instances in which the laws had totally unintended consequences. Did Congress act to end these consequences?

2. Explain the major differences between enforcement of the antitrust laws by the Department of Justice and by the Federal Trade Commission.

3. It has been suggested that the *Standard Oil* and *US Steel* decisions taken together defined an "era of dastardly deeds." Why do you think somebody made this comment? What do you think about the economic reasoning used in the majority opinion in the *US Steel* decision?

4. When an economist is hired as an expert witness by either side in an antitrust case, she must be able to argue both sides of the case from an economic standpoint. Do you think this is generally easy or difficult? Why?

5. Consider a monopolization case in which divestiture will result in a loss of some economies of scale so that average costs will be higher after divestiture. Does it follow that from an economic efficiency perspective divestiture should not be ordered in such a case?

6. If Section 2 of the Sherman Act were repealed so that it was no longer illegal "to attempt to monopolize," do you think market conduct would be affected? What about market performance? Why might Chicago School economists favor such a repeal? Why would SCP economists be less likely to support such a repeal?

7. Explain why the definition of the market is such a critical issue in Section 2 cases. Suppose Microsoft were accused of monopolizing the personal computer operating system market. How do you think the Justice Department would define the market? How do you think Microsoft would define the market? What do you think is the correct market definition?

8. Is the issue of *intent* important in monopolization cases? Should it be important? How would enforcement of the law differ if the courts had ruled that intent was not important in monopolization cases?

9. In monopolization cases the defense typically argues that divestiture will result in a significant loss of economies of scale. Should the loss of economies of scale be an absolute defense against a charge of monopolization? By absolute defense, we mean that if a monopolist could prove that there would be a significant loss of economies of scale, it could not be found to have violated Section 2 of the Sherman Act.

10. What court decision examined in this chapter makes the most sense to you in terms of economic analysis? What court decision examined in this chapter makes the least sense to you in terms of economic analysis? Explain your reasoning.

REFERENCES

1. For background historical information see Hans B. Thorelli, *The Federal Antitrust Policy: Origination of an American Tradition* (Baltimore: Johns Hopkins Press, 1955); John D. Clark, *The Federal Trust Policy* (Baltimore: Johns Hopkins Press, 1931); Albert H. Walker, *History of the Sherman Law* (New York: Equity Press, 1910); Jessie W.

Markham, "Survey of the Evidence and Findings on Mergers," in National Bureau of Economic Research, *Business Concentration and Price Policy* (New York: Arno Press, 1975), pp. 141-212; Simon N. Whitney, *Antitrust Policies: American Experience in Twenty Industries* (New York: Twentieth Century Fund, 1958), Chapter 1; and A.D. Neale and D.G. Goyder, *The Antitrust Laws of the U.S.A.* (Cambridge, England: Cambridge University Press, 1980).

2. William G. Shepherd and Clair Wilcox, *Public Policies Toward Business* (Homewood, Ill.: Irwin, 1979), p. 95.

3. *United States v. Northern Securities Co.*, 193 U.S. 197 (1904).

4. *United States v. Standard Oil Co. of New Jersey, et al.*, 221 U.S. 1 (1911).

5. John S. McGee, "Predatory Price Cutting: The Standard Oil (N.J.) Case," *Journal of Law & Economics* (October 1958): 137–69.

6. *United States v. American Tobacco Co.*, 221 U.S. 106 (1911).

7. *United States v. United States Steel Corporation, et al.*, 251 US 417 (1920).

8. *United States v. Aluminum Company of America, et al.*, 148 F.2d 416 (1945).

9. *United States v. United Shoe Machinery Corporation*, 110 F.Supp. 295 (1953), affirmed 347 U.S. 521 (1954).

10. *United States v. E.I. du Pont de Nemours & Co.*, 351 U.S. 377 (1956).

11. *United States v. Grinnell Corporation, et al.*, 384 U.S. 563 (1966).

12. *Telex Corporation v. IBM Corporation*, 510 F.2d 894 (1975).

13. *In the Matter of E.I. du Pont de Nemours & Company*, 96 F.T.C. 653 (1980).

14. *Federal Trade Commission v. Kellogg et al.*, F.T.C. Docket 8883 (1981).

15. *Aspen Skiing Company v. Aspen Highlands Skiing Corporation*, 472 US 585 (1985).

16. *Spectrum Sports, Inc. v. McQuillan*, 113 S.Ct. 884 (1993).

Chapter 19

Antitrust: Collusion

Chapter 9 analyzed a number of price-fixing agreements to determine how various firms attempted to solve the prisoner's dilemma. Government antitrust policy has addressed many of these attempts, and in this chapter we examine the effectiveness of these policies.

Explicit price-fixing agreements are the most obvious violation of Section 1 of the Sherman Act. In addition to direct price-fixing agreements, however, there are a number of more subtle restraints, including tacit agreements among oligopolists, trade association behavior, and "ethical codes" in professional organizations.

Overt Price-Fixing Agreements

Whenever firms collude to fix prices, the objective is the same: to solve the prisoner's dilemma and increase or stabilize prices. In theory, all conspiracies attempt to widen the gap between price and marginal cost, and therefore, they should all reduce economic efficiency. It is necessary, however, to examine whether there are any valid justifications for price fixing.

Several justifications have been advanced by defendant firms. First, price fixing may prevent *cutthroat competition*. This argument is particularly popular in industries characterized by high fixed costs relative to variable costs, such as the steel and railroad industries. When demand declines in these industries, marginal cost is likely to be less than average cost because each firm operates on the downward sloping portion of its average cost curve. Under such conditions, a firm's demand curve may be everywhere below its average cost curve. This situation is shown in Figure 19.1. The firm may attempt to attract new business by secret discriminatory price discounts to some purchasers. As long as price remains above marginal cost to *all* buyers and the firm is able to maintain its high price to all of its original customers, its losses will be reduced as it attracts additional customers by cutting prices. If a firm's discriminatory price cutting remains secret, this strategy may work because the price cutter is able to attract new customers away from its competitors. Secret price cuts, however, usually become public and lead to matching cuts by other firms. When this occurs, prices may fall to very low levels as each firm matches its competitors' lower prices. Widespread price cutting throughout the industry will lead to a downward price spiral and significant economic losses for all firms.

In Figure 19.1, suppose that price is initially stable at the firm's loss minimizing price P_1, and the firm is sustaining an economic loss equal to area P_1abC_1 (the gray and striped areas). If cutthroat competition developed, prices might fall below P_1 on all sales. In fact, prices might decline to marginal cost P_2 and the firm would then sustain a much greater economic loss equal to area P_2xyC_2 (the red and striped areas).

A price decline to P_2 would certainly result in economic losses and serious problems for firms in the industry. The price decline, however, should not be a major cause for society's concern or used as a justification for permitting price fixing. When price equals P_2, price equals marginal cost, which is the allocatively efficient price. The profit issue is a value judgment, not an economic efficiency issue. From an economic efficiency perspective, the short-run socially optimal price is P_2. Price fixing to maintain prices above P_2 should not be permitted.

With regard to profits, the theory of competitive markets implies that long-run economic profits will be zero, or normal, but that short-run profits will vary. During expansion periods, excess profits are likely to exist (as they often did in the railroad and steel industries), whereas during recessions and depressions, economic losses are likely to occur. True competition is often cruel, and in highly competitive markets firms periodically sustain economic losses and are forced to leave. The exiting of firms suggests that the competitive process is working, not that it is failing. One can be fairly confident that in most instances when firms complain about cutthroat competition they are really complaining about just plain old competition.

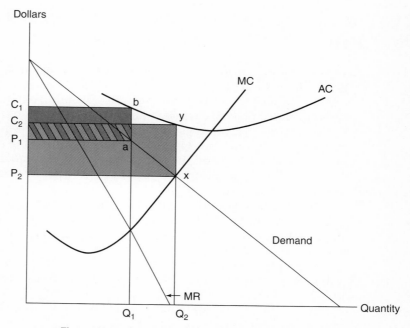

Figure 19.1 Cutthroat competition with AC above demand.

Another argument is that price fixing reduces risk, resulting in a more stable economy. According to this argument, high risk discourages investment, reduces supply, and results in higher prices. By reducing risk, price fixing may encourage investment; however, collusion that *artificially* reduces risk may create a different set of economic problems. Risk artificially reduced through collusion may result in a sluggish rate of technological advance as firms lose some of their incentive to produce new products. Furthermore, artificially reduced risk may encourage entry and capacity expansion beyond the socially optimal level.[1] An artificial reduction in risk caused by collusion, therefore, is likely to result in excess capacity and economic inefficiencies.

Finally, higher profits associated with collusion may be necessary to encourage research and development. This argument seems dubious because price fixing, by encouraging cooperation among competitors, seems unlikely to spur firms to attempt to produce new products that would make it more difficult to continue a policy of successful collusion. Furthermore, in technologically advanced industries, in which research and development expenditures are high, price-fixing agreements rarely work, because new products are developed too rapidly. It would be virtually impossible, for example, to form an effective cartel in the computer industry because new technology is developed almost daily.

Despite the preceding analysis, a few price-fixing agreements might be justified on efficiency grounds.[2] These exceptions are so few and far between, however, that an absolute ban on direct price fixing agreements probably is the optimal public policy.

Public Policy Toward Direct Price-Fixing Agreements

TRANS-MISSOURI FREIGHT CASE[3] (1897)—The first major price-fixing case to reach the Supreme Court was the *Trans-Missouri Freight Association* case. Eighteen western railroads combined to form the Trans-Missouri Freight Association. The association's stated objective was to "establish rates." Meetings were held to set rates, and penalties were imposed on carriers who broke the agreement. Penalties were even imposed for missing a rate-setting meeting. After the passage of the Sherman Act, the association continued to operate until December 6, 1892, when it was disbanded. The association was replaced, however, by a seven-member committee that continued to set rates.

The defendants never denied that they had an agreement to set rates. Instead, the main defense centered on the argument that the fixed rates were always reasonable and that in the absence of the association, cutthroat competition would destroy the industry.

The Supreme Court overturned two lower court rulings and found for the government. The opinion clearly implied that price-fixing agreements were illegal *per se*, regardless of the reasonableness of the prices established. This ruling might have been the final word on direct price-fixing agreements had it not been for the *Addyston Pipe* ruling of 1899.

ADDYSTON PIPE AND STEEL CASE[4] (1899)—The *Addyston Pipe* case involved six large producers of cast iron pipe in the Midwest and South. Beginning in 1894, the six firms, which controlled more than 65 percent of the market, entered into agreements that divided the market into exclusive *pay* territories and *free* territories. In pay territories, it was agreed that one firm would be the low bidder on all jobs. For example, Addyston Pipe was located in Cincinnati and was awarded the pay territories of Cincinnati, Ohio; Covington, Kentucky; and Newport, Kentucky. Each of the six agreed to pay "bonuses" into a common pool on all sales made in pay territories. These "bonuses" were then divided among the six defendants.

The defense argued that prices were reasonable and prevented *ruinous competition* in an industry characterized by high fixed costs relative to variable costs. The Supreme Court ruled unanimously against Addyston Pipe but, in the process, appeared to leave open the possibility that firms could sometimes use a *reasonableness* defense. The Supreme Court stated:

> We have no doubt that where the direct and immediate effect of a contract or combination among particular dealers in a commodity is to destroy competition between them and others, so that the parties to the contract or combination may obtain increased prices for themselves, such contract or combination amounts to a restraint of trade in the commodity. . . . All the facts and circumstances are, however, to be considered in order to determine the fundamental question—whether the necessary effect of the combination is to restrain interstate commerce.

This section of the decision placed a great emphasis on *higher prices* acting as a restraint of trade. It is possible to derive a corollary from this position: agreements that do not raise prices do not result in a restraint of trade and do not violate the Sherman Act. In 1927, however, the Supreme Court removed any doubt concerning the *per se* ban on direct price-fixing agreements in the *Trenton Potteries* case.

TRENTON POTTERIES CASE[5] (1927)—The *Trenton Potteries* case involved twenty-three members of the Sanitary Potters Association. The defendants controlled more than 80 percent of the vitreous pottery fixture market (better known as commodes and tubs). Competitors met through the association, set standard price lists, and attempted to persuade each other not to sell below list price. Evidence suggested that the agreements often broke down and that many sales took place at prices below list. The Supreme Court, however, stated its strong support for a *per se* ban on all price-fixing agreements.

Justice Stone delivered the majority opinion:

> The aim and result of every price-fixing agreement, if effective, is the elimination of one form of competition. The power to fix prices, whether reasonably exercised or not, involves power to control the market and to fix arbitrary and unreasonable prices. The reasonable price fixed today may through economic and business changes become the unreasonable price of tomorrow.

In the *Trenton Potteries* case the price-fixing agreements probably had little, if any, effect on price, and yet the Supreme Court majority forcefully condemned the attempt to fix prices. Despite one aberrational decision in 1933,[6] this remains the basic precedent today: Any overt attempt to fix prices is illegal *per se*.

The per se *Rule Versus The Rule of Reason*

As we just discussed, direct price-fixing agreements are illegal *per se* in the United States. In antitrust law, however, most restraints of trade come under the Rule of Reason interpretation handed down by Judge White in the *Standard Oil* case. Under a Rule of Reason interpretation a firm can argue that its "restraint of trade" is economically justified because it is a reasonable restraint.

When is a "restraint of trade" illegal *per se,* and when is a "restraint of trade" to be considered under a Rule of Reason? The answer to this question is extremely important to the American economy, because firms must know the "rules" of American competition. Failure to understand these rules will result in an excessive amount of antitrust litigation and confusion about the nature of the American economic system. The remaining sections of this chapter explore a number of restraints of trade that could fall under either a *per se* or Rule of Reason interpretation. These areas include price information exchanges between competitors without an explicit agreement to fix prices; oligopoly behavior in which firms charge identical prices without agreeing to fix prices; trade associations in which members agree to exchange a wide variety of firm and industry data; agreements to limit the freedom of commercial actions available to members of a professional organization, such as a state bar or medical association; and agreements by groups of nonprofit colleges and universities to set the terms under which member schools' sports teams can appear on television.

Price-Exchange Agreements

The basic issue of direct price-fixing agreements has been settled by the courts, but other, subtler forms of solving the prisoner's dilemma have been left open for judicial interpretation. One open area is the question of price exchanges between competitors. The Supreme Court first addressed this issue in the 1969 *Container Corporation* case.

CONTAINER CORPORATION CASE[7] (1969)—The *Container Corporation* case involved an agreement among eighteen manufacturers of cardboard containers in the southeastern United States. These firms controlled 90 percent of the relevant market. Each firm agreed to supply its competitors with price information on its most recent sales in exchange for a reciprocal agreement from each of its competitors. Despite the information exchanges, prices were generally declining throughout the period of the price exchanges. Furthermore, there was a large increase, from thirty to fifty-one, in the number of firms in the market.

The Supreme Court ruled for the government, but made it clear that price exchange agreements were not illegal *per se*. According to the Court, price exchanges would have no effect on a truly competitive market, but because the cardboard container industry was dominated by relatively few sellers, the exchanges tended to result in "price uniformity." Justice Douglas's opinion indicated that price exchanges would violate the Sherman Act if the structural characteristics of an industry led to the conclusion that prices would be affected by the exchanges.

U.S. GYPSUM CASE[8] (1978)—The fairly strong ban on price exchange agreements in the *Container Corporation* decision appeared to be modified in the 1978 *U.S. Gypsum* case. Gypsum board was sold in a highly concentrated market, with an eight-firm concentration ratio of 94. The eight leading producers had followed precisely the same price-exchange practices as the cardboard container manufacturers; however, their defense had a different twist. They argued that price verification was necessary to prevent them from violating the Robinson-Patman Act. According to this argument, price verification was simply a method of preventing illegal price discrimination by ensuring that any discriminatory prices were made in a good faith effort to meet the lower price of a competitor.

The Supreme Court rejected this Robinson-Patman Act defense, but **remanded**, or sent the case back to the lower court, for a new trial based on the issue of *intent* in criminal cases. The Supreme Court majority ruled that the jury had been improperly charged that "if the effect of the exchanges of pricing information was to raise, fix, maintain, and stabilize prices, then the parties to them are presumed, AS A MATTER OF LAW, to have intended that result." According to the Court, the determination of intent "must be established by evidence and inferences drawn therefrom and cannot be taken from the trier of fact through reliance on a legal presumption of wrongful intent from proof of an effect on prices."

While still leaving price exchange agreements vulnerable under the Sherman Act, the *U.S. Gypsum* decision significantly weakened the *Container Corporation* precedent.

Oligopolistic Behavior—Conscious Parallelism

Chapters 7 through 12 explored many different theories of oligopolistic behavior. Most of these came to a similar conclusion: for rational reasons oligopolists avoid aggressive price competition even in the absence of collusion. If these theories are correct, then a lack of price competition would be expected in oligopolistic industries. This presents an extremely difficult problem for antitrust authorities because oligopolistic behavior that, on the surface, may appear to be in restraint of trade may represent rational independent business behavior aimed at maximizing long-run profits.

The courts have defined the term **conscious parallelism** as a group of oligopolists behaving in an identical manner but with a lack of proof that the firms ever met to agree on this parallel course of behavior. *Conscious parallelism* refers to the idea that rational business behavior in a tight oligopoly will lead firms to behave identically with regard to price and other business practices. When does conscious parallelism become illegal? As the cases in this section suggest, that question has proved difficult for the courts to answer.

AMERICAN TOBACCO CASE[9] (1946)—In the 1946 *American Tobacco* case, there was no evidence of an overt conspiracy or even a tacit conspiracy. Divestiture after the 1911 *American Tobacco* case (recall from Chapter 18) had resulted in the establishment of over a dozen new tobacco companies, including Liggett & Myers and R.J. Reynolds. For about a decade, the cigarette producers competed aggressively, and then, in the early 1920s, price competition suddenly ceased. The tobacco oligopolists behaved in classic textbook fashion. The *Big 3* (as American, Liggett, and Reynolds were known) rigged the tobacco auction markets so that all three purchased tobacco at identical prices. Furthermore, they followed each other's pricing policies in lockstep.

This *consciously parallel* behavior may have been the natural outgrowth of the oligopolistic structure of the cigarette industry. Relying on strong circumstantial evidence, however, the Supreme Court ruled for the government and stated, "No formal agreement is necessary to constitute an unlawful conspiracy." Instead, the Court noted, "Where the circumstances are such as to warrant a jury in finding that the conspirators had a unity of purpose or a common design and understanding, the conclusion that a conspiracy is established is justified."

The *American Tobacco* case resulted in total fines of only $255,000 and no structural relief. This raises a serious question regarding the remedies in oligopoly cases. If a firm's behavior is the natural result of an oligopolistic market structure, then the levying of fines is unlikely to have any effect on future behavior or economic performance. In fact, behavior in the cigarette industry changed little after the 1946 decision.

The *American Tobacco* case was initially thought to be a breakthrough in antitrust policy. It was followed in 1948 by several other government victories, including a major case against Paramount and four other leading motion picture producers and distributors that resulted in the divestiture of over 65 percent of the leading producers' movie theaters.[10] In 1954, however, the courts took the first major step away from the *American Tobacco* precedent in another motion picture industry case.

THEATRE ENTERPRISES CASE[11] (1954)—After the 1948 *Paramount* decision, Theatre Enterprises built a new theater, the Crest, in suburban Baltimore, with the hope of attracting first-run motion pictures. Theatre Enterprises contacted eight major distributors and each refused to supply the Crest with first-run films, despite Theatre Enterprises' offer of substantial financial guarantees. Assuming that the refusals resulted from consciously parallel behavior, Theatre Enterprises sued.

In 1954 the Supreme Court ruled against Theatre Enterprises because of a lack of evidence that the eight distributors had an agreement, "tacit or express," to refuse to supply the Crest with films. The Court declared, "Circumstantial evidence of consciously parallel behavior may have made heavy inroads into the traditional judicial attitude toward conspiracy; but 'conscious parallelism' has not yet read conspiracy out of the Sherman Act entirely."

The *Theatre Enterprises* case represented a significant first movement away from the *American Tobacco* precedent. The movement continued with the 1970 *Pfizer* decision.

PFIZER CASE[12] (1970)—Before 1952, three drugs dominated the antibiotic market, Parke Davis's chloromycetin, American Cyanamid's aureomycin, and Pfizer's terramycin. All three drugs were protected by patents. In 1952, a Pfizer scientist developed tetracycline by dechlorinizing Cyanamid's aureomycin. As a result of publicity surrounding Pfizer's discovery, Cyanamid applied for a product and process patent for tetracycline. There were, therefore, two pending patents for tetracycline.

After some discussions, Cyanamid agreed to withdraw its patent claim, and on January 11, 1955, Pfizer received a patent on tetracycline. Meanwhile, Bristol-Myers decided to produce tetracycline through a different fermentation process and, in 1954, began to sell tetracycline to Squibb and Upjohn, which marketed Bristol's drug under the Squibb and Upjohn labels. When Pfizer received its patent in 1955, it immediately filed an infringement suit against Bristol, Squibb, and Upjohn.

Pfizer seemed to have a strong case against Bristol; however, on December 14 and 15, 1955, the CEOs of Pfizer and Bristol met, along with their patent attorneys. The government complaint charged that at the meetings the firms agreed that tetracycline would be marketed at identical prices by all sellers.

A District Court jury ruled for the government. The Second Circuit Court of Appeals, however, overturned the jury's ruling because the trial judge had misled the jury to believe that circumstantial evidence of "unreasonably high profits" was the key legal issue in the case. According to the Appeals Court, the key question was, "Did the participants at those meetings conspire to carry out the program as alleged by the government?"

In 1972, the Supreme Court, by a 3–3 split, upheld the Appeals Court ruling. Under the *Pfizer* precedent it appears that conscious parallelism alone is not enough to warrant a conviction under the Sherman Act. Instead, a government victory requires additional acts. Even under the present interpretation, however, oligopolists may be subject to antitrust attack if their behavior strongly suggests a common attempt to fix or maintain prices. Such a situation arose in the electric turbine industry between 1964 and 1976.

GENERAL ELECTRIC-WESTINGHOUSE CASE[13] (1976)—The background facts in this case were thoroughly analyzed in Chapter 9.* Recall that in May 1963, GE and Westinghouse embarked on a pricing policy whereby they both tacitly agreed to charge book prices and guaranteed these prices by using a price protection clause. The system worked very effectively and resulted in identical prices after August 1964.

GE and Westinghouse argued that their pricing policies were simply a form of conscious parallelism, which was legal under recent precedents. The Justice Department argued that their conduct went beyond simple conscious parallelism

---

*See Chapter 9, pp. 213–14, for details of the pricing policy.

and that internal documents suggested that both companies intended their policy to stabilize prices.

In 1976, the defendants agreed to a consent decree. The decree was aimed at preventing the indirect communication of price information between GE and Westinghouse. The agreement included four major methods of eliminating indirect price communication. First, the defendants were enjoined from signaling prices by making public statements regarding price. Second, they were prohibited from using the price protection plan, and they were enjoined from publishing their current price quotations. Third, the decree banned the publication of price-related information "from which a general pricing policy or strategy c[ould] be inferred." Finally, the firms were prohibited from obtaining price information about each other from buyers.

The *GE-Westinghouse* consent decree suggests that in some cases the government may still be able to attack oligopolistic behavior. But in 1984, the following Court of Appeals ruling in the *Ethyl* case made it clear that the scope of the *GE-Westinghouse* consent decree is limited

THE ETHYL CASE[14] (1984)—Recall from Chapter 9 that one of the examples of effective collusive price leadership was the market for lead-based antiknock gasoline additives in the 1970s. For many years Ethyl Corporation was a monopolist in this market, but in 1948 Du Pont entered, and in the early 1960s PPG Industries and Nalco Chemical entered. In 1974 Du Pont held a 36 percent market share, followed by Ethyl with 34 percent, PPG with 17.5 percent, and Nalco with 12.5 percent.[15]

From 1974 to 1979 there were twenty-four list price changes in the industry. In twenty of these cases all four firms changed price on the same day. In the other four cases, all four firms had identical prices a day or two apart. Such a high degree of price uniformity required a sophisticated form of price leadership. Leadership was characterized by: (1) at least 30 days advance notice of all price changes; (2) public press notices of all price changes; (3) a delivered price system that required buyers located in the same city to pay the same price (these systems are discussed in Chapter 21); and (4) the use of most favored customer clauses, whereby if one buyer received a lower price, all buyers would receive the same reduced price. Price leadership was clearly established to ensure both detection of all price cuts and punishment of cheaters.

The FTC ruled that the practices represented "unfair methods of competition" and therefore violated Section 5 of the FTC Act. The Court of Appeals, however, overturned the FTC ruling. Noting that the FTC had never argued that the practices "were the result of any agreement express or tacit," the Appeals Court argued that absent evidence of a tacit agreement the FTC carried a heavy burden of proof. According to the Court of Appeals, the FTC had to prove that there was "anticompetitive intent or purpose" on the part of the producers or that there was "an absence of an independent legitimate reason for [their] conduct."

One point omitted from our earlier analysis but emphasized by the Appeals Court was the dramatic decline in the demand for leaded gasoline that was taking place in the 1970s. As a result of greatly increased environmental regulations, unleaded gasoline was rapidly replacing leaded gasoline in the marketplace. The Court found that as a result of this decrease in demand the firms were consistently offering buyers discounts off the published list prices. According to the Court, between 1974 and 1979, Nalco and PPG discounted 80 percent and 58 percent of their sales, respectively. In the words of the Court:

> The main problem has been that market demand, due to factors uncontrolled by petitioners, is sharply declining. A dying market, which will soon dry up altogether, does not attract new entries. Absent some reasonable prospect that a price reduction would increase demand—and there is none—it is not surprising that existing producers have not engaged in as much price competition as might exist under other conditions.

Conscious parallelism remains a practice that is for the most part beyond the reach of the antitrust laws. In the absence of an explicit agreement to fix prices, only the most extreme forms of parallel behavior can be successfully fought in court.

Trade Associations

Trade associations present a unique set of problems for antitrust enforcement. Trade association practices have varied widely, from innocent information gathering and disseminating activities to sophisticated attempts to force compliance with published list prices. In highly competitive industries, it is doubtful that even aggressive attempts at price fixing by associations will be successful. In concentrated markets, however, trade associations may provide a successful vehicle for price fixing.

As precedents have developed, a Rule of Reason has evolved in trade association cases. Simple information gathering and dissemination has become viewed as reasonable, and attempts to impose prices directly or indirectly have become viewed as unreasonable.

HARDWOOD LUMBER CASE[16] (1921)—In December 1918 the American Hardwood Manufacturers Association was formed. The association's 400 members operated only 5 percent of the total hardwood lumber mills in the United States, but produced 33 percent of total output. The association developed a plan for reporting prices to the association that required daily reports on all sales including buyer and seller identification; kind, grade, and quality specifications; and prices. The reports were supplemented by monthly regional meetings to discuss prices and by contracting to have members submit their books to audits by competitors. Under the plan, prices increased sharply in 1919. When the government filed suit, the defense attributed these increases to the wartime pent-up demand for lumber and poor weather conditions.

Despite evidence that the plan had at best a limited effect on prices because 9000 independent lumber producers remained outside the association, the Supreme Court ruled that the plan went too far.

SUGAR INSTITUTE CASE[17] (1936)—We discussed the Sugar Institute in Chapter 9. Recall that the Institute consisted of fifteen manufacturers that produced more than 80 percent of the refined cane sugar in the United States and that the

Institute established a Code of Ethics that distinguished "ethical" from "unethical" types of behavior. The Justice Department filed suit, contending that the Code of Ethics went beyond the simple announcement of prices. Under the code, members refused to deal with water carriers that refused to announce freight rates or who granted price concessions to any sugar refiner; wholesalers who granted any price concessions; and any trucker, broker, or warehousemen who granted secret rebates. The Institute required sugar brokers to pledge, under oath, to adhere to the Code of Ethics. Members were also prohibited from granting quantity-based price discounts, even if the discounts were justified by lower costs. Finally, F.O.B. (freight on board) pricing, whereby buyers paid the mill price plus actual freight costs, was prohibited.

The Supreme Court condemned this behavior because "[t]he unreasonable restraints which defendants imposed lay not in advance announcements, but in the steps taken to secure adherence, without deviation, to prices and terms thus announced." According to the Court, the Sugar Institute, like the Hardwood Manufacturers Association, tried far too hard to eliminate price cutting, and it was this behavior that led to its condemnation.

TAG MANUFACTURERS CASE[18] (1949)—The Tag Manufacturers Institute consisted of thirty-one members that produced over 95 percent of all business tags. The Institute required its members to report their prices under threat of financial penalty. Relying on evidence that the required reporting of prices had no effect on actual prices, the Court of Appeals ruled in favor of the tag manufacturers.

Perhaps the most important piece of evidence in the case was the fact that the Institute's rules stated explicitly, "Nothing herein shall be construed as a limitation or restriction upon the right of each Subscriber independently to establish such price, or such terms and conditions of sale, or policies of whatever nature affecting prices or sales, as he may deem expedient." Furthermore, there was abundant evidence of continuing price competition in the industry.

The *Hardwood Lumber*, *Sugar Institute*, and *Tag Manufacturers* cases represent fairly well the state of the law with regard to trade association activities. Price reporting schemes that do little more than ask members to report prices, and which then make this information available to the public, will generally be permitted. Direct attempts to force adherence to list prices, or restrict price cutting, however, will bring an association within the reach of Section 1.

◢ *The Professions*

Until the 1970s it was common for professional societies to restrict competition by forbidding advertising or price competition. In recent years the courts have greatly limited the scope of permitted restrictions, and it is now safe to assume that the professions come well within the jurisdiction of the Sherman Act.

THE GOLDFARB CASE[19] (1975)—Recall from Chapter 9 that the Goldfarbs purchased a home in Fairfax County, Virginia.* They contacted thirty-six lawyers to obtain title insurance, and each lawyer quoted a fee of 1 percent of the value of

---

*For more details see Chapter 9, p. 219.

the property. All thirty-six lawyers consulted a fee schedule of recommended minimum prices published by the Fairfax County Bar Association. Believing that the bar association's action violated the Sherman Act, the Goldfarbs sued. The County Bar argued that the fee schedule was merely advisory and not subject to any enforcement mechanisms.

The Supreme Court, by a vote of 8-0, found in favor of the Goldfarbs. The Court ruled that the "record here . . . reveals a situation quite different from what would occur under a purely advisory fee schedule. Here a fixed, rigid price floor arose from respondents' activities: every lawyer who responded to petitioners' inquiries adhered to the fee schedule, and no lawyer asked for additional information in order to set an individualized fee." Furthermore, the Court noted that the "fee schedule was enforced through the prospect of professional discipline from the State Bar, and the desire of attorneys to comply with announced professional norms."

The Goldfarb case restricted the use of fee schedules in the legal profession. Two years later, the Supreme Court addressed another issue: advertising in the professions.

THE BATES AND O'STEEN CASE[20] (1977)—Bates and O'Steen were licensed attorneys in Arizona. In 1974, they opened a legal clinic in Phoenix for the purpose of handling simple legal cases for low fees. For two years Bates and O'Steen abided by a state bar ban on advertising and watched their practice sink toward bankruptcy. In desperation, on February 22, 1976, they placed an advertisement in the *Arizona Republic* newspaper. The advertisement helped business, but it also resulted in disciplinary action by the State Bar. When Bates and O'Steen were suspended from practicing law by the State Bar of Arizona, they decided to take the bar association to court.

Bates and O'Steen contended that the advertising ban violated the Sherman Act and the First Amendment's protection of freedom of speech. The bar association presented the following justifications for the ban:

1. Price advertising would result in excessive commercialization of the law profession, which would "undermine the attorney's sense of dignity and self-worth."
2. Advertising would inevitably be misleading with regard to the relationship between price and quality.
3. Advertising would lead to an excess demand for legal services, which would result in an excessive amount of litigation.
4. The costs of advertising would be passed on to the consumer and would result in higher fees.
5. Lawyers would advertise a given package of services for a fixed fee and then cut the quality of service to force the fee to fit the services provided.

The Supreme Court rejected each of these arguments in turn and ruled that while the state bar's ban on advertising did not violate the Sherman Act, it was unconstitutional.

Recall from Chapter 13 that informational price advertising is pro-competitive. This ruling, therefore, has undoubtedly increased the level of effective competition in several professions, including law, optometry, and dentistry.

THE ENGINEERS CASE[21] (1978)—Recall from Chapter 9 that the National Society of Professional Engineers adopted a Code of Ethics that prohibited competitive bidding. Engineers were prohibited from discussing fees until *after* a client had selected an engineer for a project.

The society's defense was that such a restriction was necessary to protect the "public health, safety, and welfare," because competitive bidding would result in low-quality engineering work. The Supreme Court did not accept the society's position and ruled that the code operated as an absolute ban on competitive bidding and therefore clearly violated the Sherman Act.

These three cases suggest that professional organizations generally cannot restrict price or advertising competition. The professions represented a major new area for antitrust action in the 1970s, and the strict interpretation adopted by a fairly conservative Supreme Court suggests that no Court is likely to significantly change the strict restrictions against agreements that affect price. This remains the clearest and strongest area in antitrust law: Direct agreements among competitors that affect price are illegal *per se*.

Nonprofit Organizations: Cases Involving Colleges and Universities

Another issue in two major Section 1 cases decided since 1984 has been whether nonprofit organizations such as colleges and universities can engage in restraints of trade that attempt to protect the missions of these institutions. In both cases, the Supreme Court ruled that restraints imposed by groups of colleges and universities typically would be decided under a Rule of Reason interpretation. Despite this Rule of Reason interpretation, however, the Court found against the schools in both cases.

THE NATIONAL COLLEGIATE ATHLETIC ASSOCIATION CASE[22] (1984)—The National Collegiate Athletic Association (NCAA) was created in 1905 to help support and regulate intercollegiate athletics. Beginning in 1952 the NCAA limited the total number of televised college football games and the number of television appearances per season for each college or university team.

The College Football Association (CFA) consisted of a group of large universities with major football programs that banded together to promote their interests in college football within the overall NCAA structure. In 1979 the CFA negotiated a separate television contract with the National Broadcasting Company (NBC) that allowed for more television appearances for each school than the NCAA permitted. In response, the NCAA announced it would discipline the members of the CFA. The members of the CFA then sued the NCAA under Section 1 of the Sherman Act and immediately obtained a court order, or an **injunction**, preventing the NCAA from taking any disciplinary action against the CFA schools. The District Court and the Court of Appeals both ruled that the NCAA television plan was a per se violation of Section 1 because the plan limited the output of televised college football games.

On appeal the Supreme Court ruled that it was inappropriate to apply a *per se* rule to the case, but nonetheless concluded that the NCAA's restrictions violated Section 1 under a Rule of Reason interpretation. The Supreme Court majority used a Rule of Reason interpretation because they believed that some horizontal restraints of trade were necessary to supply the product, college football games, at all. The Court recognized that unless the members of a football league agreed jointly to certain league rules, no games would be played. Jointly agreed to rules spanned the gambit from the size of the field and the number of players to the requirements that student-athletes not be paid and must attend classes. In the absence of such restrictions, colleges would not agree to play each other, and consumer choice would be restricted.

Turning to the specifics of the case, the NCAA argued that its plan was pro-competitive because it protected attendance at live football games and promoted competitive balance among NCAA member teams. The Supreme Court ruled that the NCAA did not appear to take either of these objectives too seriously. For one thing, the television plan allowed for broadcast of national games into local communities in which live games were simultaneously taking place. Furthermore, the NCAA did not limit the amount of money a school could spend on football or the amount of revenue it could collect from football-related activities, such as ticket and merchandise sales. Finally, the NCAA did nothing to limit the way in which those revenues could be spent by the colleges.

In the final analysis, the Supreme Court majority ruled that there were several anticompetitive effects of the NCAA's television plan. The majority opinion stated that "the record supports the District Court's conclusion that by curtailing output and blunting the ability of member institutions to respond to consumer preference, the NCAA has restricted rather than enhanced the place of intercollegiate athletics in the Nation's life."

IVY LEAGUE OVERLAP GROUP CASE[23] (1993)—In 1958 the Massachusetts Institute of Technology (MIT) and the eight Ivy League schools formed the "Ivy Overlap Group."* The purpose of the group was to meet to agree on the financial aid packages offered to students admitted to more than one of the schools. All nine schools offered admission based strictly on merit, but offered financial aid packages based strictly on need. Each April the nine schools meet and explicitly set the award packages offered to each student. Differences of $500 or less were ignored, but if there was more than a $500 disagreement about the size of a package, the schools agreed to a compromise amount.

The Justice Department charged that the Overlap Group was engaged in a price-fixing conspiracy to set the price of tuition for each and every admitted student. The eight Ivy League schools decided to sign a consent decree prohibiting them from continuing to meet to set financial aid packages. MIT, however, refused to sign the consent decree and took the Justice Department to court. The

---

*The eight Ivy League schools are Brown University, Columbia University, Cornell University, Dartmouth College, Harvard University, Princeton University, the University of Pennsylvania, and Yale University.

District Court ruled that the Overlap Group was engaged in a price-fixing conspiracy, but that because of the nonprofit status and educational mission of the schools the conspiracy was not illegal per se. Instead of a strict per se rule, the District Court decided to apply an **abbreviated Rule of Reason** to the case. The abbreviated Rule of Reason "applies in cases where *per se* condemnation is inappropriate, but in which 'no elaborate industry analysis is required to demonstrate the anticompetitive character' of an inherently suspect restraint." Under the abbreviated Rule of Reason the District Court offered MIT a chance to present a pro-competitive defense and then found for the Justice Department.

The Court of Appeals overturned the District Court, and remanded the case for a full Rule of Reason hearing. The Court of Appeals noted that it was possible that the Overlap Group meetings had no negative competitive impact. In its defense, MIT argued that the meetings improved the quality of education at the schools, increased consumer choice by making an Overlap Group education more accessible to a larger number of students, promoted competition among the members in areas other than price, and promoted socioeconomic diversity at the schools.

In the absence of the meetings, MIT feared that a bidding war for highly qualified wealthy students would leave less financial aid for qualified needy students. Because the resources available for aid are relatively fixed each year, this would result in fewer total students being offered aid and far fewer needy students, particularly minority students, being offered aid.

There never was a full Rule of Reason trial in this case because on December 22, 1993, MIT agreed to a consent decree. The settlement prohibited a return to the former practices of the Overlap Group, but permitted the colleges to agree "on general principles for determining financial aid, to award aid solely on the basis of financial need, and to exchange limited data about applicants' financial profiles."

◢ *Patents and Section 1 of the Sherman Act*

Section 1 of the Sherman Act forbids all restraints of trade. As we have discussed, the courts interpreted this as a *per se* ban on *all* direct price-fixing agreements. The Constitution, however, explicitly grants a patentee the "exclusive right to make, use, and vend the invention or discovery." Although there is no explicit constitutional right to fix prices, the exclusive right provision can be interpreted as ensuring that a patent holder has the right to fix the sale price on a patented item even if it is produced under license by another manufacturer.

Antitrust policy has attempted to limit the most obvious patent abuses of Section 1 while still permitting patent holders to obtain the basic monopoly benefits associated with the system. The first major issue addressed under the antitrust laws was the use of price-fixing clauses in patent licensing agreements. The basic precedent was set in the 1926 *General Electric* case.

THE GENERAL ELECTRIC CASE[24]—General Electric owned the three basic patents for the use of tungsten filaments in light bulbs. Without these patents it was virtually impossible to compete successfully in the light bulb market, and GE could have maintained a monopoly on light bulbs by simply refusing to license its patents. GE, however, granted Westinghouse a license on March 1, 1912. Under the terms of the license, Westinghouse agreed to follow GE's pricing and distribution policy. The licensing agreement explicitly forbade Westinghouse from underpricing GE. In the absence of patent protection, such an agreement would clearly have violated Section 1 of the Sherman Act.

The case presented a classic dilemma in patent antitrust law. If the courts prevented GE from fixing bulb prices, GE could have adopted a non-licensing policy and produced all tungsten filament bulbs itself. If the Courts permitted price fixing on the patented bulbs, however, it would eliminate some of the incentive for GE's competitors to create improved bulbs, because GE and the licensees would all lose if aggressive competition erupted after the development of a new light bulb. By permitting price fixing and encouraging more licensing, the courts might reduce GE's short-run monopoly power a bit, but they would create an environment that would be less conducive for technological change in the future. Conversely, by strictly enforcing the ban on price fixing, the courts might create an even stronger short-run monopoly for GE, but such a ruling would create an increased incentive for Westinghouse and others to invent around the tungsten filament patents.

The Supreme Court decided in favor of a bit less short-run monopoly power and ruled in favor of permitting price fixing.

> When the patentee licenses another to make and vend, and retains the right to continue to make and vend on his own account, the price at which his licensee will sell will necessarily affect the price at which he can sell his own patented goods. It would seem entirely reasonable that he should say to the licensee, "Yes, you may make and sell articles under my patent, but not so as to destroy the profit that I wish to obtain by making them and selling them myself."

The basic *General Electric* precedent has never been overturned. If a license contains an agreement to abide by the patentee's price, the courts will generally uphold the price-fixing agreement. This ruling can be defended on economic grounds, but it can also be attacked on economic grounds. Because a patentee usually holds a significant cost advantage over any licensee (by virtue of the licensee's royalty payments), a patent holder should be able to compete with its licensees without benefit of a price-fixing clause. In fact, if a licensee elects to charge a lower price than a patentee, the patentee should be able to at least match the lower price, unless the licensee is a more efficient producer. If the licensee is a more efficient producer, there is little economic justification for protecting the inefficient patentee. In other words, in those rare cases in which a licensee can produce a good at a lower social cost than a patentee, it would seem to make economic sense to prevent price-fixing and encourage the efficient licensee to charge a lower price. Of course, the licensee would still have to pay royalties to the patentee.

The General Electric precedent provided a sound defense in straightforward cases in which one patentee licensed one patent to a few firms. It quickly became clear, however, that the courts would not permit a group of firms to pool a large number of patents in an obvious attempt to use patent protection to avoid the antitrust laws. The *Hartford-Empire* case is the classic example of such an attempt to monopolize an industry through the use of a **patent pooling** arrangement.

THE HARTFORD-EMPIRE CASE[25]—The *Hartford-Empire* case involved one of the most extensive patent pools in United States history. Because patent pooling can be used to solve the prisoner's dilemma, we discussed the case extensively in Chapter 9.[26] Recall that by 1938, Hartford had acquired more than 600 glass manufacturing patents.[27] Once its control was complete, Hartford allocated each glass manufacturer a strict production quota for each specific type of glass container. As a result of a series of complex quota agreements, in 1938, 94 percent of all glass containers were produced on machines using one or more of Hartford-Empire's patents.[28]

The Supreme Court ruled against Hartford. The Court ordered the defendants to lease or license glass-making machinery to all on demand at "standard royalties and without discrimination or restrictions."

Despite the 1945 decision, the glass container industry remained highly oligopolistic. Twenty-five years of patent control enabled the leading firms to maintain their market shares well into the future.[29] The case suggests that market power built on patent control is likely to continue long after the patents expire. In the *Hartford-Empire* case, even the remedy of forced licensing had only a limited effect on market structure.

THE UNITED STATES GYPSUM CASE[30]—The *U.S. Gypsum* case, which was also examined in Chapter 9, presents another example of patent abuse. Recall that the controlling patent, the Utzman patent, was issued for the idea of covering the entire gypsum core (including the edges) with paper instead of enclosing just the two sides. This minor technological advance resulted in U.S. Gypsum's domination of the industry for a quarter century.

Between 1917 and 1929, U.S. Gypsum followed an aggressive policy of filing infringement suits against any firm that came close to infringing on the Utzman patent, and by 1929 virtually all wallboard with closed edges was produced under U.S. Gypsum's Utzman patent. On June 6, 1929, two months before the Utzman patent expired, U.S. Gypsum and its licensees met in Chicago to discuss a new licensing agreement. What eventually emerged was an agreement signed on August 6, 1929, the exact day the Utzman patent expired, that expanded U.S. Gypsum's patent control. Each licensee agreed to pay a royalty on "all plaster board and gypsum wallboard of every kind" whether made by patented processes or not. The agreement covered fifty patents and seven patent applications and was to run until the most junior patent expired. As it turned out, two patents were granted in 1937, so the agreements were to run until 1954. As in the earlier agreement, U.S. Gypsum was to fix the minimum price on all wallboard products.

The Supreme Court condemned the 1929 agreements:

> It is well settled that price fixing, without authorizing statutes, is illegal per se. . . . Patents grant no privilege to their owners of organizing the use of those patents to monopolize an industry through price control, through royalties for the patents drawn from patent-free industry products and through regulation of distribution.

An analysis of the *Hartford-Empire* and *U.S. Gypsum* cases suggests that patents can be used not only as a spur for technological advance, but as a spur for collusion. Furthermore, because collusion is likely to reduce the incentive for technological advance, abusive patent behavior of this type almost certainly reduces the rate of technological advance. The *Hartford-Empire* and *U.S. Gypsum* cases represent extreme examples of patent abuse. Other cases, however, present more difficult policy dilemmas.

THE LINE MATERIAL CASE[31]—The *Line Material* case involved price-fixing in **cross-licensing agreements**, whereby one or more firms agree to license their patents to each other. The products involved in this case were two patented "dropout fuse cutouts" (circuit breakers) and the housing suitable for use with the cutouts. Line Material held a 1935 patent on the housing that was uncontested by both parties. In March 1939, however, Southern States Equipment Corporation received a patent on a new fuse cutout that had been developed by George N. Lemmon. On October 17, 1939, Line Material received a patent on a more advanced fuse cutout based on the Lemmon patent and developed by Schultz and Steinmayer. A manufacturer could produce the best possible fuse cutout only by using *both* the Lemmon and Schultz patents.

In May 1938, the two firms agreed to a bilateral, royalty-free cross-licensing agreement. Southern States and Line Material then licensed the Lemmon and Schultz patents to ten other manufacturers. Each license contained a price-fixing clause that prevented the licensee from underpricing Southern States and Line Material.

The Supreme Court ruled that the General Electric precedent did not permit price fixing of cross-licensed patents:

> While the *General Electric* case holds that a patentee may, under certain conditions, lawfully control the price the licensee of his several patents may charge for the patented device, no case of this Court has construed the patent and anti-monopoly statutes to permit separate owners of separate patents by cross-licenses or other arrangements to fix the prices to be charged by them and their licensees for their respective products.

THE ROYAL INDUSTRIES CASE[32]—The *Royal Industries* case raised several other interesting legal questions related to the *General Electric* doctrine. In April 1963, Royal Industries obtained a patent for producing plastic bag tie strips from Gerald C. Bower, the owner of Plas-Ties Corporation. Shortly thereafter, Royal acquired 80 percent of the stock in Plas-Ties. Plas-Ties remained a separate subsidiary, however, with Bower retaining 20 percent stock ownership and Royal never produced any tie strips. In May 1963, Plas-Ties and Pollack Paper Company, a division of St. Regis Paper, signed a written licensing agreement. The license contained all the usual provisions, plus a further stipulation: "If Royal reduces its selling prices below those set forth in the attached Exhibit A, said 10% royalty shall be reduced one percentage point for each 5% reduction in the selling prices, provided however that the royalty shall not be reduced below 5%." There was, however, no explicit price-fixing clause in the written agreement.

From May 1963 until February 1966, St. Regis and Plas-Ties maintained identical prices. In February 1966, however, licensee St. Regis lowered its prices. The next month, Plas-Ties matched St. Regis's lower prices. In June 1966, St. Regis lowered its prices again, and Royal, but not Plas-Ties, complained. A conference was held, and this conference became a major point of dispute during the trial. Royal contended that a price-fixing agreement had been reached at the conference; St. Regis denied that any price-fixing agreement had been consummated. In any event, after the June conference, St. Regis raised its prices a bit, but they remained below Plas-Ties's prices. Then in May 1967 St. Regis again reduced its prices. This proved to be the last straw for Royal. In a letter dated June 8, 1967, Royal threatened that unless St. Regis raised its prices to match Plas-Ties's prices, its license would be terminated. When St. Regis refused to raise its prices, Royal terminated the license. St. Regis ignored the termination notice, and Royal then filed an infringement suit against St. Regis.

The District Court further restricted the *General Electric* precedent by ruling in favor of St. Regis. The Court noted that the patent-antitrust exception allowed under the *General Electric* precedent was very limited and did not extend to a case in which the patent owner, Royal in this case, did not compete with the licensee, St. Regis.

The *Royal Industries* ruling further restricted the *General Electric* doctrine by bringing into question several practices. The decision suggested that any price-fixing agreement made *after* an initial patent licensing agreement is likely to be viewed with deep suspicion by the courts. Furthermore, by restricting Royal, the patent holder, to act only in concert with Plas-Ties, the manufacturer of the patented good, the Circuit Court added a further restriction to the patent holder's rights.

SUMMARY

1. The Court's tough stand against direct price-fixing agreements makes economic sense. There are so few cases of economically justified price fixing that a *per se* ban, by avoiding long, complicated, and costly arguments over reasonableness, represents an optimal policy.

2. The basic issue of direct price-fixing agreements has been settled by the courts, but other more subtle forms of solving the prisoner's dilemma have been left open for judicial interpretation. One open area is price exchanges between competitors. The Supreme Court has ruled that price exchanges come under a Rule of Reason interpretation, and are illegal only if there is an intent to raise prices.

3. With regard to oligopolistic behavior, the issues are far more complex. Consciously parallel behavior is likely to remain outside the reach of the current antitrust statutes. Oligopolists follow consciously parallel behavior because it is rational. In the absence of structural remedies, it is doubtful that convictions and fines will have much impact on oligopolistic behavior.

4. Unless the Courts dramatically change their current position and order structural remedies in oligopoly cases, any long-run change in policy toward conscious parallelism would require new legislation.

5. With regard to trade associations, the continuous reporting of price information to competitors can be used to discourage price cutting be-

cause few firms wish to be identified as chiselers by their competitors, who are often also their friends. Price reporting schemes that do little more than ask members to report prices, and which then make this information available to the public, will generally be permitted. However, direct attempts to force adherence to list prices or restrict price cutting will bring an association within the reach of Section 1.

6. Until the 1970s it was common for organizations of physicians, lawyers, and other professionals to restrict competition by forbidding advertising or price competition. In the past 25 years, the courts have greatly limited the scope of permitted restrictions, and professional organizations now come within the jurisdiction of the Sherman Act.

7. In two major cases, the courts ruled that nonprofit organizations such as colleges and universities also are subject to the Sherman Act.

8. Antitrust policy has attempted to limit the most obvious patent abuses while still permitting patent holders to obtain the basic monopoly benefits associated with the system.

9. Although the courts have ruled that it is legal for a patent holder to fix the price a licensee may charge for a patented product, any attempt to extend the power of one patent into other areas, such as through a patent-pooling agreement or a conspiracy directed against one or more competitors, is on shaky grounds.

10. Overall, the antitrust laws have been fairly successful in the area of horizontal agreements. In the absence of the Sherman Act, price fixing would undoubtedly be far more common. And despite the protestations of a relatively small minority of economists, the economic inefficiencies that would result from permitting collusion would place a significant burden on society.[33]

KEY TERMS

abbreviated Rule of Reason	*per se* rule
conscious parallelism	price exchange agreement
cross-licensing agreement	remanded
injunction	Rule of Reason
overt price-fixing agreement	tacit price-fixing agreement
patent pooling	

DISCUSSION QUESTIONS

1. Discuss one economic strength and one economic weakness in the antitrust laws with regard to price fixing. Make sure you use precedents to support your position.

2. In the *Container Corporation* case the court refused to accept the argument

that declining prices are a legitimate defense in price-exchange cases. Do you believe this decision made economic sense?

3. Can you identify any examples from your local neighborhood (such as gasoline stations, food stores, or restaurants) of tacit or overt collusion? Which type of collusion do you suspect? Why?

4. Why does oligopoly present a particularly difficult problem from both an economic and legal standpoint? How have the courts dealt with this problem in this century? What one precedent do you believe makes the most economic sense? Why?

5. What are the common justifications offered by defendants in price-fixing cases? Are any of these justifications valid?

6. Do you agree or disagree with the following statement: If two small producers of bread exchanged price information over the telephone, it would not be necessary to prove that they intended to increase prices to an unreasonable level to show a criminal violation of the Sherman Act.

7. Would it be legal for a patent holder to license a single patent to one licensee with a price-fixing clause? Would it be legal for a group of firms to pool their patents, refuse to license an individual patent, and only license the entire group with price-fixing clauses?

8. Some economists have argued that the 1926 *General Electric* precedent is obsolete and should be overturned by the Supreme Court. Do you agree?

9. Suppose a hospital always receives identical secret bids to buy antibiotics from five drug companies. Would such identical bids "prove" the existence of collusion?

10. Do you agree with the initial ruling against the Ivy League Overlap Group? What group of students would most likely emerge as winners from such a ruling? What group of students would most likely emerge as losers from such a ruling? What would likely happen to the total number of students on financial aid?

11. Why might a doctor or lawyer argue that price fixing is in the interests of his or her patients and clients, respectively? Do you think an economist would be convinced by these arguments?

12. Suppose at the next national meeting of the American Economics Association, economists agreed that no new Ph.D. in economics would accept a professorship from a four-year university or college for less than $55,000 per year. Do you think such an agreement would have any significant economic impact? Would such an agreement be legal?

REFERENCES

1. Don E. Waldman, "Welfare and Collusion: Comment," *American Economic Review* 72 (March 1982): 268-71.

2. This view was common during the first 25 years of this century. See J.M. Clark, *Studies in the Economics of Overhead Costs*

(Chicago: University of Chicago Press, 1923), pp. 434–50. For a later statement of this position see Almarin Phillips, *Market Structure, Organization and Performance* (Cambridge, Mass.: Harvard University Press,1962), pp. 221–42.

3. *United States v. Trans-Missouri Freight Association*, 166 U.S. 290 (1897).
4. *Addyston Pipe and Steel Company v. United States*, 175 U.S. 211 (1899).
5. *United States v. Trenton Potteries Company et al.*, 273 U.S. 392 (1927).
6. *Appalachian Coals Inc. v. United States*, 288 US 344 (1933).
7. *United States v. Container Corporation of America et al.*, 393 U.S. 333 (1969).
8. *United States v. United States Gypsum Company et al.*, 438 U.S. 422 (1978).
9. *American Tobacco Company et al. v. United States*, 328 U.S. 781 (1946).
10. *United States v. Paramount Pictures et al.*, 334 U.S. 131 (1948).
11. *Theatre Enterprises, Inc. v. Paramount Film Distributing Corporation et al.*, 346 U.S. 537 (1954).
12. *United States v. Chas. Pfizer & Co., Inc., American Cyanamid Company and Bristol-Myers Company*, 426 F.2d 32 (1970).
13. *General Electric and Westinghouse Consent Decree*, Civil No. 28,228 E.D. Pennsylvania (December 1976).
14. *Ethyl Corporation v. FTC*, 729 F.2d 128 (1984).
15. *Ibid.*, pp. 204–5.
16. *American Column and Lumber Company et al. v. United States*, 257 U.S. 377 (1921).
17. *Sugar Institute, Inc. et al. v. United States*, 297 U.S. 553 (1936).
18. *Tag Manufacturers Institute v Federal Trade Commission*, 174 F.2d 452 (1949).
19. *Goldfarb et al. v. Virginia State Bar et al.*, 421 US 773 (1975).
20. *Bates et al. v. State Bar of Arizona*, 433 US 350 (1977).
21. *National Society of Professional Engineers v. United States*, 98 S.Ct. 1355 (1978).
22. *National Collegiate Athletic Association v. Board of Regents of University of Oklahoma*, 486 U.S. 85 (1984).
23. *United States v. Brown University*, 5 F.3d 658 (1993).
24. *United States v. General Electric Company et al.*, 272 U.S. 476 (1926).
25. *Hartford Empire Company v. United States*, 323 U.S. 386 (1945).
26. See *supra*, Chapter 9, pp. 222–23.
27. Don E. Waldman, *The Economics of Antitrust: Causes and Analysis* (Boston: Little, Brown, 1986), p. 218.
28. *Ibid.*, p. 218.
29. Don E. Waldman, *Antitrust Action and Market Structure*, (Lexington, MA: D.C. Heath, 1978), pp. 110–11.
30. *United States v. United States Gypsum Company et al.*, 333 U.S. 364 (1948).
31. *United States v. Line Material Company, Southern States Equipment Corporation et al.*, 333 U.S. 287 (1948).
32. *Royal Industries v. St. Regis Paper Company*, 1970 Trade Cases ||73,076.
33. Donald Dewey, "Information, Entry, and Welfare: The Case for Collusion," *American Economic Review* (September 1979): 588. For a rather extreme statement of this position, see Dominick T. Armentano, *Antitrust and Monopoly: Anatomy of a Policy Failure* (New York: John Wiley & Sons, 1982), Chapter 5.

Chapter 20

Antitrust: Mergers

Mergers raise some of the more intriguing policy questions in industrial organization because many mergers have positive as well as negative effects on competition and efficiency. As a result, there is a continuing debate among economists as to whether mergers generally promote greater efficiency or greater market power. It is important, therefore, to point out both the positive and negative effects of a particular merger and then to decide whether the positive or negative effects dominate.

The three broad merger categories are: horizontal, vertical, and conglomerate. **Horizontal mergers** involve firms that are *direct* competitors. The firms must compete in both the same product market and the same geographic market. **Vertical mergers** involve firms that produce at different stages of production in the same industry. If Bethlehem Steel purchased an iron ore mining company, it would be classified as a vertical merger. **Conglomerate mergers** involve companies that operate in either different product markets or the same product market but different geographic markets. Conglomerate mergers are usually subdivided into three types: **product extension mergers** between companies that produce different but related products (e.g., laundry detergent and liquid bleach); **geographic extension mergers** between companies that produce the same product in different locations (e.g., a midwestern beer producer purchases a northeastern beer producer); and **pure conglomerate mergers** between firms operating in entirely separate markets (e.g., a telephone company purchases a rental car company).

Merger History

Figure 20.1 combines data from several sources on the number of mergers in the United States since approximately the beginning of the twentieth century. The figure shows that four merger waves have influenced the structure of American industry.*

---

*The number of mergers reported for the early years is biased downward because early data sources reported only mergers between "large" firms.

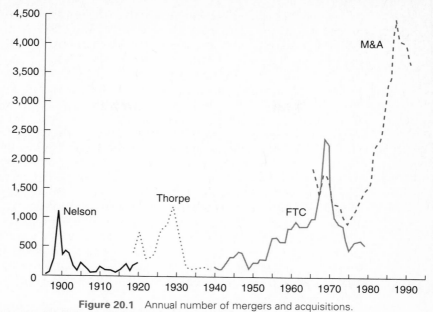

Figure 20.1 Annual number of mergers and acquisitions.

Source: Adapted from Golbe and White, Figure 9.6, in Alan J. Auerbach (ed.), *Corporate Takeovers* (Chicago: University of Chicago Press, 1988).

Spurred by the passage of the Sherman Act, the first merger wave occurred around the turn of the century. Relative to the size of the economy, this first merger wave dwarfs the others. In the peak year of the first wave, 1898, the number of mergers per dollar of real GNP was almost five times greater than in 1988, the peak year of the most recent wave that attracted so much media attention.[1] Most of the mergers during this period were horizontal, often involving several firms. In fact, 75 percent of firm disappearances during this wave resulted from mergers involving at least five firms.[2] Many of today's large firms were formed in this period, including Standard Oil of New Jersey (Exxon), Goodyear, U.S. Steel (USX), General Electric, Nabisco, and Eastman Kodak. As one economic historian stated. "It is no exaggeration to say that the structure of the modern American economy had been reshaped by the end of the first decade of the twentieth century."[3]

The second major merger wave took place in the 1920s. Stigler has called this wave the *merger to oligopoly* movement, as compared with the first *merger to monopoly* wave.[4] Mergers of this period typically combined fewer firms than the mergers of the first wave and, rather than creating the industry leader, often resulted in the formation of the second or third largest firm in an industry. Whereas most of the mergers during the first wave took place in manufacturing and mining, during the second wave, considerable merger activity occurred in other sectors, such as utilities, banking, and retailing. Horizontal mergers again were prevalent during this wave, although product extension and vertical mergers were also common.[5]

Figure 20.1 shows little merger activity from the beginning of the Great Depression until the third merger wave began sometime in the mid 1950s. More than 25,000 mergers took place in the years 1960 to 1970, with slightly more than half taking place in mining or manufacturing.[6] In large measure because passage of the Celler-Kefauver Act in 1950 made horizontal mergers subject to effective legal challenge, this merger wave differed from the earlier two waves in that the vast majority were conglomerate mergers. From 1963 to 1972 approximately 80 percent of the assets acquired were the result of conglomerate mergers. Pure conglomerate mergers, in particular, were widespread during this period.[7]

The fourth major merger wave in the United States took place during the 1980s. The large mergers in this most recent wave received considerable media attention, in part because of the large sums of money involved. For example, Philip Morris purchased Kraft in 1988 for $12.9 billion. Also, many of the mergers of the 1980s resulted from hostile tender offers, making for dramatic news reports. Unfortunately, data on mergers by type of acquisition are no longer published so it is difficult to make statistical comparisons of the fourth merger wave with the earlier waves. We can guess, however, that the proportion of mergers accounted for by horizontal combinations rose compared with the third wave.* It is also known that many oil companies used their profits from the 1970s to acquire other firms in the 1980s.

Motives for Merger

In one sense all mergers occur for the same reason: one group believes that the acquired company is worth more than the acquired company's owners believe the company is worth. No merger will take place unless this condition is fulfilled. Several major reasons are commonly advanced to explain mergers.[8] Seven of the most commonly advanced reasons are discussed below.

MARKET POWER

All three types of mergers can increase market power, and the next section of this chapter analyzes the potential anticompetitive effects in detail. Horizontal mergers are more likely than either vertical or conglomerate mergers to have serious anticompetitive effects.[9] Because horizontal mergers always increase concentration, the possibility exists that market power will increase. If General Motors acquired Ford, it is very likely that prices and profits would increase in the automobile market, even given competition from the Japanese and Europeans. Vertical mergers may result in increased entry barriers, particularly the capital barrier, or an increased likelihood of collusion. Finally, although other negative effects are

---

*One hypothesis is that the Reagan Administration adopted a more lenient antitrust policy.

possible, the most likely negative impact of a conglomerate merger is a reduction in the level of potential competition.

With regard to horizontal mergers, the Cournot-Nash model suggests that a reduction in the number of firms in an industry can result in reduced output and higher price. Recall from Chapter 7 that the equilibrium quantity in a Cournot-Nash industry with linear demand, constant marginal and average costs, and N firms is:

$$Q_{CN} = \frac{N}{N+1} Q_{comp},$$

where Q_{CN} represents total quantity produced in the Cournot-Nash industry and Q_{comp} represents the competitive output at which price equals marginal cost. Because horizontal mergers always reduce N, these mergers should reduce output and result in higher prices.

EFFICIENCY GAINS

Mergers are often motivated by a desire to increase economic efficiency, and some mergers result in significant efficiency gains. Economies of scale may result from any merger but are most common in horizontal mergers. A horizontal merger may enable the consolidated firm to reduce its production or marketing costs. In one documented example, three British bearing manufacturers were able to increase their output per employee by 40 percent after a merger.[10] Vertical mergers also may result in real economies by reducing the transactions costs associated with coordinating the different stages of production, and conglomerate mergers may improve efficiency by taking advantage of synergies in production or distribution.

All three types of mergers may improve efficiency by eliminating *x-inefficiencies*. Recall from Chapter 3 that in a world in which managers have some discretion, costs may not be minimized because of x-inefficiency. If managers are interested in living a quiet, peaceful life, they may not continually strive to find the least costly way of organizing production, handling materials, and, in general, doing business. As a result, costs are higher than necessary. Inefficient firms suffering from x-inefficiencies may be the most likely targets of takeover bids because these firms have the greatest potential for improving their profitability by replacing current managers with more efficient managers.

Although horizontal mergers may result in real economies of scale or a reduction in x-inefficiencies, one must be careful to distinguish *real* economies from *pecuniary* economies. Recall from Chapter 5 that pecuniary economies result when increased market power gives a firm the ability to obtain inputs, including capital, at lower prices than its competitors. Such pecuniary economies result in a change in the distribution of income but do not lower the opportunity costs of production. Recent evidence suggests that although many mergers, particularly horizontal mergers, result in some cost reductions, the cost savings are often small.[11]

FINANCIAL MOTIVES

A motive for merger may be speculation that the "whole is worth more than the sum of its parts." When a large conglomerate is on a roll of good purchases, its stock value will rise, and so will its price/earnings ratio. If this successful conglomerate purchases another profitable company with a lower price/earnings ratio, and finances the purchase by exchanging its stock for the acquired firm's stock, all parties may gain financially in the short run. The owners of the acquired firm gain if the conglomerate pays a premium for their stock, that is, if the conglomerate pays more than the stock is worth on the open market. In addition, the owners of the conglomerate gain because earnings per share rise when the acquired firm's profits are added to the conglomerate's profits.

Suppose for example that a large conglomerate firm, hypothetically named GEAKO, has a price/earnings ratio for its stock of 20, but a small target firm, hypothetically named WEAKO, has a much lower price/earnings ratio of 10. If the annual profits (earnings) of WEAKO are $10 million, then its current stock value is $10 \times \$10$ million = $100 million. If the annual profits of GEAKO *before* the merger are $500 million, its stock value is $20 \times \$500$ million = $10 billion. If GEAKO acquires WEAKO, GEAKO's earnings rise to $510 million and its stock value rises by $200 million to $10.2 billion. Suppose GEAKO offers to pay $125 million for WEAKO. The WEAKO stockholders receive $25 million more than the stock is valued by the stock market, and the stockholders of GEAKO still come out ahead: the price of $125 million is considerably below the $200 million increase in the value of GEAKO's stock.

This analysis may seem complicated but it boils down to a simple phenomenon: because of stock market myopia, even in the absence of any real benefits from the merger, the stock market behaves as if the acquired firm will fare better under the conglomerate's ownership. The potential problem is that if investors stop believing in the conglomerate's ability to keep growing and keep increasing its profitability, then its stock value will tumble, and existing stockholders will sustain large capital losses. By that time many of the original stockholders will have sold their stock for large short-run capital gains. This financial motive for merger was probably strongest during the merger wave of the late 1960s, when acquisitions were financed largely through stock exchanges.

Until recently the American tax code provided another financial motive for merger. Because paid-out corporate profits are taxed twice—first, as corporate profits, and then as individual income—there is an incentive for firms to retain profits and reinvest these retained profits in ways that lower their stockholders' personal income tax burden. If retained earnings are used to acquire companies, and the acquisitions result in an increase in the conglomerate's stock value, then capital gains result. Until 1989 capital gains in the United States were taxed at a lower rate than other types of personal income, and therefore, it was preferable from a tax standpoint to receive income in the form of capital gains rather than as distributed corporate profits. Until fairly recently, therefore, the tax laws resulted in an additional incentive for merger.

RISK REDUCTION

It is often argued that mergers, particularly conglomerate mergers, reduce risk, and there is some truth to the old saying: It's foolish to put all your eggs in one basket.* For a merger to reduce risk, the acquiring firm's profits must not be perfectly correlated with the acquired firm's profits. Although this technical condition is met in most mergers, a merger will not reduce risk significantly if the acquired firm operates in an industry that is highly interdependent with the acquiring firm's other business activities. In the case of considerable interdependence, when one part of the acquiring firm's business flounders, so will the acquired part.

Pure conglomerate mergers are the most likely mergers to reduce risk. Few horizontal, vertical, product extension, or geographic extension mergers significantly reduce risk, however, because they usually involve markets that are interdependent with the firm's other operations. If two coal companies merged and then the market for coal became depressed, both firms would suffer, and the merger would have done little to reduce risk. Similarly, if a hotel firm purchased a rental car company, and then because of a recession the demand for vacation travel declined, both the hotel and car rental businesses would suffer.

EMPIRE BUILDING

A factor encouraging some mergers is the desire of an individual to build a financial empire. Strange as it may seem, many mergers are primarily the result of an individual's effort at self-aggrandizement. Perhaps the two best examples were the efforts of Harold Geneen as the Chief Executive Officer (CEO) at ITT, and Charles Bluhdorn as the CEO at Gulf & Western. To these individuals, growth, pure and simple, was often sufficient motive for a merger.

FAILING FIRM

A firm on the verge of bankruptcy may attempt to find a buyer to bail it out. The Penn-Central railroad merger, which ultimately ended in bankruptcy, was a classic example. Few large mergers appear to be motivated by the existence of a failing firm, however. Defining a large merger as a merger in which the acquired firm had at least $10 million in assets, Boyle found that in only 4.8 percent of all large mergers was the acquired firm suffering from economic losses before the merger.[12]

---

*It is important to realize that diversification by a firm lowers the *firm's* risk, but *individual investors* can always select their optimal combination of returns and risk by diversifying their investment holdings.

AGING OWNERS

In some cases, a motive for merger is the age structure of the company's ownership. If a company is privately owned or controlled by an individual without heirs, or without heirs who have a desire to operate the business, then the owner will sometimes search for a buyer. A merger permits the owner to retire on the anticipated future earnings of the firm because these earnings are capitalized into the present value of the firm.

The Effects of Mergers on Competition and Welfare

HORIZONTAL MERGERS

Horizontal mergers may result in both an increase in market power and a reduction in costs because of increased economies of scale. The positive effects of increased economies must be balanced, therefore, against the negative effects of increased market power.[13] Williamson has created a model to explain this trade-off that is analyzed in Figure 20.2.* Before the merger, the industry performed com-

---

*The model was developed in O. E. Williamson, "Economies as an Antitrust Defense: The Welfare Tradeoffs," *American Economic Review* 58 (March 1968): 18–36. Williamson's analysis is static and ignores the potential dynamic impacts of mergers on the rate of technological advance. As we discovered in Chapter 14, these dynamic impacts may be more important than the static impacts analyzed by Williamson.

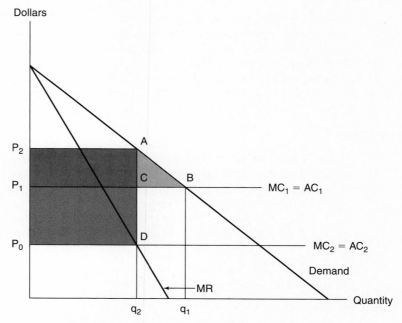

Figure 20.2   The welfare effects of a horizontal merger.

petitively, with output equal to q_1 and price equal to P_1, which equals marginal cost MC_1. The merger results in the creation of a monopoly. After the merger, marginal costs are reduced to MC_2, but because of monopoly, output declines to the level at which $MC = MR$ at q_2, and price increases to P_2. The merger reduces consumer surplus by the dark gray and light gray areas P_2ABP_1, but also reduces the costs of producing the q_2 units by the red area P_1CDP_0. The dark gray rectangle P_2ACP_1 represents the transfer from consumer surplus to producer profits that results from the merger. The light gray triangle ABC represents the deadweight loss resulting from the merger. If the light gray deadweight loss triangle ABC is larger than the red rectangle P_1CDP_0, then the merger has a *net* negative effect. If the light gray deadweight loss triangle ABC is smaller than the red rectangle P_1CDP_0, then the merger has a *net* positive effect.

Figure 20.3 shows a numerical example in which a merger takes place in an industry with demand curve $P = 100 - 0.25Q$. Before the merger, the industry performed competitively, with output equal to $q_1 = 280$ and price equal to marginal cost $MC_1 = 30$. After the merger, marginal costs fall to $MC_2 = 10$, but output declines to $q_2 = 180$, the level at which $MC = MR$, and price increases to $P_2 = 55$. The merger reduces consumer surplus by the dark gray and light gray areas $P_2ABP_1 = 180(25) + (1/2) (25 \times 100) = 5750$, but it also reduces the costs of producing the q_2 units by the red rectangle $P_1CDP_0 = 180 \times 20 = 3600$. The dark gray rectangle $P_2ACP_1 = 180 \times 25 = 4500$ represents a transfer from consumer surplus to producers profits. The light gray triangle ABC $= 1/2(25 \times 100) = 1250$ represents the deadweight loss resulting from the merger. Because the light gray deadweight loss ABC $= 1250$ is smaller than the red cost-savings area $P_1CDP_0 = 3600$, this merger has a net positive effect.

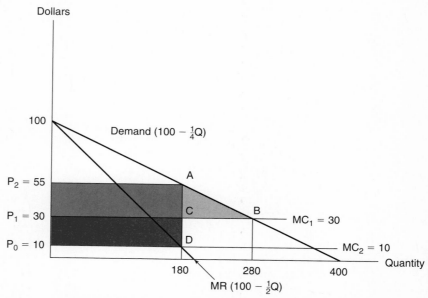

Figure 20.3   Cost-reducing merger resulting in a welfare gain.

To understand the implications of Figures 20.2 and 20.3, it is necessary to understand the trade-off of market power for cost reduction. If the effects of the cost reduction exceed the effects of the market power increase, the merger has on balance a positive effect, whereas if the effects of the market power increase exceed the effects of the cost reduction, the merger has on balance a negative effect.

VERTICAL MERGERS

We analyzed the economic impact of vertical relationships in detail in Chapter 16. At the end of that chapter, we noted that the major legal theory used by the government to oppose vertical mergers is foreclosure, which is controversial among economists but has been accepted by the courts in the past. Consider this hypothetical example: Suppose McDonald's purchased a large producer of restaurant equipment. McDonald's would then buy its equipment from its own subsidiary, and therefore, the merger would foreclose other equipment suppliers from selling to McDonald's. In theory, such a merger might result in the demise of restaurant equipment suppliers that had previously supplied McDonald's, and as a result, market structure might deteriorate in the equipment industry. Furthermore, after the merger, McDonald's fast food competitors might be forced to pay higher equipment prices, and this could ultimately result in higher fast food prices to consumers.

In Chapter 16 we showed that this argument is dependent on the existence of significant market power in at least one of the markets, either the restaurant equipment market or the fast food market. Recall that if *both* markets were competitive, increased vertical integration and foreclosure would have no negative effects on efficiency, because prices in both markets would equal marginal cost regardless of the degree of vertical integration. In addition, because of the problem of double marginalization, if both firms had monopolies in their respective markets (**bilateral monopoly**) vertical integration would have a positive effect on efficiency.

We also noted in Chapter 16 that increased vertical integration can raise the capital barrier to entry, result in price squeezes, and facilitate collusion. Vertical mergers, therefore, can have a negative economic impact.

CONGLOMERATE MERGERS

Theoretically, conglomerate mergers also may increase market power.[14] Attacks on conglomerate mergers have been based on four arguments: (1) the elimination of potential competition, (2) reciprocal buying, (3) cross-subsidization, and (4) economic forbearance.

The classic **potential competition** argument was advanced when Procter & Gamble, the nation's leading detergent producer, purchased Clorox, the leading bleach producer. In a precedent-setting antitrust case, the government argued that Procter's existence as a potential entrant into the liquid bleach market served as a check on the pricing behavior of existing liquid bleach manufacturers, because existing producers were aware that high prices and profits would encourage Procter to enter. According to this argument, once Procter purchased Clorox, this potential competition was eliminated and the price of bleach would increase.

Reciprocity refers to the possibility that a large conglomerate can encourage its suppliers to purchase inputs from another of the conglomerate's divisions. If a large food wholesaler purchased a major spice manufacturer, it might "request" that its food suppliers purchase their spice requirements from its spice division. As a result, the market power of the acquired spice manufacturer might increase, and small independent spice manufacturers might be forced to withdraw from the market.

Cross-subsidization is another argument that has been advanced against conglomerate mergers. According to this theory, conglomerates will attempt to gain an increased market share in one market by using profits earned in another market to subsidize short-run losses. It has been argued that when Philip Morris purchased Miller Beer it chose to subsidize Miller's extensive advertising campaign with profits earned in Philip Morris's other markets.[15] This practice may be both rational and anticompetitive if it results in higher concentration and increased long-run prices and profits. Few conglomerate mergers probably result in substantial subsidization because unless entry barriers are high, the short-run losses associated with subsidization will usually be greater than any potential long-run profit gains.

Some economists have also theorized that conglomerate mergers will result in **economic forbearance** between the nation's leading firms, a situation in which no conglomerate firm will rock the boat in any market because it fears retaliation in another market.[16] For instance, suppose General Motors purchased IBM, and Ford bought Compaq Computers. Ford might discourage Compaq from competing too aggressively against IBM for fear of retaliation by General Motors in the automobile market. As a result, GM and Ford might compete less aggressively in both markets.

Empirical Evidence on the Effects of Mergers

Economists have relied on three types of evidence to determine whether mergers improve economic efficiency. **Event studies** examine the impact of a proposed merger on the stock market valuation of the firm around the time of the merger. If merger targets often suffer from severe x-inefficiencies, investors should believe new owners will replace the inefficient management team with a more efficient one. As a result, the stock market evaluation of the acquired firm should increase at the time of the announcement of the merger because the anticipated higher *future* earnings should be capitalized into the value of the stock.

Some empirical evidence suggests that around the time of a merger the acquired firm experiences a significant increase in the value of its stock, which results in large capital gains for the stockholders of the acquired company. Jensen and Rubek found that positive returns at the time of the merger ranged between 16 and 30 percent for tender offers before 1980.[17] Similarly, DeAngelo, DeAngelo, and Rice found an average 27 percent gain for leveraged buyouts between 1973 and 1980.[18] Several other studies have found similar results.[19] Because these studies generally find that the stock values of the acquiring companies did not experience any significant change at the time of merger, it has been concluded that the anticipated net effect of these mergers on efficiency must be positive. This follows because a positive gain for acquired firms plus a zero change for acquiring firms sums to a positive net change.

The event study evidence exhibits several weaknesses. The greatest problem is that there is a huge difference between *anticipated* and *actual* efficiency effects of mergers. Such differences are common. Studies that stretch the time horizon beyond the actual moment of the merger have generally found that the initial gains are lost. For example, when Magenheim and Mueller analyzed stock values of the acquiring firms three years after merger, they found that the values had declined a significant 16 percent.[20] In summarizing seven different studies, Jensen and Ruback found a 5.5 percent average decline one year after merger.[21] Such results cast doubt on the implications of the event studies.

A second type of study examines the *premerger profitability* of acquired and acquiring firms. If mergers enhance efficiency, acquiring firms should be more profitable than other firms, and acquired firms should be less profitable. This follows if the acquired firms suffer from x-inefficiencies and are therefore less profitable. Acquiring firms, by contrast, should be full of highly efficient managers and should be more profitable. Perhaps the most careful study of the profitability of acquired firms was carried out by Ravenscraft and Scherer, who found that acquired firms tended to be more profitable than their competitors.[22] Table 20.1 summarizes one of their major findings. In each year the acquired firms tended to be more profitable than the benchmark firms. Ravenscraft and Scherer concluded, "When would-be acquirers 'fished' among the population of relatively small manufacturing enterprises for noncoercive acquisitions, they tended to haul in mainly the specimens with superior profit records."[23] The evidence regarding acquiring companies suggests that the acquiring firms are relatively large and tend to be growing quickly, but there is little evidence that they are particularly profitable compared with the typical firm.[24]

Although event studies and premerger studies provide some evidence concerning the efficiency impacts of mergers, the best evidence should come from postmerger studies of profitability and productivity. Postmerger studies should be able to test directly whether mergers result in improved economic performance on the part of acquired firms. The Ravenscraft and Scherer study is probably the best in terms of methodology, and their results provide little evidence that merg-

TABLE 20.1 Profitability of Acquired Firms

Acquisition Period	Number of Firms	Average Profits (%)	FTC Profit Benchmark (%)
1968	392	20.8	11.3
1971	113	19.6	8.6
1974	129	18.9	11.6
All three years	634	20.2	10.9

Source: David J. Ravenscraft and F. M. Scherer, *Mergers, Sell-Offs, and Economic Efficiency* (Washington, D.C.: Brookings Institution, 1987), p. 60.

ers result in a systematic improvement of company performance.[25] Rather, their findings seem to confirm that some mergers make things better, some make things worse, and many have little or no effect on efficiency. One of Ravenscraft and Scherer's more striking results was that just under 50 percent of all mergers eventually resulted in divestiture of the acquired operation.[26] Furthermore, acquired units were much more likely to be divested than other lines already operated by the same acquiring firms. This sell-off phenomenon was heavily emphasized by Ravenscraft and Scherer, who also found that the sell-offs were generally preceded by a period of low and declining profitability.

To summarize these empirical findings:

1. *Event Studies* often show that stock values of acquired firms rise significantly at the time of merger, suggesting that the stock market investors believe that mergers will result in increased profitability.
2. *Premerger studies* have shown no systematic evidence either that acquired firms are less profitable or that acquiring firms are more profitable than the typical firm.
3. *Postmerger studies* have suggested that many mergers ultimately fail and no evidence reveals a systematic improvement in profitability as a result of merger.

The empirical evidence suggests that policy makers should view mergers on a case-by-case basis, assuming neither positive nor negative effects. The effect of most mergers on competition and efficiency is probably quite small. In other words, most mergers are more or less neutral with regard to real economic impacts.

Actual Public Policy

HORIZONTAL MERGERS: POLICY BEFORE 1950

Chapter 18 noted that Section 1 of the Sherman Act encouraged mergers by forbidding price fixing and other restraints of trade. It was not until 1914 that Congress acted to tighten the law with the passage of the Clayton Act. Unfortunately, although the Clayton Act outlawed mergers by stock acquisition, it made no mention of asset acquisitions, in which one firm purchased the physical plant and equipment of another firm. The courts could have interpreted Congress' intent as including asset acquisitions, but on November 23, 1926, the Supreme Court seriously weakened Section 7 when it handed down three simultaneous rulings. The most significant of these was a simple two-page decision in the *Thatcher Manufacturing* case.

THATCHER MANUFACTURING CASE[27] (1926)—Thatcher was a major glass manufacturer that acquired the stock of three direct competitors, Lockport Glass, Essex Glass, and Travis Glass. After purchasing the stock, Thatcher purchased the assets of all three companies, so that as of January 13, 1921, the three firms ceased to exist. On March 1, 1921, the FTC staff filed a complaint charging Thatcher with violating the Clayton Act. The Commission ordered Thatcher to divest all of its assets that were formerly held by the three acquired firms.

The Supreme Court overturned the Commission and ruled, "The Act has no application to ownership of a competitor's property and business obtained prior to any action by the Commission, even though this was brought about through stock unlawfully held." This ruling effectively meant that as long as a firm acquired the assets, rather than the stock, of a competing company, there was nothing the government could do under the Clayton Act.

HORIZONTAL MERGERS: THE CELLER-KEFAUVER ACT OF 1950

Recall from Chapter 18 that the final major amendment to the Clayton Act occurred in 1950 with the passage of the **Celler–Kefauver Act.** The Celler-Kefauver Act amended Section 7 of the Clayton Act to include mergers through asset as well as stock acquisition, thereby closing the large loophole opened by the Supreme Court's interpretation of the original Section 7. The Celler-Kefauver Act also extended section 7 to reach vertical and conglomerate mergers as well as horizontal mergers. With the passage of the Celler-Kefauver Act, Section 7 of the Clayton Act finally had some clout in dealing with anticompetitive mergers. The first major test of the new law came in 1958 in the *Bethlehem Steel* decision.

BETHLEHEM STEEL CASE[28] (1958)—On December 11, 1956, Bethlehem Steel and Youngstown Steel entered into an agreement whereby Bethlehem obtained all of Youngstown's assets. At the time of the merger, Bethlehem ranked as the nation's second largest steel maker, with a 15 percent national market share. Youngstown ranked sixth, with a 5 percent share. U.S. Steel was the nation's leading producer with approximately a 30 percent share, and the industry was highly concentrated with a four-firm concentration ratio of 60.

Bethlehem and Youngstown defended the merger on two grounds: (1) that Bethlehem and Youngstown competed in different geographic markets and Bethlehem would never consider entry into Youngstown's market and (2) that the beneficial aspects of the merger outweighed any possible negative effects because the merger would enable Bethlehem to compete more effectively against U.S. Steel.

The District Court rejected both defenses. First, the Court found that in 1955 Bethlehem had shipped over 2 million tons of steel products into Youngstown's Mid-Continent area. This represented a 4.9 percent market share. Youngstown in the same year shipped 2,823,992 tons, or 6.7 percent of total industry shipments, into the region. These figures indicated that Bethlehem and Youngstown were competitors in the Mid-Continent market.

As for the beneficial effects outweighing any negative effects, the Court ruled that this defense did not hold up "as a matter of law." The Court went on to state that "good motives and even demonstrable benefits are irrelevant" to the law.

Bethlehem's contention that it would never enter the Midwest market *de novo* proved to be false. A few years later, Bethlehem constructed a large integrated steel complex in Burns Harbor, Indiana.

The *Bethlehem Steel* case was not appealed to the Supreme Court, but a few years later the highest court upheld its major precedents in the *Brown Shoe* case.

BROWN SHOE CASE[29] (1962)—The *Brown Shoe* case established major precedents for both horizontal and vertical mergers. In 1955 Brown Shoe purchased Kinney. Each firm was both a manufacturer and retailer of shoes. Brown was the fourth largest manufacturer with a 4 percent market share, and Kinney was the 12th largest manufacturer with a 0.5 percent share. In retailing, Kinney was the nation's largest chain retailer, operating over 350 family shoe stores, and it ranked eighth among all shoe retailers in sales. Brown was the nation's third largest shoe retailer by sales volumes.

The shoe industry was highly competitive in both sectors. In manufacturing the top twenty-four firms controlled only 35 percent. In retailing, there were virtually no entry barriers, and thousands of independents competed successfully against the large chains. Despite the almost perfectly competitive nature of the shoe retailing industry, the Supreme Court handed down a strong ruling against Brown Shoe. The decision was an obvious attempt to deter future horizontal mergers, even in competitive industries in which the potential negative effects of such mergers would be minimal or nonexistent.

The Court ruled that because in 118 cities the combined market shares of Brown and Kinney exceeded 5 percent, the merger violated the Clayton Act. Chief Justice Warren wrote:

> If a merger achieving 5% control were now approved, we might be required to approve future merger efforts by Brown's competitors seeking similar market shares. The oligopoly Congress sought to avoid would then be furthered and it would be difficult to dissolve the combinations previously approved.

The *Brown Shoe* decision established the **incipiency precedent** with regard to horizontal mergers. The incipiency precedent suggested that horizontal mergers should be banned even in competitive markets to prevent future increases in concentration. Four years later, the Supreme Court not only reinforced this precedent but also seemed to extend it in the *Von's Grocery* case.

VON'S GROCERY CASE[30] (1966)—On March 25, 1960, Von's Grocery acquired Shopping Bag Food Stores. The merger resulted in a combination between the third and sixth largest food retailers in the Los Angeles area. Von's held a 4.3 percent share, and Shopping Bag held a 3.2 percent share. Safeway was the leading firm in the area, and Von's argued that the merger would enable it to compete more effectively against Safeway. The Supreme Court ruled in favor of the government and stated, "The basic purpose of the 1950 Celler-Kefauver Act was to prevent economic concentration in the American economy by keeping a large number of small competitors in business."

The *Von's Grocery* case set a very strict standard for horizontal merger cases. Even when economic circumstances seemed to call for a reduction in the number of firms in an industry, the *Von's Grocery* decision suggested that the Supreme Court would try to stem the tide. In both the *Brown Shoe* and *Von's Grocery* cases, the social goal of maintaining a large number of competitors was considered at least as important as the economic goal of efficiency.

PHILADELPHIA NATIONAL BANK CASE[31] (1964)—In November 1960, the Philadelphia National Bank (PNB) attempted to acquire the Girard Trust Corn

Exchange Bank (Girard). The two banks ranked second and third, respectively, among Philadelphia's forty-two commercial banks, and the merger would have created the largest bank in the area. Had the merger been approved, the four-firm concentration ratio in Philadelphia would have risen to 78 percent. Unlike the *Brown Shoe* and *Von's Grocery* cases, therefore, the *PNB* case involved a highly concentrated market.

The Supreme Court held that the 30 percent combined market share of PNB and Girard Trust went well beyond the legal limit in a horizontal merger. The Court suggested that unless there were highly mitigating circumstances a horizontal merger between two large firms in a concentrated market would be considered a violation of Section 7. The *PNB* decision, combined with the *Von's Grocery* decision, made horizontal mergers almost *per se* illegal under the Supreme Court leadership of Chief Justice Warren during the 1960s. A more conservative Supreme Court under the leadership of Chief Justice Warren Burger in the 1970s, however, took a more lenient attitude.

GENERAL DYNAMICS CASE[32] (1974)—The *General Dynamics* case revolved around the activities of one of General Dynamics' acquisitions, Material Service Corporation. Material Service was a large Midwestern producer of building materials, concrete, limestone, and coal. All of Material Service's coal production was from deep-shaft mines. In 1954, Material Service began purchasing the stock of United Electric Coal. By 1959 it had acquired 34 percent of United Electric's stock, enabling Material Service to control United Electric. When General Dynamics acquired Material Service in 1959, it acquired the nation's fifth largest coal producer.

The Justice Department's complaint contended that Material Service's acquisition of United Electric substantially reduced competition in two geographic markets: the "Eastern Interior Coal Province Sales Area," consisting of Illinois and Indiana; parts of Kentucky, Tennessee, Iowa, Minnesota, Wisconsin, and Missouri; and the State of Illinois. At the time of the merger, Material Service ranked as the second largest producer in both submarkets, with a 7.6 percent share in the "Eastern Province," and a 15.1 percent share in Illinois. United Electric ranked sixth in the "Eastern Province," with a 4.8 percent share, and it ranked fifth in Illinois with an 8.1 percent share.

The defense argued that despite these market share figures, the merger was justified on two grounds. First, United Electric had only a small quantity of reserves, and therefore, without a buyer, United would cease to be a significant competitive factor in the future. Second, because United Electric operated only strip mines, it competed in an entirely different market from Material Service, which operated only deep-shaft mines.

The Supreme Court accepted both defenses and found for General Dynamics. The decision signaled that a more conservative Supreme Court would no longer side automatically with the government in all Section 7 cases. By 1984, the courts had moved even farther away from their strict interpretation of the 1960s, as indicated by the Second Circuit Court of Appeals decision in the *Waste Management* case.

WASTE MANAGEMENT CASE[33] (1984)—In 1980 Waste Management acquired Waste Resources. The two firms provided waste disposal services in many states, but the case revolved around the effect of the merger in Dallas, Texas. The District Court found that the two firms had a combined 48.8 percent share of the relevant waste disposal market in Dallas and that under the *PNB* precedent the merger should be dissolved. The Court of Appeals reversed based on an argument that entry barriers were so low that even a firm with a 48.8 percent market share could not permanently raise prices above competitive levels.

The *General Dynamics* and *Waste Management* decisions represented major shifts away from the incipiency precedent. In the 1989 *Elders Grain* case, however, the Seventh Circuit Court of Appeals dissolved a merger between two leading producers of industrial dry corn.

ELDERS GRAIN CASE[34] (1989)—On June 5, 1988, Illinois Cereal Mills (ICM), a leading producer of "industrial dry corn" used in the manufacture of corn flakes, corn bread, doughnuts, and other food products, purchased a rival, the Lincoln Grain Company, from Elders Grain. At the time of the acquisition ICM and Lincoln ranked second and fifth, respectively, in sales of industrial dry corn. The merger made ICM the leading producer with a 32 percent market share, and there were only four other manufacturers of industrial dry corn in the United States.

ICM had taken a series of legal actions to try to prevent the FTC from prohibiting the merger. The company went so far as to break up Lincoln's assets into smaller parts before the merger so that, technically, the acquisitions did not have to be reported to the FTC. In addition, ICM accelerated the acquisition date so that the FTC did not learn about the merger until June 2, 1988, just three days before the merger was consummated. On June 3, 1988, The FTC informed ICM that it intended to challenge the acquisition, but ICM went ahead with the merger anyway.

The District Court and Appeals Court both ruled that the merger had to be rescinded pending a full FTC investigation into the legality of the merger. The Appeals Court based its decision on the high likelihood that the merger violated Section 7 of the Clayton Act. The Court of Appeals noted several important industry characteristics. First, the industry was highly concentrated and had a history of attempting to fix prices through collusive activities. Second, entry was difficult and required a minimum of three years to "design, build, and start operating a new mill." In addition, the Court of Appeals took particular aim at ICM's legal maneuvers, and noted:

> To reward these tactics by holding that a district court has no power . . . to rescind a consummated transaction would go far toward rendering the statute a dead letter. Some statutes are born dead, opponents having succeeded in blocking the enactment of a viable statute. There is no indication that this statute was meant to be a stillbirth.

Despite the *General Dynamics* and *Waste Management* decisions, horizontal mergers remain an area in which the antitrust laws hold some punch. It is doubtful that the Supreme Court of the 1990s would permit a merger between two dominant firms in a highly concentrated market. However, the government could not win a case similar to the *Von's Grocery* case today. There is no longer a Supreme Court majority that believes in the *incipiency* argument, and a merger between two small firms is likely to be permitted today.

VERTICAL MERGERS

Vertical mergers are less likely to have anticompetitive effects than horizontal mergers. They can, however, increase entry barriers and the probability of collusion. From a legal standpoint, vertical merger cases have dealt primarily with one issue: **foreclosure**.

DU PONT–GENERAL MOTORS CASE[35] (1957)—The first major vertical merger case to reach the Supreme Court involved two of America's corporate giants, General Motors (GM) and Du Pont. In 1917, before General Motors became the dominant automobile producer, Du Pont began to acquire General Motors' stock, until by 1919, Du Pont controlled 23 percent of GM. Thirty years later, in 1949, the Justice Department filed a complaint under the Clayton Act charging that Du Pont's stock interest in GM foreclosed other firms from the market for paints and fabrics used by General Motors.

Du Pont contended that the government's market definition was incorrect, because automobile and appliance paints and fabrics made up a very small percentage of the total paint and fabric market. Furthermore, Du Pont argued that despite the stock link, General Motors often bought paints and fabrics from other companies besides Du Pont. Finally, Du Pont raised the obvious issue of timing. Could the government file a Section 7 case thirty years after the alleged violation?

In 1957, forty years after the stock acquisition, the Supreme Court ruled that the link between Du Pont and General Motors violated the Clayton Act. The majority emphasized that Du Pont always supplied the largest portion of GM's requirements for paints and fabrics and that this dominant position "was not gained solely on competitive merit."

In 1961 the Supreme Court ordered Du Pont to divest its General Motors stock. By then forty-four years had elapsed since the original stock acquisition. It is not surprising, therefore, that the case came to be known by a phrase used in Justice Burton's dissenting opinion as "The Sleeping Giant Case."

BROWN SHOE CASE REVISITED[36] (1962)—The *Brown Shoe* case involved a merger between the nation's fourth largest shoe manufacturer, Brown, and one of the nation's leading retailers, Kinney. Evidence suggested that after the merger Kinney had significantly increased its purchases of Brown shoes. In a highly competitive market, however, it is doubtful that this had any significant economic impact. Nevertheless, the Supreme Court ruled that the vertical elements of the merger violated the Clayton Act.

The Court's majority stated:

> [W]e cannot fail to recognize Congress' desire to promote competition through the protection of viable, small, locally owned businesses. Congress appreciated that occasional higher costs and prices might result from the maintenance of fragmented industries and markets. It resolved these competing considerations in favor of decentralization.

In this portion of the decision, the Court made a purposeful choice in favor of maintaining a large number of firms regardless of the effect on prices and costs. Such a decision seems to place a priority on social goals (a large number of small firms) over efficiency goals (lower prices and costs).

The *Du Pont* and *Brown Shoe* precedents suggested that vertical mergers violated Section 7 as long as a *reasonable probability* of foreclosure existed. A 1989 Court of Appeals ruling in the *Fruehauf* case, however, suggested a change in court interpretation.

THE FRUEHAUF CASE[37] (1989)—In the 1970s Fruehauf was the nation's leading producer of truck trailers with a 25 percent market share. The four-firm concentration ratio in the truck trailer market was 49. Fruehauf acquired Kelsey, a leading manufacturer of "heavy-duty wheels" used in the manufacture of truck trailers. Kelsey held a 15 percent market share, and the market for heavy-duty wheels was highly concentrated with a four-firm concentration ratio of approximately 70. The Federal Trade Commission ruled that the merger foreclosed a maximum of 5.8 percent of the heavy-duty wheel market and that the percentage violated Section 7 of the Clayton Act.

The Court of Appeals recognized the likelihood of some foreclosure, but reversed the FTC. According to the Appeals Court, no evidence showed that as a result of the merger competing buyers of heavy-duty wheels would be unable to obtain supplies from Kelsey or its competitors at competitive prices, or that entry into the truck trailer market would require simultaneous entry into the heavy-duty wheel market. Furthermore, the Court concluded that Fruehauf was never a serious potential entrant into the manufacturing of heavy-duty wheels.

The *Fruehauf* decision suggests that under recent interpretation of Section 7, the courts are likely to look at far more than the percentage of the market foreclosed by a vertical merger. In the *Fruehauf* case the Court closely examined all of the expected competitive impacts of the merger and concluded that there was a very small probability of significant anticompetitive effects.

CONGLOMERATE MERGERS

Conglomerate mergers have been treated more cautiously by the courts than either horizontal or vertical mergers. The government has based its relatively few legal attacks primarily on two issues: the elimination of potential competition and the possibility of reciprocal buying arrangements.

Potential Competition Cases

PROCTER & GAMBLE CASE[38] (1967)—In 1957, Procter & Gamble, the nation's leading producer of soaps and detergents, acquired Clorox, the nation's leading producer of liquid bleach. Both firms held dominant positions: Procter had a 54.4 percent share of the detergent market, and Clorox had a 48.8 percent share of the liquid bleach market. The four-firm concentration ratio was over 80 in both markets; therefore, the merger involved the leading firms in two highly concentrated and complementary markets.

The government complaint charged three major negative effects of the merger. First, the merger eliminated Procter & Gamble as a potential competitor in the liquid bleach market. Second, it further entrenched Clorox as the industry leader, because Procter, as the nation's leading advertiser, could greatly increase the advertising expenditures of Clorox. Finally, the FTC argued that smaller competitors would be hesitant to compete aggressively against large, diversified Procter & Gamble.

The Supreme Court ordered the merger dissolved because Procter was the most likely potential entrant into the liquid bleach market. The Court noted, however, that if Procter & Gamble had acquired a small bleach producer, and then competed aggressively with Clorox, such a *toehold* merger might have significantly increased the level of effective competition. A few years later, the FTC addressed the issue of a *toehold* merger in the *Bendix* case.

BENDIX CASE[39] (1970)—In 1967, Bendix, a large, diversified firm specializing in the aerospace, automotive, automation, and scientific industries, acquired Fram, a leading producer of automotive, aerospace, and water filters. The complaint revolved around the automobile filter market, which was highly concentrated, with General Motors controlling 32.4 percent, Purolator 21.7 percent, and Fram 17.2 percent. Bendix held a very small 0.35 percent market share and decided that it wanted to expand into the market on a much larger scale. After some deliberation, Bendix decided it would only expand through merger, not through internal expansion.

The FTC staff argued that the Bendix-Fram merger eliminated potential competition. The full Commission agreed but, in the process, handed down an important ruling which stated that the FTC would be inclined to permit toehold mergers between a large potential competitor and a small nondominant firm.

In 1971, the Sixth Circuit Court of Appeals overturned the Commission's ruling, not on substance, but on a legal technicality.[40] The Appeals Court ruled that because the FTC had failed to inform Bendix of its intention to use the toehold theory in its case, Bendix had not been given the opportunity to prepare an adequate defense. The Appeals Court did not rule on the legitimacy of the toehold theory.

MARINE BANCORPORATION CASE[41] (1974)—The *Marine Bancorporation* case involved a geographic extension merger by one of Washington State's largest banks. In February 1971, the National Bank of Commerce (NBC), which was a wholly owned subsidiary of Marine Bancorporation, acquired the Washington Trust Bank (WTB). The two banks operated on opposite sides of Washington, almost 300 miles apart. NBC, located in Seattle, was the state's second largest bank, and the two top Washington banks controlled 51.3 percent of the state's total deposits. WTB was the third largest bank in the Spokane area, with an 18.6 percent regional market share. The top three banks in Spokane held a 92.3 percent market share.

Entry and expansion in the banking industry was highly regulated in Washington. Some of the regulations made little economic sense; their main purpose appears to have been to protect banks from competition. For example, banks were forbidden from operating or establishing new branches outside the city or town in which they competed, except by merger with another bank in another town. Furthermore, once a bank acquired another bank's assets, it was prohibited from branching. Washington also forbade a new bank from merging with any company for ten years after its establishment.

The Supreme Court considered these regulatory restrictions and permitted the merger. The Court ruled that in states in which such stringent entry and expansion barriers exist, the "potential-competition doctrine-grounded as it is on relative freedom of entry on the part of the acquiring firm-will seldom bar a geographic market extension merger by a commercial bank."

It is interesting to note that the *Marine Bancorporation* decision was handed down at the same time as the *General Dynamics-United Electric* decision. The two decisions point clearly to a more lenient attitude to mergers by the Supreme Court under Chief Justice Burger during the 1970s.

YAMAHA MOTORS CASE[42] (1981)—In the late 1970s Brunswick, a large, diversified manufacturer, was the second largest seller of outboard motors in the United States with a market share that ranged between 19.8 and 26 percent. Despite its position as the leading seller, Brunswick did not *manufacture* outboard motors. Brunswick decided to enter into a *joint venture* with Yamaha Motors of Japan to manufacture outboard motors in the United States. Yamaha produced outboard motors in Japan but did not sell outboard motors in the United States. Under the terms of a joint venture, two firms agree to engage in a commercial activity and share in the profits. Functionally, joint ventures have been treated as mergers under the antitrust laws because the two firms combine to engage in a joint activity exactly as they would if they merged.

The Eighth Circuit Court of Appeals affirmed an FTC ruling that the joint venture violated Section 7. The Court noted that for the joint venture to violate the law it was necessary for the FTC to show that Brunswick or Yamaha had "available feasible means" for entering the American outboard motor market, and "that those means offer[ed] a substantial likelihood of ultimately producing deconcentration of that market or other significant procompetitive effects." The Appeals Court concluded that the evidence supported a finding that the joint venture significantly reduced potential competition and therefore violated Section 7.

TENNECO CASE[43] (1982)—A year after the Eighth Circuit Court of Appeals handed down the *Yamaha* decision, the Second Circuit Court of Appeals handed down a far different ruling in the *Tenneco* case. In the late 1960s and early 1970s, Tenneco had wanted to enter the shock absorber market, and it had contacted major European manufacturers concerning possible patent licensing arrangements. Tenneco went so far as to acquire a small manufacturing company that held a shock absorber patent. Tenneco then decided abruptly to change strategy and entered the shock absorber market by acquiring Monroe, a major manufacturer of shock absorbers. The FTC ruled that the acquisition violated Section 7, but the Second Circuit Court of Appeals, by a split 2-1 vote, overturned.

The Second Circuit Court ruled that there was insufficient evidence that Tenneco would have entered the market *de novo* in the absence of its purchase of Monroe. Despite the Appeals Court's finding that "[t]he record contains abundant evidence that Tenneco had both the interest and the incentive to enter the market for replacement shock absorbers," the Court ruled against the FTC. Ultimately, the Second Circuit ruling emphasized that Section 7 deals with "probabilities," not "ephemeral possibilities," and the Court found an insufficient probability that Tenneco would have entered the market either *de novo* or through a toehold acquisition.

Reciprocal Buying Cases

CONSOLIDATED FOODS CASE[44] (1964)—The *Consolidated Foods* case is the classic reciprocal buying case. In 1951, Consolidated Foods acquired Gentry. Consolidated was a food processor, wholesaler, and retailer. Gentry produced dehydrated onions and garlic in a highly concentrated market. Basic Vegetable was the industry leader with a 58 percent share, while Gentry controlled 32 percent.

The FTC complained that Consolidated had attempted to expand Gentry's market share by having its distributing division suggest to its suppliers that they purchase their requirements of dehydrated onions and garlic from Gentry. Despite these suggestions, by 1958 Gentry had increased its market share only marginally to 35 percent, hardly evidence of an overwhelmingly successful campaign. In a unanimous decision, however, the Supreme Court sided with the FTC. The Court concluded that some food processors who sold to Consolidated had given their onion and garlic business to Gentry for reciprocity reasons.

Gentry's behavior of contacting suppliers was so overtly an attempt to influence their purchasing patterns that the Court declared the merger illegal. It is interesting to note, however, that Gentry's president testified that Gentry's onions and garlics were inferior, and therefore, it is questionable whether Consolidated's behavior had much of an impact. The *Gentry* case suggests that overt attempts to influence purchasers' buying habits may be enough to condemn a merger.

ITT[45] (1970)—The *ITT-Grinnell* case involved a charge of reciprocal buying, and therefore, it is included here, but the government's case also included complaints concerning cross-subsidization, foreclosure, and economic forbearance. The forbearance charge was particularly unique because the Justice Department claimed that such a large conglomerate merger would likely have "general anticompetitive effects" and therefore should be prohibited.

The District Court found for ITT on all counts. With regard to the forbearance charge, the Court noted "that the legislative history, the statute itself and the controlling decisional law all make it clear beyond a . . . doubt that in a Section 7 case the alleged anticompetitive effects of a merger must be examined in the context of *specified product and geographic markets*."

The *ITT* case was the last major conglomerate merger case filed by the Justice Department. Unfortunately, it was not appealed to a higher court. Attorney General Mitchell and President Nixon were both strongly against an appeal. Just how strongly the President felt is indicated by the following excerpt from the famous Nixon White House tapes. On April 19, 1971, President Nixon told Deputy Attorney General Kleindienst, "The IT&T thing—stay the hell out of it. Is that clear? . . . Your—my order is to drop the goddamn thing. Is that clear?"[46]

Given the President's sentiments, it is not surprising that the Justice Department withdrew its three pending merger cases against ITT in exchange for a consent decree. Under the decree, ITT agreed to divest Grinnell's fire protection division.

Merger Guidelines and the Hart-Scott-Rodino Act

Having analyzed the courts' decisions, we now turn to the criteria used by the government to decide which mergers to challenge. In 1968 the Justice Department issued its first set of merger guidelines. The guidelines were meant to help reduce the uncertainty regarding the legality or illegality of a particular merger. Especially with regard to *horizontal mergers,* the 1968 guidelines tended to be quite strict. In an industry with a four-firm concentration ratio of over 75, the guidelines suggested that the antitrust authorities would challenge any of the mergers in Table 20.2.

With regard to *vertical mergers,* the 1968 guidelines suggested that a challenge would be forthcoming if the buyer of an input made 6 percent of the total purchases of the input *and* the supplier of the input made 10 percent of total input sales; if the supplier of the input made 20 percent of total input sales; if the buyer of the input controlled 10 percent of its market; or if there was a significant trend toward vertical integration in the industry.

With regard to *conglomerate mergers*, the 1968 guidelines suggested that a merger would be challenged if the merger eliminated a main potential entrant; if the merger created a substantial possibility of reciprocal buying arrangements; if the merger created increased leverage for the acquired firm, such as an increased advertising advantage; or if *any* of the largest 200 firms tried to acquire any other significant firm.

In keeping with the main line of economic thinking during the 1960s and the fairly tough policy toward mergers of the Supreme Court under Chief Justice Earl Warren's Court, the 1968 guidelines were quite strict. When President Reagan took office in 1980, both economic thinking and the Supreme Court's position under the leadership of Chief Justice Warren Burger had changed. Economists and the Courts had become more accepting of the economic advantages associated with mergers and less suspicious of the potential negative impacts, particularly with regard to vertical and conglomerate mergers. As a result of this new attitude, Assistant Attorney General William Baxter presided over a major rewriting of the merger guidelines in 1982.

The new guidelines were released in June 1982 and revised slightly in 1984. With regard to horizontal mergers, the new guidelines were significantly more le-

TABLE 20.2

Acquiring Firm's Market Share (%)	Acquired Firm's Market Share (%)
4	4
10	2
15	1

nient. Instead of basing the standard on traditional concentration ratio measures, the 1982 guidelines were based on the Herfindahl Index.[47] Recall from Chapter 4 that the Herfindahl Index is defined as:

$$\text{HHI} = \sum_{i=1}^{n} S_i^2$$

where S_i is the market share of the ith firm in the industry, and n is the total number of firms in the industry.

The 1982 horizontal merger guidelines suggested that the Justice Department would not challenge a merger if the postmerger industry Herfindahl would be less than 1000. If the postmerger Herfindahl would fall between 1000 and 1800, mergers causing an increase in the Herfindahl of less than 100 were unlikely to be challenged, but mergers causing an increase in the Herfindahl of more than 100 were likely to be challenged, subject to an analysis of the effects of the merger on entry barriers, the probability of collusion, and other competitive conditions. If a merger resulted in a postmerger Herfindahl greater than 1800 and caused an increase in the Herfindahl of 100, it was very likely to be challenged. If a merger resulted in a postmerger Herfindahl of more than 1800 and caused an increase in the Herfindahl of between 50 and 100, it was likely to be challenged subject to a consideration of its competitive effects. Finally, if a merger resulted in a postmerger Herfindahl of over 1800, and caused an increase in the Herfindahl of less than 50, it was unlikely to be challenged.

The 1982 guidelines were significantly more lenient than the 1968 ones. Under the old guidelines, the Von's Grocery–Shopping Bag merger would have been a borderline case for challenge. Under the 1982 guidelines, the Von's Grocery merger would not have come close to being challenged.

With regard to vertical mergers, the 1982 guidelines eliminated all mention of specific market share limitations. Instead the new guidelines listed three requirements for *consideration* of a challenge to a vertical merger. First, the merger had to make it unlikely that any entrant would enter one market (the primary market) without entering the other market (the secondary market) involved in the merger. Second, the merger had to make entry into the primary market much less likely. Third, entry barriers and other characteristics of noncompetitive performance had to exist in the primary market. The combined effect of these requirements was to make a challenge to any vertical merger unlikely. Under these guidelines, the Brown Shoe–Kinney Shoe merger and the Du Pont–General Motors merger would certainly have been permitted.

The 1982 guidelines mentioned only one reason for challenging a conglomerate merger—the elimination of potential competition. With regard to potential competition challenges, the 1982 guidelines created a tough standard. First, the market had to be highly concentrated with a Herfindahl of over 1800. This requirement alone put most conglomerate mergers beyond the reach of the guidelines. Second, entry into the market had to be difficult. Third, there had to be only a few other potential entrants into the market. Fourth, the market share of the acquired firm had to be at least 5 percent. Under these guidelines, few conglomerate mergers would be challenged.

Compared with the 1968 guidelines, the 1982 guidelines left relatively few mergers open for challenge. The 1982 guidelines suggested a retreat from an aggressive anti-merger policy.

In 1984, the Department of Justice revised the 1982 guidelines. The 1982 guidelines stated that the Department generally would *not* consider potential efficiency gains before deciding whether to challenge a merger. The 1984 guidelines explicitly recognize efficiency gains as a relevant factor in the Department's decision-making process but made it clear that efficiencies were not to be considered an absolute defense but merely one factor to be considered before a final decision was reached on a particular merger.

In 1992 the guidelines were revised again to further deemphasize the importance of simple concentration measures and to further emphasize the impact of the merger on price and entry conditions. The 1992 guidelines made it clear that the Justice Department would not rely on simple changes in concentration measures without evidence that the merger would result in higher prices or a greater likelihood of effective collusion. Furthermore, even a merger that was likely to result in higher short-run prices would be permitted as long as the higher prices were likely to induce entry within two years. Under the 1992 guidelines very few mergers will be challenged.

It is important to note one other major change in antitrust enforcement that went into effect in 1976 with the passage of the **Hart-Scott-Rodino Act** (also known as the Antitrust Improvements Act). The Hart-Scott-Rodino Act amended Section 7 of the Clayton Act to require advance notification to the Justice Department and the FTC of any major merger. Any merger in which one firm has sales or assets of at least $100 million and the other firm has sales or assets of at least $10 million must be reported to the government at least 30 days in advance. The act requires the provision of extensive data concerning the proposed merger and gives the government time to report to the potential merger partners whether a challenge will be forthcoming.

Although compliance with the Hart-Scott-Rodino Act is expensive, it has resulted in improved enforcement by enabling the government to act quickly and before the fact against proposed mergers. In fact, it is more than a coincidence that no major merger case has worked its way to the Supreme Court since the passage of the Hart-Scott-Rodino Act.

SUMMARY

1. The three types of mergers are horizontal mergers, which involve firms that are direct competitors; vertical mergers, involving firms that produce at different stages of production in the same industry; and conglomerate mergers, which involve companies that operate in either different product markets or the same product market but different geographic markets.

2. Four major merger waves have taken place in the United States. These waves occurred at the turn of the century, in the 1920s, in the 1960s and 1970s, and in the 1980s.

3. Motives for merger include market power, efficiency gains, financial gains to stockholders, risk reduction, and empire building.

4. Horizontal mergers are most likely to result in increased market power, but they also may result in efficiency gains due to economies of scale.

5. Vertical mergers may reduce transaction costs, but they also may increase barriers to entry and facilitate collusion.

6. Conglomerate mergers are least likely to reduce actual competition, but they may reduce *potential* competition.

7. Empirical evidence suggests that most mergers have little impact on profitability or efficiency. A minority of mergers result in significant efficiency gains or significant increases in market power.

8. Public policy toward horizontal mergers was lax until 1950, then strict for 25 years until the mid 1970s. Since then policy has been relaxed, but major horizontal mergers with significant effects on market structure still are subject to antitrust enforcement.

9. Public policy toward vertical mergers centers on the issue of foreclosure. Policy was strict in the 1950s and 1960s but has loosened up considerably since then.

10. Public policy toward conglomerate mergers has centered on the issues of potential competition, reciprocity, and economic forbearance. Some conglomerate mergers were successfully challenged in the 1960s, 1970s, and 1980s, but few cases would be challenged under current Department of Justice guidelines.

11. Since 1968 the Department of Justice has established merger guidelines suggesting which mergers the Department is likely to challenge. The guidelines were amended in 1982, 1984, and 1992. Each change resulted in fewer mergers that would be challenged. Under current guidelines very few vertical or conglomerate mergers are likely to be challenged. The 1992 guidelines increased the importance of potential competition in horizontal merger cases and reduced the likelihood of challenges to horizontal mergers as well.

KEY TERMS

bilateral monopoly	Hart-Scott-Rodino Act
Celler-Kefauver Act	horizontal mergers
conglomerate mergers	incipiency precedent
cross-subsidization	potential competition
economic forbearance	product extension mergers
event studies	pure conglomerate mergers
foreclosure	reciprocity
geographic extension mergers	vertical mergers

DISCUSSION QUESTIONS

1. Suppose Kellogg's, the nation's leading ready-to-eat cereal manufacturer with a 45 percent market share, purchased a leading manufacturer of cardboard packaging boxes. Should the government challenge this merger?

2. In 1986, the Federal Trade Commission challenged the mergers of Coca-Cola with Dr. Pepper and Pepsico with Seven-Up but then permitted the merger of Dr. Pepper with Seven-Up. Did these decisions make economic sense?

3. Suppose McDonald's attempted to acquire Burger King. Should the Federal Trade Commission challenge the merger?

4. What conduct theory (or theories) suggests that the elimination of a large potential entrant could have a significant effect on a market? Why does the theory suggest this outcome?

5. In major merger cases, the defendant almost always argues that a tremendous increase in costs will result if the merger is prevented. Is such a defense justified in most cases?

6. Suppose a particular horizontal merger results in some increased economies of scale. Does it follow that the merger should be permitted?

7. Consider the *Marine Bancorporation* case. In what ways does this case suggest the problems inherent in regulating banking? Did the Supreme Court decision make economic sense?

8. Suppose there were only five manufacturers of refrigerators in the world. If Sears bought the largest of these manufacturers, should the Federal Trade Commission challenge the merger?

9. Why were conglomerate mergers the main type of merger from 1960 to 1980?

10. If you could change the antitrust laws with regard to mergers, what changes would you suggest? Why?

PROBLEMS

1. Suppose an industry consists of three firms, each with costs LRMC = LRAC = 20. Industry demand is $P = 200 - Q$. The firms currently use the Cournot-Nash model in quantities. What is the current industry output and price? Assuming continuing Cournot-Nash behavior and no effect on costs, if two of these firms merge, what would happen to the industry price and output? What is the impact on economic welfare?

2. An industry is currently performing competitively with price equal to marginal cost. If demand is $P = 200 - Q$ and LRMC = LRAC = 50, what is output and price? If a series of mergers monopolizes the industry and results in lower costs such that LRMC = LRAC = 40, what happens to industry output and price? Does this merger improve welfare? If the mergers reduced the monopolist's costs to LRMC = LRAC = 20, would the merger improve welfare?

3. According to the 1982 merger guidelines, would the following horizontal mergers be challenged:

   a. An industry consists of five firms with market shares of 50, 30, 10, 5, and 5 percent, respectively, and the leading firm acquires the firm with 10 percent of the market.

   b. An industry consists of five firms with market shares of 30, 25, 20, 15, and 10 percent, respectively, and the two smallest firms merge.

   c. An industry consists of 15 firms; five firms have market shares of 10 percent each, and 10 firms have market shares of 5 percent each. Two of the firms with 10 percent market shares merge to form a company with a 20 percent market share.

REFERENCES

1. Devra L. Golbe and Lawrence J. White, "Mergers and Acquisitions in the U.S. Economy: An Aggregate and Historical Overview," in Alan J. Auerbach (ed.), *Mergers and Acquisitions*, (Chicago: University of Chicago Press, 1988), pp. 25–47.

2. Ralph L. Nelson, *Merger Movements in American Industry, 1895–1956* (Princeton, N.J.: Princeton University Press, 1959), p. 29.

3. Glenn Porter, *The Rise of Big Business, 1860–1920*, 2nd edition (Arlington Heights, Ill: Harlan Davidson, 1992), p. 84.

4. George J. Stigler, "Monopoly and Oligopoly by Merger," *American Economic Review* 40 (May 1950): 23–34; reprinted in *The Organization of Industry* (Homewood, Ill.: Irwin, 1968), pp. 95–107.

5. Carl Eis, "The 1919–1930 Merger Movement in American Industry," *Journal of Law & Economics* 12 (October 1969): 280–4.

6. Federal Trade Commission, *Economic Report on Corporate Mergers* (Washington, D.C.: U.S. Government Printing Office, 1969).

7. Bruce T. Allen, "Merger Statistics and Merger Policy," *Review of Industrial Organization* (Summer 1984); and David J. Ravenscraft and F.M. Scherer, *Mergers, Selloffs, and Economic Efficiency* (Washington, D.C.: Brookings Institution, 1987), pp. 198–9.

8. Cynthia Benzing, "Mergers—What the "Grimm" Data Tell Us," *Review of Industrial Organization* 8 (December 1993): 747–53.

9. John E. Kwoka, Jr., "The Private Profitability of Horizontal Mergers with Non-Cournot and Maverick Behavior," *International Journal of Industrial Organization* 7 (September 1989): 403–11.

10. F.M. Scherer, Alan Beckenstein, Erich Kaufer, and R.D. Murphy. *Multiplant Operation: An International Comparison Study* (Cambridge: Harvard University Press, 1975), p. 169.

11. Dennis C. Mueller (ed.), *The Determinants and Effects of Mergers* (Cambridge, UK: Oelgeschlager, Gunn & Hain, 1985); and Geoffry Meeks, *Disappointing Marriage: A Study of the Gains from Merger* (Cambridge, UK: Cambridge University Press, 1977).

12. Stanley E. Boyle, "Pre-Merger Growth and Profit Characteristics of Large Conglomerate Mergers in the United States: 1948–1968," *St. Johns Law Review*, Special Edition (Spring 1970): 160–1. For a theoretical model see Mark A. Dutz, "Horizontal Mergers in Declining Industries," *International Journal of Industrial Organization* 7 (March 1989): 11–33.

13. See Kenneth D. Boyer, "Mergers that Harm Competition," *Review of Industrial Organization* 7 (1992): 191–202; and Laurence Schumann, "Patterns of Abnormal Returns and the Competitive Effects of Horizontal Mergers," *Review of Industrial Organization* 8 (December 1993): 679–96.

14. John T. Scott, "Purposive Diversification as a Motive for Merger," *International Journal of Industrial Organization* 7 (March 1989): 35–47; and Thomas A. Wilson, "An Analysis of the Profitability of Business of Diversified Companies," *Review of Industrial Organization* 7 (1992): 151–85.

15. Kenneth G. Elzinga, "The Beer Industry," in Walter Adams (ed.), *The Structure of American Industry*, 8th edition (New York: Macmillan Publishing Company, 1990), p. 146; and "Miller's Fast Growth Upsets the

Beer Industry," *Business Week* (November 8, 1976): 58–67.

16. See Willard F. Mueller, "Conglomerates: A 'Nonindustry'" in Walter Adams (ed.), *The Structure of American Industry,* 7th edition (New York: Macmillan Publishing Company, 1986), especially pp. 377–81.

17. Michael C. Jensen and Richard R. Ruback, "The Market for Corporate Control: The Scientific Evidence," *Journal of Financial Economics* 11 (1983): 5–50.

18. Harry DeAngelo, Linda DeAngelo, and Edward M. Rice, "Going Private: Minority Freezeouts and Stockholder Wealth," *Journal of Law and Economics* 27 (1984): 367–402.

19. See also Gregg A. Jarrell, James A. Brinkley, and Jeffrey M. Netter, "The Market for Corporate Control: The Empirical Evidence Since 1980," *Journal of Economic Perspectives* 2 (1988) 49–68; and Andrei Schleifer and Robert W. Vishny, "Value Maximization and the Acquisition Process," *Journal of Economic Perspectives* 2 (1988): 7–20.

20. Ellen B. Magenheim and Dennis C. Mueller, "Are Acquiring-Firm Shareholders Better Off After an Acquisition?" in John Coffee, Jr., Louis Lowenstein, Susan Rose-Ackerman (eds.), *Knights, Raiders, and Targets: The Impact of Hostile Takeover,* (New York: Oxford University Press, 1988).

21. Michael C. Jensen, and Richard S. Ruback, "The Market for Corporate Control: The Scientific Evidence," *Journal of Financial Economics* 11 (1983): 5–50.

22. David J. Ravenscraft and F.M. Scherer, *Mergers, Sell-Offs, and Economic Efficiency* (Washington, D.C.: Brookings Institution, 1987); and David J. Ravenscraft and F.M. Scherer, "The Profitability of Mergers," *International Journal of Industrial Organization* 7 (March 1989): 101–16. See also Avi Dor and Bernard Friedman, "Mergers of Not-for-Profit Hospitals in the 1980s: Who Were the Most Likely Targets?" *Review of Industrial Organization* 9 (August 1994): 393–407; Laurence Schumann, "Patterns of Abnormal Returns and the Competitive Effects of Horizontal Mergers," *Review of Industrial Organization* 8 (December 1993): 679–96; William W. Alberts and Nikhil P. Varaiya, "Assessing the Profitability of Growth by Acquisition: A 'Premium Recapture' Approach," *International Journal of Industrial Organization* 7 (March 1989): 133–49; Rolf Bühner, "The Success of Mergers in Germany," *International Journal of Industrial Organization* 9 (December 1991): 513–32; and

Richard E. Caves, "Mergers, Takeovers, and Economic Efficiency," *International Journal of Industrial Organization* 7 (March 1989): 151–74.

23. David J. Ravenscraft and F.M. Scherer, *Mergers, Sell-Offs, and Economic Efficiency* (Washington, D.C.: Brookings Institution, 1987), p. 74.

24. See Dennis C. Mueller, *Determinants and Effects of Mergers* (Cambridge: Oelgeschlager, Gunn & Hain, 1980); G. Meeks, *Disappointing Marriage: A Study of the Gains from Mergers* (Cambridge: Cambridge University Press, 1977); for evidence from the United Kingdom see Alan Hughes, "The Impact of Merger: A Survey of Empirical Evidence for the UK," in James A. Fairburn and John A Kay (eds.), *Mergers and Merger Policy* (Oxford: Oxford University Press, 1989).

25. Other studies with similar findings include Alan Hughes, *supra* note 24; and Stephan A. Rhoades, "The Operating Performance of Acquired Firms in Banking," in R.L. Wills, J.A. Caswell, and J.D. Cuthbertson (eds.), *Issues After a Century of Competition Policy* (Lexington, MA: Lexington Books, 1987).

26. David J. Ravenscraft and F.M. Scherer, *Mergers, Sell-Offs, and Economic Efficiency* (Washington, D.C.: Brookings Institution, 1987), p. 190.

27. *Thatcher Manufacturing Company v. Federal Trade Commission,* 272 US 554 (1926).

28. *United States v. Bethlehem Steel Corporation et al.,* 168 F.Supp. 576 (1958).

29. *Brown Shoe Company v. United States,* 370 U.S. 294 (1962).

30. *United States v. Von's Grocery Company et al.,* 384 U.S. 270 (1966).

31. *United States v. Philadelphia National Bank et al.,* 374 U.S. 321 (1964).

32. *United States v. General Dynamics Corporation et al.,* 415 U.S. 486 (1974).

33. *United States v. Waste Management, Inc. and EMW Ventures Inc.,* 743 F.22d 976 (1984).

34. *FTC v. Elders Grain, Inc.,* 868 F.2d 901 (1989).

35. *United States v. E.I. du Pont de Nemours & Co. et al.,* 353 U.S. 586 (1957).

36. *Brown Shoe Company v. United States,* 370 U.S. 294 (1962).

37. *Fruehauf Corporation v. FTC,* 603 F.2d 345 (1989).

38. *Federal Trade Commission v. Procter & Gamble Co.,* 386 U.S. 568 (1967).

39. *In the Matter of The Bendix Corporation et al.,* 77 F.T.C. 731 (1970).

40. *In the Matter of The Bendix Corporation et al.,* see 450 F.2d 534 (1971).

41. *United States v. Marine Bancorporation, Inc. et al.,* 418 U.S. 602 (1974).

42. *Yamaha Motors Company v. FTC,* 657 F.2d 971 (1981); *certiorari denied* by the Supreme Court 456 U.S. 915 (1982).

43. *Tenneco, Inc. v. FTC,* 689 F.2d 346 (1982).

44. *Federal Trade Commission v. Consolidated Foods Corporation,* 380 U.S. 592 (1964).

45. *United States v. International Telephone and Telegraph Corporation,* 324 F. Supp. 19 (1970).

46. Willard F. Mueller, "The Anti-Antitrust Movement," in John V. Craven (ed.), *Industrial Organization, Antitrust, and Public Policy.* (Boston: Kluwer-Nijhoff Publishing, 1983), p. 23.

47. For a discussion of some potential problems with using the HHI see Jack Nickerson, "Durable Goods and Horizontal Merger Analysis," *Review of Industrial Organization* 10 (April 1995): 209–20.

Chapter 21

Antitrust: Price Discrimination

Chapter 15 examined the theoretical issues dealing with price discrimination. This chapter explores the public policy issues. Recall from Chapter 18 that the Robinson-Patman Act is the most controversial of the antitrust statutes. Passed during the Great Depression, its original intention was to prevent large chain store buyers from inducing suppliers to grant price concessions that were unavailable to small retailers. Ironically, Section 2(f), which is the only provision aimed directly at *buyer* behavior, has been ineffective. Instead, the Robinson-Patman Act has been directed almost entirely at sellers who grant discriminatory prices.

Sometimes called the "Magna Carta for small business," the Robinson-Patman Act often turns antitrust policy upside-down by protecting small competitors rather than the competitive process. The problem stems from the statute not adequately recognizing that price discrimination is often pro-competitive.

Although most temporary or sporadic price discrimination improves efficiency, some predatory discrimination is anti-competitive. This predatory discrimination has the specific aim of weakening or driving competitors from the market, allowing the predator to then raise price above average cost. Most predatory discrimination is systematic and carried out by dominant firms, and it is only this discrimination that offers any serious threat to competition. Unfortunately, the Robinson-Patman Act has rarely been successful in attacking predatory discrimination but, instead, has typically been directed at practices that have few negative effects on competition. Furthermore, at least in theory, true predatory behavior can be attacked under Section 2 of the Sherman Act without reference to the Robinson-Patman Act.

Robinson-Patman Act cases are grouped into either *primary-line* or *secondary-line* cases according to their effects on competition. Primary-line cases involve possible injury to a direct competitor. Most primary-line cases involve geographic price discrimination in which a national firm sells in one submarket at prices significantly below its prices elsewhere. For example, if Sealtest decided to sell ice cream at a much lower price in Montana than in the rest of the country, even though Sealtest did not manufacture ice cream in Montana, this could cause injury to small Montana dairies. Secondary-line cases involve possible injury to a competitor of a buyer who receives a lower discriminatory price. If Sealtest sold ice cream to Safeway at a lower price than to any other store, it might injure Safeway's competitors, such as A&P.

The Robinson-Patman Act forbids price discrimination:

> where the effect of such discrimination may be substantially to lessen competition or tend to create a monopoly in any line of commerce or to injure, destroy, or prevent competition with any person who either grants or knowingly receives the benefit of such discrimination, or with customers of either of them.

Unlike the other antitrust acts, which require some lessening of competition, the Robinson-Patman Act requires injury to either the competitive process or to *specific competitors*. Furthermore, the act requires only that there *may* be a substantial lessening of competition. Any price discrimination that *may* have a negative effect on any competitor at any level of competition, therefore, may be subject to Robinson-Patman Act enforcement.

Recall that the Robinson-Patman Act provided for two major defenses: cost justification and meeting competition. The act, however, left the standards for either defense wide open for judicial interpretation. Most of the major issues in the following cases revolve around the judicial standards for an acceptable defense.

Secondary Line Cases

Three of the earliest Robinson-Patman Act cases involved basing point pricing systems, such as those analyzed in Chapter 9. Two rather obvious questions arise: What does the basing point system have to do with the Robinson-Patman Act? And, why not attack these systems under the Sherman Act? Although basing point systems have been successfully challenged under the Sherman Act, the earliest cases were Robinson-Patman Act cases in which the FTC argued that buyers located close to a seller but far from a basing point paid higher mill *net* prices and, therefore, were discriminated against. The first two rulings were handed down on the same day in 1945. Both concerned the basing point system in the glucose (corn syrup) industry.

THE CORN PRODUCTS CASE[1] (1945)—The Corn Products Refining Company was a large glucose manufacturer that operated plants in Chicago and Kansas City, Missouri. It sold glucose primarily to candy manufacturers, and all sales were made at delivered prices based on a single basing point, Chicago. Candy manufacturers outside Chicago paid a higher price for glucose than Chicago buyers, even if they were located in Kansas City and purchased from Corn Products' Kansas City plant.

In 1939, the Chicago price was $2.09 per hundred pounds, and the Kansas City price was $2.49 ($2.09 + $0.40 *phantom freight* from Chicago). The FTC argued that the system discriminated against candy manufacturers located in Kansas City because the net price (net price = price − actual freight) in Kansas City was $2.49 compared with $2.09 ($2.09 − $0.00) on glucose shipped from Chicago plants to Chicago candy manufacturers.

The Federal Trade Commission argued that candy manufacturers located in Kansas City would be injured by this discrimination, and the Supreme Court agreed. The Court ruled that because glucose is a principal ingredient in low-priced candy, differences of even small fractions of a cent in the price of glucose could divert business from one manufacturer to another, and therefore, there was a "reasonable probability that the effect of the discriminations may be substantially to lessen competition."

On the same day that it handed down the *Corn Products* decision, the Supreme Court handed down a companion ruling in the *Staley* case.

THE STALEY CASE[2] (1945)—Staley was a glucose producer located in Decatur, Illinois. It competed with the Corn Products Refining Company and also followed a single basing point system based on Chicago delivered prices. When Staley entered the industry in 1920, the basing point system was well established, and Staley argued that its adoption of the system was made in "good faith" to meet competition.

The Court of Appeals upheld Staley's position but the Supreme Court reversed. The Court ruled that Staley's prices "were established not to meet equally low Chicago prices of competitors there, but in order to establish elsewhere the artificially high prices."

The *Staley* decision established two important precedents. First, the decision established that it was not an acceptable good faith defense to meet a competitor's *illegal* discriminatory price. Second, in a later section of the decision the Court established the future legal standard for judging good faith defenses as the showing "of facts which would lead a reasonable and prudent person to believe that the granting of a lower price would in fact meet the equally low price of a competitor."

THE CEMENT INSTITUTE CASE[3] (1948)—The legal death knell for basing point systems came three years later in the *Cement Institute* case when the Supreme Court ruled that the combined effect of the *Corn Products* and *Staley* decisions was to make all basing point systems illegal.*

In the *Corn Products* case, the Court held that a single basing point system was illegal, but it reserved judgment on multiple basing point price systems because of the good-faith proviso of Section 2(b) of the Robinson-Patman Act. In the *Staley* case, the Court held that a seller could not justify the adoption of a competitor's basing point price system under Section 2(b) as a good faith attempt to meet the competitor's equally low price. The combined effect of the two decisions, therefore, was to make all basing point pricing systems illegal.

For all practical purposes, the *Cement Institute* case ended legal basing point systems in the United States. The steel industry, for example, voluntarily abandoned its multiple basing point system. Illegal basing point systems, however, still occasionally arise. Recall from Chapter 9 that the plywood industry adopted a basing point system well into the 1970s.[4]

A per se ban on industry-wide systematic basing point systems seems justified. Basing point systems distort market prices and costs. Furthermore, by en-

---

*The Courts have since upheld basing point systems if freight costs play a very minor role in overall pricing decisions. See *Ethyl Corporation v. FTC,* 729 F.2d 128 (1984).

couraging firms to enter basing point industries with stable price structures, the systems may encourage excessive entry and a great deal of excess capacity.[5] Although individual producers may, from time to time, be forced to adopt a delivered pricing system to match local competition, this can be accomplished under a uniform F.O.B. pricing system, with freight absorption by the seller permitted to meet a competitor's lower price.* At the very least buyers should have the option of F.O.B. pricing with buyer pick-up at the mill. The elimination of most basing point systems has been one of the more positive effects of the Robinson-Patman Act.

MORTON SALT CASE[6] (1948)—One week after handing down the *Cement Institute* decision, the Supreme Court handed down its first major precedent in a non–basing point case. Morton Salt was the nation's leading producer of table salt. Morton followed a strict quantity-based system of price discrimination. Table 21.1 shows the price schedule used by Morton. Only five large chains, American Stores, National Tea, Kroger, Safeway, and A&P, qualified for the top discount. As a result, these five chains could sell at a retail price below the wholesale price that many independent wholesalers paid for salt. Morton argued that because the discounts were available to all purchasers, they were not discriminatory.

The Supreme Court ruled against Morton. The majority reasoned that the discounts were "theoretically" available to all, but that "functionally" they were available only to the largest chains. In another section of the decision, the Court stated that "the statute does not require that the discriminations must in fact have harmed competition, but only that there is a reasonable possibility that they 'may' have such an effect."

Two important precedents emerged from the *Morton Salt* case. First, only a *reasonable possibility* of injury to competition or competitors was required by the majority. This considerably reduced the burden of proof in Robinson-Patman Act cases because it is often possible to find a reasonable possibility that either competition or a competitor will be injured by price discrimination. Second, the *Morton Salt* case established that pure quantity-based discounts had to be *fully* cost justified.

The *Morton Salt* decision can be criticized on economic grounds. The decision highlighted the basic conflict that arises in so many Robinson-Patman Act cases. If all price discrimination is eliminated, a firm's output is likely to decline, and average costs will rise as long as economies of scale exist. Eliminating all price discrimination is likely, therefore, to raise society's average cost of producing a good. In addition, consumers may well end up paying higher prices.

In the long run, the banning of all quantity discounts may not help even the small retailers—the main focus of Congress's concern when the Robinson-Patman Act was passed. If the banning of discounts on salt encouraged the large chains to produce their own salt (that is, to vertically integrate into salt production), then Morton's output would decline, its average costs might increase, and Morton might increase its price to small retailers that were unable to produce their own salt. Under such circumstances, the difference between what large and small retailers pay for salt might increase.

---

*Under F.O.B. pricing, buyers pay the actual freight costs incurred by the seller.

TABLE 21.1 **Morton Salt's Prices for Different Quantities**

Quantity	Price per Case
Less than carload	$1.60
Carload	$1.50
5,000 Carloads/year	$1.40
50,000 Carloads/year	$1.35

STANDARD OIL OF INDIANA CASE[7] (1958)—The next major secondary-line case involved the other major defense established in the Robinson-Patman Act, the good-faith meeting of competition. Standard Oil had followed a policy of charging four large Detroit jobber-retailers prices that were 1.5 cents per gallon less than its service station customers. Each of the four jobbers sold some of their gasoline at retail, and two of the jobbers charged lower retail prices than generally prevailed for Standard's gasoline. The four jobbers took deliveries in tank-car quantities of 8,000 to 12,000 gallons, rather than the typical tank-wagon quantities of 700 to 800 gallons that were delivered to service stations. Some cost savings were associated with these large-quantity purchases; however, the Commission ruled that the *entire* 1.5 cent differential could not be cost justified.

Once its cost justification failed, Standard argued that the reductions were made in a good-faith effort to meet competition. The Commission ruled that meeting competition was not an *absolute* defense under Section 2(b). The FTC's argument was a technical one based on Section 2(a) seeming to make only the cost justification an absolute defense, while the meeting competition defense was relegated to Section 2(b), which dealt primarily with the burden of proof in Robinson-Patman Act cases (see Chapter 18).

The Supreme Court initially ruled that a good-faith meeting of competition established an absolute defense under the Robinson-Patman Act, and the case was remanded to the FTC for reconsideration of Standard's meeting competition defense. On remand the Commission ruled that Standard had not acted in "good faith," but instead was following a simple pricing system in which purchasers of over 2 million gallons a year received a lower price. The case was then appealed for a second time to the Supreme Court.

This time the Court found for Standard because it was persuaded by evidence that between 1936 and 1941 local suppliers had made numerous attempts to take business away from Standard by reducing prices to the large jobber-retailers. There is a major potential problem with this decision and with the act in general. Suppose Sunoco offered an illegal discriminatory price to one of Standard's jobbers. Should Standard be permitted to undercut Sunoco's price? Under the *Staley* precedent, one would think not. Under the *Standard Oil* precedent, however, it appears to be legitimate to match even an illegal price. Furthermore, if Standard is permitted to undercut Sunoco's price, should Texaco be permitted to cut Standard's price, and then should Shell be permitted to cut Texaco's price? In other words, after one price cut in good faith is permitted, shouldn't every subsequent price cut be permitted? If the answer is yes, then the act becomes meaningless. These are not just hypothetical questions. During the litigation period of the *Standard Oil* case, the FTC had similar suits pending against Gulf, Texaco, and Shell. However, prohibiting good-faith defenses in such cases would tend to make prices more rigid. This suggests another of the many dilemmas raised by Robinson-Patman Act enforcement.

The most important precedent emerging from the two *Standard Oil* decisions was the establishment of the good-faith meeting of competition as an absolute defense in Robinson-Patman Act cases.

THE BORDEN CASE[8] (1962)—The 1962 *Borden* case concerned the pricing practices of two major distributors of milk in Chicago: Borden and Bowman Dairy. Both firms charged prices to independent stores that included volume discounts based on daily purchases. In June 1954, Borden established the price schedule shown in Table 21.2. Furthermore, Borden granted two large chains, A&P and Jewel, a flat 8.5 percent discount. A few large independents also received a 5.5 percent discount. Bowman's discount schedule was similar, but more complex. It placed firms in one of seventeen discount groups, with discounts ranging from 3 to 8 percent. Furthermore, Bowman offered A&P and Kroger an 11 percent discount. These pricing policies placed independents into one group with their prices determined by a volume-based discount schedule, and two large chains into an entirely separate group. Both firms used a cost-justification defense, and each introduced a large volume of statistical evidence to support its cost claims.

The Supreme Court ruled for the government because Borden's and Bowman's average cost groupings were "too broad." The *Borden* decision indicates why firms have much difficulty establishing a valid cost-justification defense. First, the Court stated that price discrimination must be fully cost justified, penny for penny. According to the Supreme Court, if prices differ by $1.00 and a firm justifies a 75-cent, or even 90-cent, cost differential, the defense is likely to fail. Furthermore, cost estimates must be based on average cost estimates, not marginal cost estimates. The average cost of servicing a large buyer is likely to be much higher than marginal cost because average cost includes an allocation for overhead. Therefore requiring firms to base cost estimates on average cost sets a very stringent standard for the legitimate use of the cost-justification defense. Not surprisingly, given the extreme difficulty of establishing the cost-justification defense, only two completely successful cost-justification defenses were accepted in court between 1936 and 1954.[9]

FALLS CITY INDUSTRIES CASE[10] (1983)—Falls City Industries was a beer distributor. The company sold beer to wholesalers in Indiana, Kentucky, and eleven other states. Vanco was Falls City's only wholesaler distributor in Evansville, Indiana, and Dawson Springs was its sole distributorship in nearby Henderson, Kentucky. Because of state regulations in both Indiana and Kentucky, wholesalers could not cross state lines to sell to retailers in other states, but consumers often crossed state lines to purchase beer from the cheaper retailer. Falls City typically charged higher prices, as much as 30 percent higher, in Indiana than in Kentucky. Vanco sued Falls City, claiming that Dawson Springs passed its lower prices on to its retailers and that many consumers in Indiana then crossed the border to buy less expensive beer in Kentucky, thereby reducing Vanco's beer sales in Indiana.

TABLE 21.2 Borden's Volume Disounts (June 1954)

Average Converted Units per Day	Discount (%)
0–24	0
25–74	2
75–149	3
150 or more	4

The District Court and the Court of Appeals found that Falls City had violated the Robinson-Patman Act. In particular, both courts rejected Falls City's defense that it was meeting equally low prices in Kentucky. The courts in fact refused to consider this defense because the price discrimination was created by raising prices in Indiana rather than lowering prices in Kentucky. One unusual fact was that Indiana required brewers to charge a uniform price throughout the state. Falls City, therefore, was required by law to charge the same price to wholesalers located near the southern Indiana border with Kentucky as they charged to wholesalers hundreds of miles away in northern Indiana.

The Supreme Court remanded the case to the District Court to give Falls City an opportunity to prove that its lower prices in Kentucky were made in a good-faith effort to meet the lower prices that prevailed in Kentucky. The Supreme Court ruled that Falls City would have to show "that a reasonable and prudent businessman would believe that the lower price he charged was generally available from his competitors throughout the territory and throughout the period in which he made the lower price available."

TEXACO CASE[11] (1990)—Between 1972 and 1981, Texaco sold gasoline to twelve independent retailers in Spokane, Washington. Texaco also sold gasoline to two wholesaler-retailers of gasoline, Gull Oil Company and Dompier Oil Company. Gull sold gasoline under its own name, but Dompier sold gasoline under the Texaco brand name. Texaco sold gasoline to Gull at prices that ranged from 4 to 6 cents below its prices to the twelve independent retailers, and it sold gasoline to Dompier at prices that ranged from 3.65 to 3.95 cents below its prices to the twelve independents. For several years the independents lost sales to Gull and Dompier; then in July 1976, the twelve independents sued Texaco.

The Supreme Court ruled that Texaco's behavior violated the Robinson-Patman Act. The Court rejected Texaco's argument that Gull and Dompier were wholesalers, not retailers, and therefore that the lower prices were justified to cover the expenses associated with their wholesaler operations. It did not help Texaco's case that both Gull and Dompier generally picked up gasoline from Texaco and immediately resold it to consumers. Neither firm had substantial storage facilities. Another point working against Texaco was the company's refusal to allow the independents to haul their own gasoline from Texaco's storage tanks at lower prices.

The *Falls City* and *Texaco* cases indicate that the Robinson-Patman Act is not dead. As recently as the 1990 *Texaco* decision, the Supreme Court ruled that price discrimination that injures competitors violates the act. This ruling was handed down despite the fact that the Justice Department and the FTC filed legal briefs in the case supporting Texaco. The government's position in this case was that the Robinson-Patman Act should not apply to price differences charged to wholesalers compared with retailers. The fact that the government agencies filed briefs in support of Texaco helps explain why both the *Falls City* and *Texaco* cases were private cases filed by injured companies rather than cases filed by either the Justice Department or the FTC.

Primary-Line Cases

THE ANHEUSER-BUSCH CASE[12] (1961)—In 1954, Anheuser-Busch lowered the price of Budweiser in St. Louis below the price it charged elsewhere. The FTC ruled that this violated the Robinson-Patman Act, but the Seventh Circuit Court of Appeals held that "the threshold statutory element of price discrimination had not been established." The Circuit Court argued that because Anheuser-Busch charged the same price to all purchasers in St. Louis, there had been no price discrimination.

The Supreme Court overturned the Appeals Court. Chief Justice Warren stated "it is certain at least that Section 2(a) is violated where there is a price discrimination which deals the requisite injury to primary-line competition, even though secondary-line and tertiary-line competition are unaffected."

Having established that geographic discrimination came within the jurisdiction of the Robinson-Patman Act, the Supreme Court remanded the case to the Appeals Court for further consideration. The facts were straightforward. Before its first price decrease, Anheuser-Busch controlled 12.5 percent of the St. Louis beer market. After two price cuts, which lowered Budweiser's prices to equal its competitors' prices, Budweiser's market share increased to 39.3 percent. The price reductions lifted Budweiser from fourth place (last among the majors) to first place in the St. Louis market, but when Anheuser-Busch increased its prices in March 1955, Budweiser's market share declined to 17.5 percent.

The Circuit Court of Appeals dismissed the case for a second time, ruling that Anheuser-Busch's price discrimination had not caused any injury to competition. The Court of Appeals was persuaded by evidence that Anheuser-Busch's competitors continued to control more than three-fourths of sales in the 12 months after the price of Budweiser was voluntarily increased in St. Louis in March 1955. The Court also noted that the primary beneficiary of Anheuser-Busch's price reductions were St. Louis consumers.

The Circuit Court recognized that Anheuser-Busch's price reductions improved efficiency by bringing price closer to marginal cost and giving consumers a wider choice of popularly priced beers. Furthermore, the Court implicitly recognized that market competition on a local, rather than national, level determines beer prices. The *Anheuser-Busch* case was not appealed back to the Supreme Court. The 1967 *Utah Pie* Supreme Court decision suggested, however, that the FTC might have won such an appeal during the 1960s.

THE UTAH PIE CASE[13] (1967)—The *Utah Pie* decision is one of the most controversial antitrust decisions. Utah Pie was a small company that had been baking fresh pies for 30 years when it entered the frozen pie market in 1957. Utah Pie quickly captured 66.5 percent of the Salt Lake City market. Three large national firms, Pet Milk, Continental, and Carnation, also sold frozen pies in Utah. The case centered on the response of the three national firms to Utah Pie's domination of the Salt Lake City market.

Pet Milk produced frozen pies in California and Pennsylvania, yet its pies sometimes were selling at significantly lower prices in Salt Lake City than in markets located closer to Pet's manufacturing plant in California. Similarly, in June 1961, Continental offered its large apple pies at $2.85 per dozen in Utah, a price well below its apple pie prices in other markets. Evidence suggested that the $2.85 price may have been below "its direct cost plus an allocation for overhead." Finally, in 1959 Carnation cut its price by 60 cents per dozen in Utah, and the Supreme Court concluded that at this price, Carnation was selling pies at prices *below* average total cost.

Some evidence suggested that at some time each of the defendants attempted to cut into Utah Pie's market share by cutting prices. Utah Pie's market share did decline from 66.5 percent in 1958, to 34.3 percent in 1959, 45.5 percent in 1960, and 45.3 percent in 1961. Utah Pie, however, generally remained the leading seller. Furthermore, Utah Pie remained a profitable company throughout the four-year period under investigation.

The Circuit Court of Appeals dismissed the case, holding that the evidence failed to support a finding of *injury to competition*. The Supreme Court overturned the Appeals Court decision because of the evidence of predatory *intent* and a belief that "the Act reaches price discrimination that erodes competition as much as it does price discrimination that is intended to have immediate destructive impact."

It is easy to understand why the *Utah Pie* decision created so much controversy. The case concerned the largely unsuccessful attempt of three competitors to break a firm's 66.5 percent domination of a local market by cutting prices in a temporary and rather sporadic manner. Without question the effect of these price reductions on consumers and short-run welfare was positive, with prices reduced to levels closer to marginal cost.

There is, however, another side to the case. The Supreme Court believed that each of the three national firms showed some evidence of predatory intent. Evidence suggested that Pet Milk went so far as to send an industrial spy into Utah Pie's plant. Furthermore, although prices always covered marginal costs, there was serious doubt that they always covered average total costs. Finally, below-cost pricing can clearly be used by large national firms in local markets to attempt to destroy local competition. If such behavior is always permitted, it might result in long-run problems because a few large national firms could come to dominate many markets by establishing a tough reputation.

The *Utah Pie* decision resulted in a great deal of criticism from economists and was a major impetus for a seminal article by Professors Areeda and Turner in which they argued that only prices below *marginal* cost should be considered predatory. Furthermore, because marginal costs are difficult to calculate, Areeda and Turner advocated using *average variable cost* as a proxy for marginal cost.[14] Areeda and Turner's position was in turn criticized by many economists who argued that it was extreme.[15] Critics noted that carrying Arreda and Turner's recommendation to its logical conclusion, only prices below average variable cost are predatory, which implies that only prices below a firm's short-run shutdown price are predatory. Although such a strict standard may occasionally be breached by a firm obsessed with the destruction of a competitor, virtually all price discrimination takes place at prices well above average variable costs.

The **Areeda and Turner doctrine** has had a significant impact on some court decisions. In the *Vebco* case, for example, the Fifth Circuit Court of Appeals came close to adopting their position.

THE VEBCO CASE[16] (1975)—Vebco was primarily a distributor of air-conditioning and heating equipment in El Paso, Texas. American Excelsior (AMXCO) was the world's largest manufacturer of evaporative cooler pads for air conditioners. AMXCO's manufacturing operation was located in Arlington, Texas. Beginning in 1953 and continuing through 1969, the only cooler pads distributed by Vebco were produced by AMXCO.

In 1969 AMXCO learned of Vebco's plans to manufacture its own pads and terminated its supply relationship with Vebco. Two years later, in 1971, AMXCO offered a 25 percent discount in El Paso, which placed its El Paso prices considerably below its prices in other markets.

As a result of AMXCO's price cuts, Vebco filed a suit against AMXCO on May 28, 1971 under the Robinson-Patman Act, and it later filed a Sherman Act claim as well. Vebco's case relied on evidence of lost profits and predatory intent.

A District Court jury found in favor of AMXCO, and Vebco appealed. The Fifth Circuit Court of Appeals, relying heavily on the Areeda and Turner doctrine, affirmed the District Court decision. Judge Morgan wrote, "It is frequently quite difficult to calculate . . . marginal cost. . . . Consequently, the firm's average variable cost may be effectively substituted for marginal cost in predatory pricing analysis." Because the Court of Appeals determined that AMXCO's prices were well above average total cost, the Court dismissed the charges.

The facts in the *AMXCO* case were somewhat similar to those in the *Utah Pie* case; however, the decision relied on the Areeda and Turner doctrine instead of the *Utah Pie* precedent. Under this doctrine, Utah Pie would certainly have lost its case because its competitors' prices were always above marginal cost and average variable cost.

The *AMXCO* decision can be defended on efficiency grounds. The widespread adoption of the average variable cost test, however, might result in significant problems because even the most aggressive predatory behavior could be justified. Such a position could have its greatest impact in monopolization cases. Even the 1911 *Standard Oil* and *American Tobacco* decisions might have been overturned based on strict adherence to the Areeda and Turner doctrine.

GENERAL FOODS CASE[17] (1984)—Recall from Chapter 10 that General Foods, the producer of Maxwell House coffee, had responded aggressively to the East Coast entry of Procter & Gamble, the producer of Folgers coffee. Briefly, the facts were as follows. In 1970 General Foods held approximately a 43 percent national market share for non-instant coffee. Most of that share was held by Maxwell House.

In 1971, Procter and Gamble began to market Folgers in the East by selling in four test markets. In response to Folgers entry, General Foods greatly reduced the price of Maxwell House in the test markets. Evidence suggested that Maxwell House was sold at prices below marginal and average variable costs. In the late winter of 1974, for example, Maxwell House was sold for $2.095 per three-pound can in Pittsburgh, whereas the price of a three-pound can of unroasted green coffee beans was $2.10.

Despite the evidence of below-cost pricing, the Federal Trade Commission dismissed the case because no injury to competition had been proved. The Commission noted, "The principal effect of the heated rivalry between Folgers and Maxwell House has been to reduce the prices consumers pay for coffee and promote product quality. . . . Healthy competition does not violate the Robinson-Patman Act."

As in the *Texaco* case, the FTC seemed to take a rather limited view of the Robinson-Patman Act in the *General Foods* case. In this case evidence of prices below average variable cost were still not sufficient to result in a finding in support of the FTC staff.

THE BORDEN PRIVATE LABEL CASE[18] (1967)—The 1967 *Borden* decision concerned the issue of **private-label pricing.** Borden sold its evaporated milk under its Borden brand label (the "Elsie the Cow" label) and also under private labels such as A&P. Despite the milk being identical in physical content, Borden charged a higher price for the Borden brand.

The FTC complained that the practice violated the Robinson-Patman Act. The Fifth Circuit Court of Appeals put aside the Commission's cease and desist order on the ground that private-label milk "as a matter of law" was not of the same grade and quality as branded milk. The Supreme Court overturned the Circuit Court decision and declared that "there is nothing in the language of the statute indicating that grade, as distinguished from quality, is not to be determined by the characteristics of the product itself, but by consumer preferences, brand acceptability or what customers think of it and are willing to pay for it."

This decision could have revolutionized the private-label industry. On remand, however, the Circuit Court of Appeals ruled that Borden's private-label business had not injured competition. Judge Hutcheson stated that "where a price differential between a premium and non premium brand reflects no more than a consumer preference for the premium brand, the price difference creates no competitive advantage to the recipient of the cheaper private brand product on which injury could be predicated."

The Circuit Court opinion was clearly at odds with the Supreme Court decision. From an economic perspective, the Circuit Court's decision makes much more sense than the Supreme Court's position because consumers must consider branded products to be different from private-label products or their prices would be identical. Furthermore, as Justice Stewart pointed out in his Supreme Court dissent, the Court's position raises the possibility of some strange behavior. For example, according to the Supreme Court's reasoning, Borden could have reduced the quality of the private label milk (perhaps by adding rodent hairs) and then have legally sold it for a lower price. Fortunately, the Circuit Court's ruling saved the public from the negative implications of this Supreme Court decision.

◢ *Illegally Induced Price Discrimination*

Recall from Chapter 18 that the Robinson-Patman Act was passed in large part to prevent major chain stores with *monopsony* power from inducing lower prices from suppliers. Section 2(f) was aimed directly at this behavior; however, very few successful cases have been filed under Section 2(f). This lack of success can be traced back to the 1953 *Automatic Canteen* precedent.

AUTOMATIC CANTEEN CASE[19] (1953)—Automatic Canteen operated more than 230,000 candy vending machines, so it purchased a great deal of candy. It constantly requested lower prices from its candy suppliers under the threat of cutting off its purchases. Furthermore, Automatic Canteen would often estimate its suppliers' cost savings on large-quantity sales to Automatic Canteen and then inform its suppliers of the prices it would find acceptable.

Evidence suggested that this was a classic attempt by a large buyer to induce price concessions from suppliers. In other words, it was precisely the problem Congress had in mind when it passed the Robinson-Patman Act. The Supreme Court, however, ruled in favor of Automatic Canteen.

The Court concluded that a buyer was not liable under the Robinson-Patman Act if the induced lower prices were either "within one of the seller's defenses such as the cost justification or not known by him to be within one of those defenses." In the *Automatic Canteen* case the Court essentially stated that ignorance of the law was a defense.

By placing a heavy burden of proof on the Commission in Section 2(f) cases, the Supreme Court made successful prosecution very difficult. After the *Automatic Canteen* decision, there was little chance of an FTC victory in a Section 2(f) case, unless a seller informed a buyer that the buyer was requesting an illegal discriminatory price. The Supreme Court reinforced this position in 1979 in the *A&P* case.

THE A&P CASE[20] (1979)—In 1965 A&P solicited a bid from Borden to supply A&P's 200 Chicago stores with private-label milk. Borden offered a plan that would have saved A&P $410,000 a year, but A&P was dissatisfied with the offer and solicited a competitive bid from Bowman Dairy. Bowman made a bid that would have saved A&P $737,000 a year. A&P's Chicago buyer then informed Borden, "I have a bid in my pocket. You [Borden] people are so far out of line it is not even funny. You are not even in the ball park." A&P's buyer also told Borden that a $50,000 further reduction "would not be a drop in the bucket." Borden then offered an $820,000 a year discount. When it made this offer, Borden emphasized that it was only attempting to meet Bowman's offer.

The FTC ruled that because A&P knew that it was the beneficiary of an illegally low price, it had violated Section 2(f). The Second Circuit Court of Appeals affirmed the FTC order but the Supreme Court overturned it. Justice Stewart wrote that "since Borden had a meeting-competition defense and thus could not be liable under Section 2(b), the petitioner who did no more than accept that offer cannot be liable under Section 2(f)."

One of the ironies of the Robinson-Patman Act is the minuscule number of cases filed under Section 2(f). Between 1936 and 1966, only 30 of 1,100 Robinson-Patman Act cases, or 0.03 percent of all cases, were Section 2(f) cases.[21] One of the major Congressional concerns at the time the law was passed, therefore, has not been addressed successfully by enforcement.

Criticism of the Robinson-Patman Act by economists and judges has had a major impact on enforcement, greatly reducing the number of cases filed by the FTC. For example, although the FTC filed 219 Robinson-Patman complaints in 1963 alone, it filed only two cases in 1975, six cases between 1975 and 1982, and one case between 1983 and 1987.[22]

SUMMARY

1. Robinson-Patman Act cases are grouped into either *primary-line* or *secondary-line* cases according to their effects on competition. Primary line cases involve possible injury to a direct competitor. Secondary line cases involve possible injury to a competitor of a buyer who receives a lower discriminatory price.

2. In 1945, the Supreme Court ruled that basing point pricing systems violated the Robinson-Patman Act. These rulings against the basing point pricing system probably marked the high water mark for Robinson-Patman Act enforcement.

3. There are two defenses in Robinson-Patman Act cases: meeting competition and cost justification. The burden of proof to successfully use these defenses is high. The cost justification requires a penny-for-penny price reduction.

4. Geographic price discrimination often is pro-competitive, but the Robinson-Patman Act does not effectively distinguish pro-competitive from anti-competitive price discrimination.

5. Areeda and Turner suggested that only prices below average variable cost should violate the Robinson-Patman Act. This will rarely occur because it requires firms to charge a price below the shut-down price. Other economists have suggested that prices below average total cost might violate the Robinson-Patman Act if there is evidence of predatory intent.

6. The Robinson-Patman Act has come under increasing criticism in recent years. Much of this criticism is justified, but it may have resulted in too strong a bias in favor of dominant firms that use price discrimination to create a tough reputation and deter entry.

7. The widespread adoption of the strict Areeda and Turner Doctrine, in particular, could cause welfare problems.

8. One major result of the criticism of the Robinson-Patman Act has already been observed. The FTC is filing far fewer cases in recent years. If this trend continues, government enforcement of the Robinson-Patman Act may simply wither away.

9. Despite the government's reluctance to file cases, private suits still abound, and are likely to continue; therefore, legislative action to abolish or change the law could still have a significant impact.

10. The Robinson-Patman Act has not been entirely without its bright moments. The elimination of basing point pricing systems was a positive accomplishment. Nothing in the act prevents a firm from lowering its prices across the board to *all* buyers in response to a competitor's price reduction. In many cases an across-the-board price reduction would result in large increases in consumer welfare.

11. The costs of enforcement have been high, and the Robinson-Patman Act has resulted in far too many costly legal battles over the right of competitors to compete aggressively through the use of lower prices.

12. A pragmatic approach might be to leave the present act on the books but to limit its use to the few cases of truly anti-competitive price discrimination, particularly the use of price discrimination by dominant firms to discipline rivals. The recent reduction in FTC activity indicates a movement in this direction.

KEY TERMS

Areeda and Turner Doctrine

basing point pricing system

predatory pricing

primary-line discrimination

private-label pricing

secondary-line discrimination

DISCUSSION QUESTIONS

1. Explain the Areeda and Turner Doctrine. Has this doctrine been accepted by some federal courts? Does the doctrine make economic sense?

2. In the *Borden* case dealing with Borden's private-label evaporated milk, the Supreme Court and the Court of Appeals disagreed with each other. How did the Courts disagree? Which Court's decision do you think made more economic sense?

3. One of the original objectives of the Robinson-Patman Act was to protect small retailers from large chain stores. In the long run, does the act protect small retailers from large chain stores? Why or why not?

4. Has the government's decision to file fewer Robinson-Patman Act cases in recent years been a wise decision?

5. Every year a significant number of American college students study in London. Many of these students obtain flats (apartments) from one of a number of rental agencies specializing in finding short-term rentals for American students. Typically, the agency charges every student the same weekly rental, about £90 per week, but the quality of the flats varies greatly, ranging from luxurious flats for two in Kensington to dilapidated flats for five in Bayswater. Would an economist consider this a form of price discrimination? Would the Robinson-Patman Act consider this price discrimination? Does this suggest a problem with the law?

6. What economic inefficiencies result from successful basing point pricing systems? Why was the basing point pricing system attacked under the Robinson-Patman Act? Did the system violate any other antitrust statutes?

7. What is the difference between a primary-line and a secondary-line Robinson-Patman Act case? What type of case is more likely to result in significant negative effects on competition? Why?

8. Should the Robinson-Patman Act be repealed?

9. How might strict enforcement of the Robinson-Patman Act result in both an increase in vertical integration and a loss of economies of scale?

10. In a 1953 Robinson-Patman Act case, Champion Spark Plug Company was charged with price discrimination in the pricing of its spark plugs to Ford. Champion charged Ford 6 cents for original equipment spark plugs but sold the exact same plugs to wholesalers for 26 cents. Suggest a reason why Champion charged such a low price to Ford for original equipment plugs. The Federal Trade Commission found in favor of Champion in this case. Can you suggest a reason for the Commission's ruling?

REFERENCES

1. *Corn Products Refining Company et al. v. Federal Trade Commission*, 324 U.S. 726 (1945).
2. *Federal Trade Commission v. A.E. Staley Manufacturing Co. et al.*, 324 U.S. 746 (1945).
3. *Federal Trade Commission v. Cement Institute et al.*, 333 U.S. 683 (948).
4. See *In the Matter of Boise Cascade Corporation*, FTC Docket 8958 (1978).
5. Don E. Waldman, "Welfare and Collusion: Comment," *American Economic Review* 72 (March 1982): 268–72.
6. *Federal Trade Commission v. Morton Salt Company*, 334 U.S. 37 (1948).
7. *Standard Oil Company v. Federal Trade Commission*, 340 U.S. 231 (1951) and *Standard Oil Company v. Federal Trade Commission*, 355 U.S. 396 (1958).
8. *United States v. Borden Company et al.*, 370 U.S. 460 (1962).
9. U.S. Department of Justice, *Report of the Attorney General's National Committee to Study the Antitrust Laws* (Washington, D.C.: Government Printing Office, 1955), p. 171.
10. *Fall City Industries v. Vanco Beverage*, 460 U.S. 103 (1983).
11. *Texaco v. Hasbrouck*, 496 U.S. 543 (1990).
12. *Federal Trade Commission v. Anheuser-Busch, Inc.*, 363 U.S. 536 (1960); and *Anheuser-Busch, Inc. v. Federal Trade Commission*, 289 F.2d 835 (1961).
13. *Utah Pie Company v. Continental Baking Company et al.*, 386 U.S. 685 (1967).
14. P. Areeda and D. Turner, "Predatory Pricing and Related Practices Under Section 2 of the Sherman Act," *Harvard Law Review* (1975): 697–733.
15. See F.M. Scherer, "Predatory Pricing and the Sherman Act: Comment," *Harvard Law Review* (1976): 869–903; O. Williamson, "Predatory Pricing: A Strategic and Welfare Analysis," *Yale Law Journal* (1977): 284–340; and R. H. Koller II, "When Is Pricing Predatory," *Antitrust Bulletin* (1979): 283–306.
16. *International Air Industries Inc. and Vebco, Inc. v. American Excelsior Company*, 517 F.2d 714 (1975).
17. *In the Matter of General Foods Corp.*, 103 FTC 204 (1984).
18. *Federal Trade Commission v. Borden Company*, 383 U.S. 637 (1966); and *Federal Trade Commission v. Borden Company*, 381 F.2d 175 (1967).
19. *Automatic Canteen Company of America v. Federal Trade Commission*, 346 U.S. 61 (1953).
20. *Great Atlantic & Pacific Tea Company v. Federal Trade Commission*, 440 U.S. 69 (1979).
21. "Robinson-Patman: Dodo or Golden Rule?" *Business Week* (November 12, 1966): 66.
22. Douglas F. Greer, *Business, Government, and Society* (New York: MacMillan, 1983), p. 203; and Richard A. Whiting, "R–P: May It Rest in Peace," *Antitrust Bulletin* (Fall 1986): 711.

Chapter 22

Antitrust: Public Policy Toward Vertical Restraints of Trade and Group Boycotts

Before examining public policy toward vertical restraints, it is important to understand the discussion of vertical integration in Chapter 16. Each of the restrictions analyzed in this chapter can be considered as an alternative to increased vertical integration. The economic arguments against these practices are, therefore, similar to the arguments against vertical integration. Public policy toward five types of vertical restraints are explored, including tying agreements, exclusive dealing agreements, territorial and customer restrictions, resale price maintenance, and group boycotts.

Tying Agreements

If a firm has market power over good X, it may require that its buyers purchase another good, good Y, to obtain good X. If a film distributor has exclusive rights over a new, popular film, hypothetically entitled "Home Alone 10," and it also controls a less popular film, hypothetically entitled "The Grasshopper That Ate Cleveland," then the distributor could require that every theater that shows "Home Alone 10" must also show "The Grasshopper That Ate Cleveland." Such requirements are termed **tying agreements**; "Home Alone 10" is the **tying product** and "The Grasshopper That Ate Cleveland" is the **tied product**.

The economic impact of tying has been debated extensively over the past two decades. Opinions vary widely. Some believe that tying is never anticompetitive, and others believe that under certain circumstances tying can be an effective method of increasing monopoly power and monopoly profits.[1] Conventional wisdom rejects the extreme position that tying is never anticompetitive, but accepts that most tying agreements have few anticompetitive effects.

The possible anticompetitive impact of tying can be illustrated by examining Kodak's former policy of tying film and film processing. Before 1956, Kodak sold photographic film only on the condition that the buyer have the film processed by Kodak. Because Kodak produced superior patented film, this was an effective way to extend its power from film to processing. Kodak's practice had several anticompetitive effects. Because Kodak controlled 90 percent of the non–instant film market, it was extremely difficult for independent film processors to find any film to process. The tying arrangement thus foreclosed a huge share of the processing market, making entry into processing very difficult. Because Kodak's policy foreclosed 90 percent of the market, the only way to enter the film-processing market may have been to follow Kodak's lead and produce film as well as provide processing services. Forcing entrants to enter two markets, film and film processing, instead of one greatly increased the capital barrier to entry. Entry required not only more capital, but also large research and development expenditures to produce non-infringing film capable of competing with Kodak's film. Not surprisingly, no competitor threatened Kodak's processing market share until 1956 when Kodak agreed to a consent decree ending the tie. Shortly thereafter, the processing market became highly competitive.[2]*

Defendants have advanced two primary arguments to justify tying arrangements. First, they contend that tying is necessary for technological reasons. This argument sometimes makes sense. Often, however, this argument seems almost frivolous, as when International Salt contended that only its salt would prevent its salt dispensing machines from clogging.[3] Second, franchisors such as Carvel and Dunkin' Donuts have argued that it is necessary to tie ingredients together to maintain the high quality associated with their trademarks.[4] As the following cases indicate, these arguments have met with some success in the courts.

IBM CASE (1936)[5]—One of the government's earliest tying victories came in the 1936 *IBM* case. IBM refused to lease its tabulating machines unless the lessee agreed to purchase its entire requirements for tabulating cards from IBM. IBM had significant market power in the machine market, and this plan enabled it to control more than 80 percent of the market for both machines and cards. Remington Rand, the only other producer of tabulating machines, followed the same policy of tying its cards to its machines.

IBM argued that the tie was necessary to protect its tabulating machines from damage caused by the use of "inferior" cards. IBM stated that it was essential to the successful performance of its machines that the cards conform with relatively minute tolerances with regard to size, thickness, and freedom from defects. Its defense was undermined, however, because the United States government, under the provisions of its lease, had for years produced large quantities of its own cards that were successfully used in IBM's machines.

---

*Recently the Courts ended the restrictions placed on Kodak by this decree. With increased competition in both the film and film-processing markets in recent years, this made sound economic sense.

The Supreme Court ruled that the tying agreement violated Section 3 of the Clayton Act. Despite the decision, IBM continued to dominate the tabulating card market because its lessees continued to purchase their cards from IBM. In fact, IBM's card market share actually increased to 90 percent in 1954. In 1956, IBM agreed to a consent decree that required its market share in tabulating cards to be reduced below 50 percent.[6]

AMERICAN CAN CASE (1949)[7]—The *American Can* case dealt with the leasing practices of American Can and Continental Can. Recall from Chapter 15 that both firms adopted a policy of leasing can-closing machines for a minimum of five years, with the further restriction that the lessee purchase its entire can requirements during the five-year period exclusively from its machinery supplier. Under no circumstances would American or Continental offer machines for sale. These policies resulted in a two-firm concentration ratio of 80.

The practices had several possible anticompetitive effects. First, by placing approximately 80 percent of all can customers beyond the reach of competitors each year, the long-term leases reduced the potential market available to new can manufacturers. Second, by refusing to sell their machines, American and Continental eliminated any potential competition from a second-hand machinery market. Third, the requirement that lessees purchase their requirements of cans from their machinery supplier established a tie between machinery and cans.

These policies worked because the two firms produced superior closing machinery, and therefore, their market power in machinery was responsible for their power in cans. Recall from Chapter 15 that the tying policy enabled American and Continental to increase profitability by practicing a form of price discrimination that used can purchases to meter machinery use. Under these conditions, potential entrants into the can market were virtually forced to produce closing machinery as well as cans, and this proved to be an almost impossible barrier.

The District Court distinguished between the effect of a tying arrangement and the effect of a requirements contract and ruled that although the tying agreement was illegal, a one-year requirements contract for cans was reasonable.

The District Court's remedy eliminated most of the entry barriers created by American's policies. In addition to a lease or requirements contract being limited to one year, American was required to offer all machines for sale at *reasonable prices*. Buyers were therefore able to purchase machinery, which freed them to deal with any can manufacturer. Furthermore, American was required to charge rental rates above average cost. This encouraged buyers to purchase rather than rent machines and helped ease entry into the machinery market.

The most significant result of the decree was a dramatic increase in backward vertical integration into can production by major can users.[8] Between 1930 and 1946, only Campbell's Soup had integrated backward by purchasing a can facility from Continental Can. After the decision, self-manufacturing of cans became common. Within ten years of the decree, many large packers had entered the can industry. Backward vertical integration greatly increased the major packers' leverage in dealing with American and Continental, because large vertically integrated packers could fight price increases by threatening to increase their self-manufacturing operations.[9]

JERROLD CASE[10] (1960)—In December 1950, Jerrold Electronics installed America's first cable TV system in Lansford, Pennsylvania. After a short time the system developed technical problems that required Jerrold to develop new equipment and techniques for cable installations. Because of these problems, Jerrold decided that it would install community-wide systems only if the community agreed to purchase all the necessary equipment from Jerrold and further agreed to purchase a Jerrold service contract.

The District Court ruled that in the early years of the cable TV industry the tie was justified by technological necessity. The Court went on, however, to state that Jerrold could not continue indefinitely to sell only complete cable systems. Before the *Jerrold* decision, it appeared that tying agreements were on the verge of being declared illegal *per se*. The Supreme Court affirmed the *Jerrold* decision without comment, and thereby established an acceptable technology defense in tying cases.

THE HYDE CASE[11] (1984)—In 1984 the Supreme Court further restricted the use of the *per se* rule in tying cases. Dr. Hyde was a board-certified anesthesiologist who applied to join the staff of Jefferson Parish Hospital in New Orleans in 1976. The medical staff found Dr. Hyde to be a highly qualified anesthesiologist, but the hospital board denied him staff privileges because it had signed an exclusive contract with Roux & Associates, a group of four anesthesiologists, to provide all the hospital's anesthesia services. Hyde then sued Jefferson Parish Hospital.

The District Court ruled in favor of the hospital because the anticompetitive effects were minimal and were outweighed by economic benefits. The Court of Appeals, however, reversed, ruling that the contract involved a tying arrangement that was illegal *per se* under the Clayton Act. On appeal the Supreme Court reversed the Appeals Court. In its reversal the Supreme Court greatly restricted the use of the *per se* rule in tying cases and established a significant change in the Court's interpretation of Section 3 of the Clayton Act.

The Supreme Court recognized that the contract between Jefferson Parish Hospital and Roux & Associates established a tie between "hospital operating room services at Jefferson Parish Hospital," the tying product, and "anesthesia services of Roux & Associates," the tied product. The Court ruled, however, that because patients were free to seek services at many other hospitals in the New Orleans area, the hospital did not have sufficient market power in the tying product market, operating room services, to establish a violation of the Clayton Act. In fact, only 30 percent of the patients residing in the Jefferson Parish geographic area used Jefferson Parish Hospital for medical services. The Court noted, "there is no evidence that any patient who was sophisticated enough to know the difference between two anesthesiologists was not also able to go to a hospital that would provide him with the anesthesiologist of his choice."

In the *Hyde* decision the Supreme Court came precariously close to explicitly overturning the *per se* rule in all tying cases. Furthermore, in their concurring decision, four Justices—O'Connor, Burger, Powell, and Rehnquist—wanted to explicitly require a Rule of Reason interpretation in tying cases. The majority, however, supported the following "limited *per se*" rule.

Our cases have concluded that the essential characteristic of an invalid tying arrangement lies in the seller's exploitation of its control over the tying product to force the buyer into the purchase of a tied product that the buyer either did not want at all or might have preferred to purchase elsewhere on different terms. When such "forcing" is present, competition on the merits in the market for the tied item is restrained and the Sherman Act is violated.

The *Hyde* ruling is the Supreme Court's most recent pronouncement with regard to tying arrangements, and the decision makes it clear that a tie is illegal *per se* only if market power in the tying product is significant enough to force buyers to purchase the tied product. It is difficult to understand why this interpretation qualifies as a *per se* interpretation, because under the *Hyde* precedent defendants always have the right to attempt to prove insufficient market power over the tying product.

CASES DEALING WITH FRANCHISING AGREEMENTS

CARVEL CASE[12] (1964)—In 1955 Carvel operated a chain of 400 retail stores that sold soft ice cream. Before 1955, the franchisees were required to purchase their entire requirements of "supplies, machinery, equipment, and paper goods" from Carvel or Carvel-approved sources. In 1955 Carvel changed the standard agreement so that its dealers were required to purchase only supplies "which are a part of the end product" from Carvel. Under the new agreement, franchisees were permitted to purchase machinery, equipment, and paper goods from independent sources. The Court of Appeals ruled that Carvel's tying practices were legal because the agreements protected the Carvel trademark and affected an insubstantial amount of commerce. The *Carvel* case suggested that, although franchisers could not fix their franchisees' prices, they could protect their trademark by taking actions to ensure the quality of the products sold at each outlet. In the 1971 *Chicken Delight* case, the Ninth Circuit Court of Appeals further limited the right of the franchiser to restrict its franchisees' behavior.

CHICKEN DELIGHT CASE[13] (1971)—The facts in the *Chicken Delight* case varied little from those in the *Carvel* case. Chicken Delight operated several hundred fast food chicken outlets. It required its franchisees to purchase a specified number of chickens and all of their supplies and mixes exclusively from Chicken Delight. Because Chicken Delight received no royalties or fees, its income was completely dependent on the revenues generated from selling the tied products to its dealers.

The Circuit Court ruled that the agreement violated the Clayton Act because Chicken Delight could have effectively specified quality standards for the purchase of cooking equipment and ingredients from independent suppliers.

At first the *Carvel* and *Chicken Delight* decisions might appear to be at odds with each other; however, the two decisions simply reflect a justifiable Rule of Reason approach to franchise agreements. In the *Carvel* decision, the Court majority believed that it was impossible for Carvel to effectively police the quality of ingredients used in its ice cream products, and in the *Chicken Delight* case the

Court believed that it was possible for Chicken Delight to set quality standards for chicken and spices.

Exclusive Dealing Agreements

Under an exclusive dealing arrangement, a buyer agrees to purchase its entire requirements of some product or service from one supplier. The anticompetitive potential of a requirements contract is highly dependent on the market power of the supplier.[14] If a manufacturer with a small market share entered into a requirements contract, a relatively small share of the market would be foreclosed. However, if a dominant firm followed an exclusive dealing policy, a great deal of foreclosure could occur, and entry barriers might be significantly increased. A Rule of Reason approach, therefore, is justified with respect to exclusive dealing. Unlike tying agreements, which tend to benefit sellers but not buyers, exclusive dealing arrangements provide economic benefits to both buyers and sellers.

STANDARD OIL OF CALIFORNIA CASE[15] (1949)—The *Standard Oil* case concerned the use of requirements contracts in the retail gasoline market. Under Standard Oil's contracts, independent service stations agreed to purchase their entire supply of gasoline from Standard. Many of the contracts also required the retailers to purchase their entire supply of tires, tubes, batteries, and accessories from Standard.

Standard Oil had negotiated almost 6000 requirements contracts with independent dealers in the Southwest. The government contended that these contracts foreclosed a substantial amount of the gasoline market, thereby creating a barrier to entry into the oil refining industry. In the Justice Department's view, elimination of the contracts would encourage retailers to become *split pump* stations, that is, stations carrying more than one brand of gasoline. The government hoped that the end of requirements contracts would open the market to new independent refiners, encourage price competition, and give independent retailers more bargaining power vis-á-vis the major refiners.

Although the requirements contracts foreclosed some markets from independent refiners, it is not clear that the overall effect of the contracts was to hinder competition or hurt the independent refiners. The contracts provided both the refiner and the retailer with benefits. They assured small independent retailers of a continuing supply of gasoline and afforded some short-run protection from unforeseen price increases. An independent retailer could therefore plan its competitive strategy on the basis of known costs and avoid the risk of storing a product with a fluctuating demand. From the independent refiners' viewpoint, the contracts lowered selling costs by reducing transaction costs and reduced uncertainty by protecting refiners from a rapid reduction in demand.

The Supreme Court recognized that the requirements contracts might have net economic benefits, but nevertheless ruled that they violated the Clayton Act. According to a slim 5–4 majority, Standard's foreclosure of 6.7 percent of the market indicated a *reasonable probability* that competition would be substantially reduced. The Court majority found against Standard Oil despite a recognition that the decision might result in increased vertical integration by refiners into retailing and that such increased vertical integration might be more anticompetitive than the condemned requirements contracts.

TAMPA ELECTRIC CASE[16] (1961)—In 1955, Tampa Electric, a regulated public utility, made plans to construct six additional generating facilities. Although all the existing generating plants in peninsular Florida burned oil, Tampa Electric decided to burn coal in the first two new generators and contracted with Nashville Coal to supply its entire coal requirements for a period of 20 years. The contract set a minimum price of $6.40 per ton; the future price was to be adjusted with changes in production costs. Tampa Electric spent $3 million more to build the coal-burning plants compared with the cost of building oil-burning facilities, and Nashville spent $7.5 million preparing to meet the conditions of the contract.

In April 1957, immediately before the first scheduled coal delivery, Nashville informed Tampa Electric that the contract violated the Clayton Act, and therefore Nashville would not fulfill its conditions. Tampa Electric was then forced to purchase coal from another company at much higher prices.

Both the District Court and the Circuit Court of Appeals declared the contract void. The Supreme Court, however, overturned the Circuit Court decision. The Court ruled that because the challenged contract preempted less than 1 percent of the relevant market, it did not substantially lessen competition.

The *Tampa Electric* decision established a Rule of Reason with regard to requirements contracts and limited the reach of the 1949 Standard Oil precedent. Wisely, the Supreme Court permitted a requirements contract that had little, if any, anticompetitive effect, and which tended to be mutually beneficial to buyer and seller.

Territorial and Customer Restrictions

Manufacturers sometimes distribute goods through independent dealers who are required to sell only in certain geographic areas or only to certain customers. Although these restrictions often appear to be anticompetitive because they restrict competition among the manufacturer's dealers, they may have redeeming procompetitive effects.[17] Territorial restrictions may enable manufacturers to obtain higher-quality dealers and reduce the costs of providing retailing services. The *net* effect of territorial restrictions is highly dependent on the market power of the manufacturer and whether the restrictions increase the probability of collusion in either manufacturing or retailing. Territorial restrictions, therefore, require a Rule of Reason approach.

WHITE MOTOR CASE[18] (1963)—Before the *White Motor* decision, the Justice Department had taken the position that territorial restrictions were illegal *per se,* and based on this position, the Department had negotiated a large number of consent decrees. The White Motor Company manufactured trucks and truck parts that it distributed through dealers who agreed to abide by a territorial restriction in their contract. The restriction specified that dealers would not sell trucks to any "individual, firm, or corporation" located outside of the dealer's exclusive territory.

White Motor defended the contracts on the grounds that they enabled White to compete against larger truck manufacturers. The District Court found for the Justice Department and declared territorial restrictions a *per se* violation of the Sherman Act. The court granted a **summary judgment** for the government, which meant that it refused to even consider the evidence.

The Supreme Court overturned the summary judgment and remanded the case to the District Court for a full trial. The Supreme Court ruled that territorial restrictions come within a Rule of Reason because "We need to know more than we do about the actual impact of these arrangements on competition to decide whether they have such a 'pernicious effect on competition and lack . . . any redeeming virtue' . . . and therefore should be classified as per se violations of the Sherman Act."

A full trial based on the evidence was never held in the *White Motor* case because White Motor agreed to a consent decree under which it gave up its exclusive dealerships. The issues raised by the Supreme Court in the *White Motor* case were important factors in the 1964 *Sandura* decision of the Sixth Circuit Court of Appeals.

SANDURA CASE[19] (1964)—Sandura was a relatively small manufacturer of vinyl floor coverings. Its first vinyl floor covering, Sandran, was initially marketed in 1949 and despite a quick sales start soon developed two major problems: Sandran usually began to yellow shortly after installation, and even worse, many of the Sandran vinyls delaminated and broke apart. As a result of these problems, the company was on the verge of bankruptcy.

Having established a terrible reputation with its original Sandran, Sandura was unable to obtain quality distributors to market its "New Improved Sandran," even though it had solved the earlier problems. In an effort to attract quality distributors, Sandura offered dealers exclusive territories. After establishing the exclusive territories, Sandura was able to become competitive again, although its market share remained small, never exceeding 5 percent. Moreover, Sandura's share was dwarfed by the "Big 3" of the vinyl floor covering industry, Armstrong, Congoleum, and Pabco, which together controlled over 75 percent of capacity.

The Circuit Court, applying a Rule of Reason, found that under these circumstances Sandura's territorial restrictions were legal. The Court believed that the distributors, the dealers, and the public would all be better served if Sandura continued to be a competitive force.

The *Sandura* decision made good economic sense. The competitive impact of Sandura's restrictions was positive because the restrictions enabled Sandura to compete more effectively against giants like Armstrong and Congoleum. Three years later, however, the Supreme Court handed down a decision, which if permanently upheld, would have overturned the *Sandura* decision.

THE SCHWINN CASE[20] (1967)—In 1951, Schwinn was the leading U.S. manufacturer of bicycles, with a 22.5 percent market share. In the next decade Schwinn's share declined to 12.8 percent, and it lost its leadership position to the Murray Ohio Manufacturing Company. Murray sold primarily private label bicycles to Sears, Montgomery Ward, and other large chain retailers. By contrast, Schwinn sold some of its bikes through twenty-two wholesale distributors, who in turn sold to a large number of independent retailers, but most of Schwinn's bikes were sold directly to retailers on consignment or under the so-called *Schwinn Plan*. Under the Schwinn Plan, Schwinn shipped its bicycles to retailers but Schwinn maintained *legal* ownership, and paid the retailers a commission on each sale.

The case revolved primarily around Schwinn's requirement that its twenty-two wholesalers sell only to franchised Schwinn dealers located in the wholesaler's exclusive territory. The wholesalers, however, were not restricted to selling only Schwinn bicycles, and many carried other brands. Each franchised Schwinn retailer was authorized to buy from only one wholesaler, and the franchised retailers were forbidden from selling to unfranchised bicycle retailers.

The Supreme Court drew a careful distinction between cases in which Schwinn sold outright to wholesalers and cases in which it sold on consignment or through the Schwinn Plan. In cases of outright sale, a majority held that it was illegal per se for a manufacturer to restrict its distributors' sales territory. In the cases in which Schwinn maintained ownership over the goods, under consignment and the Schwinn Plan, the majority held that Schwinn could impose territorial restrictions under a Rule of Reason interpretation.

The legal and economic implications of the *Schwinn* decision are confusing. The decision was meant to clarify and simplify the law by placing a *per se* interpretation on most territorial restrictions. However, the *Schwinn* decision created an incentive for firms to avoid a per se ruling by setting up a consignment system of distribution and then hoping the system would pass a Rule of Reason test in court. From an economic perspective, it is hard to see how the Schwinn Plan was any more or less restrictive than the condemned wholesaler–retailer system. In 1977, the Supreme Court came to accept this view and overturned the *Schwinn* decision.

SYLVANIA CASE[21] (1977)—The confusion created by the *Schwinn* decision was decreased by the *Sylvania* case. Sylvania manufactured television sets, which before 1962 were marketed through a large number of independent retail stores and company-owned distributors. Prompted by a decline in its market share to between 1 and 2 percent, Sylvania decided to change its distribution system. Sylvania eliminated its wholesale distributors and sold directly to a limited number of franchised dealers. To improve its position vis-á-vis the industry leader RCA, which controlled over 60 percent of the market, Sylvania limited the number of franchisees in any given area and permitted its franchisees to sell only from the location(s) approved by Sylvania. The new system was an effort to attract more aggressive and competent retailers, and the strategy worked. Under the new plan, Sylvania's market share increased to 5 percent.

Continental TV was a San Francisco–based franchisee of Sylvania. In 1965, Sylvania decided to franchise another San Francisco dealer, Young Brothers, which was located approximately one mile from Continental TV. Continental TV protested that this violated Sylvania's marketing policy. When Sylvania went ahead and franchised Young Brothers, Continental TV canceled a large Sylvania order, and instead purchased a supply of televisions from one of Sylvania's competitors.

At approximately the same time that Sylvania franchised Young Brothers, Continental TV wanted to open another store in Sacramento. Sylvania refused to grant Continental TV a franchise in Sacramento because, according to Sylvania, the market was already adequately served by existing franchisees. Continental TV then informed Sylvania that it was going to move some Sylvania televisions from San Francisco to Sacramento and sell them from its Sacramento retail store, regardless of its agreement with Sylvania. Two weeks later Sylvania suddenly reduced Continental TV's credit line from $300,000 to $50,000. In response to the credit reduction, Continental TV withheld payments it owed Sylvania. Sylvania then terminated Continental TV's franchise, and Sylvania's collection agency sued Continental TV in an effort to recover payment for the unpaid Sylvania televisions that were still in Continental TV's possession.

A District Court jury trial resulted in a damage award of $1.77 million to Continental TV. The Ninth Circuit Court of Appeals reversed and held that Sylvania's restrictions were less harmful to competition than the restrictions used by Schwinn.

The Supreme Court ruled in favor of Sylvania, and in the process directly overturned the *Schwinn* decision and returned to the Rule of Reason interpretation of the *White Motor* case.

THE SONY CASE[22] (1980)—Very few cases since the *Sylvania* decision have resulted in a plaintiff successfully challenging a territorial restriction, but the *Sony* case represents one of the rare exceptions. Sony sold dictation equipment through a series of regional dealerships. Before 1975, Sony required its dealers to "primarily devote and otherwise concentrate its operations in the retail sale" of Sony products to the dealer's local area. In 1974, Eiberger began selling outside its territory. After complaints were lodged against Eiberger by other Sony retailers, Sony changed its warranty system requirements so that any sales made out of a retailer's local area required a mandatory payment of a "warranty fee" to Sony that was roughly equal to the profits the retailer earned on the sale. Sony argued that it wanted to ensure warranty coverage on all sales. By eliminating all profits on sales in other territories, however, Sony effectively eliminated any such sales.

The Court of Appeals affirmed a District Court ruling against Sony. The Court noted that the primary purpose of the warranty fee system was to eliminate intrabrand competition among Sony's retailers, and if Sony wished to ensure warranty coverage, there were far less anticompetitive methods of accomplishing that goal.

The present state of the law with regard to territorial restrictions applies the Rule of Reason to all cases. This makes economic sense because territorial restrictions of the type used by Sandura and Sylvania have a positive rather than a negative effect on competition.

Resale Price Maintenance Agreements

Resale price maintenance (RPM) is the vertical counterpart of horizontal price fixing. Recall from the discussion in Chapter 16 that under RPM agreements the manufacturer specifies either the maximum or minimum price retailers can charge.

As the following cases indicate, the courts have generally been tougher on resale price maintenance than has Congress. In 1976, however, even Congress turned against RPM and repealed the remaining "fair trade laws" that permitted resale price maintenance.

DR. MILES CASE[23] (1911)—Dr. Miles produced proprietary medicines under a group of secret formulas. The drugs were sold to wholesalers and retailers under a written agreement that they would sell at prices set by Dr. Miles. Park & Sons was a wholesaler that refused to sign the price maintenance agreement. Park induced a number of wholesalers, who had signed the agreement, to supply it with Dr. Miles' medicines at cut-rate prices. When Park advertised and sold these drugs to retailers at reduced prices, Dr. Miles sued Park.

The Supreme Court ruled that the written agreements violated the Sherman Act. Justice Hughes wrote that Dr. Miles "having sold its product at prices satisfactory to itself, the public is entitled to whatever advantage may be derived from competition in the subsequent traffic."

One of the major determining factors in the *Dr. Miles* decision was the use of a formal written agreement to maintain prices. Eight years later, the Supreme Court handed down a decision that limited the reach of the *Dr. Miles* decision to cases in which a written agreement was used to enforce resale price maintenance.

COLGATE CASE[24] (1919)—Unlike Dr. Miles, Colgate had not resorted to written agreements to maintain its retail prices. Instead Colgate announced that it would refuse to supply any wholesaler or retailer that did not abide by Colgate's suggested prices. The evidence suggested that Colgate sometimes went beyond simply announcing that it would not deal with price-cutters by using investigations to determine which companies were reducing prices and soliciting information from dealers regarding which of its retailers were reducing prices. The Supreme Court ruled that Colgate's actions did not violate the Sherman Act. According to the Court, "the act does not restrict the long recognized right of a trader or manufacturer engaged in an entirely private business, freely to exercise his own independent discretion as to parties with whom he will deal."

The *Colgate* decision created a large loophole in the Sherman Act with regard to RPM. Within three years of that decision, however, the Supreme Court twice attempted to clarify its meaning. In both *United States v. Schrader's Sons*[25] and *FTC v. Beech Nut Packing Company*,[26] the Supreme Court ruled that an express written agreement was not necessary for a resale price maintenance agreement to violate the Sherman Act. In both of these cases, the Court ruled that because the defendants had made elaborate arrangements to police their RPM agreements, the plans violated the antitrust laws. These cases limited, without overturning, the *Colgate* precedent and helped to create a political movement among small retailers to legalize RPM. In 1937, this movement paid off with the passage of the **Miller-Tydings Act**.

The Miller-Tydings Act amended the Sherman Act to permit states to pass laws legalizing resale price maintenance. The act also prevented the FTC from taking action against RPM as an "unfair method of competition." By 1941, forty-five of the forty-eight states had passed so-called fair trade laws permitting RPM. Only Texas, Missouri, Vermont, and the District of Columbia stood as exceptions.

SCHWEGMANN CASE[27] (1951)—After the Miller-Tydings Act gave states the right to permit written resale price maintenance agreements, Louisiana passed an RPM law. The Louisiana law went beyond merely permitting RPM agreements; it contained a provision that if one firm signed an RPM agreement, all other retailers in Louisiana were forced to abide by the agreement. When Schwegmann Brothers, a large New Orleans retailer, refused to sign an agreement with Calvert Distillers and continued to sell Calvert liquor at cut-rate prices, Calvert took Schwegmann to court.

The Supreme Court sided with Schwegmann and ruled that RPM agreements could not be enforced against nonsigners. According to the Court, if the Louisiana law were upheld, then "once a distributor executed a contract with a single retailer setting the minimum resale price for a commodity in the state, all other retailers could be forced into line." The Court further stated that if Congress had desired to eliminate the consensual element from RPM it would have added a nonsigner provision to the law. Following the Court's lead, Congress voted to overrule the *Schwegmann* decision in 1952 by passing the **McGuire Act**, which extended the Miller-Tydings Act to include nonsigners of an RPM agreement.

PARKE DAVIS CASE[28] (1960)—After the passage of the McGuire Act, both Virginia and the District of Columbia failed to enact fair trade laws. Parke Davis, however, announced a national policy of refusing to deal with wholesalers or retailers who sold below its suggested prices. In the summer of 1956, drug retailers in Washington, D.C., and Richmond, Virginia, advertised and sold Parke Davis's drugs below the RPM prices. To enforce its prices, Parke Davis informed its wholesalers that they would be cut off from supplies if they continued to supply price-cutting retailers. Parke Davis also informed each of the cut-rate retailers that their supplies would be eliminated if they continued to cut prices. Furthermore, each wholesaler and retailer was informed that every other wholesaler and retailer was being informed of Parke Davis's policy.

Even after being threatened by Parke, five retailers refused to abide by Parke Davis's prices. These retailers were cut off from their supplies by Parke Davis directly and by Parke Davis's wholesalers. Furthermore, supplies of all Parke Davis drugs were eliminated, including prescription drugs that were never sold below RPM prices. When the five retailers persisted in selling drugs from existing stocks below Parke Davis's list prices, Parke Davis decided to modify its policy. Each of the five price-cutters was told that shipments would be resumed if they simply stopped advertising Parke Davis drugs at cut-rate prices. When the five price-cutters agreed to stop advertising, Parke Davis resumed shipments to all five firms. Within one month, however, several retailers were once again advertising Parke Davis drugs at cut-rate prices. By this time the Justice Department, at the request of Dart Drug, had begun an investigation of Parke Davis, and therefore Parke Davis elected not to take any further action.

The District Court held that Parke Davis's actions were legal under the *Colgate* doctrine. The Supreme Court reversed because Parke Davis had involved the independent wholesalers in its actions and thereby had gone beyond the limits of the *Colgate* precedent.

The *Parke Davis* decision further eroded the importance of the *Colgate* doctrine in non–fair trade states. It was not antitrust policy, however, but economic pressures that ultimately reduced the incidence of RPM. The emergence of large discount chains and the existence of large mail-order houses in non–fair trade states combined to make the fair trade laws less and less effective. By 1975, only six states had fair trade laws that were enforceable against nonsigners, and in 1976 Congress repealed the Miller-Tydings and McGuire acts.

THE SHARP CASE[29] (1988)—Despite the repeal of the fair trade laws by Congress, the issue continued to percolate through the courts. In 1988 the Supreme Court ruled once again that RPM is not illegal *per se*. The 1988 case involved Sharp Electronics and two of its dealers in Houston, Texas. In 1968 Sharp had granted Business Electronics an exclusive franchise to market Sharp's electronic calculators (which sold for an average price of approximately $1000 per unit in 1968). In 1972, Sharp granted Hartwell a second Houston franchise. Sharp published a list of suggested retail prices, which Hartwell generally abided by. Business Electronics, however, tended to consistently maintain prices below the suggested level. In June 1973, Hartwell gave Sharp an ultimatum that it would terminate its relationship with Sharp unless Sharp terminated its relationship with Business Electronics. Within a month of the ultimatum, Sharp terminated its relationship with Business Electronics.

A District Court jury found for Business Electronics and awarded $600,000 in damages. The Court of Appeals, however, ordered a new trial because the jury had been given erroneous instructions implying that Sharp's actions could be considered illegal *per se*. The Supreme Court affirmed the Appeals Court, ordered a new trial, and declared explicitly that vertical restraints including RPM agreements are not to be considered illegal *per se* unless they include an *explicit* agreement on price between the manufacturer and the retailer.

The *Sharp* decision indicates that manufacturers still have quite a bit of latitude under the *Colgate* precedent. According to the *Sharp* decision, as long as the manufacturer avoids a direct agreement regarding what price a retailer will charge, the manufacturer can unilaterally refuse to supply any retailer.

RUSSELL STOVER CASE[30] (1983)—Much of the recent confusion surrounding resale price maintenance stems from the failure of the government to explicitly ask the Supreme Court to overturn the *Colgate* precedent. The Federal Trade Commission almost attempted to do this in a case brought against Russell Stover Candies. Russell Stover sold boxed candies through more than 18,000 retail outlets under a minimum RPM policy. Evidence indicated that over 97 percent of Russell Stover candies were sold at prices equal to or above the minimum suggested retail price, and Russell Stover eliminated supplies from price-cutting retailers. The Federal Trade Commission interpreted the *Colgate* doctrine as protecting only a manufacturer's right to initially select retailers. According to the Commission, the *Colgate* doctrine did not protect a subsequent "implied conspiracy" between those retailers and the manufacturer.

The Court of Appeals reversed the FTC and noted, "If *Colgate* no longer stands for the proposition that a 'simple refusal to sell to customers who will not sell at prices suggested by the seller is permissible . . . ,' it is for the Supreme Court, not this court, to so declare." Any hope that the case would be appealed to the Supreme Court for a decision concerning the continued relevance of the *Colgate* doctrine was eliminated when the Reagan Administration appointed several new commissioners to the Federal Trade Commission who were sympathetic to the legalization of RPM. A newly constituted Federal Trade Commission chose not to appeal the case to the Supreme Court.

Group Boycotts

Group boycotts fall into one of two general categories. In some cases, a group of firms with market power over some product or service draws up a **black list** and refuses to deal with firms on the list. In other cases, a group of firms with control over a critical resource draws up a **white list** and supplies only firms on the list with the resource. The cases below illustrate both types of boycotts. If the boycotting group has market power, such boycotts may be anticompetitive.

FASHION ORIGINATORS GUILD[31] (1941)—The Fashion Originators' Guild of America (FOGA) was an association of designers, manufacturers, and distributors of women's clothing. Guild designers complained that after their original designs entered retail channels, non-Guild members would copy the designs and market virtually identical garments. To stop this piracy, the FOGA combined to force retailers to stop marketing copied fashions. All guild members agreed not to distribute garments to any retailer who marketed pirated styles. Furthermore, the guild managed to obtain *signed* agreements from more than 12,000 retailers not to sell pirated clothing.

Because the 176 manufacturers who were guild members controlled more than 60 percent of the women's garments that wholesaled at prices above $10.75, these manufacturers had considerable market power in the high-priced ($10 was a lot of money for a dress in 1941) segment of the market. It was extremely important, therefore, for most retailers to have some access to garments produced by Guild members.

The FTC filed a complaint under Section 5 of the FTC Act, and the Supreme Court ruled unanimously that the guild's actions violated the antitrust laws. The Court made it clear that a **group boycott** could not be justified on the grounds that it was necessary to protect the group from the illegal actions of another firm(s). If the guild was concerned about pirating, it could have filed a law suit against the accused pirates, but it could not take the law into its own hands by violating the Sherman Act.

THE ASSOCIATED PRESS CASE[32] (1945)—In 1945 the Associated Press (AP) was a cooperative association of more than 1200 newspapers. According to the AP's by-laws, members were forbidden to supply news information to non-members, and they were given considerable power to block competitors from becoming AP members. If an applicant for membership did not compete with another AP member, the applicant could become a member by a simple majority vote of the Board of Directors with no financial payment to the AP. If an applicant competed with an existing AP member, however, the applicant was required: (1) to pay 10 percent of the "total amount of the regular assessments" received by the AP from members in the same competitive field during the entire period from October 1, 1900, to the time of the new member's election to the AP; (2) to relinquish all exclusive rights to any news or picture service and to make all of its news sources available to its competitors on the same terms as they were available to the applicant; and (3) to receive a majority vote of *all* regular members of the Associated Press. Because AP was the nation's largest supplier of news stories, these policies made entry into the newspaper business more difficult.

Despite the existence of competing news services, the Supreme Court held that the AP's actions violated the Sherman Act. The Court affirmed the District Court's decree and required the AP to furnish news on equal terms to both old and new AP members. The Court also ruled that members were free to furnish news to non-members.

The *Associated Press* decision suggested that if a group of firms controls a resource that is considered critical to competition, the group must make the resource available to competitors on a more or less equal basis. It is important to realize, however, that a modified Rule of Reason still applies in group boycott cases. A small group of firms, with no market power, that bands together to form a buying or selling co-operative will usually be protected from the antitrust laws as long as alternative sources of supply are readily available to non-members. If the co-operative effort confers a major competitive advantage on co-op members, however, the co-operative may have to adopt an open admissions policy.

SUMMARY

1. Unlike most horizontal agreements, most vertical restraints of trade are not illegal *per se.* Tying agreements, requirements contracts, territorial restrictions, and RPM clearly come under a Rule of Reason standard.

2. Until the *Hyde* decision in 1984, tying agreements were illegal *per se* unless they were initially required for a limited time for technological reasons. In the *Hyde* decision, the Supreme Court moved to make tying illegal only if significant market power exists in the tying product market.

3. Exclusive dealing contracts come under a Rule of Reason and are illegal only if they preempt a significant share of the relevant market demand.

4. The Supreme Court has consistently held that territorial and customer restrictions come under a Rule of Reason interpretation. The courts have permitted small nondominant firms to use territorial restrictions to acquire dealerships but have forbidden dominant firms from eliminating intraband competition by imposing territorial restrictions.

5. With regard to resale price maintenance (RPM), the basic 1919 *Colgate* doctrine still holds. This gives a manufacturer the right to unilaterally refuse to deal with a distributor. Evidence of an implied conspiracy between the manufacturer and retailer is necessary for RPM to violate the Sherman Act.

6. If one group of firms controls a resource that is critical to the economic survival of another group of firms, it is illegal for the dominant group to refuse to deal with the other group.

7. It would be hard to criticize current policy too severely because it recognizes the potential benefits associated with vertical agreements while rec-

ognizing the lack of economic justification for many tying and resale price maintenance agreements.

8. The Supreme Court has not permitted the major types of anticompetitive vertical restraints such as tying of nonpatented items to patented items or the use of long-term requirements contracts by firms with market power.

KEY TERMS

black list	summary judgment
exclusive dealing arrangements	territorial restrictions
fair trade laws	tied product
group boycotts	tying product
McGuire Act	tying agreements
Miller-Tydings Act	white list
resale price maintenance (RPM)	

DISCUSSION QUESTIONS

1. Do you agree or disagree with the following statement: The Clayton Act made tying arrangements illegal *per se* in the United States.

2. Explain how tying agreements can enable firms to practice price discrimination. Does this price discrimination tend to improve economic efficiency?

3. Under what circumstances are territorial restrictions economically justified? Have the courts recognized these circumstances?

4. In what ways are exclusive dealing arrangements and tying agreements similar? In what ways do they differ?

5. You are a small retailer of high-quality men's clothing. For years you have sold Ralph Lauren Polo menswear at the company's suggested retail prices. One day you decide to reduce these prices to 20 percent below the suggested retail price. The next month Ralph Lauren informs you that it will no longer supply you with its clothing. There is no evidence that anyone complained to Ralph Lauren about your price cuts. Is Ralph Lauren's behavior a violation of the antitrust laws? Explain your answer.

6. Do you agree with the Court of Appeals' ruling in the *Sylvania* case? If RCA, with a 60 percent share of the television market, had tried to use the same territorial restrictions as Sylvania, would a similar court ruling make economic sense?

7. Would the antitrust laws be violated if KFC announced that henceforth all of its franchisees would be required to purchase all of their paper goods,

chickens, and other ingredients from KFC? Would the courts be likely to uphold such an agreement?

8. Time-Warner is a monopolist in the cable television market in many cities, including New York City. Time-Warner also owns CNN. When Fox News entered the cable news market, Time-Warner refused it access to many of its cable systems, including in New York City. Time-Warner claimed it had no available station on which to air the Fox News. Would Fox have a legitimate antitrust claim against Time-Warner?

9. Chapter 16 showed that RPM might be used by manufacturers to prevent low-price, low-service retailers from "free riding" on the services provided by high-price, high-service retailers. When RPM was legal, some of the goods commonly sold under RPM were toiletries (e.g., toothpaste, shaving cream, mouthwash), cosmetics (e.g., cold cream, deodorant), blue jeans, men's underwear, and boxed candy. What were the services that the manufacturers of these goods were concerned about in these markets? Does this suggest the existence of another motivation for RPM in these cases? What might the motivation have been?

10. Identify a good you purchased in the last year that appeared to be sold under RMP. What "evidence" makes you believe that RPM was used in this product market?

11. Do professional sports franchises tie products together? Give an example.

REFERENCES

1. For an argument that tying agreements are never anticompetitive see Dominick T. Armentano, *Antitrust and Monopoly: Anatomy of a Policy Failure* (New York: John Wiley & Sons, 1982), pp. 198–203. For an excellent statement of the position that tying is rarely anticompetitive see Richard A. Posner, *Antitrust Law: An Economic Perspective* (Chicago: University of Chicago Press, 1976), pp. 171–84. See also William L. Baldwin and David McFarland, "Tying Agreements in Law and Economics," *Antitrust Bulletin* (September 1963); Suchan Chae, "Bundling Subscription TV Channels: A Case of Natural Bundling," *International Journal of Industrial Organization* 10 (June 1992): 213–30.

2. Don E. Waldman, *Antitrust Action and Market Structure* (Lexington, Mass.: D.C. Heath, 1978), pp. 143–50.

3. *International Salt Company v. United States,* 332 U.S. 392 (1947).

4. *Siegel v. Chicken Delight,* 448 f.2d 43 (1971); *Ungar v. Dunkin' Donuts of America,* no. 75–1625, CA3.

5. *International Business Machines v. United States,* 298 U.S. 131 (1936).

6. Waldman, *supra* note 2, p. 141.

7. *United States v. American Can Company,* 87 F.Supp. 18 (1949).

8. Waldman, *op.cit,* p. 76.

9. Charles H. Hessian, "The Metal Container Industry," in Walter Adams (ed.), *The Structure of American Industry* (New York: Macmillan, 1971), pp. 323–4.

10. *United States v. Jerrold Electronics Corporation,* 187 F.Supp. 545 (1960).

11. *Jefferson Parish Hospital District No. 2 v. Hyde,* 466 U.S. 104 (1984).

12. *Susser et al. v. Carvel Corporation,* 332 F.2d 505 (1964).

13. *Siegel et al. v. Chicken Delight,* 448 F.2d 43 (1971).

14. See Phillipe Aghion and Patrick Bolton, "Contracts as a Barrier to Entry," *American Economic Review* 77 (June 1987): 388–401; Eric B. Rasmusen, J. Mark Ramseyer, and John S. Wiley, "Naked Exclusion," *American Economic Review* 81 (December 1991): 1137–45; Robert Innes and Richard J. Sex-

ton, "Strategic Buyers and Exclusionary Contracts," *American Economic Review* 84 (June 1994): 566–84; and David Besanko and Martin K. Perry, "Exclusive Dealing in a Spatial Model of Retail Competition," *International Journal of Industrial Organization12*, (September 1994): 297–329.

15. *Standard Oil Company of California et al. v. United States*, 337 U.S. 293 (1949).
16. *Tampa Electric v. Nashville Coal*, 365 U.S. 320 (1961).
17. See L.J. White, "Vertical Restraints in Antitrust Law: A Coherent Model," *Antitrust Bulletin* (Summer 1981): 327–45.
18. *White Motor Co. v. United States*, 372 U.S. 253 (1963).
19. *Sandura v. Federal Trade Commission*, 339 F.2d 847 (1964).
20. *United States v. Arnold Schwinn & Co. et al.*, 388 U.S. 365 (1967).
21. *Continental T.V. v. GTE Sylvania Inc.*, 433 U.S. 36 (1977).
22. *Eiberger v. Sony Corporation of America*, 622 F.2d 1068 (1980).
23. *Dr. Miles Medical Company v. John Park & Sons Company*, 220 U.S. 373 (1911).
24. *United States v. Colgate & Co.*, 250 U.S. 300 (1919).
25. *United States v. Schrader's Sons*, 252 U.S. 85 (1920).
26. *FTC v. Beech Nut Packing Company*, 257 U.S. 441 (1922).
27. *Schwegmann Brothers et al. v. Calvert Distillers Corp.*, 341 U.S. 384 (1951).
28. *United States v. Parke Davis & Co.*, 362 U.S. 29 (1960).
29. *Business Electronics Corp. v. Sharp Electronics Corp.*, 485 US 717 (1988).
30. *Russell Stover Candies, Inc v. FTC*, 718 F.2d 256 (1983).
31. *Guild of America Inc., et al. v. Federal Trade Commission*, 312 U.S. 457 (1941).
32. *Associated Press et al. v. United States*, 326 U.S. 1 (1945).

Chapter 23

International Economics and Industrial Organization

Until recently, there was little overlap between the material covered in industrial organization courses and that covered in international trade courses. International trade theorists typically dealt with models of perfect competition and ignored the effects of monopoly and oligopoly. Similarly, industrial organization economists tended to treat the international sector as a minor sidelight. In the late 1970s and early 1980s, it became clear that such views were myopic. Fortunately, conditions have changed rapidly in both fields in the past fifteen years with the introduction of many industrial organization models applied to situations of international competition.

This chapter examines the rapidly expanding links between the two fields. It should become apparent that any thorough understanding of a modern industrial economy requires an understanding of the large impact of foreign competition on domestic markets. Because the concept of a global economy is now a reality, this chapter has tremendous importance in a modern course on industrial organization.

The Basic Theory of the Gains from Trade

Suppose that the United States is initially closed to all foreign trade in good X and that good X is produced in perfectly competitive markets in both the United States and the rest of the world. There are many ways to prevent trade, the most common being prohibitive tariffs or import restrictions. The Japanese, for example, have long restricted rice imports in this manner. Figure 23.1 depicts the two markets: on the left is the market in the United States, and on the right is the

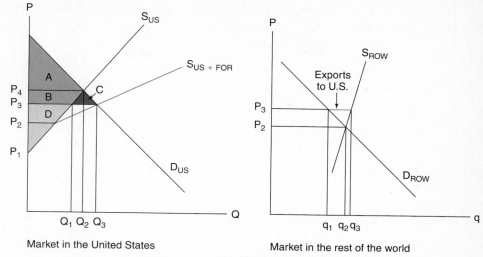

Figure 23.1   The gains from trade with competitive world markets.

market in the rest of the world (ROW). In the absence of trade between the United States and the rest of the world, the equilibrium price will be P_4 in the United States and P_2 in the rest of the world. Total consumer surplus in the United States equals the red triangle A, and total producer surplus in the United States equals the sum of gray areas B and D.

Suppose the United States decides to permit trade in good X. Because the price of good X in the United States, P_4, is greater than the price in the rest of the world, P_2, firms in the rest of the world will want to export good X to the United States. To determine how much these foreign firms will be willing to export at prices greater than P_2, take the horizontal difference between the supply curve in the rest of the world, S_{ROW}, and the demand curve in the rest of the world, D_{ROW}. For example, at a price of P_3, foreign firms are willing to export $q_3 - q_1$ units of good X (represented by the distance of the red line segment) to the United States. By adding the amount that foreign firms are willing to export to the United States at every price above P_2 to the United States supply curve without trade, S_{US}, we obtain the United States supply curve with trade, $S_{US + FOR}$.

If trade is permitted, the price in the United States will decline to P_3, where the supply curve with trade, $S_{US + FOR}$, equals the demand curve in the United States. With trade, American firms will supply Q_1 units of good X to the United States market, and foreign firms will export $Q_3 - Q_1$ units of good X, which by construction must equal $q_3 - q_1$ units of good X. The equilibrium price in the United States and the rest of the world must be equalized by free trade at P_3 or else there would be an incentive to sell more in the market with the higher price. As a result of trade, total consumer surplus in the United States has *increased* by the sum of areas B and C, so that total consumer surplus is equal to the sum of areas A, B, and C. However, total producer surplus earned by American firms equals the light gray area D, and has *declined* by the dark gray area B.

What is the net welfare effect of the decision to permit trade? Consumer surplus increased by the areas B and C, but producer surplus among American firms has decreased by the gray area B. Because the area B represents a gain to American consumers and a loss to American producers, it has no net impact on American welfare. The red area C, however, represents a net welfare gain to American consumers. The net impact on American consumers and producers of permitting trade is positive.

This positive effect will be larger if the American firms are able to form a cartel before the opening of the market to trade. In Figure 23.2 we assume that before the opening up of the market to trade the American firms have formed a cartel and increased the price above the competitive price P_4 to P_5. If free trade destroys the American cartel, the American firms will be forced to compete with the foreign firms, and price will decline to the competitive world price with free trade, P_3.

In the cartel case, in the absence of trade the equilibrium price will be P_5 in the United States and P_2 in the rest of the world. Once again, total consumer surplus in the United States equals the red triangle A, and total producer surplus in the United States equals the sum of the gray areas B and D. Trade results in an *increase* in consumer surplus by the areas B and C, an *increase* in producer surplus by the small gray triangle E, and a *decrease* in producer surplus equal to the area B. The net positive welfare change equals the triangle C plus the small gray area E.

The gains from trade in this case are often broken down into a procompetitive gain from trade and a normal gain from trade. In Figure 23.2, the increase in output from Q_0 to Q_2 is the procompetitive gain, and the increase in output from Q_2 to Q_3 is the normal gain from trade. The increase in output from Q_0 to Q_2 is called a procompetitive gain because it represents the increase in output that

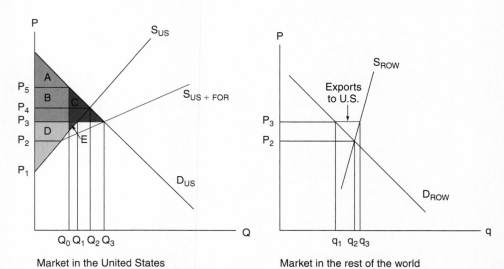

Market in the United States   Market in the rest of the world

Figure 23.2   The gains from trade with a domestic monopoly and competitive markets in the rest of the world.

would occur *without* trade if the domestic monopoly could be broken up into a perfectly competitive industry. Free trade in this case becomes a substitute for domestic policy to break up the monopoly.

The Case of a Dominant Domestic Firm and a Group of Small Foreign Firms: The Dominant Firm Price Leadership Model Revisited

The previous analysis assumed that both the American market and the rest of the world market were perfectly competitive. Now we consider the case in which the American market is controlled by a monopolist but the rest of the world market consists of a group of small competitive firms. This case is identical to that of dominant firm price leadership examined in Chapter 7.

Consider the dominant firm price leadership model analyzed in Chapter 7. Figure 23.3 shows the basic conditions in the industry and the equilibrium *without* trade. The industry demand curve D is $P = 100 - q$, and the dominant firm's marginal cost curve is $MC_d = 25 + \left(\frac{1}{3}\right)q_d$. In the absence of trade the domestic dominant firm equates $MR_d = 100 - 2q_d$ to $MC_d = 25 + \left(\frac{1}{3}\right)q_d$. Solving for q_d:

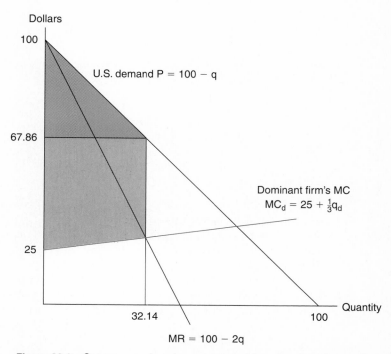

Figure 23.3 Consumer and producer surplus with monopoly and no trade.

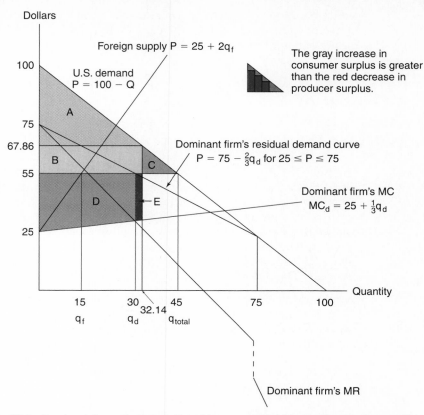

Figure 23.4 Dominant domestic monopolist with a competitive fringe of foreign firms and increased domestic welfare with trade.

$$100 - 2q_d = 25 + \frac{1}{3}q_d \quad \Rightarrow \quad 300 - 6q_d = 75 + q_d$$

$$\text{or } 7q_d = 225 \quad \Rightarrow \quad q_d = 32.14.$$

With $q_d = 32.14$, $P = 100 - 32.14 = 67.86$. Consumer surplus equals the red triangle and producer surplus equals the gray area.

Figure 23.4 depicts the equilibrium with trade. This equilibrium is identical to the equilibrium in Figure 7.12 in Chapter 7. The supply curve for the foreign "fringe" firms is $P = 25 + 2q_f$, where q_f is the quantity supplied by the foreign firms.

Recall that the dominant firm's residual demand curve is obtained by subtracting the fringe supply curve from the total demand curve at every price greater than $P = 25$. Such calculations yield the linear residual demand curve that passes through the two points $(0, 75)$ and $(75, 25)$ and has a kink at $q = 75$. The residual demand curve that passes through those two points is:

$$P = 75 - \frac{2}{3}q_d \text{ for } 25 \leq P \leq 75.$$

By the "twice as steep rule," marginal revenue is:

$$MR_d = 75 - \frac{4}{3}q_d \text{ for } 25 \leq P \leq 75.$$

Once the residual demand curve of the dominant firm is identified, the profit-maximizing output for the dominant firm can be calculated as shown in Figure 23.4. The marginal cost curve for the dominant firm is:

$$MC_d = 25 + \frac{1}{3}q_d.$$

To maximize profits, the dominant firm equates MC_d to MR_d and produces thirty units. To obtain price go up vertically to the dominant firm's residual demand curve and $P = 55$.

Once price is known, the foreign firms act as perfectly competitive price takers and supply the quantity at which the foreign supply curve intersects the horizontal line $P = 55$. In this case, $q_f = 15$. Total industry output is the sum of the dominant firm's output and the fringe's output, or $q_{total} = q_d + q_f = 30 + 15 = 45$.

Consider the changes in consumer and producer surplus that occur because of trade in Figure 23.4. In the absence of trade, consumer surplus equals the red area A and producer surplus equals the sum of areas B, D, and E. The sum of areas B, D, and E in Figure 23.4 equals the gray trapezoid in Figure 23.3. With free trade, consumer surplus increases by the sum of areas B and C, and producer surplus decreases by areas B and E. The area B is a transfer from producer to consumer surplus, and the net welfare effect is an increase in consumer surplus equal to area C combined with a decrease in producer surplus equal to the small red trapezoid E. If the area C is larger than the area E, as it is in Figure 23.4, then a net increase in welfare results from the opening up of trade.

It is possible for welfare to be reduced by the introduction of free trade. The only change in the initial market conditions in Figure 23.5 compared with Figure 23.4 is that the foreign supply has decreased to $P = 25 + 4q_f$. The residual demand curve is then:

$$P = 85 - \frac{4}{5}q_d \text{ for } 25 \leq P \leq 85.$$

By the "twice as steep rule," marginal revenue is:

$$MR_d = 85 - \frac{8}{5}q_d \text{ for } 25 \leq P \leq 85.$$

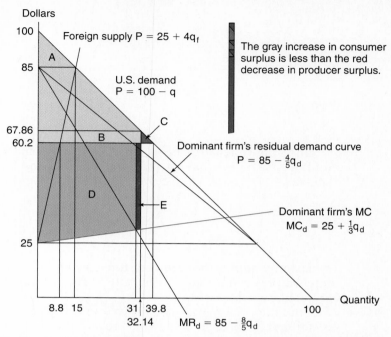

Figure 23.5 Dominant domestic monopolist with a competitive fringe of foreign firms and reduced domestic welfare with trade.

The profit-maximizing output for the dominant firm can be calculated as shown in Figure 23.5. The marginal cost curve for the dominant firm is:

$$MC_d = 25 + \frac{1}{3}q_d.$$

To maximize profits, the dominant firm equates MC_d to MR_d and produces thirty-one units.* To obtain price go up vertically on the dominant firm's residual demand curve and $P = 60.2$.

Once price is known, the foreign firms act as perfectly competitive price takers and supply the quantity for which the foreign supply curve intersects the horizontal line $P = 60.2$. In this case, $q_f = 8.8$. Total industry output is the sum of the dominant firm's output and the foreign fringe's output, or $q_{total} = q_d + q_f = 31 + 8.8 = 39.8$.

As in Figure 23.4, the net welfare effect is an increase in consumer surplus equal to the gray triangle C combined with a decrease in producer surplus equal

---

*
$$MR_d = 85 - \frac{8}{5}q_d = 25 + \frac{1}{3}q_d = MC_d.$$

Multiplying both sides of the equation by 15 yields:

$$1275 - 24q_d = 375 + 5q_d \quad \Rightarrow \quad q_d = \frac{900}{29} = 31.0.$$

to the small trapezoid E. In Figure 23.5, the area E is larger than the area C, so there is a net decrease in welfare as a result of opening up trade.

As Figures 23.4 and 23.5 indicate, the larger the foreign fringe's supply, the larger is the increase in consumer surplus in the American market, and the more likely it is that trade has a net positive welfare impact.

EMPIRICAL EXAMPLES

Steel

The steel industry in the United States shows how increased foreign trade can reduce the monopoly power of dominant domestic firms. As we discussed in Chapter 9, the steel industry was a tight oligopoly during the first half of the twentieth century. During that period there was virtually no price competition and little threat of import competition. In fact, before 1958, annual steel imports into the United States remained below 2 million tons.[1] Beginning in the late 1960s, imported steel captured a greater share of the American market, increasing from 4.7 percent in 1960 to 7.3 percent in 1964, 16.7 percent in 1967, and 26.6 percent in 1984.

Imported steel gained an advantage over American steel because U.S. producers failed to meet the demand for certain types of products and because foreign steel was often less expensive. During the initial period of import penetration, American buyers often claimed that foreign steel was of higher quality and that the service provided by foreign producers was superior. By the time America turned toward protectionism in 1969, import competition had significantly restrained prices. As noted by the Council on Wage and Price Stability, between 1959 and 1969 "there were limiting forces which operated to prevent U.S. steel companies from increasing prices and maintaining the previous higher profit levels. *Chief among these was import competition.*"[2]

Automobiles

Another example of the effect of import competition on prices can be found in the automobile industry. Immediately after World War II, the "Big 3"—General Motors, Ford, and Chrysler—dominated the American automobile industry. Imports made up less than 1 percent of American car sales in 1945. By 1987, however, imports held more than 30 percent of the American market. Foreign firms, led by the Japanese, initially concentrated their efforts on the small-car market, in which they were particularly adept at taking economic advantage of large increases in demand caused by the rise in oil prices in the 1970s. Foreign competition had a major impact on automobile pricing. For example, Adams and Brock wrote in the 1970s: "foreign competitors occupy nearly 40 percent of the [small-car] field; [and as a result] there is no recognized price leader; there is no rigid pattern of leadership-followship; and pricing exhibits the variability and unpredictability characteristic of a more competitive market."[3]

As it had done in the steel industry in 1969, the United States acted to limit Japanese automobile exports in the early 1980s. Because the Japanese were restricted to a limited number of units, they moved from exporting inexpensive small cars with small profit margins to shipping expensive large cars with large profit margins. Ironically, this resulted in a broader base of competition between the domestic and foreign automobile manufacturers. The import restrictions also led most of the major Japanese firms (Toyota, Nissan, Honda, Mazda, and Subaru) to produce automobiles in the United States.

It is safe to conclude that in both the steel and automobile industries foreign competition greatly increased effective competition in the United States after World War II. American consumer welfare undoubtedly was much higher as a result of this increased competition.

EMPIRICAL EVIDENCE OF THE EFFECT OF INCREASED IMPORT COMPETITION ON PRODUCTIVITY

In both the steel and the automobile industries, increased foreign competition resulted in reduced prices. Increased import competition may also result in improved productivity and reduced x-inefficiencies. In the early 1980s New Zealand provided an excellent opportunity to study the effects of import restrictions on productive efficiency.[4] In 1980 the New Zealand government offered foreign producers the chance to bid competitively for import licenses.

In theory, competitive bidding for the licenses should have resulted in bids that left foreign producers earning normal economic profits in New Zealand. Suppose, for example, that New Zealand firms could produce widgets for $1.00, but foreign producers could produce the same widgets for $0.90. Foreign firms, however, are forbidden from exporting widgets to New Zealand without a license. In the absence of tariffs on widgets, if New Zealand offers import licenses to the highest bidder, the bids should rise to $0.10 per widget. If a $0.03 tariff is imposed on widgets, the license would be expected to be bid up only to $0.07.

Using this theoretical rationale, Pickford examined actual bids for licenses in 189 New Zealand product lines. The bids were significantly greater than zero in 130 of the 189 product lines. The data were also aggregated by placing eighty-seven product lines into twenty-two product groups, which could be classified in the New Zealand Customs Tariff and the New Zealand Standard Industrial Classification system. Table 23.1 shows Pickford's primary results. Twenty of the twenty-two product groups had mean bids that were statistically greater than zero, ranging from a low of 8.2 percent (bottled spirits) to a high of 85.8 percent (toys and games). To understand these results, consider that the mean premium for "brushes" in Table 23.1 is 53.2 percent, which implies that foreigners would be willing to pay $5.32 for a license to export brushes priced at $10.00 to New Zealand. This in turn implies that foreigners could produce the brushes for $4.68 ($10.00 − $5.32).* Pickford's results suggest that when New Zealand producers were protected from foreign competition they tended to have much higher production costs than the most efficient foreign producers.

---

*The $5.32 figure may underestimate the cost advantage of foreign producers because foreign firms should recognize that the price would decline below $10.00 after they entered the New Zealand market.

TABLE 23.1 **Mean Premium Values Paid for Import Licenses in New Zealand**

Group of Products	Premium Paid (%)
1. Toys and games	85.8*
2. Glassware	64.9*
3. Leather goods	57.9*
4. Metal furniture	56.1*
5. Electric sound equipment	55.1*
6. Brushes	53.2*
7. Ceramics	43.3*
8. Confectionery and chocolate	42.3*
9. Jewelry	39.8*
10. Plastic consumer goods	36.6*
11. Rubber goods	36.0*
12. Sports equipment	34.8*
13. Domestic metal utensils	33.3*
14. Handknitting yarns	29.3*
15. Male clothing	26.6*
16. Carpets and mats	26.3*
17. Nonalcoholic beverages	26.3*
18. Female clothing	25.5
19. Domestic appliances	25.2*
20. Plastic intermediate goods	24.6
21. Preserved fruits and vegetables	21.7*
22. Bottled spirits	8.2*

*Statistically significant at the 5% level.

Source: M. Pickford, "A New Test for Manufacturing Industry Efficiency: An Analysis of the Results of Import License Tendering in New Zealand," *International Journal of Industrial Organization* 3 (1985): 166.

Economies of Scale and Strategic Trade Policy[5]

In recent years economists have looked closely at the potential for government intervention to improve domestic welfare in markets in which economies of scale are significant. Such intervention is often considered a game in which the government moves first and the domestic and foreign firms move second. One possible intervention would be to grant a direct or indirect **subsidy** to domestic firms. We examine the subsidy case in detail, but the same basic conclusions have been drawn using other types of government intervention such as **tariffs** and import quotas.

Using the Cournot-Nash framework presented in Chapter 7, consider a model with one domestic firm, one foreign firm, and no government intervention. To simplify the analysis, we assume that the product is sold only in the domestic market. The foreign firms, therefore, produce only for export. The demand in the domestic market is $P = 100 - q_d - q_f$. In our examples in Chapter 7, MC = AC = 10; here we set fixed costs equal to 500, so $TC_d = 500 + 10q_d$.* The existence of fixed costs does not affect marginal cost, so MC_d remains equal to 10. Reviewing the basic model from Chapter 7, we have:

$$P = 100 - q_d - q_f$$
$$TC_d = 500 + 10q_d \text{ and } MC_d = 10$$
$$MR_d = 100 - q_f - 2q_d$$

From Chapter 7 these conditions yield the following reaction functions:

$$q_d = 45 - \frac{1}{2}q_f.$$

$$q_f = 45 - \frac{1}{2}q_d.$$

Solving for the Cournot-Nash equilibrium we obtain:

$$q_d = q_f = 30.$$
$$P = 100 - 60 = 40.$$

To obtain profits for each firm, calculate TR − TC:

$$\Pi_d = \Pi_f = Pq - FC - MCq = (40 \times 30) - 500 - 10(30) = 400,$$

where Π_d represents the profits for the domestic firm and Π_f represents the profits for the foreign firm. Each firm produces thirty units of output and earns an economic profit of 400.

---

*One common method of measuring scale economies is the *function coefficient*, S, defined as the ratio of average cost to marginal cost. If S > 1, economies of scale exist; if S < 1, diseconomies of scale exist; and if S = 1, constant returns to scale exist. In Figure 23.6, S > 1 for all q > 0, and therefore, economies of scale exist for all q > 0.

These conditions establish sufficient but not necessary conditions for the existence of economies of scale, and they are used here to simplify the analysis. Economies of scale could, for example, also exist for some q > 0 if there is a fixed setup cost and increasing marginal cost or if there are decreasing marginal costs for some q > 0. For further clarification see Andreu Mas-Colell and Michael D. Whinston, *Microeconomic Theory* (New York: Oxford University Press, 1995), pp. 144–5.

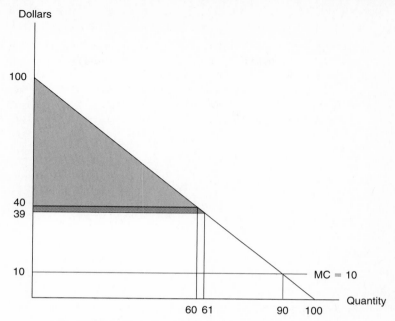

Figure 23.6　The effect of a subsidy on consumer surplus.

In Figure 23.6 the gray triangle depicts consumer surplus in the domestic market, which equals:

$$\text{Consumer Surplus} = \frac{1}{2}60^2 = \frac{3600}{2} = 1800.$$

The domestic firm earns a profit of 400, so consumer surplus plus the domestic firm's profits equals $1800 + 400 = 2200$.

Suppose the domestic government grants a subsidy, s, of 3 per unit to the domestic firm. The domestic firm's total costs become:

$$TC_d = FC + MCq_d - sq_d = 500 + (10 - 3)q_d = 500 + 7q_d$$

Effective marginal cost is now:

$$MC_d = MC - s = 10 - 3 = 7.$$

The domestic firm's reaction function is derived as follows:

$$MR_d = 100 - q_f - 2q_d = 7 = MC$$

or:

$$q_d = 46.5 - \frac{1}{2}q_f.$$

With the subsidy, the domestic firm has a cost advantage over the foreign firm. To solve for the new Cournot-Nash equilibrium, substitute the foreign firm's reaction function into the domestic firm's reaction function and obtain the domestic firm's equilibrium output:

$$q_d = 46.5 - \frac{1}{2}q_f = 46.5 - \frac{1}{2}\left(45 - \frac{1}{2}q_d\right)$$

or

$$q_d = 46.5 - 22.5 + \frac{1}{4}q_d$$

so

$$q_d = \frac{24 \cdot 4}{3} = 32.$$

The foreign firm's output is therefore:

$$q_f = 45 - \frac{1}{2}(32) = 29.$$

Total industry output is $Q = 32 + 29 = 61$, and $P = 100 - 61 = 39$.

Profits are now substantially different for each firm. The domestic firm produces more than the foreign firm and, including the subsidy, earns:

$$\Pi_d = Pq - FC - MCq + sq = (39 \times 32) - 500 - 10(32) + 3(32) = 524.$$

The foreign firm earns:

$$\Pi_f = Pq - FC - MCq = (39 \times 29) - 500 - 10(29) = 341.$$

With the subsidy, consumer surplus increases by the red area in Figure 23.6 and equals:

$$\text{Consumer Surplus} = \frac{1}{2}61^2 = \frac{3721}{2} = 1860.5.$$

Now the sum of consumer surplus and the domestic firm's profit equals $1860.5 + 524 = 2384.5$. The cost of the subsidy to taxpayers, however, equals $3(32) = 96$. Subtracting the cost of the subsidy from the sum of consumer surplus and the domestic firm's profit yields $2384.5 - 96 = 2288.5$.

Recall that in the absence of government intervention total consumer surplus plus domestic firm profits equaled 2200. With the subsidy, total consumer surplus plus domestic firm profits minus the cost of the subsidy equals 2288.5. Because 2288.5 > 2200, the domestic country is better off as a result of the subsidy.

The existence of entry barriers and presubsidy economic rents are important for this result. If there are no entry barriers and entry is easy, then the effects of a subsidy may be quite different. If we assume economies of scale in production but easy entry, profits will be normal in both the initial and final equilibrium, and a subsidy will have dramatically different impacts on the domestic and foreign economies. This is essentially the model of monopolistic competition.

To understand this different outcome, consider a market characterized by a linear demand curve, constant marginal cost, and Cournot-Nash behavior. Suppose the demand curve for good X is the familiar demand curve $P = 100 - Q$. Assume fixed costs equal 256 and marginal cost equals 20, so:

$$TC = 256 + 20q$$

In the initial equilibrium there are *two* domestic and *two* foreign firms, or a total of *four* firms. From Chapter 7 we know that the Cournot-Nash equilibrium in a market with four identical firms, linear demand, and linear marginal cost is:

$$q_1 = q_2 = q_3 = q_4 = \frac{1}{N+1}Q_{pc} = \frac{1}{5}\,80 = 16,$$

where Q_{pc} is the competitive output ($P = MC = 20$), and N is the number of firms in the industry. In this example, total output is 64 and $P = 36$. Figure 23.7 depicts the demand curve and the relevant Cournot-Nash equilibrium.

Because fixed costs equal 256, each firm earns a normal profit:

$$\Pi_1 = \Pi_2 = \Pi_3 = \Pi_4 = Pq - FC - MCq = (36 \times 16) - 256 - 20(16) = 576 - 256 - 320 = 0.$$

In the absence of government intervention, consumer surplus equals the light gray area in Figure 23.7, or:

$$\text{Consumer Surplus} = \frac{1}{2}64^2 = \frac{4096}{2} = 2048.$$

Because profits are zero, the sum of consumer surplus and domestic firms' profits also equals 2048.

If the domestic government places a subsidy of 16 per unit on good X, this effectively reduces the marginal cost of production for domestic firms from 20 to 4 ($MC - s = 20 - 16 = 4$) in Figure 23.7. Because the foreign firms earn zero economic profits before the subsidy, they will be unable to compete after the subsidy and will leave the market entirely to domestic firms. In Figure 23.7, the perfectly

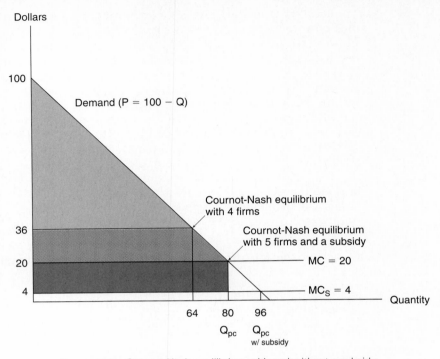

Figure 23.7 Cournot-Nash equilibrium with and without a subsidy.

competitive price with the subsidy would be 4, and the competitive output with the subsidy would be 96. Because entry is free, the subsidy will attract additional firms into the domestic market. In the final equilibrium, profits must equal zero. This occurs when three additional firms enter the domestic market, giving a total of five firms in the domestic market (the original two firms plus three domestic entrants).* The Cournot-Nash equilibrium with five domestic firms is:

$$q_1 = q_2 = q_3 = q_4 = q_5 = \frac{1}{N+1}Q_{pc} = \frac{1}{6}(96) = 16.$$

With five firms each producing an output of 16, total output is 80, and P = 20. *The price declines by the exact amount of the subsidy.* Figure 23.7 shows the new Cournot-Nash equilibrium. Furthermore, because fixed costs equal 256, each firm earns a normal profit:

*Remember that two foreign firms left the market, so that there is a net gain of one firm worldwide.

$$\Pi_1 = \Pi_2 = \Pi_3 = \Pi_4 = \Pi_5 = Pq - FC - MCq + sq =$$
$$(20 \times 16) - 256 - 20(16) + 16(16) = 320 - 256 - 320 + 256 = 0.$$

As a result of the subsidy, consumer surplus has increased by the red area in Figure 23.7, and total consumer surplus equals:

$$\text{Consumer Surplus} = \frac{1}{2}80^2 = \frac{6400}{2} = 3200.$$

The domestic firms' profits still equal zero, but the government must pay a subsidy equal to the dark gray area in Figure 23.7. The cost of the subsidy equals $qs = 80 \cdot 16 = 1280$. Consumer surplus minus the cost of the subsidy equals $3200 - 1280 = 1920$. Because total consumer surplus without the subsidy was 2048, the subsidy has resulted in a net loss for the domestic country.

In this example each of the five firms continued to produce the same output as each of the four firms produced before the implementation of the subsidy. Horstmann and Markusen have shown this to be a general result.[6] They proved that assuming a specific subsidy per unit, free entry, Cournot-Nash behavior, and linear demand curves, the post-entry equilibrium will be where each firm continues to produce the same output at the same average cost as firms produced before the subsidy.

THE EFFECTIVENESS OF INDUSTRIAL POLICY

Our theoretical analysis has yielded ambiguous results regarding the welfare effects of industrial policies such as subsidies and tariffs. Several empirical studies have found that while industrial policies may yield improvements in welfare, these improvements tend to be quite small.

U.K. Subsidies and Tariffs

Venables examined the potential effect of export subsidies and import tariffs in the United Kingdom.[7] Using data for nine industries in 1982 and making several different types of game theoretic assumptions, he found that the potential gains from industrial policy tended to be quite small. Table 23.2 presents Venables' results for export subsidies of 4 percent and 2 percent. In nineteen of thirty-six cases, the subsidy reduces welfare. Furthermore, only in the "Artificial and Synthetic Fibers" industry does a subsidy yield a gain "as large as 1 percent" of the base of consumption. Table 23.3 presents the results for import tariffs. Once again the gains tend to be small, except in the "Artificial and Synthetic Fibers" industry. Venables summarized his findings by stating that "the conclusion which emerges from the simulations is that trade models of this type provide a rather weak case for policy intervention."[8]

TABLE 23.2 **Welfare Effects of Export Subsidies Under Oligopoly: UK Industries 1982 Data (gain as a percentage of base consumption)**

	Game*	4%S	2%S
257 Pharmaceutical products	C	−0.23	−0.06
	B	−0.24	−0.08
260 Artificial and synthetic fibers	C	1.01	0.55
	B	0.06	0.07
322 Machine tools	C	−1.34	−0.25
	B	−1.31	−0.25
330 Office machinery	C	−1.09	0.23
	B	−0.63	−0.10
342 Electric motors, generators	C	−0.38	−0.05
	B	−0.36	−0.05
346 Domestic electrical appliances	C	0.22	0.14
	B	0.10	0.08
350 Motor vehicles	C	0.92	0.66
	B	0.15	0.16
438 Carpets, Linoleum	C	−0.65	0.04
	B	−0.41	0.00
451 Footwear	C	−3.49	−0.19
	B	−2.44	−0.17

*C, Courtnot-Nash assumption; B, Bertrand assumption.

Source: Anthony J. Venables, "Trade Policy Under Imperfect Competition: A Numerical Assessment," in Paul Krugman and Alasdair Smith (eds.), *Empirical Studies of Strategic Trade Policy* (Chicago: University of Chicago Press, 1994), p. 57.

The Commercial Aircraft Industry

Chapter 11 examined the commercial aircraft industry as an excellent example of an industry in which learning-by-doing is highly significant. In 1967 a British, French, and German government consortium provided subsidies to enable the Europeans to enter the commercial aircraft industry. In 1974 the first European aircraft appeared on the market, but they were a commercial failure. The three governments then decided it was necessary to produce a complete line of aircraft to compete with Boeing. This goal was finally accomplished by Airbus, the European-subsidized company, but Airbus still faced a significant cost disadvantage because of its relatively small size. This cost disadvantage resulted in a need to supply ever larger government subsidies.

TABLE 23.3 Welfare Effects of Import Tariffs Under Oligopoly: UK Industries 1982 Data (gain as a percentage of base consumption)

	Game*	5%	10%	15%	20%
257 Pharmaceutical products	C	0.59	0.96	1.15	1.20
	B	0.44	0.70	0.80	0.77
260 Artificial and synthetic fibers	C	2.23	3.93	5.07	5.64
	B	1.15	1.55	1.44	1.07
322 Machine tools	C	0.67	0.44	−0.20	−0.81
	B	0.64	0.40	−0.27	−0.90
330 Office machinery	C	1.52	2.09	1.97	1.81
	B	0.70	0.62	−0.15	−1.22
342 Electric motors, generators	C	0.76	1.04	0.96	0.65
	B	0.71	0.96	0.85	0.52
346 Domestic electrical appliances	C	1.15	1.54	1.46	1.18
	B	0.86	1.11	0.94	0.55
350 Motor vehicles	C	1.44	2.13	2.24	1.99
	B	0.90	1.22	1.09	0.64
438 Carpets, linoleum	C	0.74	0.64	0.48	0.39
	B	0.55	0.37	0.12	−0.03
451 Footwear	C	0.60	0.48	0.47	0.47
	B	0.12	−0.10	−0.14	−0.15

*C, Courtnot-Nash assumption; B, Bertrand assumption.

Source: Anthony J. Venables, "Trade Policy Under Imperfect Competition: A Numerical Assessment," in Paul Krugman and Alasdair Smith (eds.), *Empirical Studies of Strategic Trade Policy* (Chicago: University of Chicago Press, 1994), p. 52.

Klepper analyzed the commercial aircraft industry to see if these subsidies improved welfare.[9] His results, presented in Table 23.4, suggest that if Airbus's entry is compared with an alternative market structure of monopoly, presumably a Boeing monopoly, total economic welfare worldwide decreases by more than $73 billion as a result of the subsidies. Curiously, if Airbus's entry is considered an alternative market structure to duopoly, worldwide welfare is increased by $5.9 billion with the subsidy; however, all of the gains accrue to North American producers.

These results are consistent with our theoretical analysis. Because of the existence of large economies of scale, the optimal structure is a monopoly, and the entry of subsidized Airbus into a monopolized industry forces higher costs on society and results in greatly reduced producer surplus. Conversely, if the alternative structure is duopoly with both duopolists initially assumed to produce equal and suboptimal output levels, then the entry of subsidized Airbus at a small scale results in the exiting of one of the two original duopolists. However, it also results

TABLE 23.4 **Distribution of Welfare Effects of European-Supported Market Entry into Commercial Aircraft (million 1986 $US)**

	Producer Surplus	Consumer Surplus	Total
Compared with monopoly			
Europe	−2,826	10,544	7,718
North America	−107,582	12,631	−94,951
Rest of world	0	13,630	13,630
Total	−110,408	36,795	−73,613
Compared with duopoly			
Europe	−2,826	−905	−3,731
North America	11,974	−1,405	10,569
Rest of world	0	−958	−958
Total	9,148	−3,268	5,880

Source: Gernot Klepper, "Industrial Policy in the Transport Aircraft Industry," in Paul Krugman and Alasdair Smith (eds.), *Empirical Studies of Strategic Trade Policy* (Chicago: University of Chicago Press, 1994), p. 116.

in the expansion of output by the remaining North American producer. As a result, compared with duopoly, the larger scale of the one remaining North American firm results in almost a $12 billion producer surplus gain to the North American firm. Notice that consumers gain only compared with the monopoly situation.

The Case for Specialization with Economies of Scale

The Airbus example suggests the advantages of having one world monopolist in markets with very large economies of scale. In this section we expand on this theme.

Consider the case in which the United States and a foreign country produce two goods, large widgets and small widgets. One firm produces both types of widgets in each country. Furthermore, economies of scale are highly significant in the production of both large and small widgets. Finally, to simplify the analysis, we assume that demand and cost conditions are identical in both countries and for both large and small widgets.

Figure 23.8 shows the LRAC and LRMC curves for large widgets along with the demand curve for the combined United States and foreign large widget market, $D_{US + F}$. The demand curve for large widgets in each country, $D_{US} = D_F = MR_{US + F}$, is also identified, as are the marginal revenue curves for both demand curves. Note that the combined demand curve $D_{US + F}$ is twice the demand curve for each country $D_{US} = D_F$. An identical diagram could be drawn for small widgets.

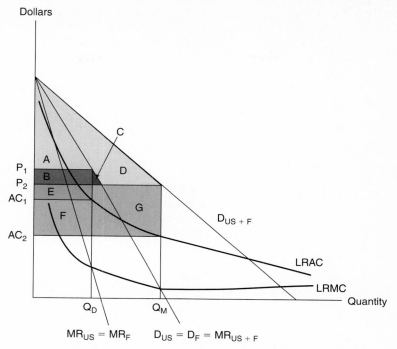

Figure 23.8   Economies of scale and monopoly specialization.

Suppose both countries decide to protect their domestic market in both large and small widgets by forbidding trade. Each monopolist would maximize profits in each market by equating $LRMC$ to $MR_{US} = MR_F$. Price in each market would be P_1, and average cost would equal AC_1. Profits earned in each market would equal the sum of the rectangles B and E in Figure 23.8, and because each domestic monopolist earns identical profits in both the large widget and the small widget markets, total profits for each monopolist would equal twice the area of rectangles B and E. Consumer surplus in each country would equal twice the red triangle A.

Suppose that the countries decided to permit trade. Rather than competing aggressively, however, each firm begins to rapidly expand its output in one market only. The American firm expands production of large widgets, and the foreign firm expands production of small widgets. In time, the American firm produces only large widgets and the foreign firm produces only small widgets. In the new equilibrium, the American firm is a monopolist in large widgets in both markets and the foreign firm is a monopolist in small widgets in both markets.

The price in each market declines to P_2, and the average cost in each market declines much more dramatically than price, to AC_2. Each firm earns much larger profits equal to the sum of the areas E, F, and G in Figure 23.8. Consumer surplus increases to the sum of the areas A, B, C, and D in each market, and therefore total consumer surplus increases to twice the sum of the areas A, B, C, and D. Both societies are unambiguously better off because profits and consumer surplus have increased in both the United States and the foreign country.

The gains from trade in this case do not result from an increase in competition because there is only one world monopolist producing each good. Instead the gains result entirely from the lower costs of production associated with economies of scale that occur when the monopolist in each market is able to expand output. The gains result from having one monopolist serve both markets at lower long-run average cost, rather than having two domestic monopolists each serve their own domestic markets at higher long-run average cost.

AN EMPIRICAL EXAMPLE: AUTOMOBILES REVISITED

Some of you may have noticed that the analysis of large and small widgets in the United States and a foreign country read remarkably like large and small automobiles in the United States and Japan. The similarity was intentional. The automobile industry provides a real-world example of the benefits of specialization. Recall from the earlier discussion of the automobile industry that in the 1960s and 1970s, Japan specialized in the export of small cars to the United States, and American firms specialized in the production of larger luxury-style automobiles. Such specialization resulted in both countries taking greater advantage of economies of scale, and American consumers were the primary beneficiaries because they had a larger selection of automobiles at lower prices.

A SIMILAR OLIGOPOLY EXAMPLE: JAPANESE CONTROL OF THE TELEVISION MARKET IN THE UNITED STATES

In 1962 the Japanese share of the American television market was less than 1 percent. By the late 1980s, no televisions were being manufactured in the United States. According to Robert Reich, "The reasons for the success of the Japanese producers relative to their American counterparts can be traced to their cost advantage, the better quality of their product, and their marketing and distribution strategies."[10]

The Japanese government's policies undoubtedly played some role as Japan became dominant in the television industry, but this example is consistent with our theoretical analysis. Japanese firms were able to take advantage of economies of scale to a greater extent than American firms in the 1950s and 1960s, and, as a result, the American firms abandoned the television market to the Japanese.

Multinational Corporations and Direct Foreign Investment

One additional issue worth examining in this chapter is **direct foreign investment** by American companies abroad and by foreign companies in the United States. Why would large multinational corporations invest directly in foreign countries instead of simply exporting to those countries from their domestic manufacturing base? The existence of tariffs and quotas provides a partial answer to this question, but even if free trade existed everywhere in the world, there would still be direct investment in foreign countries.

Before considering the advantages of direct foreign investment, it is important to recognize that there are major impediments to direct investment abroad. First, language and culture invariably create problems that are not faced by domestic producers. The language problem has been particularly apparent in the European Community (EC), where, despite a lack of tariffs and official barriers, firms have been reluctant to invest directly in other member countries. The cultural problems are indicated by anecdotal evidence such as the story of Radio Shack's entry into the Dutch market. On entry, Radio Shack advertised a big Christmas promotion right before December 25. This would have been fine in the United States, but proved to be a bit late in the Netherlands, where gifts are exchanged on December 6![11] Second, multinationals may face political and economic risks abroad that are unknown at home. In an extreme form firms may fear expropriation of property by an unfriendly government, and in a less extreme form they may fear wild exchange rate fluctuations in the foreign currency. Third, it may be costly to train and station personnel abroad, and this may force firms to pay large premiums to acquire a workforce. These potential problems are significant and limit the degree to which firms invest abroad.

Against these potential costs are a number of large potential gains. First, multinational expansion may enable firms to take advantage of economies of scale in production, distribution, and investment. Essentially, multinational expansion enables firms to take advantage of *multiplant* economies of scale. Second, direct foreign investment reduces tariffs and transportation costs and permits firms to avoid import restrictions. Third, some factor prices—wages are often used as the primary example—may be lower abroad. Fourth, multinationals may wish to move strategically to prevent the entry of domestic substitutes into the foreign market. Fifth, some less-developed countries offer very attractive tax breaks to foreign investors.

Given this list of potential advantages, it is not surprising that empirical evidence indicates that industries characterized by high concentration, high advertising, and high research and development expenditures are most likely to be the targets of multinational expansion.[12] Multinationals almost always operate in oligopolistic markets in which technology and product differentiation are significant. Consider some of the world's largest and best-known multinationals: Coca-Cola, Nestlé, IBM, Ford, Toyota, Philips, Colgate, and Electrolux. All operate in markets in which product differentiation or research and development are very important.

MULTINATIONALS AND WELFARE

There are two conflicting views of the welfare effects of direct foreign investment. Host countries gain from the transfer of capital, technology, and managerial skills. Recent examples of countries experiencing such gains include Poland and the Baltic states of Latvia, Lithuania, and Estonia after the breakup of the Soviet

Union. However, multinational investment may result in the transfer of profits from the host country to the domestic country. There is little doubt, for example, that if Japanese automobile production in the U.S. were severely restricted, American automobile manufacturers would keep a larger percentage of total United States automobile profits at home. Of course, U.S. consumers would suffer a major welfare loss as a result of such restrictions.

The true measure of the welfare effects of direct foreign investment depends on exactly what happens to the total value of output produced when real resources are transferred from the domestic to the foreign country. This says nothing about how any net benefits are distributed between the two countries, and that is an issue well beyond the scope of this book.

SUMMARY

1. With competitive domestic and world markets, free trade maximizes domestic welfare.
2. Trade may improve welfare by reducing the market power of a domestic monopolist.
3. The market power of American steel and automobile producers was significantly reduced by foreign competition.
4. Some evidence indicates that increased trade may result in significantly lower worldwide production costs.
5. The existence of signficant economies of scale opens up the possibility that trade restrictions may improve domestic welfare.
6. Industrial policies aimed at increasing domestic welfare by restricting trade often have the opposite effect and reduce domestic welfare.
7. If economies of scale are very significant, the optimal market structure may be a worldwide monopolist capable of taking full advantage of economies of scale.
8. Direct foreign investment in foreign countries has both benefits and costs for multinational corporations and host countries.
9. The net impact of direct foreign investment on a domestic economy depends on whether GDP increases as a result of the investment and how the increase in GDP is distributed between the countries.

KEY TERMS

direct foreign investment	quotas
gains from trade	strategic trade policy
industrial policy	subsidy
multinationals	tariffs

DISCUSSION QUESTIONS

1. Opponents of free trade in the United States often argue that in competitive markets (for example, clothing manufacturing) free trade "exports" American jobs abroad. Is there any truth to this position? If there is any truth to this argument, does it follow that free trade should be prevented?

2. In the absence of trade, what goods that you purchase do you think would be priced higher? Do you believe the quality of these goods would be higher or lower without trade? Why?

3. Do you agree with the following statement: Free trade is always better for domestic welfare. Domestic welfare can never be improved by interfering with free trade.

4. Why did Japan come to dominate the world color television market?

5. In what ways does the United States benefit when foreign firms invest in the United States? Are there costs to the United States of this direct foreign investment?

6. How has Japan's refusal to open up its agricultural markets to free trade affected the typical Japanese consumer?

PROBLEMS

1. (You need a calculator to answer this question.) Suppose the widget industry is perfectly competitive. Currently imports of widgets are prohibited into the United States. The U.S. demand for widgets is $P = 100 - Q$, and the supply of domestic producers of widgets is:

$$P = 25 + Q_{US}$$

If trade were permitted, foreign firms' supply of widgets to the United States would be:

$$P = 25 + 2Q_f$$

What are the welfare gains to the United States of permitting trade?

2. (You need a calculator to answer this question.) A domestic monopolist exists in the American zonker market. The U.S. demand for zonkers is $P = 100 - Q$ and the American monopolists' costs are $AC = MC = 20$. Currently there is an import ban on zonkers into the United States.

If trade were permitted, a group of small international firms would enter the U.S. zonker market, and the American monopolist would act as a dominant firm price leader. The supply in the United States of the international fringe firms would be:

$$P = 20 + q_f$$

23—International Economics and Industrial Organization

What would be the net welfare effect on the United States of permitting trade? Would American consumers benefit? Would the American monopolist benefit?

3. (You need a calculator to answer this question.) One Japanese firm produces widgets and one American firm produces widgets. Both produce with the following total costs:

$$TC = 250 + 40q$$

The only demand for widgets is in the United States and is $P = 100 - Q$. What is the Cournot-Nash equilibrium for the duopolists?

Suppose the United States government places a tariff (tax) of 10 per widget on Japanese widgets sold in the United States, while American widgets continue to be sold tax-free.

   a. Assuming Cournot-Nash behavior, what is the new equilibrium output for each firm?
   b. What is the Cournot-Nash equilibrium price?
   c. What is the impact of the tariff on American welfare?

4. (You need a calculator to answer this question.) Suppose one European firm and one American firm produce both widgets and zonkers (each firm produces both products). The total costs of production for each firm and for each product are identical, with:

$$TC_W = 500 + 20q_W \text{ and } TC_Z = 500 + 20q_Z$$

The demand for each product in the American and European markets is identical, with:

$$P_W = 100 - Q_W \text{ and } P_Z = 100 - Q_Z$$

Initially trade between Europe and the United States in both zonkers and widgets is prohibited and both firms act as monopolists in both domestic markets.

What is the current price and quantity of widgets and zonkers in each market?

Once trade is permitted, the American firm specializes in widget production and monopolizes both the American and European widget markets, and the European firm specializes in zonkers and becomes a worldwide monopolist in zonkers. With trade, the American monopolist faces the following worldwide demand for widgets:

$$P_W = 100 - \frac{1}{2}Q_W$$

With trade, the European monopolist faces the following worldwide demand for zonkers:

$$P_Z = 100 - \frac{1}{2}Q_Z$$

Both firms charge monopoly prices in their respective markets. What is the impact of permitting trade on prices of both widgets and zonkers in the United States and Europe? What is the impact of permitting trade on American and European welfare?

REFERENCES

1. Walter Adams, "The Steel Industry," in Walter Adams, ed., *The Structure of American Industry,* 4th edition (New York: Macmillan, 1971), p. 84.
2. Council on Wage and Price Stability, Staff Report, *A Study of Steel Prices* (Washington: U.S. Government Printing Office, July 1975), pp. 9–10 (emphasis ours).
3. Walter Adams and James Brock, "The Automobile Industry," in Walter Adams (ed.), *The Structure of American Industry,* 8th edition (New York: Macmillan, 1990), p. 111.
4. M. Pickford, "A New Test for Manufacturing Industry Efficiency," *International Journal of Industrial Organization* 3 (1985): 153–77.
5. Major contributions include: J.A. Brander and B.J. Spencer, "International R&D Rivalry and Industrial Strategy," *Review of Economic Studies,* 50 (1983): 707–22; J.A. Brander and B.J. Spencer, "Export Subsidies and International Market Share Rivalry," *Journal of International Economics* 18 (1985): 227–42; A.K. Dixit and G.M. Grossman, "Targeted Export Promotion with Several Oligopolistic Industries," *Journal of International Economics,* 21 (1986): 233–50; J. Eaton and G.M. Grossman, "Optimal Trade and Industrial Policy Under Oligopoly," *Quarterly Journal of Economics,* 101 (1985): 383–406; I. Horstmann and J.R. Markusen, "Up the Average Cost Curve: Inefficient Entry and the New Protectionism," *Journal of International Economics* 20 (1986): 225–48; P.R. Krugman, "Import Protection as Export Promotion: International Competition in the Presence of Oligopoly and Economies of Scale," in H. Kierzkowski (ed.), *Monopolistic Competition in International Trade.* (Oxford: Oxford University Press, 1984); and A.J. Venables, "Trade and Trade Policy with Imperfect Competition: The Case of Identical Products and Free Trade," *Journal of International Economics,* 19 (1974): 1–20.
6. I. Horstmann and J.R. Markusen, "Up the Average Cost Curve: Inefficient Entry and the New Protectionism," *Journal of International Economics* 20 (1986): 225–48.
7. Anthony J. Venables, "Trade Policy Under Imperfect Competition: A Numerical Assessment," in Paul Krugman and Alasdair Smith (eds.), *Empirical Studies of Strategic Trade Policy* (Chicago: University of Chicago Press, 1994).
8. *Ibid.,* p. 63.
9. Gernot Klepper, "Industrial Policy in the Transport Aircraft Industry," in Paul Krugman and Alasdair Smith (eds.), *Empirical Studies of Strategic Trade Policy* (Chicago: University of Chicago Press, 1994).
10. Ira C. Magaziner and Robert B. Reich, *Minding America's Business: The Decline and Rise of the American Economy,* (New York: Harcourt, Brace, Jovanovich, 1982), p. 171 (emphasis added).
11. "Radio Shack's Rough Trip," *Business Week* (May 30, 1977): 55.
12. See Richard E. Caves, Michael E. Porter, and A. Michael Spence, *Competition in the Open Economy* (Cambridge: Harvard University Press, 1980); Howard P. Marvel, "Foreign Trade and Domestic Competition," *Economic Inquiry,* 18 (1980): 103–22; Stephen G. Grubaugh, "Determinants of Direct Foreign Investment," *Review of Economics and Statistics,* 69 (1987): 149–52; and John M. Conner and Willard F. Mueller, "Manufacturing, Denationalization, and Market Structure: Brazil, Mexico, and the United States," *Industrial Organization Review,* 2 (1978): 86–105.

Chapter 24

Regulation and Deregulation

Over the past twenty years the extent of direct government regulation in the American economy has continually declined. Thirty years ago government regulation affected not only the major public utilities such as electricity, natural gas, and telecommunications, but also all transportation industries from the railroads to the airlines. Today less than 4 percent of gross national product (GNP) is produced in regulated sectors.

This chapter addresses the economic rationale for regulation and the rationale for recent deregulation. A thorough examination of economic regulation would require an entire book, so only the most important issues are addressed here. This is a useful concluding chapter because it applies a great deal of the knowledge gained throughout the book.

The Rationale for Regulation: Traditional Public Utility Regulation

The authority for regulation of private industry comes from no lesser source than the Constitution of the United States, which declared that Congress had the right to "regulate commerce . . . among the several states." Despite this constitutional mandate, for the first century of the nation's existence there was virtually no federal regulation over the day-to-day operation of business. In the latter half of the nineteenth century, however, the increasing significance of economies of scale in many sectors resulted in increased market power for some firms.[1] Nowhere was this increase in potential power more dramatic than in the railroad industry in the midwest and west. Because of the monopoly power of the railroads in sparsely populated areas, farmers were forced to either pay high shipping rates or watch their grain spoil. As economic pressures grew, two important agrarian political groups arose: the Populists and the Grangers. These groups were able to support a candidate for President and to win a number of seats in Congress. As the influence of the Populists and Grangers grew, the two major parties were forced to address their economic concerns, and two policies emerged—antitrust and regulation.

The initial economic rationale for regulation was based on the existence of large economies of scale. Previous chapters devoted a great deal of attention to economies of scale, and Chapters 2 and 5 discussed the concept of a **natural monopoly**. Recall that in natural monopolies one firm can serve the market more efficiently than more than one firm. Figure 24.1 shows a natural monopoly. The LRAC curve in Figure 24.1 is sloping downward where it intersects the demand curve at an output of q_1. Because the LRAC curve is sloping downward at q_1, LRMC must lie below LRAC at q_1. Allocative efficiency demands that output be expanded as long as price is above LRMC or, as in Figure 24.1, until output equals q_2. If a private firm were forced to expand output to q_2 and charge price P_2, price would be below LRAC and the firm would sustain an economic loss equal to the gray area C_2abP_2.

There is a policy dilemma associated with the natural monopoly depicted in Figure 24.1. If an unregulated firm were free to maximize profits, it would produce the profit-maximizing output q_m, charge the profit-maximizing price P_m, and earn excess economic profits equal to the red area C_mdcP_m. Entry would be virtually impossible because the natural monopolist would have a large first-mover advantage and could quickly expand output to q_1 if threatened with entry. The natural monopolist could, therefore, earn excess economic profits for a long

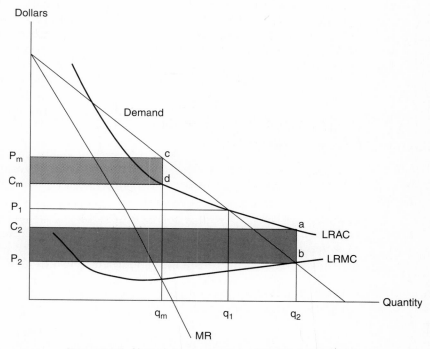

Figure 24.1 Natural monopoly as a justification for regulation.

period. In fact, in the absence of new technology, it could earn these excess profits indefinitely.

Conversely, if the government attempted to force the natural monopolist to charge the socially optimal price, P_2, at which MC = P, then the monopolist would sustain an economic loss. Under such draconian regulation, no investors would be attracted to the industry, and the industry would have to be subsidized or it would cease to exist.*

There is, however, a middle ground in Figure 24.1. Suppose the regulators attempted to set a price equal to P_1, where P = LRAC. With price equal to P_1, economic profits are normal, so investors can be attracted into the industry. Furthermore, although output is less than the socially optimal output q_2, it is considerably greater than the profit-maximizing output of q_m. The price P_1 is a compromise price known as a **Ramsey price**. The Ramsey price is the price that maximizes total social benefits subject to the requirement that profits cannot be negative. From a welfare perspective, P_1 is significantly better than the profit-maximizing price, but significantly worse than the socially optimal price. In theory, it appears to be a reasonable and workable compromise. In practice, serious problems are associated with such a compromise price. We consider the major problems in the next few sections.

The Workings of American Regulation

Although the first state regulatory boards were established in 1874, regulation at the national level did not begin until 1887 with the establishment of the Interstate Commerce Commission (ICC). The legal foundation for the ICC was an 1877 Supreme Court decision, *Munn v. Illinois*.[2] Illinois had set the maximum price to store grain in warehouses throughout the state. Munn sued, but the Supreme Court ruled in favor of the state. Chief Justice Waite wrote:

> . . . Looking, then, to the common law from whence came the right which the Constitution protects, we find that when private property is "affected with a public interest it ceases to be *juris privati* only."
>
> . . . When, therefore, one devotes his property to a use in which the public has an interest, he, in effect, grants to the public an interest in that use and must submit to be controlled by the public for the common good to the extent of the interest he has thus created.

The *Munn* decision eventually led to the establishment of many regulatory commissions in the United States. Commissioners are appointed by the executive branch of government, the President at the federal level, or the governor at the state level. Most commissions are dominated by lawyers and former politicians and include few, if any, economists. Furthermore, although a few commissioners are well trained in economics, most are not.

Public utility commissions have several major tasks. Commissions have the difficult job of simultaneously setting the permitted level of profits, the price

---

*There is one exception to this conclusion. Price discrimination could enable a monopolist to charge the socially optimal price and still earn an economic profit. This point is discussed later.

level, the price structure, and the rate base. None of these tasks is more important than setting the "correct" level of profits. The target profit level is typically set as a permitted rate of return on invested capital. Profit rates must be high enough to ensure a flow of capital, but not so high as to generate large excess profits. In establishing a price structure, the commission must decide how much price discrimination to permit. Finally, the commission must determine the **rate base**, or the value of the firm's invested capital to be used to calculate profits. As we will see shortly, a decision to allow too much capital into the rate base calculation will result in profits being excessive, and a decision to squeeze the rate base will prevent needed capital from entering the industry.

SETTING THE PERMITTED RATE OF RETURN

The commission must set the permitted rate of return r, the permitted price structure p, and the permitted rate base K in the following equation:*

$$r = \frac{TR - TC}{K},$$

where r represents the rate of return on invested capital, TR represents total revenue, TC represents total costs, and K represents the value of the firm's invested capital or the *rate base*.

If r is fixed at "too low" a level, investors will stay away from the utility's stocks and bonds, and capacity may lag behind demand requirements. Insufficient capacity could cause a regulator's worst nightmare—a service interruption. However, if r turns out to be "too high," output will be restricted below a more socially optimal level, and high profits may cause a public outcry against both the commission and the utility.

The value of r goes a long way toward determining the stock value of the company and therefore is extremely important to the firm. Suppose, for example, that a utility's stock is worth ten times its annual profit flow; that is, the utility's price/earnings ratio equals 10. If the target value of r is set at 10 percent and K = $10 million, then targeted annual profits (TR − TC) are $1 million. The utility's stock value should then be 10 times $1 million, or $10 million. Now suppose the utility convinces the commission to raise the target r to 11 percent. If K remains fixed at $10 million, permitted target profits increase to $1.1 million, and the value of the utility's stock should increase to 10 times $1.1 million, or $11 million. There is an immediate $1 million capital gain to stockholders because of the increase in the target value of r. It is obviously worth a great deal of time and effort on the part of stockholders to lobby for an increase in r.

---

*This equation is often described as:

$$TR = OC + Dep + r(RB),$$

where TR represents total revenues, OC is operating costs, Dep is depreciation, r is the permitted rate of return, and RB is the rate base.

How does a commission set the targeted r? Commissions have generally considered three criteria: the cost of raising capital; the utility's capital attraction requirements (that is, whether the utility should be expanding or contracting its capacity); and comparable returns in other "equal risk" industries that would permit the utility to earn a normal economic profit. Historically, commissions have often relied on the concept of comparable returns, which means that the utility should earn a rate of return equal to the average in "similar industries." Although this criterion may initially seem to make economic sense, one realizes on second thought that there are no *unregulated* industries that are comparable to public utilities. Risk to a public utility is so fundamentally different from risk to a firm in an unregulated industry that it is virtually impossible to compare the two. For instance, even if General Motors typically earns a 15 percent rate of return, it still runs a risk of sustaining an economic loss in any given year. If Consolidated Edison is targeted to earn a "comparable rate of return" of 15 percent, it runs virtually no risk of sustaining an economic loss in any year.

Because of the problems associated with using comparable returns, economists have argued that it makes more sense to rely on the cost of raising capital and the firm's capital attraction requirements when setting the target r. The cost of capital is calculated as a weighted average of the firm's cost of raising capital through the three standard securities: bonds, preferred stocks, and common stocks. Bonds and preferred stocks pay fixed interest rates, and therefore the cost of capital raised through these instruments is easy to calculate.

The cost of capital raised through the sale of common stocks is more complicated to determine because the cost is directly related to expected future profits. If the utility expects to pay stockholders a fixed dividend per share equal to D every year, and if the price of a share of common stock equals P, then the cost of capital raised by selling a share of common stock is s in the following equation:*

$$P = \frac{D}{(1 + s)} + \frac{D}{(1 + s)^2} + \ldots + \frac{D}{(1 + s)^n} \qquad [24.1]$$

To understand Eq. 24.1, recall from the discussion of present value in Chapter 8 that if $n \rightarrow \infty$ in Eq. 24.1, then:

$$P = \frac{D}{s} \ \text{ or } \ s = \frac{D}{P}.$$

If, for example, D = $15 and P = $100, then s = 15 percent.

A weighted average of the cost of bonds, preferred stocks, and common stocks is the preferred measure of the cost of capital, but it may not be the optimal permitted rate of return r. The commission also must consider the utility's capital attraction requirements. In a declining industry (e.g., the railroads in 1960), an optimal rate of return should encourage the *withdrawal of capital*, and therefore, the target r should be set at a low level below the normal rate of return

---

*The assumption that dividends D are constant is highly questionable, and commissions typically assume some rate of growth in dividend payments over time.

in the economy. The cost of capital calculation, therefore, is not the optimal way to calculate r in all cases. It is, however, a good first approximation.

Efficiency Problems Associated with Rate of Return Regulation

X-INEFFICIENCY

Rate of return regulation causes serious efficiency problems. With r guaranteed, there is little incentive for the utility to minimize costs, and this encourages x-inefficiency.[3] Because x-inefficiencies increase total costs and cause r to fall below the permitted level, x-inefficiencies may precipitate a request to increase prices. Although a commission can deny a price hike if it determines that x-inefficiencies exist, most price increase requests are approved.

An institutional check against x-inefficiency is **regulatory lag**. Regulatory lag exists whenever costs increase or decrease. If costs increase, the utility cannot immediately raise prices. It must first request a price increase. Until the price hike is approved, the utility will earn a rate of return less than r. Similarly, if costs decrease, the utility will earn a rate of return greater than r until a price reduction is approved. Regulatory lag punishes x-inefficiency and rewards improved efficiency.

THE AVERCH-JOHNSON EFFECT

Another efficiency problem associated with public utility regulation was first suggested by Averch and Johnson.[4] They theorized that if r is greater than the market cost of capital, s, the utility has an incentive to use too much capital relative to other inputs. If r = 10 percent and s = 8 percent, for example, then every $1 increase in K costs the utility 8 cents but results in a 10-cent increase in permitted profits. The utility is guaranteed an extra 2 cents in profits for every additional $1 it invests in capital. Averch and Johnson hypothesized that the utility would consider its cost of capital to be approximately 6 percent, 8 percent minus the 2 percent "discount" the utility receives in the form of permitted profits above the market cost of capital. According to Averch and Johnson, therefore:

$$\text{The utility's cost of capital} = s - (r - s) = 2s - r$$

The **Averch-Johnson effect** is shown in Figure 24.2.* The red **isoquants** labeled Q_1 and Q_2 in Figure 24.2 show the combinations of labor and capital that the regulated firm can use to produce outputs of Q_1 and Q_2, respectively. In the absence of regulation, each red **isocost line** has a negative slope equal to the ratio of the price of labor over the price of capital, $-w/s$. To minimize the cost of producing any quantity, a firm must produce at a point on the relevant isoquant at

---

*It is necessary to have studied intermediate microeconomic theory to understand Figure 24.2.

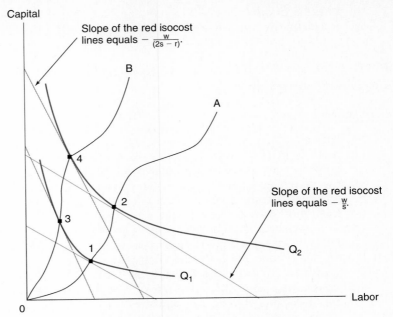

Figure 24.2 The Averch-Johnson effect.

which the isocost line is tangent to the isoquant. For an output of Q_1 the cost-minimizing point is point 1, and for an output of Q_2 the cost-minimizing point is point 2. The **input expansion path**, OA, shows all the possible cost-minimizing combinations of labor and capital in the absence of regulation. Because the line OA identifies the lowest possible social cost of producing any possible output, it is the *socially optimal input expansion path*.

The Averch-Johnson effect suggests that the cost of capital to the utility is $2s - r$, which is lower than the social cost of capital, s. In Figure 24.2, each black isocost line represents an isocost line faced by a regulated firm. The black isocost lines are steeper than the red isocost lines; the slope of the black lines equals $-w/(2s - r)$. Given the black isocost lines faced by a regulated utility, the optimal input expansion path is OB. For an output of Q_1 the cost-minimizing point is point 3, and for an output of Q_2 the cost-minimizing point is point 4. For any output, a regulated firm uses more capital and less labor along expansion path OB than along the socially optimal expansion path OA. According to Averch and Johnson, the regulated utility will invest in too much capital and select a non-optimal combination of inputs.

Although testing empirically for the Averch-Johnson effect is difficult, the following evidence suggests that regulated firms have attempted to increase their rate bases by using too much capital:[5]

1. Utilities avoided using **peak-load pricing**.[6] Under peak-load pricing systems, firms charge higher prices during peak demand periods and lower prices during off-peak periods. Because marginal costs are higher during peak periods,

peak-load pricing is efficient. By reducing the quantity demanded during peak periods, peak-load pricing reduces capacity requirements and lowers the utility's rate base. By avoiding peak-load pricing, utilities increase their capital requirements.

2. Utilities invested in capacity that exceeded demand even during peak demand periods.[7]
3. Instead of forming regional power pools to share electricity, power companies preferred to invest in enough capacity to meet their peak requirements.[8]
4. Utilities delayed the introduction of less capital-intensive technologies. In the late 1960s, for example, AT&T continued to invest in capital-intensive transcontinental cables between the United States and Europe when less capital-intensive satellite communications were available.[9] To meet winter peak demand in the northeastern United States, the natural gas industry built capital-intensive pipelines instead of less capital-intensive underground storage facilities.[10]
5. Regulated utilities refused to lease facilities even if leasing reduced costs because leased facilities are not included in a firm's rate base. In the communications industry, common carriers refused to lease satellite communications from Comstat (Communications Satellite Corporation) even though Comstat was established by the government as the official corporation for installing an international satellite communications network.[11] Similarly, electric utilities have been hesitant to lease fuel cores for nuclear power plants.[12]
6. Public utilities set too high a standard of service reliability. By attempting to prevent all possible service interruptions, utilities were able to increase their capital expenditures and rate bases.[13]
7. Utilities permitted, even encouraged, outside suppliers to sell inputs at high prices.[14] In the 1950s when the electrical equipment manufacturers were fixing prices, the electric utilities not only failed to identify the conspiracy but also were less than vigorous in pressing damage claims. The utilities had an incentive to be exploited because high input prices increased their rate bases.
8. Utilities invested in capital-intensive areas that increased their rate bases even if the investments resulted in economic losses. In the 1960s, for example, AT&T invested in its TELPAK multichannel business service and its TWX teletype service in competition with Western Union. Its rate of return was very low on both services compared with its return on regulated interstate telephone activities.[15]

This empirical evidence in support of the Averch-Johnson effect all occurred before the early 1970s. From the end of World War II until the early 1970s, the marginal cost of capital tended to be fairly constant because of relatively low inflation and the Federal Reserve's **Regulation Q**, which limited the interest rates that banks could pay on all deposits, including large certificates of deposits (CDs). In the early 1970s two factors changed. First, high energy prices resulted in increased inflation, which increased interest rates and the marginal cost of capital. Second, the Federal Reserve suspended Regulation Q, which caused a dramatic increase in the rate of return on CDs and resulted in a large increase in the marginal cost of capital. With interest rates on CDs rising from 7 percent in 1972 to 12 percent in 1974, the marginal cost of capital suddenly exceeded the permitted rate of return, r, for most utilities.[16] Given this new cost structure, the incentive to invest in excessive capital was eliminated for most utilities.

During the 1950s and 1960s, the Averch-Johnson effect may have had a redeeming feature. Each of these distortions increased costs, but each distortion also increased output. Recall from Figure 24.1 that regulation restricts output below the socially optimal level at which price equals marginal cost. The Averch-Johnson effect encourages regulated utilities to increase output beyond q_1 and to invest in riskier investments. By increasing output and encouraging risk-taking, the Averch-Johnson effect partially offsets two of the major problems associated with regulation. This has led Alfred Kahn to suggest that "as an offset to monopoly, the [Averch-Johnson] distortion probably does more good than harm."[17]

Not all economists have accepted the Averch-Johnson hypothesis. Several economists have theorized that regulation results in the use of too few units of capital relative to other inputs.[18] One alternative hypothesis suggests that firms may underinvest in capital because they fear that future regulations will be tightened. Tighter future regulation would cause a lower permitted rate of return on invested capital.[19] By underinvesting in capital, regulated firms limit the potential damage associated with a lower rate of return in the future. Some empirical studies have failed to find evidence of an Averch-Johnson effect, and at least one study found evidence of undercapitalization.[20]

SETTING THE PRICE STRUCTURE

The Price Structure with Decreasing Costs

From the end of World War II through the early 1970s, utilities faced declining long-run average cost curves like those shown in Figure 24.1. Under these cost conditions, commissions used second-degree and third-degree price discrimination to increase output and decrease average costs. In Figure 24.1 if the utility sets price at P_1, profits are normal but output is below the socially optimal level q_2. To increase output toward q_2, commissions permitted the use of second-degree price discrimination. Recall from Chapter 15 that with second-degree price discrimination all buyers are offered the same price schedule and they self-select into different groups.

Figure 24.3 shows how, under conditions of decreasing LRAC, price discrimination can enable a utility to produce the socially optimal output and earn a normal profit. Buyers are offered a price schedule that gives a rate reduction for large purchases. In response, customers divide themselves into three groups, residential buyers, small commercial buyers, and large commercial buyers. Residential buyers pay the highest price P_1, small commercial buyers pay a lower price P_2, and large commercial buyers pay a price equal to marginal cost P_{mc}. The quantity purchased by residential consumers is q_1, the quantity purchased by small commercial users is $q_2 - q_1$, and the quantity purchased by large commercial users is $q_3 - q_2$. Because total output is q_3, the average cost of production is $AC = P_2$ for *all* units produced. The utility earns a positive economic profit equal to the red area P_1abP_2 on sales to residential users, earns a normal profit on sales to small commercial users, and sustains an economic loss equal to the gray area cdef on sales to large commercial buyers. If the red area P_1abP_2 equals the gray area cdef, the

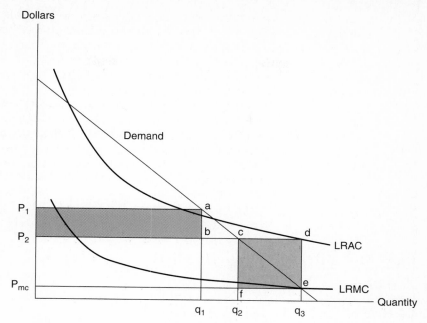

Figure 24.3 The use of price discrimination to improve economic efficiency.

utility earns a normal economic profit and output is equal to the socially optimal output.

Commissions have also permitted third-degree price discrimination. In the telecommunications industry, for example, customers have been separated into business and residential buyers. Business customers have a more inelastic demand and pay higher rates.

The Price Structure with Increasing Costs

Recall that in the early 1970s cost conditions changed dramatically as the price of oil and other fossil fuels increased and Regulation Q was suspended by the Federal Reserve System. Electric utilities suddenly faced an entirely new cost structure as variable fuel costs became a significant component of total costs and conservation became a high national priority. In addition, high inflation and interest rates increased the cost of expanding capacity. Almost overnight marginal costs and average costs were *increasing* instead of decreasing, and the optimal pricing structure no longer called for discrimination in favor of large users but, instead, required efforts to reduce demand.

After 1974 the marginal cost of generating electricity was significantly higher during peak demand periods when the last kilowatt-hour of generating capacity had to be brought on line. A typical electric utility, for example, would use only its low-cost hydroelectric or nuclear power capacity during off-peak periods. As demand increased during the day, newer fossil fuel facilities would be used. Finally, as demand reached peak, aging and inefficient facilities would be brought on line. With each increase in demand, therefore, the marginal cost of generating a kilowatt-hour of electricity would increase. The entire cost of operating the last inefficient units of generating capacity, including depreciation, should be allocated to those last units of peak demand.

Figure 24.4 shows the post-1974 cost structure. Suppose demand equals D_P during the peak period from 8:00 AM to 10:00 PM, and demand equals D_{OP} during the off-peak period from 10:00 PM to 8:00 AM. Efficient pricing requires charging P_P during the peak period and P_{OP} during the off-peak period.

The first electric utility to adopt a peak-load pricing system was the Wisconsin Power & Light Company in 1977.* Wisconsin Power & Light charged commercial users 2.03 cents per kilowatt-hour between 8:00 AM and 10:00 PM and 1.013 cents per kilowatt-hour between 10:00 PM and 8:00 AM.[21] Since 1977 many states have implemented peak-load pricing schemes into their price structures.[22]

The Spread of Regulation into Other Markets

THE CAPTURE THEORY OF REGULATION

The existence of large economies of scale was used to justify regulation in the railroad industry and the traditional public utilities, such as electricity, gas, and telecommunications. But why did regulation spread to markets in which economies of scale were not significant? Why, for example, did the government regulate trucking rates, airline fares, and the well-head price of natural gas? One possible explanation is that the regulated firms "captured" control of the regulatory commissions. According to this **capture theory**, once the railroads were regulated, the commissions came to view their primary responsibility as protecting the regulated firms from "too much" competition, rather than protecting consumers from monopoly prices.

Stigler first suggested that regulation is supplied in response to interest group lobbying pressure to protect the group from competition.[23] Peltzman expanded on Stigler's theory by suggesting that legislators select regulatory policies that maximize the legislators' political support.[24] Interest groups provide votes, campaign contributions, and other campaign resources to the legislators. In turn, the legislators provide support in the form of wealth transfers to the interest groups that provide the most votes and resources.

To formalize the model, suppose there are n firms in an industry that benefits from regulation. Assume the following:

1. Regulation results in a wealth transfer of T from consumers to the n firms.

---

*Long before the electric utilities moved to a peak-load pricing structure, AT&T charged higher long-distance rates during the peak demand period on weekdays from 8:00 AM to 5:00 PM. In 1984 AT&T offered a 40 percent rate reduction on weekdays from 5:00 PM to 11:00 PM and a 60 percent reduction on weekends, holidays, and on weekdays from 11:00 PM to 8:00 AM.

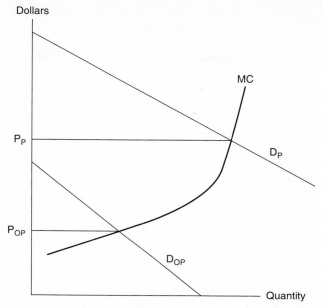

Figure 24.4 Peak-load pricing in a regulated utility.

2. The cost of organizing firms to lobby is a function of the number of firms n, and equals C(n). The cost function C(n) is a positive function of n because it is more difficult and costly to organize a large group than a small group.
3. The incentive for consumers to lobby against regulation increases with an increase in the total number of consumers negatively impacted by regulation and an increase in the intensity of consumers' feelings.

Given these assumptions, the per capita net benefits of regulation for each firm i, B_i, equal:

$$B_i = \frac{T - C(n)}{n} = \frac{T}{n} - \frac{C(n)}{n}.$$

As n decreases, T/n increases, C(n) decreases, and C(n)/n may increase, decrease, or remain constant. If C(n)/n decreases or remains constant, the net benefits of regulation must increase with a decrease in n. Even if C(n)/n increases, it is likely that the increase in T/n will be greater than the increase in C(n)/n.* Reducing n is

---

*In the term T/n, only the denominator declines as n declines. In the term C(n)/n, both the numerator and denominator decline as n declines. If follows that the increase in the term T/n associated with a decrease in n is likely to be greater than any decrease in the term C(n)/n associated with a decrease in n.

likely, therefore, to increase the net benefits associated with regulation and increase the intensity of the groups' lobbying effort.*

The model is perhaps best understood through an example.[25] Suppose that as a result of government price supports and import restrictions on peanuts, consumers pay $349 million more for peanut products each year. If there are 44,000 peanut farmers, then:

$$\frac{T}{n} = \frac{\$349 \text{ million}}{44,000} = \$7,931.82;$$

each farmer gains almost $8000 from the government intervention. If there are 250 million American consumers, the program costs each consumer on average ($349 million/250 million) = $1.40. In terms of which group is likely to organize, there is a tremendous asymmetry. Few consumers will spend any time attempting to save $1.40, but peanut farmers will be willing to invest a great deal of time, effort, and money to gain $8000 in benefits.

One of the major implications of the Peltzman model is that regulation tends to benefit small, well-organized groups with strong feelings (e.g., regulated firms) at the expense of large, unorganized groups with weak feelings (e.g., consumers). The history of regulation of transportation industries is consistent with the Stigler/Peltzman theory: the railroads were a well-organized, small group with a great deal to gain from expanded regulation into the trucking, busing, water carrier, and airline industries. Ironically, as time passed, regulation came to favor the trucking industry at the expense of the railroads.

Occupational licensing in the professions provides another powerful example of how the regulatory process can be captured and brought under the control of those being regulated. Professional organizations of doctors, lawyers, electricians, engineers, and plumbers have been able to convince state legislatures to establish licensing regulations and to then allow the professional organizations to set the licensing rules themselves. Doctors, for example, decide who can practice medicine, and lawyers decide who can practice law. It should come as no surprise that these self-imposed regulations typically make entry difficult and result in higher incomes for those already licensed.[26]

Additional evidence in support of the capture theory is provided by the aggressive opposition of regulated firms to deregulation. AT&T fought deregulation of the telecommunications industry, and the major air carriers led the fight against airline deregulation.[27] If regulation were detrimental to regulated firms and served the interests of consumers, regulated firms would welcome deregulation. In fact, few regulated firms have supported deregulation.

---

*Similarly, as n increases, T/n decreases, whereas C(n)/n may increase, decrease, or remain constant. If C(n)/n increases or remains constant, the net benefits of regulation must decrease with an increase in n. Even if C(n)/n decreases, it is likely that the decrease in T/n will be greater than the decrease in C(n)/n. Increasing n is likely, therefore, to decrease the net benefits associated with regulation and decrease the groups' intensity of lobbying effort.

The Movement from Regulation to Deregulation

Recently there has been a dramatic trend away from regulation. As new technologies have reduced the incidence of natural monopoly in the modern economy, the number of justified areas for regulation has decreased. In this section we address the important movements away from regulation that have occurred in the major regulated industries during the past two decades.

SURFACE TRANSPORTATION

Despite the the Interstate Commerce Commission's (ICC) efforts to protect the railroads, their competitive position declined after World War II. The development of the interstate highway system combined with the growth of the commercial airline industry destroyed the railroads' passenger business, which declined from 50 billion passenger miles in 1940 to 22 billion in 1960 and 10 billion in 1975.[28] The railroads argued that the government unfairly subsidized competing modes of transportation. For example, while the government built the interstate highway system and new airports, the railroads had to use their own funds to build and maintain their rail beds. Furthermore, the government permitted truck carriers to use collusion and price discrimination to compete with the railroads, and the ICC was slow to allow the railroads to reduce rates in response to discriminatory price cutting by truckers.*

By 1960 the railroads were in deep financial trouble. The ICC responded by encouraging mergers and permitting service reductions, but the commission still refused to permit major rate cuts. Under pressure from the railroads to deregulate, in 1976 Congress passed the Railroad Revitalization and Regulatory Reform Act, which: (1) provided $1.6 billion in government subsidies; (2) increased price flexibility; (3) accelerated the pace of merger approvals; and (4) expedited the closing of low-volume rail routes. The 1976 act did not go far enough, however, and in 1980 Congress passed the Staggers Act, which authorized more subsidies, eliminated antitrust immunity, and permitted greater price flexibility.

Deregulation resulted in immediate improvements in the railroads' economic performance. First, the railroads eliminated many unprofitable routes. Between 1975 and 1982, the railroads abandoned 17.2 percent of their track miles.[29] Deregulation enabled the railroads to increase rates in markets in which they had a comparative advantage, such as the transportation of bulky commodities such as coal, and decrease prices in markets in which they faced stiff competition. Overall, rail prices decreased by 17.5 percent between 1975 and 1983.[30]

To level the playing field, in 1980 Congress also passed the Motor Carrier Act, which partially deregulated the trucking industry. This act, which was strongly

---

*The Reed-Bullwinkle Act of 1948 legalized the establishment of cartels, or rate bureaus, in the railroad, trucking, airline, and water carrier industries.

TABLE 24.1 **Entry Requests and Approved Requests of Carriers**

	Entry Authority Applications from Carriers		Percentage of Applications Approved		
Year	Existing	New	Existing (%)	New (%)	Number of Carriers
1975	2,822	276	55	61	16,005
1976	6,406	586	61	62	16,462
1977	8,622	558	65	72	16,606
1978	12,983	703	69	78	16,874
1979	20,687	974	69	80	17,083
1980	18,788	1,490	73	86	18,129
1981	19,135	4,576	88	85	22,270
1982	9,150	4,925	84	55	25,722

Source: Thomas Gale Moore, "Rail and Trucking Deregulation," in Leonard W. Weiss and Michael W. Klass (eds.), *Regulatory Reform: What Actually Happened* (Boston: Little, Brown, 1986), p. 31.

opposed by the large truck carriers, eased entry and allowed greater price flexibility. Before 1980, regulation prevented entry into trucking if existing truckers could meet demand. Given this restriction, most entry requests were denied. Table 24.1 shows the dramatic impact of the 1980 Motor Carrier Act on entry. Requests for entry authority by truckers increased dramatically after deregulation, and the percentage of requests granted increased as well. One striking figure is the 60.7 percent increase in the number of carriers between 1975 and 1982. Entry caused rates for truckload carriers to decline by 25 percent in this period.[31] As prices fell, profits were squeezed, and the number of trucking bankruptcies increased 400 percent between 1980 and 1985.[32]

Deregulation of surface transportation resulted in improved economic efficiency.[33] Inefficient firms closed down, costs fell, and rates declined. Railroad profits increased, and trucking profits decreased. These results were a direct consequence of increased interindustry competition.

AIRLINE REGULATION AND DEREGULATION

Regulation of the airline industry began in the 1920s, when the United States Postal Service was authorized to award mail routes and set rates. In 1934, the ICC took over the regulation of mail carriage and set up a competitive bidding system to allocate routes. To ensure a flow of mail traffic, the airlines continuously bid under cost, and soon many were on the verge of bankruptcy.[34] Congress responded to this threat to the airlines by passing the Civil Aeronautics Act of 1938, which established the Civil Aeronautics Authority. In 1940 the Civil Aeronautics Authority became the Civil Aeronautics Board (CAB). The CAB controlled the industry until the early 1980s and had complete control over rates, entry, exit, and safety. In 1958 the authority over safety was transferred to the Federal Aviation Authority (FAA).

The CAB set fares to earn a target rate of return on investment, and the fares had little relationship to costs. Average costs per passenger mile were significantly higher on short routes than on long routes. Fares, however, were related primarily to distance, so they were maintained well above average cost on long routes. These high fares subsidized below-average cost fares on short routes. Price changes tended to be across-the-board, and the CAB discouraged price competition. Entry was approved only if it would not harm existing carriers. Finally, inefficient carriers that were in danger of sustaining economic losses were rewarded with new, profitable routes to keep them from going bankrupt.

Between 1949 and 1969, passenger miles increased at an average annual rate of 14 percent, while the average fare per mile decreased by 2 percent.[35] During this period, the Consumer Price Index (CPI) increased by 50 percent.[36] The decline in real air fares resulted from a 22 percent decrease in the average cost per passenger mile.[37] In the late 1960s the impact of regulation first came into serious question when it was discovered that fares on unregulated *intrastate* routes were much lower than fares on comparable regulated routes.[38]

In the absence of price competition, the airlines turned to various forms of nonprice competition, which took the form of increased frequency of flights and more amenities. As the airlines kept adding extra flights, empty seats abounded and load factors were low. In 1969, for example, only 50.3 percent of available seats were filled.[39] These low load factors increased average costs and reduced profits.

In 1976 the CAB took its first tentative steps toward deregulation when it permitted charter flight operators to reduce fares on advance purchase tickets with a minimum stay requirement. In 1977 the CAB allowed certain major carriers to lower fares by 45 percent on "Super Saver" transcontinental flights if the tickets were purchased at least thirty days in advance and were for a minimum seven-day stay. When economist Alfred Kahn became chair of the CAB in June 1977, he announced that his goal was to eliminate all regulation of fares and entry and to ultimately disband the CAB.[40] Under Kahn the CAB began permitting fare reductions of up to 70 percent and fare increases of up to 10 percent.

Over the protests of the major airlines, Congress passed the Airline Deregulation Act (ADA) in October 1978.[41] The ADA ended the CAB's route authority effective December 1980 and its fare authority effective January 1983. The act also abolished the CAB at the end of 1984 and transferred the CAB's remaining authority over antitrust and international matters to the Department of Transportation (DOT).

Deregulating the industry in 1979 proved to be unfortunate. In 1979 the Shah of Iran was overthrown, causing oil prices to increase to $34 a barrel, an all-time high. As a result, the price of jet fuel jumped from 40 cents to over 60 cents per gallon. High oil prices precipitated a severe worldwide recession that greatly reduced the demand for air travel.

Despite these economic problems, entry occurred after deregulation. Midway entered in 1979, New York Air in 1980, and People Express in 1981. Furthermore, several of the larger carriers, such as Pacific Southwest Airlines and Southwest Airlines, entered the interstate market. In addition, most of the major airlines expanded into new territories. The effect was an explosion of new competition.

The new carriers had significantly lower costs than the established airlines and were able to compete effectively based on lower fares. One major advantage for the new airlines was a non-unionized labor force. In 1985, for example, pilots for non-unionized People Express earned between $22,000 and $70,000, compared with an average of $90,000 at the unionized major airlines. The major carriers were also saddled with a large fleet of 747 and DC-10 jumbo jets, which could not be used efficiently on the more price-competitive middle- and short-distance routes. In addition, the entrants reduced maintenance costs by relying on one or two types of aircraft, and they squeezed more seats into their planes. Further cost reductions were achieved by reducing in-flight amenities. People Express even charged for soft drinks and snacks. Between 1976 and 1983, the ratio of flight attendants to passengers decreased by 16 percent. Under deregulation airline travel began to resemble bus travel, with low prices and low amenities.

The increase in competition and reduction in costs led to a sharp decline in fares in those large cities in which a new low-cost airline entered. Between 1975 and 1983, after adjusting for inflation, the average price per passenger-mile declined by 8.5 percent.[42] The major carriers left the smaller markets, and small-market fares tended to increase. The increase in small-market fares was expected because regulation had highly subsidized service to small cities. The overall fare reductions forced several large carriers into bankruptcy. Victims included Braniff and Continental. Continental took advantage of bankruptcy to destroy its unions, reduce costs, and reemerge as a low-cost, low-price carrier.

One of the most dramatic impacts of deregulation was the development of the hub-and-spoke system.[43] Under regulation, many passengers were forced to change airlines on medium or long trips. Under deregulation the airlines quickly learned that passengers preferred to stay with one carrier. By creating hubs and channeling passengers into and out of these hubs, the airlines could prevent most passengers from changing airlines. The hub-and-spoke system also reduced costs by allowing the airlines to rely on smaller, more efficient planes. Before long, all of the successful airlines were structured around a hub-and-spoke system. The system enabled several regional airlines, such as USAir and Piedmont, to expand into national carriers.

Deregulation has had many positive effects. Fares have declined, the number of flights has increased, productivity has improved, and capacity utilization has increased.[44] Problems, however, have appeared in recent years as concentration has increased. Recall from Chapter 10 that the major carriers were very aggressive in fighting entry and succeeded in eliminating most of the new firms from the market. Concentration also increased because the Department of Transportation (DOT) failed to prevent a number of anticompetitive mergers even after the Department of Justice (DOJ) opposed them. In 1986, for example, the TWA–Ozark and Northwest–Republic mergers were both opposed by the Department of Justice but were approved by the Department of Transportation. In just the three short years of 1985 to 1987, twenty mergers were approved. The Department of Transportation has consistently acted as though the airline industry is perfectly contestable, yet as we saw in Chapter 5, this is not the case.[45] As Alfred Kahn has noted:[46]

> . . . the reconcentration of the industry reflects in part the deplorable failure of the Department of Transportation to disallow even one merger, or, in all but one case, even to set conditions to mitigate potential anticompetitive consequences. The DOT seems to have no appreciation whatever of the dangers our antitrust laws were set up almost a century ago to forestall.

A good deal of empirical evidence indicates that increasing airline concentration is correlated with higher fares.[47] The cost of the DOT's failure to enforce the antitrust laws, therefore, has been substantial. Some of the gains from deregulation may be lost if the trend toward increasing concentration continues.

REGULATION OF TELECOMMUNICATIONS AND BROADCASTING

Telecommunications

The history of telecommunications began with the invention of the telephone by Alexander Graham Bell in 1876. Bell founded the American Telephone and Telegraph Company (AT&T) and aggressively attempted to monopolize the communications industry by driving out small local telephone companies.* AT&T refused to sell equipment to independent telephone companies, refused to connect independents to its long-distance lines, and used predatory pricing when necessary. By 1940 AT&T controlled more than 85 percent of the nation's telephones.

There was no federal regulation of the industry until the ICC was given limited authority to regulate telephone service in 1910. The ICC, however, did not control the growth of AT&T. Early in the century, state commissions were established, but they too were passive. The Communications Act of 1934 established the Federal Communications Commission (FCC) to regulate telephone service and radio broadcasting. The FCC studied the industry for four years, and in 1939 issued a report that put the Commission's seal of approval on the existing market structure. Over the next twenty years the FCC undertook few important regulatory actions regarding the telephone industry.

State commissions had no legal authority to regulate interstate commerce, and therefore, state commissions had no authority over long-distance interstate rates and tended to be passive. With a few exceptions, such as California and New York, states spent few resources on telephone regulation. The national Bell system, consisting of a series of regional monopolies that cut across state lines, greatly complicated the state commissions' tasks. Southwestern Bell Telephone, for example, provided service to five states with over 40 million telephones. The interstate composition of the regional Bell companies made it difficult for state commissions to separate intrastate from interstate costs, which made it virtually impossible to regulate effectively.

---

*There were actually three conflicting legal claims to invention of the telephone. After many years in court, in 1888 Bell finally won out over the claims of Elisha Gray and Daniel Drawbaugh by a 4–3 Supreme Court decision.

Early regulation served the interests of AT&T well. The FCC established long-distance rates based on data supplied and interpreted by AT&T. Long-distance rates declined, not because of effective FCC oversight, but because of technological advances and economies of scale. AT&T's profits were high, and it was secure in its monopoly position because the Commission prevented entry.

Under regulation, AT&T kept long-distance rates high to subsidize local service. This pricing policy made entry into long-distance service look particularly attractive. With the development of microwave technology in the 1940s, potential competitors filed with the FCC to enter the long-distance market. The FCC consistently refused to grant licenses to use the microwave radio band for long-distance telecommunications. After a three-year review, the FCC finally ruled in 1959 that it would permit limited private use of the microwave band.[48] The Commission, however, refused to authorize use of the microwave band by common carriers, and AT&T refused to allow private line users to interconnect with the AT&T system. To compete against the development of private microwave lines, AT&T slashed the price of its TELPAK business service, and the FCC found that AT&T's TELPAK rates were below cost.

In 1963, Microwave Communications Inc. (MCI) filed for common carrier status to build a microwave system for privately leased lines between Chicago and St. Louis. AT&T opposed the request and stated that it would refuse interconnection for the new system. AT&T argued that the proposal was a form of **cream-skimming**, which would allow MCI to steal AT&T's best corporate customers and lead to higher rates for AT&T's subsidized local customers. In 1969 the FCC approved MCI's request, and in 1971 the Commission expanded its ruling to approve interconnection with the AT&T system. AT&T, however, continued to fight interconnection.[49] It was not until 1976 that the FCC granted MCI unlimited interconnection privileges for its private lines.

MCI's legal battle did not end there. In 1975 MCI began to offer limited dial-up long-distance service. Once again AT&T argued this was cream-skimming that would harm local residential customers. This time the FCC agreed with AT&T and refused to permit MCI to offer dial-up service. MCI appealed the FCC ruling to the federal courts and in 1977 the Court of Appeals overturned the Commission.[50] In 1978 the Supreme Court refused to reconsider the Court of Appeals' decision, and discount long-distance dial-up service became available for many customers.[51] Long-distance rates between cities served by MCI declined dramatically. AT&T's monopoly over long-distance service had been broken by a series of FCC and court decisions, but the major industry changes were yet to come.

Recall from Chapter 18 that in 1974, the Justice Department filed an antitrust suit against AT&T. On January 8, 1982, AT&T signed a consent decree that permitted AT&T to keep Western Electric, Long Lines, and Bell Labs. AT&T's twenty-two local operating companies, however, had to be divested. Furthermore, AT&T was given permission to enter unregulated markets. This decree resulted in the largest divestiture in antitrust history, over $87 billion in assets.

The combined effect of the 1978 Supreme Court ruling in favor of MCI and the consent decree was a monumental change in market structure. In 1979 AT&T held a 96 percent share of long-distance revenues; by 1987 that share had declined to approximately 70 percent.[52] Rates declined dramatically as well. A 10-minute daytime call from New York to Chicago that cost $4.49 in December 1983 was only $2.23 in December 1988, and a 10-minute call from New York to Los Angeles declined from $5.15 to $2.32.[53] AT&T remained the dominant firm in terms of market share, but it was unable to use this dominance to raise long-distance rates. Furthermore, until 1989 continued regulation made it impossible for AT&T to cut rates in a predatory manner, allowing MCI and Sprint to gain footholds in the long-distance market.[54]

In 1989, the FCC replaced traditional rate of return regulation with **price cap** regulation.[55] Price cap regulation allows firms to raise prices a maximum amount based on the following formula:

$$\text{permitted price increase} = \text{increase in CPI} - X$$

In theory, price cap regulation provides an incentive for firms to improve efficiency because they must keep price increases below the increase in the Consumer Price Index (CPI). In the long-distance telecommunications industry, however, the price cap was essentially meaningless because AT&T wanted to *reduce* rates in response to lower costs and increased competition. The 1989 policy change, therefore, effectively deregulated long-distance rates.

The breakup of AT&T resulted in the creation of seven large regional telephone companies to replace the twenty-two AT&T local operating companies.* Local telephone rates have increased since the breakup of AT&T.[56] Three primary factors have combined to cause local rate increases. First, after divestiture the local companies could no longer use profits earned on long-distance service to subsidize losses on local service. Second, large users have been able to set up their own communications systems, bypassing the local companies entirely. Third, under regulation AT&T had used slow depreciation of its equipment, which left the operating companies greatly underdepreciated at the time of divestiture. After divestiture, the local companies pressed for accelerated depreciation, which increased their short-run costs. Immediately after divestiture, local rates increased dramatically, rising at an 8.7 percent annual rate.[57] In 1985, Pacific Bell requested a 94 percent increase in its basic monthly rate, and Bell of Pennsylvania requested a 66 percent increase.[58] Later in the decade, however, the rate of price increases slowed down considerably.[59]

Broadcasting

Regulation of broadcasting began shortly after the introduction of radio broadcasting in 1920. Because of the limited number of available wavelengths in the radio spectrum, without regulation the airwaves would have turned into a veritable Tower of Babel with stations crowding each other on the spectrum. The Radio Act of 1927 established the Federal Radio Commission to control access to the radio spectrum. With the passage of the Communications Act of 1934, the FCC took over the responsibilities of the Radio Commission. The FCC has had three

---

*The seven regional companies are NYNEX, Bell Atlantic, Bell South, Ameritech, Southwestern Bell, U.S. West, and Pacific Telesis.

primary responsibilities.: (1) allocating the radio spectrum in a way that maintains a clarity of signals; (2) controlling the ownership structure to achieve a diversity of opinions; and (3) ensuring that broadcasters keep the public informed. Although the FCC was passive in its regulation of telecommunications, it was aggressive in its regulation of the more glamorous broadcasting industry.

No company can operate an over-the-air broadcast station without a license from the FCC. Licenses are terminated automatically after five years, and broadcasters must apply for renewals. It is rare for a renewal request to be denied. The fundamental guideline used by the FCC to allocate licenses is that a licensee must operate for the "public interest, convenience and necessity." To say the least, this is a vague guideline.

The limited number of VHF television stations (channels 2 through 13) available created market power for those companies fortunate enough to obtain a VHF license. In 1975, the average pretax return on invested capital in a VHF television station was 67 percent, and in the largest cities it was generally above 100 percent.[60] In the 1950s and 1960s, the FCC protected VHF stations from competition with cable television by limiting cable service to rural areas that could not receive clear over-the-air television signals. When this FCC position became untenable in the late 1960s, the Commission added a series of restrictions on cable services. The FCC limited the number of stations a cable system could carry, required the provision of free public access channels for local government and educational use, and prevented entry into large cities.

With the national movement toward deregulation in the early 1980s, many restrictions on cable television were lifted. The cable industry, however, came under new regulation in 1984, when Congress passed the Cable Communications Act. The 1984 law gave local governments the power to license and control cable companies, which were viewed as natural monopolies. Although the Cable Communications Act of 1984 gave cable companies increased price flexibility, it continued to require cable systems to set aside stations for public and educational access.

To ensure a diversity of opinions in a free and open society, the FCC has ownership restrictions that limit the number of stations any one person or company can own. Until 1996 no one person or company could own more than twelve television stations, twelve AM radio stations, and twelve FM radio stations. Furthermore, the twelve television stations could not reach more than 25 percent of the national population, and no one company could own more than one station in the same market.

The Telecommunications Act of 1996

On February 8, 1996, President Clinton signed into law sweeping changes in the communications industry. The Telecommunication Act of 1996 dramatically reduced regulation in telecommunications, television and radio broadcasting, and cable television. Key provisions of the bill included:

1. Local telephone companies, long-distance telephone companies, and cable television companies were allowed to enter each other's markets.
2. Broadcasting ownership regulations were liberalized, permitting television companies to own over-the-air stations reaching up to 35 percent of national

viewers. The number of radio stations that could be controlled by one company was also increased, and the ban on ownership of a television station and cable company in the same market was lifted.

3. The bill phased in deregulation of cable television rates by 1999, and many rates were deregulated effective January 8, 1996.

4. Cable and telephone companies were forbidden from acquiring more than a 10 percent interest in each other's operations, except in small communities with a population below 35,000.

5. The bill made it illegal to transmit indecent materials (pornography) across the Internet. This section of the bill came under immediate First Amendment challenge in the courts and was declared unconstitutional.

6. The act expanded FCC jurisdiction to include satellite services.

7. Television manufacturers were required to install a "v-chip" in all new televisions larger than 13 inches. The v-chip allows parents to block out violent or sexually explicit programming. The television industry was required to develop a rating system within one year warning of violent and sexual content.

The bill should revolutionize telecommunications by blurring the distinctions between markets. AT&T, MCI, and Sprint are now free to enter local telephone markets, and the seven regional phone companies can supply long-distance services. On the day the bill was signed into law, the chair of AT&T announced that AT&T would offer local phone service nationally and would enter the television services industry.[61] The president of Bell Atlantic, one of the regional local monopolies, announced that Bell Atlantic would immediately offer long-distance service outside its market.[62] There was speculation that the act would result in a huge merger wave. Bell Atlantic, for example, indicated that it would attempt to merge with NYNEX. Cable companies indicated that they would enter local telephone markets by offering combined cable and telephone services.

Opponents of the bill predicted that it would result in higher telephone and cable rates because only limited competition would develop.[63] Consumer groups worried that without antitrust enforcement large mergers would consolidate the industry in the hands of a few large multimedia giants and result in the loss of tens of thousands of jobs.

As of this writing there is no way to know what the final impact of the 1996 Telecommunication Act will be, but the industry is certain to be changed forever. Given the history of telephone deregulation, one virtual certainty is that increased competition will speed up the rate of technological advance in all sectors.

Electricity

In 1935 Congress passed the Public Utility Act, establishing the Federal Power Commission (FPC) to regulate the interstate aspects of the electricity industry. The Department of Energy Organization Act of 1977 transferred authority over interstate electricity regulation to the Federal Energy Regulatory Commission (FERC).

Vertical integration is extremely important in the electricity industry. There are three vertical stages: generation, transmission, and distribution. Economies of scale are significant at the transmission and distribution stages, but less significant at the generation stage. Unlike the transportation and communications industries, there is a significant amount of government ownership in electricity. The federal government owns facilities that generate approximately 10 percent of all electricity. The Tennessee Valley Authority (TVA) is the most famous of the federal government's operations. State and local governments control approximately 10 percent of distribution services. Nebraska has a statewide distribution utility, and the tiny hamlet of Hamilton, New York, population 3,600, has a village electric utility.

Given current cost structures, there is little disagreement that the transmission and distribution sectors are still natural monopolies. The debate over deregulation is centered on the generation stage, in which economies of scale are much less significant. Generation typically has accounted for over 50 percent of total industry costs, so deregulation of generation would have a significant impact.[64] If vertical integration were dissolved, resulting in independent generation, transmission, and distribution companies, most regions could support multiple generation companies and a reasonable level of competition.[65]

Vertical disintegration and increased competition would likely result in lower industrial rates relative to residential rates because generating companies would compete for large commercial accounts. Deregulation also might result in entry by large, private bulk-power users. For deregulation to benefit residential consumers it would have to be accompanied by watchful antitrust policies aimed at preventing mergers that would increase regional concentration. Generating companies also would have to be guaranteed interconnection to transmission lines.

Natural Gas Industry

Vertical integration is also very important in the natural gas industry, in which there are also three vertical stages: production at the well-head, transportation through pipelines, and distribution. Although economies of scale are highly significant in transportation and distribution, they are insignificant at the production stage. Before 1938 the Federal Power Commission had no authority to regulate the price of natural gas, and the Supreme Court had ruled that state and local commissions could not set the price of interstate gas. In 1938 Congress passed the Natural Gas Act, which gave the FPC the power to set interstate pipeline rates but exempted producing and gathering operations at the well-head from regulation.

In 1954, in *Phillips Petroleum v. Wisconsin,* the Supreme Court ordered the FPC to begin to regulate the well-head price of natural gas.[66] Phillips was the largest nonintegrated gas producer in the county. When Phillips raised its rates to the state of Wisconsin, Wisconsin complained to the FPC. The Commission claimed it had no regulatory authority over gas prices, and Wisconsin then sued Phillips. The Supreme Court ruled that although the 1938 act had exempted producing and gathering operations, it had not exempted the subsequent sale of natural gas across state lines. The Supreme Court ordered the FPC to expand its authority into pricing at the well-head.

Initially the FPC attempted to regulate gas prices using traditional rate of return regulation, but because gas and oil are usually produced together (gas was actually a wasted by-product of oil production for decades), it was virtually impossible to separate the costs of gas production from the costs of oil production. Rate cases became hopelessly backlogged before the FPC. In desperation the Commission turned to setting regional well-head prices. The FPC divided the country into twenty-three producing areas and announced temporary price ceilings in each area. A distinction was made between gas produced from "old" wells and "new" wells. The price ceiling was higher on "new" gas to provide an incentive for exploration.

Regulation of the well-head price of natural gas never made economic sense, and this became abundantly clear with the onset of the energy crisis of 1973–74. As OPEC increased oil prices, regulation kept the price of natural gas artificially low. This resulted in an excess demand for natural gas as consumers rationally attempted to switch from expensive oil and electricity to artificially low-priced natural gas. Price controls also reduced the incentive for exploration.

In 1978 Congress passed the Natural Gas Policy Act. The act gradually deregulated the price of natural gas at the well-head. Price ceilings were removed from deep-well gas (wells more than 5000 feet deep) in November 1979 and from "new" gas in January 1985. "Old" gas remained under price control until July 1989. Today the well-head price of natural gas is unregulated.

SUMMARY

1. Direct regulation of business began in the United States in markets in which economies of scale were very significant, such as the railroads, electricity and natural gas, and telecommunications.

2. Many government commissions were established to control these industries. Often these commissions were captured by the firms they were meant to regulate.

3. Regulated industries attempted to suppress competition by convincing commissions to expand their regulatory authority into new markets such as trucking, airlines, and cable television.

4. Commissions were primarily concerned with ensuring that service was provided at reasonable rates and with few service interruptions.

5. Regulations centered on establishing a permitted rate of return, a price structure, and a rate base.

6. Effective regulation probably lowered prices, but also resulted in x-inefficiencies and the use of too much capital relative to other inputs.

7. In recent years there has been a movement away from direct regulation of business and toward the use of increased competition to improve economic efficiency.

8. New product technology has tended to create new competition for most regulated industries. Trucking and air travel destroyed the power of the railroads, microwave systems undermined AT&T's control of long-distance telephone service, and cable television weakened the power of over-the-air television stations.

9. More recently, rapid technological change is leading to competition among local telephone, long-distance telephone, and cable television companies in many markets.

10. Although regulation will continue to exist in the few remaining areas of natural monopoly, such as the transmission and local distribution of electricity and gas, the primary lesson from America's history of regulation is that, over time, it is technology and competition that move an economy forward.

11. Creative destruction is a more powerful force than any government policy aimed at protecting consumers from high prices or industries from competition.

KEY TERMS

Averch-Johnson effect

capture theory of regulation

cream-skimming

input expansion path

isocost lines

isoquants

natural monopoly

peak-load pricing

price cap

Ramsey price

rate base

Regulation Q

regulatory lag

DISCUSSION QUESTIONS

1. Describe the conditions that result in natural monopoly. What industries remain natural monopolies today? In the past 25 years has the number of natural monopolies in the United States increased or decreased? Why has this change occurred?

2. In what ways can rate of return regulation result in a nonoptimal use of capital? *Ceteris paribus,* would this distortion increase or decrease with an increase in the permitted rate of return r?

3. Under traditional rate of return regulation, would regulated firms prefer rapid rates of depreciation or slow rates of depreciation? Why?

4. Why do you believe that AT&T agreed to divest most of its assets? Do you think AT&T would have agreed to keep the local operating companies and divest the rest of its operations? Why or why not?

5. When cable television was first introduced, the over-the-air broadcasting industry welcomed the innovation; however, recently the broadcasting industry has opposed deregulation of the cable television industry. Why do you think the industry's position changed?

6. What were the historical similarities and differences in the origins of regulation in the railroads and trucking? In which industry was the economic rationale for regulation greater?

7. Entry restrictions were very important in the regulatory history of the trucking and airline industries, but much less important in the railroad industry. Why?

8. Has deregulation of the airline industry been a *complete* success?

9. What problems were caused by the continued regulation of the price of natural gas during the energy crisis of the early 1970s?

PROBLEMS

1. Consider a regulated natural monopoly with the following demand and cost conditions:

$$\text{Demand: } P = 100 - Q$$

$$\text{Total Costs: } TC = 1800 + 10Q$$

$$AC = \frac{TC}{Q} = \frac{1800}{Q} + \frac{10Q}{Q} = \frac{1800}{Q} + 10$$

$$MC = 10$$

a. If a regulatory commission sets the price at the Ramsey price at which P = AC, what would be the regulated price? Show this result on a graph. [*Hint:* Set AC equal to demand and find the two roots of the quadratic equation. The AC curve "cuts" the demand curve at two outputs, but the Ramsey price is set at the larger quantity.]

b. What is consumer surplus plus profit at the Ramsey price? Show this on your graph.

c. If price were set at marginal cost, what would be the industry output? What would be the value of consumer surplus plus industry profits? Show these areas on your graph.

d. Which price results in greater economic welfare (that is, the sum of consumer surplus plus economic profit)? What area on your graph represents the change in welfare? Explain.

2. Consider the same regulated natural monopoly from question 1 with the following demand and cost conditions:

$$\text{Demand: } P = 100 - Q$$

$$\text{Total Costs: } TC = 1800 + 10Q$$

$$AC = \frac{TC}{Q} = \frac{1800}{Q} + \frac{10Q}{Q} = \frac{1800}{Q} + 10$$

$$MC = 10$$

Suppose a regulatory commission established the following price structure: The first 60 units are sold at a price of 40, and the next 30 units are sold at a price of 10.

   a. Is this price structure allocatively efficient?

   b. What are the profits earned by the regulated firm?

3. Suppose a regulated utility faces the following demand curves:

$$\text{Demand Off-Peak: } P = 50 - Q$$

$$\text{Demand Peak: } P = 110 - Q$$

Marginal costs are:

$$MC = 20 + \frac{1}{2}Q$$

   a. What are the socially optimal peak and off-peak prices?

   b. Suppose the regulatory commission sets $P = 30$ during both peak and off-peak periods. What is the social cost of such a pricing policy?

   c. Suppose the regulatory commission sets $P = 40$ during both peak and off-peak periods. What is the social cost of such a pricing policy?

REFERENCES

1. For historical background see I.L. Sharfman, *The Interstate Commerce Commission, A Study in Administrative Law and Procedure,* (New York: The Commonwealth Fund, 1931–1937); Gabriel Kolko, *Railroads and Regulation, 1877–1916,* (Princeton: Princeton University Press, 1965); Alfred E. Kahn, *The Economics of Regulation: Principles and Institutions,* (Cambridge, MA: MIT Press, 1988), particularly, vol. II, pp. 26–8. For related background on the passage of the Sherman Act in 1890 see H.B. Thorelli, *The Federal Antitrust Policy: Organization of an American Tradition* (Baltimore: Johns Hopkins Press, 1955); J.D. Clark, *The Federal Trust Policy* (Baltimore: Johns Hopkins Press, 1931); A.H. Walker, *History of the Sherman Law* (New York: Equity Press, 1910); A.D. Neale and D.G. Goyder, *The Antitrust Laws of the U.S.A.* (Cambridge, U.K.: Cambridge University Press, 1980).

2. *Munn v. Illinois,* 94 US 113 (1877).

3. Walter J. Primeaux, "An Assessment of X-Efficiency Gained Through Competition," *Review of Economics and Statistics* 59 (February 1977): 105–8; and Rodney E. Stevenson, "X-Efficiency and Interfirm Rivalry: Evidence in the Electric Utility Industry," *Land Economics* 58 (February 1982): 52–66.

4. Harvey Averch and Leland L. Johnson, "Behavior of the Firm Under Regulatory Constraint," *American Economic Review* (December 1962): 1052–69. Stanislaw Wellisz is often given credit for simultaneously presenting the same theory; see Stanislaw H. Wellisz, "Regulation of Natural Gas Pipeline Companies: An Economic Analysis," *Journal of Political Economy* (February 1963): 30–43.

5. The following list is adapted from Alfred E. Kahn, *The Economics of Regulation: Principles and Institutions* (Cambridge, MA: MIT Press, 1988), vol. II, pp. 50–4. The empirical evidence has been mixed; see Leland L. Johnson, "The Averch-Johnson Hypothesis after Ten Years," in William G. Shepherd and Thomas G. Gies (eds.), *Regulation in Further Perspective* (Cambridge, MA: Ballinger Publishing Co., 1974), pp. 67–78. For evidence suggesting that the Averch-Johnson effect does not exist, see Charles W. Smithson, "The Degree of Regulation and the Monopoly Firm: Further Empirical Evidence," *Southern Economic Journal* 44 (1978): 568–80; David P. Baron and Robert A. Taggart Jr., "A Model of Regulation Under Uncertainty and a Test of Regulatory Bias," *The Bell Journal of Economics* 8

(1977): 151–67; and W.J. Boyes, "An Empirical Examination of the Averch-Johnson Effect," *Economic Inquiry* (March 1976).

6. William G. Shepherd and Thomas G. Gies, *Utility Regulation: New Directions in Theory and Practice* (New York: Random House, 1966), p. 265; William G. Shepherd, "Marginal-Cost Pricing in American Utilities," *Southern Economic Journal* 33 (July 1966): 61–4; Ralph K. Davidson, *Price Discrimination in Selling Gas and Electricity* (Baltimore: Johns Hopkins Press, 1955), pp. 150–1; and Stanislaw H. Wellisz, "Regulation of Natural Gas Pipeline Companies: An Economic Analysis," *Journal of Political Economy* 71 (February 1963): 30–43.

7. Harold H. Wein, "Fair Rate of Return and Incentives—Some General Considerations," in Harry M. Trebing (ed.), *Performance Under Regulation* (East Lansing, MI: Michigan State University Press, 1968), pp. 42–53.

8. Alfred E. Kahn, *The Economics of Regulation: Principles and Institutions,* (Cambridge, MA: MIT Press, 1988), vol. II, pp. 50–1.

9. Merton J. Peck, "The Single-Entity Proposal for International Communications," *American Economic Review* 60 (May 1970): 199–201.

10. Kahn, *op cit.,* vol. II, p. 51.

11. Kahn, *op cit.,* vol. II, pp. 51–2.

12. "Utilities' Embrace of Nuclear Fuel Stalled by Its Classification as a Current Asset," *Wall Street Journal* (November 12, 1968): 4.

13. Kahn, *op cit.,* vol. II, p. 53.

14. Kahn, *op cit.,* vol. II, pp. 53–4.

15. 70 *Public Utilities Reports* (3rd series), 129, 143 (November 1967).

16. J.O. Light and William L. White, *The Financial System* (Homewood, IL: Irwin, 1979), p. 268.

17. Kahn, *op cit.,* vol. II, p. 107.

18. See Elizabeth E. Bailey, *Economic Theory of Regulatory Constraint* (Lexington, MA: Heath, 1973), Chapter 5; Richard J. Gilbert and David M. Newbery, "Regulatory Games," Department of Economics Working Paper no. 8879, Berkeley: University of California, Berkeley; and W. Davis Dechert, "Has the Averch-Johnson Effect been Theoretically Justified?" *Journal of Economic Dynamics and Control* 8 (1984): 1–17.

19. Gilbert and Newbery, *op cit.*

20. Smithson found no evidence of a tendency for regulated firms to invest in too much or too little capital; see Charles W. Smithson, "The Degree of Regulation and the Monopoly Firm: Further Empirical Evidence," *Southern Economic Journal* 44 (1978): 568–80. Baron and Taggart found

evidence of undercapitalization; see David P. Baron and Robert A. Taggart Jr., "A Model of Regulation Under Uncertainty and a Test of Regulatory Bias," *The Bell Journal of Economics* 8 (1977): 151–67.

21. Sanford Berg (ed.), *Innovative Electric Rates* (Lexington, MA: Lexington Books, 1983).

22. Berg, *ibid,* p. 305.

23. George Stigler, "The Theory of Economic Regulation," *Bell Journal of Economics and Management Science* 2 (Spring 1971): 3-21. Not all economists have accepted this theory. See Clifford Nowell and John Tschirhart, "Testing Theories of Regulatory Behavior," *Review of Industrial Organization* 8 (December 1993): 653–68.

24. Sam Peltzman, "Toward a More General Theory of Regulation," *Journal of Law and Economics* 19 (August 1976): 211–40.

25. This example is derived from Bruce Ingersoll, "Peanut Quota System Comes Under Attack for Distorting Market," *Wall Street Journal* (May 1, 1990).

26. William G. Shepherd, *Public Policies Toward Business* (Homewood, IL: Irwin, 1991), pp. 427–8; and Lawrence Shephard, "Licensing Restrictions and the Cost of Dental Care," *Journal of Law and Economics* 21 (April 1971): 187-202.

27. AT&T consistently fought deregulation; see *Allocation of Microwave Frequencies Above 890 Mc.,* 27 FCC 359 (1959); *In the Matter of Microwave Communications Inc.,* 18 FCC 953 (1969); and *United States Independent Telephone Association v. MCI Telecommunications Corporation et al.; American Telephone and Telegraph Company v. MCI Telecommunications Corporation et al.;* and *Federal Communication Commission v. MCI Telecommunications Corporation et al.,* 580 F2d 590 (1977). With regard to the airlines, see Pablo T. Spiller, "The Differential Impact of Airline Regulation on Individual Firms and Markets: An Empirical Analysis," *Journal of Law and Economics* 26 (1983): 655-89; and Daniel P. Kaplan, "The Changing Airline Industry," in L. W. Weiss and M. W. Klass, *Regulatory Reform: What Actually Happened* (Boston: Little, Brown, 1986), p. 45.

28. William G. Shepherd and Clair Wilcox, *Public Policies Toward Business* (Homewood, IL: Irwin, 1979), p. 377.

29. Theodore E. Keeler, *Railroads, Freight, and Public Policy* (Washington, D.C.: Brookings Institution, 1983), pp. 105–7.

30. Thomas Gale Moore, "Rail and Trucking Deregulation," in Leonard W. Weiss and Michael W. Klass, *Regulatory Reform: What Actually Happened* (Little, Brown, 1986), p. 25.

31. Moore, *ibid.,* p. 32.

32. Kenneth Labich, "Blessings by the Truck-load," *Fortune* (November 11, 1985): 138.

33. For an argument that these gains will be maintained in the long run see James N. Giordano, "Deregulation Without Apology: A Truncated Survivor Analysis of Long-Run Efficiency Gains in the U.S. Trucking Industry," *Review of Industrial Organization* 10 (October 1995): 635–50.

34. W. Kip Viscusi, John M. Vernon, and Joseph E. Harrington, Jr., *Economics of Regulation and Antitrust* (Lexington, MA: Heath, 1992), pp. 526–7.

35. Kaplan, *supra* note 27, p. 41.

36. Kaplan, *ibid.*

37. Kaplan, *ibid.,* p. 42.

38. T.E. Keeler, "Airline Regulation and Market Performance," *Bell Journal of Economics* 3 (Autumn 1972): 399–424; Simat, Helliesen and Eichner, Inc., "The Intrastate Air Regulation Experience in Texas and California," in Paul W. MacAvoy and John W. Snow (eds.), *Regulation of Passenger Fares and Competition Among the Airlines* (Washington: American Enterprise Institute for Public Policy Research, 1977); and *Civil Aeronautics Board Practices and Procedures,* Report of the Subcommittee on Administrative Practice and Procedure, U.S. Senate, 1975, p. 41.

39. Kaplan, *op cit.,* p.43.

40. Alfred E. Kahn, "Surprises of Airline Deregulation," *American Economic Review* (May 1988): 316–22; and Alfred E. Kahn, "Airline Deregulation—A Mixed Bag, but a Clear Success Nevertheless," *Transportation Law Journal* 16 (1988): 229–52; William G. Shepherd, "The Airline Industry," in Walter Adams, ed., *The Structure of American Industry* (New York: Macmillan, 1990), p. 219.

41. Kaplan, *op cit.,* p. 45.

42. Thomas G. Moore, "U.S. Airline Deregulation," *Journal of Law & Economics* (April 1986): 1-28.

43. For a theoretical justification of the hub-and-spoke system as a solution to an optimization problem see Ken Hendricks, Michele Piccione, and Guofu Tan, "The Economics of Hubs: The Case of Monopoly," *Review of Economic Studies* 62 (January 1995): 83-99. The effects of the hub-and-spoke system are analyzed in Robert A. Sinclair, "An Empirical Model of Entry and Exit in Airline Markets," *Review of Industrial Organization* 10 (October 1995): 541–57; and Jan K. Brueckner and Pablo T. Spiller, "Competition and Mergers in Airline Networks," *International Journal of Industrial Organization* 9 (September 1991): 323–42.

44. Alfred E. Kahn, "Surprises of Airline Deregulation," *American Economic Review* (May 1988): 316–22; Alfred E. Kahn, "Airline Deregulation—A Mixed Bag, but a Clear Success Nevertheless," *Transportation Law Journal* 16 (1988): 229–52; John R. Meyer and Clinton V. Oster, Jr., *Deregulation and the Future of Intercity Passenger Travel.* (Cambridge, MA: MIT Press, 1987); Steven Morrison and Clifford Winston, *The Evolution of the Airline Industry,* (Washington, D.C.: Brookings Institution, 1994); Douglas W. Caves, Laurtis R. Christensen, Michael W. Tretheway, and Robert J. Windle, "An Assessment of the Efficiency Effects of U.S. Airline Deregulation via an International Comparison," in Elizabeth E. Bailey (ed.), *Public Regulation: New Perspectives on Institutions and Policies* (Cambridge, MA: MIT Press, 1987); and Thomas Gale Moore, "U.S. Airline Deregulation: Its Effects on Passengers, Capital, and Labor," *Journal of Law and Economics* 29 (April 1986): 1-28.

45. See also Amy D. Abramowitz and Stephen M. Brown, "Market Share and Price Determination in the Contemporary Airline Industry," *Review of Industrial Organization* 8 (August 1993): 419–33; and Andrew S. Joskow, Gregory J. Werden, and Richard L. Johnson, "Entry, Exit, and Performance in Airline Markets," *International Journal of Industrial Organization* 12 (December 1994): 457–71.

46. Alfred E. Kahn, "I Would Do It Again," *Regulation* 2 (1988): 22–8.

47. See E. Han Kim, and Vijay Singal, "Mergers and Market Power: Evidence from the Airline Industry," *American Economic Review* 83 (June 1993): 549–69; Thomas G. Moore, "U.S. Airline Deregulation," *Journal of Law and Economics* (April 1986): 1-28; and Gloria J. Hurdle, Richard L. Johnson, Andrew S. Joskow, Gregory J. Werden, and Michael A. Williams, "Concentration, Potential Entry, and Performance in the Airline Industry," *Journal of Industrial Economics* (December 1989): 135. See also Severin Borenstein, "Hubs and High Fares: Dominance and Market Power in the U.S. Airline Industry," *Rand Journal of Economics* (Autumn 1989): 344–65; and E.E. Bailey, D.R. Graham, and D.P. Kaplan, *Deregulating the Airlines* (Cambridge, MA: MIT Press, 1985), pp. 169–71.

48. *Allocation of Microwave Frequencies Above 890 Mc.,* 27 FCC 359 (1959).

49. *In the Matter of Microwave Communications Inc.,* 18 FCC 953 (1969).

50. *United States Independent Telephone Association v. MCI Telecommunications Corporation et al.; American Telephone and Telegraph Company v. MCI Telecommunications Corporation et al.;* and *Federal Communication Commission v. MCI Telecommunications Corporation et al.,* 580 F2d 590 (1977).

51. *United States Independent Telephone Association v. MCI Telecommunications Corporation et al.; American Telephone and Telegraph Company v. MCI Telecommunications Corporation et al.;* and *Federal Communication Commission v. MCI Telecommunications Corporation et al., Certiorari* denied 439 US 980 (1978).

52. See Michael E. Porter, "Competition in the Long Distance Telecommunications Market: An Industry Structure Analysis" (Cambridge, MA: Monitor, October, 1987); and Leonard Waverman, "U.S. Interexchange Competition," in Robert W. Crandall and Kenneth Flamm (eds.), *Changing the Rules* (Washington, D.C.: Brookings Institution, 1989).

53. "Cheers, Jeers Still Ringing," *USA Today* (December 30, 1988).

54. Yu Hsing and Franklin G. Mixon, Jr., "Price Convergence in Contestable Market Structures: The Impact of Time and Price-Caps on Intercity Telecommunications Rates," *International Journal of Industrial Organization* 9 (December 1994): 813–22.

55. For a discussion of alternatives to traditional rate of return regulation see David M. Sappington, "Designing Incentive Regulation," *Review of Industrial Organization* 9 (June 1994): 245–72.

56. Fuhr found that although local rates have increased since divestiture, there was no evidence that rural rates had increased more rapidly than the average of all residential rates. Joseph P. Fuhr, Jr., "Rural Telephony Since Divestiture," *Review of Industrial Organization* 6 (1991): 89–95.

57. Manley R. Irwin, "The Telecommunications Industry," in Walter Adams (ed.), *The Structure of American Industry* (New York: Macmillan, 1990), p. 257.

58. Douglas F. Greer, *Business, Government, and Society* (New York: Macmillan, 1987), p. 328.

59. Irwin, *op cit.,* p. 257.

60. R.H. Coase, "Payola in Radio and Television Broadcasting," *Journal of Law and Economics* (October 1979): 269–328.

61. "Communications Bill Signed and the Battles Begin Anew," *New York Times* (January 9, 1996): 1.

62. *Ibid.,* p. D16.

63. "Static Erupts as Law Is Signed," *Syracuse Post-Standard* (February 9, 1996): B-6.

64. Leonard W. Weiss, *Case Studies in American Industry* (New York: John Wiley & Sons, 1980), p.92

65. Leonard W. Weiss, "Antitrust in the Electric Power Industry," in A. Phillips (ed.), *Promoting Competition in Regulated Markets* (Washington, D.C.: Brookings Institution, 1975), pp. 135–73; Paul L. Joskow and Richard Schmalensee, *Markets for Power* (Cambridge, MA: MIT Press, 1983).

66. *Phillips Petroleum Company v. Wisconsin et al.,* 342 US 672 (1954).

Glossary

abbreviated rule of reason: A limited form of the Rule of Reason which "applies in cases where *per se* condemnation is inappropriate, but where 'no elaborate industry analysis is required to demonstrate the anticompetitive character' of an inherently suspect restraint."

absolute cost advantage: A cost advantage one firm has over another firm that results in one firm producing any given level of output at a lower average cost.

accounting costs: The costs reported by firms in their financial reports following various bookkeeping conventions. For some inputs, particularly capital and labor, accounting costs and economic costs typically differ considerably, creating problems for the measurement of economic profits.

advertising response function: A function $Q = f(A)$, where Q is sales and A is the number of advertising messages. For a typical entrant, the advertising response function is first horizontal, then rises at an increasing rate, then rises at a decreasing rate, and finally decreases.

aggregate concentration: A measure of the role played by large companies in the economy as a whole, commonly measured by the percentage of total assets controlled by the largest 50, 100, or 200 firms in an economy.

allocative efficiency: A state in which the marginal benefit of producing another unit of output is equal to its marginal cost. If this condition is satisfied, the socially optimal quantity of the good is being produced, meaning that there is no way to reallocate resources to make one consumer or firm better off without hurting another.

applied research: Research aimed at obtaining knowledge with the objective of using that knowledge for commercial purposes. A chemist working on an AIDS vaccine in a pharmaceutical company's laboratory is doing applied research.

appropriability: The ability of a firm to maintain exclusive control over its technology without seeing that technology lost to competitors.

Areeda and Turner doctrine: An argument advanced by Professors Areeda and Turner suggesting that only prices below marginal cost should be considered predatory. Furthermore, because marginal costs are difficult to calculate, average variable cost should be used as a proxy for marginal cost.

asset specificity: The degree to which some assets are of value primarily to one firm. Asset specificity can arise due to geographic location, physical characteristics, or specialized human capital.

average cost: Total cost divided by the level of output.

average fixed cost: Fixed cost divided by the level of output.

average variable cost: Variable cost divided by the level of output.

Averch-Johnson effect: A theory suggesting that if a public utility is permitted to earn a rate of return greater than the market cost of capital, the utility will utilize too much capital relative to other inputs and therefore produce inefficiently from a social standpoint.

avoidable cost: The sum of variable cost and the recoverable part of fixed cost. Avoidable costs are those that the firm will not have to pay if it produces zero output in the short run.

barometric price leadership: A form of price leadership in which price changes are initiated by a relatively small firm with no ability to enforce them.

basic research: Research aimed at gaining knowledge for its own sake. For example, a research scientist at a major university working on quantum physics is engaged in basic research.

basing point pricing system: A delivered price system under which one or more geographic locations are established as basing points, and buyers are charged prices that include standard freight charges from the nearest basing point, even if the seller's manufacturing plant is located far from the basing point.

Bertrand model: A model developed by Joseph Bertrand in 1883 that criticized Cournot's result by showing that if firms assumed that all other firms hold their prices constant, Cournot's logic results in an entirely different outcome with price equal to marginal cost.

bilateral monopoly: A vertically integrated industry in which there is an independent monopolistic producer in both the downstream and upstream markets.

black list: A list of firms that a firm(s) with market power refuses to buy from or sell to.

bounded rationality: Limits on knowledge based on limited ability of individuals to solve complex problems and envision and understand all future possibilities due to constraints on knowledge, foresight, skill, and time.

capture theory of regulation: A theory that regulated firms gain control over the regulatory commissions that are supposed to be their regulators. According to the capture theory, once an industry is regulated, the commission comes to view its primary responsibility as protecting the regulated firms from "too much" competition, rather than protecting consumers from monopoly prices.

Celler-Kefauver Act: A 1950 law that amended Section 7 of the Clayton Act to include mergers through asset as well as stock acquisition. The Celler-Kefauver Act also extended Section 7 to reach vertical and conglomerate, as well as horizontal, mergers.

certain information: If a game includes nature, but nature never moves after any other player moves, then the game is said to be of certain information.

chain-store paradox: The paradox that in a repeated prisoner's dilemma game of any number of finite rounds with perfect, complete, certain, and symmetric information, firms defect in every round.

Chicago School of economics: A school of industrial organization economists who believe that price theory models should be the primary tool for analyzing markets. Followers of the Chicago School rely heavily on price theory models to make predictions about expected conduct and performance and to analyze economic welfare.

Clayton Act: A 1914 law aimed at preventing certain specific types of anti-competitive business conduct, such as price discrimination, tying agreements, exclusive dealing arrangements, mergers reducing competition, and interlocking directorates.

collusive price leadership: A form of price leadership in which a few large firms in an oligopoly lead price changes and expect that all price changes will be followed by competitors.

complete information: If a game includes nature, but nature does not move first, or nature's first move is observed by all players, the game is of complete information.

concentration ratio: The cumulative share of the K largest firms in the market, where typical values of K are 4, 8, and 20. Thus, the four-firm concentration ratio (CR4) is the sum of the market shares of the largest four firms in the industry. The most common measure of market size is sales, but concentration ratios can also be calculated using other measures of size, such as value added, employment, or assets.

conglomerate mergers: Mergers involving companies that operate in either different product markets or the same product market but different geographic markets.

conscious parallelism: An antitrust law term meaning that a group of oligopolists behave in an identical manner, but there is a lack of proof that the firms ever met to agree on this parallel course of behavior. Conscious parallelism refers to the idea that rational business behavior in a tight oligopoly will lead firms to behave identically with regard to price and other business practices.

consumer surplus: The difference between the maximum amount a consumer is willing to pay for a good and the amount he or she actually pays. Adding consumer surplus over many individuals gives a measure of the aggregate benefit consumers receive from buying a good.

contestable market: A theory developed in the early 1980s which states that potential competition may be more important than actual competition. According to this theory, even a monopolized market may perform as though it were competitive if there is sufficient potential competition.

convenience goods: Consumer goods that are relatively inexpensive items and are purchased on a regular basis, such as soft drinks, cigarettes, and gasoline.

correlation coefficient: A commonly used statistical measure of the strength of the relationship between two variables. The correlation coefficient ranges from 1 to -1. If the coefficient equals 1, a perfect linear relationship exists between the two variables. A correlation coefficient equal to -1 also indicates a perfect linear relationship; in this case the relationship is inverse. If the coefficient equals zero, there is no relationship between the variables.

Cournot-Nash Model: A quantity-based model of oligopoly behavior. In the Cournot model, firms assume that the output of all other firms in the industry will remain constant.

cream-skimming: The practice wherein unregulated firms reduce rates to attract the best customers from regulated firms.

creative destruction: The theory of Joseph Schumpeter that capitalism moves forward in major technological leaps that destroy the old economic order and create a new order.

credible threat: A strategy to deter entry that appears rational from the standpoint of the potential entrant.

cross-licensing agreement: A patent licensing agreement in which one or more firms agree to license their patents to each other.

cross-subsidization: The practice of conglomerate firms attempting to gain an increased market share in one market by using profits earned in another market to subsidize short-run losses.

deadweight loss: Losses of consumer and producer surplus that are not transferred to other parties. Deadweight loss is a measure of the misallocation of resources resulting from problems such as imperfect competition or taxation.

dependent variable: The variable whose values are predicted in a regression equation; the left-hand side variable.

depreciation: A measure of the decrease in economic value that occurs during a period when an asset, such as a machine, is in use.

diffusion: The stage of technological advance in which a technological innovation comes into common use.

direct foreign investment: Investment in productive assets by a domestic firm in a foreign country.

discount rate: The rate at which an individual or firm is willing to trade future income for current income. For example, if an individual's discount rate is 10 percent, the individual is willing to trade $1.10 of future income for $1.00 of current income.

discounting: The process of evaluating future dollars as being worth less than their face value today. For example, because X dollars invested today at an interest rate i would increase in value to $X (1 + i)$ dollars in one year, $X (1 + i) (1 + i) = X (1 + i)^2$ in two years, and $X (1 + i)^t$ in t years, the promise to pay X dollars t years from today has a discounted present value of:

$$\text{discounted present value} = \frac{X}{(1 + i)^t}$$

diseconomies of scale: Also called *decreasing returns to scale*. A production function exhibits diseconomies of scale if a proportionate increase in all inputs results in a less than proportionate increase in output. In this case, with constant per-unit input prices, long-run average costs increase as the quantity of output produced increases.

dominant firm price leadership model: A model assuming an industry with one dominant firm and a group of fringe firms, in which the dominant firm maximizes profits subject to the constraint imposed by the fringe firms' output.

dominant strategy: In game theory, a strategy that outperforms any other strategy no matter what strategy an opponent selects.

dominated strategy: In game theory, a strategy that is always worse than some other strategy.

Dorfman-Steiner model: One of the earliest formal models of the relationship between market structure and advertising. The model suggests that the advertising to sales ratio in an industry is directly related to the price-cost margin and inversely related to the price elasticity of demand.

double marginalization: A problem that exists with bilateral monopoly in a vertically structured industry, in which each successive vertical stage of monopoly causes a greater price distortion compared with a vertically integrated firm.

downstream: In a vertically structured industry, a later stage of production.

dynamic games: Games that are sequential, in which Firm 1 moves, then Firm 2 responds, then Firm 1 responds to Firm 2's response, and so on, and so on . . .

dynamic performance: How an industry performs over time, with an emphasis on whether or not the rate of technological advance is optimal.

economic cost: The payment required to keep a resource in its present employment. Economic cost is closely related to *opportunity cost.*

economic forbearance: An argument against conglomerate mergers between the nation's leading firms, based on the theory that no conglomerate firm will rock the boat in any market because it fears retaliation in another market. For instance, suppose General Motors purchased IBM, and Ford bought Compaq Computers. Ford might discourage Compaq from competing too aggressively against IBM for fear of retaliation by General Motors in the automobile market.

economies of scale: Also called *increasing returns to scale.* A production function exhibits economies of scale if a proportionate increase in all inputs results in a more than proportionate increase in output. In this case, with constant per-unit input prices, long-run average costs decrease as the quantity of output produced increases.

economies of scope: A production function exhibits economies of scope if it is less costly for one firm to perform two activities than it is for two firms to perform the activities separately.

efficiency in production: A cost condition in which firms are producing output at the lowest possible average cost.

engineering studies: An approach to estimate economies of scale in production by using interviews, questionnaires, and surveys to gather information from engineers who are responsible for designing and planning new plants.

entry barriers: Any factor that prevents long-run entry into a market.

event studies: Statistical studies that examine the impact of a proposed merger on the stock market valuation of the acquired or acquiring firm around the time of the merger.

excess capacity: An industry with more capacity than is required to meet industry demand.

excess return on sales: The ratio of economic profits to sales revenue. Assuming that firms are in long-run equilibrium and operating in the range of their production functions with constant returns to scale, the excess profit rate on sales $\left(\frac{TR - TC}{TR}\right)$ will, on average, across all products produced by the firm, equal the Lerner index.

exclusive dealing arrangements: An agreement in which a retailer agrees to carry only one manufacturer's products.

exit barriers: Any cost that a firm must incur to leave an industry.

experience goods: Goods whose qualities can be identified only through trial after buying the good. Common examples include consumer nondurable convenience goods such as beer, toothpaste, soap, toiletries, and cereal; and consumer durable goods including such household appliances as refrigerators and washing machines.

explanatory variable: Also called an *independent variable;* a right-hand side variable in a regression equation. The values of an explanatory variable are known and are used to predict the value of the *dependent variable.*

explicit collusion: Collusion in which a group of competitors discuss and set prices and/or quantities. The term is synonymous with *overt collusion.*

extensive form of a game: The game tree representation of a dynamic game.

failing firm: A firm on the verge of bankruptcy.

fair trade laws: A euphemistic term referring to laws that permit the use of resale price maintenance.

fast-second innovator: A dominant firm that responds quickly to the technological advances of small competitors.

Federal Trade Commission (FTC): The regulatory commission established by the Federal Trade Commission Act of 1914. The FTC is charged with regulating firms to prevent "unfair methods of competition."

Federal Trade Commission Act: A 1914 law that established the Federal Trade Commission (FTC) as an independent antitrust agency to prevent "unfair methods of competition."

first-degree price discrimination: Price discrimination where each consumer pays his or her reservation price for the good. Often called *perfect discrimination.*

first-mover advantage: An advantage accruing to the first firm to enter an industry that later entrants have great difficulty overcoming. A common example is the product differentiation advantage associated with being the first firm to enter a consumer good industry.

fixed costs: The costs of those inputs, such as land, buildings, and equipment, whose level of usage cannot be changed in the short run. Fixed costs do not vary with the level of output but are the same regardless of whether the firm produces a large or small amount of output.

Folk theorem: A theorem that was part of the oral tradition among game theorists long before it was published. The *grim strategy* is an example.

followship demand curve: A firm's demand curve drawn on the assumption that all firms in an industry charge the same price.

foreclosure: In a vertically structured industry, a situation in which downstream firms have difficulty obtaining inputs or upstream firms have difficulty finding buyers.

franchise fee: A fixed fee charged by a manufacturer for the right to sell its product.

free-rider problem: A situation in which either consumers consume a good but other consumers pay for the good or a group of sellers use the services provided by another group of sellers without paying for the services. For example, low-priced dealers obtain a free ride on the services provided by high-priced dealers.

gains from trade: The welfare increase in a domestic country associated with a change from a restrictive trade policy to a free trade policy. There are always gains from trade in competitive markets.

game theory: The study of how interdependent decision makers make choices. A game must include players, actions, information, strategies, payoffs, outcomes, and equilibria.

game tree: A diagram that represents a dynamic game as a sequence of possible moves. The game tree representation of a game is also known as the *extensive form* of the game.

geographic extension mergers: A conglomerate merger between companies that produce the same product in different locations. For example, a midwestern beer producer purchases a northeastern beer producer.

grim strategy: A firm's strategy in an infinitely repeated game played with the following behavioral rules: start by cooperating and charging the collusive price; continue to charge the collusive price unless a competitor lowers price, in which case, you charge the Bertrand equilibrium price, $P = MC$, forever. See also *trigger price strategy*.

group boycotts: An agreement among a group of firms with market power to refuse to deal with firms on a *black list* or to deal only with firms on a *white list*.

Hart-Scott-Rodino Act: A 1976 law amending Section 7 of the Clayton Act by requiring advanced notification to the Justice Department and the Federal Trade Commission of any major merger.

Herfindahl-Hirshman Index (HHI): An index of market power that takes into account both the number of firms and the inequality of market shares. The HHI is defined as the sum of the squares of individual firms' market shares, expressed mathematically as:

$$HHI = S_1^2 + S_2^2 + S_3^2 + \ldots + S_K^2 = \sum_{i=1}^{K} S_i^2$$

where S_i is the market share of the ith firm and K is the number of firms in the industry.

horizontal mergers: A merger involving firms that are direct competitors. The firms must compete in both the same product and geographic markets.

horizontal product differentiation: Differentiation between brands based on different product characteristics but not on different overall quality. For example, a McDonald's Quarter Pounder is somewhat different from a Burger King Whopper or a Wendy's Single, but the overall quality of the three burgers is similar.

incipiency precedent: A legal antitrust precedent that horizontal mergers should be banned even in competitive markets to prevent future increases in concentration.

independent variable: Also called an *explanatory variable*; a right-hand side variable in a regression equation. The values of an independent variable are known and are used to predict the value of the *dependent variable*.

industrial policy: The policy of restricting free trade through tariffs and quotas in an attempt to increase domestic welfare.

infinite game: A static game that is repeated an infinite number of times.

informational advertising: Advertising that provides consumers with truthful information about price, location, or quality.

injunction: A court order preventing a person or firm from carrying out a given activity or ordering a given activity to be undertaken.

innovation: The stage in the research and development process consisting of the first commercial application of an invention. Innovation requires refinement of an invention to "get the bugs out" and develop a marketable product.

input expansion path: In an isoquant-isocost diagram, the locus of points showing all the possible cost-minimizing combinations of inputs for producing any possible output.

invention: The discovery of an idea that "should" work. In the invention stage of research and development the idea passes through its first rough tests, which indicate whether it will work.

isocost lines: In an isoquant-isocost diagram, the lines that represent the input combinations that it is possible to purchase at the current input prices for a given total cost.

isoquants: Given a production function relating inputs to output, the isoquants are a series of curves that identify input combinations that yield equal outputs.

learning by doing: The process whereby, because of production experience, firms lower their average costs as cumulative output increases.

Lerner index: Mathematically:

$$\frac{P - MC}{P}$$

The Lerner index is a measure of the degree of *market power* that a firm possesses.

limit pricing: A strategy of charging a price below the short-run profit-maximizing price to deter entry.

location game: A game in which firms choose between different locations for their manufacturing plants or retail outlets or between different possible characteristics for their products.

low-price guarantees: A promise made to a buyer that the seller "will not be undersold and will match or beat any competitor's price."

marginal cost: The additional cost of producing one more unit of output.

marginal product: With a short-run production function, the extra output obtained by adding one additional unit of a variable input.

marginal rate of technical substitution: The rate at which a firm can substitute one input for another input without changing output.

marginal revenue: The change in total revenue resulting from selling one additional unit of output.

market for corporate control: A mechanism by which shirking by managers is limited. If managers use their discretion to further their own interests rather than to maximize profits, an outsider will perceive an opportunity to purchase the poorly run firm, replace the existing managers, and realize a profit.

market power: The ability of a firm to set price above marginal cost.

McGuire Act: A 1952 law that extended the *Miller-Tydings Act* to include non-signers of a resale price maintenance agreement.

Miller-Tydings Act: A 1937 law that gave the States the right to legalize resale price maintenance in the United States.

minimax strategy: A solution to a zero-sum game in which a firm calculates the maximum outcome for each of its opponent's possible plays and then selects the strategy that minimizes its opponent's maximum possible outcome.

minimum efficient scale: The lowest level of output for which a firm's long-run average cost is minimized.

mixed strategy game: A game with no pure strategy equilibrium in which an optimal strategy is for each player to randomly select its actions with given probabilities that maximize its expected payoff, given the randomly selected strategies being played by its opponents.

monopolistic competition: A market structure characterized by easy entry, product differentiation, and long-run profits equal to zero.

monopoly: A market controlled by one firm.

most favored customer guarantee: A guarantee made by a firm that if it lowers the price to any one buyer it will retroactively offer that price to any other buyer that purchased the good in the past during some specified period, such as six months or a year. Also known as a *price protection clause*.

multicollinearity: A situation in which two or more of the independent variables in a regression are highly correlated, meaning that they tend to move together. Multicollinearity makes it hard to separate the independent effects of the variables, with the result that estimated coefficients have large standard errors and low t-statistics.

multinationals: Corporations that operate in many different countries.

Nash equilibrium: An equilibrium in a game where both players are doing the best they can given the choice of their opponent(s).

natural monopoly: A market in which one firm can serve the market more efficiently than more than one firm.

non-followship demand curve: Firm 1's demand curve drawn on the assumption that all other firms maintain price while only Firm 1 either lowers or raises price.

numbers equivalent: The ratio of 10,000 over the *Herfindahl-Hirshman Index* (*HHI*), that is, N in the following equation:

$$N = \frac{10{,}000}{HHI}.$$

A measure of the number of equal-sized firms that could "fit" in an industry.

oligopoly: A market structure characterized by the domination of a few firms.

opportunism: The assumption that individuals maximize their utility in a guileful way, misleading, deceiving, and confusing others if it is to their advantage to do so and if such activities cannot be detected easily.

opportunity cost: The value of the resources used to produce a particular good had those resources been used in their best alternative use. Opportunity cost measures foregone possibilities.

overt collusion: A method of collusion in which a group of competitors sit down to discuss and set prices or quantities. The term is synonymous with *explicit collusion.*

parameters: Descriptive measures of a population. In an equation, the coefficients of the independent variables are the parameters; least squares regression is the most common methodology in economics for obtaining estimates of parameters.

parametric price: A price that is considered fixed by sellers or buyers.

patent pooling: An agreement by a group of firms to share a large number of patents in an attempt to monopolize a market.

patent race game: A game in which a group of firms attempt to be the first to obtain a patent. Patent races typically result in too many resources being spent to obtain the patent and a reduction in economic welfare.

peak-load pricing: A pricing system in which firms charge higher prices during high-demand periods and lower prices during low-demand periods.

pecuniary economies: Savings that are purely redistributive, increasing the welfare of one group and reducing the welfare of another.

***per se* rule:** A legal precedent that an action is "intrinsically" illegal regardless of any proposed defense.

perfect collusion: Collusion that results in the joint profit-maximizing price.

perfect competition: An economic model that assumes each firm in a market recognizes that its effect on the overall market is insignificant. Therefore, firms do not view other firms as rivals; they make business decisions without considering the actions or reactions of other firms in the industry.

perfect discrimination: Another term for *first-degree price discrimination*. With perfect discrimination each consumer pays his or her reservation price for the good.

perfect information: A game in which each player knows every move that has been made by the other players before taking any action.

persuasive advertising: Advertising designed to create a subjective positive reaction to a product. Much of the advertising on television is persuasive. For example, beautiful people drive fast, good-looking automobiles.

phantom freight: Under the basing point pricing system, charges for freight that are not incurred as costs by the supplier. These charges are paid by buyers located far from a basing point but close to a seller's manufacturing plant.

phases of the moon system: A collusive pricing system used in the electrical equipment industry in the 1950s. Under the system, each company was awarded a target percentage of the switchgear market, and the low bidder rotated into the low-bid position based on the current phase of the moon.

pooling equilibrium: An equilibrium in a dynamic game with asymmetric information in which all types of players select the same strategy. For example, an equilibrium where both high-cost and low-cost monopolists charge the same price in period 1 and, therefore, the potential entrant learns nothing about the monopolist's costs unless it enters.

potential competition: Competition provided by firms that are not in an industry but may enter the industry if there is a sufficiently large incentive to enter.

predatory pricing: A strategy of charging a very low price with the objective of driving a competitor(s) out of the market.

present value: The value today of future income. See also *discounting*.

price cap: Public utility regulation allowing firms to raise price a maximum amount based on the following formula:

$$\text{Permitted Price Increase} = \text{Increase in CPI} - X$$

Under price cap regulation there is an incentive for firms to improve efficiency because they must keep price increases below the increase in the CPI.

price-cost margin: A measure of performance used in numerous industrial organization studies. The price-cost margin is:

$$\frac{P - AVC}{P}$$

The price-cost margin is typically calculated from data available in the *Census of Manufactures*.

(price) elasticity of demand: The percentage change in the quantity demanded of a good in response to a 1 percent change in its price.

price exchange agreement: An agreement among a group of competitors to provide price information to each other.

price discrimination: The practice of charging different consumers different price-marginal cost margins for the same product.

price protection clause: A guarantee made by a firm that if it lowers the price to any buyer it will retroactively offer that price to any other buyer that purchased the good in the past during some specified period, such as six months or a year. Also known as a *most favored customer guarantee.*

price squeeze: A pricing policy by a vertically integrated firm in which a firm simultaneously increases the price of an input and decreases the price of a finished good.

primary-line competition: Competition between sellers in a market in which the sellers practice price discrimination.

primary-line discrimination: Price discrimination that involves possible injury to a direct competitor.

prisoner's dilemma game: A game of collusion in which both players would be better off colluding, but defecting is a dominant strategy.

private-label brand: A product that is sold under a store brand label.

producer surplus: The difference between the revenue a producer receives from selling a product and the minimum amount the producer would be willing to sell the product for; the amount producers receive for a good in excess of the opportunity costs of producing it.

product extension merger: A conglomerate merger between companies that produce different but related products. For example, a laundry detergent producer purchases a liquid bleach producer.

product proliferation: The strategic decision to preempt potential entrants by creating brands to fill every available product niche.

production function: The mathematical relationship between inputs and outputs indicating the maximum possible output that can be produced from a given set of inputs.

profits: Total revenue minus total costs.

pure conglomerate mergers: A conglomerate merger between firms operating in entirely separate markets. For example, a telephone company purchases a light bulb company.

quotas: A restriction on the number of units of a good that can be imported into a country.

raising rivals' costs: Any strategy that attempts to increase rivals' production costs to make entry more difficult.

Ramsey price: The price that maximizes total social benefits subject to the requirement that profits cannot be negative.

rate base: The value of a regulated firm's invested capital, used by a regulatory commission to calculate profits.

rate of return on assets: A measure of profitability calculated as $\dfrac{\pi - T + I}{A}$, where π is profits, T is the tax on profits, I is interest payments to debtholders, and A is total assets.

rate of return on stockholders' equity: A measure of profitability calculated as $\dfrac{\pi - T}{E}$, where π is profits, T is the tax on profits, and E is stockholders' equity. This measure is attractive because it corresponds to what individual investors are trying to maximize. Competitive industries with the same risk will have the same rate of return on equity in the long run.

reaction function: A function that shows the optimal output (price) that one firm will produce (charge) in response to any output (price) produced (charged) by competitors.

real economies: Cost savings that reflect actual savings of resources, such as a reduction in transaction costs.

reciprocity: A practice whereby a large conglomerate encourages its suppliers to purchase inputs from another of the conglomerate's divisions.

regression analysis: The most widely used statistical technique in economics. The technique involves developing a mathematical equation that describes the relationship between a variable to be forecast and the variable(s) believed to be related to the forecast variable.

Regulation Q: The Federal Reserve System's regulation that limited the interest rates banks could pay on all deposits, including large certificates of deposits (CDs).

regulatory lag: When costs increase under regulation, a utility cannot immediately raise prices. Instead, a regulated utility must first request a price increase. Until the price hike is approved, the utility will earn a rate of return less than the permitted rate of return, r. Similarly if costs decrease, the utility will earn a rate of return greater than r until a price reduction is approved. Regulatory lag punishes *x-inefficiency* and rewards improved efficiency.

remanded: A legal decision by a higher court to send a case back to a lower court for review.

repeated game: A static game that is played more than once.

replacement cost: A method of evaluating the cost of capital based on the long-run cost of buying a capital asset of comparable quantity.

resale price maintenance: A pricing policy in which a manufacturer sets a minimum or maximum price for which the product may be sold at retail. Also referred to as *RPM*.

residual demand curve: A demand curve derived by assuming that a firm faces a demand curve that is left over, or residual, after the other firms in the industry have chosen their outputs.

returns to scale: The rate at which output increases in response to proportional increases in all inputs. If returns to scale are increasing, output increases more than proportionately; with constant returns to scale, output increases at the same rate as inputs. The third case is *decreasing* returns to scale, in which a proportionate increase in all inputs leads to a less than proportionate increase in output.

risk-adjusted rate of return: The return a competitive firm would earn if its projects carried the same level of risk as the firm being examined.

Robinson-Patman Act: A 1936 law that amended Section 2 of the Clayton Act by more strictly limiting the use of price discrimination.

RPM: A pricing policy under which a manufacturer sets a minimum or maximum price for which a product may be sold at retail. Same as *resale price maintenance*.

Rule of Reason: The precedent in antitrust law that only unreasonable attempts to monopolize violate the Sherman Act.

rule-of-thumb pricing: A pricing system under which a firm follows a formula to determine its price. A firm may, for example, set a target rate of return on its invested capital or set price as a fixed mark-up over invoice costs.

sales maximization: An alternative objective of managers, as opposed to profit maximization. Subject to a minimum profit constraint of stockholders, a sales-maximizing manager will choose to produce and sell an additional unit of output as long as marginal revenue is positive.

satisficing: Managerial behavior such that the manager sets a minimum acceptable level of performance below which he or she does not want to fall, rather than trying to maximize profits. Managers might settle for satisficing because of organizational size and complexity.

search goods: Goods whose qualities can be judged before purchase through pre-purchase testing. Search goods include fresh fruits and vegetables, which can be squeezed and smelled to test for freshness; fresh meats, which can be viewed; shoes, which can be tried on; and sofas and chairs, which can be sat upon.

second-degree price discrimination: Price discrimination where all consumers are offered the same price schedule and consumers self-select into the different price categories. Consumers pay different prices, but every consumer who buys within the same price category pays the same price.

secondary-line competition: Competition between the buyers of a good.

secondary-line discrimination: Price discrimination involving possible injury to a competitor of a buyer who receives a lower discriminatory price.

separating equilibrium: An equilibrium in a dynamic game with asymmetric information in which different players select different strategies. For example, high-cost and low-cost monopolists charge different prices in period 1; therefore, the monopolist's price in time period 1 fully reveals whether it is a high- or low-cost producer.

separation of ownership and control: A feature of many corporations in which the people who make the day-to-day decisions, the managers, are not the owners, those who receive profits from the firm's operations. Some economists hypothesize that separation of ownership and control results in managers pursuing objectives other than maximizing profits.

Sherman Act: The first national antitrust law passed in 1890. The Sherman Act banned restraints of trade and attempts to monopolize.

shopping goods: Goods that are relatively expensive and are purchased intermittently, such as appliances, automobiles, and televisions.

shutdown price: The price below which a firm will choose to produce no output in the short run. Assuming that no fixed costs are recoverable, the shutdown price for a perfectly competitive firm is the minimum of its average variable cost.

SIC code: The Standard Industrial Classification (SIC) code system used by the federal government in the United States to define manufacturing industries.

simultaneity bias: A statistical bias that may result in studies where it is impossible to identify the direction of the relationship between a dependent variable and an independent variable. For example, advertising may erect an entry barrier that enables firms to earn high profits, or alternatively, high profits may enable firms to spend large amounts on advertising.

Stackelberg follower: The firm that moves second in the *Stackelberg model.*

Stackelberg leader: The firm that moves first in the *Stackelberg model.*

Stackelberg model: A quantity-based model that considers what happens if the Cournot model is viewed as a two-stage sequential game in which one firm, the Stackelberg leader, moves first. In equilibrium the Stackelberg leader selects the output on the Stackelberg follower's reaction function that maximizes the Stackelberg leader's profits.

static game: A game in which the players move simultaneously.

static models: Models that deal with a moment in time. For example, when short-run marginal and average cost curves are drawn in a textbook, the curves take a snapshot of the industry at a precise moment in time.

statistical cost analysis: Regression analysis aimed at measuring the significance of economies of scale. In the regression, cost is the dependent variable and output volume is one of the independent variables. To control for the effects of other factors that influence costs, variables such as the age of the equipment, the capacity utilization rate, and input prices must also be included as independent variables in the regression.

stockholder revolt: A decision by stockholders to turn against the management of a company. Some argue that this form of indirect owner control encourages managers to treat stockholders carefully and keep their interests in mind.

strategic barriers to entry: Behavioral barriers to entry based on the notion that existing firms deliberately behave in ways that decrease the probability of entry by other firms.

strategic trade policy: Government intervention in trade policy aimed at improving domestic welfare.

strong incumbent: An incumbent firm that is always predatory in response to entry.

structural barriers to entry: Elements of basic market structure that act to deter entry. The major structural barriers are economies of scale, absolute cost advantages, capital cost requirements, and product differentiation advantages.

Structure-Conduct-Performance Paradigm: An industrial organization paradigm that is primarily empirical in its orientation. The paradigm was developed in the 1940s and 1950s by Professors Mason and Bain, who hypothesized that a direct relationship exists among market structure, market conduct, and market performance.

subsidy: A payment from the government to a consumer or firm aimed at encouraging a behavior considered socially beneficial.

summary judgment: A court ruling in favor of one party, where the court believes there is no reason to even consider the evidence.

survivor test: A test of economies of scale based on the idea that, over time, the firms that survive in an industry, supplying constant or increasing fractions of an industry's total output, must be efficient. A decreasing share of output over time is evidence of relative inefficiency; firms or plants of this size are not surviving.

sunk cost: That portion of fixed costs that is not recoverable.

symmetric information: A game in which all players have exactly the same information when each player moves.

tacit collusion: A method of collusion in which firms set identical prices without ever meeting to discuss prices because of a "meeting of the minds."

takeover: A purchase of one firm's stock by another firm or group of investors. The threat of a takeover constrains managers from straying too far from profit-maximizing strategies.

tariff: A tax placed on an imported good.

technological opportunity: The inherent inter-industry differences in ability to make major technological progress. For example, some industries, such as the computer or the drug industry, have many scientific opportunities to make progress, whereas others, such as the brick or the glass bottle industry, have far fewer scientific opportunities.

territorial restrictions: Restrictive agreements under which manufacturers distribute goods through independent dealers who are required to sell only in certain geographic areas or only to certain customers.

third-degree price discrimination: Price discrimination where consumers are separated into two or more groups according to their elasticities of demand, and groups with more inelastic demand face higher price-marginal cost margins.

tie-in sales: A tie-in exists when a firm with market power over good X requires its buyers to purchase another good, good Y, in order to obtain good X. Also known as a *tying agreement*.

tied product: In a tying agreement the product over which the seller does not have market power.

tit-for-tat strategy: A strategy in a prisoner's dilemma game in which the tit-for-tat player starts off in the first round cooperating, and in every subsequent round N > 1, adopts his/her opponent's strategy in the previous round (i.e., the opponent's strategy in round N − 1).

Tobin's q: A measure of profitability using the ratio of the market value of the firm to the replacement value of its assets. In a perfectly competitive industry in long-run equilibrium, the value of q would be 1; the market value of the firm would just equal what it would cost to rebuild it.

total cost: In the short run, the sum of fixed costs and variable costs. In the long run, all costs are variable and are included in total cost.

total revenue: The same as sales. Total revenue is equal to price times quantity.

total variable cost: The costs associated with inputs that can be varied in the short run. Often called simply *variable cost*.

transaction costs: The costs of using the market to make a transaction and to gather the information to make those transactions.

trigger price strategy: A firm's strategy in an infinitely repeated game played with the following behavioral rules: Start by cooperating and charging the joint profit-maximizing price; continue to charge the joint profit-maximizing price unless a competitor lowers price, in which case, charge the Bertrand equilibrium price, $P = MC$, forever. See also *grim strategy*.

two-part tariff: A two-part tariff consists of a lump-sum payment (for example, a copier machine rental) combined with a per-unit charge (for example, a per-copy charge).

tying agreements: A tying agreement exists when a firm with market power over good X requires its buyers to purchase another good, good Y, to obtain good X. Also known as a *tie-in sale*.

tying product: In a tying agreement, the product over which the seller has market power.

uniform density: A distribution function in which a variable is equally spaced over all possible preferences or locations. For example, consumers are equally spaced over all possible locations.

upstream: In a vertically structured industry, an earlier stage of production.

vertical merger: A merger involving firms that produce at different stages of production in the same industry.

vertical product differentiation: Differentiation in the actual quality of two brands. For example, Ben & Jerry's ice cream and Häagen Dazs ice cream have a higher fat content than Breyers ice cream, which has a higher fat content than the typical store brand of ice cream.

vertical restraints: A variety of methods used by manufacturers to limit the ways in which retailers can market their products. Examples include resale price maintenance, exclusive dealing arrangements, and tying agreements.

warranted concentration ratio: A way to interpret the information on minimum efficient scale (MES) in industries by considering the percent of national output that would be produced by four firms if each firm operated one MES plant. A high figure suggests that, to realize economies of scale, an industry can consist of only a few large firms, whereas a low figure indicates that there is "room" for a large number of firms.

weak incumbent: An incumbent firm that will only be predatory in one market if it believes predatory pricing will increase its profits in future markets to compensate for the lost profits as a result of its predatory behavior.

white list: A list of firms that a firm(s) with market power will only buy from or sell to.

x-inefficiency: A situation in which less than the maximum output is produced from a given set of inputs. X-inefficiency might exist, for example, if managers are interested in living a quiet life and therefore do not continually strive to find the least costly way of doing business.

Answers to Odd-Numbered Problems

CHAPTER 2

1. a. The two total cost functions are:

$$TC_1 = 200 + q$$
$$TC_2 = 40 + 5q$$

b. The two average cost and marginal cost functions are:

$$AC_1 = \frac{200}{q} + \frac{q}{q} = \frac{200}{q} + 1 \qquad MC_1 = 1$$

$$AC_2 = \frac{40}{q} + \frac{5q}{q} = \frac{40}{q} + 5 \qquad MC_2 = 5$$

c. The smallest number of acres for which she should buy the tractor is identified by the number of acres where $AC_1 = AC_2$.

$$AC_1 = \frac{200}{q} + 1 = \frac{40}{q} + 5 = AC_2$$

$$200 + q = 40 + 5q \Rightarrow 4q = 160 \Rightarrow q = 40$$

She should choose the tractor only if the number of acres mowed is greater than or equal to 40.

d. If the tractor has a positive resale value, this would reduce the AC of using the tractor. If RV represents the tractor's resale value, then:

$$AC_1 = \frac{200}{q} + 1 - \frac{RV}{q}$$

With lower average costs for the tractor she would select the tractor to mow fewer than 40 acres. The exact number of acres is not known unless the value of RV is known.

3. a. The firm should produce 30 units of output because:

$$P = 60 = 2q = MC$$

$$q = 30$$

b. Profits, π, equal:

$$\pi = TR - TC = 30\,(60) - [(30)^2 + 100] = 800$$

c. The marginal cost curve above the average variable cost curve is the supply curve for the firm. The MC curve is everywhere above the AVC curve (AVC = q), so the supply curve is identical to the MC curve, and is:

$$P = 2q$$

d. If q_f represents a firm's quantity supplied, and q_i represents the industry's quantity supplied, then with 100 identical firms the supply curve is:

$$q_f = \frac{P}{2} \Rightarrow q_i = \frac{100P}{2} \Rightarrow q_i = 50P$$

solving for P yields:

$$P = \frac{1}{50}q$$

The answer can also be obtained by horizontally summing 100 firm demand curves. This yields a supply curve with an intercept of zero and a slope of (1/50).

5. a. $MR = 96 - 12Q$

   b. $MC = 4Q = 96 - 12Q \Rightarrow 16Q = 96 \Rightarrow Q = 6$
      $$P = 96 - 6(6) = 60$$

   c. $\pi = TR - TC = 6(60) - 2(6)^2 = 360 - 72 = 288$

CHAPTER 4

1. a. The four-firm concentration ratio is:

$$30 + 20 + 12 + 10 = 72$$

   b. The Herfindahl-Hirshman Index is:

$$(900 + 400 + 144 + 100 + 100 + 64 + 49 + 9) = 1766$$

3. The answers to question 2 are:

   a. Four-firm concentration ratio = 72

   b. The HHI = 1518

   The concentration ratio suggests that both industries have the same structure, but the HHI indicates a difference. The HHI is much more sensitive to large market shares of the top firms. In this case, the industry in question 1 is identified as being less competitive than the industry in question 2.

5. For industry A:

$$HHI = 4900 + 100 + 100 + 100 = 5200$$

For industry B:

$$HHI = 625 + 625 + 625 + 625 = 2500$$

These values suggest that industry A is less competitive than industry B. The four-firm concentration ratio, however, equals 100 in both industries. Only the HHI indicates a difference in market structure.

The HHI is very sensitive to large market shares of the leading firms. In this case, the 70 percent market share of the leading firm in industry A has a greater impact on the HHI than on the four-firm concentration ratio.

CHAPTER 6

1. Sales would still be split in half with Waldman getting 50 percent and Other Truck getting 50 percent.

   This is *not* a Nash equilibrium because each ice cream truck could gain sales by moving toward the middle of the parade route if the other truck remained parked 1/4 mile from the middle.

   Society is better off because the total travel time to obtain ice cream is reduced by the action of the local police. With both trucks parked in the middle, some consumers would walk a half mile to obtain ice cream, but with each parked 1/4 mile from one end, the farthest any consumer would walk is 1/4 mile.

3. There is no dominant strategy in this game. There is no Nash equilibrium in this game because there is always an incentive for one of the players to move from a cell. The firms would adopt a mixed strategy.

CHAPTER 7

1. There are two methods for solving this problem: using reaction functions, and using the total output rule for two firms with linear demand and marginal cost. We show both solutions below.

   Using reaction functions:

$$P = a - b(q_1 + q_2) \quad \text{or} \quad MR_1 = (a - bq_2) - 2bq_1$$

$$\text{to maximize profits}$$

$$MR_1 = (a - bq_2) - 2bq_1 = c = MC \implies 2bq_1 = (a - c) - bq_2$$

$$\text{solving for } q_1$$

$$q_1 = \frac{(a - c) - bq_2}{2b} = \frac{(a - c)}{2b} - \frac{1}{2}q_2$$

By symmetry $q_2 = \dfrac{(a - c)}{2b} - \dfrac{1}{2}q_1$

Therefore, $q_1 = \dfrac{(a - c)}{2b} - \dfrac{1}{2}\left[\dfrac{(a - c)}{2b} - \dfrac{1}{2}q_1\right]$

and $q_1 = \dfrac{1}{2}\left[\dfrac{(a - c)}{2b}\right] + \dfrac{1}{4}q_1 \Rightarrow \dfrac{3}{4}q_1 = \dfrac{(a - c)}{4b}$

or $q_1 = \dfrac{(a - c)}{3b}$

By symmetry:

$$q_2 = \dfrac{(a - c)}{3b}$$

Using the rule that the Cournot-Nash equilibrium with linear demand and linear marginal cost is equal to 2/3 of the competitive output, we first find the competitive output.

$$P = a - bq = c = MC$$

$$q = \dfrac{(a - c)}{b}$$

Since the Cournot-Nash total output is 2/3 of q:

$$q_{CN} = \dfrac{2(a - c)}{3b}$$

Therefore, $q_1 = q_2 = \dfrac{(a - c)}{3b}$

Notice how much simpler it is to use the second method.

3. First identify the follower's reaction function:

$$MR_2 = (60 - 2q_1) - 4q_2 = 20 = MC_2 \Rightarrow 4q_2 = 40 - 2q_1$$

$$q_2 = 10 - \dfrac{1}{2}q_1$$

Next substitute Firm 2's reaction function in Firm 1's demand curve and maximize profits.

$$P_1 = \left[60 - 2\left(10 - \dfrac{1}{2}q_1\right)\right] - 2q_1 = 40 + q_1 - 2q_1 = 40 - q_1$$

$$MR_1 = 40 - 2q_1 = 10 = MC_1$$

$$q_1 = \dfrac{30}{2} = 15$$

Therefore, $q_2 = 10 - \dfrac{1}{2}q_1 = 10 - \dfrac{1}{2}(15) = 10 - (7.5) = 2.5$

5. In Figure Problem 7.5 the foreign firm's initial marginal cost curve is MC_F, after the unit tax marginal cost increases to MC_T. As a result of the tax the dominant foreign firm decreases output from q_4 to q_3 and increases price from P_3

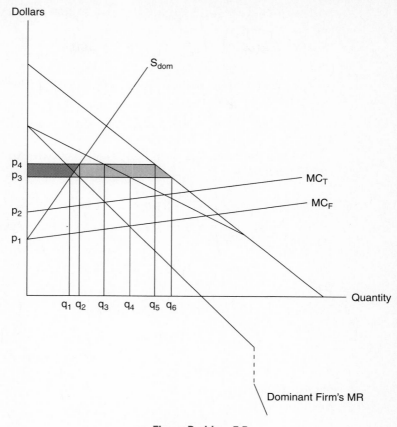

Figure Problem 7.5

to P_4. The domestic firms increase output from q_1 to q_2. Domestic consumer surplus decreases by the sum of the shaded gray area and the red area. Domestic producer surplus increases by the red area. Because the reduction in consumer surplus is greater than the increase in domestic firms' producer surplus, domestic welfare is reduced by the tax.

CHAPTER 8

1. The present value of a promise to pay $1,000 in two years at a discount rate of 10 percent is:

$$PV = \frac{\$1,000}{(1.1)^2} = \frac{\$1,000}{1.21} = \$846.45$$

   The present value of a promise to pay $1,000 for the next 100 years at a discount rate of 10 percent is:

$$PV = \frac{\$1,000}{.10} = \$10,000$$

The present value of a promise to pay \$1,000 in two years at a discount rate of 5 percent is:

$$PV = \frac{\$1,000}{(1.05)^2} = \frac{\$1,000}{1.1025} = \$907.03$$

The present value of a promise to pay \$1,000 for the next 100 years at a discount rate of 5 percent is:

$$PV = \frac{\$1,000}{.05} = \$20,000$$

The present value of a promise to pay \$1,000 in two years at a discount rate of 20 percent is:

$$PV = \frac{\$1,000}{(1.2)^2} = \frac{\$1,000}{1.44} = \$694.44$$

The present value of a promise to pay \$1,000 for the next 100 years at a discount rate of 20 percent is:

$$PV = \frac{\$1,000}{.20} = \$5,000$$

3. a. To maximize profits Firm 1 would set:

$$mr_1 = 100 - 4q_1 = 10 + 2q_1 = mc_1$$
$$6q_1 = 90 \Rightarrow q_1 = 15 \text{ and } p_1 = 70$$

b. For Firm 2:

$$mr_2 = 100 - 4q_2 = 22 + 2q_2 = mc_2$$
$$6q_1 = 78 \Rightarrow q_2 = 13 \text{ and } p_2 = 74$$

c. For quantities greater than 6 and marginal costs greater than 22, it is necessary to add the *quantities* to obtain the combined marginal cost curve as follows:

$$q_1 = \frac{1}{2}mc - 5 \text{ and } q_2 = \frac{1}{2}mc - 11$$
$$Q = q_1 + q_2 = \frac{1}{2}mc - 5 + \frac{1}{2}mc - 11 = mc - 16$$
$$\text{or } mc = 16 + Q$$

To maximize profits:

$$MR = 100 - 2Q = 16 + Q = MC$$
$$3Q = 84 \text{ or } Q = 28$$

With $Q = 28$, $P = 100 - 28 = 72$, and $MC = 16 + 28 = 44$.

Since MC = 44 for each firm, for joint profit maximization:

$$mc_1 = 10 + 2q_1 = 44 \Rightarrow q_1 = \frac{34}{2} = 17$$

$$mc_2 = 22 + 2q_1 = 44 \Rightarrow q_2 = \frac{22}{2} = 11$$

CHAPTER 10

1. a. The limit price is 60 because the potential entrant's marginal cost and average cost equal 60.

   b. Setting MR = MC, the profit-maximizing price is:

   $$MR = 200 - 2Q = 50 = MC \Rightarrow Q = 75 \Rightarrow P = 125$$

   Profits equal:

   $$\pi = TR - TC = PQ - 50Q = (125)(75) - 50(75) = 9375 - 3750 = 5625$$

   c. At the limit price, profits equal:

   $$\pi = TR - TC = PQ - 50Q = (60)(140) - 50(140) = 8400 - 7000 = 1400$$

3. a.

Time of Switch to Limit Price	Profits at $t = 1$	Profits at $t = 2$	Profits at $t = 3$	Profits at $t = 4$	Profits at $t = 5 \ldots t = n$
$t = 0$	900[1]	900	900	900	900
$t = 1$	2,500[2]	700	700	700	700
$t = 2$	2,500	1,500[3]	500	500	500
$t = 3$	2,500	1,500	500[4]	500	500
$t = 4$	2,500	1,500	500	500	500

1. $\pi = Q(P - AC) = 90(20 - 10) = 900$
2. Entrants produce a quantity of 0 at $t = 0$, so total quantity equals 50 and $P = 60$. Therefore, $\pi = Q(P - AC) = 50(60 - 10) = 2,500$ at $t = 1$.
3. Entrants produce a quantity of 20 at $t = 1$, so total quantity equals 70 and $P = 40$. Therefore, $\pi = Q(P - AC) = 50(40 - 10) = 1,500$ at $t = 2$.
4. Entrants produce a quantity of 40 at $t = 2$, so total quantity equals 90 and $P = 20$ (the limit price). Therefore, $\pi = Q(P - AC) = 50(20 - 10) = 500$ at $t = 3$.

b.

Discount Rate	Switch to Limit Price at t = 0	Switch to Limit Price at t = 1	Switch to Limit Price at t = 2	Switch to Limit Price at t = 3	Switch to Limit Price at t = 4
i = 10%	**9,000**[1]	8,633[2]	7,645[3]	7,645	7,645
i = 15%	6,000[4]	**6,232**[5]	5,829[6]	5,829	5,829

1. $\pi = \dfrac{900}{.10} = 9,000$

2. $\pi = \dfrac{2,500}{1.1} + \dfrac{700}{.10} - \dfrac{700}{1.1} = 2,272.72 + 7,000 - 636.36 = 8,633.36$

3. $\pi = \dfrac{2,500}{1.1} + \dfrac{1,500}{(1.1)^2} + \dfrac{500}{.10} - \dfrac{500}{1.1} - \dfrac{500}{(1.1)^2} = 2,272.72 + 1,239.67 + 5,000 - 454.54$

   $- 413.22 = 7,644.63$

4. $\pi = \dfrac{900}{.15} = 6,000$

5. $\pi = \dfrac{2,500}{1.15} + \dfrac{700}{.15} - \dfrac{700}{1.15} = 2,173.91 + 4,666.66 - 608.70 = 6,231.87$

6. $\pi = \dfrac{2,500}{1.15} + \dfrac{1,500}{(1.15)^2} + \dfrac{500}{.15} - \dfrac{500}{1.15} - \dfrac{500}{(1.15)^2} = 2,173.91 + 1,134.22 + 3,333.33 - 434.78$

   $- 378.07 = 5,828.61$

c. The increase in output by entrants shortens the optimal time to switch to a limit pricing policy. At a discount rate of 10 percent the optimal time to switch is now at t = 0 compared with t = 2 in Table 10.2, and the optimal time to switch at a discount rate of 15 percent is t = 1 compared with t = 3 in Table 10.2. The more output produced by entrants, the earlier will be the optimal time to switch to a limit pricing policy.

5. a. The new game would be played as follows:

Round	p_n	b^n	b^{n-1}	Monopolist's Action	Potential Entrant's Action
10	1/4	1/1024	1/512	Fight	Stay Out
9	1/4	1/512	1/256	Fight	Stay Out
8	1/4	1/256	1/128	Fight	Stay Out
7	1/4	1/128	1/64	Fight	Stay Out
6	1/4	1/64	1/32	Fight	Stay Out
5	1/4	1/32	1/16	Fight	Stay Out
4	1/4	1/16	1/8	Fight	Stay Out
3	1/4	1/8	1/4	Fight	Stay Out
2	1/4	1/4	1/2	Mixed Strategy with: $\mu_2 = 1/3$ $(1 - \mu_2) = 2/3$	Mixed Strategy with: $\theta_2 = 1/2$ $(1 - \theta_2) = 1/2$
1	0 (incumbent never fights in n = 1)	1/2	1	Not Fight	Enter

The incumbent continues to fight entry longer and the potential entrant stays out longer in this version of the game.

Intuitively this makes sense because the initial probability that the incumbent is strong has increased, and this would be expected to have an additional deterrent effect.

b. The new game is played as follows:

Round	p_n	b^n	b^{n-1}	Monopolist's Action	Potential Entrant's Action
10	1/10	1/1048576	1/262144	Fight	Stay out
9	1/10	1/262144	1/65536	Fight	Stay out
8	1/10	1/65536	1/16384	Fight	Stay out
7	1/10	1/16384	1/4096	Fight	Stay out
6	1/10	1/4096	1/1024	Fight	Stay out
5	1/10	1/1024	1/256	Fight	Stay out
4	1/10	1/256	1/64	Fight	Stay out
3	1/10	1/64	1/16	Fight	Stay out
2	1/10	1/16	1/4	Mixed Strategy with: $\mu_2 = 1/3$ $(1 - \mu_2) = 2/3$	Stay out
1	0	1/4	1	Not fight	Enter

The incumbent continues to fight entry longer and the potential entrant stays out longer in this version of the game.

Intuitively this makes sense because the potential entrant has less incentive to enter because the potential profits to be earned on entry have been cut in half.

CHAPTER 11

1. The incumbent could produce with a SRAC curve that minimizes cost at Q_{LP}, but its short-run profit-maximizing price would then be above the limit price of P_{LP}. To ensure that the incumbent charges the limit price, it is necessary to produce with $SRAC_2$ so that $SRMC = MR$ for the output Q_{LP}. It is possible, however, for an incumbent to produce with a SRAC curve that minimizes cost at Q_{LP}, charge a price above P_{LP}, and use predatory pricing to deter entry.

3. With

$$LRAC\ (q) = 50 + \frac{100}{10^{\lambda q}}$$

If $\lambda = 0$, then:

$$LRAC = 50 + \frac{100}{10^{0q}} = 50 + 100 = 150$$

Because LRAC is constant, learning-by-doing is not significant. Early entrants would have no cost advantage over latecomers, and the long-run equilibrium price should equal 150.

If $\lambda = \infty$, then:

$$\text{LRAC} = 50 + \frac{100}{10^{\infty q}} = 50 + 0 = 50$$

Because LRAC is constant, learning-by-doing is not significant. Early entrants would have no cost advantage over latecomers, and the long-run equilibrium price should equal 50.

With $\lambda = 0$, a competitive market structure would likely emerge because LRAC = 150. With $\lambda = 1$, however, learning-by-doing is important and the first-movers in the industry should maintain an advantage over later entrants. Therefore, more firms should be in this industry in the long-run if $\lambda = 0$.

CHAPTER 12

1. If the fixed costs of production of sickeningly sweet corn flakes were $100 instead of $60, Big G would not enter the sickeningly sweet corn flakes market when demand tripled because Eq. 12.2 would become:

$$\pi_{pv}^{G3d} = \frac{7.50}{.10} - \frac{100}{1.1^1} = 75 - 90.91 = -15.91 < 0$$

Because profits are negative with the higher fixed costs, Big G would stay out of the market and there would be no need to use product proliferation to deter entry.

If fixed costs were $55 instead of $60, then all the profit functions in Figure 12.4 would be higher. As a result, t* would occur at an earlier time, and product proliferation would take place earlier. Using a calculator it's possible to show that:

$$\pi_G = \sum_{t=t_G}^{0} \frac{2.50}{(1.1)^t} + \sum_{t=1}^{\infty} \frac{7.50}{(1.1)^t} - \frac{55}{(1.1)^{t_G}}$$

$$= \sum_{t=t_G}^{0} \frac{2.50}{(1.1)^t} + 75.00 - \frac{55}{(1.1)^{t_G}}$$

for $t_G = -6$, $\pi_{pv}^G = 23.72 + 75.00 - 97.44 = 1.28$

while for $t_G = -7$, $\pi_{pv}^G = 28.59 + 75.00 - 107.18 = -3.49$

Therefore, $-7 < t^* < -6$, and product proliferation would occur between $t = -7$ and $t = -6$. In the text, for fixed cost of $60, $-5 < t^* < -4$, so product proliferation would occur between $t = -5$ and $t = -4$.

3. a. A pooling equilibrium exists because:

$$\rho_H \pi_2^H + (1 - \rho_H) \pi_2^L = 0.75 (75) + 0.25 (-300) = 56.25 - 75 = -18.75 < 0$$

Therefore, a high-cost monopolist would limit price and charge P = 55, the optimal price for a low-cost monopolist, in period 1.

b. A low-cost monopolist would charge its profit-maximizing price P = 55 in period 1.

c. The high-cost monopolist limits prices in period 1 and charges its profit-maximizing price in period 2; therefore, total profits for a high-cost monopolist would be:

$$\pi_H = 45\,(55 - 25) + \frac{37.5\,(62.5 - 25)}{1.1} = 1{,}350 + 1{,}278.41 = 2{,}628.41$$

d. The low-cost monopolist charges its profit-maximizing price in periods 1 and 2; therefore, total profits for a low-cost monopolist would be:

$$\pi_L = 45\,(55 - 10) + \frac{45\,(55 - 10)}{1.1} = 2{,}025 + 1{,}840.91 = 3{,}865.91$$

CHAPTER 13

1. a. Product differentiation is *less* significant because an increase of 1 in the price of good 2 increases the quantity demanded of good 1 by only 1/2 unit instead of 1 unit.

b. Because product differentiation is less significant, the equilibrium price would be expected to be lower.

c.

$$2p_1 = 96 + \frac{1}{2}p_2 - q_1$$

$$p_1 = \left(48 + \frac{1}{4}p_2\right) - \frac{1}{2}q_1$$

$$MR_1 = \left(48 + \frac{1}{4}p_2\right) - q_1$$

For profit maximization:

$$MR_1 = \left(48 + \frac{1}{4}p_2\right) - q_1 = 12 = MC$$

$$q_1 = 36 + \frac{1}{4}p_2$$

By symmetry:

$$q_2 = 36 + \frac{1}{4}p_1$$

To obtain Firm 1's reaction function solve for p_1:

$$q_1 = 96 - 2p_1 + \frac{1}{2}p_2 = 36 + \frac{1}{4}p_2$$

$$p_1 = 30 + \frac{1}{8}p_2$$

By symmetry, Firm 2's reaction function is:

$$p_1 = 30 + \frac{1}{8}p_2$$

To solve for p_1:

$$p_1 = 30 + \frac{1}{8}\left(30 + \frac{1}{8}p_1\right)$$

$$p_1 = 30 + \frac{30}{8} + \frac{1}{64}p_1$$

$$p_1 - \frac{1}{64}p_1 = \frac{63}{64}p_1 = 33.75$$

$$p_1 = \frac{33.75 \times 64}{63} = 34.29$$

3. a. In long-run equilibrium firms must earn economic profits equal to zero. Therefore,

$$\pi = 0 = 10 - \frac{1}{10}n \Rightarrow n = 100$$

b. With 100 firms:

$$\pi + CS = 10 - \frac{1}{10}(100) + \sqrt{100} = 10 - 10 + 10 = 10$$

This is not the socially optimal number of firms, because a decrease in the number of firms increases $\pi + CS$. For example, for $n = 90$:

$$\pi + CS = 10 - \frac{90}{10} + \sqrt{90} = 10 - 9 + (9.49) = 10.49$$

c. Using calculus, set the first derivative of $\pi + CS$ equal to zero:

$$\pi + CS = 10 - \frac{1}{10}n + n^{\frac{1}{2}}$$

$$\frac{d(\Pi + CS)}{dn} = -\frac{1}{10} + \frac{1}{2}n^{-\frac{1}{2}} = -\frac{1}{10} + \frac{1}{2\sqrt{n}} = 0$$

$$2\sqrt{n} = 10 \Rightarrow \sqrt{n} = 5 \Rightarrow n = 25$$

CHAPTER 14

1. In Figure Problem 14.1(a) patents slow down the rate of technological advance, but in Figure Problem 14.1(b) only with patent protection do the firm's benefits exceed costs. In this figure, the technological advance is developed only with patent protection.

3. a. & b. There is not a unique Nash equilibrium in this game. There are, however, two Nash equilibria (innovate, imitate) and (imitate, innovate).

c. If Firm A plays innovate with a probability of 75 percent and imitate with a probability of 25 percent, then Firm B always earns an expected profit equal to 4. For example, consider:

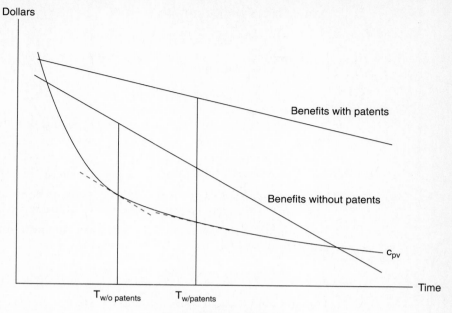

Figure Problem 14.1(a)

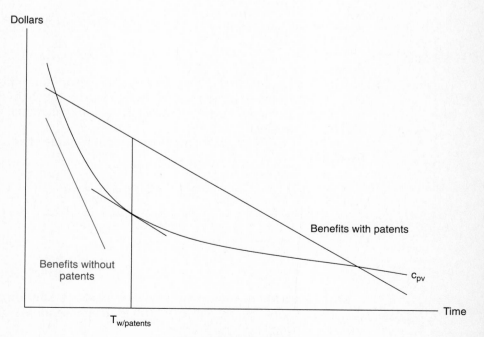

Figure Problem 14.1(b)

Firm B always plays innovate:

$$E(\pi_B) = (.75)(4) + (.25)(4) = 3 + 1 = 4$$

Firm B always plays imitate:

$$E(\pi_B) = (.75)(5) + (.25)(1) = (3.75) + (.25) = 4$$

Firm B plays innovate 50 percent of the time and imitate 50 percent of the time:

$$E(\pi_B) = (.75)(.5)(4) + (.25)(.5)(4) + (.75)(.5)(5) + (.25)(.5)(1)$$
$$= (1.5) + (.5) + 1.875 + (.125) = 4$$

No matter what strategy Firm B selects, it always earns an expected profit equal to 4. This suggests an optimal mixed strategy for Firm A.

d. Non-optimal outcomes are (innovate, innovate) and (imitate, imitate). The probability of (innovate, innovate) equals:

$$\frac{3}{4}\frac{3}{4} = \frac{9}{16}$$

The probability of (imitate, imitate) equals:

$$\frac{1}{4}\frac{1}{4} = \frac{1}{16}$$

The probability of a non-optimal outcome is:

$$\frac{9}{16} + \frac{1}{16} = \frac{10}{16} = \frac{5}{8} = .625 = 62.5\%$$

CHAPTER 15

1. The socially optimal fare is 40 because from an economic efficiency perspective, an additional passenger should be allowed on the flight as long as she/he is willing to pay a price greater than or equal to the marginal cost of adding another passenger.

    It is first necessary to calculate the marginal revenue of adding stand-by passengers.

Quantity	Price	Total Revenue (PQ)	Marginal revenue (ΔTR)/(ΔQ)
10	200	2000	2000/10 = 200
25	100	2500	500/15 = 33.33
40	40	1600	(−900)/15 = (−60)

Because the MR of adding the 25th passenger is greater than marginal cost, the airline should charge a price of 100 to maximize profits. The socially optimal result would not be achieved.

3. The marginal cost of an additional patron is zero; therefore, to maximize profits the symphony should equate marginal revenue to zero in each market or:

$$MR_A = 100 - 4q_A = 0 \quad \text{so} \quad q_A = 25$$
$$MR_c = 50 - 4q_c = 0 \quad \text{so} \quad q_c = 12.5$$

Because it is impossible to seat half a child, the profit-maximizing quantities would be 25 adults and 12 children. Prices would be:

$$p_A = 100 - 2(25) = 50$$
$$p_c = 50 - 2(12) = 26$$

If price discrimination were illegal it would be necessary to add the two demand curves to obtain the total demand for tickets as shown in Figure Problem 15.3. Setting MR = MC = 0:

$$MR = 75 - 2q = 0 \quad \text{so} \quad q = 37.5$$

Because it is necessary to seat whole people in the theater, the profit-maximizing number of tickets would be 37 and price would equal 38 (p = 75 − 37 = 38).

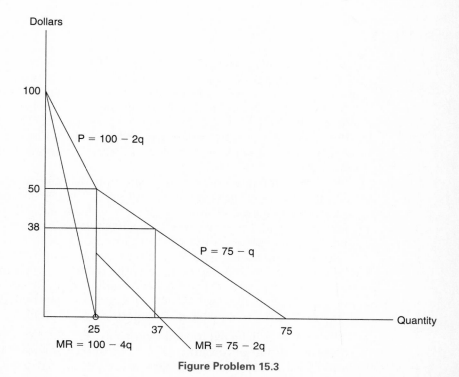

Figure Problem 15.3

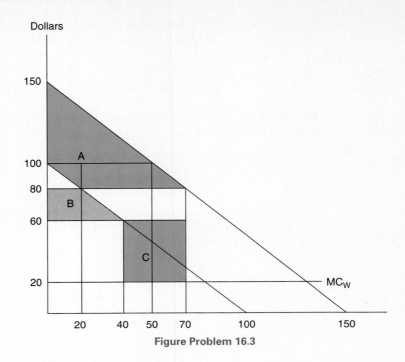

Figure Problem 16.3

CHAPTER 16

1. Consider a profit-maximizing franchisee. The royalty on profits will not affect the franchisee's profit-maximizing behavior, because whatever output maximized profits before the royalty on profits will maximize profits after the imposition of the royalty. Before and after the royalty on profits the franchisee charges the same price and produces the same output. The royalty does not affect consumer surplus or joint profits for the franchisor and franchisee. The royalty affects only the distribution of the profits between the franchisor and franchisee.

   To answer the question we must determine whether a percentage royalty on revenues has an impact on output and price. The percentage revenue royalty reduces the marginal revenue for the franchisee from selling additional units of the good and, therefore, results in a lower marginal revenue curve and reduced output for the franchisee. With lower output, price is increased, and consumer surplus decreases. In addition, combined profits for the franchisee and franchisor are reduced because of the reduction in output.

   Because both consumer surplus and combined profits are lower with a royalty based on a percentage of total revenues, economic efficiency is reduced compared with a royalty based on a percentage of profits.

3. The situation is depicted in Figure Problem 16.3. RPM results in an increase in consumer surplus of the red area A, a loss of consumer surplus of the gray area B, and a gain in profits to the manufacturer of the red area C.

The red area A has been broken down into two small triangles, one large triangle, and one rectangle. Area B has been broken down into a rectangle and a triangle.

The areas are:

$$\text{Area C} = (40)\,(30) = 1200$$

$$\text{Area B} = (20)\,(20) + \frac{1}{2}\,(20)\,(20) = 400 + 200 = 600$$

$$\text{Area A} = \frac{1}{2}\,(50)\,(50) + (20)\,(30) + \frac{1}{2}\,(20) + (20) + \frac{1}{2}\,(20)\,(20)$$

$$= 1250 + 600 + 200 + 200 = 2250$$

The net welfare change is: $1200 - 600 + 2250 = 2850$
In this case, RPM improves economic welfare.

CHAPTER 20

1. In this industry the perfectly competitive quantity is:

$$P = 200 - Q = 20 = MC$$

$$Q = 180 \quad \text{and} \quad P = 20$$

The Cournot-Nash equilibrium with three firms is:

$$Q_{CN} = \frac{3}{4}Q_{PC} = \frac{3}{4}180 = 135$$
$$\text{Therefore, } P = 65$$

If two firms merge, the Cournot-Nash equilibrium would be:

$$Q_{CN} = \frac{2}{3}Q_{PC} = \frac{2}{3}180 = 120$$
$$\text{Therefore, } P = 80$$

In Figure Problem 20.1, as a result of the merger consumer surplus declines more than profits increase, so economic welfare declines as a result of the merger.

Change in consumer surplus:
$$\text{New CS} - \text{Old CS} = \frac{1}{2}\,(120)\,(120) - \frac{1}{2}\,(135)\,(135) = 7200 - 9112.5 = -1912.5$$

Change in profits:
$$\text{New Profits} - \text{Old Profits} = 120\,(80 - 20) - 135\,(65 - 20) = 7200 - 6075 = 1125$$

The net change in consumer surplus plus profits is:
$$-1912.5 + 1125 = -787.5$$

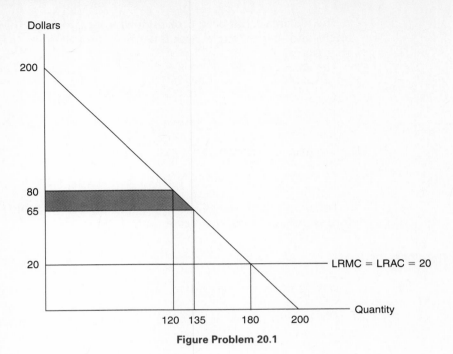

Figure Problem 20.1

3. a. The HHI before the merger was:

$$\text{HHI} = 50^2 + 30^2 + 10^2 + 5^2 + 5^2 = 2500 + 900 + 100 + 25 + 25 = 3550$$

After the merger the HHI is:

$$\text{HHI} = 60^2 + 30^2 + 5^2 + 5^2 = 3600 + 900 + 25 + 25 = 4550$$

Because the original HHI was greater than 1800 and the merger resulted in an increase in the HHI of more than 100, the merger is very likely to be challenged under the merger guidelines.

b.   The HHI before the merger was:

$$\text{HHI} = 30^2 + 25^2 + 20^2 + 15^2 + 10^2 = 900 + 625 + 400 + 225 + 100 = 2250$$

After the merger the HHI is:

$$\text{HHI} = 30^2 + 25^2 + 25^2 + 20^2 = 900 + 625 + 625 + 400 = 2555$$

Once again, because the original HHI was greater than 1800 and the merger resulted in an increase in the HHI of over 100, the merger is very likely to be challenged under the merger guidelines.

c. The HHI before the merger was:

$$HHI = 5\,(10^2) + 10\,(5^2) = 500 + 250 = 750$$

After the merger the HHI is:

$$HHI = 20^2 + 3\,(10^2) + 10\,(5^2) = 400 + 300 + 250 = 950$$

Because the postmerger HHI is less than 1000, this merger is very unlikely to be challenged.

CHAPTER 23

1. As indicated in Figure Problem 23.1, without trade the equilibrium price and quantity are:

$$Demand = 100 - Q_{US} = 25 + Q_{US} = Supply$$
$$solving\ for\ Q_{US}\ yields\ Q_{US} = 37.5$$
$$P = 100 - Q_{US} = 62.5$$

With trade the total supply curve is the sum of the U.S. supply and the foreign supply in the United States:

$$Q_{US} = P - 25\ and\ Q_f = \frac{1}{2}P - 12.5$$

$$\Rightarrow Q_{total} = Q_{US} + Q_f = (P - 25) + (\frac{1}{2}P - 12.5) = \frac{3}{2}P - 37.5$$

$$\Rightarrow \frac{3}{2}P = 37.5 + Q_{total} \Rightarrow P = 25 + \frac{2}{3}Q_{total}$$

The equilibrium with trade:

$$Demand = 100 - Q = 25 + \frac{2}{3}Q = Supply$$

$$\frac{5}{3}Q = 75 \Rightarrow Q = 45$$

With trade, Q = 45, P = 55.

Welfare changes to the United States as a result of free trade are identified below.

Consumer surplus without trade was:

$$CS_{w/o\ trade} = \frac{1}{2}\,(37.5)^2 = 703.125$$

Producer surplus without trade was:

$$PS_{w/o\ trade} = \frac{1}{2}\,(37.5)^2 = 703.125$$

Without trade, CS + PS = 703.125 + 703.125 = 1406.25

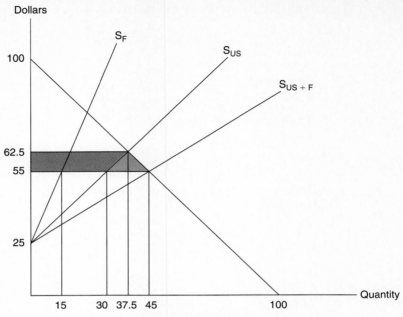

Figure Problem 23.1

Consumer surplus with trade is:

$$CS_{w/trade} = \frac{1}{2}(45)^2 = 1012.5$$

The domestic firms' producer surplus with trade is:

$$PS_{w/trade} = \frac{1}{2}(30)^2 = 450$$

With trade, CS + PS = 1012.5 + 450 = 1462.5
The net welfare gain to the United States from trade is:

$$1462.5 - 1406.25 = 56.25$$

3. The Cournot-Nash equlibrium for the duopolists is obtained by finding the intersection of the two reaction functions. Because of symmetry, each firm has the same reaction function. The American firm's reaction function is:

$$P = 100 - q_J - q_{US} \quad \text{and} \quad MC_{US} = 40$$
$$MR_{US} = (100 - q_J) - 2q_{US} = 40$$
$$q_{US} = 30 - \frac{1}{2}q_J$$

By symmetry the Japanese firm's reaction function is:

$$q_J = 30 - \frac{1}{2}q_{US}$$

The Cournot-Nash equlibrium is:

$$q_{US} = 30 - \frac{1}{2}q_J = 30 - \frac{1}{2}(30 - \frac{1}{2}q_{US}) = 15 + \frac{1}{4}q_{US}$$

$$q_{US} = \frac{15 \times 4}{3} = 20$$

By symmetry $q_J = 20$ and total quantity $q = 40$; therefore, $P = 60$.

a. With the tariff, the Japanese firm's reaction function changes to:

$$P = 100 - q_{US} - q_J \quad \text{and} \quad MC_J = 50$$
$$MR_J = (100 - q_{US}) - 2q_J = 50$$
$$q_J = 25 - \frac{1}{2}q_{US}$$

The American firm's Cournot-Nash ouput is then:

$$q_{US} = 30 - \frac{1}{2}q_J = 30 - \frac{1}{2}(25 - \frac{1}{2}q_{US}) = 17.5 + \frac{1}{4}q_{US}$$

$$q_{US} = \frac{17.5 \times 4}{3} = 23.33$$

The Japanese firm's Cournot-Nash output is then:

$$q_J = 25 - \frac{1}{2}q_{US} = 25 - \frac{1}{2}(23.33) = 25 - (11.67) = 13.33$$

b. Total output with the tariff is $23.33 + 13.33 = 36.66$, and price is $P = 63.34$.

c. Before the tariff:

$$CS_{US} = \frac{1}{2}(40)^2 = 800$$

$$\pi_{US} = TR - TC = (20 \times 60) - (250 + 20(40)) = 1200 - 1050 = 150$$

$$\text{and } CS_{US} + \pi_{US} = 800 + 150 = 950$$

After the tariff:

$$CS_{US} = \frac{1}{2}(36.66)^2 = 671.98$$

$$\pi_{US} = TR - TC = (23.33 \times 64.34) - [250 + 40(23.33)]$$
$$= (1501.05) - (1183.2) = 317.85$$

In addition, the government gains tax revenue equal to:

$$\text{Tax Revenue} = 10 \times 13.33 = 133.33$$

$$CS_{US} + \pi_{US} + \text{Tax Revenue} = 671.98 + 317.85 + 133.33 = 1123.16$$

American welfare increases by $1123.16 - 950 = 173.16$

CHAPTER 24

1. a. To find the Ramsey price set AC = Demand:

$$AC = \frac{1800}{Q} + 10 = P = 100 - Q \Rightarrow \frac{1800}{Q} + 10 = 100 - Q$$

$$\frac{1800}{Q} = 90 - Q \Rightarrow Q^2 - 90Q + 1800 = 0$$

$$(Q - 60)(Q - 30) = 0 \Rightarrow Q = 30 \quad \text{and} \quad Q = 60$$

The regulated quantity would be Q = 60, and the Ramsey price is P = 40.

b. With P = 40 and Q = 60, consumer surplus CS is:

$$CS = \frac{1}{2}(60)^2 = 1800$$

Profits are zero because P = AC. The red triangle A in Figure Problem 24.1 represents the sum of CS plus profits.

c. If P = MC = 10, then Q = 90. Consumer surplus CS equals:

$$CS = \frac{1}{2}(90)^2 = 4050$$

With Q = 90, AC = (1800/90) + 10 = 20 + 10 = 30. Economic profits, π, are negative and equal to:

$$\pi = Q(P - AC) = 90(10 - 30) = -1800$$

Total CS + π = 4050 − 1800 = 2250.
In Figure Problem 24.1, CS is represented by the *sum* of areas A, B, C, D, and E. The economic loss is represented by the *sum* of areas D, E, and F.

d. Price equal to marginal cost results in greater economic welfare by 450 (2250 − 1800).
  The change in welfare in Figure Problem 24.1 is represented by the triangle composed of the areas C and E. This is so because the gain in consumer surplus is equal to the sum of areas B, C, D, and E, whereas the economic loss is represented by the sum of areas D, E, and F. The economic loss area equals 90 × 20 = 1800. The sum of areas B and D also equals the economic loss, that is, 60 × 30 = 1800. It follows that the gain in consumer surplus, equal to the sum of areas B, C, D, and E, *minus* the economic loss equal to the sum of areas B and D, equals the triangle made up of areas C and E.

3. a. The socially optimal prices are set where P = MC during each period. During the off-peak period:

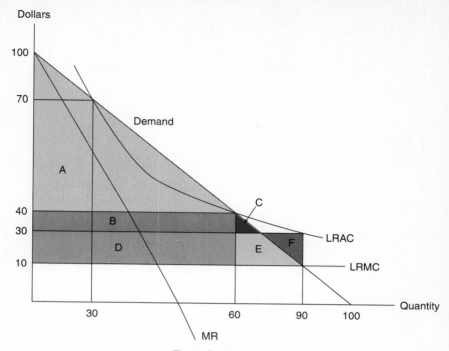

Figure Problem 24.1

$$P = 50 - Q = 20 + \frac{1}{2}Q$$

$$\frac{3}{2}Q = 30 \Rightarrow Q = \frac{2}{3}30 = 20$$

$$P = 50 - 20 = 30$$

During the peak period:

$$P = 110 - Q = 20 + \frac{1}{2}Q$$

$$\frac{3}{2}Q = 90 \Rightarrow Q = \frac{2}{3}90 = 60$$

$$P = 110 - 60 = 50$$

b. There is no social cost during the off-peak period because P = 30 is the optimal price during off-peak periods.

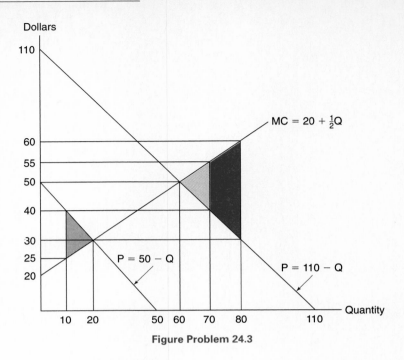

Figure Problem 24.3

During peak periods the social cost is equal to the solid and shaded red triangle area in Figure Problem 24.3. This area equals:

$$\text{Social Cost} = \frac{1}{2}\,(20 \times 30) = 300$$

b. During peak periods the social cost is equal to the small shaded red triangle in the figure. This area equals:

$$\text{Social Cost} = \frac{1}{2}\,(10 \times 15) = 75$$

During off-peak periods the social cost is equal to the gray triangle in the figure. This area equals:

$$\text{Social Cost} = \frac{1}{2}\,(10 \times 15) = 75$$

The total social cost of setting P = 40 is 150.

Author Index

Legal Case Index

Subject Index

Cournot-Nash equilibrium, 154–161, 166
  duopoly and, 158
  empirical evidence, 161
  with three or more firms, 158–160
Cournot-Nash model, 625
  international trade and, 576–582, 583
Court cases. *See* Legal Case Index.
Crazy Eddie, 214–215
Cream-skimming, 610, 625
Creative destruction, 344–346, 625
Credible threat, 241, 625
Cross-licensing agreements, 499, 625
  in glass industry, 222–223
Cross-section studies, 432–433. *See also*
    Structure-conduct-performance
    paradigm
Cross-subsidization, 625
  antitrust litigation, 524
  theory, 513
Customer restrictions
  effects, 554
  litigation, 554–557
Cutthroat competition, 482–483

Dawson Springs, 538–539
Dead-weight loss, 625
  calculating, 38–39
Dead-weight loss triangle, 37–39
Decisions, legal. *See* Legal Case Index.
Defection, 179
Demand curve, 26–27
  dominant firm, 170–171
  followship, 188, 189
  linear, 36, 154
  non-followship, 188, 189
  residual, 150, 151
Demand growth, 197
Department of Energy Organization
    Act, 613
Department of Transportation
  airlines mergers and, 608–609
  responsibilities, 607
Dependent variable, 43, 625
Depreciation, 436, 625
Deregulation, 605–615
  airline industry, 607–609
  electricity industry, 614
  market concentration and, 90
  natural gas industry, 615
  surface transportation, 605–606
  telecommunications, 610–611,
    612–613
Diffusion, as R&D stage, 347, 625
Direct foreign investment, 586–587, 625
Discount rate, 181, 235, 625
Discounting, 180, 625
Discrimination
  predatory, 533
  price, 384–400. *See also* Price discrimi-
    nation
Diseconomies of scale, 21, 23–24, 625
Dominant firm, 169–174
  price leadership. *See* Dominant firm
    price leadership
  productivity, import competition
    and, 574–575

R&D and, 355–356
  small foreign firms and, 569–574
Dominant firm price leadership,
    169–174, 625
  collusion under, examples, 203–207
  decline in, 174
  in international market, 569–573
Dominant strategy, 137, 626
Dominated strategy, 142, 626
Dompier Oil Company, 539
Dorfman-Steiner model, 319–320, 626
DOT. *See* Department of Transportation
Double marginalization, 406–409, 626
Douglas, 269–270
Downstream, 406, 626
Dr. Miles decision, 558
Drug industry, 489, 558, 559–560
Du Pont
  antitrust litigation, 473, 474, 475,
    490, 520, 526
  collusive price leadership example,
    209
  limit pricing, 243
Dump-the-surplus discrimination,
    398–399
Dynamic efficiency, 345–346
Dynamic game, 139, 144, 626
Dynamic performance, 9, 626

Economic cost, 626
  versus accounting cost, 14–15
Economic forbearance, 513, 626
  antitrust litigation, 524
Economic theory, 9, 13–47
  cost concepts, 14–24. *See also* Costs
  monopoly, 33–37, 40–41. *See also* Mo-
    nopoly
  perfect competition, 24–32. *See also*
    Perfect competition
  policymaking cautions and, 42
  profit-maximization, 13–14
  statistical tools, 42–47
  welfare economics, 32–33
Economies of scale, 101–108, 575–586,
    626
  in advertising, 115–116
  aircraft industry and, 582–584
  Cournot-Nash framework, 576–582,
    583
  diseconomies of scale, sources, 23–24
  in electricity industry, 613–614
  empirical estimates, 102–108
  as entry barrier, 101–102, 103,
    118–119
  in limit pricing, 238–239
  market concentration and, 90
  measurement, 576
  in natural gas industry, 614
  regulation and, 593
  sources, 21–23
  specialization with, 584–586
Economies of scope, 55, 108–109, 626
Efficiency
  collusion versus, 449–451
  market structure and, 345–346
  mergers and, 507–508, 513–515

in production, 32, 626
  rate of return regulation problems,
    597–602
Efficiency gains, 507–508
Eiberger, 557
EIC (Enterprise Industrial Categories),
    91–93
Elasticity
  collusion and, 197
  of demand. *See* Price elasticity of de-
    mand
Elders Grain, 519
Electrical equipment industry
  antitrust litigation, 499
  barometric price leadership, 211–212
  learning curve and market entry,
    272–273
  low-price guarantees, 213–214
  market division schemes, 220–222
Electricity industry
  antitrust litigation, 554
  regulation and deregulation, 613–614
Electronics industry
  antitrust litigation, 560
  collusion, 214
Empire building, 509
Empire Machine Company, 222–223
Engineering studies, 104–105, 626
Engineers, society of. *See* National Soci-
    ety of Professional Engineers
Enterprise Industrial Categories, 91–93
Entertainment industry, 488–489
Entry, 98–127
  advertising and. *See* Advertising
  barriers. *See* Entry barriers
  contestable markets and, 124–127
  deterrents. *See* Entry deterrents
  empirical evidence, 117–122
  exit and, 123–124
  expected profitability and, 116–117
  incentives, 116–117
  market growth and, 117
  patterns, 98–99
  sunk costs and, 123–124
Entry barriers, 6, 99–101, 99–114,
    441–442, 626
  absolute cost advantage as, 110–111
  advertising as, 114–116, 330–331
  Bain's evidence on, 118–120
  capital costs as, 111–113, 420
  and concentration and profit,
    443–444
  economies of scale as, 101–108
  economies of scope and, 108–109
  empirical evidence, 117–122
  product differentiation as, 113–116
  specific, relative heights, 118
  static/structural, 101–114
Entry deterrents, 232–280
  excess capacity as, 261–263
  game theory, 285–298
  learning curve and, 267–273
  limit pricing as, 232–245. *See also*
    Limit pricing
  predatory pricing as, 245–252
  price and nonprice strategies,
    278–280

National Society of Professional Engineers
  antitrust litigation, 494
  competitive bidding restriction, 219–220
Natural Gas Act, 614
Natural gas industry, 614–615
Natural Gas Policy Act, 615
Natural monopoly, 42, 630
  regulation and, 593–594
NCAA (National Collegiate Athletic Association), 494–495
NEIO (new empirical industrial organization), 455
Neoclassical firm, 53–54
New empirical industrial organization, 455
New Zealand, 574–575
Newmark & Lewis, 214–215
Newspaper industry, 561–562
Nice behavior, 186
Non-followship demand curve, 188, 189, 630
Non-zero sum games, 139–140
Nonmanufacturing industries, market concentration, 79, 90–93. *See also specific industry or company*
Nonprice strategies, 278–280
Northern Securities, 470
Numbers equivalent, 83, 631

Oil industry
  antitrust litigation, 466, 470–471, 537–538, 539, 553–554
  predatory pricing, 248, 249
  price leadership, 202–205, 212
Oligopoly, 3–4, 149–174, 631
  advertising and, 321–325
  Bertrand model, 167–169
  conscious parallelism and, 487–488
  Cournot model, 149–154
  Cournot-Nash equilibrium, 154–161
  dominant firm price leaders and, 174
  dominant firm price leadership model and, 169–174
  entry deterrence. *See* Entry barriers; Entry deterrents
  game theory, 8, 135–146. *See also* Game theory
  Japanese, television production, 586
  mergers and, 505
  price determination models, 167–174
  quantity determination models, 149–167
  R&D under, 349–354
  Stackelberg model, 161–167, 636
  United Kingdom, subsidies and tariffs and, 582, 583
OPEC. *See* Organization of Petroleum Exporting Countries
Opportunism, 56, 631
Opportunity cost, 14, 631
Organization of Petroleum Exporting Countries
  excess capacity, 225
  price-fixing, 203–205
Outboard motor production, 523

Overseas trade. *See* International trade
Overt collusion, 178, 631
Overt price-fixing agreement, 482–484
Owens-Illinois, 222–223
Owners, aging, 510
Ownership, separating control from, 59

Parameters, 43, 631
Parametric price, 203, 631
Paramount, 488
Pareto efficiency, 384
Park & Sons, 558
Parke Davis, 559–560
Patent cartels, 222–224
Patent litigation
  circuit breakers, 499
  glass containers, 498
  light bulbs, 496–498
  plastic bag tie strips, 499–500
  under Sherman Act, 496–500
  sorbothane, 478
  tetracycline, 489
  Utzman, 498
Patent pooling, 223–224, 498, 631
Patent race game, 357, 381–383, 631
Patents
  economics of, 366–369
  effectiveness, 369–375
  game theory, 357, 381–383
  lawsuits. *See* Patent litigation
  as measure of innovation, 361
  patent-dependency, 368, 370–371, 372
Peak-load pricing, 598–599, 631
  adoption, 602
  in regulated utility, 601, 602
Pecuniary economies, 23, 631
Per se rule, 631
  Hyde case, 551–552
  versus the Rule of Reason, 486
Perfect collusion, 179, 631
Perfect competition, 3, 24–32, 631
  assumptions, 25–27
  equilibrium and, 29–32
  versus monopoly, R&D under, 347–350, 354, 355
  supply curve and, 27–31
  welfare effects, 37–40
Perfect discrimination, 385, 631. *See also* First-degree price discrimination
Perfect information, 138, 631
Performance, dynamic, 9, 626
Performance measures, in SCP studies, 434–440. *See also* Structure-conduct-performance paradigm
Persuasive advertising, 315, 632
Pet Milk, 541
Pfizer, 489
Phantom freight, 215–217, 632
Phases of the moon system, 221, 632
Philadelphia National Bank, 517–518
Piracy litigation, 561
Pittsburgh Plus system, 215–216
Plas-Ties, 499–500
Plywood industry, 217–218
Policy
  industrial, effectiveness in international trade, 581–584

natural monopoly and, 593–594
  public, litigation reflecting. *See* Antitrust laws; Litigation; *specific case, litigant, or industry*
Pooling equilibrium, 287, 632
Postmerger studies, 514–515
Potential competition, 632
  antitrust litigation, 512, 521–524
Pottery production, 485–486
PPG Industries, 490–491
Pre-sale services, in vertical integration
  ensuring, 417
  insufficient, 410–413, 414
Predatory discrimination, 533
Predatory prices, 193
Predatory pricing, 245–252, 632. *See also* Price discrimination
  airline industry, 250–252
  American Tobacco Company, 248–249
  empirical evidence, 248–252
  Kreps and Wilson model, 257–260
  Maxwell House Coffee, 250
  ReaLemon, 249–250
  Standard Oil of New Jersey, 248, 249
Premerger studies, 514, 515
Present value, 180, 632
  of profits, 181, 232
Price/pricing. *See also* Cost; Price discrimination
  antitrust litigation, 484–487
  basing point system. *See* Basing point pricing system
  concentration and, 453–455
  elasticity, 26–27, 36–37
  of inputs, in vertical integration, 418–419
  leadership. *See* Price leadership
  limit, 232–245. *See also* Limit pricing
  marginal revenue and, 33–36
  parametric, 203
  peak-load, 598–599
  predatory. *See* Predatory pricing
  price-cost margins. *See* Price-cost margins
  price-exchange agreement. *See* Price-exchange agreements
  price-fixing agreement. *See* Price-fixing agreements
  product differentiation and, 304–307
  profitability, relationship with, 453–454
  Ramsey price, 594
  R&D and, 356–358
  RPM agreements. *See* Resale price maintenance agreement
  rule-of-thumb, 63–65
  structure, setting, 600–602
Price cap, 611, 632
Price-cost margins, 632
  annual, concentration regressions, 452
  as measurement in SCP studies, 437–438
Price determination models, 149–167
Price discrimination, 384–400, 632
  basing point pricing and, 395–396
  clear-the-stock, 399

franchising agreements, 552–553
group boycotts, 561–562
RPM agreements, 557–561. *See also*
    Resale price maintenance agreement
territorial and customer restrictions,
    554–557
tying agreements, 548–553
Vinyl floor industry, 555
Von's Grocery, 517, 526

Warranted concentration ratio, 107,
    638
Warren, Chief Justice, 517, 518, 540
Washington Trust Bank, 522–523
Waste Management, 518–519
Waste Resources, 518–519

Weak incumbent, 246–247, 638
Welfare economics, 32–33
Welfare effects
  of advertising, 332–338
  of international trade, 568–569,
    571–575, 581–584
  multinational corporations and,
    587–588
  in perfect competition vs. monopoly,
    37–40
  of price discrimination, 388–393,
    404–405
Westinghouse
  antitrust litigation, 213, 489–490, 497
  barometric price leadership, 211–212
  low-price guarantees, 213–214
  market division scheme, 220–222
White, Chief Justice, 594

White list, 561, 638
White Motor Company, 554–555
Wholesale industry, market concentration, 91, 92–93
World markets. *See* International trade

X-inefficiency, 39, 62, 597, 638
Xerox, 244

Yamaha Motors, 523
Youngstown Steel, 516

Zero-sum games, 136–138

Credits

Table 4.3: From Devra L. Golbe and Lawrence J. White, "A Time Series Analysis of Mergers and Acquisitions in the U.S. Economy" in Alan J. Auerbach, CORPORATE TAKEOVERS: CAUSES AND CONSEQUENCES, Chicago: University of Chicago Press, ©1988. Reprinted with permission. *Tables 5.2 and 5.3:* Reprinted by permission of the publisher from BARRIERS TO NEW COMPETITION by Joe S. Bains, Cambridge, Mass.: Harvard University Press, Copyright ©1956 by the President and Fellows of Harvard College. *Page 221:* From J.G. Fuller, THE GENTLEMAN CONSPIRATORS (NY: Grove, 1962), p. 66. Reprinted with permission. *Table 10.6:* Daniel P. Kaplan, "The Changing Airline Industry," in Leonard W. Weiss & Michael W. Klass, eds., REGULATORY REFORM: WHAT ACTUALLY HAPPENED, ©1986, p. 59. Reprinted by permission of Addison-Wesley Educational Publishers Inc. *Tables 11.1 and 11.2:* David C. Mowery & Nathan Rosenberg, "The Commercial Aircraft Industry," in Richard R. Nelson, ed., GOVERNMENT AND TECHNICAL PROGRESS: A CROSS-INDUSTRY ANALYSIS, Pergamon Press, 1982, pp. 107, 111. Reprinted with permission of Richard R. Nelson. *Table 11.5:* From Robert Smiley, "Empirical Evidence on Strategic Entry Deterrence," INTERNATIONAL JOURNAL OF INDUSTRIAL ORGANIZATION 6, 1980, p. 172. Reprinted with permission. *Table 13.1:* Reprinted with permission from the September 28, 1994 issue of ADVERTISING AGE. Copyright, Crain Communications Inc. 1994. *Tables 14.4, 14.5, 14.7, and 14.8:* From Richard C. Levin et al., "Appropriating the Returns from Industrial Research and Development," BROOKINGS PAPERS ON ECONOMIC ACTIVITY, No. 3 (Washington: Brookings Institution, 1987), pp. 794, 797, 809, 810. Reprinted with permission. *Table 14.6:* From Edwin Mansfield, "Patents and Innovation," MANAGEMENT SCIENCE, February 1986, p. 175. Reprinted with permission of INFORMS. *Pages 345–346:* From Joseph A. Schumpeter, CAPITALISM, SOCIALISM AND DEMOCRACY, ©1950. Reprinted by permission of Addison-Wesley Educational Publishers Inc. *Table 17.4:* From Ian Domowitz et al., "Business Cycles and the Relationship Between Concentration and Price-Cost Margins," RAND JOURNAL OF ECONOMICS, Spring 1986, Table 2. Copyright ©1986. Reprinted by permission of RAND. *Table 20.1:* From David J. Ravenscraft and F.M. Scherer, MERGERS, SELL-OFFS, AND ECONOMIC EFFICIENCY (Washington: Brookings Institution, 1987), p. 60. Reprinted with permission. *Table 23.1:* From M. Pickford, "A New Test for Manufacturing Industry Efficiency: An Analysis of the Results of Import License Tendering in New Zealand," INTERNATIONAL JOURNAL OF INDUSTRIAL ORGANIZATION 3, 1985, p. 166. Reprinted with permission. *Tables 23.2 and 23.3:* From Anthony J. Venables, "Trade Policy Under Imperfect Competition: A Numerical Assessment," in Paul Krugman and Alasdair Smith, eds., EMPIRICAL STUDIES OF STRATEGIC TRADE POLICY, Chicago: University of Chicago Press, ©1994, pp. 52, 57. Reprinted with permission. *Table 23.4:* From Gernot Klepper, "Industrial Policy in the Transport Aircraft Industry," in Paul Krugman and Alasdair Smith, eds., EMPIRICAL STUDIES OF STRATEGIC TRADE POLICY, Chicago: University of Chicago Press, ©1994, p. 116. Reprinted with permission. *Table 24.1:* From Thomas Gale Moore, "Rail and Trucking Deregulation," in Leonard W. Weiss and Michael W. Klass, eds., REGULATORY REFORM: WHAT ACTUALLY HAPPENED, ©1986, p. 31. Reprinted by permission of Addison-Wesley Educational Publishers Inc. *Page 599:* Adapted from Alfred E. Kahn, THE ECONOMICS OF REGULATION: PRINCIPLES AND INSTITUTIONS (Cambridge, Mass.: MIT Press, 1988), vol. II, pp. 50–54. Reprinted with permission.